Readings in the Philosophy of Religion

Readings in the Philosophy of Religion

third edition

EDITED BY KELLY JAMES CLARK

broadview press

BROADVIEW PRESS — www.broadviewpress.com
Peterborough, Ontario, Canada

Founded in 1985, Broadview Press remains a wholly independent publishing house. Broadview's focus is on academic publishing; our titles are accessible to university and college students as well as scholars and general readers. With over 600 titles in print, Broadview has become a leading international publisher in the humanities, with world-wide distribution. Broadview is committed to environmentally responsible publishing and fair business practices.

The interior of this book is printed on 100% recycled paper.

Library and Archives Canada Cataloguing in Publication

Readings in the philosophy of religion / edited by Kelly James Clark. — Third edition.

Includes bibliographical references.
ISBN 978-1-55481-276-9 (softcover)

1. Religion—Philosophy. I. Clark, Kelly James, 1956–, editor

BL51.R42 2017   210   C2017-901905-8

Broadview Press handles its own distribution in North America
PO Box 1243, Peterborough, Ontario K9J 7H5, Canada
555 Riverwalk Parkway, Tonawanda, NY 14150, USA
Tel: (705) 743-8990; Fax: (705) 743-8353
email: customerservice@broadviewpress.com

Distribution is handled by Eurospan Group in the UK, Europe, Central Asia, Middle East, Africa, India, Southeast Asia, Central America, South America, and the Caribbean. Distribution is handled by Footprint Books in Australia and New Zealand.

Canada

Broadview Press acknowledges the financial support of the Government of Canada through the Canada Book Fund for our publishing activities.

Copy edited by Michel Pharand
Cover design by George Kirkpatrick
Interior design and typesetting by Jennifer Blais

PRINTED IN CANADA

TO NICHOLAS WOLTERSTORFF
friend and philosopher (in that order)

Contents

Part Six
CHINESE PHILOSOPHY OF RELIGION   409

Introduction   411

Chapter 29: The Ancient Texts   421

Chapter 30: "Confucian" Religion   435

Chapter 31: Religion in the *Daode Jing*   463

Chapter 32: Ritual, Religion, and Naturalism   474

Suggestions for Further Study   498

Permissions Acknowledgements   499

Preface

The most significant addition to the Third Edition is a section on Chinese Philosophy of Religion. In order to make room for this section, several essays were eliminated. The First Edition's section on Asian religion was not included in the Second Edition because professors indicated that they were not assigning it to their students. Perhaps because of changes in the world, reviewers insisted on its inclusion in a new edition. Since one of my areas of expertise is early Chinese thought, I was only too eager to reintroduce students to the topic.

Western students know considerably less about non-Western thought, and non-Western philosophy of religion has not seen the scholarly explosion witnessed in the Christian world. Philosophy of religion for the past fifty years has seen a tremendous resurgence, but it has mostly been, truth be told, philosophy of Christianity. The essays in this textbook mainly reflect that resurgence. The new section on Chinese philosophy aims to rectify that parochialism.

But we can't rectify everything at once. So I decided not to include a section on Asian philosophy. Asia is a cultural construct which covers too many acres and eras to be meaningfully captured in a phrase or a short section of a book. There is simply no way (or no simple way) to cover the variety and subtlety of beliefs and practices from sixth-century BCE Mahājanapada (in what we now call India) to twenty-first-century Tokyo. So I decided to focus on what I know best: Chinese philosophy and religion.

Similar problems afflict China and the Chinese. There's no "Chinese mind" that captures some distinctly and uniformly "oriental" way of thinking. In early China, different people had different thoughts at different places at different times. There are, however, historically significant texts which subsequent thinkers systematized and reflected on. We'll focus on just a few of those texts from early China, texts attributed to Confucius in various ways, for example, and Laozi.

To help the reader understand those texts, I have done two things in the section on Chinese Philosophy of Religion. First, the section begins with a selection of primary texts so that students have some sense of the original source material. Second, I include a substantial introduction to early Chinese philosophy and religion, locating the texts within their socio-cultural background. Unlike the other chapters, I've front-loaded the discussion and so have not included a final, concluding essay on the topic overall (as one finds in the previous sections). I hope teachers and students alike will rise to the occasion of attempting to understand a tradition that is not their own. It is, I think, worth the effort.

Finally, I have included two new essays on the cognitive science of religion. Since Richard Dawkins declared God a delusion based on findings in the cognitive science of religion, it seems worth taking the time to understand (a) just what the cognitive science of religion has "discovered," and (b) what are the implications of the cognitive science of religion for the rationality of religious belief.

Introduction

THE RENAISSANCE OF PHILOSOPHY OF RELIGION

During the past thirty years, there has been a remarkable renaissance in philosophy of religion. Due to the influence of Alvin Plantinga, J.L. Mackie, William Alston, Antony Flew, George Mavrodes, Ludwig Wittgenstein (and the Wittgensteinians), Nicholas Wolterstorff, Robert and Marilyn Adams, Norman Kretzman and Eleonore Stump (to name a few), philosophy of religion has redeployed. The theistic arguments have been dusted off, developed and criticized; new forms of arguments for the existence of God have sprung up. While the daunting deductive argument from evil has been generally conceded to be unsound, new versions of the problem of evil, as well as new theodicies, have been introduced. Philosophers of religion have given up their defensive stance and have pushed ahead with distinctively religious projects in such areas as God and morality, God and human knowledge, and the nature of God; philosophers are using their technical and intuitive abilities to discuss distinctively religious questions such as "Why pray?" and "Is there a hell?" And increasing recognition of non-theistic religions has forced discussion of, for example, religious pluralism and Buddhist philosophy of religion.

The rebirth of philosophy of religion is especially noteworthy given the reigning anti-religious philosophies. In the heyday of logical positivism, for example, religious belief was reduced to emotive utterances or unimportant nonsense. Religious claims were considered beyond the pale of intelligibility. The rejection of religious belief as nonsensical was not rooted in a deep awareness of divine transcendence; rather it was rooted in intellectual imperialism: to a prior and restrictive commitment to the "world of science."

Logical positivism has been shown for the will-o-the-wisp that it was: prejudice masquerading as cool and detached reason. Even if one granted its initial assumptions, it could not, on its own terms, rationally justify the world it hoped to inhabit. Logical positivism died a well-deserved death but its facile dismissal of religious belief held sway in philosophical circles. After all, hadn't Hume shown the arbitrariness of religious hypotheses to account for the design of the universe? Didn't Nietzsche, Freud, and Marx reveal the ignoble sources of religious belief? Hadn't the problem of evil demonstrated the impossibility of an omniscient, omnipotent, wholly good being, given the fact of evil?

For most ordinary believers around the world, news of the demise of the divine would have come as a shock. Blissfully unaware of the latest views on this or that, ordinary religious believers struggle to accept and maintain their religious beliefs, as they have for millennia. Professional philosophical reflection has grown more and more distant from ordinary people's believing experience and it has gotten increasingly technical and inaccessible to even the most well-educated laypersons.

This collection of essays is an attempt to take seriously the experience of non-professional philosophical religious believers (and unbelievers). The essays have been tried out on undergraduate students for over two decades. Those that students have found to be esoteric, pedantic, or incomprehensible have been eliminated. Those that students have found to be disconnected from their own lived experience have been removed. The essays that have survived are potent in terms of both clarity and import. Not every essay will appeal to every student, of course, and some are more difficult than others. Nonetheless, for those who are interested in critical reflection on the most fundamental religious concerns, there is ample opportunity here in these essays. And who does not want to know what kind of God, if any at all, exists?

The essays in this collection are by both historical and contemporary authors. Few have reflected on the divine so well and so thoroughly as Thomas Aquinas. Even where one disagrees, Aquinas (as well as other medievals) is a good place to start. Most of the essays are from the past twenty years or so; they demonstrate the remarkable fertility of recent philosophy of religion.

Arguments for the Existence of God

Part One

Introduction

Introduction. Attempts to prove the existence of God (or the gods or a deity or an ultimate divine reality) are as ancient as philosophy itself. In Western philosophy, the best developed theistic argument was offered by Aristotle in the fourth century BCE. So compelling was Aristotle's argument that Thomas Aquinas, the great Christian philosopher, reaffirmed it in 1300 CE. Variations on Aristotle's argument were developed into the so-called cosmological argument. The cosmological argument begins with the existence of the universe itself and asks for an explanation of the universe. Although the argument typically (in modern times) begins from the general fact of the existence of the universe, versions of the cosmological argument are also based on motion and change.

The cosmological argument belongs to a broader class of arguments that are called *a posteriori*. *A posteriori* arguments rely on premises that are known or knowable through experience. The *a posteriori* premises in cosmological arguments include: some things are in motion, things change, and the universe exists. Other prominent *a posteriori* arguments are based on the design of the universe, alleged religious experiences, and our sense of right and wrong. *A priori* arguments, on the other hand, are based on premises that are known or knowable independent of experience. The most significant *a priori* argument for the existence of God is the ontological argument. This argument attempts to establish the existence of God by way of the definition or essence of God.

Arguments for the existence of God are part of the project of natural theology. *Natural theology* is the attempt to prove the existence of God without reference to information gained from reputed divine revelation. Natural theology relies not on revelation but on reason and experience to establish the existence of God. The grand tradition of natural theology attempted to prove the existence of God from premises that are universally known. *Classical natural theology* is the attempt to prove the existence of God on the basis of premises that all rational creatures are obliged to accept. If one could make an easy inference to the existence of God on the basis of universally acceptable (and, reputedly, obvious) premises, then belief in God would be a requirement of reason.

The project of classical natural theology is a failure for two reasons. The first is, I believe, more important. First, there are few universally acceptable premises, at least in matters of fundamental human concern. Rational people, we have learned, rationally disagree. In areas of deep human concern—for example, ethics, politics, and human nature—some reasonable people simply judge fundamental truths differently from other reasonable people. The attempt to justify *any* philosophical argument to everyone's rational satisfaction is a snare and a delusion. The second problem is not unrelated to the first. It is difficult to decide, upon reflection, on the truth or falsity of key premises in all of the arguments. Although *a posteriori* arguments are rooted in experience, they almost always rely on a controversial metaphysical truth which is distant from experienceable reality, difficult to grasp and resistant to a simple determination of truth. All of this is not to deny, of course, that each premise is really true or false; all that follows is that not everyone will see its truth or falsity in any easy way. Rational people, I'll say it again, rationally disagree. I have stated this as if the crux of the matter for theistic arguments is that there is legitimate disagreement about the truths of the premises. It should be recognized, of course, that some philosophers believe that the crucial premises in all theistic arguments are false.

Let us turn to brief introductions of the arguments and their critiques that are presented in each section.

The ontological argument. The ontological argument is perhaps the most beguiling of the arguments for the existence of God. First developed by Anselm, it received the immediate criticism of the monk, Gaunilo. While the logic of the argument is straightforward, its conclusion comes as a surprise. The argument begins with the definition of God as the greatest possible being and concludes that God exists. How can a mere definition (idea) be used to prove the existence (reality) of something? In its barest form the argument goes as follows:

1. God has every perfection.

2. Existence is a perfection.

3. God exists.

What does it mean to say that God has every perfection? The medievals believed that there are great-making properties, those properties that are better to have than not. So, for example, it's better to be able to move oneself than to be immobile. It is better to know things than to be ignorant or without consciousness. It is better to be able to be moral than not; it is better to be morally perfect than morally less than perfect or evil. Etc., etc. So self-locomotion, knowledge, and goodness are great-making properties. And it is better to exist than not, and to exist forever than to begin to exist or to cease existing; that is, existence is a great-making property. So, if a being has every great making property then that being must exist. Anselm's own argument proceeds more indirectly. His understanding of God's perfection: God is that being than which none greater can be conceived. Anselm supposes that God, that being than which none greater can be conceived, does not exist and then draws an absurd consequence. By *reductio ad absurdum* (reducing an assumption to absurdity by showing it entails a contradiction) Anselm deduces his conclusion: God exists.

Gaunilo's criticism is straightforward. By using a similar line of reasoning, we can prove the existence of the greatest possible anything, such as the most perfect island. He is using the *reductio ad absurdum* strategy on Anselm's argument. Without showing where Anselm's argument goes wrong, he tries to show that the argument form entails absurdities and so must be unsound. Anselm does not reply directly to this argument. Rather, he says that if his reasoning can be applied to the lost island, then the lost island exists. Of course, he's assuming that his reasoning can't be applied to islands but applies to God (and maybe to other necessarily existing metaphysical entities such as numbers).

Although the argument has been widely thought to have been unmasked by Immanuel Kant, who alleged that it illegitimately moves from thought to reality, it has found new life in the twentieth century, especially with the development of modal logic (the logic of possibility and necessity). Rather than move from a definition of God to the reality of God, these arguments begin with the possibility of a perfect being and contend that this entails the necessity of God's existence. The best developed version of the modal ontological argument was developed by Alvin Plantinga. Laura Garcia, after a brief excursus to help us gain an understanding of the language and logic of possibility and necessity, takes us through Plantinga's ontological argument. Plantinga's argument is simple but deep, relying on axioms of modal logic: if a maximally great being is possible, then a maximally great being is necessary. As one might expect, Plantinga's argument has elicited many criticisms, which Garcia takes up in turn.

The cosmological argument. We begin with Thomas Aquinas's famous (or infamous!) Five Ways or five arguments for the existence of God. The first three arguments are, roughly, cosmological arguments. The first relies upon the indisputable fact of motion and the second upon the fact of change (from potency to act—say from cold but potentially hot to actually hot). Both, in turn, depend upon the claim that an infinite regress of movers or changers is impossible. There must be, according to these arguments, a first mover or changer. The third way is intuitively more difficult. It is based on possibility (something that exists but might not have, or doesn't exist but might have) and necessity (something that cannot fail to exist). The assumption that everything is merely possible, according to Aquinas, leads to the absurd conclusion that nothing exists now. But, of course, something does exist now, so our assumption must have been false—not everything is merely possible or, in other words, a necessary being (God?) exists. The fourth way is based on gradations of goodness. And the fifth way, typically called "The Teleological Argument," is based on the simple fact that things work towards ends. These things that attain their ends, but are stupid, must be guided or directed toward that end by something outside of themselves and this guide or director is God. In our day most people believe that Aquinas's arguments rely on an outdated Aristotelian science (Ways 1, 2, and 5) or are simply fallacious (Way 3).

Leibniz's version of the cosmological argument has supporters even today. This argument is simple:

1. The universe exists.

2. There is a sufficient explanation of the existence of everything.

3. God is the sufficient explanation of the existence of the universe.

Leibniz's argument depends upon the controversial principle of sufficient reason: for every positive fact or truth there is a sufficient reason for its existence or its truth. The principle of sufficient reason does not deny that some things are self-explanatory—that carry their own explanation, so to speak, within themselves. God, of course, is just such a self-explanatory being—he carries his existence within his own nature.

A new version of the cosmological argument is based on an older, Arabic argument called the Kalaam argument. William Lane Craig argues that an actual infinity is impossible. Since an eternally existing universe would be an actual infinity, an eternal universe is impossible; the universe had a beginning in time. He contends that God is the only adequate explanation of the beginning of the universe (although I omit his arguments in support of God).

The argument from design. The argument from design is probably the most intuitively appealing of all the arguments for the existence of God. Many people are taken with the wonder and beauty of the world or some feature of it and contend that it simply could not have occurred by accident or unintentionally. This may be formalized:

1. The world is designed.

2. Design implies a designer.

3. Hence, the world is designed.

Critiques of the argument attack either or both of the premises.

This section begins with William Paley's famous argument from design which had the misfortune of being published 23 years after David Hume's powerful critique. Paley's argument begins with the famous analogy of stumbling upon a watch in the wilderness. Rejecting a variety of possible explanations, Paley contends that the only reasonable explanation of the existence and design of the watch is that it had a watchmaker. Paley completes the analogy by demonstrating that the universe relevantly resembles a watch. The portion of his book that I have chosen focuses (no pun intended) on the eye. The watch-like character of such parts of the universe implies that the universe was designed.

Hume's famous critique of the argument from design was published posthumously. Some people consider this work the definitive critique of all natural theology. After carefully presenting the argument, Hume notes its essential reliance on analogy—the universe is like a machine. At first, Hume accepts the analogy and demonstrates that we are not led by reason to affirm the existence of God. Second, Hume offers reasons to reject the analogy—there are relevant disanalogies between the universe and machines. And, finally, Hume suggests that given sufficient time and limited possibilities, the apparent design of the universe would come into existence (without the necessity of divine forethought).

Hume merely suggested that the universe, with all of its remarkable but merely apparent design, could have arisen by chance. But it was not until Darwin that a mechanism was offered to account for "design." As a young student Darwin was deeply impressed with the arguments of Paley. His subsequent research, however, led him to reject the notion of a supernatural designer in favour of a purely natural explanation of "design"—natural selection.

The so-called "Fine-Tuning" argument takes a step back from design of parts of the universe—like the eye, the wing or the cell—and asks what conditions are necessary for the existence of (human) life at all. Physical constants, such as the law of gravity and the initial explosive forces of the big bang, are precisely fine-tuned for the existence of life. Even the slightest of variations of such constants (and there are many of them) would not have permitted the existence of life. The evidence of fine-tuning suggests, so Robin Collins argues, the existence of a being who intended to create a world which permitted the existence of human agents capable of responding to him.

Moral arguments. Moral arguments for the existence of God are both simple and initially appealing:

1. Right and wrong are objective properties.

2. The best explanation of the existence of objective moral properties is their agreement or disagreement with the will of God.

3. Hence, there is a God.

As early as Plato, this divine command theory of morality was critiqued. Plato asked the following questions: Are things good because the gods will them? Or do the gods will them because they are good? If things are good simply because God wills them, then morality seems arbitrary (God could have willed just anything). But if the latter is true, that God wills things because they are good, then God seems irrelevant to morality (he simply recognizes an independent standard and wills it).

Robert Merrihew Adams offers a defense of the divine command theory which avoids the charge of arbitrariness. He believes that the arbitrariness problem is resolved by locating the source of morality in the will of a loving God who couldn't and, hence, wouldn't will cruelty. Adams also defends a Kantian approach to morality: the theist has a better reason to be moral, and this provides a practical reason to believe in God.

Linda Zagzebski presents a moral argument for the rationality of theistic belief. If all one has to go on morally are one's own moral intuitions and reasoning and those of others, one is rationally led to skepticism, both about the possibility of moral knowledge and about one's moral effectiveness. This skepticism is extensive, amounting to moral despair. But such despair cannot be rational. It follows that the assumption of the argument must be false and one must be able to rely on more than one's own human powers and those of others in attempting to live a moral life. The Christian God has such a function. Hence, Zagzebski contends, if it is rational to attempt a moral life, it is rational to believe in the Christian God.

Religious experience. People have long contended that their religious experiences, their experiences of God, ipso facto demonstrate the existence of God. If an experience is of God, then there is a god. Many reject arguments from religious experience because they claim that it is not valid to infer the objective reality of God from a subjective religious experience. Further, there are no tests or checking procedures to determine if an alleged religious experience is veridical (as opposed to illusory).

Perhaps the most important contemporary defender of religious experience is William Alston, who favourably compares religious experience with sensory experience. We routinely take sensory experience to provide reliable information about an empirical reality independent of our minds; likewise Alston contends that religious experience provides reliable information about a divine reality independent of our minds. Alston's strategy is to respond to objections to his claim that religious experience relevantly resembles ordinary sensory experience.

The self-refutation of naturalism. Plantinga's intriguing essay develops the nagging thought, called Darwin's doubt, that evolutionary naturalism can account only for the survival value of our beliefs and not the truth of our beliefs. Can evolutionary naturalism provide the resources to trust the reliability of our cognitive faculties? Starting with the undeveloped worries of prominent naturalists, Plantinga develops a sophisticated probabilistic argument against the reliability of our cognitive faculties given the hypotheses of naturalism and evolution. If, given those hypotheses, our cognitive faculties can't be trusted, then they can't be trusted in defense of naturalism and evolution. Theism, of the Christian-Jewish-Muslim variety, however, has the resources adequately to account for the reliability of our cognitive faculties. While the theist can consistently maintain the reliability of her cognitive faculties, the naturalist-evolutionist can do so only on pain of irrationality.

In this and the preceding two sections I have included some of the recent, novel defenses of religious belief without the usual instant "refutation" by a non-theist critic. I have done so for two reasons. First, I want to leave the reader with the (correct) impression that recent philosophy of religion has demonstrated the rich fertility of the project of theistic arguments. Second, I have allotted an entire section to critiques of God, which critiques themselves shall go uncriticized. There have been and will continue to be criticisms of moral arguments, arguments from religious experience and Plantinga's critique of naturalism. But these arguments will be revised in light of legitimate criticism, new arguments will be developed, and new criticisms will be offered.

The balance of probabilities. We have considered various individual arguments for the existence of God. That is, we have considered diverse phenomena—the sheer existence of the universe, the alleged design of the universe, morality, religious experience, and the reliability of our cognitive faculties—separately as evidence for the existence of God. One of the most prominent recent developments in theistic arguments is to consider all of this apparently disparate evidence conjointly rather than singly. Relying on developments in the probabilistic analysis of, for example, scientific theories, these new sorts of arguments ask the following question: what is the best explanation of all of the relevant data taken together? Defenders of these so-called "cumulative case arguments" contend that God is the best explanation of, for example, the sheer existence of the universe, the alleged design of the universe, morality, religious experience, and the reliability of our cognitive faculties.

Richard Swinburne is perhaps the best-known defender of cumulative case arguments for the existence of God. He contends that all of the traditional arguments provide some evidence for God's existence but that, when they are taken together (cumulatively), they make it more probable than not that God exists.

Atheist J.L. Mackie argues that the evidence, when taken cumulatively, makes it overall unlikely that God exists. There are, he contends, adequate naturalistic explanations of all of the phenomena that the theist takes as evidence. Likewise there is the significant improbability of God's existence given the fact of evil. So, given all of the available evidence, it is unlikely that God exists.

Reflections. As in the preceding section, we are faced with the remarkable fact of rational disagreement. Brilliant thinkers, with no obvious cognitive defects (but, perhaps with religious axes to grind), disagree concerning the most fundamental of human questions: Does God exist?

Alvin Plantinga offers up quite a few theistic arguments. While confessing that the project of classical natural theology was a failure, nonetheless the existence and design of the universe do constitute some reason to believe in God. Likewise, other sorts of reasons are on offer: for example, the success of our cognitive equipment, music, and love. In addition, Plantinga offers a rebuttal to Mackie's claim that the existence of God is impossible or unlikely given the fact of evil. Finally, Plantinga briefly defends the thesis that belief in God is rational without the support of an argument.

When it comes to theistic arguments, why do apparently rational people disagree? William Wainwright contends that believing involves not only the intellect but also the will and the passions. Wainwright contrasts the Lockean view of reason (which opposes the influence of the will and the passions on right reason) with the view of Jonathan Edwards (which both admits and affirms that reason cannot function, in some cases, without the influence of the will). Wainwright comes out on the side of Edwards and shows the significance of this view on the assessment of theistic arguments.

Both Wainwright and Plantinga nudge us toward our next section: What makes belief in God rational? In the next section we will consider in detail one such new approach to theistic arguments. I leave it to the reader to consider whether or not theistic arguments have been defended to such an extent that religious belief is rational. I will leave it to another section to discuss whether or not theistic arguments are essential for rational religious belief.

Chapter 1

The Ontological Argument

THE ONTOLOGICAL ARGUMENT

ST. ANSELM AND GAUNILO*

Anselm's argument. *Truly there is a God, although the fool hath said in his heart, There is no God.*

AND SO, Lord, do thou, who dost give understanding to faith, give me, so far as thou knowest it to be profitable, to understand that thou art as we believe; and that thou art that which we believe. And indeed, we believe that thou art a being than which nothing greater can be conceived. Or is there no such nature, since the fool hath said in his heart, there is no God? (Psalms xiv. 1). But, at any rate, this very fool, when he hears of this being of which I speak—a being than which nothing greater can be conceived—understands what he hears, and what he understands is in his understanding; although he does not understand it to exist.

For, it is one thing for an object to be in the understanding, and another to understand that the object exists. When a painter first conceives of what he will afterwards perform, he has it in his understanding, but he does not yet understand it to be, because he has not yet performed it. But after he has made the painting, he

___

* St. Anselm (1033–1109) was a priest, philosopher and theologian. He was appointed Archbishop of Canterbury in 1093. Gaunilo of Marmoutier (near Tours, France) was an eleventh-century monk best known for his critique of Anselm's ontological argument.

both has it in his understanding, and he understands that it exists, because he has made it.

Hence, even the fool is convinced that something exists in the understanding, at least, than which nothing greater can be conceived. For, when he hears of this, he understands it. And whatever is understood, exists in the understanding. And assuredly that, than which nothing greater can be conceived, cannot exist in the understanding alone. For, suppose it exists in the understanding alone: then it can be conceived to exist in reality; which is greater.

Therefore, if that, than which nothing greater can be conceived, exists in the understanding alone, the very being, than which nothing greater can be conceived, is one, than which a greater can be conceived. But obviously this is impossible. Hence, there is no doubt that there exists a being, than which nothing greater can be conceived, and it exists both in the understanding and in reality.

Gaunilo's criticism. It is said that somewhere in the ocean is an island, which, because of the difficulty, or rather the impossibility, of discovering what does not exist, is called the lost island. And they say that this island has an inestimable wealth of all manner of riches and delicacies in greater abundance than is told of the Islands of the Blest; and that having no owner or inhabitant, it is more excellent than all other countries, which are inhabited by mankind, in the abundance with which it is stored.

Now if some one should tell me that there is such an island, I should easily understand his words, in which there is no difficulty. But suppose that he went on to say, as if by a logical inference: "You can no longer doubt that this island which is more excellent than all lands exists somewhere, since you have no doubt that it is in your understanding. And since it is more excellent not to be in the understanding alone, but to exist both in the understanding and in reality, for this reason it must exist. For if it does not exist, any land which really exists will be more excellent than it; and so the island already understood by you to be more excellent will not be more excellent."

If a man should try to prove to me by such reasoning that this island truly exists, and that its existence should no longer be doubted, either I should believe that he was jesting, or I know not which I ought to regard as the greater fool: myself, supposing that I should allow this proof; or him, if he should suppose that he had established with any certainty the existence of this island. For he ought to show first that the hypothetical excellence of this island exists as a real and indubitable fact, and in no wise as any unreal object, or one whose existence is uncertain, in my understanding.

Anselm's reply. But, you say, it is as if one should suppose an island in the ocean, which surpasses all lands in its fertility, and which, because of the difficulty, or the impossibility, of discovering what does not exist, is called a lost island; and should say that there can be no doubt that this island truly exists in reality, for this reason, that one who hears it described easily understands what he hears.

Now I promise confidently that if any man shall devise anything existing either in reality or in concept alone (except that than which a greater be conceived) to which he can adapt the sequence of my reasoning, I will discover that thing, and will give him his lost island, not to be lost again.

But it now appears that this being than which a greater is inconceivable cannot be conceived not to be, because it exists on so assured a ground of truth; for otherwise it would not exist at all.

Hence, if any one says that he conceives this being not to exist, I say that at the time when he conceives of this either he conceives of a being than which a greater is inconceivable, or he does not conceive at all. If he does not conceive, he does not conceive of the non-existence of that of which he does not conceive. But if he does conceive, he certainly conceives of a being which cannot be even conceived not to exist. For if it could be conceived not to exist, it could be conceived to have a beginning and an end. But this is impossible.

He, then, who conceives of this being conceives of a being which cannot be even conceived not to exist; but he who conceives of this being does not conceive that it does not exist; else he conceives what is inconceivable. The non-existence, then, of that than which a greater cannot be conceived is inconceivable.

Discussion

1. To whom does Anselm address his remarks? What do we ordinarily call what he is doing? How does this affect your understanding of the argument?

2. What does he ask God to grant him? What does this imply about his view of the relationship of reason to faith?

3. How does Anselm define God? What does this imply about God?

4. What is the heart of Gaunilo's criticism?

5. What is the heart of Anselm's reply?

ONTOLOGICAL ARGUMENTS FOR GOD'S EXISTENCE

LAURA GARCIA*

Background. The search for a sound proof of the existence of God, using premises that can be known independently of experience, has inspired philosophers from St. Anselm in the eleventh century to Norman Malcolm and Alvin Plantinga in recent decades. While Anselm's argument began from the definition of God as the greatest conceivable being ("that than which none greater can be conceived") and sought to show that a being so conceived must exist, Malcolm and Plantinga begin from the possibility of a perfect being and argue that, given the standard theistic understanding of God, for God's existence to be possible is for it to be necessary. The common element in so-called *ontological proofs* is that they attempt to prove the actual being or existence of God beginning from God's conceivability or possibility. It's easy to see that, typically anyway, arguments of the form *X possibly exists, therefore X exists* are invalid. Such arguments could prove the actual existence of anything from unicorns to jackalopes. But defenders of ontological arguments hold that, in the case of God, reasoning similar to this one can be logically sound.[1]

A *modal argument* for God's existence is one that employs the notions of logical possibility and necessity, as these have been described by philosophers as types or modes of propositions. For example, mathematical propositions like *three is greater than two* are necessarily true, while many scientific claims, such as *salt dissolves in water*, are contingently true (while true, they could have been false). Similarly, some falsehoods are contingently false (while false, they could have been true); for example *humans can run a mile in three minutes*; finally, some propositions are impossible or

necessarily false, e.g., *Barbara is older than herself*. Here we will consider a modal version of the ontological argument proposed by Alvin Plantinga which begins from the possibility of a certain kind of perfect being and concludes that a perfect being exists necessarily, that is, that its nonexistence is impossible. In order to evaluate this argument, we need some understanding of the concepts and principles he employs.

Preliminary definitions. Recent work in *modal logic* (which studies the relationships among modal propositions) appeals to the notion of possible worlds to interpret modal concepts like "possible" and "necessary." To understand possible worlds, we need to know what is meant by a *state of affairs*. A state of affairs corresponds to a proposition in the following way: if the proposition *p* is true, then the state of affairs *S* "picked out" by *p* obtains. For instance, the proposition that *the Chicago Cubs win the World Series in 2004* picks out the state of affairs of the Cubs winning the league pennant and then the World Series in 2004. This happens to be a state of affairs that does not obtain (is not part of the actual world).

It is a separate question whether unrealized states of affairs *exist*, but many philosophers (including Plantinga) argue that they do. Just as false propositions may still exist in some sense (since we refer to them and assign them a truth-value), so states of affairs that don't obtain might still exist. They are not part of the world of concrete entities, however, and do not causally interact with it. If they are entities of some sort, they are *abstract entities*. The state of affairs described above, though it does not obtain and seemed less than probable at the beginning of the 2004 season even to diehard Cubs fans, is nevertheless a possible state of affairs. It is one that might have obtained. Perhaps its obtaining is even consistent with the physical laws of the universe remaining as they are (though this might be open to debate; some would have seen a World Series trophy for the Cubs as a certifiable miracle), but

---

*   Laura Garcia teaches Philosophy at Boston College.

that is a separate question. One way of putting the possibility involved here is by saying that in some possible world (different from the actual world) it is true that the Cubs win the World Series in 2004; in that world, the state of affairs of a Cubs world championship in 2004 obtains.

A *possible world* can be defined as a maximal, consistent state of affairs. Two states of affairs S1 and S2 are consistent with each other if it's possible for them to obtain together or be co-instantiated. Any world with states of affairs that cannot obtain together would clearly not be a *possible* world; it would not be one that could itself obtain or be actual. Further, a possible world must be maximal, in that it says something about everything. For every possible word W and every proposition *p*, either *p* is true in *W* or *it's not the case that p* is true in *W*. In the actual world, it is false that unicorns exist, but there are possible worlds where they do exist. Numbers, on the other hand, exist in every possible world, since in every world it will be true that *four and four are eight*, and square circles exist in no possible world. If square circles are impossible beings, then, a *necessary being* is a being that exists in every possible world.

The terminology of possible worlds enables us to distinguish between a wider and narrower sense of the word "necessary." Some philosophers restrict this term to mathematical propositions and propositions such that their denials generate a contradiction within first-order logic. But numerous necessary propositions fall into neither of these categories. Examples include definitional truths (*No bachelor is married*), necessities of ontological category (*No prime minister is a prime number*), necessities of identity (*Dr. Jekyll is Mr. Hyde*), and necessities of composition (*Water is H_2O*). Some necessary truths are *a priori* in that they can be known independently of actual experience of the world, but some are *a posteriori*, such as the last two examples given above. The wider notion of necessity, *broadly logical necessity*, includes all those states of affairs that obtain in every possible world and every proposition that is true in every possible world.

Conceivable does not entail possible. What is logically necessary in the broad sense cannot always be determined simply by examining our concepts, then. Similarly, what is logically possible will depend not just on what we can conceive, but on what is in fact compatible with all (broadly) necessary truths. Surely if a state of affairs obtains then it must be a possible state of affairs, so that is one way of determining what is possible. But we cannot move from the claim that a state of affairs is conceivable to the claim that is a possible state of affairs. It is conceivable that water should have had some other molecular composition, yet *Water is H_2O* is a necessary truth. Further, some mathematical claims, such as Goldbach's Conjecture (every even number is the sum of two prime numbers), have been neither proved nor disproved, so it is conceivable that *Goldbach's Conjecture is true* and also conceivable that *Goldbach's Conjecture is false*. But since mathematical theorems are necessary propositions (either necessarily true or necessarily false), if Goldbach's Conjecture is possibly true, it is necessarily true, and if it is false, it is necessarily false (impossible). So we cannot move from *conceivably p* to *possibly p* in this case without winding up in a contradiction—Goldbach's Conjecture will be necessarily true and necessarily false at the same time.

In many cases it may be that we have little more to guide us in determining the modal status of a proposition other than our intuitions about whether the concepts involved are internally compatible. We might propose that *conceivably p* justifies an inference to *it is prima facie possible that p*, recognizing that what is conceivable may still turn out to be impossible, since it might conflict with some necessary truths in ways we did not anticipate. It might be internally possible, so to speak, but not "compossible" with all the necessary features of reality that there are. On the other hand, the inference from *p is inconceivable* to *p is logically impossible* seems safe enough, since it picks out a kind of internal incoherence or incompatibility that is accessible *a priori*. But for reasons just given, not every impossible state of affairs will be inconceivable.

A final comment before we look at Plantinga's proof for God. Plantinga assumes, along with most philosophers, that possibility and necessity are fixed or stable properties of the propositions or states of affairs they modify. Could what is necessary have been merely contingent, or even impossible? It seems not, since this would lead to a deep incoherence in our reasoning. It is inconceivable that something should be red but not colored, or that two and two should add up to five— we cannot make sense out of the idea that what is in fact impossible somehow might have been possible. An occasional philosopher (e.g., René Descartes) has been attracted to the idea that the laws of logic and all other truths are subject to the will of God, so that God could bring it about that two and two are five or that God himself both exists and doesn't exist at the same time. But this would lead to such a deep skepticism about the trustworthiness of our reasoning faculties that it's hard to know even how to defend this view, or how to differentiate it from the opposing view. (After all, both could be true if Descartes is right.) Plantinga rejects the Cartesian proposal, then, and assumes that what is possible is necessarily possible and, more important for our purposes, that what is possibly necessary (or necessary in some possible world) is simply necessary. What is necessary cannot vary from one possible world to another (nor can what is contingent or what is impossible vary in this way).

Anselm's ontological argument. One of St. Anselm's insights is that things that don't (actually) exist have no level of greatness at all; they have no actual perfections (non-existent "things" have no properties or perfections at all). In order to have a certain level of power or knowledge or goodness or beauty, a thing must first exist. If there are no unicorns (if the property being-a-unicorn is not instantiated), there is obviously no fastest or strongest unicorn. Many athletes have impressive abilities in the actual world, but there are possible worlds where they are slow or flabby, and possible worlds where they do not exist at all. Anselm's point is that just as Patriots' quarterback Tom Brady has zero passing ability in worlds in which he doesn't exist, so the greatest conceivable being must at least exist in order to be the greatest being. Anselm's proof begins from a definition of God as the *greatest conceivable being*, or the most perfect being possible, and concludes to the actual existence of this being. The greatest being we can conceive of would have such perfections as omniscience, omnipotence, and moral perfection, of course. But since any being that does not actually exist cannot be the greatest possible being, God must actually exist.[2]

Many criticize Anselm's proof for failing to distinguish between what belongs to God *by definition* and what belongs to God *in fact* (in the actual world). Graham Oppy argues that all such definitional arguments for God's existence are either logically invalid (the conclusion does not follow from the premises) or they beg the question (in that no one would accept the premises who did not already accept the conclusion). Oppy represents the typical definitional argument for God as taking the following form:

(1) God is an existent supremely perfect being. (By definition of "God")

(2) Hence, according to the preceding definition, God exists. (From (1))

(3) Hence, God exists.

If we assume that in (1) the name "God" refers to an (actually) existing being, then no one would accept (1) who doesn't already accept (3). If instead we take

(1) as simply a definition that leaves open the question of whether God exists (in the actual world), then (3) does not follow from (1). What follows is simply that God must exist in order to be God; but this is trivially true, and is true even of things that don't exist. In order to be a fox, a creature has to at least exist, but that doesn't tell us whether or not there are (in the actual world) any foxes. So including existence within the definition of "God" does not yield a persuasive proof of God's existence. An objection similar to this one is often attributed to the eighteenth-century German philosopher Immanuel Kant.

Modal arguments for God's existence. Plantinga concludes from Kantian-style objections to the ontological argument that Anselm may have intended to put forward a different argument, one that relies on the point that necessary existence is greater than contingent existence. Anselm does suggest, in the passages following his initial statement of the argument, that God exists so truly that he cannot be conceived not to exist. Perhaps a better way of putting this would be that God's nonexistence is impossible, or that God is by definition a necessary being. Adding necessary existence to the list of perfections in the definition of "God" means that if it is possible that God exists, God's existence is necessary. Recall that what is possibly necessary is necessary. Thus, if there is any possible world in which God exists necessarily, God exists necessarily; he will exist in every possible world, including the actual world. Norman Malcolm, writing in 1960, capitalized on this hint in Anselm's work to formulate a modal argument for God:

(1) It's possible that there is a being that is omnipotent, omniscient, and morally perfect and exists necessarily. (Premise)

(2) Hence, there exists in every possible world a being that is omnipotent, omniscient, and

morally perfect. (From (1) and theorems of modal logic)[3]

Alvin Plantinga applauds the modal approach, but criticizes Malcolm's argument for failing to account for the fact that a being's properties may vary from world to world (recall the Tom Brady example). In the present case, even if the argument shows that in some possible world W^* there exists a being that *in that world* has necessary existence, omnipotence, omniscience, and moral perfection, the being might be ignorant or morally weak in worlds other than W^*. It might *exist* in every possible world, that is, but without carrying with it the divine perfections in every world. This leads Plantinga to formulate his own version of the modal argument for God, one that includes in the definition of a most perfect being that the being must have its perfections essentially. Features *essential* to a being are those it has in every possible world in which it exists. Being human is essential to Socrates, let's assume, so Socrates is human in every possible world in which he exists. If omniscience, omnipotence and moral perfection are essential to God, he has them in every possible world in which he exists. Theists typically hold that God's perfections belong to him essentially in this way—that God doesn't just happen to be all-powerful or morally perfect but he could not fail to be so. Plantinga combines these three perfections in the property of *maximal excellence*: a being exemplifies maximal excellence if it exemplifies omniscience, omnipotence and moral perfection. An even more robust property is *maximal greatness*: a being exemplifies maximal greatness if it exemplifies maximal excellence in every possible world. Maximal greatness entails necessary existence, since a being cannot exemplify maximal excellence in a world without existing in that world. A being that exemplifies maximal excellence in every possible world must exist in every possible world.

With these definitions in hand, we can state Plantinga's modal proof concisely as follows:

(P) Possibly there is a maximally great being.

(C) Necessarily there is a maximally great being. (From P)[4]

If a maximally great being exists in any possible world, then there exists in that world a being that has maximal excellence in every possible world (and so exists in every possible world). Maximal greatness cannot be exemplified anywhere, as it were, without being exemplified everywhere. It follows from (C) of course that there is a maximally great being in the actual world, and hence that God (defined as a maximally great being) exists.

Objections to Plantinga's modal argument. Attacks on formal proofs of this kind take two forms: either the proof is *logically invalid* (the conclusion does not follow logically from the premises) or the proof is *logically unsound* (either it is invalid or the premise is false or dubious). Some challenge the validity of Plantinga's argument based on a denial of the axiom of modal logic that states that possibility and necessity cannot vary from one possible world to another—that they are necessarily what they are. Without this axiom, of course, (C) does not follow from (P). But since turning possibility and necessity into contingent features of things leads to incoherence, it's not clear that this objection carries much serious weight.

Another attack on the argument relies on the claim that there can't be any such thing as a necessary being, so any argument that concludes to the existence of such a being must be unsound. This attack relies on restricting the concept of necessity to *a priori* propositions along logical truths, mathematical truths, and other clear conceptual truths. But as we have seen, such a restriction overlooks necessities of other kinds. If reflecting on the concepts involved leads one to believe that (P) is indeed true, then there is at least *prima facie* reason to accept it. Recall our earlier principle that conceivability supports *prima facie* possibility.

Mark Strasser proposes a related objection to Plantinga's argument. If one grants the conclusion of that argument, this entails that *maximal excellence is necessarily exemplified*. From this it follows, Strasser says, that "we are committed to the inconceivability of the non-existence of maximal excellence."[5] But in fact that stronger claim does not follow. Accepting that a proposition *p* is necessary (or that a certain concept is necessarily exemplified) commits one to the *impossibility* of *not-p*, but not the *inconceivability* of *not-p*. According to Saul Kripke, the claim that *the Morning Star is not the Evening Star* is impossible but conceivable; indeed, many believed it to be true until advances in astronomy indicated otherwise. The same holds for many other necessities of identity, of ontological category, and of composition. As Strasser points out, if the conclusion of Plantinga's argument is that God's nonexistence is *inconceivable*, then anyone who can conceive of God's nonexistence must deny the conclusion of the argument (and reject the premise as well). So if he is right, even most theists would have to reject the argument, since most believe that God's nonexistence is at least conceivable. But just as *conceivably p* does not entail *possibly p*, *not possibly p* does not entail *p is inconceivable*.[6]

More formidable criticisms of the modal argument focus on the plausibility of the premise. Plantinga himself raised some difficulties for (P) in the section just after he presents the modal proof. One problem is that there are premises similar to (P), in that they describe properties which are either necessarily instantiated or necessarily not instantiated, and that seem to have the same kind of initial plausibility that (P) has. But if they are true, then (P) is necessarily false, and if (P) is true, then these rival premises are necessarily false. One example Plantinga gives is:

(N) No-maximality is possibly exemplified. [No-maximality is possessed by any entity that exists in a world in which there is no maximally great being.]

If (N) is true, then in some possible world there exists a being that is in less than perfect company, since in that world there is no maximally great being. But if there is no maximally great being in some possible world, there is no maximally great being in any possible world—maximal greatness must be exemplified in every possible world or in none.

To make matters worse, there are a number of other rival premises, similar to that are likewise incompatible with (P). Plantinga discusses the property of near-maximality, which is exemplified by any being which does not exist in every world but has a degree of greatness not exceeded by any being in any world. If near-maximality is possibly exemplified, then of course maximal greatness is not possibly exemplified, for there will be a possible world in which there is a less-than-perfect being whose greatness is unsurpassed by any being in any possible world.

Finally, parodies of the ontological argument can be produced for an infinite number of lesser deities, beings that lack one or more of the perfections dear to Anselmian philosophers and theologians. One could replace (P) with claims like the following:

(Q1) It's possible that there is a being that exists necessarily and is essentially omniscient and essentially omnipotent and essentially morally imperfect (or perhaps just contingently perfect).

(Q2) It's possible that there is a being that exists necessarily and is essentially morally perfect and essentially omniscient but essentially has only power of degree n.

Especially in the case of (Q2), we seem in danger of proving the existence of an infinite number of deities of varying degrees of power (or knowledge or goodness), so that the ontological argument becomes in effect too successful. Also, some considerations favoring the plausibility of (P), that it is conceivably true for example, work just as well to support the rival premises. If there is no reason to prefer (P) to the alternatives, then although one could still endorse Plantinga's argument, one would have no rational grounds for refusing to endorse the parallel arguments, which seems to commit one to a universe populated by an alarming number of deities or near-deities (in the case of the Q-family of arguments) or to contradictory conclusions (in the case of no-maximality and near-maximality).

Replies to the objections. We should first consider Plantinga's reply to the sorts of arguments that render maximal greatness impossible. Even though it is rational (Plantinga thinks) for someone to accept one of the rival premises, it is also rational to accept (P) itself, and hence to reject any proposition incompatible with it. Here Plantinga cites an analogy with another modal claim, Leibniz's Law (sometimes called "The Indiscernibility of Identicals"):

(LL) Necessarily, for any objects x and y and property P, if x=y, then x has P if and only if y has P.

Plantinga suggests, as part of the justification for believing (LL) and similar claims, that if we "carefully ponder" the proposition and the objections to it, "if we consider its connections with other propositions we accept or reject and still find it compelling, we are within our rights in accepting it—and this whether or not we can convince others."[7] If someone considers (P) and it seems plausible to her, even after considering other propositions she accepts, then she is within her (epistemic) rights in accepting (P). Further, if she accepts (C) because it follows from (P), then she is rational in accepting theism. If (P) and its rival premises seem to her to be situated exactly similarly with respect to everything she knows and seem equally plausible to her, then perhaps she should withhold belief for the time being, though even this might be debated.[8] Plantinga's claim for the modal argument, then, is that it can render belief in God rational, even if it does not render unbelief irrational. Earlier defenders of the ontological proof (like Anselm) thought it could be shown that anyone who denies the existence of God is foolish or irrational, but Plantinga does not make this stronger claim for his version of the argument.

Still, some critics deny that Plantinga has succeeded even in the more modest goal of showing belief in God to be rational. Graham Oppy claims that it is rational to accept the theistic conclusion on the basis of (P) only if it is rational to accept (P). He then notes that applying Plantinga's strategy above, that is, considering the connections of (P) with other propositions one accepts or rejects, will likely lead theists to consider whether there is (in fact) a being that possesses maximal greatness (recall that whatever is actual is possible). But then their acceptance of (P) will not be suitably independent of their acceptance of the conclusion (C), so that Plantinga's argument will not make accepting (C) any more rational for theists than it was before. Their belief in God will be just as rational or irrational as it was without this argument.[9]

In reply to Oppy, it might be urged that a person could consider the premise of Plantinga's argument without having an opinion about the conclusion, and could then come to accept theism on that basis. Oppy concedes that this is possible in principle, but he refuses to grant that such a person (call him Sam) is automatically rational in believing in God, since we do not yet know whether he is rational in accepting (P). Further, even if Sam is rational in arriving at (C) initially (because of Plantinga's argument), he might not

be rational in continuing to believe (C) once he considers the parallel arguments mentioned above. This last constraint on rationality seems much too strong, however. Surely a positive assessment of Sam's rationality need not be put on hold until he has opportunity to consider all possible objections to his beliefs. So unless Sam accepts (P) for bad reasons (or no reasons at all), we can assume Sam is rational in accepting (C) on the basis of (P).

What then of the person who is familiar with Oppy's objection to the modal argument, that exactly parallel arguments can be constructed to prove an infinite number of pseudo-deities? Here I think the obvious response is to claim that there is an asymmetry between the premise of Plantinga's argument and premises proposing the possibility of lesser beings. With respect to (N) and its kind, one might find the idea of no-maximality inherently implausible, since no-maximality is a sort of *ad hoc* property that renders maximal greatness impossible without showing any internal incoherence in it or pointing to any necessary features of reality that would in some way exclude it (other than no-maximality itself). With respect to (Q)-style arguments, it might be intuitively plausible to hold that maximal greatness is possibly exemplified and intuitively implausible that lesser perfections (or imperfections) could be combined with necessary existence in a personal being. These intuitions would render (P) much more plausible than any of the rival hypotheses. Unless appeals to intuition are out of bounds when considering modal claims like (P), then someone with these intuitions who accepts theism on the basis of Plantinga's argument is certainly within her epistemic rights and is (so far) rational.[10] (Note that her acceptance of (P) here is based on intuitions about necessary existence and perfection, not on her prior acceptance of (C).) Oppy is right to point out that the argument remains "dialectically impotent" against anyone who does not share these modal intuitions with respect to (P). But, as Plantinga points out, "the same goes for any number of philosophical claims and ideas. Indeed, philosophy contains little else. Were we to believe only [that] for which there are incontestable arguments from uncontested premises, we should find ourselves with a pretty slim and pretty dull philosophy."[11]

In a further attempt to discredit the rationality of accepting Plantinga's premise, William Rowe argues that whenever we encounter a deep-seated (seemingly unresolvable) conflict of intuitions, the only acceptable stance is to withhold belief. Since there is deep-seated disagreement about the plausibility of (P), the rational person will withhold belief in (P) pending further input. But withholding belief in a claim that is intuitively obvious may be psychologically impossible in some cases, and in any event it's not clear that philosophy would progress very far if we restricted our beliefs according to Rowe's rule. After all, some philosophers claim to have the intuition that the law of non-contradiction could be false, and according to Aristotle, there is no way to demonstrate from prior principles that these people are wrong. Surely we don't have to withhold belief in this law until we have convinced all comers of its truth and necessity.[12]

Similar considerations show that R. Kane is mistaken in claiming that the defender of Plantinga's argument must *prove* its major premise, perhaps by proving: "(N*) By definition, all beings having necessary existence are perfect."[13] Suppose Ann simply considers (N*) and finds it plausible, and so finds (P) more plausible than any of its rivals. Or suppose she simply considers (P) and the rival premises and (P) just seems more plausible in its own right. Then surely Ann is rational to accept (P) even in the absence of a demonstration either of (P) or (N*). Rowe thinks this is insufficient for calling Ann rational, however. He claims that we need a theory about when accepting a claim because it seems true (or plausible, or more probable than not) is rational and when it isn't.[14] Again, this demand is too strong. It's true that Ann's belief may not qualify as rational if it has been accepted on a whim or out of spite or to impress a friend, and even if her belief is rational initially, it might cease to be so once she considers various objections or if she begins to doubt the reliability of her reasoning faculties. This is why Plantinga describes the standard believer in (P) as someone who has "pondered" it, considered criticisms, reflected on its relationships to other propositions he believes, and the like. But it's hard to imagine any full theory of the rationality of intuitions that will rule out the acceptance of (P) while leaving in place the acceptance of other philosophically contested claims. And few philosophers feel the need to develop any such theory before they commit themselves to a belief in Leibniz's Law, say, or to the axioms of modal logic, or to a host of other such philosophical "starting points."

One could accept Kane's challenge, of course, and try to provide an argument for (P) along the lines he suggests, proving that any necessary (concrete) being must exemplify maximal excellence. St. Thomas Aquinas argues in the *Summa Theologica*, for example, that a being that exists necessarily is one whose essence is to exist, and such a being must also be omnipotent, omniscient, and perfectly good. It might be some support for (P) in fact, to urge that it is the only one of the competing premises considered here that is compatible with the conclusion of standard cosmological arguments, assuming that these have some plausibility of their own. Alternatively, one might appeal to a principle of simplicity to defend the greater plausibility of (P) over its rivals. Richard Swinburne argues that the hypothesis of a being with infinite power and knowledge is simpler than the hypothesis of a being with finite perfections, since the latter requires further explanations as to why the being has precisely this range of power or knowledge rather than a little more or a little less.

In one further creative approach to justifying (P), Thomas Morris urges the dismissal of (Q)-style deities by appealing to additional modal intuitions. He argues for the intuitive plausibility of:

(D) Any non-divine created person has a *prima facie* duty to be thankful to God for his existence.

And it might be a conceptual truth that:

(T) Thankfulness is possible only for what could have been otherwise.

Since there cannot be any obligation to do what is impossible, it must be possible for any non-divine person to be thankful to God for his or her existence. Hence (by (T)) it must be possible that he or she might not have existed. This would render all (Q)-style deities in Oppy's examples impossible, since each is a non-divine person who is said to exist necessarily.[15] It's true that Morris's strategy risks bringing in further controversial elements, but as Plantinga reminds us, philosophy flourishes only when we are willing to take a few risks.

Notes

1. Many philosophers (including Alvin Plantinga) deny that there are *possible beings*, preferring to speak instead of *properties that are possibly exemplified*. For example, *Frodo is a possible being* translates into *Being-identical-with-Frodo is possibly exemplified*. Properties like being-identical-with-Frodo must be exemplified by one and the same being in every possible world in which they are exemplified at all. Such properties are sometimes called individual essences or *haecceities*. Throughout this chapter, I will continue to speak of possible beings, as this locution is more colloquial and can always

be translated into language about possibly instantiated properties.

2. Some argue that God's perfections cannot be co-exemplified, since (for example) omnipotence requires the power to do evil and moral perfection requires that one *cannot* do evil. These problems might be resolved by defining the perfections in such a way that they do not entail any contradictory claims. On the definition of "omnipotence," see Alfred Freddoso and Thomas Flint, "Maximal Power," in Alfred Freddoso, ed. *The Existence and Nature of God* (Notre Dame: U of Notre Dame P, 1983).

3. See "Anselm's Ontological Arguments," *Philosophical Review* 9 (1960): 41–62.

4. In more precise language, the argument reads: (P) Possibly maximal greatness is exemplified; therefore (C) Necessarily maximal greatness is exemplified. The argument relies on an axiom of modal logic which states that what is possible is necessarily possible.

5. "Leibniz, Plantinga and the Test for Existence in a Possible World," *International Journal for Philosophy of Religion* 18 (1985): 153–59. Strasser here speaks of maximal excellence existing, though it would be more accurate to speak instead of its being exemplified, since in a platonist metaphysics, even unexemplified properties exist.

6. Logically, the first of these claims reads: *Possibly (Cp and not Pp)*, or *it is possible that* p *is conceivable but not possible*. The second claim is: *Possibly (not Pp and Cp)*, or *it is possible that* p *is impossible but still conceivable*. The claims are logically equivalent.

7. *God, Freedom and Evil* (London: Allen and Unwin, 1974), pp. 220–21.

8. In a famous and much-anthologized essay, William James argues that when faced with an option between two beliefs, where the option is live, forced, and momentous, and reason cannot decide the matter, our passional nature (our desires, including our desire for happiness) may lawfully enter in to determine our commitment to one side or the other. See *The Will to Believe* (New York: Longmans, Green & Co., 1897), reprinted (in part) in Louis Pojman, ed. *Philosophy of Religion: An Anthology*, 3rd ed. (Belmont, CA: Wadsworth, 1998), pp. 404–12.

9. See Oppy's *Ontological Arguments and Belief in God* (New York: Cambridge, 1995), pp. 191–92.

10. For an argument on the other side, see William Rowe, "Modal Versions of the Ontological Argument," in Louis Pojman, ed. *Philosophy of Religion: An Anthology*, 3rd ed. (Belmont, CA: Wadsworth, 1998), pp. 88–92. Rowe's intuitions are that (N) is *a priori* more plausible than (P) because (1) it is narrower in scope in that it only makes a claim about *one* possible world (though of course it has implications for every possible world) and (2) it is simpler, in positing fewer beings than (P) does. These claims in turn presuppose that the *a priori* probability of a theory (or claim) is enhanced if it has the features Rowe mentions, and that (N) rates higher with respect to these than does (P). Not everyone will agree with Rowe on these claims.

11. Op. cit., p. 220.

12. See "An Examination of the Cosmological Argument," in Louis Pojman, ed. *Philosophy of Religion: An Anthology*, 3rd ed. (Belmont, CA: Wadsworth, 1998), pp. 15–24. Concerning the Principle of Sufficient Reason, Rowe says that "a number of very able philosophers fail to apprehend its truth, and some even claim that the principle is false. It is doubtful, therefore, that many of us, if any, know intuitively that PSR is true" (p. 23). On the other hand, Rowe grants that PSR may be a presupposition of reason; it's just that we cannot be certain that what reason presupposes is in fact true. It's hard to see how either of these considerations would convince someone who finds PSR intuitively evident, or who takes presuppositions of reason to be as good an indicator of truth as any we are likely to find, that belief in PSR is unjustified or doesn't qualify as at least *rational*. Showing that those with different intuitions should accept it is another matter, of course.

13. See R. Kane, "The Modal Ontological Argument," *Mind* 93 (1984): 336–50.

14. Rowe says that to *establish* that theistic belief based on Plantinga's modal argument is rational, "requires that we become clear that its premise satisfies all the circumstances (whatever they are) that are required for it to be permissible to believe a proposition even though we cannot prove it and don't have any good evidence for it." ("Modal Versions of the Ontological Argument," p. 92). But it's not obvious that the burden of proof rests on Plantinga to develop a criterion of rationality, acceptable to every philosopher, according to which someone in Ann's circumstances is "evidently" rational in believing (P). (For one

thing, if it seems evident to Plantinga that Ann's accepting (P) in these circumstances is rational, presumably any criterion that renders her belief irrational would be suspect for him.) Perhaps the burden of proof is on Rowe to develop a universally-accepted theory of rationality according to which Ann's acceptance of (P) is *not* rational. After all, the claim that someone's belief is rational is a relatively modest one.

15. For Morris's argument, see "Necessary Beings," *Mind* 94 (1985): 263–72. With respect to supposed necessary entities that are material objects, Morris suggests appealing either to the intuition that no material object can exist necessarily or to a companion principle to (D), namely: (D) It is possible for a created non-divine person to be thankful to God for any part of his natural causal environment.

Discussion

1. In your own words: What is a possible world?

2. What is the property of maximal greatness?

3. If a maximally great being is possible, a maximally great being is necessary. Rewrite this in possible worlds language.

4. Present one objection to Plantinga's argument and the response.

Chapter 2

The Cosmological Argument

THE FIVE WAYS

THOMAS AQUINAS*

Claim. The existence of God can be proved in five ways.

The argument from motion. The first and more manifest way is the argument from motion. It is certain, and evident to our senses, that in the world some things are in motion. Now whatever is in motion is put in motion by another, for nothing can be in motion except it is in potentiality to that towards which it is in motion; whereas a thing moves inasmuch as it is in act. For motion is nothing else than the reduction of something from potentiality to actuality. But nothing can be reduced from potentiality to actuality, except by something in a state of actuality. Thus that which is actually hot, as fire, makes wood, which is potentially hot, to be actually hot, and thereby moves and changes it. Now it is not possible that the same thing should be at once in actuality and potentiality in the same respect, but only in different respects. For what is actually hot cannot simultaneously be potentially hot; but it is simultaneously potentially cold. It is therefore impossible that in the same respect and in the same way a thing should be both mover and moved, i.e., that it should move itself. Therefore, whatever is in motion must be put in motion by another. If that by which it is put in motion be itself put in motion, then this also must needs be put in motion by another, and that by another again. But this cannot go on to infinity, because then there would be no first mover, and, consequently, no other mover; seeing that subsequent movers move only inasmuch as they are put in motion by the first mover; as the staff moves only because it is put in motion by the hand. Therefore it is necessary to arrive at a first mover, put in motion by no other; and this everyone understands to be God.

Argument from the nature of efficient causes. The second way is from the nature of the efficient cause. In the world of sense we find there is an order of efficient causes. There is no case known (neither is it, indeed, possible) in which a thing is found to be the efficient cause of itself; for so it would be prior to itself, which is impossible. Now in efficient causes it is not possible to go on to infinity, because in all efficient causes following in order, the first is the cause of the intermediate cause, and the intermediate is the cause of the ultimate cause, whether the intermediate cause be several, or only one. Now to take away the cause is to take away the effect. Therefore, if there be no first cause among efficient causes, there will be no ultimate, nor any intermediate cause. But if in efficient causes it is possible to go on to infinity, there will be no first efficient cause, neither will there be an ultimate effect, nor any intermediate efficient causes; all of which is plainly false. Therefore it is necessary to admit a first efficient cause, to which everyone gives the name of God.

---

* Thomas Aquinas (1225–74), an Italian philosopher-theologian, taught at the University of Paris.

Argument from possibility. The third way is taken from possibility and necessity, and runs thus. We find in nature things that are possible to be and not to be, since they are found to be generated, and to corrupt, and consequently, they are possible to be and not to be. But it is impossible for these always to exist, for that which is possible not to be at some time is not. Therefore, if everything is possible not to be, then at one time there could have been nothing in existence. Now if this were true, even now there would be nothing in existence, because that which does not exist only begins to exist by something already existing. Therefore, if at one time nothing was in existence, it would have been impossible for anything to have begun to exist; and thus even now nothing would be in existence—which is absurd. Therefore, not all beings are merely possible, but there must exist something the existence of which is necessary. But every necessary thing either has its necessity caused by another, or not. Now it is impossible to go on to infinity in necessary things which have their necessity caused by another, as has been already proved in regard to efficient causes. Therefore we cannot but postulate the existence of some being having of itself its own necessity, and not receiving it from another, but rather causing in others their necessity. This all men speak of as God.

The argument from gradation. The fourth way is taken from the gradation to be found in things. Among beings there are some more and some less good, true, noble and the like. But "more" and "less" are predicated of different things, according as they resemble in their different ways something which is the maximum, as a thing is said to be hotter according as it more nearly resembles that which is hottest; so that there is something which is truest, something best, something noblest and, consequently, something which is uttermost being; for those things that are greatest in truth are greatest in being, as it is written in *Metaph.*

ii. Now the maximum in any genus is the cause of all in that genus; as fire, which is the maximum heat, is the cause of all hot things. Therefore there must also be something which is to all beings the cause of their being, goodness, and every other perfection; and this we call God.

The teleological argument. The fifth way is taken from the governance of the world. We see that things which lack intelligence, such as natural bodies, act for an end, and this is evident from their acting always, or nearly always, in the same way, so as to obtain the best result. Hence it is plain that not fortuitously, but designedly, do they achieve their end. Now whatever lacks intelligence cannot move towards an end, unless it be directed by some being endowed with knowledge and intelligence; as the arrow is shot to its mark by the archer. Therefore some intelligent being exists by whom all natural things are directed to their end; and this being we call God.

Discussion

1. Which of Aquinas's Five Ways seems, at first glance, the most plausible? Why?

2. Do any of the arguments give you the impression that Aquinas is playing a logical trick? Where do you think the "trick" is located?

3. What exactly would each argument, if cogent, prove about the *nature* of God?

4. Suppose that you, like Aquinas, wished to argue for the existence of God based on the best scientific knowledge (*scientia*) of your day. Where do you think you might start? Are there items of knowledge which you think are best explained by the existence of God?

ON THE ULTIMATE ORIGINATION OF THINGS

GOTTFRIED WILHELM LEIBNIZ*

The sufficient reason for existence. Besides the world or aggregate of finite things we find a certain Unity which is dominant, not only in the sense in which the soul is dominant in me, or rather in which the self or *I* is dominant in my body, but also in a much more exalted manner. For the dominant Unity of the universe not only rules the world, but also constructs or makes it; and it is higher than the world and, if I may so put it, extramundane; it is thus the ultimate reason of things. Now neither in any one single thing, nor in the whole aggregate and series of things, can there be found the sufficient reason of existence. Let us suppose the book of the elements of geometry to have been eternal, one copy always having been written down from an earlier one; it is evident that, even though a reason can be given for the present book out of a past one, nevertheless out of any number of books taken in order going backwards we shall never come upon a full reason; though we might well always wonder why there should have been such books from all time—why there were books at all, and why they were written in this manner. What is true of the books is true also of the different states of the world; for what follows is in some way copied from what precedes (even though there are certain laws of change). And so, however far you go back to earlier states, you will never find in those states a full reason why there should be any world rather than none, and why it should be such as it is.

What if the world were eternal? Indeed, even if you suppose the world eternal, as you will still be supposing

nothing but a succession of states and will not in any of them find a sufficient reason, nor however many states you assume will you advance one step towards giving a reason, it is evident that the reason must be sought elsewhere. For in things which are eternal, though there may be no cause, nevertheless there must be known a reason; which reason in things that are permanent is necessity itself or essence, but in the series of changeable things (if this be supposed to be an eternal succession from an earlier to a later) it will be, as will be presently understood, the prevailing of inclinations, in a sphere where reasons do not necessitate (by an absolute or metaphysical necessity, in which the contrary implies a contradiction), but incline. From this it is evident that even by supposing the world to be eternal we cannot escape the ultimate, extra-mundane reason of things, or God.

The metaphysically necessary being. The reasons of the world then lie in something extra-mundane, different from the chain of states, or series of things, whose aggregate constitutes the world. And so we must pass from physical or hypothetical necessity, which determines the subsequent things of the world by the earlier, to something which is of absolute or metaphysical necessity, for which itself no reason can be given. For the present world is necessary physically or hypothetically, but not absolutely or metaphysically. In other words, when once it is determined that it shall be such and such, it follows that such and such things will come into being. Since then the ultimate root must be in something which is of metaphysical necessity, and since there is no reason of any existent thing except in an existent thing, it follows that there must exist some one Being of metaphysical necessity, that is, from whose essence existence springs; and so there must exist something different from the plurality of beings, that is the world, which, as we have allowed and have shown, is not of metaphysical necessity.

---

* Gottfried Wilhelm Leibniz (1646–1716) was a German philosopher, scientist, mathematician, and diplomat.

Discussion

1. Leibniz's argument relies on *the principle of sufficient reason*: for every positive fact there is a sufficient reason why that fact obtains. Do you think this principle is true? What would have to be the case if the principle of sufficient reason were false?

2. The principle of sufficient reason does not claim that we can *know* the explanation of every fact, but it claims that there *is* an adequate explanation of every fact. Do you think there are facts that have no explanation? Try to think of an unexplainable fact.

3. Reflect on Leibniz's claim that if the world (the universe) were eternal, it would still require an extra-mundane explanation of its eternal existence. Does that seem right to you? Why or why not?

THE KALAAM VERSION OF THE COSMOLOGICAL ARGUMENT

WILLIAM LANE CRAIG*

Why is there something? "The first question which should rightly be asked," wrote the great German philosopher and mathematician Gottfried Wilhelm Leibniz, "is: Why is there something rather than nothing?" Think about that for a moment. Why *does* anything exist at all, rather than nothing? Why does the universe, or matter, or anything at all exist, instead of just empty space?

Many great minds have been puzzled by this problem. For example, in his biography of the renowned philosopher Ludwig Wittgenstein, Norman Malcolm reports,

> . . . He said that he sometimes had a certain experience which could best be described by saying that "when I have it, *I wonder at the existence of the World.* I am then inclined to use such phrases as 'How extraordinary that anything should exist!' or 'How extraordinary that the world should exist!'"[1]

Similarly, the Australian philosopher J.J.C. Smart has said, ". . . My mind often seems to reel under the immense significance this question has for me. That anything exists at all does seem to me a matter for the deepest awe."[2]

Why *does* something exist instead of nothing? Unless we are prepared to believe that the universe simply popped into existence uncaused out of nothing, then the answer must be: Something exists because there is an eternal, uncaused being for which no further explanation is possible. But who or what is this eternal, uncaused being? Leibniz identified it with God. But many modern philosophers have identified it with the universe itself.

Now this is exactly the position of the atheist, that the universe itself is uncaused and eternal, or, as Russell remarks, ". . . The universe is just there, and that's all." But this means, of course, that our lives are without ultimate significance, value or purpose, and that we are therefore abandoned to futility and despair. Indeed, Russell himself acknowledges that life can be faced only upon the "firm foundation of unyielding despair."[3]

Are there reasons to believe that the universe is not eternal and uncaused, that there is something more? I think that there are. . . . I want to . . . expound two philosophical arguments for why I believe that the universe had a beginning.

An actual infinite? Here is the first philosophical argument:

1. An actual infinite cannot exist.

2. A beginningless series of events in time is an actual infinite.

3. Therefore, a beginningless series of events in time cannot exist.

Let's first examine step one: *an actual infinite cannot exist.* I need to explain what I mean by an actual infinite. A collection of things is said to be actually infinite only if a part of it is equal to the whole of it. For example, which is greater:

1, 2, 3, . . .

or

0, 1, 2, 3, . . .?

---

* William Lane Craig is an itinerant philosopher who is affiliated with Talbot School of Theology.

According to prevailing mathematical thought, they are equivalent because they are both actually infinite. This seems strange because there is an extra number in one series that cannot be found in the other. But this only goes to show that in an actually infinite collection, a part of the collection is equal to the whole of the collection.

For the same reason, mathematicians state that the series of even numbers is the same size as the series of all natural numbers, even though the series of all natural numbers contains all the even numbers plus an infinite number of odd numbers as well:

1, 2, 3, . . .

2, 4, 6, . . .

So a collection is actually infinite if a part of it equals the whole of it.

Now the concept of an *actual* infinite needs to be sharply distinguished from the concept of a *potential* infinite. A potential infinite is a collection that is increasing without limit but is at all times finite. The concept of potential infinity usually comes into play when we add to or subtract from something without stopping. Thus, a finite distance may be said to contain a potentially infinite number of smaller finite distances. This does not mean that there actually is an infinite number of parts in a finite distance; rather it means that one can keep on dividing endlessly and never reach an "infinitieth" division. Infinity merely serves as the limit to which the process approaches. Thus, a potential infinite is not truly infinite. It is simply indefinite. It is at all points finite but always increasing.

To sharpen the distinction between an actual and a potential infinite, we can draw some comparisons between them. The concept of actual infinity is used in set theory to designate a set which has an actually infinite number of members . . . But the concept of

potential infinity finds no place in set theory, because the members of a set must be definite, whereas a potential infinite is indefinite and acquires new members as it grows. Thus, set theory has only finite or actually infinite sets.

The proper place for the concept of the potential infinite is found in mathematical analysis, as in infinitesimal calculus. There a process may be said to increase or diminish to infinity, in the sense that that process can be continued endlessly with infinity as its terminus . . . The concept of actual infinity does not pertain to these operations because an infinite number of operations is never actually made.

According to the great German mathematician David Hilbert, the chief difference between an actual and a potential infinite is that a potential infinite is always something growing toward a limit of infinity, while an actual infinite is a completed totality with an actually infinite number of things.[4]

A good example contrasting these two types of infinity is the series of past, present and future events. If, as the atheist claims, the universe is eternal, then there have occurred in the past an actually infinite number of events. But from any point in the series of events, the number of future events is potentially infinite. Thus, if we pick 1845, the birth-year of Georg Cantor, who discovered infinite sets, as our point of departure, we can see that past events constitute an actual infinity while future events constitute a potential infinity:

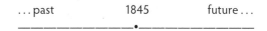

. . . past   1845   future . . .

This is because the past is realized and complete, whereas the future is never fully actualized, but is always finite and always increasing. In the following discussion, it will be exceedingly important to keep the concepts of actual infinity and potential infinity distinct and not to confuse them.

A second clarification that I must make concerns the word "exist." When I say that an actual infinite cannot exist, I mean "exist in the real world" or "exist outside the mind." I am not in any way questioning the legitimacy of using the concept of actual infinity in the realm of mathematics, which is a realm of thought only. What I am arguing is that an actual infinite cannot exist in the real world of stars and planets and rocks and men.

Absurdities. Let me use a few examples to illustrate the absurdities that would result if an actual infinite could exist in reality. Suppose we have a library which contains an actually infinite number of books. Imagine there are only two colors of books, black and red, and these are placed on the shelves alternately: black, red, black, red and so forth. Now if somebody told us that the number of black books equals the number of red books, we would probably not be too surprised. But would we believe someone who told us that the number of black books equals the number of black books plus red books? For in this latter collection we find all the black books plus an infinite number of red books as well.

Or imagine there are three colors of books, or four or five or a hundred. Would you believe someone who claimed that there are as many books in a single color as there are in the entire collection?

Or imagine that there are an infinite number of colors of books. You might assume that there would be one book per color in the infinite collection. But you would be wrong. According to mathematicians, if the collection is actually infinite, there could be for each of the infinite colors an infinite number of books. So you would have an infinity of infinities. And yet it would still be true that if you took all the books of all the colors and added them together, you wouldn't have any more books than if you had taken just the books of a single color.

Let's continue. Suppose each book had a number printed on its spine. Because the collection is actually infinite, *every possible number* is printed on some book. So we could not add another book to the library, for what number would we assign to it? All the numbers have been used up! Thus, the new book could not have a number. But this is absurd, since objects in reality can be numbered.

If an infinite library could exist, it would be impossible to add another book to it. But this conclusion is obviously false, for all we have to do is tear out a page from each of the first hundred books, add a title page, stick them together and put this new book on the shelf. It would be that easy to add to the library. So the only conclusion left to us is that an actually infinite library could not exist.

But suppose we could add to the library, and I put a book on the shelf. According to mathematicians, the number of books in the collection is the same as before. How can this be? If I put the book on the shelf, there is one more book in the collection; if I take it off the shelf, there is one less. I can see myself add and remove the book. Am I really to believe that when I add the book there are no more books in the collection and when I remove it there are no fewer books? Suppose I add an infinity of books to the collection. Am I seriously to believe that there are no more books in the collection than before? What if I add an infinity of infinities of books to the collection? Is there now not one single book more in the collection than before? I find this hard to believe.

Now let's reverse the process and loan out some of the books. Suppose we loan out book number one. Isn't there now one fewer book in the collection? Let's loan out all the odd-numbered books. We have loaned out an infinite number of books, and yet mathematicians would say there are no fewer books in the collection. When we loaned out all these books, a great number of gaps were left behind on the shelves. Suppose we push all the books together again to close the gaps. All those gaps added together would add up to an infinite distance. But, according to mathematicians, the shelves would still be full, the same as before you loaned any out!

Now suppose we loaned out book numbers 4, 5, 6 . . . out to infinity. At a single stroke, the collection would be virtually eliminated, the shelves emptied, and the infinite library reduced to finitude. And yet, we have removed exactly the same number of books this time as when we first loaned out all the odd numbered books! Does anybody believe such a library could exist in reality?

These examples serve to illustrate that an actual infinite cannot exist in the real world. Again I want to underline the fact that what I have argued in no way threatens the theoretical system bequeathed by Cantor to modern mathematics. Indeed, some of the most eager enthusiasts of transfinite mathematics, such as David Hilbert, are only too ready to agree that the concept of actual infinity is an idea only and has no relation to the real world. So we can conclude the first step: an actual infinite cannot exist.

Beginningless series = actual infinity. The second step is: *a beginningless series of events in time is an actual infinite.* By "event" I mean something that happens. Thus, this step is concerned with change and holds that, if the series of past events or changes goes back and back and never had a beginning, then, considered all together, these events constitute an actually infinite collection.

Let me provide an example. Suppose we ask someone where a certain star came from. He replies that it came from an explosion in a star that existed before it. Then we ask, where did *that* star come from? Well, it came from another star before that. And where did that star come from? From another, previous star, and so on and so on. This series of stars would be an example of a beginningless series of events in time.

Now if the universe has existed forever, then the series of all past events taken together constitutes an actual infinite, because every event in the past was

preceded by another event. Thus, the series of past events would be infinite. It would not be potentially infinite, for we have seen that the past is complete and actual; only the future can be described as a potential infinite. It seems obvious, therefore, that a beginningless series of events in time is an actual infinite.

But that brings us to our conclusion: *a beginningless series of events in time cannot exist.* We know that an actual infinite cannot exist in reality. Since a beginningless series of events in time is an actual infinite, such a series cannot exist. So the series of all past events must be finite and have a beginning. But the universe *is* the series of all events, so the universe must have had a beginning.

Let me give you a few examples to make the point clear. We know that, if an actual infinite could exist in reality, it would be impossible to add to it. But the series of events in time is being added to every day, or at least, so it appears. If the series were actually infinite, then the number of events that have occurred up to the present moment is no greater than the number of events up to, say, 1789, or any point in the past, no matter how long ago it might be.

Take another example. Suppose Earth and Jupiter have been orbiting the sun from eternity. Suppose that it takes the Earth one year to complete one orbit, and it takes Jupiter three years to complete one orbit. So for every one orbit Jupiter completes, Earth completes three. Here is the question: If they have been orbiting from eternity, which has completed more orbits? The answer is: They are equal. Now this seems absurd, since the longer they went, the farther and farther Jupiter would fall behind. How could they possibly be equal?

Or, finally, suppose we meet a man who claims to have been counting from eternity and now he is finishing: . . . -5, -4, -3, -2, -1, 0. Now this is impossible, for we may ask, why didn't he finish counting yesterday or the day before or even the year before? By then an infinity of time had already elapsed, so that he should have finished. The fact is we would never find anyone completing such a task because at any previous point in time he would have already finished. There would never be a point in the past at which we could find him counting at all, for he would have already finished. But if, no matter how far back in time we go, we never find him counting, then it cannot be true that he has been counting from eternity. This illustrates once more that the series of past events could not be without a beginning, for if you could not count numbers from eternity, neither could you have events from eternity.

These examples underline the absurdity of a beginningless series of events in time. Because such a series is an actual infinite, and an actual infinite cannot exist, a beginningless series of events in time cannot exist. This means that the universe began to exist, which is the point that we set out to prove.

The second argument: the impossibility of traversing the infinite. Let's look now at the second philosophical argument for the beginning of the universe. Here it is:

1. The series of events in time is a collection formed by adding one member after another.

2. A collection formed by adding one member after another cannot be actually infinite.

3. Therefore, the series of events in time cannot be actually infinite.

This argument does not debate the existence of an actual infinite. But it does argue that an actual infinite cannot come to exist by adding the members of a collection one after the other.

Let's look at the first step: *The series of events in time is a collection formed by adding one member after another.* This point is pretty obvious. When we consider the collection of all past events, it is clear that those events did not exist simultaneously, but they existed one after

another in time. So we have one event, then another after that, then another, and so on. So when we talk about the collection of "all past events," we are talking about a collection that has been formed by adding one member after another.

The second step is the crucial one: *A collection formed by adding one member after another cannot be actually infinite.* Why? Because no matter how many members a person added to the collection, he could always add one more. Therefore he could never arrive at infinity.

Sometimes this is called the impossibility of counting to infinity. No matter how many numbers you count, you could always count one more. You would never arrive at infinity.

Or sometimes this is referred to as the impossibility of traversing the infinite. You could never cross an infinite distance. Imagine a man running up a flight of stairs and every time his foot strikes the top step, another step appears above it. It is clear that the man could run forever, but he would never cross all the steps because you could always add one more step.

Now notice that this impossibility has nothing to do with the amount of time available. The very nature of the infinite requires that it cannot be formed by adding one member after another, regardless of the amount of time available. Thus, an infinite collection could come to exist in the real world only if all the members were created simultaneously. For example, if our library of infinite books were to exist in the real world, it would have to be created instantaneously by God. God would say, "Let there be . . .!" and the library would come into existence all at once. But forming the library by adding one book at a time would be impossible, because you would never arrive at infinity.

Therefore, our conclusion must be: *The series of events in time cannot be actually infinite.* If there were an infinite number of days prior to today, then today would never arrive. It is impossible to "cross" an infinite number of days to reach today. But, obviously, today has arrived. So we know that prior to today, there cannot have been an infinite number of days. Therefore the number of days is finite, and the universe must have had a beginning.

Contemporary philosophers have shown themselves incapable of refuting this reasoning.[5] Thus, one of them asks: "If an infinite series of events has preceded the present moment, how did we get to the present moment? How could we get to the present moment—where we obviously are now—if the present moment was preceded by an infinite series of events?"[6] Concluding that this difficulty has not been overcome and that the issue is still in dispute, he passes on to another subject, leaving the argument unrefuted. Similarly, another philosopher comments rather weakly, "It is difficult to show exactly what is wrong with this argument," and with that remark moves on without further ado.[7]

Conclusion. So we have two philosophical arguments to prove that the universe had a beginning. First, we argued that an actual infinite cannot exist. Since a beginningless universe would involve an actually infinite number of past events, the universe must have had a beginning. Second, we argued that an actually infinite collection cannot be formed by adding one member after another. Since the series of past events has been formed by adding one event after another, it cannot be infinite, and the universe must have had a beginning. [Which, he argues in the remainder of the book, is God.]

Notes

1. Norman Malcolm, *Ludwig Wittgenstein: A Memoir* (London: Oxford UP, 1958), p. 70.

2. J.J.C. Smart, "The Existence of God," *Church Quarterly Review* 156 (1955), p. 194.

3. Bertrand Russell and F.C. Copleston, "The Existence of God," in *The Existence of God*, ed. with an Introduction by John Hick, Problems of Philosophy Series (New York: Macmillan and Co., 1964), pp. 174, 176.

4. David Hilbert, "On the Infinite," in *Philosophy of Mathematics*, ed. with an Introduction by Paul Benacerraf and Hilary Putnam (Englewood Cliffs, NJ: Prentice Hall, 1964), pp. 139, 141.

5. For an in-depth discussion of this, see my book, *The Kalaam Cosmological Argument* (London: Macmillan, 1979; New York: Barnes & Noble, 1979), Appendixes 1 and 2.

6. John Hospers, *An Introduction to Philosophical Analysis*, 2nd ed. (London: Routledge & Kegan Paul, 1967), p. 434.

7. William L. Rowe, *The Cosmological Argument* (Princeton, NJ: Princeton UP, 1975), p. 122.

Discussion

1. Has your mind ever reeled at the sheer wonder of the existence of the universe? Why or why not?

2. What makes Craig's argument that an actual infinite cannot really exist *seem* so persuasive? *Is* it persuasive?

3. It is impossible, according to Craig's first argument, for the universe to be an actual infinite. But if there is a God, he surely has existed forever. How could an eternally existent God be a better explanation of the existence of the universe than simply postulating an eternally existent universe?

Chapter 3

The Argument from Design

THE WATCH AND THE WATCHMAKER

WILLIAM PALEY*

The watch. In crossing a heath, suppose I pitched my foot against a *stone*, and were asked how the stone came to be there, I might possibly answer, that for any thing I knew to the contrary it had lain there for ever; nor would it, perhaps, be very easy to show the absurdity of this answer. But suppose I had found a *watch* upon the ground, and it should be inquired how the watch happened to be in that place, I should hardly think of the answer which I had before given, that for any thing I knew the watch might have always been there. Yet why should not this answer serve for the watch as well as for the stone; why is it not as admissible in the second case as in the first? For this reason, and for no other, namely, that when we come to inspect the watch, we perceive—what we could not discover in the stone—that its several parts are framed and put together for a purpose, e.g., that they are so formed and adjusted as to produce motion, and that motion so regulated as to point out the hour of the day; that if the different parts had been differently shaped from what they are, or placed after any other manner or in any other order than that in which they are placed, either no motion at all would have been carried on in the machine, or none which would have answered the use that is now served by it. To reckon up a few of the plainest of these parts and of their offices, all tending to one result: We see a cylindrical box containing a coiled elastic spring, which, by its endeavor to relax itself, turns round the box. We next observe a flexible chain—artificially wrought for the sake of flexure—communicating the action of the spring from the box to the fusee. We then find a series of wheels, the teeth of which catch in and apply to each other, conducting the motion from the fusee to the balance and from the balance to the pointer, and at the same time, by the size and shape of those wheels, so regulating that motion as to terminate in causing an index, by an equable and measured progression, to pass over a given space in a given time. We take notice that the wheels are made of brass, in order to keep them from rust; the springs of steel, no other metal being so elastic; that over the face of the watch there is placed a glass, a material employed in no other part of the work, but in the room of which, if there had been any other than a transparent substance, the hour could not be seen without opening the case. This mechanism being observed—it requires indeed an examination of the instrument, and perhaps some previous knowledge of the subject, to perceive and understand it; but being once, as we have said, observed and understood, the inference we think is inevitable, that the watch must have had a maker—that there must have existed, at some time and at some place or other, an artificer or artificers who formed it for the purpose which we find it actually to answer, who comprehended its construction and designed its use.

---

*   William Paley (1743–1805) was an English philosopher and theologian.

Anticipated objections. Nor would it, I apprehend, weaken the conclusion, that we had never seen a watch made—that we had never known an artist capable of making one—that we were altogether incapable of executing such a piece of workmanship ourselves, or of understanding in what manner it was performed; all this being no more than what is true of some exquisite remains of ancient art, of some lost arts, and, to the generality of mankind, of the more curious productions of modern manufacture. Does one man in a million know how oval frames are turned? Ignorance of this kind exalts our opinion of the unseen and unknown artist's skill, if he be unseen and unknown, but raises no doubt in our minds of the existence and agency of such an artist, at some former time and in some place or other. Nor can I perceive that it varies at all the inference, whether the question arise concerning a human agent or concerning an agent of a different species, or an agent possessing in some respects a different nature.

Neither, secondly, would it invalidate our conclusion that the watch sometimes went wrong, or that it seldom went exactly right. The purpose of the machinery, the design, and the designer might be evident, and in the case supposed, would be evident, in whatever way we accounted for the irregularity of the movement, or whether we could account for it or not. It is not necessary that a machine be perfect, in order to show with what design it was made: still less necessary, where the only question is whether it were made with any design at all.

Nor, thirdly, would it bring any uncertainty into the argument, if there were a few parts of the watch, concerning which we could not discover or had not yet discovered in what manner they conduced to the general effect; or even some parts, concerning which we could not ascertain whether they conduced to that effect in any manner whatever. For, as to the first branch of the case, if by the loss, or disorder, or decay of the parts in question, the movement of the watch were found in fact to be stopped, or disturbed, or retarded, no doubt would remain in our minds as to the utility or intention of these parts, although we should be unable to investigate the manner according to which, or the connection by which, the ultimate effect depended upon their action or assistance; and the more complex the machine, the more likely is this obscurity to arise. Then, as to the second thing supposed, namely, that there were parts which might be spared without prejudice to the movement of the watch, and that we had proved this by experiment, these superfluous parts, even if we were completely assured that they were such, would not vacate the reasoning which we had instituted concerning other parts. The indication of contrivance remained, with respect to them, nearly as it was before.

Nor, fourthly, would any man in his senses think the existence of the watch with its various machinery accounted for, by being told that it was one out of possible combinations of material forms; that whatever he had found in the place where he found the watch, must have contained some internal configuration or other; and that this configuration might be the structure now exhibited, namely, of the works of a watch, as well as a different structure.

Nor, fifthly, would it yield his inquiry more satisfaction, to be answered that there existed in things a principle of order, which had disposed the parts of the watch into their present form and situation. He never knew a watch made by the principle of order; nor can he even form to himself an idea of what is meant by a principle of order, distinct from the intelligence of the watchmaker.

Sixthly, he would be surprised to hear that the mechanism of the watch was no proof of contrivance, only a motive to induce the mind to think so:

And not less surprised to be informed, that the watch in his hand was nothing more than the result of the laws of *metallic* nature. It is a perversion of language to assign any law as the efficient, operative cause of any thing. A law presupposes an agent; for it is only the mode according to which an agent proceeds: it implies a power; for it is the order according to which that power acts. Without this agent, without this power, which are both distinct from itself, the *law* does nothing, is nothing. The expression, the "law of metallic nature," may sound strange and harsh to a philosophic ear; but it seems quite as justifiable as some others which are more familiar to him, such as "the law of vegetable nature," "the law of animal nature," or, indeed, as "the law of nature" in general, when assigned as the cause of phenomena, in exclusion of agency and power, or when it is substituted into the place of these.

Neither, lastly, would our observer be driven out of his conclusion or from his confidence in its truth, by being told that he knew nothing at all about the matter. He knows enough for his argument; he knows the utility of the end; he knows the subserviency and adaptation of the means to the end. These points being known, his ignorance of other points, his doubts concerning other points, affect not the certainty of his reasoning. The consciousness of knowing little need not beget a distrust of that which he does know. . . .

The eye. . . . [E]very indication of contrivance, every manifestation of design which existed in the watch, exists in the works of nature, with the difference on the side of nature of being greater and more, and that in a degree which exceeds all computation. I mean, that the contrivances of nature surpass the contrivances of art, in the complexity, subtilty, and curiosity of the mechanism; and still more, if possible, do they go beyond them in number and variety; yet, in a multitude of cases, are not less evidently mechanical, not less evidently contrivances, not less evidently accommodated to their end or suited to their office, than are the most perfect productions of human ingenuity.

I know no better method of introducing so large a subject, than that of comparing a single thing with a single thing: an eye, for example, with a telescope. As far as the examination of the instrument goes, there is precisely the same proof that the eye was made for vision, as there is that the telescope was made for assisting it. They are made upon the same principles; both being adjusted to the laws by which the transmission and refraction of rays of light are regulated. I speak not of the origin of the laws themselves; but such laws being fixed, the construction in both cases is adapted to them. For instance, these laws require, in order to produce the same effect, that the rays of light, in passing from water into the eye, should be refracted by a more convex surface than when it passes out of air into the eye. Accordingly we find that the eye of a fish, in that part of it called the crystalline lens, is much rounder than the eye of terrestrial animals. What plainer manifestation of design can there be than this difference? What could a mathematical instrument maker have done more to show his knowledge of his principle, his application of that knowledge, his suiting his means to his end? . . .

But this, though much, is not the whole: by different species of animals, the faculty we are describing is possessed in degrees suited to the different range of vision which their mode of life and of procuring their food requires. *Birds*, for instance, in general, procure their food by means of their beak; and the distance between the eye and the point of the beak being small, it becomes necessary that they should have the power of seeing very near objects distinctly. On the other hand, from being often elevated much above the ground, living in the air, and moving through it with great velocity, they require for their safety, as well as for assisting them in descrying their prey, a power of seeing at a great distance—a power of which, in birds of rapine, surprising examples are given. The fact accordingly is, that two peculiarities are found in the eyes of birds, both tending to *facilitate* the change upon which the adjustment of the eye to different distances depends. The one is a bony, yet, in most species, a flexible rim or hoop, surrounding the broadest part of the eye, which confining the action of the muscles to that part, increases the effect of their lateral pressure upon the orb, by which pressure its axis is elongated for the purpose of looking at very near objects. The other is an additional muscle called the marsupium, to draw, on occasion, the crystalline lens *back*, and to fit the same eye for the viewing of very distant objects. By these means, the eyes of birds can pass from one extreme to another of their scale of adjustment, with more ease and readiness than the eyes of other animals.

The eyes of *fishes* also, compared with those of terrestrial animals, exhibit certain distinctions of structure adapted to their state and element. We have already observed upon the figure of the crystalline compensating by its roundness the density of the medium through which their light passes. To which we have to add, that the eyes of fish, in their natural and indolent state, appear to be adjusted to near objects, in this respect differing from the human eye, as well as those of quadrupeds and birds. The ordinary shape of the fish's eye being in a much higher degree convex than that of land animals, a corresponding difference attends its muscular conformation, namely, that it is throughout calculated for *flattening* the eye.

The *iris* also in the eyes of fish does not admit of contraction. This is a great difference, of which the probable reason is, that the diminished light in water is never strong for the retina.

In the *eel*, which has to work its head through sand and gravel, the roughest and harshest substances, there is placed before the eye, and at some distance from it, a transparent, horny, convex case or covering, which, without obstructing the sight, defends the organ. To such an animal could any thing be more wanted or more useful?

Thus, in comparison, the eyes of different kinds of animals, we see in their resemblances and distinctions one general plan laid down, and that plan varied with the varying exigencies to which it is to be applied. . . .

In considering vision as achieved by the means of an image formed at the bottom of the eye, we can never reflect without wonder upon the smallness yet correctness of the picture, the subtlety of the touch, the fineness of the lines. A landscape of five or six square leagues is brought into a space of half an inch diameter, yet the multitude of objects which it contains are all preserved, are all discriminated in their magnitudes, positions, figures, colors. The prospect from Hampstead-hill is compressed into the compass of a sixpence, yet circumstantially represented. A stagecoach, travelling at an ordinary speed for half an hour, passes in the eye only over one-twelfth of an inch, yet is this change of place in the image distinctly perceived throughout its whole progress; for it is only by means of that perception that the motion of the coach itself is made sensible to the eye. If any thing can abate our admiration of the smallness of the visual tablet compared with the extent of vision, it is a reflection which the view of nature leads us every hour to make, namely, that in the hands of the Creator, great and little are nothing.

Sturmius held that the examination of the eye was a cure for atheism. Besides that conformity to optical principles which its internal constitution displays, and which alone amounts to a manifestation of intelligence having been exerted in the structure—besides this, which forms, no doubt, the leading character of the organ, there is to be seen, in every thing belonging to it and about it, an extraordinary degree of care, an anxiety for its preservation, due, if we may so speak, to its value and its tenderness. It is lodged in a strong, deep, bony socket, composed by the junction of seven different bones, hollowed out at their edges. In some few species, as that of the coatimondi, the orbit is not bony throughout; but whenever this is the case, the upper, which is the deficient part, is supplied by a cartilaginous ligament, a substitution which shows the same care. Within this socket it is embedded in fat, of all animal substances the best adapted both to its repose and motion. It is sheltered by the eyebrows—an arch of hair which, like a thatched penthouse, prevents the sweat and moisture of the forehead from running down into it.

But it is still better protected by its *lid*. Of the superficial parts of the animal frame, I know none which, in it, office and structure, is more deserving of attention than the eyelid. It defends the eye; it wipes it; it closes it in sleep. Are there in any work of art whatever, purposes more evident than those which this organ fulfils; or an apparatus for executing those purposes more intelligible, more appropriate, or more mechanical? If it be overlooked by the observer of nature, it can only be because it is obvious and familiar. This is a tendency to be guarded against. We pass by the plainest instances, while we are exploring those which are rare and curious; by which conduct of the understanding we sometimes neglect the strongest observations, being taken up with others which, though more recondite and scientific, are, as solid arguments, entitled to much less consideration.

In order to keep the eye moist and clean—which qualities are necessary to its brightness and its use—a wash is constantly supplied by a secretion for the purpose; and the superfluous brine is conveyed to the nose through a perforation in the bone as large as a goose-quill. When once the fluid has entered the nose, it spreads itself upon the inside of the nostril, and is evaporated by the current of warm air which in the course of respiration is continually passing over it. Can any pipe or outlet for carrying off the waste liquor from a dye-house or distillery, be more mechanical than this is? It is easily perceived that the eye must want moisture; but could the want of the eye generate the gland which produces the tear, or bore the hole by which it is discharged—a hole through a bone? . . .

The argument cumulative. Were there no example in the world of contrivance except that of the eye, it would be alone sufficient to support the conclusion which we draw from it, as to the necessity of an intelligent Creator. It could never be got rid of, because it could not be accounted for by any other supposition which did not contradict all the principles we possess of knowledge—the principles according to which things do, as often as they can be brought to the test of experience, turn out to be true or false. Its coats and humors, constructed as the lenses of a telescope are constructed, for the refraction of rays of light to a point, which forms the proper action of the organ; the provision in its muscular tendons for turning its pupil to the object, similar to that which is given to the telescope by screws, and upon which power of direction in the eye the exercise of its office as all optical instrument depends; the further provision for its defence, for its constant lubricity and moisture, which we see in its socket and its lids, in its glands for the secretion of the matter of tears, its outlet or communication with the nose for carrying off liquid after the eye is washed with it; these provisions compose altogether an apparatus, a system of parts, a preparation of means, so manifest in their design, so exquisite in their contrivance, so successful in their issue, so precious, and so infinitely beneficial in their use, as, in my opinion, to bear down all doubt that can be raised upon the subject. And what I wish, under the title of the present chapter, to observe, is, that if other parts of nature were inaccessible to our inquiries, or even if other parts of nature presented nothing to our examination but disorder and confusion, the validity of this example would remain the same. If there were but one watch in the world, it would not be less certain that it had a maker. If we had never in our lives seen any but one single kind of hydraulic machine, yet if of that one kind we understood the mechanism and use, we should be as perfectly assured that it proceeded from the hand and thought and skill of a workman, as if we visited a museum of the arts, and saw collected there twenty different kinds of machines for drawing water, or a thousand different kinds for other purposes. Of this point each machine is a proof independently of all the rest. So it is with the evidence of divine agency. The proof is not a conclusion which lies at the end of a chain of reasoning, of which chain each instance of contrivance is only a link, and of which, if one link fail, the whole fails; but it is an argument separately supplied by every separate example. An error in stating an example affects only that example. The argument is cumulative in the fullest sense of that term. The eye proves it without the ear; the ear without the eye. The proof in each example is complete; for when the design of the part, and the conduciveness of its structure to that design is shown, the mind may set itself at rest; no future consideration can detract any thing from the force of the example. . . .

The designer. Contrivance, if established, appears to me to prove every thing which we wish to prove. Among other things, it proves the *personality* of the Deity, as distinguished from what is sometimes called nature, sometimes called a principle which terms, in the mouths of those who use them philosophically, seem to be intended to admit and to express an efficacy, but to exclude and to deny a personal agent. Now, that which can contrive, which can design, must be a person. These capacities constitute personality, for they imply consciousness and thought. They require that which can perceive an end or purpose, as well as the power of providing means and directing them to their end. They require a centre in which perceptions unite, and from which volitions flow; which is mind. The acts of a mind prove the existence of a mind; and in whatever a mind resides, is a person. The seat of intellect is a person. We have no authority to limit the properties of mind to any particular corporeal form, or to any particular circumscription of space. These

properties subsist, in created nature, under a great variety of sensible forms. Also, every animated being has its *sensorium*; that is, a certain portion of space, within which perception and volition are exerted. This sphere may be enlarged to an indefinite extent—may comprehend the universe; and being so imagined, may serve to furnish us with as good a notion as we are capable of forming, of the *immensity* of the divine nature, that is, of a Being, infinite, as well in essence as in power, yet nevertheless a person. . . .

Wherever we see marks of contrivance, we are led for its cause to an *intelligent* author. And this transition of the understanding is founded upon uniform experience. We see intelligence constantly contriving; that is, we see intelligence constantly producing effects, marked and distinguished by certain properties—not certain particular properties, but by a kind and class of properties, such as relation to an end, relation of parts to one another and to a common purpose. We see, wherever we are witnesses to the actual formation of things nothing except intelligence producing effects so marked and distinguished. Furnished with this experience, we view the productions of nature. We observe *them* also marked and distinguished in the same manner. We wish to account for their origin. Our experience suggests a cause perfectly adequate to this account. No experience, no single instance or example, can be offered in favor of any other. In this cause, therefore, we ought to rest; in this cause the common-sense of mankind has, in fact, rested, because it agrees with that which in all cases is the foundation of knowledge—the undeviating course of their experience. . . .

Discussion

1. Consider a watch and a rock. Which one does the world more relevantly resemble? How would the conclusion of Paley's argument

differ if you were to believe that the universe is more like the rock?

2. Now reconsider the watch and compare it with an eye. Do you find it easy or difficult to resist the inclination to believe that the eye was designed?

3. Are there any adequate, non-supernatural, explanations of the apparent design of things like the human eye?

CRITIQUE OF THE ARGUMENT FROM DESIGN

DAVID HUME*

Cleanthes. Look round the world: contemplate the whole and every part of it: You will find it to be nothing but one great machine, subdivided into an infinite number of lesser machines, which again admit of subdivisions to a degree beyond what human senses and faculties can trace and explain. All these various machines, and even their most minute parts, are adjusted to each other with an accuracy which ravishes into admiration all men who have ever contemplated them. The curious adapting of means to ends, throughout all nature, resembles exactly, though it much exceeds, the productions of human contrivance; of human designs, thought, wisdom, and intelligence. Since, therefore, the effects resemble each other, we are led to infer, by all the rules of analogy, that the causes also resemble; and that the Author of Nature is somewhat similar to the mind of man, though possessed of much larger faculties, proportioned to the grandeur of the work which he has executed. By this argument *a posteriori*, and by this argument alone, do we prove at once the existence of a Deity, and his similarity to human mind and intelligence. . . .

Philo. What I chiefly scruple in this subject, said Philo, is not so much that all religious arguments are by Cleanthes reduced to experience, as that they appear not to be even the most certain and irrefragable of that inferior kind. That a stone will fall, that fire will burn, that the earth has solidity, we have observed a thousand and a thousand times; and when any new instance of this nature is presented, we draw without hesitation the accustomed inference. The exact

similarity of the cases gives us a perfect assurance of a similar event; and a stronger evidence is never desired nor sought after. But wherever you depart, in the least, from the similarity of the cases, you diminish proportionably the evidence; and may at last bring it to a very weak analogy, which is confessedly liable to error and uncertainty. . . .

If we see a house, Cleanthes, we conclude, with the greatest certainty, that it had an architect or builder; because this is precisely that species of effect which we have experienced to proceed from that species of cause. But surely you will not affirm, that the universe bears such a resemblance to a house, that we can with the same certainty infer a similar cause, or that the analogy is here entire and perfect. The dissimilitude is so striking, that the utmost you can here pretend to is a guess, a conjecture, a presumption concerning a similar cause; and how that pretension will be received in the world, I leave you to consider.

Cleanthes. It would surely be very ill received, replied Cleanthes; and I should be deservedly blamed and detested, did I allow, that the proofs of a Deity amounted to no more than a guess or conjecture. But is the whole adjustment of means to ends in a house and in the universe so slight a resemblance? The economy of final causes? The order, proportion, and arrangement of every part? Steps of a stair are plainly contrived, that human legs may use them in mounting; and this inference is certain and infallible. Human legs are also contrived for walking and mounting; and this inference, I allow, is not altogether so certain, because of the dissimilarity which you remark; but does it, therefore, deserve the name only of presumption or conjecture? . . .

Philo. Experience alone can point out to him the true cause of any phenomenon. Now, according to this method of reasoning . . . it follows, (and is, indeed, tacitly allowed by Cleanthes himself), that order,

---

* David Hume (1711–76) was a Scottish philosopher best known for his skeptical views.

arrangement, or the adjustment of final causes, is not of itself any proof of design; but only so far as it has been experienced to proceed from that principle. For aught we can know *a priori*, matter may contain the source or spring of order originally within itself, as well as mind does; and there is no more difficulty in conceiving, that the several elements, from an internal unknown cause, may fall into the most exquisite arrangement, than to conceive that their ideas, in the great universal mind, from a like internal unknown cause, fall into that arrangement. The equal possibility of both these suppositions is allowed. But, by experience, we find, (according to Cleanthes), that there is a difference between them. Throw several pieces of steel together, without shape or form; they will never arrange themselves so as to compose a watch. Stone, and mortar, and wood, without an architect, never erect a house. But the ideas in a human mind, we see, by an unknown, inexplicable economy, arrange themselves so as to form the plan of a watch or house. Experience, therefore, proves, that there is an original principle of order in mind, not in matter. From similar effects we infer similar causes. The adjustment of means to ends is alike in the universe, as in a machine of human contrivance. The causes, therefore, must be resembling....

But can you think, Cleanthes, that your usual phlegm and philosophy have been preserved in so wide a step as you have taken, when you compared to the universe houses, ships, furniture, machines, and, from their similarity in some circumstances, inferred a similarity in their causes? Thought, design, intelligence, such as we discover in men and other animals, is no more than one of the springs and principles of the universe, as well as heat or cold, attraction or repulsion, and a hundred others, which fall under daily observation.... But, allowing that we were to take the operations of one part of nature upon another, for the foundation of our judgement concerning the origin of the whole, (which never can be admitted), yet why

select so minute, so weak, so bounded a principle, as the reason and design of animals is found to be upon this planet? What peculiar privilege has this little agitation of the brain which we call thought, that we must thus make it the model of the whole universe? Our partiality in our own favour does indeed present it on all occasions; but sound philosophy ought carefully to guard against so natural an illusion....

But to show you still more inconveniences, continued Philo, in your Anthropomorphism, please to take a new survey of your principles. *Like effects prove like causes.* This is the experimental argument; and this, you say too, is the sole theological argument. Now, it is certain, that the liker the effects are which are seen, and the liker the causes which are inferred, the stronger is the argument. Every departure on either side diminishes the probability, and renders the experiment less conclusive. You cannot doubt of the principle; neither ought you to reject its consequences.

Now, Cleanthes, said Philo, with an air of alacrity and triumph, mark the consequences. First, By this method of reasoning, you renounce all claim to infinity in any of the attributes of the Deity. For, as the cause ought only to be proportioned to the effect, and the effect, so far as it falls under our cognisance, is not infinite; what pretensions have we, upon your suppositions, to ascribe that attribute to the Divine Being?...

Secondly, You have no reason, on your theory, for ascribing perfection to the Deity, even in his finite capacity, or for supposing him free from every error, mistake, or incoherence, in his undertakings. There are many inexplicable difficulties in the works of Nature, which, if we allow a perfect author to be proved *a priori*, are easily solved, and become only seeming difficulties, from the narrow capacity of man, who cannot trace infinite relations. But according to your method of reasoning, these difficulties become all real....

But were this world ever so perfect a production, it must still remain uncertain, whether all the excellences of the work can justly be ascribed to the workman. If we survey a ship, what an exalted idea must we form of the ingenuity of the carpenter who framed so complicated, useful, and beautiful a machine? And what surprise must we feel, when we find him a stupid mechanic, who imitated others, and copied an art, which, through a long succession of ages, after multiplied trials, mistakes, corrections, deliberations, and controversies, had been gradually improving? Many worlds might have been botched and bungled, throughout an eternity, ere this system was struck out; much labour lost, many fruitless trials made; and a slow, but continued improvement carried on during infinite ages in the art of world-making. In such subjects, who can determine, where the truth; nay, who can conjecture where the probability lies, amidst a great number of hypotheses which may be proposed, and a still greater which may be imagined?

And what shadow of an argument, continued Philo, can you produce, from your hypothesis, to prove the unity of the Deity? A great number of men join in building a house or ship, in rearing a city, in framing a commonwealth; why may not several deities combine in contriving and framing a world?

To multiply causes without necessity, is indeed contrary to true philosophy: but this principle applies not to the present case. Were one deity antecedently proved by your theory, who were possessed of every attribute requisite to the production of the universe; it would be needless, I own, (though not absurd), to suppose any other deity existent. But while it is still a question, Whether all these attributes are united in one subject, or dispersed among several independent beings, by what phenomena in nature can we pretend to decide the controversy? Where we see a body raised in a scale, we are sure that there is in the opposite scale, however concealed from sight, some counterpoising weight equal to it; but it is still allowed to doubt, whether that weight be an aggregate of several distinct bodies, or one uniform united mass. And if the weight requisite very much exceeds any thing which we have

ever seen conjoined in any single body, the former supposition becomes still more probable and natural. An intelligent being of such vast power and capacity as is necessary to produce the universe, or, to speak in the language of ancient philosophy, so prodigious an animal exceeds all analogy, and even comprehension. . . .

And why not become a perfect Anthropomorphite? Why not assert the deity or deities to be corporeal, and to have eyes, a nose, mouth, ears, &c.? Epicurus maintained, that no man had ever seen reason but in a human figure; therefore the gods must have a human figure. And this argument, which is deservedly so much ridiculed by Cicero, becomes, according to you, solid and philosophical.

In a word, Cleanthes, a man who follows your hypothesis is able perhaps to assert, or conjecture, that the universe, sometime, arose from something like design: but beyond that position he cannot ascertain one single circumstance; and is left afterwards to fix every point of his theology by the utmost license of fancy and hypothesis. . . .

Discussion

1. Clearly outline the argument from design as offered by Cleanthes in the first paragraph.

2. This argument is an argument from analogy and relies on the principle that *like effects prove like causes*. If it were a good analogy, what would follow about God?

3. Hume suggests that the argument might rely on a bad analogy. In what respects is the universe like and unlike a machine?

4. Hume offers an explanation of the "design" of the universe that does not appeal to God. Can you find it? Is it an equally adequate explanation?

A SCIENTIFIC ARGUMENT FOR THE EXISTENCE OF GOD: THE FINE-TUNING DESIGN ARGUMENT

ROBIN COLLINS*

Introduction. Suppose we went on a mission to Mars, and found a domed structure in which everything was set up just right for life to exist. The temperature, for example, was set around 70°F and the humidity was at 50%; moreover, there was an oxygen recycling system, an energy gathering system, and a whole system for the production of food. Put simply, the domed structure appeared to be a fully functioning biosphere. What conclusion would we draw from finding this structure? Would we draw the conclusion that it just happened to form by chance? Certainly not. Instead, we would unanimously conclude that it was designed by some intelligent being. Why would we draw this conclusion? Because an intelligent designer appears to be the only plausible explanation for the existence of the structure. That is, the only alternative explanation we can think of—that the structure was formed by some natural process—seems extremely unlikely. Of course, it is *possible* that, for example, through some volcanic eruption various metals and other compounds could have formed, and then separated out in just the right way to produce the "biosphere," but such a scenario strikes us as extraordinarily unlikely, thus making this alternative explanation unbelievable.

The universe is analogous to such a "biosphere," according to recent findings in physics. Almost everything about the basic structure of the universe—for example, the fundamental laws and parameters of physics and the initial distribution of matter and energy—is balanced on a razor's edge for life to occur. As the eminent Princeton physicist Freeman Dyson notes, "There

are many . . . lucky accidents in physics. Without such accidents, water could not exist as liquid, chains of carbon atoms could not form complex organic molecules, and hydrogen atoms could not form breakable bridges between molecules"[1]—in short, life as we know it would be impossible.

Scientists call this extraordinary balancing of the parameters of physics and the initial conditions of the universe the "fine-tuning of the cosmos." It has been extensively discussed by philosophers, theologians, and scientists, especially since the early 1970s, with hundreds of articles and dozens of books written on the topic. Today, it is widely regarded as offering by far the most persuasive current argument for the existence of God. For example, theoretical physicist and popular science writer Paul Davies—whose early writings were not particularly sympathetic to theism—claims that with regard to basic structure of the universe, "the impression of design is overwhelming."[2] Similarly, in response to the life-permitting fine-tuning of the nuclear resonances responsible for the oxygen and carbon synthesis in stars, the famous astrophysicist Sir Fred Hoyle declares that:

> I do not believe that any scientists who examined the evidence would fail to draw the inference that the laws of nuclear physics have been deliberately designed with regard to the consequences they produce inside stars. If this is so, then my apparently random quirks have become part of a deep-laid scheme. If not then we are back again at a monstrous sequence of accidents.[3]

The evidence of fine-tuning. A few examples of this fine-tuning are listed below:

1. If the initial explosion of the big bang had differed in strength by as little as 1 part in 1060, the universe would have either quickly collapsed back on itself, or

---

* Robin Collins is Professor of Philosophy at Messiah College.

expanded too rapidly for stars to form. In either case, life would be impossible.[4]

2. Calculations indicate that if the strong nuclear force, the force that binds protons and neutrons together in an atom, had been stronger or weaker by as little as 5%, life would be impossible.[5]

3. Calculations by Brandon Carter show that if gravity had been stronger or weaker by 1 part in 1040, then life-sustaining stars like the sun could not exist. This would most likely make life impossible.[6]

4. If the neutron were not about 1.001 times the mass of the proton, all protons would have decayed into neutrons or all neutrons would have decayed into protons, and thus life would not be possible.[7]

5. If the electromagnetic force were slightly stronger or weaker, life would be impossible, for a variety of different reasons.[8]

Imaginatively, one could think of each instance of fine-tuning as a radio dial: unless all the dials are set exactly right, life would be impossible. Or, one could think of the initial conditions of the universe and the fundamental parameters of physics as a dart board that fills the whole galaxy, and the conditions necessary for life to exist as a small one-foot wide target: unless the dart hits the target, life would be impossible. The fact that the dials are perfectly set, or the dart has hit the target, strongly suggests that someone set the dials or aimed the dart, for it seems enormously improbable that such a coincidence could have happened by chance.

Although individual calculations of fine-tuning are only approximate and could be in error, the fact that the universe is fine-tuned for life is almost beyond question because of the large number of independent instances of apparent fine-tuning. As philosopher John Leslie has pointed out, "clues heaped upon clues can constitute weighty evidence despite doubts about each element in the pile."[9] What is controversial, however, is the degree to which the fine-tuning provides evidence for the existence of God. As impressive as the argument from fine-tuning seems to be, atheists have raised several significant objections to it. Consequently, those who are aware of these objections, or have thought of them on their own, often will find the argument unconvincing.... My goal in this chapter, therefore, is to make the fine-tuning argument as strong as possible. This will involve developing the argument in as objective and rigorous a way as we can, and then answering the major atheist objections to it. Before launching into this, however, we will need to make a preliminary distinction.

A preliminary distinction. To rigorously develop the fine-tuning argument, we will find it useful to distinguish between what I shall call the *atheistic single-universe hypothesis* and the *atheistic many-universes hypothesis*. According to the atheistic single-universe hypothesis, there is only one universe, and it is ultimately an inexplicable, "brute" fact that the universe exists and is fine-tuned. Many atheists, however, advocate another hypothesis, one which attempts to explain how the seemingly improbable fine-tuning of the universe could be the result of chance. This hypothesis is known as the *atheistic many-worlds hypothesis*, or the *atheistic many-universes hypothesis*. According to this hypothesis, there exists what could be imaginatively thought of as a "universe generator" that produces a very large or infinite number of universes, with each universe having a randomly selected set of initial conditions and values for the parameters of physics. Because this generator produces so many universes, just by chance it will eventually produce one that is fine-tuned for intelligent life to occur.

General principle of reasoning used. We will formulate the fine-tuning argument against the atheistic single-universe hypothesis in terms of what I will call *the prime principle of confirmation*. The prime principle of confirmation is a general principle of reasoning which tells us when some observation counts as evidence in favor of one hypothesis over another. Simply put, the principle says that *whenever we are considering two competing hypotheses, an observation counts as evidence in favor of the hypothesis under which the observation has the highest probability (or is the least improbable)*. (Or, put slightly differently, the principle says that whenever we are considering two competing hypotheses, H1 and H2, an observation, O, counts as evidence in favor of H1 over H2 if O is more probable under H1 than it is under H2.) Moreover, the degree to which the evidence counts in favor of one hypothesis over another is proportional to the degree to which the observation is more probable under the one hypothesis than the other.

For example, the fine-tuning is much, much more probable under theism than under the atheistic single-universe hypothesis, so it counts as strong evidence for theism over this atheistic hypothesis. In the next major subsection, we will present a more formal and elaborated rendition of the fine-tuning argument in terms of the prime principle. First, however, let's look at two illustrations of the principle and then present some support for it.

For our first illustration, suppose that I went hiking in the mountains, and found underneath a certain cliff a group of rocks arranged in a formation that clearly formed the pattern "Welcome to the mountains Robin Collins." One hypothesis is that, by chance, the rocks just happened to be arranged in that pattern—ultimately, perhaps, because of certain initial conditions of the universe. Suppose the only viable alternative hypothesis is that my brother, who was in the mountains before me, arranged the rocks in this way. Most of us would immediately take the arrangements of rocks

to be strong evidence in favor of the "brother" hypothesis over the "chance" hypothesis. Why? Because it strikes us as extremely *improbable* that the rocks would be arranged that way by chance, but *not improbable* at all that my brother would place them in that configuration. Thus, by the prime principle of confirmation we would conclude that the arrangement of rocks strongly supports the "brother" hypothesis over the chance hypothesis.

Or consider another case, that of finding the defendant's fingerprints on the murder weapon. Normally, we would take such a finding as strong evidence that the defendant was guilty. Why? Because we judge that it would be *unlikely* for these fingerprints to be on the murder weapon if the defendant was innocent, but *not unlikely* if the defendant was guilty. That is, we would go through the same sort of reasoning as in the above case.

Several things can be said in favor of the prime principle of confirmation. First, many philosophers think that this principle can be derived from what is known as the *probability calculus*, the set of mathematical rules that are typically assumed to govern probability. Second, there does not appear to be any case of recognizably good reasoning that violates this principle. Finally, the principle appears to have a wide range of applicability, undergirding much of our reasoning in science and everyday life, as the examples above illustrate. Indeed, some have even claimed that a slightly more general version of this principle undergirds all scientific reasoning. Because of all these reasons in favor of the principle, we can be very confident in it.

The argument developed. Let us summarize the fine-tuning argument by explicitly listing its two premises and its conclusion:

Premise 1. The existence of the fine-tuning is not improbable under theism.

Premise 2. The existence of the fine-tuning is very improbable under the atheistic single-universe hypothesis.

Conclusion: From premises (1) and (2) and the prime principle of confirmation, it follows that the fine-tuning data provides strong evidence in favor of the design hypothesis over the atheistic single-universe hypothesis.

At this point, we should pause to note two features of this argument. First, the argument does not say that the fine-tuning evidence proves that the universe was designed, or even that it is likely that the universe was designed. In order to justify these sorts of claims, we would have to look at the full range of evidence both for and against the design hypothesis, something we are not doing in this chapter. Rather, the argument merely concludes that the fine-tuning strongly *supports* theism *over* the atheistic single-universe hypothesis.

In this way, the evidence of the fine-tuning argument is much like fingerprints found on the gun: although they can provide strong evidence that the defendant committed the murder, one could not conclude merely from them alone that the defendant is guilty; one would also have to look at all the other evidence offered. Perhaps, for instance, ten reliable witnesses claimed to see the defendant at a party at the time of the shooting. In this case, the fingerprints would still count as significant evidence of guilt, but this evidence would be counterbalanced by the testimony of the witnesses. Similarly the evidence of fine-tuning strongly supports theism over the atheistic single-universe hypothesis, though it does not itself show that, everything considered, theism is the most plausible explanation of the world. Nonetheless, as I argue in the conclusion of this chapter, the evidence of fine-tuning provides a much stronger and more objective argument for theism (over the atheistic

single-universe hypothesis) than the strongest atheistic argument does against theism.

The second feature of the argument we should note is that, given the truth of *the prime principle of confirmation*, the conclusion of the argument follows from the premises. Specifically, if the premises of the argument are true, then we are guaranteed that the conclusion is true: that is, the argument is what philosophers call *valid*. Thus, insofar as we can show that the premises of the argument are true, we will have shown that the conclusion is true. Our next task, therefore, is to attempt to show that the premises are true, or at least that we have strong reasons to believe them.

Support for the premises. Premise (1) is easy to support and fairly uncontroversial. The argument in support of it can be simply stated as follows: *since God is an all good being, and it is good for intelligent, conscious beings to exist, it is not surprising or improbable that God would create a world that could support intelligent life.* Thus, the fine-tuning is not improbable under theism, as premise (1) asserts.

Premise (2) may be defended as follows. Upon looking at the data, many people find it very obvious that the fine-tuning is highly improbable under the atheistic single-universe hypothesis. And it is easy to see why when we think of the fine-tuning in terms of the analogies offered earlier. In the dart-board analogy, for example, the initial conditions of the universe and the fundamental parameters of physics are thought of as a dart-board that fills the whole galaxy, and the conditions necessary for life to exist as a small one-foot wide target. Accordingly, from this analogy it seems obvious that it would be highly improbable for the fine-tuning to occur under the atheistic single-universe hypothesis—that is, for the dart to hit the board by chance.

Some objection to the fine-tuning argument. As powerful as the core version of the fine-tuning argument is, several major objections have been raised to it by both atheists and theists. In this section, we will consider these objections in turn.

Objection 1: *More Fundamental Law Objection.* One criticism of the fine-tuning argument is that, as far as we know, there could be a more fundamental law under which the parameters of physics *must* have the values they do. Thus, given such a law, it is not improbable that the known parameters of physics fall within the life-permitting range.

Besides being entirely speculative, the problem with postulating such a law is that it simply moves the improbability of the fine-tuning up one level, to that of the postulated physical law itself. Under this hypothesis, what is improbable is that of all the conceivable fundamental physical laws there could be, the universe just happens to have the one that constrains the parameters of physics in a life-permitting way. Thus, trying to explain the fine-tuning by postulating this sort of fundamental law is like trying to explain why the pattern of rocks below a cliff spell "Welcome to the mountains Robin Collins" by postulating that an earthquake occurred and that all the rocks on the cliff face were arranged in just the right configuration to fall into the pattern in question. Clearly this explanation merely transfers the improbability up one level, since now it seems enormously improbable that of all the possible configurations the rocks could be in on the cliff face, they are in the one which results in the pattern "Welcome to the mountains Robin Collins."

A similar sort of response can be given to the claim that the fine-tuning is not improbable because it might be *logically necessary* for the parameters of physics to have life-permitting values. That is, according to this claim, the parameters of physics must have life-permitting values in the same way 2 + 2 must equal 4, or the interior angles of a triangle must add up to 180 degrees in Euclidian geometry. Like the "more fundamental law" proposal above, however, this postulate

simply transfers the improbability up one level: of all the laws and parameters of physics that conceivably could have been logically necessary, it seems highly improbable that it would be those that are life-permitting.

Objection 2: *Other Forms of Life Objection.* Another objection people commonly raise to the fine-tuning argument is that as far as we know, other forms of life could exist even if the parameters of physics were different. So, it is claimed, the fine-tuning argument ends up presupposing that all forms of intelligent life must be like us. The answer to this objection is that most cases of fine-tuning do not make this presupposition. Consider, for instance, the case of the fine-tuning of the strong nuclear force. If it were slightly larger or smaller, no atoms could exist other than hydrogen. Contrary to what one might see on Star Trek, an intelligent life form cannot be composed merely of hydrogen gas: there is simply not enough stable complexity. So, in general the fine-tuning argument merely presupposes that intelligent life requires some degree of stable, reproducible organized complexity. This is certainly a very reasonable assumption.

Objection 3: *Anthropic Principle Objection.* According to the weak version of the so-called *anthropic principle*, if the laws of nature were not fine-tuned, we would not be here to comment on the fact. Some have argued, therefore, that the fine-tuning is not really *improbable or surprising* at all under atheism, but simply follows from the fact that we exist. The response to this objection is to simply restate the argument in terms of our existence: our existence as embodied, intelligent beings are extremely unlikely under the atheistic single-universe hypothesis (since our existence requires fine-tuning), but not improbable under theism. Then, we simply apply the prime principle of confirmation to draw the conclusion that *our existence* strongly confirms theism over the atheistic single-universe hypothesis.

To further illustrate this response, consider the following "firing-squad" analogy. As John Leslie (1988,

p. 304) points out, if fifty sharp shooters all miss me, the response "if they had not missed me I wouldn't be here to consider the fact" is not adequate. Instead, I would naturally conclude that there was some reason why they all missed, such as that they never really intended to kill me. Why would I conclude this? Because my continued existence would be very improbable under the hypothesis that they missed me by chance, but not improbable under the hypothesis that there was some reason why they missed me. Thus, by the prime principle of confirmation, my continued existence strongly confirms the latter hypothesis.

Objection 4: *The "Who Designed God?" Objection.* Perhaps the most common objection that atheists raise to the argument from design, of which the fine-tuning argument is one instance, is that postulating the existence of God does not solve the problem of design, but merely transfers it up one level. Atheist George Smith, for example, claims that:

> If the universe is wonderfully designed, surely God is even more wonderfully designed. He must, therefore, have had a designer even more wonderful than He is. If God did not require a designer, then there is no reason why such a relatively less wonderful thing as the universe needed one.[10]

Or, as philosopher J.J.C. Smart states the objection:

> If we postulate God in addition to the created universe we increase the complexity of our hypothesis. We have all the complexity of the universe itself, and we have in addition the at least equal complexity of God. (The designer of an artifact must be at least as complex as the designed artifact).... *If the theist can show the atheist that postulating God actually reduces the complexity of one's total world view, then the atheist should be a theist.*[11]

The first response to the above atheist objection is to point out that the atheist claim that the designer of an artifact must be as complex as the artifact designed is certainly not obvious. But I do believe that their claim has some intuitive plausibility: for example, in the world we experience, organized complexity seems only to be produced by systems that already possess it, such as the human brain/mind, a factory, or an organism's biological parent.

The second, and better, response is to point out that, at most, the atheist objection only works against a version of the design argument that claims that all organized complexity needs an explanation, and that God is the best explanation of the organized complexity found in the world. The version of the argument I presented against the atheistic single-universe hypothesis, however, only required that the fine-tuning be more probable under theism than under the atheistic single-universe hypothesis. But this requirement is still met even if God exhibits tremendous internal complexity, far exceeding that of the universe. Thus, even if we were to grant the atheist assumption that the designer of an artifact must be as complex as the artifact, the fine-tuning would still give us strong reasons to prefer theism over the atheistic single-universe hypothesis.

To illustrate, consider the example of the "biosphere" on Mars presented at the beginning of this paper. As mentioned above, the existence of the biosphere would be much more probable under the hypothesis that intelligent life once visited Mars than under the chance hypothesis. Thus, by the prime principle of confirmation, the existence of such a "biosphere" would constitute strong evidence that intelligent, extraterrestrial life had once been on Mars, even though this alien life would most likely have to be much more complex than the "biosphere" itself.

The final response theists can give to this objection is to show that a super-mind such as God would not require a high degree of unexplained organized complexity to create the universe....

The many-universes hypothesis. In response to theistic explanation of fine-tuning of the cosmos, many atheists have offered an alternative explanation, what I will call the atheistic *many-universes hypothesis*. (In the literature it is more commonly referred to as the *Many Worlds hypothesis*, though I believe this name is somewhat misleading.) According to this hypothesis, there are a very large—perhaps infinite—number of universes, with the fundamental parameters of physics varying from universe to universe. Of course, in the vast majority of these universes the parameters of physics would not have life-permitting values. Nonetheless, in a small proportion of universes they would, and consequently it is no longer improbable that universes such as ours exist that are fine-tuned for life to occur.

Advocates of this hypothesis offer various types of models for where these universes came from. We will present what are probably the two most popular and plausible, the so-called *vacuum fluctuation* models and the *oscillating Big Bang* models. According to the vacuum fluctuation models, our universe, along with these other universes, were generated by quantum fluctuations in a pre-existing superspace.[12] Imaginatively, one can think of this pre-existing superspace as an infinitely extending ocean full of soap, and each universe generated out of this superspace as a soap-bubble which spontaneously forms on the ocean.

The other model, the oscillating Big Bang model, is a version of the *Big Bang* theory. According to the Big Bang theory, the universe came into existence in an "explosion" (that is, a "bang") somewhere between 10 and 15 billion years ago. According to the *oscillating* Big Bang theory, our universe will eventually collapse back in on itself (what is called the "Big Crunch") and then from that "Big Crunch" will arise another "Big Bang," forming a new universe, which will in turn itself collapse, and so on. According to those who use this model to attempt to explain the fine-tuning, during every cycle, the parameters of physics and the initial conditions of the universe are reset at random. Since this process of collapse, explosion, collapse, and explosion has been going on for all eternity, eventually a fine-tuned universe will occur, indeed infinitely many of them.

In the next section, we will list several reasons for rejecting the atheistic many-universes hypothesis.

Reasons for rejecting the many-universes hypothesis. The first reason for rejecting the atheistic many-universes hypothesis, and preferring the theistic hypothesis, is the following general rule: *everything else being equal, we should prefer hypotheses for which we have independent evidence or that are natural extrapolations from what we already know.* Let's first illustrate and support this principle, and then apply it to the case of the fine-tuning.

Most of us take the existence of dinosaur bones to count as very strong evidence that dinosaurs existed in the past. But suppose a dinosaur skeptic claimed that she could explain the bones by postulating a "dinosaur-bone-producing-field" that simply materialized the bones out of thin air. Moreover, suppose further that, to avoid objections such as that there are no known physical laws that would allow for such a mechanism, the dinosaur skeptic simply postulated that we have not yet discovered these laws or detected these fields. Surely, none of us would let this skeptical hypothesis deter us from inferring the existence of dinosaurs. Why? Because although no one has directly observed dinosaurs, we do have experience of other animals leaving behind fossilized remains, and thus the dinosaur explanation is a *natural extrapolation* from our common experience. In contrast, to explain the dinosaur bones, the dinosaur skeptic has invented a set of physical laws, and a set of mechanisms that is *not* a natural extrapolation from anything we know or experience.

In the case of the fine-tuning, we already know that minds often produce fine-tuned devices, such as

Swiss watches. Postulating God—a supermind—as the explanation of the fine-tuning, therefore, is a natural extrapolation from what we already observe minds to do. In contrast, it is difficult to see how the atheistic many-universes hypothesis could be considered a natural extrapolation from what we observe. Moreover, unlike the atheistic many-universes hypothesis, we have some experiential evidence for the existence of God, namely religious experience. Thus, by the above principle, we should prefer the theistic explanation of the fine-tuning over the atheistic many-universes explanation, everything else being equal.

A second reason for rejecting the atheistic many-universes hypothesis is that the "many-universes generator" seems like it would need to be designed. For instance, in all current worked-out proposals for what this "universe generator" could be—such as the oscillating big bang and the vacuum fluctuation models explained above—the "generator" itself is governed by a complex set of physical laws that allow it to produce the universes. It stands to reason, therefore, that if these laws were slightly different the generator probably would not be able to produce any universes that could sustain life. After all, even my bread machine has to be made just right in order to work properly, and it only produces loaves of bread, not universes! Or consider a device as simple as a mouse trap: it requires that all the parts, such as the spring and hammer, be arranged just right in order to function. It is doubtful, therefore, whether the atheistic many-universes theory can entirely eliminate the problem of design the atheist faces; rather, at least to some extent, it seems simply to move the problem of design up one level. . . .

A third reason for rejecting the atheistic many-universes hypothesis is that it cannot explain other features of the universe that seem to exhibit apparent design, whereas theism can. For example, many physicists, such as Albert Einstein, have observed that the basic laws of physics exhibit an extraordinary degree of beauty, elegance, harmony, and ingenuity. Nobel Prize-winning physicist Steven Weinberg, for instance, devotes a whole chapter of his book *Dreams of a Final Theory*[13] to explaining how the criteria of beauty and elegance are commonly used to guide physicists in formulating the right laws. . . .

Now such beauty, elegance, and ingenuity make sense if the universe was designed by God. Under the atheistic many-universes hypothesis, however, there is no reason to expect the fundamental laws to be elegant or beautiful. As theoretical physicist Paul Davies writes, "If nature is so 'clever' as to exploit mechanisms that amaze us with their ingenuity, is that not persuasive evidence for the existence of intelligent design behind the universe? If the world's finest minds can unravel only with difficulty the deeper workings of nature, how could it be supposed that those workings are merely a mindless accident, a product of blind chance?"[14]

This brings us to the final reason for rejecting the atheistic many-universes hypothesis, which may be the most difficult to grasp: namely, neither the atheistic many-universes hypothesis (nor the atheistic single-universe hypothesis) can at present adequately account for the improbable initial arrangement of matter in the universe required by the second law of thermodynamics. To see this, note that according to the second law of thermodynamics, the entropy of the universe is constantly increasing. The standard way of understanding this entropy increase is to say that the universe is going from a state of order to disorder. We observe this entropy increase all the time around us: things, such as a child's bedroom, that start out highly organized tend to "decay" and become disorganized unless something or someone intervenes to stop it.

Now, for purposes of illustration, we could think of the universe as a Scrabble board that initially starts out in a highly ordered state in which all the letters are arranged to form words, but which keeps getting randomly shaken. Slowly, the board, like the universe, moves from a state of order to disorder. The problem for the atheist is to explain how the universe could have started out in a highly ordered state, since it is extraordinarily improbable for such states to occur by chance. If, for example, one were to dump a bunch of letters at random on a Scrabble board, it would be very unlikely for most of them to form into words. At best, we would expect groups of letters to form into words in a few places on the board.

Now our question is, Could the atheistic many-universes hypothesis explain the high degree of initial order of our universe by claiming that given enough universes, eventually one will arise that is ordered and in which intelligent life occurs, and so it is no surprise that we find ourselves in an ordered universe? The problem with this explanation is that it is overwhelmingly more likely for local patches of order to form in one or two places than for the whole universe to be ordered, just as it is overwhelmingly more likely for a few words on the Scrabble board randomly to form words than for all the letters throughout the board randomly to form words. Thus, the overwhelming majority of universes in which intelligent life occurs will be ones in which the intelligent life will be surrounded by a small patch of order necessary for its existence, but in which the rest of the universe is disordered. Consequently, even under the atheistic many-universes hypothesis, it would still be enormously improbable for intelligent beings to find themselves in a universe such as ours which is highly ordered throughout.[15]

Conclusion. In the above sections we showed we have good, objective reasons for claiming that the fine-tuning provides strong evidence for theism. We first presented an argument for thinking that the fine-tuning provides strong evidence for preferring theism over the atheistic single-universe hypothesis, and then presented a variety of different reasons for rejecting the atheistic many-universes hypothesis as an explanation of the fine-tuning.

Notes

1. Freeman Dyson, *Disturbing the Universe* (New York: Harper & Row, 1979), p. 251.

2. Paul Davies, *The Cosmic Blueprint: New Discoveries in Nature's Creative Ability to Order the Universe* (New York: Simon and Schuster, 1988), p. 203.

3. Fred Hoyle, quoted in John Barrow and Frank Tipler, *The Anthropic Cosmological Principle* (Oxford: Oxford UP, 1986), p. 22.

4. Paul Davies, *The Accidental Universe* (Cambridge: Cambridge UP, 1982), pp. 90–91.

5. John Leslie, "How to Draw Conclusions from a Fine-Tuned Cosmos," *Physics, Philosophy and Theology: A Common Quest for Understanding*, ed. Robert Russell, et al. (Vatican City State: Vatican Observatory P, 1988), pp. 4, 35; Barrow and Tipler, p. 322.

6. Paul Davies, *Superforce* (Touchstone, 1985), p. 242.

7. John Leslie, *Universes* (New York: Routledge, 1989), pp. 39–40.

8. Leslie, "How to Draw Conclusions," p. 299.

9. Leslie, "How to Draw Conclusions," p. 300.

10. George Smith, "Atheism: The Case Against God," *An Anthology of Atheism and Rationalism*, ed. Gordon Stein (Prometheus Press, 1980), p. 56.

11. J.J.C. Smart, "Laws of Nature and Cosmic Coincidence," *The Philosophical Quarterly* 35, 140: 275–76; italics mine.

12. For example, see Quentin Smith, "World Ensemble Explanations," *Pacific Philosophical Quarterly* 67 (1986): 82.

13. Steven Weinberg, *Dreams of a Final Theory* (New York: Vintage Books, 1994), Chapter 6, "Beautiful Theories."

14. Davies, *Superforce*, pp. 235–36.

15. See Lawrence Sklar, *Physics and Chance: Philosophical Issues in the Foundation of Statistical Mechanics* (Cambridge: Cambridge UP, 1993), Chapter 8, for a review of the non-theistic explanations for the ordered arrangement of the universe and the severe difficulties they face.

Discussion

1. You might not understand all of the science to which Collins appeals. Suppose we assume that what he says is roughly true. How unlikely is it that the universe would have just the right physical constants to permit the evolution of human life?

2. What are some reasons for rejecting some of the non-theistic explanations of the existence of human life? Do you think Collins has made a strong case for rational belief in God? Why or why not?

3. Does Collins's argument avoid Hume's criticisms?

Chapter 4

Moral Arguments

EUTHYPHRO

PLATO*

Socrates. Come, then, and let us examine what we are saying. That thing or person which is dear to the gods is pious, and that thing or person which is hateful to the gods is impious, these two being the extreme opposites of one another. Was not that said?

Euthyphro. It was . . .

Soc. And further, Euthyphro, the gods were admitted to have enmities and hatreds and differences?

Euth. Yes, that was also said.

Soc. And what sort of difference creates enmity and anger? . . . I will suggest that these enmities arise when the matters of difference are the just and unjust, good and evil, honourable and dishonourable. Are not these the points about which men differ, and about which when we are unable satisfactorily to decide our differences, you and I and all of us quarrel, when we do quarrel?

Euth. Yes, Socrates, the nature of the differences about which we quarrel is such as you describe.

Soc. And the quarrels of the gods, noble Euthyphro, when they occur, are of a like nature?

Euth. Certainly they are.

Soc. They have differences of opinion, as you say, about good and evil, just and unjust, honourable and dishonourable: there would have been no quarrels among them if there had been no such differences— would there now?

Euth. You are quite right.

Soc. Does not every man love that which he deems noble and just and good, and hate the opposite of them?

Euth. Very true.

Soc. But, as you say, people regard the same things, some as just and others as unjust,—about these they dispute; and so there arise wars and fightings among them.

Euth. Very true.

Soc. Then the same things are hated by the gods and loved by the gods, and are both hateful and dear to them?

Euth. True.

Soc. And upon this view the same things, Euthyphro, will be pious and also impious?

Euth. So I should suppose.

Soc. Then, my friend, I remark with surprise that you have not answered the question which I asked. For I certainly did not ask you to tell me what action is both pious and impious: but now it would seem that what is loved by the gods is also hated by them. And therefore, Euthyphro, in thus chastising your father you may very likely be doing what is agreeable to Zeus but disagreeable to Cronos or Uranus, and what is acceptable to Hephaestus but unacceptable to Hera, and there may be other gods who have similar differences of opinion.

Euth. But I believe, Socrates, that all the gods would be agreed as to the propriety of punishing a murderer: there would be no difference of opinion about that. . . .

---

* Plato founded the first school of philosophy (in the western world) in the fourth century BCE.

Soc. . . . There was a notion that came into my mind while you were speaking; I said to myself: "Well, and what if Euthyphro does prove to me that all the gods regarded the death of the serf as unjust, how do I know anything more of the nature of piety and impiety? For granting that this action may be hateful to the gods, still piety and impiety are not adequately defined by these distinctions, for that which is hateful to the gods has been shown to be also pleasing and dear to them." And therefore, Euthyphro, I do not ask you to prove this; I will suppose, if you like, that all the gods condemn and abominate such an action. But I will amend the definition so far as to say that what all the gods hate is impious, and what they love pious or holy; and what some of them love and others hate is both or neither. Shall this be our definition of piety and impiety?

Euth. Why not, Socrates?

Soc. Why not! certainly, as far as I am concerned, Euthyphro, there is no reason why not. But whether this admission will greatly assist you in the task of instructing me as you promised, is a matter for you to consider.

Euth. Yes, I should say that what all the gods love is pious and holy, and the opposite which they all hate, impious.

Soc. Ought we to enquire into the truth of this, Euthyphro, or simply to accept the mere statement on our own authority and that of others? What do you say?

Euth. We should enquire; and I believe that the statement will stand the test of enquiry.

Soc. We shall know better, my good friend, in a little while. The point which I should first wish to understand is whether the pious or holy is beloved by the gods because it is holy, or holy because it is beloved of the gods.

Euth. I do not understand your meaning, Socrates. . . .

Soc. And what do you say of piety, Euthyphro: is not piety, according to your definition, loved by all the gods?

Euth. Yes.

Soc. Because it is pious or holy, or for some other reason?

Euth. No, that is the reason.

Soc. It is loved because it is holy, not holy because it is loved?

Euth. Yes.

Soc. And that which is dear to the gods is loved by them, and is in a state to be loved of them because it is loved of them?

Euth. Certainly.

Soc. Then that which is dear to the gods, Euthyphro, is not holy, nor is that which is holy loved of God, as you affirm; but they are two different things.

Euth. How do you mean, Socrates?

Soc. I mean to say that the holy has been acknowledged by us to be loved of God because it is holy, not to be holy because it is loved.

Euth. Yes.

Soc. But that which is dear to the gods is dear to them because it is loved by them, not loved by them because it is dear to them.

Euth. True.

Soc. But, friend Euthyphro, if that which is holy is the same with that which is dear to God, and is loved because it is holy, then that which is dear to God would have been loved as being dear to God; but if that which is dear to God is dear to him because it is loved by him, then that which is holy would have been holy because it is loved by him. But now you see that the reverse is the case, and that they are quite different from one another. For one is of a kind to be loved because it is loved, and the other is loved because it is of a kind to be loved. Thus you appear to me, Euthyphro, when I ask you what is the essence of holiness, to offer an attribute only, and not the essence—the attribute of being loved by all the gods. But you still refuse to explain to me the nature of holiness. And therefore, if you please, I will ask you not to hide your treasure, but to tell me once more what holiness or piety really is, whether dear to the gods or not (for that is a matter about which we will not quarrel) and what is impiety?

Euth. I really do not know, Socrates, how to express what I mean. For some-how or other our arguments, on whatever ground we rest them, seem to turn round and walk away from us.

Discussion

1. Suppose you believe that morality depends upon God. Which alternative would you find more palatable—arbitrariness or superfluousness? Why?

2. What are the religious motivations for maintaining that morality depends upon God?

3. If morality depends upon God, in what sense is God good? That is, if there is a criterion of goodness that stands over and judges people, in what sense is God good if the standard of goodness does not stand over him?

MORAL ARGUMENTS FOR THEISTIC BELIEF

ROBERT MERRIHEW ADAMS*

Introduction. Moral arguments were the type of theistic argument most characteristic of the nineteenth and early twentieth centuries. More recently they have become one of philosophy's abandoned farms. The fields are still fertile, but they have not been cultivated systematically since the latest methods came in. The rambling Victorian farmhouse has not been kept up as well as similar structures, and people have not been stripping the sentimental gingerbread off the porches to reveal the clean lines of argument. This essay is intended to contribute to the remedy of this neglect. It will deal with quite a number of arguments, because I think we can understand them better if we place them in relation to each other. This will not leave time to be as subtle, historically or philosophically, as I would like to be, but I hope I will be able to prove something more than my own taste for Victoriana.

An argument from the nature of right and wrong. Let us begin with one of the most obvious, though perhaps never the most fashionable, arguments on the farm: an Argument from the Nature of Right and Wrong. We believe quite firmly that certain things are morally right and others are morally wrong (for example, that it is wrong to torture another person to death just for fun). Questions may be raised about the nature of that which is believed in these beliefs: what does the rightness or wrongness of an act consist in? I believe that the most adequate answer is provided by a theory that entails the existence of God—specifically, by the theory that moral rightness and wrongness consist in agreement and disagreement, respectively, with the

will or commands of a loving God. One of the most generally accepted reasons for believing in the existence of anything is that its existence is implied by the theory that seems to account most adequately for some subject matter. I take it, therefore that my metaethical views provide me with a reason of some weight for believing in the existence of God.

Perhaps some will think it disreputably "tenderminded" to accept such a reason where the subject matter is moral. It may be suggested that the epistemological status of moral beliefs is so far inferior to that of physical beliefs, for example, that any moral belief found to entail the existence of an otherwise unknown object ought simply to be abandoned. But in spite of the general uneasiness about morality that pervades our culture, most of us do hold many moral beliefs with almost the highest degree of confidence. So long as we think it reasonable to argue at all from grounds that are not absolutely certain, there is no clear reason why such confident beliefs, in ethics as in other fields, should not be accepted as premises in arguing for the existence of anything that is required for the most satisfactory theory of their subject matter.[1]

Advantages. The divine command theory of the nature of right and wrong combines two advantages not jointly possessed by any of its nontheological competitors. These advantages are sufficiently obvious that their nature can be indicated quite briefly to persons familiar with the metaethical debate, though they are also so controversial that it would take a book-length review of the contending theories to defend my claims. The first advantage of divine command metaethics is that it presents facts of moral rightness and wrongness as objective, nonnatural facts—objective in the sense that whether they obtain or not does not depend on whether any human being thinks they do, and nonnatural in the sense that they cannot be stated entirely in the language of physics, chemistry, biology, and human or animal psychology.

---

* Robert Merrihew Adams is Professor Emeritus in the Department of Philosophy at Yale University.

For it is an objective but not a natural fact that God commands, permits, or forbids something. Intuitively this is an advantage....

Alleged disadvantages. What we cannot avoid discussing, and at greater length than the advantages, are the alleged disadvantages of divine command metaethics. The advantages may be easily recognized, but the disadvantages are generally thought to be decisive. I have argued elsewhere, in some detail, that they are not decisive. Here let us concentrate on ... the gravest objection to the more extreme forms of divine command theory [which] is that they imply that if God commanded us, for example, to make it our chief end in life to inflict suffering on other human beings, for no other reason than that he commanded it, it would be wrong not to obey. Finding this conclusion unacceptable, I prefer a less extreme, or modified, divine command theory, which identifies the ethical property of wrongness with the property of being contrary to the commands of a *loving* God. Since a God who commanded us to practice cruelty for its own sake would not be a loving God, this modified divine command theory does not imply that it would be wrong to disobey such a command....

Our discussion of the Argument from the Nature of Right and Wrong may be concluded with some reflections on the nature of the God in whose existence it gives us some reason to believe. (1) The appeal of the argument lies in the provision of an explanation of moral facts of whose truth we are already confident. It must therefore be taken as an argument for the existence of a God whose commands—and presumably, whose purposes and character as well—are in accord with our most confident judgments of right and wrong. I have suggested that he must be a loving God. (2) He must be an intelligent being, so that it makes sense to speak of his having a will and issuing commands. Maximum adequacy of a divine command theory surely requires that God be supposed

to have enormous knowledge and understanding of ethically relevant facts, if not absolute omniscience. He should be a God "unto whom all hearts are open, all desires known, and from whom no secrets are hid." (3) The argument does not seem to imply very much about God's power, however—certainly not that he is omnipotent. (4) Nor is it obvious that the argument supports belief in the unity or uniqueness of God. Maybe the metaethical place of divine commands could be taken by the unanimous deliverances of a senate of deities, although that conception raises troublesome questions about the nature of the morality or quasi-morality that must govern the relations of the gods with each other.

Kantian arguments. The most influential moral arguments for theistic belief have been a family of arguments that may be called Kantian. They have a common center in the idea of a moral order of the universe and are arguments for belief in a God sufficiently powerful to establish and maintain such an order. The Kantian family has members on both sides of one of the most fundamental distinctions in this area: the distinction between theoretical and practical arguments. By "a theoretical moral argument for theistic belief" I mean an argument having an ethical premise and purporting to prove the *truth*, or enhance the *probability*, of theism. By "a practical argument for theistic belief" I mean an argument purporting only to give ethical or other practical reasons for *believing* that God exists. The practical argument may have no direct bearing at all on the truth or probability of the belief whose practical advantage it extols.

Arguments from the Nature of Right and Wrong are clearly theoretical moral arguments for theistic belief. Kant, without warning us of any such distinction, gives us sometimes a theoretical and sometimes a practical argument (in my sense of "theoretical" and "practical," not his). His theoretical argument goes roughly as follows:

(A) We ought (morally) to promote the realization of the highest good.

(B) What we ought to do must be possible for us to do.

(C) It is not possible for us to promote the realization of the highest good unless there exists a God who makes the realization possible.

(D) Therefore, there exists such a God.

Kant was not clear about the theoretical character of this argument, and stated as its conclusion that "it is morally necessary to assume the existence of God."[2] Its premises, however, plainly imply the more theoretical conclusion that God exists.

(C) needs explanation. Kant conceived of the highest good as composed of two elements. The first element, moral virtue, depends on the wills of moral agents and does not require divine intervention for its possibility. But the second element, the happiness of moral agents in strict proportion to their virtue, will not be realized unless there is a moral order of the universe. Such an order, Kant argues, cannot be expected of the laws of nature, without God.

Doubts may be raised whether Kant's conception of the highest good is ethically correct and whether there might not be some nontheistic basis for a perfect proportionment of happiness to virtue. But a more decisive objection has often been made to (A): In any reasonable morality we will be obligated to promote only the best attainable approximation of the highest good. For this reason Kant's theoretical moral argument for theism does not seem very promising to me.

Elsewhere Kant argues quite differently. He even denies that a command to promote the highest good is contained in, or analytically derivable from, the moral law. He claims rather that we will be "hindered" from doing what the moral law commands us to do unless we can regard our actions as contributing to the realization of "a final end of all things" which we can also make a "final end for all our actions and abstentions." He argues that only the highest good can serve morally as such a final end and that we therefore have a compelling moral need to believe in the possibility of its realization.[3] This yields only a practical argument for theistic belief. Stripped of some of its more distinctively Kantian dress, it can be stated in terms of "demoralization," by which I mean a weakening or deterioration of moral motivation.

(E) It would be demoralizing not to believe there is a moral order of the universe, for then we would have to regard it as very likely that the history of the universe will not be good on the whole, no matter what we do.

(F) Demoralization is morally undesirable.

(G) Therefore, there is moral advantage in believing that there is a moral order of the universe.

(H) Theism provides the most adequate theory of a moral order of the universe.

(I) Therefore, there is a moral advantage in accepting theism.

What is a moral order of the universe? I shall not formulate any necessary condition. But let us say that the following is *logically sufficient* for the universe's having a moral order: (1) A good world-history requires something besides human virtue (it might, as Kant thought, require the happiness of the virtuous); but (2) the universe is such that morally good actions will probably contribute to a good world-history. (I use "world" as a convenient synonym for "universe.")

Avoiding demoralization. Theism has several secular competitors as a theory of a moral order of the universe in this sense. The idea of scientific and cultural progress has provided liberal thinkers, and Marxism has provided socialists, with hopes of a good world-history without God. It would be rash to attempt to adjudicate this competition here. I shall therefore not comment further on the truth of (H) but concentrate on the argument from (E) and (F) to (G). It is, after all, of great interest in itself, religiously and in other ways, if morality gives us a reason to believe in a moral order of the universe.

Is (E) true? Would it indeed be demoralizing not to believe there is a moral order of the universe? The issue is in large part empirical. It is for sociologists and psychologists to investigate scientifically what are the effects of various beliefs on human motivation. . . . But I have the impression there has not yet been very much hard, empirical research casting light directly on the question whether (E) is true. . . . Lacking scientifically established answers to the empirical aspects of our question, we may say, provisionally, what seems plausible to us. And (E) does seem quite plausible to me. Seeing our lives as contributing to a valued larger whole is one of the things that gives them a point in our own eyes. The morally good person cares about the goodness of what happens in the world and not just about the goodness of his own actions. If a right action can be seen as contributing to some great good, that increases the importance it has for him. Conversely, if he thinks that things will turn out badly no matter what he does, and especially if he thinks that (as often appears to be the case) the long-range effects of right action are about as likely to be bad as good, that will diminish the emotional attraction that duty exerts on him. Having to regard it as very likely that the history of the universe will not be good on the whole, no matter what one does, seems apt to induce a cynical sense of futility about the moral life, undermining one's moral resolve and one's interest in moral considerations. My

judgment on this issue is subject to two qualifications, however.

(1) We cannot plausibly ascribe more than a demoralizing tendency to disbelief in a moral order of the universe. There are certainly people who do not believe in such an order, but show no signs of demoralization.

(2) It may be doubted how much most people are affected by beliefs or expectations about the history of the universe as a whole. . . .

Some will object that those with the finest moral motivation can find all the inspiration they need in a tragic beauty of the moral life itself, even if they despair about the course of history. The most persuasive argument for this view is a presentation that succeeds in evoking moral emotion in connection with the thought of tragedy: Bertrand Russell's early essay "A Free Man's Worship"[4] is an eloquent example. But I remain somewhat skeptical. Regarded aesthetically, from the outside, tragedy may be sublimely beautiful; lived from the inside, over a long period of time, I fear it is only too likely to end in discouragement and bitterness, though no doubt there have been shining exceptions.

Defending practical arguments. But the main objection to the present argument is an objection to all practical arguments. It is claimed that none of them give justifying reasons for believing anything at all. If there are any practical advantages that are worthy to sway us in accepting or rejecting a belief, the advantage of not being demoralized is surely one of them. But can it be right, and intellectually honest, to believe something, or try to believe it, for the sake of any practical advantage, however noble?

I believe it can. This favorable verdict on practical arguments for theoretical conclusions is particularly plausible in "cases where faith creates its own verification," as William James puts it,[5] or where your wish is at least more likely to come true if you believe it will. Suppose you are running for Congress and an unexpected misfortune has made it doubtful whether you still have a good chance of winning. Probably it will at least be clear that you are more likely to win if you continue to believe that your chances are good. Believing will keep up your spirits and your alertness, boost the morale of your campaign workers, and make other people more likely to take you seriously. In this case it seems to me eminently reasonable for you to cling, for the sake of practical advantage, to the belief that you have a good chance of winning.

Another type of belief for which practical arguments can seem particularly compelling is trust in a person. Suppose a close friend of mine is accused of a serious crime. I know him well and can hardly believe he would do such a thing. He insists he is innocent. But the evidence against him, though not conclusive, is very strong. So far as I can judge the total evidence (including my knowledge of his character) in a cool, detached way, I would have to say it is quite evenly balanced. I want to believe in his innocence, and there is reason to think that I ought, morally, to believe in it if I can. For he may well be innocent. If he is, he will have a deep psychological need for someone to believe him. If no one believes him, he will suffer unjustly a loneliness perhaps greater than the loneliness of guilt. And who will believe him if his close friends do not? Who will believe him if I do not? Of course I could try to pretend to believe him. If I do that I will certainly be less honest with him, and I doubt that I will be more honest with myself, than if I really cling to the belief that he is innocent. Moreover, the pretense is unlikely to satisfy his need to be believed. If he knows me well and sees me often, my insincerity will probably betray itself to him in some spontaneous reaction.

The legitimacy of practical arguments must obviously be subject to some restrictions. Two important restrictions were suggested by William James.

(1) Practical arguments should be employed only on questions that "cannot . . . be decided on intellectual grounds."[6] There should be a plurality of alternatives that one finds intellectually plausible. (The option should be "living," as James would put it.) Faith ought not to be "believing what you know ain't so." It also ought not to short-circuit rational inquiry; we ought not to try to settle by practical argument an issue that we could settle by further investigation of evidence in the time available for settling it. (2) The question to be decided by practical argument should be urgent and of practical importance ("forced" and "momentous," James would say). If it can wait or is pragmatically inconsequential, we can afford to suspend judgment about it and it is healthier to do so. . . .

Similarly I think that the rationality of trying for moral reasons to believe in a moral order of the universe depends in large measure on the antecedent strength of one's commitment to morality. If one is strongly committed, so that one wishes to be moral even if the world is not, and if one seeks, not reasons to be moral, but emotional undergirding for the moral life, then it may well be rational to be swayed by the practical argument for the belief. . . .

Self-interest and morality. Both Kantian and Christian theism imply that true self-interest is in harmony with morality. Kant believed that in the long run one's happiness will be strictly proportioned to one's virtue. And if that would be denied by many Christian theologians for the sake of the doctrine of grace, they would at least maintain that no one can enjoy the greatest happiness without a deep moral commitment and that every good person will be very happy in the long run. They believe that the most important parts of a good person's self-interest are eternally safe, no matter how much his virtue or saintliness may lead him to sacrifice here below. The truth of these beliefs is surely another logically sufficient condition of the universe's having a moral order. (I assume that virtue is not so richly its own reward as to be sufficient in itself for happiness.)

There are both theoretical and practical arguments for theistic belief which are first of all arguments for faith in a moral world order that harmonizes self-interest with morality. As such, they belong to the Kantian type. For obvious reasons, let us call them "individualistic," by contrast with Kant's own, more "universalistic," arguments. The practical arguments of this individualistic Kantian type depend on the claim that it would be demoralizing not to believe in a harmony of self-interest with virtue.... The conviction that every good person will be very happy in the long run has often contributed, in religious believers, to a cheerfulness and single-heartedness of moral devotion that they probably would not have had without it. This integration of motives may be regarded as morally advantageous even if its loss does not lead to criminality.

I anticipate the objection that self-interest has no place in the highest ethical motives, and that belief in the harmony of self-interest with morality therefore debases rather than elevates one's motivation. What could be nobler than the virtuous sacrifice of what one regards as one's only chance for great happiness? Yet such sacrifice is rendered impossible by faith in the sure reward of virtue.

I have two replies: (1) Self-interest remains a powerful motive in the best of us; a life of which that was not true would hardly be recognizable as human. It is not obvious that a hardwon victory over even the most enlightened self-interest is morally preferable to the integration of motives resulting from the belief that it will be well with the righteous in the long run. Those who hold that belief still have plenty of victories to win over shorter-sighted desires. And it is plausible to suppose—though I do not know that anyone has proved it—that we are more likely to attain to the goodness that is possible through an integration of motives, than to win a death struggle with our own deepest self-interest, since the latter is so hard.

(2) It is not only in our own case that we have to be concerned about the relation between self-interest and virtue. We influence the actions of other people and particularly of people we love. Morally, no doubt, we ought to influence them in the direction of always doing right (so far as it is appropriate to influence them deliberately at all). But as we care about their self-interest too, our encouragement of virtue in them is apt to be more wholehearted and therefore more effective, if we believe that they will be happy in the long run if they do right. It is hard to see any ground for a charge of selfishness in this aspect of faith in the sure reward of virtue. It is not unambiguously noble (though it might be right) to encourage someone else—even someone you love—to make a great and permanent sacrifice of his true self-interest. We have no reason to regret the loss of opportunities to influence others so sadly....

I have focused, as most philosophical discussion of the moral arguments has, on the connections of theism with the nature of right and wrong and with the idea of a moral order of the universe. I am keenly aware that they form only part of the total moral case for theistic belief. Theistic conceptions of guilt and forgiveness,[7] for example, or of God as a friend who witnesses, judges, appreciates, and can remember all of our actions, choices, and emotions, may well have theoretical and practical moral advantages at least as compelling as any that we have discussed.

God's goodness. Perhaps moral arguments establish, at most, subsidiary advantages of belief in God's existence. They are more crucial to the case for his goodness. Causal arguments from the existence and qualities of the world may have some force to persuade us that there is a God, but they plainly have much less support to offer the proposition,

(K) If there is a God, he is morally very good.

(Here I define "a God" as a creator and governor of the whole universe, supreme in understanding and knowledge as well as in power, so that (K) is not a tautology.)

There is a powerful moral argument for (K). Belief in the existence of an evil or amoral God would be morally intolerable. In view of his power, such belief would be apt to carry with it all the disadvantages, theoretical and practical, of disbelief in a moral order of the universe. But I am even more concerned about the consequences it would have in view of his knowledge and understanding. We are to think of a being who understands human life much better than we do—understands it well enough to create and control it. Among other things, he must surely understand our moral ideas and feelings. He understands everyone's point of view, and has a more objective, or at least a more complete and balanced view of human relationships than any of us can have. He has whatever self-control, stability, and integration of purpose are implied in his having produced a world as constant in its causal order as our own. And now we are to suppose that that being does not care to support with his will the moral principles that we believe are true. We are to suppose that he either opposes some of them, or does not care enough about some of them to act on them. I submit that if we really believed there is a God like that, who understands so much and yet disregards some or all of our moral principles, it would be extremely difficult for us to continue to regard those principles with the respect that we believe is due them. Since we believe that we ought to pay them that respect, this is a great moral disadvantage of the belief that there is an evil or amoral God. . . .

Conclusion. In closing, I shall permit myself an argument *ad hominem.* The hypothesis that there is an amoral God is not open to the best known objection to theism, the argument from evil. Whatever may be said against the design argument for theism, it is at least far from obvious that the world was not designed. Yet hardly any philosopher takes seriously the hypothesis that it was designed by an amoral or evil being. Are there any good grounds for rejecting that hypothesis? Only moral grounds. One ought to reflect on that before asserting that moral arguments are out of place in these matters.

Notes

1. Cf. Henry Sidgwick, *The Methods of Ethics*, 7th ed. (New York: Dover, 1966), p. 509.

2. Immanuel Kant, *Critique of Practical Reason*, trans. L.W. Beck (New York: Liberal Arts Press, 1956), p. 130 (p. 125 of the Prussian Academy edition).

3. Immanuel Kant, *Religion within the Limits of Reason Alone*, trans. T.M. Greene and H.H. Hudson (New York: Harper, 1960), pp. 5–7. (The long footnote is particularly important.) In the *Critique of Practical Reason*, pp. 147–51 (142–46, Prussian Academy edition).

4. 1903, reprinted in Bertrand Russell, *Why I Am Not a Christian, and Other Essays on Religion and Related Subjects* (New York: Simon and Schuster, n.d.).

5. William James, "The Sentiment of Rationality," in his *The Will to Believe and Other Essays in Popular Philosophy* (New York: Dover Publications, 1956), p. 97.

6. William James, *The Will to Believe*, ibid., p. 11.

7. A theistic argument from the nature of guilt has been offered by A.E. Taylor, *The Faith of a Moralist*, vol. I (London: Macmillan, 1930), pp. 206–10. Cf. also H.P. Owen, *The Moral Argument for Christian Theism* (London: George Allen & Unwin, 1965), pp. 57–59.

Discussion

1. How does Adams attempt to solve the Euthyphro problem? Do you think he is successful?

2. Adams claims that the most adequate explanation of right and wrong is the agreement or disagreement with the commands of God. What are some other explanations of the nature of right and wrong? Is God's will more adequate?

3. Why does Adams think that the pursuit of morality, on some accounts of the nature of morality, would be demoralizing? How does theism improve on those competing accounts?

DOES ETHICS NEED GOD?

LINDA ZAGZEBSKI*

Why study ethics? Whenever anyone begins a study of ethics, a natural question to ask is why should we undertake such a study at all. I am satisfied with the answer that ethics teaches us how to be moral and anyone who understands what morality is will thereby want to live by it, just as anyone who understands the meaning of an analytic proposition will thereby see its truth. But wanting to be moral, I believe, is not sufficient to justify either the study of ethics or the attempt to practice morality. The question, "Should I try to be moral?" is not the same as the classic question, "Why be moral?" The latter question is sufficiently answered by the response that morality is its own justification. Morality aims at the good and anyone who understands what good means will see that its pursuit is justified. It is much harder, though, to answer the question, "Should I try to be moral?" This is because there is no point in trying to do something I cannot do. It is not enough to know that morality is intrinsically worthy of pursuit. There is simply no reason for me to pursue something unless I have good reason to think that I am capable of pursuing it successfully. So it is not rational to attempt to lead a moral life without a strong response to the fear of moral impotence, a fear which, I will argue, is rationally motivated and not easy to meet. In what follows I will attempt to show that it is not rational to try to be moral unless it is rational to believe that the attempt has a reasonable chance for success. But it is not rational to believe success is reasonably likely unless one believes there is a factor which explains how. A providential God is such a factor. Since it is rational to try to be moral, it is rational to believe in a providential God.

Is the moral life futile? One source of the fear of attempting to lead a moral life is the vague suspicion that the whole enterprise is futile. To see what generates this fear we ought to look at what the point of morality and moral studies is. It is, clearly, a practical one, and in this respect the study of ethics is quite different from other academic studies and even other branches of philosophy. The point is not simply to know certain things, to satisfy one's intellectual curiosity; it is not even to become wise. The purpose is to produce good and to prevent evil and to make oneself into a virtuous person. Of course, most philosophers have pointed out the practical end of ethics, though some have thought it exhausted in the doing of right acts and the avoidance of wrong acts or in the attainment of happiness. It seems to me that in producing good and avoiding evil I am primarily aiming at producing something independent of myself, so morality is not just practical, but creative. In this way it is like art. Art also aims at producing something independent of oneself, though it is creations of beauty rather than creations of good. But while almost anybody would agree that art is worthy of pursuit, some individual might reasonably conclude that there is no point in her trying to pursue it if she doubts her ability to do it successfully. The same point applies to a host of other worthwhile activities—Olympic-level gymnastics, a career as a solo cellist, finding a cure for leukemia—each is obviously worth doing, but knowing that it is worth doing is not sufficient to provide me with a rational motivation for attempting it, even if I want to do it very much. Similarly, it is not enough for me to know that morality is worthwhile in order for me to see the point in trying to pursue it myself. I need some assurance that my chances of success are not too remote.

The problem is intensified when we realize that the moral life involves more than time and effort.

---

*   Linda Zagzebski is the Kingfisher College Chair of Philosophy of Religion and Ethics at the University of Oklahoma.

At least some of the time it involves the sacrifice of self-interest. It is not rational, however, to give up a known good unless it is probable that the sacrifice really is for a greater good. This means that I need assurance on several counts. First, I need confidence that I can have moral knowledge. That is, I need good reasons to believe that my individual moral judgments, both about obligations and about values, are correct. Second, I need confidence in my moral efficacy, both in the sense that I can overcome moral weakness, and in the sense that I have the causal power to bring about good in the world. Third, insofar as many moral goals require cooperation, I need confidence in the moral knowledge and moral efficacy of other people.

The argument I will present can be cast in the form of a *reductio ad absurdum*. If all I have to go on morally is my own moral intuitions and reasoning and the intuitions and reasoning of others, then I am rationally led to skepticism about the possibility of moral knowledge. Furthermore, my experience and that of others leads me to be skeptical of a person's ability to follow moral beliefs. In addition, it is rational to be skeptical of human moral power in the sense that we can, by acting individually and collectively, bring about good and prevent evil in the world. The assumption of this argument therefore leads me to a very extensive moral skepticism, amounting actually to moral despair. But such despair cannot be rational. Therefore, the assumption of the argument must be false and I must be able to rely on more than my own human powers and those of others in attempting to live a moral life.

Moral skepticism? The first step of the argument is that a considered use of my moral and perceptual faculties and reasoning leads me to be skeptical of the possibility of attaining moral knowledge using these faculties alone. This skepticism is, I think, the most rational and fair-minded response to moral pluralism. I am not denying that there are many cases of moral agreement, even cross-culturally. Moral agreements typically involve general principles about the promotion of certain goods and the prevention of certain evils where no conflicts with other values arise. So almost anybody anywhere would accept a principle prohibiting the infliction of gratuitous suffering, or a principle advocating the acquisition of knowledge when no other good need be sacrificed. But when it is said that we ought to join the moral endeavor, this is not taken to mean that we ought to limit our efforts to the non-controversial cases. Our efforts are in fact required in the large areas in which there is considerable controversy.

In almost every area of morality it is a common human experience to find that people make very different moral judgments. The differences arise at every level of belief—at the level of judging the rightness or wrongness of particular acts, at the level of general principles of obligation, at the level of basic moral values, at the metaethical level. In some cases these differences are resolvable. Some are due to differences in beliefs about circumstances or causal relationships. So a moral disagreement about withholding medical treatment might reduce to a disagreement about a patient's chances of recovery, or a disagreement about some method of famine relief might turn on the question of whether it would cause more famine later. Another kind of resolvable moral difference arises when one party to the dispute makes a fallacious inference in reasoning. Since a part of reasoning has been codified into fairly clear and commonly-accepted rules disputes involving the violation of one of these rules should be easy to resolve. Still another kind of difference is one in which one disputant is lacking in sensitivity to a basic value. Some people may be incapable of appreciating a particular good and some of the time this can be detected. Perhaps he does not put much value in beauty or knowledge or love. We think of such a person as having a cognitive or emotional defect, and at least some of the time we may even reach general agreement on such a judgment.

All these cases, though resolvable, are rather uninteresting, and perhaps they are uninteresting precisely because they are resolvable. The really interesting cases of moral disputes are those which fall under none of these categories. They are disputes which cannot be blamed on factual error or error in logic or insensitivity to value. These are the cases that are not rationally decidable. This is not to say that in such cases no error in reasoning has been made, nor is it to say that no mistake has been made in the detection of value. What I am claiming is that there are cases in which we have no non-question-begging procedure for deciding where the error lies. Whenever I find significant disagreement with one of my moral judgments I could, of course, simply claim that the people who disagree with me are irrational or insensitive to good and evil, or have made some factual error, or any combination of these defects. But if I am honest, shouldn't I admit that I have no right to use correspondence with what seems to me to be rational and intuitively correct as a way of deciding the trustworthiness of others when my own trustworthiness is presumably also open to question?

Descartes remarks in the opening lines of the *Discourse on Method* that good sense must be more equally distributed than anything else since everyone is content with his share. It seems true that each person is content with his share of good judgment, in moral as well as in non-moral matters, but I do not see that it follows that such judgment is equally shared by all. People not so well endowed with practical wisdom might not be aware of their limitations. In fact, I suspect they usually are not. This is because the lack of practical wisdom involves the inability to judge character and moral ability, including one's own. So if I were lacking in the ability to make good moral judgments, I would not know it. How am I, then, to know that I am one of the luckier, more morally gifted ones? On the other hand, suppose Descartes's point is right and good judgment in moral matters really *is* equally distributed among people. Again many moral differences would be irresolvable. So regardless of the way good moral judgment is distributed among people, some moral disputes are undecidable. Either they are undecidable because such judgment is equal and so no one person's judgment counts more than another's, or they are undecidable because such judgment is unequal, but there is no non-question-begging procedure I can use to determine who has the better judgment. I conclude that in cases in which there is considerable moral disagreement which cannot be resolved by a commonly-accepted procedure, I ought to mistrust the judgments on both sides of the dispute, including my own.

The skepticism I am talking about is extensive and drastic, not the innocuous amount of skepticism that is healthy and no doubt required by intellectual honesty and modesty. To see how serious the problem is, we should address two further questions: (1) How widespread are the disagreements of the kind I have called undecidable, and (2) How strong a doubt should a rational person adopt as the result of these disagreements? The answer to both questions, I think, is that it is considerable.

To take the first question first, what reasons do we have to think that undecidable moral disagreements are widespread? It is obvious that there are very many moral disagreements. It is probably almost as obvious that in very many cases these disagreements have not been resolved to the satisfaction of most interested, rational people. But, of course, the fact that so many moral disagreements remain unresolved does not entail that they are unresolvable. Philosophers and others spend a lot of effort at attempting to resolve such disputes. Surely they must think it is possible to settle these matters; otherwise, they would not attempt it. If I am right, wouldn't this make most professional ethics, as well as most moral deliberation, misguided? Since the point of my argument is to save moral reasoning and action from being misguided, I do want to say that the reliance on our human faculties is not sufficient to save it from hopeless skepticism. However, an activity can be saved from hopelessness by something about which some of its practitioners are unaware. I am attempting to give a moral argument for the rationality of theistic belief. If I am right, then God's existence makes the moral life rational. God's existence does this whether the people who deliberate about and attempt to live a moral life know it or not.

Let us now consider the second question. Why should the fact that there are very many moral issues which are undecidable lead to such extreme skepticism? Perhaps a person could admit that many moral disputes are undecidable, but instead of concluding that such disputes have no resolution which has been adequately shown to be rational enough to support action, he might conclude instead that they're all rationally justified, or, at least, that many of them are.[1] This position seems reasonable when applied to disagreements about such things as scientific or historical theories, where one has little or nothing to lose if one is wrong, but it seems extremely implausible when applied to morality. It would be very odd to tell a woman contemplating an abortion that her position is rationally justified and that she ought to go ahead and act on it, but add that the contrary position is equally justified. I would think such information would be unhelpful in the extreme and would no doubt give her no motivation to act one way or the other.

Another way we might consider avoiding the consequence of accepting despair from this skeptical argument is to embrace a more benign form of skepticism, such as that of David Hume. This type of skepticism does not have any practical effect on the way one lives one's life, nor even on one's tendency to acquire and keep beliefs. Hume argues, for example, for skepticism about the existence of enduring physical objects, the existence of an enduring self, and the justification of induction. However, he admits that his skepticism has no effect on our tendency to believe

in the existence of enduring objects and a self or to make inductive inferences. When he says these beliefs are not rationally justified, he does not mean that we ought not to believe them. This is because it cannot be the case that we ought not to do something we cannot help doing, and Hume says we cannot help having these beliefs. My moral case is quite different, however. We have a strong natural motivation to be moral, but unlike Humean doubt, moral beliefs are very vulnerable to the doubt I have described, and it is not true that we cannot help having them. Skepticism does not take away the natural desire to be moral, but it does take away the motivating force because morality is intimately connected with feelings, commitments, sacrifices, expectations, and hopes. The moral life involves risk, both because of the personal sacrifices it requires and because of the emotional commitment it involves. This makes it very vulnerable to skepticism; hence, the despair.

The argument that moral pluralism rationally leads to moral skepticism depends in part on the assumption that the acquisition of knowledge is social. Though I do not intend to defend it here, this assumption seems to me to be true and to be applicable to knowledge in the moral sphere. We learn the meaning and application of moral terms socially; we have our moral sensitivities socially educated; we learn the trustworthiness of our moral reasoning, as we do all other forms of reasoning, by the responses of others; and we learn the validity of those perceptual and other factual beliefs which we use in making specific moral judgments by comparing them with the judgments of others. This is not to say, of course, that the reasoning and judgments of others are always the last word, but it is to say that they must be taken into account and the reliability of our own moral judgments is significantly weakened when they conflict with those of others. They are, at least, unless we have some reasonable explanation of the conflict which settles the disagreement in our favor.

Skepticism about our moral efficacy? So far I have argued that if all we have to go on in moral deliberation is our human faculties, then the existence of moral pluralism makes many moral disagreements undecidable and this ought to lead us rationally into an extensive skepticism about moral knowledge. The skepticism we are rationally led to, though, is not limited to knowledge of moral truths. If we are rational, we must also doubt our moral efficacy. In the first place, the predominance of moral weakness ought to lead us to lack trust in our own moral powers and those of others. Furthermore, even when moral weakness is not a problem, there is good reason to doubt our moral efficacy in the sense of our causal power over good and evil. People have been struggling to promote good and to prevent evil for as long as people have had a moral sense at all, but is there good evidence that good is increasing and evil decreasing? Even when good is produced or evil eliminated, do we have good reason to think that it is usually the result of a conscious, morally-motivated human choice? Of course, some of the time it probably is, but if I impartially consider the probability that on any given occasion I can, by my efforts, produce good or eliminate evil, would I calculate that the probability is sufficiently great to be worth the emotional risk and personal sacrifice of making the effort? If I were certain that my judgment about what is good and how to attain it were true, the doubt about my moral efficacy might still leave it rational to act on my moral judgment and take the risk of being ineffective. But when doubt about the judgment itself is added to doubt about my ability to act on it effectively, the result is a very serious degree of skepticism, making it irrational in many cases to accept the sacrifices of attempting to be moral. In deciding whether or not to attempt a moral life, I must weigh the probability that a certain quantity of good will be produced by my efforts against the probability that a sacrifice of a certain quantity of good will result.

Let i = the increase in the probability that a good will obtain as a result of my efforts.

s = the probability that my efforts will result in a sacrifice of certain lesser goods.

$V1$ = the value of the good I might produce by attempting a moral life.

$V2$ = the value of the good I would sacrifice.

We could then calculate the expected value of the attempt to be moral as:

$$VM \text{ (value of moral effort)} = i \times V1 - s \times V2.$$

It should be recognized that part of the value $V1$ will be internal goods which accrue to me simply in virtue of my efforts at being moral. The probability that this part of $V1$ will obtain may be very high. However, I have argued that the value i, which is the overall probability that I can produce $V1$, might be so much lower than the probability value s, it could easily happen that the value VM is negative, even though we would expect $V1$ to be much greater than $V2$.

I have argued that if all we have to go on morally are our human faculties, then we are rationally led to extensive moral skepticism, both about the possibility of moral knowledge and about moral efficacy. If one's actions are consistent with one's beliefs such skepticism would have a devastating effect on the attempt to lead a moral life. It rationally leads to moral despair. But moral despair cannot be rational since we know the attempt to lead a moral life is rational. The assumption of the argument, that our human faculties alone make the rational attempt to practice morality possible, must therefore be false.

A kind of *reductio*. This argument is, as I have pointed out, a kind of *reductio ad absurdum*. It is not, however, a *reductio* in the usual logician's sense of a reduction to a logical contradiction. The absurdity is of a different kind. Total and unrelenting moral despair, I presume, is an absurd state. It cannot be rational to be in such a state, though I do not intend to argue for this. There may be people influenced by some aspects of existentialism, who believe that life is absurd and simply accept it. This essay is not intended for those people. It is intended for those people who believe that if life is truly absurd, it ought not to be lived. Since it ought to be lived, it must not be absurd. I am assuming that nihilism is neither natural nor rational, and in spite of Nietzsche, it is certainly not comforting.

In the famous essay, "A Free Man's Worship," Bertrand Russell attempted to exalt human life on a foundation of moral despair by endowing it with the beauty of tragedy. He thought the right attitude toward the moral history of the universe is complete resignation, but the morally sensitive person with sufficient imagination can find all the motivation he needs to live a morally worthy life in the purely aesthetic qualities of such a life, and in this there is a kind of freedom. That there are people who can find sufficient motivation to live in such a manner may be possible, but whether it is rational or even praiseworthy to give up lesser goods in what is thought to be a vain attempt to obtain greater goods is dubious, even if the attempt itself is beautiful.

Ethics and God. If moral despair is irrational, then we must be able to trust more than our own human faculties of perception, reasoning and intuition in attempting to lead a moral life. What kind of trust do we need in order to avoid such despair? I argued that skepticism faces us at several points in attempting to be moral. First, there is skepticism about the possibility of attaining moral knowledge. In attempting to live morally we need to trust that there is something beyond our human cognitive and moral faculties which can provide guidance in knowing moral truth. The Christian God has such a function. Second, I argued that there is skepticism about moral efficacy in the sense of moral weakness. This suggests that the attempt to lead a moral life requires trust in something that can help us overcome such weakness. The Christian notion of grace serves such a function. Third, there is skepticism about moral causal power, both my own and that of others. This means that the attempt to live morally requires trust that the ultimate goal of morality can be reached, that good can be created and preserved and evil can be prevented or eliminated, in spite of the fact that people differ greatly in their moral judgments and often seem to be acting at cross-purposes. The Christian notion of divine providence serves this requirement for the moral life.

I conclude that it is only rational to do ethics and attempt to lead a moral life if there is something we can trust which will save us from these three forms of moral skepticism. I have not argued that the Christian God is the only thing that can serve the need for trust in living the moral life, but the Christian God does serve these needs. It is therefore more rational for a person who believes in the rationality of the attempt to live morally to believe in such a God than not to believe in anything in which she can put such trust.

The argument can be summarized as follows: It is not rational to try to be moral unless it is rational to believe the attempt likely to be successful. At least, the likelihood of its success must not be outweighed by the sacrifices such an attempt entails. But it is not rational to believe such an attempt likely to be successful if all we have to go on in the moral life are our own faculties. This is because those faculties rationally lead us to extensive skepticism both about moral knowledge and about moral efficacy. Since it is rational to try to be moral, we must have more to go on in the moral life than our own human faculties. In particular, the possibility of success in the moral life requires something which enables us to get out of skepticism. The Christian God has such a function.

Objections. An objector might say that though the Christian concepts of grace and providence are adequate to forestall skepticism about moral efficacy, how does the existence of God prevent skepticism about moral knowledge? Isn't the theist as much faced with the problem of moral pluralism as is the non-theist? In response, it seems to me that it is certainly true that the theist is faced with a certain amount of skepticism about his own particular moral judgments. Theism does not guarantee the possession of moral truth to the believer. However, the theist has a better way of dealing with the problem of moral pluralism than the non-theist in two ways. First, the theist has another source of moral knowledge in divine revelation and the teachings of the Church, and second, the theist's trust in divine providence gives him reason to believe in moral progress, not only with respect to moral efficacy, but also with respect to moral knowledge. This is not to suggest that the theist has no problems with doubt about the interpretation of God's will. Such a suggestion would be naive. But again, the Christian concept of providence provides confidence that these problems are resolvable.

There is one more way in which my conclusion might be blocked. It might be agreed that the assumption of my argument rationally leads to despair, that such despair is not rational, and that therefore it is rational to have trust in attempting to be moral. But perhaps the human need for trust is its own justification; it is not necessary to bring in the existence of a providential God to justify it. If the human need for trust is strong enough, it might outweigh the skepticism I have defended. We might call this the alternative of blind trust, or trust out of the sheer need to avoid despair. Such trust would be, I think, more rational than despair, but some trust can be more rational than others, and the trust I have defended is a trust with a set of beliefs which explains its rationality. This seems to be far more rational than blind trust.

Conclusion. I have given a moral argument for the rationality of belief in the Christian God. I have assumed that it is rational to try to be moral, but given certain problems in the moral life, it is not rational unless certain conditions obtain—those conditions which free a person from the three forms of skepticism I have discussed. The argument is Kantian in its general structure since, like Kant, the claim is that moral endeavor presupposes the existence of something like God as a condition for the rational possibility of its achievement. Theistic belief is, therefore, justified in the practical domain of reason. I have not argued, though, that belief in the Christian God is the only conceivable way to provide the conditions necessary for making moral effort rational, but it has no competitors that I know of. It follows that the theist is acting more rationally than the non-theist when they both act on their moral beliefs and claim that those beliefs are justified. Since most non-theists do not hesitate to do this, it follows that it would be more rational for them to believe in God than not to.

Note

1. This seems to be the position of Richard W. Miller in "Ways of Moral Learning," *Philosophical Review* XCIV, 4 (October 1985). See esp. pp. 507–09, 548–56, and fn. 33, p. 539.

Discussion

1. Why should we become moral skeptics if we are left to our own reason and insight and that of others?

2. How would moral skepticism and a sense of moral impotence affect your moral life?

3. How would the Christian God serve to resolve the problems of moral skepticism and moral impotence?

4. Suppose the moral life is possible only if God exists. Does that prove God's existence? Does it make belief in God rational?

Chapter 5

Religious Experience

THE EXPERIENTIAL BASIS OF THEISM

WILLIAM P. ALSTON*

Background issues. I will try to explain, so far I can in the space allotted, why I think it is rational to be a theist. Rather than being equally sketchy about everything, I will select one or two issues for special consideration.

First, a word as to how I understand "theism." Rather than tailoring the term to an exact fit with the details of my own beliefs, I will give it a latitudinarian reading. Theism is the view that there is a single, ultimate and supremely perfect source of being, on which all other than itself depends at every moment for its existence, and which appears to us as personal. (The last clause is designed to include those who hold that the ultimate source of being is only "analogically" or "symbolically" describable in personalistic terms.) Theism is only an abstract aspect of elaborate religious systems, but it may be usefully singled out for discussion. However, the involvement of theism in a larger context, comprising not only a richer matrix of belief but a "form of life," is crucial for the ensuing discussion. I will make no attempt to defend the rationality of theism as a philosophical theory, embraced outside of participation in the life of a theistic religion. I conceive theistic belief to rest on twin pillars of unequal strength. First, there are the very general

considerations of "natural theology," accessible to any sufficiently intelligent and reflective person; they give some support to the belief. Of the traditional arguments for the existence of God, I take most seriously the cosmological and ontological arguments. Without claiming for them anything like coercive proof, it seems to me that the cosmological argument, properly construed, provides a significant support for the view that the physical universe depends for its existence on a necessarily existing source of all being other than itself. And the ontological argument, properly construed, provides significant support for the view that this necessarily existing source of all being is an absolutely perfect being.

The other pillar is the experience of God. It is reasonable to believe in the existence of God because we have experienced His presence and activity in our lives. I consider this to be the more massive pillar. As I see it, the proper role of natural theology is not to bear the whole weight, or even most of it, but to provide basis for reassurance, in moments of doubt, that what we take to be our experience of God is not merely a projection of our needs and fears. I am not concerned to argue that a theistic belief resting wholly on natural theology is a rational belief. Because of this, and because I feel that I have something more distinctive to say about the experiential pillar, I will confine my discussion to that side of the matter.

Experiential support. My first task is to explain how I am thinking of this experiential support. Many discussions of the "argument from religious experience" treat

* William P. Alston (1921–2009) was Professor of Philosophy at Syracuse University.

this as one more piece of natural theology. Like the teleological or moral arguments it begins with certain data, in this case religious experiences; and the question is whether an adequate *explanation* of these data requires an appeal to God. That is *not* the way I am thinking of an experiential support for theism. I am thinking of it as analogous to the experiential support all of us have for the existence of the physical world. Here it is not a matter of gathering data, in the form of sensory experiences, and then claiming that they are best explained by supposing that they are due to the action of the physical world on us. It is rather that we take ourselves, *in* these experiences, to be aware of the physical world. No explanatory issues are involved. To be sure, a few philosophers have attempted to carry through the explanatory argument just mentioned, but they have been conspicuously unsuccessful; and in any event that is not our normal stance. By analogy, I am claiming that a participant in a theistic religion takes herself to be aware of God at various times, that it is rational for her to do so, and that because of this theistic belief is rational for her.

Note that I have compared the experiential support for theistic belief to our experiential support for belief in the physical world, not to our experiential support for belief in, e.g., trees, much less to my experiential support for the belief that there is now a tree in front of me. With respect to the range of experience I am considering (call it "theistic experience" *faute de mieux*) God is not one of the items disclosed among others. We don't consult our experience of, e.g., leading the Christian life, to determine whether God is there, rather than someone or something else the way I "consult" my visual experience, i.e., take a look to see whether that Mercedes sedan is still in front of my house. Similarly, we don't take a closer look or carry out more extensive observations to determine whether there is a physical world. The supposition that there is a physical world (that there are physical things spread out in space, exhibiting various perceivable qualities)

is constitutive of the practice of forming particular beliefs about particular physical things on the basis of sense experience in the way we usually do. (Call this "perceptual practice.") To be sure, this very abstract belief in the existence of the "physical world" is not disengaged and explicitly assented to at the earlier stages of mental development. Nevertheless, in learning to form physical-object beliefs on the basis of sense experience we are, at least implicitly and in practice, accepting the proposition that the physical world exists (and that we are aware of it in sense experience). Thus the question of the rationality of this belief *is* the question of the rationality of perceptual practice. Since, for us at any rate, to accept that belief is to engage in that practice, the belief is rational *if* the practice is. Analogously, the relatively abstract belief that God exists is constitutive of the doxastic practice of forming particular beliefs about God's presence and activity in our lives on the basis of theistic experience. (Call this "theistic practice.") Here, too, the question of the rationality of that belief, insofar as it rests on experiential support, *is* the question of the rationality of that practice. In neither case is there any question of using particular experiences to settle the question one way or the other, the way I use particular experiences to settle the question of whether my wife is in the kitchen or of whether God told me that I am handling this problem in the right way.

This is not to say that we can't, or don't, *discover* God, or the physical world, by experience. We can discover one or the other by coming to participate, reasonably, in one or the other doxastic practice. By learning to engage in the practice we discover various particular facts about God or the physical world; and *thereby* come to discover God or the physical world. The present point is just that these discoveries are much more global affairs than the discovery of some scientific fact about God or the physical world; they are tied to the practice as a whole rather than to certain particular exercises thereof.

This talk of doxastic practices is reminiscent of talk of language games and the like; and lest I find myself tarred with such dreadful appellations as "Wittgensteinian fideism" let me hasten to make it explicit that I am thinking of these practices in a "realistic" fashion, rather than in an idealist, "pragmatist," culturally relativist, or linguistically solipsistic way. I am not supposing that we create divine or physical "worlds" in Goodmanian fashion by engaging in these practices. I am not supposing that the realities we encounter therein depend for their existence in any way on our conceptual or linguistic activities. Nor am I supposing that the question of their existence can be raised only within the practice in question. (My limited reliance on natural theology is an indication of this.) For better or for worse, I believe that in sensory experience and in theistic experience we encounter and learn about realities that could be just as they are had we not been around to record the fact.

I should say a word about the scope of my term "theistic experience." I mean it to range over all experiences that are taken by the experiencer to be an awareness of God (where God is thought of theistically). I impose no restrictions on its phenomenal quality. It could be a rapturous loss of conscious self-identity in the mystical unity with God; it could involve "visions and voices"; it could be an awareness of God through the experience of nature, the words of the Bible, or the interaction with other persons; it could be a background sense of the presence of God, sustaining one in one's ongoing activities. Thus the category is demarcated by what cognitive significance the subject takes it to have, rather than by any distinctive phenomenal feel.

The theistic doxastic practice. We have seen that the rationality of theistic belief, insofar as that rests on an experiential base, depends on the rationality of a certain "doxastic" practice, what we have called "theistic practice." But how do we decide that? The evaluation of doxastic practices is a thorny matter, indeed,

and I shall only be able to touch on a few points in this chapter.

The first point is that where we are dealing with what we might call a *basic* practice, one that constitutes our basic or most direct cognitive access to a subject matter, it is not to be expected that we can show it to be rational or irrational in a non-circular way, by using only the output of other practices. Very roughly, the reason for that judgment is this. The most important consideration in deciding on the rationality of a doxastic practice is its reliability, the extent to which it can be depended on to yield true rather than false beliefs. But if the practice in question, P, is our basic access to its subject matter, we will have no independent way of comparing P's deliverance with the real facts of the matter, so as to determine the accuracy of P's deliverance. I believe that a survey of attempts to establish, from the outside, the reliability, or unreliability, of doxastic practices plausibly taken as basic, like sense perception and introspection, will support this judgment. Thus we should not suppose that unless we can establish the reliability of theistic practice on the basis of premises taken from other practices we will have to deem it irrational. If we imposed that requirement across the board we would be jettisoning sense perception, introspection, rational intuition, and deductive and inductive reasoning; we should be bereft of belief. And how could we justify making this demand of theistic practice alone?

Well, then, what *can* we do to assess the rational status of a basic doxastic practice? The obvious alternative is to look at its internal "coherence," ways in which it might be self-supporting. This can be illustrated by some of the ways in which perceptual practice is self-supporting. Engaging in this practice and relying on its outputs, we discover (a) that perceptual beliefs formed by a subject at a time can be confirmed by other subjects or by the same subject at other times; and (b) that by relying on its inputs as a basis for reasoning we can discover regularities, thereby putting us in a position to effectively anticipate the course of events and exercise control over them. This does *not* constitute a non-circular argument for the rationality or reliability of perceptual practice. It is only by relying on the outputs of this practice that we get our reasons for supposing that the practice exhibits these features. (We don't learn this from ESP or from divine revelation.) Nevertheless there *are* ways in which perceptual practice supports itself from the inside; they are fruits of the practice that encourage us to engage in it and to take it seriously as a source of information. Nor is this self-support a trivial matter. It is conceivable that our perceptual beliefs and what is based on them should not hang together in this way; hence the fact that they do so is a mark in its favor.

Now it is clear that theistic practice does not exhibit these kinds of self-support. Its deliverances do not put us in a position to predict the doings of God, much less control them. Nor is the same sort of intersubjective corroboration possible. This latter point divides into two. First, the community of practitioners is much less extensive. And second, even within that community there are no definite criteria of confirmation. If I suppose that I have seen an airplane flying over my house at a certain moment there are principles that determine what kinds of sensory experiences by observers in what spatio-temporal locations will confirm or disconfirm my belief. But there are no such principles governing the intersubjective confirmation of my supposition that I was keenly aware of God's sustaining love at a certain moment. If no one else was aware of it at that moment, what is that supposed to show?

These disanalogies, and others that might have been mentioned, have been taken by some philosophers to discredit the claims of theistic practice to be a cognitive access to an objective reality. But this is no more than a piece of epistemic imperialism, as much so as the requirement that the reliability of theistic practice be established in other practices, or the requirement that the existence of God be shown by other practices to be the best explanation of theistic experience. It is only that the imperialism is not quite so easy to detect here. In this guise the imperialism consists in taking the mode of self-support exhibited by perceptual practice to be the standard for all other doxastic practices, at least all other experiential doxastic practices, practices of forming beliefs on the basis of experience. If a practice does not hang together in this way, it is to be dismissed; this mode of success is taken to be a necessary as well as a sufficient condition of rationality.

To see what is wrong with this we need to reflect on the point that what features of a doxastic practice betoken reliability are a function of the nature of the subject matter and our relation thereto. If the subject matter is maximally stable, as in mathematics, then always yielding the same beliefs about the same objects is an indication of reliability; but if the subject matter is in constant flux that same feature would rather betoken unreliability. If the subject matter is inorganic nature, the formation of beliefs concerning intelligible communications from the objects would indicate unreliability, but not if the subject matter is persons. What features indicate reliability depends on what features are such that they *could* be expected to be present if the practice yields mostly truths, given the nature of the subject matter and our relation to it. And how do we tell what the subject matter is like? If the practice in question is a basic one, we have to rely on it to tell us. Thus, a practice sets its own standards for judging its reliability, as well as providing the data for that judgment. It not only grades its own exams; it even provides the criteria for grade assignment.

Perceptual and theistic practices. Let's apply this to the present issue. The picture of the physical world and our perceptual relation thereto that is built upon the basis of sense perception is that of a realm of items that behave and interact (including interactions involving human percipients) in lawful ways that are, to a considerable extent at least, humanly discoverable. This picture provides grounds for supposing that any veridical perceptual experience will be lawfully related to the perceptual experiences of others in specifiable ways that form an effective basis for intersubjective testing. Moreover, the picture suggests that the predictive capacity one gains from a knowledge of general laws is a reasonable expectation, one of the ways in which the by and large veridicality of perceptual beliefs would show themselves. But, by contrast, the picture of God and God's relations to the world that is built up on the basis of theistic practice is quite different. God is too transcendent, too "wholly other" for us to expect to be able to predict, much less control, His behavior, however accurate our particular experiences of His presence. And it is part of that unpredictability that we cannot expect to ascertain lawful regularities in His manifestations to our experience. Even if our particular readings of God's presence were 100% accurate, we could not expect to discover the general conditions under which a human being would experience a certain divine activity if it were really taking place. Insofar as we have any idea of what conditions are required for an individual's being aware of God, they have to do with subtle factors like openness and purity of heart, factors for the presence of which we hardly have an effective test. Therefore, since there is no reason to expect these achievements, however reliable the practice, their absence is no reason to brand it as unreliable, or even to doubt its reliability. It is a further and very important question, into which I will not have time to go into in this paper, how theistic practice, if reliable, could be expected to display that reliability, what fruits of the practice are such that, if they are forthcoming, the practice can be considered self-supporting in a way appropriate to it.

I take these considerations to be a decisive refutation of the claim that theistic practice can be branded as unreliable and/or irrational because it fails to exhibit the kind of self-support characteristic of perceptual practice. Nevertheless, the tendency to take sense perception as our model of a veridical experiential access to reality is so deeply rooted that it will be worthwhile to consider the matter from another angle. I believe that it will help us to cast a critical eye on this tendency if we try the experiment of looking at perceptual practice from the standpoint of other doxastic practices and consider what judgment on its rationality might be indicated from those other perspectives. Nor do we have to rely on our own imaginations alone for this task. We only have to remember the low esteem in which sense perception has been held by many philosophers from Parmenides to Descartes. Plato, for example, held that sense perception cannot be regarded as a source of knowledge because its objects lack the stability required for true knowledge; moreover they are not fully determinate; there is no definite truth about them. We may, I think, take Plato to be using the standards of mathematics to judge perceptual practice. Since it is incapable of the achievements of mathematics, we cannot take its output as serious candidates for knowledge. In like fashion inductive reasoning has often been denigrated because it cannot meet the requirements of deductive reasoning by displaying a necessary connection between premises and conclusion. I would ask those who reject theistic practice for the reasons we have been considering, why we should take their strictures any more seriously than we do those of Plato against perception. In both cases the critic condemns a doxastic practice for not meeting expectations that are appropriate to a different practice. Of course, in both cases the critic is free to choose not to play the game unless it gives him what his favorite game provides. But why should the rest of us take these preferences seriously?

Here is another way of seeing the essential arbitrariness of my opponent's view. Sense perception, though certainly a useful guide to the physical environment, does not rank as high as it might conceivably rank, even on its own chosen dimensions. There are several respects in which sense perception is less than perfect. First, its deliverances can't all be accurate since there are contradictions among them. Second, though its deliverances have provided a basis for the discovery of regularities that serve as a basis for prediction and control, that achievement has been slow in coming, given the whole stretch of human life on earth, and even now it is spotty. We can certainly envisage a cognitive faculty that would reveal the regularities, along with the particular exemplifications, much more obviously and unerringly. Third, if we are to trust contemporary science, which itself is ultimately based on the deliverances of sense perception, our perceptual beliefs, though useful as a guide to action, rather badly misrepresent the intrinsic character of their objects. Most perceivers take physical things to be intrinsically qualified by the colors they display to our visual awareness: we perceive rocks, tables and leaves as continuously filled in, whereas actually they are mostly empty space with a few particles floating around; and so on. In all these respects perceptual practice is less ideal than it might conceivably be as a source of information about the physical environment. This being the case, why should we take its actual achievement level to be the norm for experiential sources of belief? Why shouldn't we take perceptual practice itself to be irrational for failing to come up to some higher standard? Isn't it just arbitrary to fasten on the level actually achieved by perceptual practice, rather than some higher or lower level? What warrant do we have for supposing that this is the level marked out by the nature of things as the one required for rational acceptance? Once we confront this issue squarely, we will realize that we proceed in this fashion only because we are so thoroughly immersed in perceptual practice that we are irresistibly led to take it as our measuring stick for other experiential sources of belief. But on reflection we can see that we have no rational warrant for doing so. This is just one more form of epistemic imperialism, judging one doxastic practice from the standpoint of another.

Conclusion. Much more needs to be said about these issues. But I hope that I have said enough to show at least that there is an arguable case for regarding what I have called theistic practice as a rational mode of belief formation, and hence that there is an experiential support for the rationality of theistic belief.

Discussion

1. In what ways is religious experience like sensory experience?

2. In what ways is religious experience unlike sensory experience?

3. How does Alston respond to the alleged dissimilarities? Do you think his responses are adequate?

4. What do you consider the most powerful objection to the veridicality of religious experience? Can ordinary sensory experience overcome this sort of objection?

Chapter 6

Naturalism Refuted?

THE SELF-REFUTATION OF NATURALISM

ALVIN PLANTINGA*

Proper function. . . . Most of us think (or would think on reflection) that at least a function or purpose of our cognitive faculties is to provide us with true beliefs. Moreover, we go on to think that when they function properly, in accord with our design plan, then for the most part they do precisely that. . . .

. . . Over a vast area of cognitive terrain we take it both that the purpose (function) of our cognitive faculties is to provide us with true or verisimilitudinous beliefs and that, for the most part, that is just what they do. We suppose, for example, that most of the deliverances of memory are at least approximately correct. True, if you ask five witnesses how the accident happened, you may get five different stories. Still, they will agree that there was indeed an *accident* and that it was an *automobile* accident (as opposed, say, to a naval disaster or a volcanic eruption); there will usually be agreement as to the number of vehicles involved (particularly if it is a small number), as well as the rough location of the accident (Aberdeen, Scotland, as opposed to Aberdeen, South Dakota), and so on. And all this is against the background of massive and much deeper agreement: that there are automobiles; that they do not disappear when no one is looking; that if

released from a helicopter they fall down rather than up, that they are driven by people who use them to go places, that they are seldom driven by three-year-olds, that their drivers have purposes, hold beliefs, and often act on those purposes and beliefs, that few of them (or their drivers) have been more than a few miles from the surface of the earth, that the world has existed for a good long time—much longer than ten minutes, say—and a million more such Moorean truisms. (Of course, there is the occasional dissenter—in the grip, perhaps, of cognitive malfunction or a cognitively crippling philosophical theory.)

We think our faculties much better adapted to reach the truth in some areas than others; we are good at elementary arithmetic and logic, and the perception of middle-sized objects under ordinary conditions. We are also good at remembering certain sorts of things: I can easily remember what I had for breakfast this morning, where my office was located yesterday, and whether there was a large explosion in my house last night. Things get more difficult, however, when it comes to an accurate reconstruction of what it was like to be, say, a fifth-century BCE Greek (not to mention a bat), or whether the axiom of choice or the continuum (hypothesis) is true; things are even more difficult, perhaps, when it comes to figuring out how quantum mechanics is to be understood, and what the subnuclear realm of quark and gluon is really like, if indeed there really is a subnuclear realm of quark and gluon. Still, there remains a vast portion of our cognitive terrain where we think that our cognitive faculties do furnish us with truth.

---

* Alvin Plantinga is John A. O'Brien Professor, Emeritus of Philosophy at the University of Notre Dame.

The problem. But isn't there a problem, here, for the naturalist? At any rate for the naturalist who thinks that we and our cognitive capacities arrived upon the scene after some billions of years of evolution (by way of natural selection, genetic drift, and other blind processes working on such sources of genetic variation as random genetic mutation)? Richard Dawkins (according to Peter Medawar, "one of the most brilliant of the rising generation of biologists") once leaned over and remarked to A.J. Ayer at one of those elegant, candle-lit, bibulous Oxford college dinners, that he couldn't imagine being an atheist before 1859 (the year Darwin's *Origin of Species* was published); "although atheism might have been logically tenable before Darwin," said he, "Darwin made it possible to be an intellectually fulfilled atheist."[1]

Now Dawkins thinks Darwin made it possible to be an intellectually fulfilled atheist. But perhaps Dawkins is dead wrong here. Perhaps the truth lies in the opposite direction. If our cognitive faculties have originated as Dawkins thinks, then their ultimate purpose or function (if they *have* a purpose or function) will be something like *survival* (of individual, species, gene, or genotype); but then it seems initially doubtful that among their functions—ultimate, proximate, or otherwise—would be the production of true beliefs. Taking up this theme, Patricia Churchland declares that the most important thing about the human brain is that it has evolved; hence, she says, its principal function is to enable the organism to *move* appropriately:

> Boiled down to essentials, a nervous system enables the organism to succeed in the four F's: feeding, fleeing, fighting and reproducing. The principle chore of nervous systems is to get the body parts where they should be in order that the organism may survive. . . . Improvements in sensorimotor control confer an evolutionary advantage: a fancier style of representing is advantageous *so long as it is geared to the*

> *organism's way of life and enhances the organism's chances of survival* [Churchland's emphasis]. Truth, whatever that is, definitely takes the hindmost.[2]

Her point, I think, is that (from a naturalistic perspective) what evolution guarantees is (at most) that we *behave* in certain ways—in such ways as to promote survival, or survival through childbearing age. The principal function or purpose, then, (the 'chore' says Churchland) of our cognitive faculties is not that of producing true or verisimilitudinous beliefs, but instead that of contributing to survival by getting the body parts in the right place. What evolution underwrites is only (at most) that our *behavior* be reasonably adaptive to the circumstances in which our ancestors found themselves; hence (so far forth) it does not guarantee mostly true or verisimilitudinous beliefs. Of course our beliefs *might* be mostly true or verisimilitudinous (hereafter I'll omit the "verisimilitudinous"); but there is no particular reason to think they *would* be: natural selection is interested not in truth, but in appropriate behavior. What Churchland says suggests, therefore, that naturalistic evolution—that is, the conjunction of metaphysical naturalism with the view that we and our cognitive faculties have arisen by way of the mechanisms and processes proposed by contemporary evolutionary theory—gives us reason to doubt two things: (a) that a *purpose* of our cognitive systems is that of serving us with true beliefs, and (b) that they *do*, in fact, furnish us with mostly true beliefs.

W.V.O. Quine and Karl Popper, however, apparently demur. Popper argues that since we have evolved and survived, we may be pretty sure that our hypotheses and guesses as to what the world is like are mostly correct.[3] And Quine says he finds encouragement in Darwin:

> What does make clear sense is this other part of the problem of induction: why does our innate subjective spacing of qualities accord so well with

the functionally relevant groupings in nature as to make our inductions tend to come out right? Why should our subjective spacing of qualities have a special purchase on nature and a lien on the future?

There is some encouragement in Darwin. If people's innate spacing of qualities is a gene-linked trait, then the spacing that has made for the most successful inductions will have tended to predominate through natural selection. Creatures inveterately wrong in their inductions have a pathetic but praiseworthy tendency to die before reproducing their kind.[4]

Indeed, Quine finds a great deal more encouragement in Darwin than Darwin did: "With me," says Darwin,

the horrid doubt always arises whether the convictions of man's mind, which has been developed from the mind of the lower animals, are of any value or at all trustworthy. Would any one trust in the convictions of a monkey's mind, if there are any convictions in such a mind?[5]

So here we appear to have Quine and Popper on one side and Darwin and Churchland on the other. Who is right? But a prior question: what, precisely, is the issue? Darwin and Churchland seem to believe that (naturalistic) evolution gives one a reason to doubt that human cognitive faculties produce for the most part true beliefs: call this "Darwin's Doubt." Quine and Popper, on the other hand, apparently hold that evolution gives us reason to believe the opposite: that human cognitive faculties *do* produce for the most part true beliefs. How shall we understand this opposition?

Darwin's doubt. One possibility: perhaps Darwin and Churchland mean to propose that a certain objective

conditional probability is relatively low: the probability of human cognitive faculties' being reliable (producing mostly true beliefs), given that human beings *have* cognitive faculties (of the sort we have) and given that these faculties have been produced by evolution (Dawkins's blind evolution, unguided by the hand of God or any other person). If metaphysical naturalism and this evolutionary account are both true, then our cognitive faculties will have resulted from blind mechanisms like natural selection, working on such sources of genetic variation as random genetic mutation. Evolution is interested, not in true belief, but in survival or fitness. It is therefore unlikely that our cognitive faculties have the production of true belief as a proximate or any other function, and the probability of our faculties' being reliable (given naturalistic evolution) would be fairly low. Popper and Quine on the other side, judge that probability fairly high.

The issue, then, is the value of a certain conditional probability: $P(R/ (N\&E\&C))$.[6] Here N is metaphysical naturalism. It isn't easy to say precisely what naturalism *is*, but perhaps that isn't necessary in this context; prominent examples would be the views of (say) David Armstrong, the later Darwin, Quine and Bertrand Russell. (Crucial to metaphysical naturalism, of course, is the view that there is no such person as the God of traditional theism.) E is the proposition that human cognitive faculties arose by way of the mechanisms to which contemporary evolutionary thought directs our attention; and C is a complex proposition whose precise formulation is both difficult and unnecessary, but which states what cognitive faculties we have—memory, perception, reason, Reid's sympathy—and what sorts of beliefs they produce. R, on the other hand, is the claim that our cognitive faculties are reliable (on the whole, and with the qualifications mentioned), in the sense that they produce mostly true beliefs in the sorts of environments that are normal for them. And the question is: what is the probability of R on N&E&C? (Alternatively, perhaps the interest of *that* question lies in its bearing on *this* question: what is the probability that a belief produced by human cognitive faculties is *true*, given N&E&C?) And if we construe the dispute in this way, then what Darwin and Churchland propose is that this probability is relatively low, whereas Quine and Popper think it fairly high. . . .

The doubt developed. . . . In order to avoid irrelevant distractions, suppose we think, first, not about ourselves and our ancestors, but about a hypothetical population of creatures a lot like ourselves on a planet similar to Earth. (Darwin proposed that we think about another species, such as monkeys.) Suppose these creatures have cognitive faculties, hold beliefs, change beliefs, make inferences, and so on; and suppose these creatures have arisen by way of the selection processes endorsed by contemporary evolutionary thought. What is the probability that their faculties are reliable? What is $P(R/(N\&E\&C))$, specified not to us, but to them? According to Quine and Popper, the probability in question would be rather high: belief is connected with action in such a way that extensive false belief would lead to maladaptive behavior, in which case it is likely that the ancestors of those creatures would have displayed that pathetic but praiseworthy tendency Quine mentions.

But now for the contrary argument. First, perhaps it is likely that their *behavior* is adaptive; but nothing follows about their *beliefs*. We aren't given, after all, that their beliefs are so much as causally connected with their behavior; for we aren't given that their beliefs are more than mere epiphenomena, not causally involved with behavior at all. Perhaps their beliefs neither figure into the causes of their behavior, nor are caused by that behavior. (No doubt beliefs would be caused by *something* in or about these creatures, but it need not be by their behavior.). . . .

A second possibility is that the beliefs of these creatures are not among the *causes* of their behavior, but are *effects* of that behavior, or effects of proximate causes that also cause behavior. Their beliefs might be like a sort of decoration that isn't involved in the causal chain leading to action. Their waking beliefs might be no more causally efficacious, with respect to their behavior, than our dream beliefs are with respect to ours. . . . Under these conditions, of course, their beliefs could be wildly false. It *could* be that one of these creatures believes that he is at that elegant, bibulous Oxford dinner, when in fact he is slogging his way through some primeval swamp, desperately fighting off hungry crocodiles. Under this possibility, as under the first, beliefs would not have (or need not have) any purpose or function; they would be more like unintended by-products. Under this possibility as under the first, the probability that their cognitive faculties are reliable is low.

A third possibility is that beliefs do indeed have causal efficacy with respect to behavior, but not by virtue of their *content*; to put it in currently fashionable jargon, this would be the suggestion that while beliefs are causally efficacious, it is only by virtue of their *syntax*, not by virtue of their *semantics*. . . . I read a poem very loudly, so loudly as to break a glass; the sounds I utter have meaning, but their meaning is causally irrelevant to the breaking of the glass. In the same way it might be that these creatures' beliefs have causal efficacy, but not by way of the content of those beliefs. A substantial share of probability must be reserved for this option; and under this option, as under the preceding two, the likelihood that the beliefs of these creatures would be for the most part true would be low. . . .

A [fourth] (and final) possibility is that the beliefs of our hypothetical creatures are indeed both causally connected with their behavior and also adaptive. Assume, then, that our creatures have belief systems and that these systems are adaptive: they produce adaptive behavior, and at not too great a cost in terms of resources. What is the probability (on this assumption together with N&E&C) that their cognitive faculties are reliable; and what is the probability that a belief produced by those faculties will be true?

Not as high as you might think. For, of course, beliefs don't causally produce behavior *by themselves*; it is beliefs, desires, and other things that do so together. Suppose we oversimplify a bit and say that my behavior is a causal product just of my beliefs and desires. Then the problem is that clearly there will be any number of *different* patterns of belief and desire that would issue in the same action; and among those there will be many in which the beliefs are wildly false. Paul is a pre-historic hominid; the exigencies of survival call for him to display tiger-avoidance behavior. There will be many behaviors that are appropriate: fleeing, for example, or climbing a steep rock face, or crawling into a hole too small to admit the tiger, or leaping into a handy lake. Pick any such appropriately specific behavior *B*. Paul engages in *B*, we think, because, sensible fellow that he is, he has an aversion to being eaten and believes that *B* is a good means of thwarting the tiger's intentions.

But clearly this avoidance behavior could be a result of a thousand other belief–desire combinations: indefinitely many other belief–desire systems fit *B* equally well.... Perhaps Paul very much *likes* the idea of being eaten, but whenever he sees a tiger, always runs off looking for a better prospect, because he thinks it unlikely that the tiger he sees will eat him. This will get his body parts in the right place so far as survival is concerned, without involving much by way of true belief. (Of course we must postulate other changes in Paul's ways of reasoning, including how he changes belief in response to experience, to maintain coherence.) Or perhaps he thinks the tiger is a large, friendly, cuddly pussycat and wants to pet it; but he also believes that the best way to pet it is to run away from it. Or perhaps he confuses running *toward* it with running *away* from it, believing of the action that is really running away from it, that it is running toward it; or perhaps he thinks the tiger is a regularly recurring illusion, and, hoping to

keep his weight down, has formed the resolution to run a mile at top speed whenever presented with such an illusion; or perhaps he thinks he is about to take part in a sixteen-hundred-meter race, wants to win, and believes the appearance of the tiger is the starting signal; or perhaps.... Clearly there are any number of belief-cum-desire systems that equally fit a given bit of behavior where the beliefs are mostly false. Indeed, even if we fix desire, there will still be any number of systems of belief that will produce a given bit of behavior: perhaps Paul does not want to be eaten, but (a) thinks the best way to avoid being eaten is to run toward the tiger, and (b) mistakenly believes that he is running toward it when in fact he is running away.

But these possibilities are wholly preposterous, you say. Following Richard Grandy, you point out that when we ascribe systems of belief and desire to persons, we make use of "principles of humanity," whereby we see others as resembling what we take ourselves to be.[7] You go on to endorse David Lewis's suggestion that a theory of content requires these "principles of humanity" in order to rule out as "deeply irrational" those nonstandard belief–desire systems; the contents involved are "unthinkable," and are hence disqualified as candidates for someone's belief–desire structure.[8] Surely you (and Grandy and Lewis) are right: in ascribing beliefs to others, we *do* think of them as like what we think we are. (This involves, among other things, thinking that the (a) purpose or function of their cognitive systems, like that of ours, is the production of true beliefs.) And a theory of content ascription does indeed require more than just the claim that the content of my beliefs must fit my behavior and desires: that leaves entirely too much latitude as to what that content, on a given occasion, might in fact be. These principles of humanity will exclude vast hordes of logically possible belief–desire systems as systems (given human limitations) no human being *could* have.... These principles will also exclude some systems as systems we think no properly functioning human being *would* have: accordingly, I will not attribute to Paul the view that emeralds are grue, or the belief that it would be good to have a nice saucer of mud for lunch.[9]

These points are quite correct; but they do not bear on the present question. It is true that a decent theory of content ascription must require more than that the belief fit the behavior; for a decent theory of content ascription must also respect or take for granted what we ordinarily think about our desires, beliefs, and circumstances and the relations between these items. But in the case of our hypothetical population, these "principles of humanity" are not relevant. For we are not given that its members are human; more important, we are not given that those principles of humanity, those commonsense beliefs about how their behavior, belief, and desire are related, are true of them. We can't assume that their beliefs, for given circumstances, would be similar to what *we* take it we would believe in those circumstances. We must ask what sorts of belief–desire systems are *possible* for these creatures, given only that they have evolved according to the principles of contemporary evolutionary theory; clearly these gerrymanders are perfectly possible. So perhaps their behavior has been adaptive, and their systems of belief and desire such as to fit that adaptive behavior; those beliefs could nonetheless be wildly wrong. There are indefinitely many belief–desire systems that fit adaptive behavior, but where the beliefs involved are not for the most part true. A share of probability has to be reserved for these possibilities as well.

Our question was this: given our hypothetical population along with N&E&C, what is the probability that the cognitive systems of beliefs these creatures display is reliable? Suppose we briefly review. First, on the condition in question, there is some probability that their beliefs are not causally connected with behavior at all. It would be reasonable to suppose, on that condition, that the probability of a given belief's being true would not be far from ½, and hence reasonable to suppose that the probability

that their cognitive faculties are reliable (produce a substantial preponderance of verisimilitudinous beliefs) is very low. Second, there is some probability that their beliefs are causally connected with behavior, but only as epiphenomenal effect of causes that also cause behavior; in that case too it would be reasonable to suppose that the probability of their cognitive systems' being reliable is very low. Third, there is the possibility that belief is only "syntactically," not "semantically," connected with behavior; on this possibility too, there would be a low probability that their cognitive faculties are reliable.... [Fourth], there is also some probability that their beliefs are causally connected with their behavior, and are adaptive; as we saw, however, there are indefinitely many belief–desire systems that would yield adaptive behavior, but are unreliable. Here one does not quite know what to say about the probability that their cognitive systems would produce mainly true beliefs, but perhaps it would be reasonable to estimate it as somewhat more than ½. These possibilities are mutually exclusive and jointly exhaustive; if we had definite probabilities for each of the five cases and definite probabilities for R on each of them, then the probability of R would be the weighted average of the probabilities for R on each of those possibilities—weighted by the probabilities of those possibilities. (Of course we don't have definite probabilities here, but only vague estimates; it imparts a spurious appearance of precision to so much as mention the relevant formula.)

Trying to combine these probabilities in an appropriate way, then, it would be reasonable to suppose that the probability of R, of these creatures' cognitive systems being reliable, is relatively low, somewhat less than ½. More exactly, a reasonable posture would be to think it very unlikely that the statistical probability of their belief-producing mechanisms' being reliable, given that they have been produced in the suggested way, is very high; and rather likely that (on N&E&C) R is less probable than its denial.

Now return to Darwin's Doubt. The reasoning that applies to these hypothetical creatures, of course, also applies to *us*; so if we think the probability of R with respect to *them* is relatively low on N&E&C, we should think the same thing about the probability of R with respect to *us*. Something like this reasoning, perhaps, is what underlay Darwin's doubt. . . . So taken, his claim is that P(R/(N&E&C)) (specified to us) is rather low, perhaps somewhat less than ½. Arguments of this sort are less than coercive; but it would be perfectly sensible to estimate these probabilities in this way.

An argument against naturalism. Suppose you do estimate these probabilities in roughly this way: suppose you concur in Darwin's Doubt, taking P(R/(N&E&C)) to be fairly low. But suppose you also think, as most of us do, that in fact our cognitive faculties *are* reliable (with the qualifications and nuances introduced previously). Then you have a straightforward probabilistic argument against naturalism—and for traditional theism, if you think these two the significant alternatives. According to Bayes's Theorem,

$$P((N\&E\&C)/R) = \frac{P(N\&E\&C) \times P(R/(N\&E\&C))}{P(R)}$$

where P(N&E&C) is your estimate of the probability for N&E&C independent of the consideration of R. You believe R, so you assign it a probability near 1 and you take P(R/(N&E&C)) to be no more than ½. Then P((N&E&C)/R) will be no greater than ½ times P(N&E&C), and will thus be fairly low. You believe C (the proposition specifying the sorts of cognitive faculties we have); so you assign it a very high probability; accordingly P((N&E)/R) will also be low. No doubt you will also assign a very high probability to the conditional *if naturalism is true, then our faculties have arisen by way of evolution*; then you will judge that P(N/R) is also low. But you do think R is true; you therefore have evidence against N. So your belief that

our cognitive faculties are reliable gives you a reason for rejecting naturalism and accepting its denial. The same argument will not hold, of course, for traditional theism; on that view the probability that our cognitive faculties are reliable will be much higher than ½; for, according to traditional (Jewish, Christian, Moslem) theism, God created us in his image, a part of which involves our having knowledge over a wide range of topics and areas.[10] So (provided that for you the prior probabilities of traditional theism and naturalism are comparable) P(traditional theism/R) will be considerably greater than P(N/R). . . .

The argument developed. By way of brief review: Darwin's Doubt can be taken as the claim that the probability of R on N&E&C is fairly low; as I argued, that is plausible. But Darwin's Doubt can also be taken as the claim that the rational attitude to take, here, is agnosticism about that probability; that is more plausible. Still more plausible is the disjunction of these two claims: either the rational attitude to take toward this probability is the judgment that it is low, or the rational attitude is agnosticism with respect to it. But then the devotee of N&E has a defeater for any belief B he holds. Now the next thing to note is that *B might be N&E itself*; our devotee of N&E has an undercutting defeater for N&E, a reason to doubt it, a reason to be agnostic with respect to it. (This also holds if he isn't agnostic about P(R/(N&E&C)) but thinks it low, as in the preliminary argument; he has a defeater either way.) If he has no defeater for this defeater and no independent evidence—if his reason for doubting N&E, remains undefeated—then the rational course would be to reject belief in N&E. . . .

What we have seen so far, therefore, is that the devotee of N&E has a defeater for any belief he holds, and a stronger defeater for N&E itself. If he has no defeater for this defeater, and no independent evidence, then the rational attitude toward N&E would be one of agnosticism.

... [T]he friend of N&E is ... likely to suggest that we consult the scientific results on the matter—what does science tell us about the likelihood that our cognitive faculties are reliable? But this can't work either. For consider any argument from science (or anywhere else) he might produce. This argument will have premises; and these premises, he claims, give him good reason to believe R (or N&E). But note that he has the very same defeater for each of those premises that he has for R and for N&E; and he has the same defeater for his belief that those premises constitute a good reason for R (or N&E). For that belief, and for each of the premises, he has a reason for doubting it, a reason for being agnostic with respect to it. This reason, obviously, cannot be defeated by an ultimately undefeated defeater. For every defeater of this reason he might have, he knows that he has a defeater-defeater: the very undercutting defeater that attached itself to R and to N&E in the first place.

·We could also put it like this: any argument he offers, for R, is in this context delicately circular or question-begging. It is not *formally* circular; its conclusion does not appear among its premises. It is instead (we might say) *pragmatically* circular in that it purports to give a reason for trusting our cognitive faculties, but is itself trustworthy only if those faculties (at least the ones involved in its production) are indeed trustworthy. In following this procedure and giving this argument, therefore, he subtly assumes the very proposition he proposes to argue for. Once I come to doubt the reliability of my cognitive faculties, I can't properly try to allay that doubt by producing an *argument*; for in so doing I rely on the very faculties I am doubting. The conjunction of evolution with naturalism gives its adherents a reason for doubting that our beliefs are mostly true; perhaps they are mostly wildly mistaken. But then it won't help to *argue* that they can't be wildly mistaken; for the very reason for mistrusting our cognitive faculties generally will be a reason for mistrusting

the faculties generating the beliefs involved in the argument. . . .

What we really have here is one of those nasty dialectical loops to which Hume calls our attention.[11]. . . When the devotee of N&E notes that he has a defeater for R, then at that stage he also notes (if apprised of the present argument) that he has a defeater for N&E; indeed, he notes that he has a defeater for anything he believes. Since, however, his having a defeater for N&E depends upon some of his beliefs, what he now notes is that he has a defeater for his defeater of R and N&E; so now he no longer *has* that defeater for R and N&E. So then his original condition of believing R and assuming N&E reasserts itself: at which point he again has a defeater for R and N&E. But then he notes that *that* defeater is also a defeater of the defeater of R and N&E; hence. . . . So goes the paralyzing dialectic. After a few trips around this loop, we may be excused for throwing up our hands in despair, or disgust, and joining Hume in a game of backgammon. The point remains, therefore: one who accepts N&E (and is apprised of the present argument) has a defeater for N&E, a defeater that cannot be defeated by an ultimately undefeated defeater. And isn't it irrational to accept a belief for which you know you have an ultimately undefeated defeater?

Hence the devotee of N&E has a defeater D for N&E—a defeater, furthermore, that can't be ultimately defeated; for obviously D attaches to any consideration one might bring forward by way of attempting to defeat it. If you accept N&E, you have an ultimately undefeated reason for rejecting N&E: but then the rational thing to do is to reject N&E. If, furthermore, one also accepts the conditional *if N is true, then so is E*, one has an ultimately undefeated defeater for N. One who contemplates accepting N, and is torn, let's say, between N and theism, should reason as follows: if I were to accept N, I would have good and ultimately undefeated reason to be agnostic about N; so I should not accept it. Unlike the preliminary argument, this is not an argument for the *falsehood* of naturalism and thus (given that naturalism and theism are the live options) for the truth of theism; for all this argument shows, naturalism might still be true. It is instead an argument for the conclusion that (for one who is aware of the present argument) accepting naturalism is irrational. It is like the self-referential argument against classical foundationalism: classical foundationalism is either false or such that I would be unjustified in accepting it; so (given that I am aware of this fact) I can't justifiably accept it.[12] But of course it does not follow that classical foundationalism is not *true*; for all this argument shows, it could be true, though not rationally acceptable. Similarly here; the argument is not for the falsehood of naturalism, but for the irrationality of accepting it. The conclusion to be drawn, therefore, is that the conjunction of naturalism with evolutionary theory is self-defeating: it provides for itself an undefeated defeater. Evolution, therefore, presents naturalism with an undefeated defeater. But if naturalism is true, then, surely, so is evolution. Naturalism, therefore, is unacceptable.

Proper function and belief in God. The traditional theist, on the other hand, isn't forced into that appalling loop. On this point his set of beliefs is stable. He has no corresponding reason for doubting that it is a purpose of our cognitive systems to produce true beliefs, nor any reason for thinking that $P(R/(N\&E\&C))$ is low, nor any reason for thinking the probability of a belief's being true, given that it is a product of his cognitive faculties, is no better than in the neighborhood of ½. He may indeed endorse some form of evolution; but if he does, it will be a form of evolution guided and orchestrated by God. And *qua* traditional theist— *qua* Jewish, Moslem, or Christian theist—he believes that God is the premier knower and has created us human beings in his image, an important part of which involves his endowing them with a reflection of his powers as a knower. . . .

Once again, therefore, we see that naturalistic epistemology flourishes best in the garden of supernaturalistic metaphysics. Naturalistic epistemology conjoined with naturalistic metaphysics leads *via* evolution to skepticism or to violation of canons of rationality; conjoined with theism it does not. The naturalistic epistemologist should therefore prefer theism to metaphysical naturalism.[13]

Notes

1. Richard Dawkins, *The Blind Watchmaker* (New York: Norton, 1986), pp. 6, 7.

2. Patricia Churchland, *Journal of Philosophy* 84 (October 1987), p. 548.

3. Karl Popper, *Objective Knowledge: An Evolutionary Approach* (Oxford: Clarendon P, 1972), p. 261.

4. W.V.O. Quine, "Natural Kinds," in *Ontological Relativity and Other Essays* (New York: Columbia UP, 1969), p. 126.

5. Letter to William Graham Down, July 3, 1881, in *The Life and Letters of Charles Darwin Including an Autobiographical Chapter*, ed. Francis Darwin (London: John Murray, Albermarle Street, 1887), 1:315–16.

6. We could think of this probability in two ways: as a conditional *epistemic* probability, or as a conditional *objective* probability. Either will serve for my argument, but I should think the better way to think of it would be as objective probability; for in this sort of context epistemic probability, presumably, should follow known (or conjectured) objective probability.

7. Richard Grandy, "Reference, Meaning and Belief," *Journal of Philosophy* 70 (1973): 443ff.

8. David Lewis, *On the Plurality of Worlds* (Oxford: Basil Blackwell, 1986), pp. 38ff., 107–08.

9. See Elizabeth Anscombe's *Intention* (Oxford: Basil Blackwell, 1957), sec. 38.

10. Thus, for example, Thomas Aquinas:

> Since human beings are said to be in the image of God in virtue of their having a nature that includes an intellect, such a nature is most in the image of God in virtue of being most able to imitate God. (*Summa Theologiae*, Ia, q. 93, a. 4)
>
> Only in rational creatures is there found a likeness of God which counts as an image. . . . As far as a likeness of the divine nature is concerned, rational creatures seem somehow to attain a representation of [that] type in virtue of imitating God not only in this, that he is and lives, but especially in this, that he understands. (*Summa Theologiae*, Ia, q. 93, a. 6)

11. David Hume, *A Treatise of Human Nature*, with an analytical index, ed. L.A. Selby-Bigge (Oxford: Clarendon Press, 1888), I, IV, i, p. 187.

12. See my "Reason and Belief in God," in *Faith and Rationality: Reason and Belief in God* (Notre Dame, IN: U of Notre Dame P, 1983).

13. Victor Reppert reminds me that the argument of this chapter bears a good bit of similarity to arguments to be found in chapters III and XIII of C.S. Lewis's *Miracles* (New York: Macmillan 1947); the argument also resembles Richard Taylor's argument in Chapter X of his *Metaphysics*.

Discussion

1. Try to state the point of Plantinga's argument against naturalism in a clear paragraph. Is Plantinga's argument an argument against evolution? Why or why not?

2. What is the alleged advantage of theism when it comes to explaining the proper functioning of our cognitive faculties?

3. Does Plantinga's argument provide adequate grounds for rational belief in God? Why or why not?

Chapter 7

The Balance of Probabilities

A CUMULATIVE CASE FOR THE EXISTENCE OF GOD

RICHARD SWINBURNE*

The justification of religious belief. . . . [O]nce I had seen what makes scientific theories meaningful and justified, I saw that any metaphysical theory, such as the Christian theological system, is just a superscientific theory. Scientific theories each seek to explain a certain limited class of data: Kepler's laws sought to explain the motions of the planets; natural selection seeks to explain the fossil record and various present features of animals and plants. But some scientific theories are on a higher level than others and seek to explain the operation of the lower-level theories and the existence in the first place of the objects with which they deal. Newton's laws explained why Kepler's laws operated; chemistry has sought to explain why primitive animals and plants existed in the first place. A metaphysical theory is a highest-level-of-all theory. It seeks to explain why there is a universe at all, why it has the most general laws of nature that it does (especially such laws as lead to the evolution of animals and humans), as well as any particular phenomena that lower-level laws are unable to explain. Such a theory is meaningful if it can be stated in ordinary words, stretched a bit in meaning perhaps. And it is justified if it is a simple theory and leads you to expect

the observable phenomena when you would not otherwise expect them. Once I had seen this, my program was there—to use the criteria of modern natural science, analyzed with the careful rigor of modern philosophy, to show the meaningfulness and justification of Christian theology.

At this time I discovered that someone else had attempted to use the best science and philosophy of his day rigorously to establish Christian theology. I read part one of the Summa Theologiae of Thomas Aquinas. He too started from where the secular world was in his day—the thirteenth century—and used the best secular philosophy available, that of Aristotle, instead of the initially more Christian-looking philosophy of Plato; and he sought to show that reflection on the observable world, as described by Aristotelian science, led inescapably to its creator God. The Summa doesn't start from faith or religious experience or the Bible; it starts from the observable world. After an introductory question, its first main question is Utrum Deus Sit, whether there is a God; and it provides five "ways" or arguments from the most evident general phenomena of experience: that things change, that things cause other things, and so on—to show that there is. I do not think that those five ways work too well in detail; and it is interesting that often where the argument goes wrong it is not because Aquinas had relied unjustifiably on Christian theology but because he had relied too much on Aristotelian science. While I realized that the details were not always satisfactory, it seemed to me that the approach of the Summa was 100 percent right. I came to see that the irrationalist

* Richard Swinburne is Emeritus Nolloth Professor of the Philosophy of the Christian Religion, Oxford University.

spirit of modern theology was a modern phenomenon, a head-in-the-sand defensive mechanism. In general, I believe, it is the spirit of St. Thomas rather than the spirit of Kierkegaard that has been the more prevalent over two millennia of Christian theology. But each generation must justify the Christian system by using the best secular knowledge of its own day; and that is why true disciples of St. Thomas cannot rely on the Summa—they have to carry out Thomas's program, using the knowledge of their own day. . . .

Scientific versus personal explanation. The basic idea of The Existence of God[1] is that the various traditional arguments for theism—from the existence of the world (the cosmological argument), from its conformity to scientific laws (a version of the teleological argument), and so on—are best construed not as deductive arguments but as inductive arguments to the existence of God. A valid deductive argument is one in which the premises (the starting points) infallibly guarantee the truth of the conclusion; a correct inductive argument is one in which the premises confirm the conclusion (that is, make it more probable than it would otherwise be). Science argues from various limited observable phenomena to their unobservable physical causes, and in so doing it argues inductively. My claim was that theism is the best justified of metaphysical theories. The existence of God is a very simple hypothesis that leads us to expect various very general and more specific phenomena that otherwise we would not expect; and for that reason it is rendered probable by the phenomena. Or rather, as with any big scientific theory, each group of phenomena adds to the probability of the theory—together they make it significantly more probable than not. When explaining phenomena we have available two different kinds of explanation.

One is *scientific explanation*, whereby we explain a phenomenon E in terms of some prior state of affairs F (the cause) in accordance with some regularity or natural law L that describes the behavior of objects involved in F and E. We explain why a stone took two seconds to fall from a tower to the ground (E) by its having been liberated from rest at the top of the tower 64 feet from the ground (F) and by the regularity derivable from Galileo's law of fall that all bodies fall toward the surface of the earth with an acceleration of 32 ft/sec^2 (L); E follows from F and L. And, as I noted earlier, science can also explain the operation of a regularity or law in some narrow area in terms of the operation of a wider law. Thus it can explain why Galileo's law of fall holds for small objects near the surface of the earth. Galileo's law follows from Newton's laws, given that the earth is a body of a certain mass far from other massive bodies and the objects on its surface are close to it and small in mass in comparison.

The other way that we use all the time and see as a proper way of explaining phenomena is what I call *personal explanation*. We often explain some phenomenon E as brought about by a person P in order to achieve some purpose or goal G. The present motion of my hand is explained as brought about by me for the purpose of picking up a glass. The motion of my legs earlier toward a room is explained by my purpose of going there to give a lecture. In these cases I bring about a state of my body that then itself causes some state of affairs outside my body. But it is I (P) who brings about the bodily state (E) conducive to producing that further state (G) rather than some other.

The kind of explanation involved here is a different way of explaining things from the scientific. Scientific explanation involves laws of nature and previous states of affairs. Personal explanation involves persons and purposes. In each case the grounds for believing the explanation to be correct are, as stated earlier, the fact that to explain the cited phenomenon and many other similar phenomena we need few entities (for example, one person rather than many), few kinds of entities with few, easily describable properties, behaving in mathematically simple kinds of ways (such as a person having certain capacities and purposes that do not change erratically) that give rise to many phenomena. In seeking the best explanation of phenomena we may seek explanations of either kind, and if we cannot find a scientific one that satisfies the criteria, we should look for a personal one.

We should seek explanations of all things; but we have seen that we have reason for supposing that we have found one only if the purported explanation is simple and leads us to expect what we find when that is otherwise not to be expected. The history of science shows that we judge that the complex, miscellaneous, coincidental and diverse needs explaining, and that it is to be explained in terms of something simpler. The motions of the planets (subject to Kepler's laws), the mechanical interactions of bodies on earth, the behavior of pendula, the motions of tides, the behavior of comets and so forth formed a pretty miscellaneous set of phenomena. Newton's law of motion constituted a simple theory that led us to expect these phenomena, and so was judged a true explanation of them. The existence of thousands of different chemical substances combining in different ratios to make other substances was complex. The hypothesis that there were only a hundred or so chemical elements of which the thousands of substances were made was a simple hypothesis that led us to expect the complex phenomena. When we reach the simplest possible starting point for explanation that leads us to expect the phenomena that we find, there alone we should stop and believe that we have found the ultimate brute fact on which all other things depend.

The cosmological argument. The cosmological argument argues from the existence of a complex physical universe (or something as general as that) to God who keeps it in being. The premise is the existence of our universe for so long as it has existed (whether a finite time or, if it has no beginning, an infinite time). The universe is a complex thing with lots and lots of separate chunks. Each of these chunks has a different finite and not very natural volume, shape, mass and so forth—consider the vast diversity of galaxies, stars and planets, and pebbles on the seashore. Matter is inert and has no powers that it can choose to exert; it does what it has to do. There is a limited amount of it in any region, and it has a limited amount of energy and velocity. There is a complexity, particularity and finitude about the universe that looks for explanation in terms of something simpler.

The existence of the universe is something evidently inexplicable by science. For, as we saw, a scientific explanation as such explains the occurrence of one state of affairs in terms of a previous state of affairs and some law of nature that makes states like the former bring about states like the latter. It may explain the planets being in their present positions by a previous state of the system (the sun and planets being where they were last year) and the operation of Kepler's laws, which postulate that states like the latter are followed a year later by states like the former. And so it may explain the existence of the universe this year in terms of the existence of the universe last year and the laws of cosmology. But either there was a first state of the universe or there has always been a universe. In the former case, science cannot explain why there was the first state; and in the latter case it still cannot explain why any matter exists (or, more correctly, matter-energy) for the laws of nature to get a grip on, as it were. By its very nature science cannot explain why there are any states of affairs at all.

But a God can provide an explanation. The hypothesis of theism is that the universe exists because there is a God who keeps it in being and that laws of nature operate because there is a God who brings it about that they do. He brings it about that the laws of nature operate by sustaining in every object in the universe its liability to behave in accord with those laws (including the law of the conservation of matter, that at each moment what was there before continues to exist). The universe exists because at each moment of finite or infinite time, he keeps in being objects with this liability. The hypothesis of theism is like a hypothesis that a person brings about certain things for some purpose. God acts directly on the universe, as we act directly on our brains, guiding them to move our limbs (but the universe of course is not his body).

As we have seen, personal explanation and scientific explanation are the two ways we have of explaining the occurrence of phenomena. Since there cannot be a scientific explanation of the existence of the universe, either there is a personal explanation or there is no explanation at all. The hypothesis that there is a God is the hypothesis of the existence of the simplest kind of person that there could be. A person is a being with *power* to bring about effects, *knowledge* of how to do so and *freedom* to choose which effects to bring about. God is by definition an omnipotent (that is, infinitely powerful), omniscient (that is, all-knowing) and perfectly free person: he is a person of infinite power, knowledge and freedom; a person to whose power, knowledge and freedom there are no limits except those of logic. The hypothesis that there exists a being with infinite degrees of the qualities essential to a being of that kind is the postulation of a very simple being. The hypothesis that there is one such God is a much simpler hypothesis than the hypothesis that there is a god who has such and such limited power, or the hypothesis that there are several gods with limited powers. It is simpler in just the same way that the hypothesis that some particle has zero mass or infinite velocity is simpler than the hypothesis that it has 0.32147 of some unit of mass or a velocity of 221,000 km/sec. A finite limitation cries out for an explanation of why there is just that particular limit, in a way the limitlessness does not. God provides the simplest stopping-point for explanation.

That there should exist anything at all, let alone a universe as complex and as orderly as ours, is exceedingly strange. But if there is a God, it is not vastly unlikely that he should create such a universe. A universe such as ours is a thing of beauty, a theater in which humans and other creatures can grow and work out their destiny, a point that I shall develop further below. So the argument from the universe to God is an argument from a complex phenomenon to a simple entity, which leads us to expect (thought does not guarantee) the existence of the former far more than it would be expected otherwise. Therefore, I suggest, it provides some evidence for its conclusion.

The argument from design. The teleological argument, or argument from design, has various forms. One form is the argument from temporal order. This has as its premises the operation of the most general laws of nature, that is, the orderliness of nature in conforming to very general laws. What exactly these laws are, science may not yet have discovered; perhaps they are the field equations of Einstein's general theory of relativity, or perhaps there are some yet more fundamental laws. Now, as we have seen, science can explain the operation of some narrow regularity or law in terms of a wider or more general law. But what science by its very nature cannot explain is why there are the most general laws of nature that there are; for *ex hypothesi*, no wider law can explain their operation.

The conformity of objects throughout endless time and space to simple laws cries out for explanation. For let us consider to what this amounts. Laws are not things, independent of material objects. To say that all objects conform to laws is simply to say that they all behave in exactly the same way. To say, for example, that the planets obey Kepler's laws is just to say that each planet at each moment of time has the property of moving in the ways that Kepler's laws state. There is, therefore, this vast coincidence in the behavioral properties of objects at all times and in all places. If all the coins of some region have the same markings, or all the papers in a room are written in the same handwriting, we seek an explanation in terms of a common source of these coincidences. We should seek a similar explanation for that vast coincidence which we describe as the conformity of objects to laws of nature—such as the fact that all electrons are produced, attract and repel other particles, and combine with them in exactly the same way at each point of endless time and space.

That there is a universe and that there are laws of nature are phenomena so general and pervasive that we tend to ignore them. But there might so easily not have been a universe at all, ever. Or the universe might so easily have been a chaotic mess. That there is an *orderly* universe is something very striking, yet beyond the capacity of science ever to explain. Science's inability to explain these things is not a temporary phenomenon, caused by the backwardness of twentieth-century science. Rather, because of what a scientific explanation is, these things will ever be beyond its capacity to explain. For scientific explanations by their very nature terminate with some ultimate natural law and ultimate physical arrangement of physical things, and the question with which I am concerned is why there are natural laws and physical things at all.

There is available again the simple explanation of the temporal orderliness of the universe, that God makes protons and electrons move in an orderly way, just as we might make our bodies move in the regular patterns of a dance. He has *ex hypothesi* the power to do this. But why should he choose to do so? The orderliness of the universe makes it a beautiful universe, but, even more importantly, it makes it a universe that humans can learn to control and change. For only if there are simple laws of nature can humans

predict what will follow from what—and unless they can do that, they can never change anything. Only if they know that by sowing certain seeds, weeding and watering them, they will get corn, can they develop an agriculture. And humans can acquire that knowledge only if there are easily graspable regularities of behavior in nature. It is good that there are human beings, embodied minicreators who share in God's activity of forming and developing the universe through their free choice. But if there are to be such, there must be laws of nature. There is, therefore, some reasonable expectation that God will bring them about; but otherwise that the universe should exhibit such very striking order is hardly to be expected.

The form of "argument from design" that has been most common in the history of thought and was very widely prevalent in the eighteenth and early nineteenth centuries is the argument from spatial order. The intricate organization of animals and plants that enabled them to catch the food for which their digestive apparatus was suited and to escape from predators suggested that they were like very complicated machines and hence that they must have been put together by a master machine-maker, who built into them at the same time the power to reproduce. The frequent use of this argument in religious apologetic came to an abrupt halt in 1859, when Darwin produced his explanation of why there were complexly organized animals and plants, in terms of the laws of evolution operating on much simpler organisms. There seemed no need to bring God into the picture.

That reaction was, however, premature. For the demand for explanation can be taken back a further stage. Why are there laws of evolution that have the consequence that over many millennia simple organisms gradually give rise to complex organisms? No doubt because these laws follow from the basic laws of physics. But then why do the basic laws of physics have such a form as to give rise to laws of evolution? And why were there primitive organisms in the first place? A plausible story can be told of how the primeval "soup" of matter-energy at the time of the "big bang" (a moment some 15,000 million years ago at which, scientists now tell us, the universe, or at least the present stage of the universe, began) gave rise over many millennia, in accordance with physical laws, to those primitive organisms. But then why was there matter suitable for such evolutionary development in the first place?

With respect to the laws and with respect to the primeval matter, we have again the same choice: saying that these things cannot be further explained or postulating a further explanation. Note that the issue here is not why there are laws at all (the premise of the argument from temporal order) or why there is matter-energy at all (the premise of the cosmological argument), but why the laws and the matter-energy have this peculiar character of being already wound up to produce plants, animals and humans. Since the most general laws of nature have this special character, there can be no scientific explanation of why they are as they are. And although there might be a scientific explanation of why the matter at the time of the big bang had the special character it did, in terms of its character at some earlier time, clearly if there was a first state of the universe, it must have been of a certain kind; or if the universe has lasted forever, its matter must have had certain general features if at any time there was to be a state of the universe suited to produce plants, animals and humans. Scientific explanation comes to a stop. The question remains whether we should accept these particular features of the laws and matter of the universe as ultimate brute facts or whether we should move beyond them to a personal explanation in terms of the agency of God.

What the choice turns on is how likely it is that the laws and initial conditions should by chance have just this character. Recent scientific work has drawn attention to the fact that the universe is fine tuned.

The matter-energy at the time of the big bang has to have a certain density and a certain velocity of recession; increase or decrease in these respects by one part in a million would have had the effect that the universe was not life-evolving. For example, if the big bang had caused the quanta of matter-energy to recede from each other a little more quickly, no galaxies, stars or planets, and no environment suitable for life would have been formed. If the recession had been marginally slower, the universe would have collapsed in on itself before life could be formed. Similarly, the constants in the laws of nature needed to lie within very narrow limits if life was to be formed. It is, therefore, most unlikely that laws and initial conditions should have by chance a life-producing character. God is able to give matter and laws this character. If we can show that he would have reason to do so, then that gives support to the hypothesis that he has done so. There is available again the reason (in addition to the reason of its beauty) that was a reason why God would choose to bring about an orderly universe at all—the worthwhileness of the sentient embodied beings that the evolutionary process would bring about, and above all of humans who can themselves make informed choices as to what sort of a world there should be.

The cumulative case. A similar pattern of argument from various other phenomena such as the existence of conscious beings, the providential ordering of things in certain respects, the occurrence of certain apparently miraculous events in history and the religious experiences of many millions is . . . available to establish theism (when all the arguments are taken together) as overall significantly more probable than not.

Note

1. Richard Swinburne, *The Existence of God* (Oxford: Clarendon P, 1979).

Discussion

1. The simplicity of hypotheses plays a major role in Swinburne's arguments. Do you think the simple, all things considered, is a sign of the true? Why or why not?

2. Consider your favourite scientific hypothesis. Does Swinburne's account of the justification of scientific hypotheses make sense?

3. Is the case for theism strengthened when one considers the cosmological argument together with, for example, the argument from design, religious experience, apparently miraculous events, etc.? Why or why not?

4. Has Swinburne ignored any relevant counter-evidence?

THE BALANCE OF PROBABILITIES

J.L. MACKIE*

Bad arguments. We can now bring together the many different arguments for theism which we have discussed, and consider their combined effect. . . . [T]here is at least one interesting and important possibility of consilience, namely that which would bring together (1) reported miracles, (2) inductive versions of the design and consciousness arguments, picking out as "marks of design" both the fact that there are causal regularities at all and the fact that the fundamental natural laws and physical constants are such as to make possible the development of life and consciousness, (3) an inductive version of the cosmological argument, seeking an answer to the question "Why is there any world at all?," (4) the suggestion that there are objective moral values whose occurrence likewise calls for further explanation, and (5) the suggestion that some kinds of religious experience can be best understood as direct awareness of something supernatural. These various considerations might be held jointly to support the hypothesis that there is a personal or quasipersonal god.

The cumulative argument. In evaluating this possibility, we must note how in principle a hypothesis can be supported by the consilience of different considerations, each of which, on its own, leaves the balance of probabilities against that hypothesis. Suppose that there are several pieces of evidence, e_1, e_2, and e_3, each of which would fit in with a hypothesis h, but each of which, on its own, is explained with less initial improbability on some other grounds, say by g_1, g_2, and g_3 respectively. Yet if the improbability involved in postulating h is less than the *sum* of the improbabilities involved in the rival explanations g_1, g_2, and g_3, though it is greater than each of these improbabilities separately, the balance of probabilities when we take e_1, e_2, and e_3 together will favour the hypothesis h. It is important that it is just the one initial improbability of h that is weighed in turn against the improbabilities of g_1, g_2, and g_3 and then against the sum of these.

But the supposed consilience of theistic arguments does not satisfy the requirements of this formal pattern. As we have seen, the first and fifth of these considerations are extremely weak: all the evidence that they can muster is easily explained in natural terms, without any improbabilities worth taking into account. Consciousness and the actual phenomena of morality and valuing as a human activity are explained without further improbabilities, given that the natural world is such as to allow life to evolve, so the only improbabilities to be scored against the naturalistic kind of explanation are whatever may be involved in there being causal regularities, the fundamental laws and physical constants being as they are, and there being any world at all. Against the rival theistic hypothesis we should have to score the (significant) improbability that if there were a god he (or it) would create a world with causal laws, and one with our specific causal laws and constants, but also the great improbability of there being a process of the unmediated fulfilment of will, and, besides, the basic improbability of there being a god at all. For while the naturalist had admittedly no reply to Leibniz's question "Why is there a world at all?," the theist, once deprived of the illusory support of the ontological argument, is equally embarrassed by the question "Why is there a god at all?". Whatever initial improbability there may be in the unexplained brute fact that there is a world, there is a far greater initial improbability in what the theist has to assert as the unexplained brute fact that there is a god capable of creating a world.

---

* J.L. Mackie (1917–81) taught at Oxford University.

In the end, therefore, we can agree with what Laplace said about God: we have no need of that hypothesis. This conclusion can be reached by an examination precisely of the arguments advanced in favour of theism, without even bringing into play what have been regarded as the strongest considerations on the other side, the problem of evil and the various natural histories of religion. When these are thrown into the scales, the balance tilts still further against theism. Although we could not . . . rule out the possibility that some acceptable modification of traditional theism might enable it to accommodate the occurrence of evils, we saw that no sound solution of this sort has yet been offered; the extreme difficulty that theism has in reconciling *its own* doctrines with one another in this respect must tell heavily against it. Also, although the clear possibility of developing an adequate natural explanation of the origin, evolution, and persistence of religious belief is not a primary argument against theism, and could be brushed aside if there were any cogent positive case for the existence of a god, yet, since there is no such case, it helps to make the negative case still more conclusive. It removes the vague but obstinate feeling that where so many people have believed so firmly—and sometimes fervently—and where religious thought and organization have been so tenacious and so resilient "there must be something in it." We do not need to invoke the "higher causes" by which Machiavelli (with his tongue in his cheek) said that ecclesiastical principalities are upheld.[1] The occurrence, even the continuing occurrence, of theism is not, in Hume's phrase, a continued miracle which subverts all the principles of our understanding.

Conclusion. The balance of probabilities, therefore, comes out strongly against the existence of a god. . . . There is . . . no easy way of defending religion once it is admitted that the literal, factual, claim that there is a god cannot be rationally sustained.

Note

1. N. Machiavelli, *The Prince* (many editions), Chapter 11.

Discussion

1. Is all of the evidence *easily* explainable, as Mackie alleges, in naturalistic terms? Why or why not?

2. Compare Mackie's with Swinburne's cumulative argument. Give several reasons for preferring one argument over the other.

3. What sorts of evidence does Mackie think count against God's existence? Do you find his claims compelling?

Chapter 8

Reflections on Arguments for the Existence of God

ARGUING FOR GOD

ALVIN PLANTINGA*

Introduction. Some two-thirds of the world's population of approximately five billion people profess belief in God—the God of Abraham, Isaac, and Jacob, God as he is conceived of by Jews, Moslems, Christians, and others. So thought of, God is an immaterial person who is all-knowing, all-powerful, perfectly good, and the creator and sustainer of the world.... This characterization of God is what we might call *standard theism*....

[I]n contemporary philosophy (contemporary Western philosophy anyway), perhaps the most widely discussed philosophical problem about belief in God is... something like this: is it rational, or reasonable, or sensible, or intellectually acceptable, or in accord with one's intellectual obligations to believe in God? (This question has been very much with us for at least the last couple of hundred years, ever since the Enlightenment.) Many apparently think not; they think contemporary science, or modern historical methods, or perhaps just what those who are enlightened and in the know now think—they think these things make it unreasonable to believe in God or at any

rate unreasonable for those who are sufficiently aware of contemporary science and culture. This question—the reasonableness or rationality of belief in God—is the topic of this [essay].

Traditional arguments for the existence of God. The most widely accepted method of approaching this question is to consider the arguments for and against belief in God. What is more natural than to look at the evidence? If the arguments *for* the existence of God (theistic arguments, as they are called) are stronger than the arguments *against* his existence, then it is rational or reasonable to believe in God; on the other hand, if the arguments against theism outweigh the arguments for it, then the rational procedure is to reject belief in God in favor of atheism or agnosticism.... As I say, this procedure seems initially, sensible; and... I shall briefly consider some of these arguments....

There are many arguments for the existence of God; they have been discussed for a long time by many acute philosophers and theologians; here it won't be possible to do more than barely indicate some of the most important arguments and some of the most important lines of discussion. Theistic arguments go back at least to the time of Aristotle (and perhaps considerably further back than that). Such arguments were extensively studied and discussed in the Middle Ages; one thinks particularly of Anselm's Ontological Argument and of Thomas Aquinas's celebrated five

---

* Alvin Plantinga is John A. O'Brien Professor, Emeritus of Philosophy at the University of Notre Dame.

ways (five theistic proofs) at the beginning of his massive and monumental *Summa Theologiae*. In the Middle Ages, the principal reason for constructing theistic proofs was not to convince people that there really is such a person as God (then, as now, most people already believed that) but to show that we human beings can *know* that there is such a person, can have *scientific* or *demonstrative* knowledge of the existence of God. Early modern philosophy and the Enlightenment saw a great flurry of theistic proofs; Descartes, Locke, Leibniz, Malebranche, Berkeley, Paley, and many others all offered proofs or arguments for the existence of God (prompting the remark that nobody doubted the existence of God until the philosophers tried to prove it). Here the aim wasn't so much to show that we can have demonstrative knowledge of the existence of God as to show that it is reasonable or rational to accept theistic belief. This attempt to provide good theistic arguments continues to the present day.

Immanuel Kant, one of the greatest commentators on the theistic arguments, divided them into three large categories: *Ontological Arguments, Cosmological Arguments*, and *Teleological Arguments*.

In some ways the most interesting of these is the utterly fascinating Ontological Argument, first offered in the eleventh century by Anselm of Canterbury (1033–1109). . . . Anselm's argument has been the subject of enormous controversy ever since he had the temerity to spring it on an unsuspecting world. It has fascinated nearly every great philosopher from Anselm's day to the present. Many utterly reject it; Kant claimed to have finally and definitively refuted it; Schopenhauer thought it was a charming joke; many philosophers since have thought it was a joke alright, but more like a *dumb* joke. And indeed the argument does have about it a suggestion of trumpery and deceit. Nonetheless there have been and are many who think some version of this argument a perfectly valid argument for the existence of God; it does not lack for contemporary defenders.[1]

Turn now to *Cosmological Arguments*. These arguments typically proceed from some very general fact about the world—that there is *motion* for example, or *causation*; they then move to the conclusion that there must be a first unmoved mover or first uncaused cause—a being that is not itself caused to exist by anything else, but causes everything else to exist. An interesting variant is presented by the argument from *contingency*. This argument begins from the fact that there are many, contingent beings—beings that (like you and me) *do* exist, but could have *failed* to exist; it moves to the conclusion that there is a *necessary* being, a being such that it is not possible that it fail to exist. (It would remain to be shown that such a being would be God.) Perhaps the strongest version of the Cosmological Arguments would combine the argument from contingency with first cause and first mover arguments.[2]

The third kind of argument, says Kant, is the *Teleological Argument* or argument from design— more exactly, the teleological arguments, since there are several different arguments of this type. A fine formulation of such an argument is given by David Hume (who, however, does not himself accept it). . . . Many facets of the universe strongly suggest that it has been created or designed: the delicate articulated beauty of a tiny flower, the night sky viewed from the side of a mountain, the fact that the cosmological constants (including in particular the rate of expansion of the universe) must be extremely accurately adjusted if there is to be intelligent life in the universe, and so on.

The nature of proof. Now these classical arguments as classically presented typically take the form of *conclusive* or *coercive* arguments, or rather would-be conclusive or coercive arguments. They take the form of attempted *demonstrations*; the idea is that any rational person who is intellectually honest will believe the premises and will see that the premises do indeed entail the intended conclusions. Taken as coercive demonstrations, it is fair to say, I think, that they fail. None of these arguments seems to be a real demonstration. None seems to be the sort of argument which (like, say, the Pythagorean Theorem . . .) really leaves no room for doubt or disagreement. Taken as *demonstrations*, the theistic arguments fail. But why should they be taken like that? After all, scarcely any arguments for any serious philosophical conclusion qualify as real demonstrations—are really such that anyone who understands them is obliged to accept them on pain of irrationality or intellectual dishonesty. Take your favorite argument for any serious philosophical conclusion; there will be plenty of people who don't accept that argument, and are not thereby shown to be either unusually dense or intellectually dishonest. So why should it be different with theistic arguments? Even if there aren't any knockdown drag-out *demonstrations* for the existence of God, there might still be plenty of good arguments. A good argument would be one that started from premises many people rationally accept (or are inclined to accept) and proceeds via steps many people reasonably endorse to the conclusion that there is such a person as God. Perhaps there aren't any demonstrations; it doesn't follow that there aren't any good arguments. As a matter of fact, I think we can see that there are a host of good theistic arguments. . . .

So suppose we take these theistic proofs in a different spirit (in the spirit appropriate to philosophical arguments generally): not as knockdown drag-out arguments which no sane person can honestly reject, but instead as arguments whose premises and inferential moves will be found attractive by many who reflect on the matter. Then I think we must conclude that the ontological argument, even in the forms in which it commits no fallacies, doesn't have a great deal of force (despite the fact that, as I think, it is a perfectly valid argument). Perhaps it has *some* force; but probably not many who reflect on the argument and understand it will find the premise—that it is possible that there be a greatest possible being—plausible unless they already accept the conclusion. The cosmological argument, however, is much stronger, and the teleological arguments, stronger yet.

Non-traditional arguments. So far the traditional arguments. In addition to these, however, there are also a large number of other theistic arguments, some of which resist easy statement and don't fall easily under the traditional rubrics. There is . . . a wide variety of *epistemological* arguments, arguments that take their premises or starting points in some fact about human knowledge. Consider, for example, *The Argument from the Confluence of Proper Function and Reliability*, which goes as follows. Most of us assume that when our intellectual or cognitive faculties are functioning properly (in the right sort of environment, the sort of environment for which they seem to be designed), they are for the most part reliable; for the most part the beliefs they produce are true. According to theism, God has created us in his image; he has created us in such a way as to resemble him in being able to know the truth over a wide range of topics and subjects. This provides an easy, natural explanation of the fact (as we see it) that when our cognitive faculties are not subject to dysfunction, the beliefs they produce are for the most part true.

And this explanation has no real competitors (at least among beliefs that are live options for us). It is sometimes suggested that nontheistic evolutionism is such a competitor; but this is a mistake. First, there is the problem I noted above: we don't have an evolutionary explanation of human cognitive capacities, and we don't even know that it is possible that there be one. But second, non-theistic evolution would at best explain our faculties' being reliable with respect to beliefs that have survival value. (That would exclude [among others] beliefs involving reasonably recondite mathematical truths, relativity theory, and quantum mechanics, and, more poignantly, scientific beliefs of the sort involved in thinking evolution is a plausible explanation of the flora and fauna we see around us.) "At best," I say; but it wouldn't really explain even that. True beliefs *as such* don't have survival value; they have to be linked with the right kind of dispositions to behavior. What evolution really requires is that our *behavior* have survival value, not necessarily that our beliefs be true; it is sufficient for the demand of evolution that we be programmed to act in adaptive ways. But there are many ways in which our behavior could be adaptive, even if our beliefs were for the most part false. (For example, our whole belief structure might be a sort of by-product or epiphenomenon, having no real connection with truth, and no real connection with our action.) So there is no explanation in evolution for the confluence of proper function and reliability. As Patricia Churchland (not noted as a defender of theism) puts it, from an evolutionary point of view, "The principal chore of nervous systems is to get the body parts where they should be in order that the organism may survive. . . . Truth, whatever that is, definitely takes the hindmost."[3]

The argument from the confluence of reliability and proper function is one epistemological theistic argument; but there are many more. For example, there are arguments from the nature of warrant or positive epistemic status, from induction, from the rejection of global skepticism, from reference, from modal intuition, and from intuition generally. But there are also a variety of *moral* arguments, arguments from the phenomena of morality. Among the best are Robert Adams's favored version[4] which, stated in simple fashion, goes as follows. A person might find herself utterly convinced (as I do) that (1) morality is objective, not dependent upon what human beings know or think, that (2) the rightness or wrongness of an action (for example, the wrongness of the action of killing someone just for the thrill of it) cannot be explained in terms of any "natural" facts about human beings or

other things—that is, it can't ultimately be explained in terms of physical, chemical, or biological facts, and that (3) there couldn't *be* such objective non-natural moral facts unless there were such a person as God who, in one way or another, brings them into being, or legislates them. This is the obverse side of the thought that in a naturalistic universe, objective moral facts somehow wouldn't make sense, wouldn't fit in.[5]

In addition to moral, epistemological, and metaphysical arguments, there are several others that don't fit well into those categories. For example, there are arguments from love, from beauty and the appreciation of beauty, from play, enjoyment, humor, and adventure. (At bottom, these arguments claim that love in its many manifestations, or a Mozart piano concerto, or a great adventure have a kind of value that can't be explained in naturalistic terms.) There are also arguments from colors and flavors, and from the meaning of life.

The most important thing to see here, I think, is this. Once we recognize that a good theistic argument doesn't have to be a proof that will coerce any reasonable intellect (once we apply the same standards to theistic arguments that we apply to other arguments), we see that there are a large number of good theistic arguments—in fact it is extremely difficult to think of any other important philosophical thesis for which there are so many importantly different arguments. Indeed, the fact that there *are* so many different arguments (the fact that theism is of explanatory value in so many, and so many different areas of thought) is itself still another argument in its favor.

Anti-theistic arguments. . . . [B]y far the most important atheological argument [is] the celebrated argument from evil. This argument goes all the way back to Epicurus.[6] The objector begins by reminding us of the sheer *extent* of suffering and evil in the world, and indeed there is an enormous amount of it. There is also the cruelly ironic character of some evil; a man who drives a cement mixer truck comes home for lunch, lingers a bit too long in the warmth and love of his family, hurriedly jumps into his truck, backs out—and kills his three-year-old daughter who had been playing behind the wheels. Why didn't God prevent something so savagely ironic? A woman in a Nazi concentration camp is compelled to choose which of her two children shall go to the gas chamber and which shall be saved; here we have evil naked and unalloyed; and if God is what theists claim he is—omnipotent and wholly good—then why does he permit such abominations in his world?...

So the objector begins with this question: if God is omnipotent and wholly good, then why is there all this evil? The theist must concede, I think, that she doesn't know—that is, she doesn't know in any detail. On a quite general level, she may know or think she knows that God permits evil because he can achieve a world he sees as better by permitting evil than by preventing it; and what God sees as better is, of course, better. But we cannot see why *our* world, with all its ills, would be better than others we think we can imagine, nor what, in any detail, is God's reason for permitting a given specific evil. Not only can we not see this, we can't, I think, envision any very good possibilities. And here I must remark that most of the attempts to explain why God permits evil—*theodicies*, as we might call them—seem to me tepid and shallow.

Of course the fact that the theist can't answer Epicurus's question—the fact that for many or most specific evils, she has no real idea what God's reason for permitting that specific evil might be—that fact does not in itself prove much of anything. Our grasp of the fundamental way of things is at best limited; there is no reason to think that if God *did* have a reason for permitting the evil in question, we would be the first to know. Something further must be added, if the objector is to make a worthwhile point. Granted: we don't know why God permits evil; but where, so far, is the problem?

Here the objector is quick to oblige. And (at least until recently) his most popular response has been to offer some version of the *deductive anti-theistic argument from evil* . . . [J.L. Mackie, for example,] claims that the existence of evil—and of course the theist will himself agree that there is evil—entails that there is no God, or at any rate no God as conceived by standard theism. Mackie puts the claim as follows: ". . . [I]t can be shown, not merely that religious beliefs lack rational support, but that they are positively irrational, that the several parts of the essential theological doctrine are inconsistent with one another."[7] He goes on to argue that the existence of God is incompatible with the existence of evil; he concludes that since the theist is committed to both God and evil, theistic belief is irrational. It ought to be discouraged; and those who accept it, presumably, ought to give it up.

At present, I think, it is fairly widely conceded (contrary to Mackie's claim) that there is nothing like straightforward contradiction or inconsistency or necessary falsehood in the joint affirmation of God and evil. It is logically possible that God should have a reason for permitting all the evil there is; but if so, then the existence of God is not incompatible with the existence of the evil the world displays. This suggestion is developed, for example, in the Free Will Defense, according to which God must put up with at least some evil if he is to create genuinely free creatures. The Free Will Defense goes all the way back to Augustine in the fifth century and is widely accepted at present.[8]

Accordingly, atheologians have turned from deductive to *probabilistic* arguments from evil. The typical atheological claim at present is not that the existence of God is logically *incompatible* with that of evil. The claim is instead that

(1) there is an omnipotent, omniscient and perfectly good God

is *improbable* or *unlikely* with respect to

(2) There are 10^{13} turps of evil (where the *turp*, is the basic unit of evil).

According to William Rowe, for example, it is probable that

(3) "There exist instances of intense suffering which an omnipotent, omniscient being could have prevented without thereby losing some greater good or permitting some evil equally bad or worse."[9]

This is probable, he says, because

> It seems quite unlikely that *all* the instances of intense suffering occurring daily in our world are intimately related to the occurrence of greater goods or the prevention of evils at least as bad; and even more unlikely, should they somehow all be so related, that an omnipotent omniscient being could not have achieved at least some of these goods (or prevented some of those evils) without permitting the instances of intense suffering that are supposedly related to them.

The atheologian, therefore, claims that (1) is improbable with respect to (2). But he doesn't make this point for the sheer academic charm of it all; something further is supposed to follow. The fact, if it is a fact, that (1) is thus improbable is supposed to show that there is something wrong or misguided about belief in God, that it is irrational, or intellectually irresponsible, or noetically second class, or not such as to measure up to the appropriate standards for proper belief.

But *is* (1) improbable on (2) (or some other reasonably plausible proposition about evil)? Why should we think so? Rowe's claim is that there is much *apparently pointless* evil; there is much which is such that we have no idea what reason God (if there is such a person) could have for permitting it. He considers a

hypothetical state of affairs in which a fawn is burned in a forest fire and refers to the fawn's "apparently pointless" suffering; this suffering he says, "was preventable, and so far as we can see, pointless." He seems to be arguing that (1) is improbable with respect to (2) because

(3) Many cases of evil are apparently pointless,

that is, many cases of evil are apparently not such that an omniscient and omnipotent God would be obliged to put up with them in order to achieve a world as good as ours.

But how shall we understand Rowe here? In particular, how shall we understand this "apparently pointless" evil? Here there are two possibilities. First, he may be holding that

(4) In fact there *are* many cases of evil such that *it is apparent that* an omnipotent and omniscient God, if he existed, would not have a reason for permitting them.

But this is much too strong. There aren't cases of evil such that it is just *obvious* or *apparent* that God could have no reason for permitting them. The most we can sensibly say is that there are many cases of evil such that we can't think of any good reason why he would permit them; but of course that doesn't mean that it is apparent to us that he doesn't *have* a reason. As Stephen Wykstra quite properly points out,[10] we could sensibly claim this latter only if we had reason to think that if such a God *did* have a reason for permitting such evils, we would be likely to have some insight into what it is. But why think *that*? There is no reason to think that if there is such a person as God, and if he had a reason for permitting a particular evil state of affairs, *we* would have a pretty good idea of what that reason might be. On the theistic conception our cognitive powers, as opposed to God's, are a bit slim for that. God might have reasons we cannot so much as understand; he might have reasons involving other creatures—angels, devils, the principalities and powers of whom St. Paul speaks—creatures of whose nature and activities we have no knowledge.

Shall we take (3) as pointing out, then, that there are many evils such that we have no idea what God's reason, if any, is for permitting them? That seems right; but why suppose it shows that (1) is improbable with respect to (2)? We could sensibly claim *that* only if we had good reason to think that we would be privy to God's reasons for permitting evil, if he had some; but of course we don't have good reason to think that. We know very little of God's alternatives; perhaps, for example, we and our suffering figure into transactions involving beings we know nothing at all about. . . .

Say that an evil is *inscrutable* if it is such that we can't think of any reason God (if there is such a person) could have for permitting it. Clearly, the crucial problem for this probabilistic argument from evil is just the fact that nothing much follows from the fact that some evils are inscrutable; if theism is true, we would expect that there would be inscrutable evil. Indeed, it is only *hubris* which would tempt us to think that we could so much as grasp God's plans here, even if he proposed to divulge them to us. But then the fact that there is inscrutable evil does not make it improbable that God exists. The argument from evil, therefore, may have some degree of strength, but its weaknesses are evident.

Is argument required for belief in God? As I said at the beginning, perhaps the most widely discussed philosophical question having to do with belief in God is the question whether such belief is rational, or reasonable, or intellectually up to snuff, or such that a person who was reasonable and well informed could accept it. And the typical way of approaching this question has been to examine the arguments for and against the existence of God. But is it really clear that

discussing those arguments is the only or best way to approach this question of the rational justification of theistic belief? The assumption seems to be that if the arguments for theism are stronger than those for atheism, then belief in God is rational; but if the arguments for atheism are stronger, then atheism, or at any rate agnosticism, is the more reasonable attitude. But why suppose that the rational status of theistic beliefs—its reasonability or intellectual acceptability—depends upon whether there are good theistic arguments available? Consider an analogy. We all believe that there has been a past and that we know something about it. As Bertrand Russell pointed out, however, it is possible (possible in the broadly logical sense) that the world is only five minutes old, having been created just five minutes ago complete with all its apparent traces of the past, all the apparent memories, dusty books, faded pictures, crumbling mountains, massive oak trees, and the like. So what about the belief that there has been a substantial past, that the world has been here for more than five minutes? Surely that belief is rational, justified, and reasonable. But is there a good non-circular, non-question begging *argument* for it? (Of course if we are content with *circular* arguments, the theist can produce plenty of such arguments for theism.) It is certainly hard to see what they might be; no one, so far as I know, has ever come up with much of a candidate. So our belief in the past is rational or justified even though we don't have a good non-circular argument for it; so a belief can be justified in the absence of such reason; so why suppose we need arguments or evidence (evidence in the sense of other supporting beliefs) for the existence of God? Why can't belief in God be properly basic?

We can approach this same question from a slightly different direction. Many philosophers (and others as well) object that theistic belief is irrational or intellectually sub par because, as they say, there is *insufficient evidence* for it. Bertrand Russell was once asked what he would say if, after dying, he were brought into the presence of God and asked why he hadn't been a believer. Russell's reply: "I'd say 'Not enough evidence God! Not enough evidence!'"[11] We needn't speculate as to how such a reply would be received; what is clear is that Russell held theistic belief to be unreasonable because there is insufficient evidence for it. W.K. Clifford, that "delicious *enfant terrible*" as William James called him, insisted that it is wrong, immoral, wicked, and monstrous to accept a belief for which you don't have sufficient evidence. As he puts it in his characteristically restrained fashion, "Whoso would deserve well of his fellows in this matter will guard the purity of his belief with a very fanaticism of jealous care, lest at anytime it should rest on an unworthy object, and catch a stain which can never be wiped away"; and he concludes by saying, "To sum up: it is wrong always, everywhere, and for anyone to believe anything upon insufficient evidence."[12] So it is wrong to accept belief in God without sufficient evidence; numberless hordes of philosophers have joined Clifford in this opinion, and in the further opinion that indeed there is not sufficient evidence for belief in God.[13]

So the evidentialist objection has two premises:

(a) It is irrational to believe in God unless there is sufficient evidence (good arguments) for theistic belief

and

(b) there is no evidence, or at least no sufficient evidence, for theistic belief.

Now I have already argued that (b) is at best dubious. There are many good theistic arguments, and putting them all together results in an impressive case indeed. But our present concern is the *other* premise of the objector's argument: the claim that in the absence of evidence, belief in God is irrational or unjustifiable or

intellectually unacceptable. Why should we believe a thing like that? Why do those who offer the evidentialist objection believe it? We don't think the same thing about belief in other minds, the past, material objects. So why here? One answer, I think, is that those who think thus, think of theism as a *scientific hypothesis*, or a quasi-scientific hypothesis, or relevantly *like* a scientific hypothesis—something like Special Relativity, for example, or Quantum Mechanics, or the Theory of Evolution. According to J.L. Mackie, for example, "Against the rival theistic hypothesis we should have to score the (significant) improbability that if there were a god he (or it) would create a world with causal laws, and one with our specific causal laws and constants, but also the great improbability of there being a process of the unmediated fulfillment of will." And speaking of religious experience, he makes the following characteristic remark: "Here, as elsewhere, the supernaturalist hypothesis fails because there is an adequate and much more economical naturalistic alternative."[14] Clearly these remarks are relevant only if we think of belief in God as or like a sort of scientific hypothesis, a theory designed to explain some body of evidence, and acceptable to the degree that it explains that evidence. On this way of looking at the matter, there is a relevant body of evidence shared by believer and unbeliever alike; theism is a hypothesis designed to explain that body of evidence; and theism is rationally defensible only to the extent that it is a good explanation thereof.

But why should we think of theism like this? Clearly there are perfectly sensible alternatives. Consider our beliefs about the past: one could take a Mackie-like view here as well. One could hold that our beliefs about the past are best thought of as like a scientific hypothesis, designed to explain such present phenomena as (among other things) apparent memories; and if there were a more "economical" explanation of these phenomena that did not postulate past facts, then our usual beliefs in the past "could not be rationally defended." But here this seems clearly mistaken (not to say silly); the availability of such an "explanation" wouldn't in any way tell against our ordinary belief that there has really been a past. Why couldn't the same hold for theism?

In responding to Hume, Thomas Reid brilliantly discusses a similar network of questions. Here the topic under discussion is not God, but material objects or an external world. Suppose it is proposed that my belief in material objects is "rationally defensible" only if it is more probable than not with respect to a body of knowledge that includes no physical object propositions but only, say, self-evident truths together with experiential propositions specifying how I am being appeared to. Add (as the history of modern philosophy strongly suggests) that it is impossible to show that physical object statements *are* more probable than not with respect to such a body of evidence; or add, more strongly, that in fact physical object propositions are *not* more probable than not with respect to such propositions. What would follow from that? One of Reid's most important and enduring contributions was to point out that nothing of much interest would follow from that. In particular it would not follow that belief in physical objects ought to be discouraged as somehow improper, or irrational, or intellectually out of order.

But why, then, should we think it follows in the case of theism? Suppose theistic belief is not more probable than not with respect to the body of beliefs shared by theists and nontheists: why should we conclude that it is not rationally defensible? Perhaps it is perfectly rational to take belief in God in the way we ordinarily take belief in other minds, material objects, the past, and the like. Why isn't it perfectly sensible to *start with* belief in God? Why does belief in God have to be probable with respect to some *other* body of evidence in order to be rationally defensible? . . .

Conclusion. So the question about the rationality of theistic belief can't anywhere nearly be settled just by paying attention to the arguments for and against belief in God. At least as important is the question whether belief in God is properly basic—whether, that is, proper and rational belief in God can resemble (say) memory beliefs in not ordinarily being accepted by way of reliance upon arguments or evidential support from other beliefs. The most promising way to investigate that question, I think, is to consider what rationality, or warrant, or positive epistemic status *is*; once we are clear about that, then we can ask whether basic belief in God can have it. I myself believe such investigation reveals that belief in God taken in the basic way is perfectly proper, and rational, and acceptable; indeed, I think we can *know* that God exists without believing on the basis of arguments. But that is a topic for another time.

Notes

1. See, for example, Charles Hartshorne's *Man's Vision of God* (New York: Harper and Row, 1941); and Norman Malcolm's "Anselm's Ontological Arguments" (*Philosophical Review*, 1960). There is a development and defense of a version of this argument in my *God, Freedom and Evil* (Grand Rapids: W.B. Eerdmans, 1978) and *The Nature of Necessity* (Oxford UP, 1974).

2. As in David Braine's *The Reality of Time and the Existence of God* (Oxford: Oxford UP, 1988).

3. Patricia Churchland, "Epistemology in the Age of Neuroscience," *Journal of Philosophy* 84 (October 1987), p. 548.

4. See Robert Merrihew Adams, "Moral Arguments for Theistic Belief" [see chapter 4].

5. See George Mavrodes, "Religion and the Queerness of Morality," in *Rationality, Religious Belief and Moral Commitment*, ed. by Robert Audi and William Wainwright (Ithaca, NY: Cornell UP, 1986).

6. Diogenes Laertius, *Lives of Eminent Philosophers*, trans. by R.D. Hicks (Cambridge: Harvard UP, 1979), 8K. x, 80–82.

7. "Evil and Omnipotence," *Mind* 64 (1955). In Mackie's posthumous *The Miracle of Theism* (Oxford: Oxford UP, 1982), Mackie wavers between his earlier claim that the existence of God is straightforwardly inconsistent with that of evil, and the claim that the existence of evil is powerful but not conclusive evidence against the existence of God. (See pp. 150–75, and see my "Is Theism Really a Miracle?" in *Faith and Philosophy* 3 (April 1986), pp. 298–313.

8. And (as I see it) rightly so; see my *The Nature of Necessity* (Oxford: Clarendon P, 1974), Chap. IX, and *God, Freedom and Evil* (New York: Harper and Row, 1974; and Grand Rapids: W.B. Eerdmans, 1980), pp. 7–64.

9. William Rowe, "The Problem of Evil and Some Varieties of Atheism" [see chapter 20].

10. Stephen Wykstra, "The Humean Obstacle to Evidential Arguments from Suffering: On Avoiding the Evils of Appearance," *International Journal for the Philosophy of Religion* 16 (1984), p. 85.

11. Bertrand Russell, quoted in W. Salmon's "Religion and Science: A New Look at Hume's Dialogues," *Philosophical Studies* 33 (1978), p. 176.

12. W.K. Clifford, "The Ethics of Belief" [see chapter 9].

13. For example, Brand Blanshard, *Reason and Belief* (London: Allen and Unwin, 1974), pp. 400 ff.; Antony Flew, *The Presumption of Atheism* (London: Pemberton, 1976), pp. 87 ff.; Bertrand Russell, "Why I am not a Christian," in *Why I Am not a Christian* (New York: Simon and Schuster, 1957), pp. 3 ff.; J.L. Mackie, *The Miracle of Theism* (Oxford: Clarendon P, 1982); Michael Scriven, *Primary Philosophy* (New York: McGraw Hill, 1966) pp. 87 ff.; and many others. This objection is even more popular in the oral tradition than in published work; and it ordinarily has the character of an unspoken assumption more than that of an explicit objection.

14. Mackie, *The Miracle of Theism*, pp. 252–53. Ibid., p. 198.

Discussion

1. Plantinga distinguishes between coercive demonstrations and arguments which some reasonable people find attractive. Defend the view that the latter is adequate for theistic arguments. Or defend the view that

non-coercive, non-demonstrative arguments are not intellectually adequate.

2. How might one develop an argument for the existence of God based on, as Plantinga suggests, love, beauty and the appreciation of beauty, play, enjoyment, humour and adventure?

3. Plantinga's loosening of the criteria for arguments and widening of the phenomena that might best be explained by God makes theism more intellectually respectable. Explain your agreement or disagreement with this statement.

THE NATURE OF REASON

WILLIAM J. WAINWRIGHT*

The Lockean background. In *An Essay Concerning Human Understanding*, John Locke defines reason as "the discovery of the certainty or probability of such propositions or truths, which the mind arrives at by deduction made from such ideas, which it has got by the use of its natural faculties; viz. by sensation or reflection" (4.18.2).[1] Rational belief is proportionate to the strength of the evidence at one's disposal. "The mind, if it *will proceed rationally*, ought to examine all the grounds of probability, and see how they make more or less for or against any proposition, before it assents to or dissents from it; and upon a due balancing of the whole, reject or receive it, with more or less firm assent, proportionably to the preponderancy of the greater grounds of probability on one side or the other" (iv. 15.5). What is true of beliefs in general is true of religious beliefs in particular. They are rational only if (1) they are properly basic (immediately grounded in the mind's intuitive awareness of its own ideas), or (2) inferred from those ideas by sound deductive or inductive standards, or (3) are the content of a revelation whose credentials are certified by beliefs meeting the first or second condition. While modern intellectuals may doubt whether religious beliefs meet these standards, Locke did not. God's existence can be demonstrated, and the evidence at our disposal makes it probable that the Bible is God's revelation.

Richard Swinburne would agree with the substance of Locke's remarks. His books *The Existence of God* and *Faith and Reason* persuasively argue that the evidence at our disposal makes God's existence probable and the Christian revelation credible.[2] Swinburne's work as a whole is informed by a conception of reason which is similar to Locke's in spirit if not always in letter. "To believe that *p* is to believe that *p* is more probable than any alternative.... The kind of probability at stake here is ... epistemic probability," and "epistemic probability is relative to evidence" (*FR* 18)....

Swinburne recognizes, of course, that apparently rational people differ over such things as the prior probability of hypotheses.... Swinburne also notes that people's beliefs in reports of experience, deliverances of reason, and other basic propositions differ "in the degrees of confidence with which they hold" them.... People's inferential standards also differ.... Finally, people's assessments of the *overall* probability of theories and hypotheses differ....

Swinburne admits that these disagreements are very much the product of our "upbringing," but insists that if progress is to be made in rational enquiry, "we must make the judgments which seem to us to be intuitively right." The relativity of our understanding "does not mean that our understanding is in error" (*EG* 56).

I believe that this is correct. But I also think that differences over prior probability, the overall probability of a hypothesis, and so on, are differences in judgment, and that differences in judgment are typically affected by what William James called our "willing" or "passional" nature—our temperament, needs, concerns, fears, hopes, passions, and "divinations." Simplicity, for example, is partly a matter of intelligibility or naturalness. But the conviction that a hypothesis is intelligible or natural is partly a product of familiarity, and is affected by our attachments and attitudes. A hypothesis that seems intelligible or natural to a traditional Christian theist like Swinburne may not seem intelligible or natural to a [confirmed and critical atheist like] J.L. Mackie.

Our assessments of the overall probability of a hypothesis like theism are also affected by our passional nature; for when it comes to "the question, what is to come of the evidence, being what it is," each of us must finally decide "according to (what is called)

---

*   William Wainwright is Distinguished Professor Emeritus of Philosophy at the University of Wisconsin, Milwaukee.

the state of his heart."[3] In the last analysis, I can only view the evidence "in the medium of *my* primary mental experiences, under the aspects which they spontaneously present to *me*, and with the aid of *my* best illative [inferential] sense."[4] Our assessments of the evidence depend on our view of prior probabilities, of the evidence's overall weight, and so on. But because these "have no definite ascertained value and are reducible to no scientific standard, what are such to each individual, depends on his moral temperament" and personal history, as well as investigation and argument.[5]

Swinburne would not deny that our willing nature affects our judgment, but would, I think, insist that its influence is epistemically harmful.... This attitude towards the effect of "passion" on reason is hardly unusual. But is it correct? [I] will offer a partial defense of the claim that the influence of the heart can be epistemically benign.

Cognitive faculties rightly disposed. The position I will defend was once a Christian commonplace: that reason is capable of knowing God—but only when one's cognitive faculties are rightly disposed. It should be distinguished from two others which have dominated modern thought. The first claims that God can be known by "objective reason"—that is, by an understanding that systematically excludes "passional factors" from the process of reasoning. The other insists that God can be known only "subjectively," or by the heart. Both views identify reason with ratiocination. They also assume that reasoning is objective only when unaffected by wants, interests, and desires. The tradition I will discuss steers between these two extremes. It places a high value on proofs, arguments, and inferences, yet also believes that a properly disposed heart is needed to see their force. The most articulate spokesman for this position is Jonathan Edwards.

Edwards was strongly influenced by Continental rationalists like Malebranche, by some of the Cambridge Platonists (Henry More, for example),

and by the empiricists (especially Locke). He was also excited by Newton and the new science. Although these traditions were diverse, they had an important common feature—an almost uncritical confidence in reason's power and scope. Edwards's practice reflects this confidence. Philosophical arguments are deployed to demolish critics, justify the principal Christian doctrines, and erect a speculative metaphysics (a subjective idealism like Berkeley's). But Edwards was also a Calvinist who shared the Reformed tradition's distrust of humanity's natural capacities and its skepticism about natural theology.

These diverse strands are reflected in the apparent ambiguity of Edwards's remarks on reason. Thus, he can say, on the one hand, that "arguing for the being of a God according to the natural powers from everything we are conversant with is short, easy, and what we naturally fall into" (Misc. 268, T 78), and yet, on the other hand, insist that, in thinking about God, reason is baffled by "mystery," "paradox," and "seeming inconsistence."...[6]

... [A]lthough reason *can* prove God's existence, determine the nature of many of his attributes, discern our obligations to him, and establish the credibility of Scripture, grace is needed to help "the natural principles against those things that tend to stupify [*sic*] it and to hinder its free exercise" (Misc. 626, T 111). It is also needed to "sanctify the reasoning faculty and assist it to see the clear evidence there is of the truth of religion in rational arguments" (Misc. 628, T 251)....

Edwards on "reason." Edwards uses "reason" in two closely related senses. Sometimes the term refers to "ratiocination, or a power of inferring by arguments" (DSL 18). At others it refers to "the power ... an intelligent being has to judge of the truth of propositions ... immediately by only looking on the propositions" as well as to ratiocination (Misc. 1340, T 219). The difference between these characterizations isn't important; in both cases, "reason's work is to perceive truth and not excellency" (DSL 18). Excellency and what pertains to it are perceived by the heart. While Edwards concedes that there is a more extended sense in which "reason" refers to "the faculty of mental perception in general" (DSL 18), he clearly prefers the stricter usage. His official view is that of other modern philosophers who deny that reason has an affective dimension (a love of the good, for example, or a delight in excellence).

Grace affects reason as well as the heart. "Common grace" helps the faculties "to do that more fully which they do by nature," strengthening "the natural principles [for example, conscience] against those things that tend to stupify it and to hinder its free exercise." "Special grace," on the other hand, "causes those things to be in the soul that are above nature; and causes them to be in the soul habitually" (Misc. 626, T 111). Special grace sanctifies by infusing benevolence or true virtue—namely, the love of being in general. Infused benevolence is the basis of a new epistemic principle; a sense of the heart which tastes, relishes, and perceives the beauty of holiness (that is, benevolence). By its means, the sanctified acquire a new simple idea (the idea of "true beauty") which the unredeemed lack. Because this idea is needed to properly understand divine matters, the "saints" are in a superior epistemic position. One can't rightly understand God's moral attributes, for example, if one doesn't perceive their beauty. Nor can one adequately grasp truths which logically or epistemically depend on God's holiness and its splendor such as the infinite heinousness of sin or the appropriateness of God's aiming at his own glory. The saints also behold old data with new eyes. They perceive the stamp of divine splendor on the world's order and design and upon the events recorded in sacred history. They thereby acquire a more accurate sense of this evidence's force and impressiveness.

[Let us consider an] epistemic effect of special grace. The new principle that God infuses

sanctifies the reasoning faculty and assists it to see the clear evidence there is of the truth of religion in rational arguments, and that in two ways, viz., as it removes prejudices and so lays the mind more open to the force of arguments, and also secondly, as it positively enlightens and assists it to see the force of rational arguments ... by adding greater light, clearness and strength to the judgment. (Misc. 628, T 251)

There is nothing intrinsically supernatural about many of these benefits. The *cause* of the mind's reasoning soundly is supernatural, but the effect (sound reasoning) often is not; the spirit simply helps us use our natural epistemic faculties rightly.

What sorts of "prejudices" interfere with reason's "free exercise"? "Opinions arising from imagination" are one example. They

take us as soon as we are born, are beat into us by every act of sensation, and so grow up with us from our very births; and by that means grow into us so fast that it is almost impossible to root them out, being as it were so incorporated with our very minds that whatsoever is objected to them, contrary thereunto, is as if it were dissonant to the very constitution of them. Hence, men come to make what they can actually perceive by their senses, or immediate and outside reflection into their own souls, the standard of possibility and impossibility. ("Prejudices" 196)

Biases arising from temperament, education custom and fashion furnish other examples. . . .

Sin's essence is a failure to obey the love commandment. Those who don't love being in general love "private systems." Their loves are partial, extending to only some beings. They are also inordinate; lives are centered on the self or more extensive private systems rather than on God (who is "in effect" being in general) and the creatures who are absolutely dependent on him and reflect his glory.

Sin has noetic consequences. Edwards refers, for example, to "the great subjection of the soul in its fallen state to the external senses" (Misc. 782, T 122). (This subjection is presumably a consequence of the soul's inordinate love of temporal goods.) Again, self-love blinds us to everything that doesn't bear on immediate self-interest (OS 145–57). . . .

Our corrupt inclinations even affect our sense of what is and isn't reasonable. "Common inclination or the common dictates of inclination, are often called common sense." A person who says that the doctrine of eternal damnation offends common sense is using the expression in this way. But the inclinations behind this judgment have been shaped by an insensibility to "the great evil of sin." They are therefore corrupt (Misc. Obs. 253). . . .

Grace frees the mind from these "prejudices." An unprejudiced reason, however, isn't dispassionate. For it is affected by *epistemically benign* feelings and inclinations. A love of wider systems alone checks self-interest. Nor is it sufficient to replace hostility towards religion with indifference or neutrality; the heart must be receptive to it. An unprejudiced reason is also affected by natural motions of the heart—gratitude for one's being, for example, or a sense that it would be unfitting for the injustice that evades human tribunals to escape punishment. And since our love of temporal goods is inordinate because it isn't subordinate to a love of eternity, the latter is needed to correct it.

Another point is relevant as well. Natural reason reveals many truths about God and our relation to him. Yet even at the level of nature these truths aren't properly understood if the heart lacks a due sense of the natural good and evil in them (a proper sense of the natural unfittingness of disobeying the world's sovereign, for example, and a horror of the natural evils consequent upon offenses against him, or a proper sense

of the natural benefits he has bestowed upon us and of the obligations these gifts create).

I conclude, then, that *common* grace not only inhibits the action of passional factors corrupting reason; it (at least temporarily) causes better affections to influence it. *Sanctifying* grace replaces the effects of corrupt affections by the influences of true benevolence. A reason that is exercising itself "freely" and without "prejudice," therefore, is affected by passional factors.

But grace does more than remove the impediments ("prejudices") hindering reason's free exercise by restructuring our affections. . . .

It should by now be clear how sin affects reasoning. Our immersion in temporal concerns distracts us so that we don't attend to our ideas. Our subjection to the senses aggravates the tendency to substitute words and other sensible signs for ideas, and our disordered lives make it difficult for us to appreciate even the natural goods and evils associated with religion. (For example, our blunted conscience blinds us to the natural fittingness of obeying God's commands, and our inordinate attachment to the present life leads us to neglect more important natural goods that extend beyond it.) A lack of true benevolence (which is sin's essence) makes it impossible to understand God's holiness (which consists in it) or to appreciate its beauty.

We are now also in a position to understand why rational arguments for religious truths aren't always convincing. Miscellanies 201 (T 246 ff.) and 408 (T 249 ff.) imply that a conviction of reality is created (1) by an idea's clarity and liveliness, (2) by its internal coherence and its coherence with our other ideas, and (3) by its agreement with "the nature and constitution of our minds themselves." Why, then, do religious ideas so often fail to carry conviction? Partly because the clarity and intensity of spiritual ideas is a function of "the practice of virtue and holiness" (Misc. 123, T 246) and our own practice falls woefully short, and partly because the "tempers" or "frames" of the ungodly aren't suited to them. . . . It is possible that those without spiritual frames can't even discern their coherence. . . .

Special, or sanctifying, grace remedies these defects by enabling us to attend more easily to the actual ideas that the words of religion stand for and by disposing the heart to be suitably affected by the natural and supernatural good and evil associated with them. Common grace has similar effects, but (because it doesn't replace the love of private systems with true benevolence) doesn't furnish the mind with actual ideas of true virtue and true beauty, affecting it only with a sense of the relevant *natural* goods and evils.

The sense of divine beauty alone is intrinsically supernatural. A reason which has been freed from the bonds of imagination, prejudice, and narrow self-interest, attends to ideas of God's being, power, knowledge, justice, munificence, and other "natural" attributes, and is suitably affected by the natural good and evil associated with them isn't functioning above its nature. A reason which has been strengthened in these ways is capable, however, of seeing the force of rational arguments for the truths of "natural religion"—that is, truths about God which neither logically nor epistemically depend on the ideas of holiness and true beauty. A suitably disposed natural reason is thus capable of establishing God's existence and general nature. Truths which depend on the ideas of holiness and true beauty can also be established by rational arguments, but the force of these can be appreciated only by people with spiritual frames.

Desires and beliefs. Edwards was the philosophical heir to rationalists, and empiricists whose confidence in reason was relatively unqualified. He was the theological heir to a Reformed tradition which distrusted humanity's natural capacities. Did he succeed in coherently weaving these apparently inconsistent strands together? The answer, I believe, is a qualified "Yes."

The key is a distinction between good rational arguments and the conditions necessary for their acceptance. I may have a good argument against smoking, for example, but my desire to smoke may prevent me from appreciating its force. What is needed isn't a better argument, but a reorientation of my desires.

Edwards's position is roughly this. While reason is capable of generating good rational arguments for God's existence, his providential government of human affairs, predestination, and many other theological and metaphysical doctrines, self-deception, prejudice, self-interest, and other passional factors make it difficult for us to see their force. These faults can't be corrected by applying Descartes's rules for correct thinking, Locke's "measures . . . to regulate our assent and moderate our persuasion,"[7] or other methods of this sort. What is needed is a set of epistemic excellences which are themselves expressions of morally desirable character traits and rightly ordered affections. The defects distorting human reasoning are deeply rooted in human nature, and can only be eliminated by the appropriate virtues.

Two features of Edwards's position are especially significant. First, the epistemic virtues aren't merely negative; they involve more than the exclusion of the passions and selfish partialities which subvert reason. Nor are the epistemic virtues confined to noncontroversial excellences like the love of truth. They include properly ordered natural affections such as gratitude and a love of being in general which God infuses into the hearts of his elect. These affections not only cast out others which adversely affect reasoning; they affect it themselves. Under their influence, we reason differently and more accurately.

The other significant feature is this. Two views should be distinguished. One is that there are circumstances in which it is legitimate for people's passions and affections to make up deficiencies in the evidence. Although the (objective) evidence isn't sufficient to warrant belief, one is entitled to let one's passional nature tip the balance. The other is that a person's passional nature is sometimes needed to evaluate the evidence properly (to accurately assess its force). The first view is often attributed to James. Edwards holds the second.

Edwards's position differs significantly from the more familiar positions of James, Kierkegaard, and others who appeal to passional factors. Edwards is an evidentialist. A proper, and therefore rational, religious belief must be self-evident or based on adequate evidence. But, unlike most evidentialists, Edwards believes that passional factors are needed to appreciate the evidence's *force*. Only those with properly disposed hearts can read the evidence rightly.

Edwards's view thus also differs from Locke's and Swinburne's. Fully rational judgments are determined not only by one's evidence and inductive standards; they are also determined by feelings and attitudes that express theological virtues. . . .

True benevolence's assessment of the evidence isn't a nonrational ground for belief in this sense. It doesn't lead the saints to construct new inductive standards, to forget about some of the evidence, or to engage in selective investigation. Nor does it provide them with a *reason* for doing so. True benevolence isn't a nonrational ground for belief in Swinburne's sense, because it isn't a *ground* for belief at all, although its presence *does* partially explain why the saints hold the beliefs they do. In the same way, a good scientist's impartiality, intellectual honesty, and desire for truth help explain why she holds the beliefs she does and not the views of some less scrupulous or more credulous colleague. But they aren't *grounds* for her belief.

The position Edwards represents must be distinguished, then, from other more familiar views. Is it true or plausible? I am not sure. But I am convinced that the two strongest objections to it are inconclusive. I will discuss the more serious of the two in the following section.

Defending the passions. That passional factors *should* affect reasoning strikes most philosophers as epistemically, or even morally, objectionable. [This objection] rest[s] on a common assumption that our passional nature isn't a reliable guide to objective truth. Since Edwards (and also, I think, Pascal, Kierkegaard, and James) denies this, th[is] objection begs the question.

Let me begin with two preliminary comments. First, people like Edwards aren't recommending that we cultivate certain beliefs by viewing the evidence selectively. Edwards isn't advising us to *ignore* evidence, but to view *all* the evidence (assess its force) in a certain way. Second, the sort of partiality exhibited by those with holy dispositions doesn't exclude other intellectual virtues closely associated with impartiality. . . . The truly benevolent *are* partial in the sense that they allow their judgments to be influenced by their new wants and interests. Whether this sort of selectivity or partiality is undesirable is another matter. . . .

The best argument against cognitive voliting [knowingly allowing one's beliefs to be influenced by passional factors] is inductive. Extensive experience has shown that need, desire, and other passional factors can adversely affect judgment. It has also shown that methodical efforts to reduce their influence can serve the cause of truth. Science is the most impressive example.

This argument, however, is also inconclusive. Edwards would agree with James. "Almost always" in science, "and even in human affairs in general," we should "save ourselves from any chance of believing falsehood, by not making up our minds at all till objective evidence has come." They would agree, in other words, that passional considerations are out of order in most cases *like those in the sample*. Both would deny that we can legitimately extrapolate from these cases to others with different subject-matters (the metaphysical and moral structure of reality, for example, or things of the spirit). As we have just seen, they have arguments purporting to show that, with respect to these subject-matters, some passional factors *are* reliable guides to truth. To simply assume that the generalization concerning the adverse effects of passional factors can be extended to areas like these begs the question. It may not, for example, apply to ethics. Aristotle argued that moral reasoning goes astray when it isn't informed by a correct understanding of the good life. The latter, however, depends on properly cultivated dispositions as well as sound reasoning. If one's emotional temper is defective or has been perverted by corrupt education, one can't appreciate the good. As a result, one misconstrues the nature of the good life, and one's practical deliberations miscarry. Now according to classical theism, God is the good. One would therefore expect a properly cultivated heart to be a necessary condition for grasping truths about him.

If theism is true, and if it is also true that subjective qualifications would be needed to know God if God existed, then there is reason to think that cognitive voliting is sometimes reliable. In refusing to allow our passional nature to affect our judgment on religious matters, we may, therefore, be prejudging the case against people like Edwards. . . .

The relevance of Edwards. Why should Edwards's account of the proper use of our epistemic faculties still interest us? For two reasons. First, his account is the most carefully articulated version known to me of an epistemic theory deeply embedded in important strands of the Christian tradition. Calvin, for example, thought that rational arguments for the authority of Scripture "will not obtain full credit in the hearts of men until they are sealed by the inward testimony of the Spirit."[8] And while Aquinas believed that there is good evidence for the divine origin of Christian teaching, he didn't think that it was sufficient to compel assent without the inward movement of a will grounded in a "supernatural principle."[9] . . . The notion that a proper disposition is needed to appreciate the force of rational arguments for the authority of the Gospel can be easily extended to rational arguments for the truths of "natural religion" when these, too, come under attack. . . .

The other reason for taking Edwards seriously is this. I suggest that theists who think that there are rational arguments for the truths of religion and who, in the light of their beliefs, think through the implications of their disagreements with intelligent, well-informed, honest, and philosophically astute critics will be forced to draw similar conclusions. They believe that these critics' assessment of the overall force of the evidence is in error. This error can't plausibly be attributed to such things as lack of intelligence, unfamiliarity with relevant evidence, obvious prejudice, or an unwillingness to consider counterclaims. Edwards would ascribe it to a failure of the heart. Modern theists may be reluctant to agree. (Partly because of their respect for these critics.) Yet if theism *is* true, and there *is* good evidence for it, what other explanation could there be of the failure of so many to appreciate its force?

Notes

1. John Locke, *An Essay Concerning Human Understanding* (2 vols., New York: Dover, 1959).

2. *The Existence of God* (Oxford: Clarendon P, 1979); *Faith and Reason* (Oxford: Clarendon P, 1981); hereafter *EG* and *FR* respectively.

3. John Henry Newman, "Love the Safeguard of Faith against Superstition," in *University Sermons* (Westminster, MD: Christian Classics, 1966), p. 227.

4. Newman, *Grammar of Assent* (Garden City, NY: Image Books, 1955), p. 318.

5. Newman, "Faith and Reason Contrasted as Habits of Mind," in *University Sermons*, p. 191.

6. Edwards's principal discussions of reason are located in the "Miscellanies" (a number of which can be found in *The Philosophy of Jonathan Edwards from His Private Notebooks*, ed. Harvey G. Townsend (Eugene, OR: University of Oregon monographs, 1955), hereafter Misc., T; "A Divine and Supernatural Light" and "Miscellaneous Observations," in *The Works of President Edwards* (1968 repr. of Leeds ed. reissued with a 2-vol. supplement in Edinburgh, 1847), p. viii, hereafter DSL and Misc. Obs., respectively; "The Mind," "Subjects to Be Handled in the Treatise on the Mind," and "Of the Prejudices of Imagination," in *Scientific and Philosophical Writings*, ed. Wallace E. Anderson (New Haven, CT: Yale UP, 1980), hereafter "Mind," "Subjects" and "Prejudices" respectively, and *Original Sin* (New Haven, CT: Yale UP, 1970), hereafter OS. Other relevant material can be found in *Religious Affections* (New Haven, CT: Yale UP, 1959), hereafter RA; *The Nature of True Virtue*, in *Ethical Writings*, ed. Paul Ramsey (New Haven, CT: Yale UP,

1989), hereafter *TV*; *History of the Work of Redemption* (New Haven, CT: Yale UP, 1989); and *Freedom of the Will*, hereafter *FW*.

7. Locke, *Essay*, introduction, p. 3.

8. John Calvin, *Institutes of the Christian Religion* (Grand Rapids, MI: Eerdmans, 1957), 1.1, 7.4.

9. St. Thomas Aquinas, *The Summa Theologica* (New York: Benziger Bros.), vol. 2, part II–II, q. 6, a. 1.

Discussion

1. What is Wainwright's explanation of disagreement concerning the power of theistic arguments?

2. If you disagree with Wainwright, what is your alternative explanation?

3. Suppose we concede that desires and aversions play a role in the assessment of arguments. How can we tell who is being misled by their improper desires and aversions?

Part One

Suggestions for Further Study

Alston, William. *Perceiving God*. Ithaca, NY: Cornell UP, 1991.

Brooke, J.H., F. Watts, and R.R. Manning, eds. *The Oxford Handbook of Natural Theology*. Oxford UP, 2013.

Clark, Kelly James. *Return to Reason*. Grand Rapids, MI: Eerdmans, 1990.

Craig, William Lane, and Quentin Smith. *Theism, Atheism and Big Bang Cosmology*. Oxford: Clarendon P, 1993.

Craig, William Lane, and J.P. Moreland, eds. *The Blackwell Companion to Natural Theology*. Hoboken, NJ: Wiley-Blackwell, 2012.

Davis, Stephen. *God, Reason and Theistic Proofs*. Grand Rapids, MI: Eerdmans, 1997.

Evans, C. Steven. *Natural Signs and Knowledge of God: A New Look at Theistic Arguments*. Oxford UP, 2012.

Helm, Paul, ed. *Divine Commands and Morality*. Oxford: Oxford UP, 1981.

Le Poidevin, Robin. *Arguing for Atheism*. New York: Routledge, 1996.

Leslie, John. *Universes*. New York: Routledge, 1989.

Manson, Neil, ed. *God and Design: The Teleological Argument and Modern Science*. Routledge, 2003.

Martin, Michael. *Atheism: A Philosophical Justification*. New York: Temple UP, 1990.

Murray, Michael. *Reason for the Hope Within*. Grand Rapids, MI: Eerdmans, 1999.

Newman, John Henry. *A Grammar of Assent*. Notre Dame: U of Notre Dame P, 1979.

O'Connor, Timothy. *Theism and Ultimate Explanation: The Shape of Contingency*. Hoboken, NJ: Wiley-Blackwell, 2012.

Rowe, William. *The Cosmological Argument*. Princeton: Princeton UP, 1975.

Rowe, William. *Philosophy of Religion: An Introduction*. Belmont: Wadsworth, 1978.

Swinburne, Richard. *The Existence of God*. Oxford: Clarendon P, 1979.

Wielenberg, Erik. *Value and Virtue in a Godless Universe*. Cambridge: Cambridge UP, 2005.

Reason and Belief in God

Part Two

Introduction

Introduction. There is a tremendous variety of positions concerning the relationship of faith to reason. One extreme contends that rational faith demands proof of a rather stringent sort and the other extreme claims that faith should be maintained contrary to or even in defiance of reason. While there is certainly a philosopher or two who have held such extreme positions, most philosophers locate themselves somewhere in the middle.

The most hotly contended recent debate on faith and reason centers around *evidentialism*, which maintains that one must have evidence or arguments for one's beliefs (in God) to be rational. Since the time of the Enlightenment, many people have felt the demand to hold all beliefs, including belief in God, up to the searching light of reason. A belief is rational, according to this view, only if it can be supported by evidence or argument.

Atheistic or agnostic evidentialists have generated a popular objection to the rationality of religious belief, *the evidentialist objection to belief in God*, which holds that it is irrational to believe in God without sufficient evidence or argument. They also claim that there is not sufficient evidence or argument for the existence of God. Hence, it is irrational to believe in God (even if God were to exist). While the evidentialist objection does not attempt to *disprove* belief in God, it does attempt to *discredit* belief in God.

There have been several responses to the evidentialist objection to belief in God. Some theists endorse *theistic evidentialism*, which contends that belief in God is rational only if there is sufficient evidence for the existence of God and holds that there *is* sufficient evidence for the existence of God (either in the form of the traditional theistic arguments or based on religious experience).

Theistic evidentialism views come in extreme forms and in more moderate forms. The most extreme view would insist that each and every person is under some sort of obligation to become a quasi-philosopher—carefully studying all of the alleged proofs and disproofs of God's existence. The more moderate view has been fetchingly called by its creator, Stephen Wykstra, "sensible evidentialism" (opposing "stupid" evidentialism?!). *Sensible evidentialism* is the view that belief in God is rational because someone in the theistic community has evidence for the truth of her beliefs; sensible evidentialism concedes that there is a need for evidence for belief to be rational. Both theistic and sensible evidentialism accept the basic contention of evidentialism—that rational belief in God requires the support of evidence or argument.

Fideism holds that belief in God ought to be accepted and maintained in the absence of or contrary to reason. If reason opposes faith, so much the worse for reason. It is difficult to find many recent defenses of fideism—it is a term as unpopular in Western philosophy as "communist" or "fundamentalist." Tertullian (c. 155–c. 240 CE) is alleged to be a fideist with respect to Christian belief due to his claim, "I believe because it is absurd." Soren Kierkegaard, the nineteenth-century Danish philosopher, is likewise branded a fideist for endorsing, embracing even, the leap of faith. Both allegations are disputed by scholars.

The most intriguing recent development in matters of faith and reason is the so-called "Reformed epistemology." This view has been developed by, among others, Alvin Plantinga and Nicholas Wolterstorff, who have been influenced by John Calvin, one of the Protestant Reformers (hence the name). *Reformed epistemology* holds that one can perfectly rationally believe in God without the support of propositional evidence. One need not have carefully considered a theistic argument and refuted the counter-arguments to maintain rational belief in God. Belief in God is *properly basic*: a rational, foundational belief that one reasons *from* and not *to*. Reformed epistemology, as you might imagine, has been subject to tremendous criticism from the philosophical community, which prizes reason, perhaps inordinately (if Reformed epistemology is correct).

The need for evidence. No recent textbook in philosophy of religion is complete without the contribution of W.K. Clifford. It is difficult to resist his impassioned demand for evidence. His potent illustration of the corrupt ship-owner suggests that just as there is an ethics of action, there is also an ethics of belief. All beliefs, in every circumstance, for every person, require (morally) the support of evidence. It is wrong, so Clifford's famous maxim goes, always and everywhere for anyone to believe anything on insufficient evidence.

Reformed epistemology. We have already mentioned the major tenets of Reformed epistemology: belief in God is perfectly proper without the support of a theistic argument. Clark defends Reformed epistemology by illustrating how actual people actually acquire beliefs. A great many of our beliefs are acquired without evidential support. Belief properly begins with trust, not suspicion; beliefs are innocent until proven guilty. So, too, belief in God may be accepted without adequate propositional evidence (unless or until one has adequate reason to give up belief in God).

Wittgensteinian fideism. I stated earlier that few contemporary philosophers defend fideism. Nonetheless, contemporary philosophers have been accused of endorsing fideism. One such position has been called "Wittgensteinian fideism." Ludwig Wittgenstein's later works both noticed and affirmed the tremendous variety of our beliefs that are not held because of reasons—such beliefs are, according to Wittgenstein, groundless. A curious number of Wittgenstein's most prominent students are religious believers, many of whom applied his general insights into the structure of human belief to religious belief. Norman Malcolm favourably compares belief in God to the belief that things don't vanish into thin air. Both are part of the untested and untestable framework of human belief. These framework beliefs are ones that we are inculcated into from the earliest ages. They form the system of beliefs *within which* testing of other beliefs can take place. While we can justify beliefs within the framework, we cannot justify the framework itself. The giving of reasons must come to an end. And then we believe, groundlessly.

Pragmatic justification of religious belief. Suppose it simply cannot be decided on the basis of the evidence whether or not God exists. Since it is nonetheless possible that God exists, there may yet be consequences for belief or unbelief; indeed, such consequences may be eternal. Pascal's famous wager relies on the undecidability of belief in God on the basis of the evidence as well as the potential consequences of belief and unbelief. At the time of his death, Pascal left a series of notes that he had intended to complete in a full and final defense of Christian belief. These intriguing notes were published in 1600 as Pascal's *Pensées*. The best that these suggestive notes can provide are hints and guesses about Pascal's final project.

Pascal's wager, the most famous portion of the *Pensées*, is intended to show that even though there is not sufficient evidence for or against the existence of

God, it is better to gain the potential benefits of eternal bliss and to avoid the potential costs of eternal damnation by committing oneself to belief in God.

I have included other sections to demonstrate that this is not all that Pascal had to say about rational religious belief. He seemed concerned to shock uninterested and easily distracted people into caring about the most important matters—their eternal destiny. He also seemed to believe that there is adequate evidence for the truth of Christianity but that one must care about the evidence in order to see it; that is, one's passions need to be properly ordered to comprehend the truth.

Calling Clifford a "delicious *enfant terrible*," William James defends the right to believe in God in the absence of sufficient evidence. His attack on Clifford, and the incessant Enlightenment demand for evidence, is two-pronged. He first argues that the person who accepts Clifford's rules of truth-seeking has made a passional (i.e., non-rational) decision. All of us, he argues, have the right to choose our own risks concerning our approach to belief-acquisition. One can be a Cliffordian who avoids false beliefs at all costs but misses out on many true beliefs. Or one can be more, shall we say, Jamesian—generously accepting many true beliefs (without adequate evidence) and so running the risk of admitting many false beliefs. James concludes his essay by demonstrating the deficiencies of Clifford's belief policies in matters of fundamental human concern: personal relationships, morality, and God. The belief policy that is most likely to secure what we want in these areas is to commit ourselves ahead of or in the absence of sufficient evidence.

Debunking arguments. Cognitive science is a relatively new discipline that unites psychology, neuroscience, computer science, and philosophy into the study of the operations of the mind/brain. It is concerned with how the mind processes information—how it is acquired, stored, retrieved, ordered, and used. The scientific study of the thinking mind has considered, among many other things, perception, attention, memory, pattern recognition, concept formation, consciousness, reasoning, problem-solving, language-processing, and forgetting. Cognitive science has also studied the ways in which we acquire and sustain religious beliefs; this subdiscipline in cognitive science is called the cognitive science of religion (CSR). Every culture seems to have deeply entrenched beliefs in spiritual beings and even an afterlife. And just as universal human traits such as language and emotion are explained by a mind-brain disposed to language and emotion, it is now widely accepted that universally occurring spiritual beliefs indicate that humans are naturally disposed to spiritual beliefs. Paul Bloom, and Aku Visala and David Leech explore the cognitive faculties implicated in belief in God such as the Agency Detecting Device (ADD) and the Theory of Mind (TOM). But, since ADD and TOM are aimed at understanding mates, enemies, and predators, their application outside of these mundane domains seems dubious. Does uncovering the cause of religious beliefs show that religious beliefs are fanciful expressions of hidden cognitive mechanisms? According to Bloom, religion is "an incidental by-product of cognitive functioning gone awry." Visala and Leech critically develop and assess the claim that CSR debunks (undermines) rational religious belief.

Reflections. How might all of this be relevant to the life of a person struggling to reconcile reason with belief in God? To answer this question, Raymond VanArragon considers the case of a hypothetical theist named Sadie who wants to ensure that her belief in God is rational. VanArragon leads her through an encounter with Clifford's demand for evidence, and argues that even though she may be unsuccessful in her attempt to meet that demand, she doesn't need to do so in order for her belief in God to be rational. Next she ponders some possible reasons for doubting that

God exists; but VanArragon suggests that Sadie could very well find those reasons less compelling than some thinkers take them to be. Finally, VanArragon supposes that Sadie finds herself unsure of what to believe after exposure to the blizzard of arguments for and against God's existence. Here he suggests Pascal and James as resources: while they do not present evidence that God exists, their reasons for believing may nonetheless be sufficient to ensure that Sadie's belief in God is rational. VanArragon concludes that reason and belief in God can be reconciled, though perhaps not as simply and decisively as some believers might wish them to be.

Chapter 9

The Need for Evidence

THE ETHICS OF BELIEF

W.K. CLIFFORD*

The shipowner. A Shipowner was about to send to sea an emigrant-ship. He knew that she was old, and not over-well built at the first; that she had seen many seas and climes, and often had needed repairs. Doubts had been suggested to him that possibly she was not seaworthy. These doubts preyed upon his mind and made him unhappy; he thought that perhaps he ought to have her thoroughly overhauled and refitted, even though this should put him to great expense. Before the ship sailed, however, he succeeded in overcoming these melancholy reflections. He said to himself that she had gone safely through many voyages and weathered so many storms that it was idle to suppose she would not come safely home from this trip also. He would put his trust in Providence, which could hardly fail to protect all these unhappy families that were leaving their fatherland to seek for better times elsewhere. He would dismiss from his mind all ungenerous suspicions about the honesty of builders and contractors. In such ways he acquired a sincere and comfortable conviction that his vessel was thoroughly safe and seaworthy; he watched her departure with a light heart, and benevolent wishes for the success of the exiles in their strange new home that was to be;

and he got his insurance money when she went down in mid-ocean and told no tales.

What shall we say of him? Surely this, that he was verily guilty of the death of those men. It is admitted that he did sincerely believe in the soundness of his ship; but the sincerity of his conviction can in no wise help him, because *he had no right to believe on such evidence as was before him.* He had acquired his belief not by honestly earning it in patient investigation, but by stifling his doubts. And although in the end he may have felt so sure about it that he could not think otherwise, yet inasmuch as he had knowingly and willingly worked himself into that frame of mind, he must be held responsible for it.

Let us alter the case a little, and suppose that the ship was not unsound after all; that she made her voyage safely, and many others after it. Will that diminish the guilt of her owner? Not one jot. When an action is once done, it is right or wrong for ever; no accidental failure of its good or evil fruits can possibly alter that. The man would not have been innocent, he would only have been not found out. The question of right or wrong has to do with the origin of his belief, not the matter of it; not what it was, but how he got it; not whether it turned out to be true or false, but whether he had a right to believe on such evidence as was before him. . . .

It may be said, however, that . . . it is not the belief which is judged to be wrong, but the action following upon it. The shipowner might say, "I am perfectly certain that my ship is sound, but still I feel it my duty to have her examined, before trusting the lives of so many people to her." . . .

---

*   W.K. Clifford (1845–79) was a British physicist and mathematician.

Belief and actions. . . . [I]t is not possible so to sever the belief from the action it suggests as to condemn the one without condemning the other. . . . Nor is that truly a belief at all which has not some influence upon the actions of him who holds it. He who truly believes that which prompts him to an action has looked upon the action to lust after it, he has committed it already in his heart. If a belief is not realized immediately in open deeds, it is stored up for the guidance of the future. It goes to make a part of that aggregate of beliefs which is the link between sensation and action at every moment of all our lives, and which is so organized and compacted together that no part of it can be isolated from the rest, but every new addition modifies the structure of the whole. No real belief, however trifling and fragmentary it may seem, is ever truly insignificant; it prepares us to receive more of its like, confirms those which resembled it before, and weakens others; and so gradually it lays a stealthy train in our inmost thoughts, which may some day explode into overt action, and leave its stamp upon our character for ever.

And no one man's belief is in any case a private matter which concerns himself alone. Our lives are guided by general conception of the course of things which has been created by society for social purposes. Our words, our phrases, our forms and processes and modes of thought, are common property, fashioned and perfected from age to age; an heirloom which every succeeding generation inherits as a precious deposit and a sacred trust to be handed on to the next one, not unchanged but enlarged and purified, with some clear marks of its proper handiwork. Into this, for good or ill, is woven every belief of every man who has speech of his fellows. An awful privilege, and an awful responsibility, that we should help to create the world in which posterity will live.

All beliefs and believers. In the . . . case which [has] been considered, it has been judged wrong to believe on insufficient evidence, or to nourish belief by suppressing doubts and avoiding investigation. The reason of this judgment is not far to seek: it is that . . . the belief held by one man was of great importance to other men. But forasmuch as no belief held by one man, however seemingly trivial the belief, and however obscure the believer, is ever actually insignificant or without its effect on the fate of mankind, we have no choice but to extend our judgment to all cases of belief whatever. Belief, that sacred faculty which prompts the decisions of our will, and knits into harmonious working all the compacted energies of our being, is ours not for ourselves, but for humanity. It is rightly used on truths which have been established by long experience and waiting toil, and which have stood in the fierce light of free and fearless questioning. Then it helps to bind men together, and to strengthen and direct their common action. It is desecrated when given to unproved and unquestioned statements, for the solace and private pleasure of the believer; to add a tinsel splendour to the plain straight road of our life and display a bright mirage beyond it; or even to drown the common sorrows of our kind by a self-deception which allows them not only to cast down, but also to degrade us. Whoso would deserve well of his fellows in this matter will guard the purity of his belief with a very fanaticism of jealous care, lest at any time it should rest on an unworthy object, and catch a stain which can never be wiped away.

It is not only the leader of men, statesman, philosopher, or poet, that owes this bounden duty to mankind. Every rustic who delivers in the village alehouse his slow, infrequent sentences, may help to kill or keep alive the fatal superstitions which clog his race. Every hard-worked wife of an artisan may transmit to her children beliefs which shall knit society together, or rend it in pieces. No simplicity of mind, no obscurity of station, can escape the universal duty of questioning all that we believe.

It is true that this duty is a hard one, and the doubt which comes out of it is often a very bitter thing. It leaves us bare and powerless where we thought that we were safe and strong. To know all about anything is to know how to deal with it under all circumstances. We feel much happier and more secure when we think we know precisely what to do, no matter what happens, than when we have lost our way and do not know where to turn. And if we have supposed ourselves to know all about anything, and to be capable of doing what is fit in regard to it, we naturally do not like to find that we are really ignorant and powerless, that we have to begin again at the beginning, and try to learn what the thing is and how it is to be dealt with—if indeed anything can be learnt about it. It is the sense of power attached to a sense of knowledge that makes men desirous of believing, and afraid of doubting.

Duty to mankind. This sense of power is the highest and best of pleasures when the belief on which it is founded is a true belief, and has been fairly earned by investigation. For then we may justly feel that it is common property, and holds good for others as well as for ourselves. Then we may be glad, not that I have learned secrets by which I am safer and stronger, but that *we men* have got mastery over more of the world; and we shall be strong, not for ourselves, but in the name of Man and in his strength. But if the belief has been accepted on insufficient evidence, the pleasure is a stolen one. Not only does it deceive ourselves by giving us a sense of power which we do not really possess, but it is sinful, because it is stolen in defiance of our duty to mankind. That duty is to guard ourselves from such beliefs as from a pestilence, which may shortly master our own body and then spread to the rest of the town. What would be thought of one who, for the sake of a sweet fruit, should deliberately run the risk of bringing a plague upon his family and his neighbours?

And, as in other such cases, it is not the risk only which has to be considered; for a bad action is always bad at the time when it is done, no matter what happens afterwards. Every time we let ourselves believe for unworthy reasons, we weaken our powers of self-control, of doubting, of judicially and fairly weighing evidence. We all suffer severely enough from the maintenance and support of false beliefs and the fatally wrong actions which they lead to, and the evil born when one such belief is entertained is great and wide. But a greater and wider evil arises when the credulous character is maintained and supported, when a habit of believing for unworthy reasons is fostered and made permanent. If I steal money from any person, there may be no harm done by the mere transfer of possession; he may not feel the loss, or it may prevent him from using the money badly. But I cannot help doing this great wrong towards Man, that I make myself dishonest. What hurts society is not that it should lose its property, but that it should become a den of thieves; for then it must cease to be society. This is why we ought not to do evil that good may come; for at any rate this great evil has come, that we have done evil and are made wicked thereby. In like manner, if I let myself believe anything on insufficient evidence, there may be no great harm done by the mere belief; it may be true after all, or I may never have occasion to exhibit it in outward acts. But I cannot help doing this great wrong towards Man, that I make myself credulous. The danger to society is not merely that it should believe wrong things, though that is great enough; but that it should become credulous, and lose the habit of testing things and inquiring into them; for then it must sink back into savagery.

The harm which is done by credulity in a man is not confined to the fostering of a credulous character in others, and consequent support of false beliefs. Habitual want of care about what I believe leads to habitual want of care in others about the truth of what is told to me. Men speak the truth to one another when each reveres the truth in his own mind and in the other's mind; but how shall my friend revere the truth in my mind when I myself am careless about it, when I believe things because I want to believe them, and because they are comforting and pleasant? Will he not learn to cry, "Peace," to me, when there is no peace? By such a course I shall surround myself with a thick atmosphere of falsehood and fraud, and in that I must live. It may matter little to me, in my cloud-castle of sweet illusions and darling lies; but it matters much to Man that I have made my neighbours ready to deceive. The credulous man is father to the liar and the cheat; he lives in the bosom of this his family, and it is no marvel if he should become even as they are. So closely are our duties knit together, that whoso shall keep the whole law, and yet offend in one point, he is guilty of all.

The ethics of belief. To sum up: it is wrong always, everywhere, and for any one, to believe anything upon insufficient evidence.

If a man, holding a belief which he was taught in childhood or persuaded of afterwards, keeps down and pushes away any doubts which arise about it in his mind, purposely avoids the reading of books and the company of men that call in question or discuss it, and regards as impious those questions which cannot

easily be asked without disturbing it—the life of that man is one long sin against mankind. . . .

Inquiry into the evidence of a doctrine is not to be made once for all, and then taken as finally settled. It is never lawful to stifle a doubt; for either it can be honestly answered by means of the inquiry already made, or else it proves that the inquiry was not complete.

"But," says one, "I am a busy man; I have no time for the long course of study which would be necessary to make me in any degree a competent judge of certain questions, or even able to understand the nature of the arguments." Then he should have no time to believe.

Discussion

1. Give three reasons for thinking that beliefs ought to be supported by evidence.

2. If you were to adhere to Clifford's ethics of belief, how would your beliefs be different?

3. Criticize Clifford's views on reason.

Chapter 10

Reformed Epistemology

WITHOUT EVIDENCE OR ARGUMENT

KELLY JAMES CLARK*

Introduction. Suppose a stranger, let's call him David, sends you a note that declares that your wife is cheating on you. No pictures are included, no dates or times, no names. Just the assertion of your wife's unfaithfulness. You have had already fifteen good, and so far as you know, faithful years with your wife. Her behavior hasn't changed dramatically in the past few years. Except for David's allegation, you have no reason to believe there has been a breach in the relationship. What should you do? Confront her with what you take to be the truth, straight from David's letter? Hire a detective to follow her for a week and hope against hope the letter is a hoax? Or do you simply remain secure in the trust that you have built up all those years?

Suppose, even worse, that your son Clifford comes home after taking his first philosophy course in college. He persuades you of the truth of the so-called "problem of other minds." How do you know that other minds and, therefore, other people exist? How do you know that people are not simply cleverly constructed robots with excellent makeup jobs? How do you know that behind the person facade lies a person—someone with thoughts, desires and feelings? You can't experience another person's feelings; you can't see another person's

thoughts (even if you were to cut off the top of their head and peer into their brain); and even Bill Clinton can't really feel another person's pain. Yet thoughts, desires, and feelings are all essential to being a person. So you can't tell from the outside or just by looking, so to speak, if someone is a person. I can know that *I* am a person because I experience my own thoughts, feelings and desires. But I can't know, because I don't have any access to your inner-experience, if you, or anyone else, is a person.

Since you can't know if anyone else is a person, you rightly infer that you can't know if your wife is a person. Unsure that your wife is a person, how do you treat her? Do you hire a philosophical detective to search the philosophical literature for a proof that people-like things really are people? Do you avoid cuddling in the meantime, given your aversion to snuggling with machines? Or do you simply trust your deep-seated conviction that, in spite of the lack of evidence, your wife is a person and deserves to be treated as such?

Two final "Supposes." Suppose that you come to believe that there is a God because your parents taught you from the cradle up that God exists. Or suppose that you are on a retreat or on the top of a mountain and have a sense of being loved by God or that God created the universe. You begin to believe in God, not because you are persuaded by the argument from design—you are simply taken with belief in God. You just find yourself believing, what you had heretofore denied, that God exists. Now you have come across the writings of David Hume and W.K. Clifford who insist that you base all of your beliefs on evidence.

*   Kelly James Clark is Senior Research Fellow at the Kaufman Interfaith Institute of Grand Valley State University.

Hume raises a further point: your belief in an all-loving, omnipotent God is inconsistent with the evil that there is in the world. Given the fact of evil, God cannot exist. To meet this demand for evidence, do you become a temporary agnostic and begin perusing the texts of Aquinas, Augustine and Paley for a good proof of God's existence? Do you give up belief in God because you see Hume's point and can't see how God and evil could be reconciled? Or do you remain steady in your trust in God in spite of the lack of evidence and even in the face of counter-evidence?

My Suppose-This and Suppose-That Stories are intended to raise the problem of the relationship of our important beliefs to evidence (and counter-evidence). Since the Enlightenment, there has been a demand to expose all of our beliefs to the searching criticism of reason. If a belief is unsupported by the evidence, it is irrational to believe it. It is the position of Reformed epistemology (likely the position that Calvin held) that belief in God, like belief in other persons, does not require the support of evidence or argument in order for it to be rational. This view has been defended by some of the world's most prominent philosophers including Alvin Plantinga, Nicholas Wolterstorff, and William Alston.[1]

The claim that belief in God is rational without the support of evidence or argument is startling for many an atheist or theist. Most atheist intellectuals feel comfort in their disbelief in God because they judge that there is little or no evidence for God's existence. Many theistic thinkers, however, insist that belief in God requires evidence and that such a demand should and can be met. So the claim that a person does not need evidence in order to rationally believe in God runs against the grain for atheist thinkers and has raised the ire of many theists. In spite of the vitriolic response to Reformed epistemology, I believe it is eminently defensible. In order to defend it, let us examine its critique of the Enlightenment demand for evidence.

The demand for evidence. W.K. Clifford, in an oft-cited article, claims that it is wrong, always and everywhere, for anyone to believe anything on insufficient evidence. Such a strong claim makes one speculate on Clifford's childhood: one imagines young W.K. constantly pestering his parents with "Why? Why? Why? . . ." It is this childish attitude toward inquiry and the risks that belief requires that leads William James to chastise Clifford as an *enfant terrible*. But, rather than disparage his character, let's examine the deficiencies of his claim that everything must be believed only on the basis of sufficient evidence (Relevance: If everything must be based on sufficient evidence, so must belief in God).

The first problem with Clifford's universal demand for evidence is that it cannot meet its own demand. Clifford offers two fetching examples (a shipowner who knowingly sends an unseaworthy ship to sea and, in the first example, it sinks and, in the second example, it makes the trip) in support of his claim. The examples powerfully demonstrate that in cases like the example, rational belief requires evidence. No one would disagree: some beliefs require evidence for their rational acceptability. But *all* beliefs in *every* circumstance? That's an exceedingly strong claim to make and, it turns out, one that cannot be based on evidence.

Consider what someone like Clifford might allow us to take for evidence: beliefs that we acquire through sensory experience and beliefs that are self-evident like logic and mathematics. Next rainy day, make a list of all of your experiential beliefs: The sky is blue, grass is green, most trees are taller than most grasshoppers, slugs leave a slimy trail. . . . Now add to this list all of your logical and mathematical beliefs: 2 + 2 = 4, every proposition is either true or false, all of the even numbers that I know of are the sum of two prime numbers, in Euclidean geometry the interior angles of triangles equal 180 degrees. From these propositions, try to deduce the conclusion that it is wrong, always and everywhere, for anyone to believe anything on insufficient evidence. None of the propositions that are allowed as evidence have anything at all to do with the conclusion. So Clifford's universal demand for evidence cannot satisfy its own standard! Therefore, by Clifford's own criterion, it must be irrational. More likely, however, the demand is simply false and it is easy to see why.

We, finite beings that we are, simply cannot meet such a demand. Consider all of the beliefs that you currently hold. How many of those have met Clifford's strict demand for evidence? Clifford intends for all of us, like a scientist in a laboratory, to test all of our beliefs all of the time. Could your beliefs survive Clifford's test? Think of how many of your beliefs, even scientific ones, are acquired *just because someone told you.* Not having been to Paraguay, I only have testimonial evidence that Paraguay is a country in South America. For all I know, all of the mapmakers have conspired to delude us about the existence of Paraguay (and even South America!). And, since I have been to relatively few countries around the world, I must believe in the existence of most countries (and that other people inhabit them and speak in that language) without support of evidence. I believe that $e=mc^2$ and that matter is made up of tiny little particles not because of experiments in a chemistry or physics lab (for all of my experiments failed) but because my science teachers told me so. Most of the beliefs that I have acquired are based on my trust in my teachers and not on careful consideration of what Clifford would consider adequate evidence. And in this busy day and age, I don't really have the time to live up to Clifford's demand for evidence! If we had the leisure to test all of our beliefs, perhaps we could meet the demand. But since we cannot meet that demand, we cannot be obligated to do so.

Even if we had the time, however, we could not meet this universal demand for evidence. The demand for evidence simply cannot be met in a large number of cases with the cognitive equipment that we have. No one, as mentioned above, has ever been able to prove the existence of other persons. No one has ever been able to prove that we were not created five minutes ago with our memories intact. No one has been able to prove the reality of the past or that, in the future, the sun will rise. This list could go on and on. There is a limit to the things that human beings can prove. A great deal of what we believe is based on faith, not on evidence or arguments.

I use the term "faith" here but that is misleading. I don't mean to oppose faith to knowledge in these instances. For surely we know that the earth is more than five minutes old and that the sun will rise tomorrow (although, maybe not in cloudy Grand Rapids!) and that Paul converted to Christianity (and lots of other truths about the past), etc., etc., etc. In these cases, we know lots of things but we cannot prove them. We have to trust or rely on the cognitive faculties which produce these beliefs. We rely on our memory to produce memory beliefs (I remember having coffee with my breakfast this morning). We rely on an inductive faculty to produce beliefs about the veracity of natural laws (If I let go of this book, it will fall to the ground). We rely on our cognitive faculties when we believe that there are other persons, there is a past, there is a world independent of our mind, or what other people tell us. We can't help but trust our cognitive faculties.

It is easy to see why. Reasoning must start somewhere. Suppose we were required to offer evidence or arguments for all of our beliefs. If we offer statements 1–4 as evidence for 5, we would have to offer arguments to support 1–4. And then we would have to offer arguments in support of the arguments that are used to support 1–4. And then we would need arguments.... You get the point. Reasoning must start somewhere. There have to be some truths that we can just accept and reason from. Why not start with belief in God?

Without evidence or argument. We have been outfitted with cognitive faculties that produce beliefs that we can reason from. The number of beliefs we do and must reason to is quite small compared to the number of beliefs that we do and must accept without the aid of a proof. That's the long and short of the human believing condition. We, in most cases, must rely on our God-given intellectual equipment to produce beliefs, without evidence or argument, in the appropriate circumstances. Is it reasonable to believe that God has created us with a cognitive faculty which produces belief in God without evidence or argument?

There are at least three reasons to believe that it is proper or rational for a person to accept belief in God without the need for an argument. First, there are very few people who have access to or the ability to assess most theistic arguments. It is hard to imagine, therefore, that the demand for evidence would be a requirement of reason. My grandmother, a paradigm of the non-philosophical believer, would cackle if I informed her that her belief in God was irrational because she was unable to understand Aquinas's second Way or to refute Hume's version of the argument from evil. The demand for evidence is an imperialistic attempt to make philosophers out of people who have no need to become philosophers. It is curious that very few philosophers (like most ordinary folk) have come to belief in God on the basis of theistic arguments. I commissioned and published a collection of spiritual autobiographies from prominent Christian philosophers just to see if philosophers were any different from my grandmother on this count. They weren't.[2]

Second, it seems that God has given us an awareness of himself that is not dependent on theistic arguments. It is hard to imagine that God would make rational belief as difficult as those that demand evidence contend. I encourage anyone who thinks that evidence is required for rational belief in God, to study very carefully the theistic arguments, their refutations and counter-refutations, and their increasing subtlety yet decreasing charm. Adequate assessment of these arguments would require a lengthy and torturous tour

through the history of philosophy and may require the honing of one's logical and metaphysical skills beyond the capacity of most of us. Why put that sort of barrier between us and God? John Calvin believed that God had provided us with a sense of the divine. He writes:

> There is within the human mind, and indeed by natural instinct, an awareness of divinity. This we take to be beyond controversy. To prevent anyone from taking refuge in the pretense of ignorance, God himself has implanted in all men a certain understanding of his divine majesty. Ever renewing its memory, he repeatedly sheds fresh drops. . . . Indeed, the perversity of the impious, who though they struggle furiously are unable to extricate themselves from the fear of God, is abundant testimony that this conviction, namely that there is some God, is naturally inborn in all, and is fixed deep within, as it were in the very marrow. From this we conclude that it is not a doctrine that must first be learned in school, but one of which each of us is master from his mother's womb and which nature itself permits no one to forget.[3]

Calvin contends that people are accountable to God for their unbelief not because they have failed to submit to a convincing theistic proof, but because they have suppressed the truth that God has implanted within their minds. It is natural to suppose that if God created us with cognitive faculties which by and large reliably produce beliefs without the need for evidence, he would likewise provide us with a cognitive faculty which produces belief in him without the need for evidence.

Third, belief in God is more like belief in a person than belief in a scientific theory. Consider the examples that started this essay. Somehow the scientific approach—doubt first, consider all of the available evidence, and believe later—seems woefully inadequate or inappropriate to personal relations. What seems manifestly reasonable for physicists in their laboratory is desperately deficient in human relations. Human relations demand trust, commitment and faith. If belief in God is more like belief in other persons than belief in atoms, then the trust that is appropriate to persons will be appropriate to God. We cannot and should not arbitrarily insist that the scientific method is appropriate to every kind of human practice. The fastidious scientist, who cannot leave the demand for evidence in her laboratory, will find herself cut off from relationships that she could otherwise reasonably maintain—with friends, family and, perhaps even God.

With or without evidence. I haven't said that belief in God could not or, in some cases, should not be based on evidence or argument. Indeed, I am inclined to think that the theistic arguments do provide some, non-coercive, evidence of God's existence. By non-coercive, I mean that the theistic arguments aren't of such power and illumination that they should be expected to persuade all rational creatures. Rational people could rationally reject the theistic proofs. Rational people, and this is a fact that we must live with, rationally disagree. Nonetheless, I believe that someone could rationally believe in God on the basis of theistic arguments, but no one needs to.[4]

Reformed epistemologists also believe, like Calvin, that the natural knowledge of himself that God has implanted within us has been overlaid by sin. Part of the knowledge process may require the removal of the effects of sin on our minds. Attention to theistic arguments might do that. Also, some of the barriers to religious belief—such as the problem of evil or the alleged threat of science to religion—may need to be removed before one can see the light that has been shining within all along.

But the scales can fall from the "mind's eye" in a wide variety of means: on a mountaintop or at the ocean, looking at a flower, through a humbling experience, or by reading *The Chronicles of Narnia*. The list

goes on yet a certain common feature should be noticed (and not the fact that few people have ever acquired belief in God as a result of the study of theistic proofs). The primary obstacle to belief in God seems to be more moral than intellectual. On the mountains one may feel one's smallness in relation to the grandness of it all. The flower may arouse one's sense of beauty. The loss of a job or a divorce may reveal one's unjustified pride. And *The Chronicles of Narnia* may awaken the dormant faith of a child. In all of these cases, the scales slide off the mind's eye when the overweening self is dethroned (not to mix too many metaphors!). Humility, not proofs, may be necessary to the realization of belief in God.

Conclusion. This approach to belief in God has been rather descriptive. We need to pay a lot more attention to how actual people actually acquire beliefs. The psychology of believing may tell us a lot about our cognitive equipment. The lessons learned from observing people and their beliefs support the position that I have defended: rational people may rationally believe in God without evidence or argument.

Notes

1. Alvin Plantinga, "Reason and Belief in God," Nicholas Wolterstorff, "Can Belief in God Be Rational If It Has No Foundations?" and William Alston, "Christian Experience and Christian Belief" in *Faith and Rationality*, Plantinga and Wolterstorff, eds. (Notre Dame: U of Notre Dame P, 1983); William Alston, *Perceiving God* (Ithaca, NY: Cornell UP, 1991); Alvin Plantinga, *Warranted Christian Belief* (New York and Oxford: Oxford UP, 1999).

2. See Kelly James Clark, *Philosophers Who Believe* (Downers Grove, IL: InterVarsity P, 1993).

3. *Institutes of the Christian Religion*, Bk. 1, Ch. 3.

4. I argue this in some detail in my *Return to Reason* (Grand Rapids, MI: Eerdmans, 1990).

Discussion

1. How much of what you believe was acquired because someone told you?

2. What beliefs (other than belief in God) might be held without evidence or argument?

3. Could Reformed epistemology be used to defend any wacky belief?

4. Defend or criticize Clark's descriptive (as opposed to evidentialism's more normative) approach to a theory of knowledge.

Chapter 11

Wittgensteinian Fideism

THE GROUNDLESSNESS OF BELIEF

NORMAN MALCOLM*

Groundless believing. In his final notebooks Wittgenstein wrote that it is difficult "to realize the groundlessness of our believing."[1] He was thinking of how much mere acceptance, on the basis of no evidence, forms our lives. This is obvious in the case of small children. They are told the names of things. They accept what they are told. They do not ask for grounds. A child does not demand a proof that the person who feeds him is called "Mama." Or are we to suppose that the child reasons to himself as follows: "The others present seem to know this person who is feeding me, and since they call her 'Mama' that probably is her name"? It is obvious on reflection that a child cannot consider evidence or even doubt anything until he has already learned much. As Wittgenstein puts it: "The child learns by believing the adult. Doubt comes *after* belief" (*OC*, 160).

What is more difficult to perceive is that the lives of educated, sophisticated adults are also formed by groundless beliefs. I do not mean eccentric beliefs that are out on the fringes of their lives, but fundamental beliefs. Take the belief that familiar material things (watches, shoes, chairs) do not cease to exist without some physical explanation. They don't "vanish in thin air." It is interesting that we do use that very

expression: "I *know* I put the keys right here on this table. They must have vanished in thin air!" But this exclamation is hyperbole; we are not speaking in literal seriousness. I do not know of any adult who would consider, in all gravity, that the keys might have inexplicably ceased to exist. . . .

The framework of thinking. Our attitude in this matter is striking. We would not be willing to consider it as even improbable that a missing lawn chair had "just ceased to exist." We would not entertain such a suggestion. If anyone proposed it we would be sure he was joking. It is no exaggeration to say that this attitude is part of the foundations of our thinking. I do not want to say that this attitude is *un*reasonable; but rather that it is something that we do not *try* to support with grounds. It could be said to belong to "the framework" of our thinking about material things.

Wittgenstein asks: "Does anyone ever test whether this table remains in existence when no one is paying attention to it?" (*OC*, 163). The answer is: Of course not. Is this because we would not call it "a table" if that were to happen? But we do call it "a table" and none of us makes the test. Doesn't this show that we do not regard that occurrence as a possibility? People who did so regard it would seem ludicrous to us. One could imagine that they made ingenious experiments to decide the question; but this research would make us smile. Is this because experiments were conducted by our ancestors that settled the matter once and for all? I don't believe it. The principle that material things do not cease to exist without physical cause is an

* Norman Malcolm (1911–90), a student and friend of Ludwig Wittgenstein, taught at Cornell University.

unreflective part of the framework within which physical investigations are made and physical explanations arrived at. . . .

A "system" provides the boundaries within which we ask questions, carry out investigations, and make judgments. Hypotheses are put forth and challenged, *within* a system. Verification, justification, the search for evidence, occur *within* a system. The framework propositions of the system are not put to the test, not backed up by evidence. This is what Wittgenstein means when he says, "Of course there is justification; but justification comes to an end" (*OC*, 192); and when he asks "Doesn't testing come to an end?" (*OC*, 164); and when he remarks that "whenever we test anything we are already presupposing something that is not tested" (*OC*, 163).

Beginning with trust. That this is so is not to be attributed to human weakness. It is a conceptual requirement that our inquiries and proofs stay within boundaries. . . . We are taught, or we absorb, the systems within which we raise doubts, make inquiries, draw conclusions. We grow into a framework. We don't question it. We accept it trustingly. But this acceptance is not a consequence of reflection. We do not decide to accept framework propositions. We do not decide that we live on the earth, any more that we decide to learn our native tongue. We do come to adhere to a framework proposition, in the sense that it forms the way we think. The framework propositions that we accept, grow into, are not idiosyncrasies but common ways of speaking and thinking that are pressed on us by our human community. For our acceptances to have been withheld would have meant that we had not learned how to count, to measure, to use names, to play games, or even *to talk*. Wittgenstein remarks that "a language-game is only possible if one trusts something." Not *can* but *does* trust something (*OC*, 509). I think he means by this trust or acceptance what he calls belief "in the sense of religious belief" (*OC*, 459). What does he

mean by belief "in the sense of religious belief"? He explicitly distinguishes it from *conjecture*. I think this means that there is nothing tentative about it, it is not adopted as a hypothesis that might later be withdrawn in the light of new evidence. This also makes explicit an important feature of Wittgenstein's understanding of belief, in the sense of "religious belief," namely, that it does not rise or fall on the basis of evidence or grounds: it is "groundless."

Evidentialism. In our Western academic philosophy, religious belief is commonly regarded as unreasonable and is viewed with condescension or even contempt. It is said that religion is a refuge for those who, because of weakness of intellect or character, are unable to confront the stern realities of the world. The objective, mature, *strong* attitude is to hold beliefs solely on the basis of *evidence*.

It appears to me that philosophical thinking is greatly influenced by this veneration of evidence. We have an aversion to statements, reports, declarations, beliefs, that are not based on grounds. . . .

"WHY? Why? why?" Suppose that a pupil has been given thorough training in some procedure, whether it is drawing patterns, building fences, or proving theorems. But then he has to carry on by himself in new situations. How does he know what to do? Wittgenstein presents the following dialogue: "'However you instruct him in the continuation of a pattern—how can he *know* how he is to continue by himself?'—Well, how do *I* know?—If that means 'Have I grounds?', the answer is: the grounds will soon give out. And then I shall act, without grounds" (*PI*, 211). Grounds come to an end. Answers to How-do-we-know? questions come to an end. Evidence comes to an end. We must speak, act, live, without evidence. This is so, not just on the fringes of life and language, but at the center of our most regularized activities. We do learn rules and learn to follow them.

But our training was in the past! We had to leave it behind and proceed on our own.

It is an immensely important fact of nature that as people carry on an activity in which they have received a common training, they do largely *agree* with one another, accepting the same examples and analogies, taking the same steps. We agree in what to say, in how to apply language. We agree in our responses to particular cases.

As Wittgenstein says: "That is not agreement in opinions but in form of life" (*PI*, 241). We cannot explain this agreement by saying that we are just doing what the rules tell us—for our agreement in applying rules, formulae, and signposts is what gives them their *meaning*.

One of the primary pathologies of philosophy is the feeling that we must *justify* our language-games. We want to establish them as well-grounded. But we should consider here Wittgenstein's remark that a language-game "is not based on grounds. It is there—like our life" (*OC*, 559).

Within a language-game there is justification and lack of justification, evidence and proof, mistakes and groundless opinions, good and bad reasoning and correct measurements and incorrect ones. One cannot properly apply these terms to a language-game itself. It may, however, be said to be "groundless," not in the sense of a groundless opinion, but in the sense that we accept it, we live it. We can say, "This is what we do. This is how we are."

In this sense religion is groundless and so is chemistry. Within each of these two systems of thought and action there is controversy and argument. Within each there are advances and recessions of insight into the secrets of nature or the spiritual condition of humankind and the demands of the Creator, Savior, Judge, Source. Within the framework of each system there is criticism, explanation, justification. But we should not expect that there might be some sort of rational justification of the framework itself. . . .

It is intellectually troubling for us to conceive that a whole system of thought might be groundless, might have no rational justification. We realize easily enough, however, that grounds soon give out—that we cannot go on giving reasons for our reasons. There arises from this realization the conception of a reason that is *self-justifying*—something whose credentials as a reason cannot be questioned. . . .

There is nothing wrong with this. How else could we have disciplines, systems, games? But our fear of groundlessness makes us conceive that we are under some logical compulsion to terminate at *those particular* stopping points. We imagine that we have confronted the self-evident reason, the self-justifying explanation, the picture or symbol whose meaning cannot be questioned. This obscures from us the *human* aspect of our concepts—the fact that what we call "a reason," "evidence," "explanation," "justification" is what appeals to and satisfies *us*.

God and the proofs. The desire to provide a rational foundation for a form of life is especially prominent in the philosophy of religion, where there is an intense preoccupation with purported proofs of the existence of God. In American universities there must be hundreds of courses in which these proofs are the main topic. We can be sure that nearly always the critical verdict is that the proofs are invalid and consequently that, up to the present time at least, religious belief has received no rational justification.

Well, of course not! The obsessive concern with the proofs reveals the assumption that in order for religious belief to be intellectually respectable it *ought* to have a rational justification. *That* is the misunderstanding. It is like the idea that we are not justified in relying on memory until memory has been proved reliable. . . .

The groundlessness of religious belief. Religion is a form of life; it is language embedded in action—what

Wittgenstein calls a "language-game." Science is another. Neither stands in need of justification, the one no more than the other. . . .

Note

1. Ludwig Wittgenstein, *On Certainty*, ed. G.E.M. Anscombe and G.H. von Wright; English translation by D. Paul and G.E.M. Anscombe (Oxford, 1969), paragraph 166. Henceforth I include references to his work in the text, employing the abbreviation "*OC*" followed by paragraph number. . . . References to his *Philosophical Investigations*, ed. G.E.M. Anscombe and R. Rhees; English translation by Anscombe (Oxford, 1967)

are indicated by "*PI*" followed by paragraph number. In *OC* and *PI*, I have mainly used the translations of Paul and Anscombe but with some departures.

Discussion

1. Are the foundations of our beliefs self-justifying or simply convenient stopping points? Defend your view.

2. If belief in God is groundless, could unbelief be groundless? If so, how?

3. Suppose our beliefs are ultimately groundless. What would follow about our grasp of reality?

Chapter 12

Pragmatic Justification of Religious Belief

THE WAGER

BLAISE PASCAL*

184. A letter to incite to the search after God.

And then to make people seek Him among the philosophers, sceptics, and dogmatists, who disquiet him who inquires of them.

187. . . . Men despise religion; they hate it and fear it is true. To remedy this, we must begin by showing that religion is not contrary to reason; that it is venerable, to inspire respect for it; then we must make it lovable, to make good men hope it is true; finally, we must prove it is true. . . .

194. . . . The immortality of the soul is a matter which is of so great consequence to us and which touches us so profoundly that we must have lost all feeling to be indifferent as to knowing what it is. All our actions and thoughts must take such different courses, according as there are or are not eternal joys to hope for, that it is impossible to take one step with sense and judgment unless we regulate our course by our view of this point which ought to be our ultimate end.

Thus our first interest and our first duty is to enlighten ourselves on this subject, whereon depends all our conduct. Therefore among those who do not believe, I make a vast difference between those who

strive with all their power to inform themselves and those who live without troubling or thinking about it.

I can have only compassion for those who sincerely bewail their doubt, who regard it as the greatest of misfortunes, and who, sparing no effort to escape it, make of this inquiry their principal and most serious occupation.

But as for those who pass their life without thinking of this ultimate end of life, and who, for this sole reason that they do not find within themselves the lights which convince them of it, neglect to seek them elsewhere, and to examine thoroughly whether this opinion is one of those which people receive with credulous simplicity, or one of those which, although obscure in themselves, have nevertheless a solid and immovable foundation, I look upon them in a manner quite different.

This carelessness in a matter which concerns themselves, their eternity, their all, moves me more to anger than pity; it astonishes and shocks me; it is to me monstrous. I do not say this out of the pious zeal of a spiritual devotion. I expect, on the contrary, that we ought to have this feeling from principles of human interest and self-love; for this we need only see what the least enlightened persons see. We do not require great education of the mind to understand that here is no real and lasting satisfaction; that our pleasures are only vanity; that our evils are infinite; and, lastly, that death, which threatens us every moment, must infallibly place us within a few years under the

---

* Blaise Pascal (1623–62) was a French mathematician and philosopher.

dreadful necessity of being for ever either annihilated or unhappy. . . .

Nothing is so important to man as his own state, nothing is so formidable to him as eternity; and thus it is not natural that there should be men indifferent to the loss of their existence, and to the perils of everlasting suffering. They are quite different with regard to all other things. They are afraid of mere trifles; they foresee them; they feel them. And this same man who spends so many days and nights in rage and despair for the loss of office, or for some imaginary insult to his honour, is the very one who knows without anxiety and without emotion that he will lose all by death. It is a monstrous thing to see in the same heart and at the same time this sensibility to trifles and this strange insensibility to the greatest objects. It is an incomprehensible enchantment, and a supernatural slumber. . . .

198. The sensibility of man to trifles, and his insensibility to great things, indicates a strange inversion.

205. When I consider the short duration of my life, swallowed up in the eternity before and after, the little space which I fill and even can see, engulfed in the infinite immensity of spaces of which I am ignorant and which know me not, I am frightened and am astonished at being here rather than there; for there is no reason why here rather than there, why now rather than then. Who has put me here? By whose order and direction have this place and time been allotted to me? . . .

Objection of atheists: "But we have no light."

This is what I see and what troubles me. I look on all sides, and I see only darkness everywhere. Nature presents to me nothing which is not matter of doubt and concern. If I saw nothing there which revealed a Divinity, I would come to a negative conclusion; if I saw everywhere the signs of a Creator, I would remain peacefully in faith. But, seeing too much to deny and too little to be sure, I am in a state to be pitied. . . .

233. . . . "God is, or He is not." But to which side shall we incline? Reason can decide nothing here. . . . A game is being played at the extremity of this infinite distance where heads or tails will turn up. What will you wager? According to reason, you can do neither the one thing nor the other; according to reason, you can defend neither of the propositions. . . .

Yes; but you must wager. It is not optional. You are embarked. Which will you choose then? Let us see. Since you must choose, let us see which interests you least. You have two things to lose, the true and the good; and two things to stake, your reason and your will, your knowledge and your happiness; and your nature has two things to shun, error and misery. Your reason is no more shocked in choosing one rather than the other, since you must of necessity choose. This is one point settled. But your happiness? Let us weigh the gain and the loss in wagering that God is. Let us estimate these two chances. If you gain, you gain all; if you lose, you lose nothing. Wager, then, without hesitation that He is. "That is very fine. Yes, I must wager; but I may perhaps wager too much." Let us see. Since there is an equal risk of gain and of loss, if you had only to gain two lives, instead of one, you might still wager. But if there were three lives to gain, you would have to play (since you are under the necessity of playing), and you would be imprudent, when you are forced to play, not to chance your life to gain three at a game where there is an equal risk of loss and gain. But there is an eternity of life and happiness. And this being so, . . . you would still be right in wagering one to win two, and you would act stupidly, being obliged to play, by refusing to stake one life against three at a game. . . . But there is here an infinity of an infinitely happy life to gain, a chance of gain against a finite number of chances of loss, and what you stake is finite. It is all divided; wherever the infinite is and there is not an infinity of chances of loss against that of gain, there is no time to hesitate, you must give all. . . . For it is no use to say it is uncertain if we will gain, and it is certain that we risk, and that the infinite distance between the certainly of what is staked and the uncertainty of what will be gained, equals the finite good which is certainly staked against the uncertain infinite. It is not so, as every player stakes a certainty to gain an uncertainty....

"I confess it, I admit it. But, still, is there no means of seeing the faces of the cards?" Yes, Scripture and the rest, etc. "Yes, but I have my hands tied and my mouth closed; I am forced to wager, and am not free. I am not released, and am so made that I cannot believe. What, then, would you have me do?"

True. But at least learn your inability to believe, since reason brings you to this, and yet you cannot believe. Endeavour, then, to convince yourself, not by increase of proofs of God, but by the abatement of your passions. You would like to attain faith and do not know the way; you would like to cure yourself of unbelief and ask the remedy for it. Learn of those who have been bound like you, and who now stake all their possessions. These are people who know the way which you would follow, and who are cured of an ill of which you would be cured. Follow the way by which they began; by acting as if they believed, taking the holy water, having masses said, etc. Even this will naturally make you believe, and deaden your acuteness. "But this is what I am afraid of." And why? What have you to lose? But to show you that this leads you there, it is this which will lessen the passions, which are your stumbling-blocks.

The end of this discourse.—Now, what harm will befall you in taking this side? You will be faithful, humble, grateful, generous, a sincere friend, truthful. Certainly you will not have those poisonous pleasures, glory and luxury; but will you not have others? I will tell you that you will thereby gain in this life, and that, at each step you take on this road, you will see so great certainty of gain, so much nothingness in what you risk, that you will at last recognise that you have wagered for something certain and infinite, for which you have given nothing....

253. Two extremes: to exclude reason, to admit reason only....

564. The prophecies, the very miracles and proofs of our religion, are not of such a nature that they can be said to be absolutely convincing. But they are also of such a kind that it cannot be said that it is unreasonable to believe them. Thus there is both evidence and obscurity to enlighten some and confuse others. But the evidence is such that it surpasses, or at least equals, the evidence to the contrary; so that it is not reason which can determine men not to follow it, and thus it can only be lust or malice of heart. And by this means there is sufficient evidence to condemn, and insufficient to convince; so that it appears in those who follow it that it is grace, and not reason, which makes them follow it; and in those who shun it, that it is lust, not reason, which makes them shun it.

Discussion

1. How much of your life is focussed on trivialities? On considering your eternal destinies? What would it take to make you care about eternity?

2. What would motivate one to believe on the basis of the wager? Are such motivations adequate grounds for genuine faith?

3. Pascal seems to think that our passions, emotions, and pride can hinder the perception of the truth. Can you think of other beliefs that are affected by our passions, emotions, and pride?

THE WILL TO BELIEVE

WILLIAM JAMES*

Introduction. I have long defended to my own students the lawfulness of voluntarily adopted faith; but as soon as they have got well imbued with the logical spirit, they have as a rule refused to admit my contention to be lawful philosophically, even though in point of fact they were personally all the time chock-full of some faith or other themselves. I am all the while, however, so profoundly convinced that my own position is correct, that your invitation has seemed to me a good occasion to make my statements more clear. . . .

Hypotheses and options. Let us give the name of *hypothesis* to anything that may be proposed to our belief; and just as the electricians speak of live and dead wires, let us speak of any hypothesis as either *live* or *dead*. A live hypothesis is one which appeals as a real possibility to him to whom it is proposed. If I asked you to believe in the Mahdi, the notion makes no electric connection with your nature,—it refuses to scintillate with any credibility at all. As an hypothesis it is completely dead. To an Arab, however (even if he be not one of the Mahdi's followers), the hypothesis is among the mind's possibilities: it is alive. This shows that deadness and liveness in an hypothesis are not intrinsic properties, but relations to the individual thinker. They are measured by his willingness to act. The maximum of liveness in an hypothesis, means willingness to act irrevocably. Practically, that means belief; but there is some believing tendency wherever there is willingness to act at all.

---

* William James (1842–1910) was a Harvard psychologist and philosopher.

Next, let us call the decision between two hypotheses an *option*. Options may be of several kinds. They may be—1. *living* or *dead*; 2. *forced* or *avoidable*; 3. *momentous* or *trivial*; and for our purposes we may call an option a *genuine* option when it is of the forced, living, and momentous kind.

1. A living option is one in which both hypotheses are live ones. If I say to you: "Be a theosophist or be a Mohammedan," it is probably a dead option, because for you neither hypothesis is likely to be alive. But if I say: "Be an agnostic or be a Christian," it is otherwise: trained as you are, each hypothesis makes some appeal, however small, to your belief.

2. Next, if I say to you: "Choose between going out with your umbrella or without it," I do not offer you a genuine option, for it is not forced. You can easily avoid it by not going out at all. Similarly, if I say, "Either love me or hate me," "Either call my theory true or call it false," your option is avoidable. You may remain indifferent to me, neither loving nor hating, and you may decline to offer any judgment as to my theory. But if I say, "Either accept this truth or go without it," I put on you a forced option, for there is no standing place outside of the alternative. Every dilemma based on a complete logical disjunction, with no possibility of not choosing, is an option of this forced kind.

3. Finally, if I were Dr. Nansen and proposed to you to join my North Pole expedition, your option would be momentous; for this would probably be your only similar opportunity, and your choice now would either exclude you from the North Pole sort of immortality altogether or put at least the chance of it into your hands. He who refuses to embrace a unique opportunity loses the prize as surely as if he tried and failed. *Per contra*, the option is trivial when the opportunity is not unique, when the stake is insignificant, or when the decision is reversible if it later proves unwise. Such trivial options abound in the scientific life. A chemist finds an hypothesis live enough

to spend a year in its verification: he believes in it to that extent. But if his experiments prove inconclusive either way, he is quit for his loss of time, no vital harm being done.

It will facilitate our discussion if we keep all these distinctions well in mind. . . .

Clifford's Maxim. . . . [T]hat delicious *enfant terrible* Clifford writes: "Belief is desecrated when given to unproved and unquestioned statements for the solace and private pleasure of the believer. . . . Whoso would deserve well of his fellows in this matter will guard the purity of his belief with a very fanaticism of jealous care, lest at any time it should rest on an unworthy object, and catch a stain which can never be wiped away. . . . If [a] belief has been accepted on insufficient evidence," [even though the belief be true, as Clifford on the same page explains] "the pleasure is a stolen one. . . . It is sinful because it is stolen in defiance of our duty to mankind. That duty is to guard ourselves from such beliefs as from a pestilence which may shortly master our own body and then spread to the rest of the town. . . . It is wrong always, everywhere, and for every one, to believe anything upon insufficient evidence."

James's thesis. . . . The thesis I defend is, briefly stated, this: *Our passional nature not only lawfully may, but must, decide an option between propositions, whenever it is a genuine option that cannot by its nature be decided on intellectual grounds; for to say, under such circumstances, "Do not decide, but leave the question open," is itself a passional decision,—just like deciding yes or no,—and is attended with the same risk of losing the truth.* . . .

Two different sorts of risk. . . . There are two ways of looking at our duty in the matter of opinion,—ways entirely different, and yet ways about whose difference the theory of knowledge seems hitherto to have

shown very little concern. *We must know the truth;* and *we must avoid error,*—these are our first and great commandments as would-be knowers; but they are not two ways of stating an identical commandment, they are two separable laws. . . .

Believe truth! Shun error—these, we see, are two materially different laws; and by choosing between them we may end by coloring differently our whole intellectual life. We may regard the chase for truth as paramount, and the avoidance of error as secondary; or we may, on the other hand, treat the avoidance of error as more imperative, and let truth take its chance. Clifford, in the instructive passage which I have quoted, exhorts us to the latter course. Believe nothing, he tells us, keep your mind in suspense forever, rather than by closing it on insufficient evidence incur the awful risk of believing lies. You, on the other hand, may think that the risk of being in error is a very small matter when compared with the blessings of real knowledge, and be ready to be duped many times in your investigation rather than postpone indefinitely the chance of guessing true. I myself find it impossible to go with Clifford. . . .

For my own part, I have also a horror of being duped; but I can believe that worse things than being duped may happen to a man in this world: so Clifford's exhortation has to my ears a thoroughly fantastic sound. It is like a general informing his soldiers that it is better to keep out of battle forever than to risk a single wound. Not so are victories either over enemies or over nature gained. Our errors are surely not such awfully solemn things. In a world where we are so certain to incur them in spite of all our caution, a certain lightness of heart seems healthier than this excessive nervousness on their behalf. . . .

The risks of belief. . . . Wherever the option between losing truth and gaining it is not momentous, we can throw the chance of *gaining truth* away, and at any rate save ourselves from any chance of *believing false-hood*, by not making up our minds at all till objective evidence has come. In scientific questions, this is almost always the case; and even in human affairs in general, the need of acting is seldom so urgent that a false belief to act on is better than no belief at all. Law courts, indeed, have to decide on the best evidence attainable for the moment. . . . But in our dealings with objective nature we obviously are recorders, not makers, of the truth; and decisions for the mere sake of deciding promptly and getting on to the next business would be wholly out of place. Throughout the breadth of physical nature facts are what they are quite independently of us, and seldom is there any such hurry about them that the risks of being duped by believing a premature theory need be faced. The questions here are always trivial options, the hypotheses are hardly living (at any rate not living for us spectators), the choice between believing truth or falsehood is seldom forced. The attitude of skeptical balance is therefore the absolutely wise one if we would escape mistakes. What difference, indeed, does it make to most of us whether we have or have not a theory of the Rontgen rays, whether we believe or not in mind-stuff, or have a conviction about the causality of conscious states? It makes no difference. Such options are not forced on us. On every account it is better not to make them, but still keep weighing reasons *pro et contra* with an indifferent hand.

I speak, of course, here of the purely judging mind. For purposes of discovery such indifference is to be less highly recommended, and science would be far less advanced than she is if the passionate desires of individuals to get their own faiths confirmed had been kept out of the game. . . . The most useful investigator, because the most sensitive observer, is always he whose eager interest in one side of the question is balanced by an equally keen nervousness lest he become deceived.[1]

Science has organized this nervousness into a regular *technique*, her so-called method of verification; and she has fallen so deeply in love with the method that one may even say she has ceased to care for truth by itself at all. It is only truth as technically verified that interests her. The truth of truths might come in merely affirmative form, and she would decline to touch it. Such truth as that, she might repeat with Clifford, would be stolen in defiance of her duty to mankind. Human passions, however, are stronger than technical rules. "Le coeur a ses raisons," as Pascal says, "que la raison ne connait pas"; and however indifferent to all but the bare rules of the game the umpire, the abstract intellect, may be, the concrete players who furnish him the materials to judge of are usually, each one of them, in love with some pet "live hypothesis" of his own. Let us agree, however, that wherever there is no forced option, the dispassionately judicial intellect with no pet hypothesis, saving us, as it does, from dupery at any rate, ought to be our ideal.

The question next arises: Are there not somewhere forced options in our speculative questions, and can we (as men who may be interested at least as much in positively gaining truth as in merely escaping dupery) always wait with impunity till the coercive evidence shall have arrived? It seems *a priori* improbable that the truth should be so nicely adjusted to our needs and powers as that. In the great boarding-house of nature, the cakes and the butter and the syrup seldom come out so even and leave the plates so clean. . . .

Faith may bring forth its own verification. *Moral questions* immediately present themselves as questions whose solution cannot wait for sensible proof. A moral question is a question not of what sensibly exists, but of what is good, or would be good if it did exist. Science can tell us what exists; but to compare the *worths*, both of what exists and of what does not exist, we must consult not science, but what Pascal calls our heart. Science herself consults her heart when she lays it down that the infinite ascertainment of fact and correction of false belief are the supreme goods for man. . . .

Turn now from these wide questions of good to a certain class of questions of fact, questions concerning personal relations, states of mind between one man and another. *Do you like me or not?*—for example. Whether you do or not depends, in countless instances, on whether I meet you half-way, am willing to assume that you must like me, and show you trust and expectation. The previous faith on my part in your liking's existence is in such cases what makes your liking come. But if I stand aloof, and refuse to budge an inch until I have objective evidence, until you shall have done something apt, . . . ten to one your liking never comes. . . . The desire for a certain kind of truth here brings about that special truth's existence; and so it is in innumerable cases of other sorts. Who gains promotions, boons, appointments, but the man in whose life they are seen to play the part of live hypotheses, who discounts them, sacrifices other things for their sake before they have come, and takes risks for them in advance? His faith acts on the powers above him as a claim, and creates its own verification.

A social organism of any sort whatever, large or small, is what it is because each member proceeds to his own duty with a trust that the other members will simultaneously do theirs. Wherever a desired result is achieved by the co-operation of many independent persons, its existence as a fact is a pure consequence of the precursive faith in one another of those immediately concerned. A government, an army, a commercial system, a ship, a college, an athletic team, all exist on this condition, without which not only is nothing achieved, but nothing is even attempted. . . . There are, then, cases where a fact cannot come at all unless a preliminary faith exists in its coming. *And where faith in a fact can help create the fact*, that would be an insane logic which should say that faith running ahead of

scientific evidence is the "lowest kind of immorality" into which a thinking being can fall. Yet such is the logic by which our scientific absolutists pretend to regulate our lives!

Logical conditions of religious belief. In truths dependent on our personal action, then, faith based on desire is certainly a lawful and possibly an indispensable thing.

But now, it will be said, these are all childish human cases, and have nothing to do with great cosmical matters, like the question of religious faith. Let us then pass on to that. Religions differ so much in their accidents that in discussing the religious question we must make it very generic and broad. What then do we now mean by the religious hypothesis? Science says things are; morality says some things are better than other things; and religion says essentially two things.

First, she says that the best things are the more eternal things. . . . The second affirmation of religion is that we are better off even now if we believe her first affirmation to be true.

Now, let us consider what the logical elements of this situation are *in case the religious hypothesis in both its branches be really true*. . . . So proceeding, we see, first, that religion offers itself as a *momentous* option. We are supposed to gain, even now, by our belief, and to lose by our nonbelief, a certain vital good. Secondly, religion is a *forced* option, so far as that good goes. We cannot escape the issue by remaining skeptical and waiting for more light, because, although we do avoid error in that way *if religion be untrue*, we lose the good, *if it be true*, just as certainly as if we positively chose to disbelieve. It is as if a man should hesitate indefinitely to ask a certain woman to marry him because he was not perfectly sure that she would prove an angel after he brought her home. Would he not cut himself off from that particular angel-possibility as decisively as if he went and married someone else? Skepticism, then, is not avoidance of option; it is option of a certain particular kind of risk. *Better risk loss of truth than chance of error,*—that is your faith-vetoer's exact position. He is actively playing his stake as much as the believer is; he is backing the field against the religious hypothesis, just as the believer is backing the religious hypothesis against the field.

To preach skepticism to us as a duty until "sufficient evidence" for religion be found, is tantamount therefore to telling us, when in presence of the religious hypothesis, that to yield to our fear of its being error is wiser and better than to yield to our hope that it may be true. It is not intellect against all passions, then; it is only intellect with one passion laying down its law. And by what, forsooth, is the supreme wisdom of this passion warranted? Dupery for dupery, what proof is there that dupery through hope is so much worse than dupery through fear? I, for one, can see no proof; and I simply refuse obedience to the scientist's command to imitate his kind of option, in a case where my own stake is important enough to give me the right to choose my own form of risk. If religion be true and the evidence for it be still insufficient, I do not wish, by putting your extinguisher upon my nature (which feels to me as if it had after all some business in this matter), to forfeit my sole chance in life of getting upon the winning side,—that chance depending, of course, on my willingness to run the risk of acting as if my passional need of taking the world religiously might be prophetic and right.

. . . Now to most of us religion comes in a still further way that makes a veto on our active faith even more illogical. The more perfect and more eternal aspect of the universe is represented in our religions as having personal form. The universe is no longer a mere *It* to us, but a *Thou,* if we are religious; and any relation that may be possible from person to person might be possible here. . . . To take a trivial illustration: just as a man who in a company of gentlemen made no advances, asked a warrant for every concession, and believed no one's word without proof, would cut himself off by such churlishness from all the social rewards that a more trusting spirit would earn,—so here, one who should shut himself up in snarling logicality and try to make the gods extort his recognition willy-nilly, or not get it at all, might cut himself off forever from his only opportunity of making the gods' acquaintance. . . . I, therefore, for one, cannot see my way to accepting the agnostic rules for truth-seeking, or willfully agree to keep my willing nature out of the game. I cannot do so for this plain reason, that *a rule of thinking which would absolutely prevent me from acknowledging certain kinds of truth if those kinds of truth were really there, would be an irrational rule.* That for me is the long and short of the formal logic of the situation, no matter what the kinds of truth might materially be.

Conclusion. I confess I do not see how this logic can be escaped. But sad experience makes me fear that some of you may still shrink from radically saying with me, *in abstracto,* that we have the right to believe at our own risk any hypothesis that is live enough to tempt our will. . . . When I look at the religious question as it really puts itself to concrete men, and when I think of all the possibilities which both practically and theoretically it involves, then this command that we shall put a stopper on our heart, instincts, and courage, and *wait*—acting of course meanwhile more or less as if religion were *not* true—till doomsday, or till such time as our intellect and senses working together may have raked in evidence enough,—this command, I say, seems to me the queerest idol ever manufactured in the philosophic cave.

Note

1. Compare Wilfrid Ward's Essay, "The Wish to Believe," in his *Witness to the Unseen* (Macmillan & Co.), 1893.

Discussion

1. Clifford says that it is wrong to believe without sufficient evidence. James says that we are within our rights to believe (certain propositions) without sufficient evidence. Defend one or the other view.

2. What prevents someone who follows James's beliefs policies from believing anything they want?

3. How have your judgments about how to approach beliefs changed now that you are fully apprised of the risks?

Chapter 13

Debunking Belief in God?

IS GOD AN ACCIDENT?

PAUL BLOOM*

God is not dead. When I was a teenager my rabbi believed that the Lubavitcher Rebbe, who was living in Crown Heights, Brooklyn, was the Messiah, and that the world was soon to end. He believed that the earth was a few thousand years old, and that the fossil record was a consequence of the Great Flood. He could describe the afterlife and was able to answer adolescent questions about the fate of Hitler's soul.

My rabbi was no crackpot; he was an intelligent and amiable man, a teacher and a scholar. But he held views that struck me as strange, even disturbing. Like many secular people, I am comfortable with religion as a source of spirituality and transcendence, tolerance and love, charity and good works. Who can object to the faith of Martin Luther King, Jr., or the Dalai Lama—at least as long as that faith grounds moral positions one already accepts? I am uncomfortable, however, with religion when it makes claims about the natural world, let alone a world beyond nature. It is easy for those of us who reject supernatural beliefs to agree with Stephen Jay Gould that the best way to accord dignity and respect to both science and religion is to recognize that they apply to "non-overlapping magisterial": science gets the realm of facts, religion the realm of values.

---

* Paul Bloom is Professor of Psychology & Cognitive Science at Yale University.

For better or worse, though, religion is much more than a set of ethical principles or a vague sense of transcendence. The anthropologist Edward Burnett Tylor got it right in 1871, when he noted that the "minimum definition of religion" is a belief in spiritual beings, in the supernatural. My rabbi's specific claims were a minority view in the culture in which I was raised, but those *sorts* of views—about the creation of the universe, the end of the world, the fates of souls—define religion as billions of people understand and practice it.

The United States is a poster child for supernatural belief. Just about everyone in this country—96 per cent in one poll—believes in God. Well over half of Americans believe in miracles, the devil, and angels. Most believe in an afterlife—and not just in the mushy sense that we will live on in the memories of other people, or in our good deeds; when asked for details, most Americans say they believe that after death they will actually reunite with relatives and get to meet God. Woody Allen once said, "I don't want to achieve immortality through my work. I want to achieve it through not dying." Most Americans have precisely this expectation.

But America is an anomaly, isn't it? These statistics are sometimes taken as yet another indication of how much this country differs from, for instance, France and Germany, where secularism holds greater sway. Americans are fundamentalists, the claim goes, isolated from the intellectual progress made by the rest of the world.

There are two things wrong with this conclusion. First, even if a gap between America and Europe exists, it is not the United States that is idiosyncratic. After all, the rest of the world—Asia, Africa, the Middle East—is not exactly filled with hard-core atheists. If one is to talk about exceptionalism, it applies to Europe, not the United States.

Second, the religious divide between Americans and Europeans may be smaller than we think. The sociologists Rodney Stark, of Baylor University, and Roger Finke, of the Pennsylvania State University, write that the big difference has to do with church attendance, which really is much lower in Europe. (Building on the work of the Chicago-based sociologist and priest Andrew Greeley, they argue that this is because the United States has a rigorously free religious market, in which churches actively vie for parishioners and constantly improve their product, whereas European churches are often under state control and, like many government monopolies, have become inefficient.) Most polls from European countries show that a majority of their people are believers. Consider Iceland. To judge by rates of churchgoing, Iceland is the most secular country on earth, with a pathetic two per cent weekly attendance. But four out of five Icelanders say that they pray, and the same proportion believe in life after death.

In the United States some liberal scholars posit a different sort of exceptionalism, arguing that belief in the supernatural is found mostly in Christian conservatives—those infamously described by the *Washington Post* reporter Michael Weisskopf in 1993 as "largely poor, uneducated, and easy to command." Many people saw the 2004 presidential election as pitting Americans who are religious against those who are not.

An article by Steven Waldman in the online magazine *Slate* provides some perspective on the divide: "As you may already know, one of America's two political parties is extremely religious. Sixty-one per cent of this party's voters say they pray daily or more often. An astounding 92 per cent of them believe in life after death. And there's a hard-core subgroup in this party

of super-religious Christian zealots. Very conservative on gay marriage, half of the members of this subgroup believe Bush uses too *little* religious rhetoric, and 51 per cent of them believe God gave Israel to the Jews and that its existence fulfills the prophecy about the second coming of Jesus."

The group that Waldman is talking about is Democrats; the hard-core subgroup is African-American Democrats.

Finally, consider scientists. They are less likely than non-scientists to be religious—but not by a huge amount. A 1996 poll asked scientists whether they believed in God, and the pollsters set the bar high—no mealy-mouthed evasions such as "I believe in the totality of all that exists" or "in what is beautiful and unknown"; rather, they insisted on a real biblical God, one that believers could pray to and actually get an answer from. About 40 per cent of scientists said yes to a belief in this kind of God—about the same percentage found in a similar poll in 1916. Only when we look at the most elite scientists—members of the National Academy of Sciences—do we find a strong majority of atheists and agnostics.

These facts are an embarrassment for those who see supernatural beliefs as a cultural anachronism, soon to be eroded by scientific discoveries and the spread of cosmopolitan values. They require a new theory of why we are religious—one that draws on research in evolutionary biology, cognitive neuroscience, and developmental psychology.

Opiates and fraternities. One traditional approach to the origin of religious belief begins with the observation that it is difficult to be a person. There is evil all around; everyone we love will die; and soon we ourselves will die—either slowly and probably unpleasantly or quickly and probably unpleasantly. For all but a pampered and lucky few, life really is nasty, brutish, and short. And if our lives have some greater meaning, it is hardly obvious.

So perhaps, as Marx suggested, we have adopted religion as an opiate, to soothe the pain of existence. As the philosopher Susanne K. Langer has put it, man "cannot deal with Chaos"; supernatural beliefs solve the problem of this chaos by providing meaning. We are not mere things; we are lovingly crafted by God, and serve his purposes. Religion tells us that this is a just world, in which the good will be rewarded and the evil punished. Most of all, it addresses our fear of death. Freud summed it all up by describing a "threefold task" for religious beliefs: "they must exorcise the terrors of nature, they must reconcile men to the cruelty of Fate, particularly as it is shown in death, and they must compensate them for the sufferings and privations which a civilized life in common has imposed on them."

Religions can sometimes do all these things, and it would be unrealistic to deny that this partly explains their existence. Indeed, sometimes theologians use the foregoing arguments to make a case for why we should believe: if one wishes for purpose, meaning, and eternal life, there is nowhere to go but toward God.

One problem with this view is that, as the cognitive scientist Steven Pinker reminds us, we don't typically get solace from propositions that we don't already believe to be true. Hungry people don't cheer themselves up by believing that they just had a large meal. Heaven is a reassuring notion only insofar as people believe such a place exists; it is this belief that an adequate theory of religion has to explain in the first place.

Also, the religion-as-opiate theory fits best with the monotheistic religions most familiar to us. But what about those people (many of the religious people in the world) who do not believe in an all-wise and just God? Every society believes in spiritual beings, but they are often stupid or malevolent. Many religions simply don't deal with metaphysical or teleological questions; gods and ancestor spirits are called upon only to help cope with such mundane problems as how to prepare food and what to do with a corpse—not to elucidate

the Meaning of It All. As for the reassurance of heaven, justice, or salvation, again, it exists in some religions but by no means all. (In fact, even those religions we are most familiar with are not always reassuring. I know some older Christians who were made miserable as children by worries about eternal damnation; the prospect of oblivion would have been far preferable.) So the opiate theory is ultimately an unsatisfying explanation for the existence of religion.

The major alternative theory is social: religion brings people together, giving them an edge over those who lack this social glue. Sometimes this argument is presented in cultural terms, and sometimes it is seen from an evolutionary perspective: survival of the fittest working at the level not of the gene or the individual but of the social group. In either case the claim is that religion thrives because groups that have it outgrow and outlast those that do not.

In this conception religion is a fraternity, and the analogy runs deep. Just as fraternities used to paddle freshmen on the rear end to instill loyalty and commitment, religions have painful initiation rites—for example, snipping off part of the penis. Also, certain puzzling features of many religions, such as dietary restrictions and distinctive dress, make perfect sense once they are viewed as tools to ensure group solidarity.

The fraternity theory also explains why religions are so harsh toward those who do not share the faith, reserving particular ire for apostates. This is clear in the Old Testament, in which "a jealous God" issues commands such as these:

"Should your brother, your mother's son, or your son or your daughter or the wife of your bosom or your companion who is like your own self incite you in secret, saying 'Let us go and worship other gods' . . . you shall surely kill him. Your hand shall be against him first to put him to death and the hand of all the people last. And you shall stone him and he shall die, for he sought to thrust you away from the LORD your God who brought you out of the land of Egypt, from the house of slaves." (Deuteronomy 13, 7:11)

This theory explains almost everything about religion—except the religious part. It is clear that rituals and sacrifices can bring people together, and it may well be that a group that does such things has an advantage over one that does not. But it is not clear why a *religion* has to be involved. Why are gods, souls, an afterlife, miracles, divine creation of the universe, and so on brought in? The theory doesn't explain what we are most interested in, which is belief in the supernatural.

Bodies and souls. Enthusiasm is building among scientists for a quite different view—that religion emerged not to serve a purpose but by accident.

This is not a value judgment. Many of the good things in life are, from an evolutionary perspective, accidents. People sometimes give money, time, and even blood to help unknown strangers in faraway countries whom they will never see. From the perspective of one's genes this is disastrous—the suicidal squandering of resources for no benefit. But its origin is not magical; long-distance altruism is most likely a by-product of other, more adaptive traits, such as empathy and abstract reasoning. Similarly, there is no reproductive advantage to the pleasure we get from paintings or movies. It just so happens that our eyes and brains, which evolved to react to three-dimensional objects in the real world, can respond to two-dimensional projections on a canvas or a screen.

Supernatural beliefs might be explained in a similar way. This is the religion-as-accident theory that emerges from my work and the work of cognitive scientists such as Scott Atran, Pascal Boyer, Justin Barrett, and Deborah Kelemen. One version of this theory begins with the notion that a distinction between the physical and the psychological is fundamental to human thought. Purely physical things, such as rocks and trees, are subject to the pitiless laws of Newton. Throw a rock, and it will fly through space on a certain path; if you put a branch on the ground, it will not disappear, scamper away, or fly into space. Psychological things, such as people, possess minds, intentions, beliefs, goals, and desires. They move unexpectedly, according to volition and whim; they can chase or run away. There is a moral difference as well: a rock cannot be evil or kind; a person can.

Where does the distinction between the physical and the psychological come from? Is it something we learn through experience, or is it somehow pre-wired into our brains? One way to find out is to study babies. It is notoriously difficult to know what babies are thinking, given that they can't speak and have little control over their bodies. (They are harder to test than rats or pigeons, because they cannot run mazes or peck levers.) But recently investigators have used the technique of showing them different events and recording how long they look at them, exploiting the fact that babies, like the rest of us, tend to look longer at something they find unusual or bizarre.

This has led to a series of striking discoveries. Six-month-olds understand that physical objects obey gravity. If you put an object on a table and then remove the table, and the object just stays there (held by a hidden wire), babies are surprised; they expect the object to fall. They expect objects to be solid, and contrary to what is still being taught in some psychology classes, they understand that objects persist over time even if hidden. (Show a baby an object and then put it behind a screen. Wait a little while and then remove the screen. If the object is gone, the baby is surprised.) Five-month-olds can even do simple math, appreciating that if first one object and then another is placed behind a screen, when the screen drops there should be two objects, not one or three. Other experiments find the same numerical understanding in nonhuman primates, including macaques and tamarins, and in dogs.

Similarly precocious capacities show up in infants' understanding of the social world. Newborns prefer to look at faces over anything else, and the sounds they most like to hear are human voices—preferably their mother's. They quickly come to recognize different emotions, such as anger, fear, and happiness, and respond appropriately to them. Before they are a year old they can determine the target of an adult's gaze, and can learn by attending to the emotions of others; if a baby is crawling toward an area that might be dangerous and an adult makes a horrified or disgusted face, the baby usually knows enough to stay away.

A skeptic might argue that these social capacities can be explained as a set of primitive responses, but there is some evidence that they reflect a deeper understanding. For instance, when twelve-month-olds see one object chasing another, they seem to understand that it really is chasing, with the goal of catching; they expect the chaser to continue its pursuit along the most direct path, and are surprised when it does otherwise. In some work I've done with the psychologists Valerie Kuhlmeier, of Queen's University, and Karen Wynn, of Yale, we found that when babies see one character in a movie help an individual and a different character hurt that individual, they later expect the individual to approach the character that helped it and to avoid the one that hurt it.

Understanding of the physical world and understanding of the social world can be seen as akin to two distinct computers in a baby's brain, running separate programs and performing separate tasks. The understandings develop at different rates: the social one emerges somewhat later than the physical one. They evolved at different points in our prehistory; our physical understanding is shared by many species, whereas our social understanding is a relatively recent adaptation, and in some regards might be uniquely human.

That these two systems are distinct is especially apparent in autism, a developmental disorder whose dominant feature is a lack of social understanding. Children with autism typically show impairments in communication (about a third do not speak at all), in imagination (they tend not to engage in imaginative play), and most of all in socialization. They do not seem to enjoy the company of others; they don't hug; they are hard to reach out to. In the most extreme cases children with autism see people as nothing more than objects—objects that move in unpredictable ways and make unexpected noises and are therefore frightening. Their understanding of other minds is impaired, though their understanding of material objects is fully intact.

At this point the religion-as-accident theory says nothing about supernatural beliefs. Babies have two systems that work in a cold-bloodedly rational way to help them anticipate and understand—and, when they get older, to manipulate—physical and social entities. In other words, both these systems are biological adaptations that give human beings a badly needed head start in dealing with objects and people. But these systems go awry in two important ways that are the foundations of religion. First, we perceive the world of objects as essentially separate from the world of minds, making it possible for us to envision soulless bodies and bodiless souls. This helps explain why we believe in gods and an afterlife. Second, as we will see, our system of social understanding overshoots, inferring goals and desires where none exist. This makes us animists and creationists.

Natural-born dualists. For those of us who are not autistic, the separateness of these two mechanisms, one for understanding the physical world and one for understanding the social world, gives rise to a duality of experience. We experience the world of material things as separate from the world of goals and desires. The biggest consequence has to do with the way we think of ourselves and others. We are dualists; it seems intuitively obvious that a physical body and a conscious entity—a mind or soul—are genuinely distinct. We don't feel that we *are* our bodies. Rather, we feel that we *occupy* them, we *possess* them, we *own* them.

This duality is immediately apparent in our imaginative life. Because we see people as separate from their bodies, we easily understand situations in which people's bodies are radically changed while their personhood stays intact. Kafka envisioned a man transformed into a gigantic insect; Homer described the plight of men transformed into pigs; in *Shrek 2* an ogre is transformed into a human being, and a donkey into a steed; in *Star Trek* a scheming villain forcibly occupies Captain Kirk's body so as to take command of the *Enterprise*; in *The Tale of the Body Thief*, Anne Rice tells of a vampire and a human being who agree to trade bodies for a day; and in *13 Going on 30* a teenager wakes up as thirty-year-old Jennifer Garner. We don't think of these events as real, of course, but they are fully understandable; it makes intuitive sense to us that people can be separated from their bodies, and similar transformations show up in religions around the world.

This notion of an immaterial soul potentially separable from the body clashes starkly with the scientific view. For psychologists and neuroscientists, the brain is the source of mental life; our consciousness, emotions, and will are the products of neural processes. As the claim is sometimes put, *The mind is what the brain does*. I don't want to overstate the consensus here; there is no accepted theory as to precisely how this happens, and some scholars are skeptical that we will ever develop such a theory. But no scientist takes seriously Cartesian dualism, which posits that thinking need not involve the brain. There is just too much evidence against it.

Still, it *feels* right, even to those who have never had religious training, and even to young children. This became particularly clear to me one night when I was arguing with my six-year-old son, Max. I was telling him that he had to go to bed, and he said, "You can make me go to bed, but you can't make me go to sleep. It's *my* brain!" This piqued my interest, so I began to ask him questions about what the brain does and does not do. His answers showed an interesting split. He insisted that the brain was involved in perception—in seeing, hearing, tasting, and smelling—and he was adamant that it was responsible for thinking. But, he said, the brain was not essential for dreaming, for feeling sad, or for loving his brother. "That's what *I* do," Max said, "though my brain might help me out."

Max is not unusual. Children in our culture are taught that the brain is involved in thinking, but they interpret this in a narrow sense, as referring to conscious problem solving, academic rumination. They do not see the brain as the source of conscious experience; they do not identify it with their selves. They appear to think of it as a cognitive prosthesis—there is Max the person, and then there is his brain, which he uses to solve problems just as he might use a computer. In this commonsense conception the brain is, as Steven Pinker puts it, "a pocket PC for the soul."

If bodies and souls are thought of as separate, there can be bodies without souls. A corpse is seen as a body that used to have a soul. Most things—chairs, cups, trees—never had souls; they never had will or consciousness. At least some nonhuman animals are seen in the same way, as what Descartes described as "beast-machines," or complex automata. Some artificial creatures, such as industrial robots, Haitian zombies, and Jewish golems, are also seen as soulless beings, lacking free will or moral feeling.

Then there are souls without bodies. Most people I know believe in a God who created the universe, performs miracles, and listens to prayers. He is omnipotent and omniscient, possessing infinite kindness, justice, and mercy. But he does not in any literal sense have a body. Some people also believe in lesser noncorporeal beings that can temporarily take physical form or occupy human beings or animals: examples include angels, ghosts, poltergeists, succubi, dybbuks, and the demons that Jesus so frequently expelled from people's bodies.

This belief system opens the possibility that we ourselves can survive the death of our bodies. Most people believe that when the body is destroyed, the soul lives on. It might ascend to heaven, descend to hell, go off into some sort of parallel world, or occupy some other body, human or animal. Indeed, the belief that the world teems with ancestor spirits—the souls of people who have been liberated from their bodies through death—is common across cultures. We can imagine our bodies being destroyed, our brains ceasing to function, our bones turning to dust, but it is harder—some would say impossible—to imagine the end of our very existence. The notion of a soul without a body makes sense to us.

Others have argued that rather than believing in an afterlife because we are dualists, we are dualists because we want to believe in an afterlife. This was Freud's position. He speculated that the "doctrine of the soul" emerged as a solution to the problem of death: if souls exist, then conscious experience need not come to an end. Or perhaps the motivation for belief in an afterlife is cultural: we believe it because religious authorities tell us that it is so, possibly because it serves the interests of powerful leaders to control the masses through the carrot of heaven and the stick of hell. But there is reason to favor the religion-as-accident theory.

In a significant study the psychologists Jesse Bering, of the University of Arkansas, and David Bjorklund, of Florida Atlantic University, told young children a story about an alligator and a mouse, complete with a series of pictures, that ended in tragedy: "Uh oh! Mr. Alligator sees Brown Mouse and is coming to get him!" [The children were shown a picture of the alligator eating the mouse.] "Well, it looks like Brown Mouse got eaten by Mr. Alligator. Brown Mouse is not alive anymore."

The experimenters asked the children a set of questions about the mouse's biological functioning—such as "Now that the mouse is no longer alive, will he ever need to go to the bathroom? Do his ears still work? Does his brain still work?"—and about the mouse's mental functioning, such as "Now that the mouse is no longer alive, is he still hungry? Is he thinking about the alligator? Does he still want to go home?"

As predicted, when asked about biological properties, the children appreciated the effects of death: no need for bathroom breaks; the ears don't work, and neither does the brain. The mouse's body is gone. But when asked about the psychological properties, more than half the children said that these would continue: the dead mouse can feel hunger, think thoughts, and have desires. The soul survives. And *children believe this more than adults do*, suggesting that although we have to learn which specific afterlife people in our culture believe in (heaven, reincarnation, a spirit world, and so on), the notion that life after death is possible is not learned at all. It is a by-product of how we naturally think about the world.

We've evolved to be creationists. This is just half the story. Our dualism makes it possible for us to think of supernatural entities and events; it is why such things make sense. But there is another factor that makes the perception of them compelling, often irresistible. We have what the anthropologist Pascal Boyer has called a hypertrophy of social cognition. We see purpose, intention, design, even when it is not there.

In 1944 the social psychologists Fritz Heider and Mary-Ann Simmel made a simple movie in which geometric figures—circles, squares, triangles—moved in certain systematic ways, designed to tell a tale. When shown this movie, people instinctively describe the figures as if they were specific types of people (bullies, victims, heroes) with goals and desires, and repeat pretty much the same story that the psychologists intended to tell. Further research has found that bounded figures aren't even necessary—one can get much the same effect in movies where the "characters" are not single objects but moving groups, such as swarms of tiny squares.

Stewart Guthrie, an anthropologist at Fordham University, was the first modern scholar to notice the importance of this tendency as an explanation for religious thought. In his 1993 book *Faces in the Clouds*, Guthrie presents anecdotes and experiments showing that people attribute human characteristics to a striking range of real-world entities, including bicycles, bottles, clouds, fire, leaves, rain, volcanoes, and wind. We are hypersensitive to signs of agency—so much so that we see intention where only artifice or accident exists. As Guthrie puts it, the clothes have no emperor.

Our quickness to over-read purpose into things extends to the perception of intentional design. People have a terrible eye for randomness. If you show them a string of heads and tails that was produced by a random-number generator, they tend to think it is rigged—it looks orderly to them, too orderly. After 9/11 people claimed to see Satan in the billowing smoke from the World Trade Center. Before that some people were stirred by the Nun Bun, a baked good that bore an eerie resemblance to Mother Teresa. In November of 2004 someone posted on eBay a ten-year-old grilled cheese sandwich that looked remarkably like the Virgin Mary; it sold for $28,000. (In response pranksters posted a grilled cheese sandwich bearing images of the Olsen twins, Mary-Kate and Ashley.) There are those who listen to the static from radios and other electronic devices and hear messages from dead people—a phenomenon presented with great seriousness in the Michael Keaton movie *White Noise*. Older readers who lived their formative years before CDs and MPEGs might remember listening intently for the significant and sometimes scatological messages that were said to come from records played backward.

Sometimes there really are signs of nonrandom and functional design. We are not being unreasonable when we observe that the eye seems to be crafted for seeing, or that the leaf insect seems colored with the goal of looking very much like a leaf. The evolutionary biologist Richard Dawkins begins *The Blind Watchmaker* by conceding this point: "Biology is the study of complicated things that give the appearance of having been designed for a purpose." Dawkins goes on to suggest that anyone before Darwin who did not believe in God was simply not paying attention.

Darwin changed everything. His great insight was that one could explain complex and adaptive design without positing a divine designer. Natural selection can be simulated on a computer; in fact, genetic algorithms, which mimic natural selection, are used to solve otherwise intractable computational problems. And we can see natural selection at work in case studies across the world, from the evolution of beak size in Galápagos finches to the arms race we engage in with many viruses, which have an unfortunate capacity to respond adaptively to vaccines.

Richard Dawkins may well be right when he describes the theory of natural selection as one of our species' finest accomplishments; it is an intellectually satisfying and empirically supported account of our own existence. But almost nobody believes it. One poll found that more than a third of college undergraduates believe that the Garden of Eden was where the first human beings appeared. And even among those who claim to endorse Darwinian evolution, many distort it in one way or another, often seeing it as a mysterious internal force driving species toward perfection. (Dawkins writes that it appears almost as if "the human brain is specifically designed to misunderstand Darwinism.") And if you are tempted to see this as a "red state–blue state" issue, think again: although it's true that more Bush voters than Kerry voters are creationists, just about half of Kerry voters believe that God created human beings in their present form, and most of the rest believe that although we evolved from less-advanced life forms, God guided the process.

Most Kerry voters want evolution to be taught either alongside creationism or not at all.

What's the problem with Darwin? His theory of evolution does clash with the religious beliefs that some people already hold. For Jews and Christians, God willed the world into being in six days, calling different things into existence. Other religions posit more physical processes on the part of the creator or creators, such as vomiting, procreation, masturbation, or the molding of clay. Not much room here for random variation and differential reproductive success.

But the real problem with natural selection is that it makes no intuitive sense. It is like quantum physics; we may intellectually grasp it, but it will never feel right to us. When we see a complex structure, we see it as the product of beliefs and goals and desires. Our social mode of understanding leaves it difficult for us to make sense of it any other way. Our gut feeling is that design requires a designer—a fact that is understandably exploited by those who argue against Darwin.

It's not surprising, then, that nascent creationist views are found in young children. Four-year-olds insist that everything has a purpose, including lions ("to go in the zoo") and clouds ("for raining"). When asked to explain why a bunch of rocks are pointy, adults prefer a physical explanation, while children choose a functional one, such as "so that animals could scratch on them when they get itchy." And when asked about the origin of animals and people, children tend to prefer explanations that involve an intentional creator, even if the adults raising them do not. Creationism—and belief in God—is bred in the bone.

Religion and science will always clash. Some might argue that the preceding analysis of religion, based as it is on supernatural beliefs, does not apply to certain non-Western faiths. In his 2004 book, *The End of Faith*, the neuroscientist Sam Harris mounts a fierce attack on religion, much of it directed at Christianity and Islam, which he criticizes for what he sees as ridiculous factual claims and grotesque moral views. But then he turns to Buddhism, and his tone shifts to admiration—it is "the most complete methodology we have for discovering the intrinsic freedom of consciousness, unencumbered by any dogma." Surely this religion, if one wants to call it a religion, is not rooted in the dualist and creationist views that emerge in our childhood.

Fair enough. But while it may be true that "theologically correct" Buddhism explicitly rejects the notions of body-soul duality and immaterial entities with special powers, actual Buddhists believe in such things. (Harris himself recognizes this; at one point he complains about the millions of Buddhists who treat the Buddha as a Christ figure.) For that matter, although many Christian theologians are willing to endorse evolutionary biology—and it was legitimately front-page news when Pope John Paul II conceded that Darwin's theory of evolution might be correct—this should not distract us from the fact that many Christians think evolution is nonsense.

Or consider the notion that the soul escapes the body at death. There is little hint of such an idea in the Old Testament, although it enters into Judaism later on. The New Testament is notoriously unclear about the afterlife, and some Christian theologians have argued, on the basis of sources such as Paul's letters to the Corinthians, that the idea of a soul's rising to heaven conflicts with biblical authority. In 1999 the pope himself cautioned people to think of heaven not as an actual place but, rather, as a form of existence—that of being in relation to God.

Despite all this, most Jews and Christians, as noted, believe in an afterlife—in fact, even people who claim to have no religion at all tend to believe in one. Our afterlife beliefs are clearly expressed in popular books such as *The Five People You Meet in Heaven* and *A Travel Guide to Heaven*. As the *Guide* puts it,

"Heaven is *dynamic*. It's bursting with excitement and action. It's the ultimate playground, created purely for our enjoyment, by someone who knows what enjoyment means, because He invented it. It's Disney World, Hawaii, Paris, Rome, and New York all rolled up into one. And it's *forever*! Heaven truly is the vacation that never ends."

(This sounds a bit like hell to me, but it is apparently to some people's taste.)

Religious authorities and scholars are often motivated to explore and reach out to science, as when the pope embraced evolution and the Dalai Lama became involved with neuroscience. They do this in part to make their world view more palatable to others, and in part because they are legitimately concerned about any clash with scientific findings. No honest person wants to be in the position of defending a view that makes manifestly false claims, so religious authorities and scholars often make serious efforts toward reconciliation—for instance, trying to interpret the Bible in a way that is consistent with what we know about the age of the earth.

If people got their religious ideas from ecclesiastical authorities, these efforts might lead religion away from the supernatural. Scientific views would spread through religious communities. Supernatural beliefs would gradually disappear as the theologically correct version of a religion gradually became consistent with the secular world view. As Stephen Jay Gould hoped, religion would stop stepping on science's toes.

But this scenario assumes the wrong account of where supernatural ideas come from. Religious teachings certainly shape many of the specific beliefs we hold; nobody is born with the idea that the birthplace of humanity was the Garden of Eden, or that the soul enters the body at the moment of conception, or that martyrs will be rewarded with sexual access to scores of virgins. These ideas are learned. But the universal themes of religion are not learned. They emerge as accidental by-products of our mental systems. They are part of human nature.

Discussion

1. What is the religion-as-opiate theory (and what are some religion-as-opiate theories) and why does Bloom reject it?

2. What is the religion is a fraternity theory and why does Bloom reject it?

3. What is the religion-as-accident theory and why does Bloom favour it?

4. How do intuitive dualism and agency detection contribute to the development of religious belief?

5. If beliefs in supernatural agents are accidents, are they no longer rationally tenable?

NATURALISTIC EXPLANATION FOR RELIGIOUS BELIEF

AKU VISALA AND DAVID LEECH*

Introduction. Recent naturalistic explanations of religion downplay earlier appeals to socio-economic factors (Marxist) and human needs (Freudian) as causes of religious belief, and claim to have better empirical support than the predecessor theories.[1] These new cognitive-evolutionary explanations have led some commentators to suppose that these new approaches might be the final nail in the coffin of reasonable religious commitment (e.g., Dennett, 2006). In this essay, we will firstly outline some of the main contemporary naturalistic explanations of religious belief that have emerged in the last 20 years. Following Jeffrey Schloss (2009) we will divide contemporary explanations of religious belief into three types: (1) cognitive explanations, (2) evolutionary explanations, and (3) co-evolutionary explanations, and examine each type of explanation in its corresponding section. We will then survey some recent debates about the relevance of such naturalistic explanations for the rationality of religious belief.

Naturalistic explanations of religious belief. The contemporary naturalistic explanations of religious belief in which we are interested draw on recent scientific developments in biology, psychology, anthropology and cognitive science (see Haines, 2007; Laland and Brown, 2002). These explanations posit only causes, effects, powers and entities that can be understood in terms of current theories of natural and behavioral sciences when explaining religious belief.[2] These new naturalistic explanations of religious beliefs

suppose that religious belief is part of our nature as human beings, as opposed to something culturally constructed: it might serve a biological function or it might be a by-product of our cognition, but nevertheless the tendency to form religious beliefs is a part of universal human nature, rather than simply being a product of religious individuals' history and cultural environment.

The question that naturalistic explanations of religious belief attempt to answer is how do pan-human tendencies to form religious beliefs emerge and persist? Answers come in three different types: (1) cognitive explanations, (2) evolutionary explanations, and (3) co-evolutionary explanations. Many see the fault line between these approaches as lying in the way in which they understand the relationship of religious belief to natural selection: some claim that religious belief has never had an adaptive biological function, but is a pure by-product of the evolution of cognition (Boyer, 2001), whereas others claim that religious belief has indeed been favored by natural selection because it has provided (or provides) certain survival advantages (e.g., D.S. Wilson, 2002). This parallels the better-known division in evolutionary biology between "adaptationists" who hold that all—or at least, all important—physical and behavioral traits are governed by natural selection, and "pluralists" who hold that certain seemingly functional traits of an organism might be accidental consequences ("spandrels," or "by-products") of some other traits. The split, however, is not as clean as this and we will return to it later.

Cognitive explanations. Most cognitive explanations of religion are presented under the rubric of what is now called "the cognitive science of religion" (CSR), which includes a host of different theories including cognitive, evolutionary and co-evolutionary explanations and theorists (e.g., Scott Atran [2002], Pascal Boyer [1994, 2001], Justin Barrett [1999, 2000, 2004],

* Aku Visala is Research Fellow of the Finnish Academy, University of Helsinki, Finland. David Leech is Lecturer in Philosophy at the University of Bristol.

Robert McCauley and E. Thomas Lawson [Lawson and McCauley 1990, 2002], and Harvey Whitehouse [2000, 2004]). The starting point of CSR is that the basic functions of the human mind do not vary across cultures. This is due to the fact that human minds emerge from similar biological foundations (brains) in basically uniform natural environments. Further, our cognitive systems shape or "constrain" the content of our beliefs and perceptions: our minds select and transform information. Due to such processes, human cognition produces recurrent patterns in human thinking and behavior across cultures by constraining and informing possible ways of thinking and acting. The most salient religious beliefs (e.g., beliefs about morally interested gods and spirits) can be explained by invoking these systems.

Several hypotheses and theories have been presented within CSR to explain how the normal operations of human psychological mechanisms explain the observable recurrent patterns in religious belief. These together make up what Michael Murray and Andrew Goldberg (2009) have helpfully called the "standard model of CSR," as found more or less in Atran, Barrett and Boyer. The standard model starts from the assumption that human cognitive architectures are modular in structure and their components were selected for in the Pleistocene. These modular cognitive mechanisms are then presented as working conjointly to generate religious belief and behavior cross-culturally as a by-product of their normal functioning. More specifically, religious beliefs are held to arise and persist for the following three reasons.

Firstly, they are *counterintuitive* in ways that make them optimally suited for recall and transmission. Religions are communal, so religious ideas have to spread beyond individuals to become believed by whole communities. This means that they must have properties that make them memorable and which make them transmit successfully from one mind to another. The minimal-counterintuitiveness

hypothesis (MCI) states that human minds are such that some ideas are more "catching" than others. In particular, human minds find strange or counterintuitive ideas very memorable and interesting. But this hypothesis predicts that only certain sorts of counterintuitive ideas will have high memorability and transmit well, namely those which involve only a few rather than many violations of humans' innate "ontological categories" (Boyer, 1994, 2001).

Secondly, religious beliefs spring from cognitive mechanisms that generate beliefs about *agents* and *agency* (Barrett, 2004). Religious beliefs arise in the first place with the help of the so-called *hypersensitive agency detection device* (HADD). HADD is based on the observation that humans tend to interpret ambiguous stimuli as having been produced by agents, and that this perceptual bias would be adaptive, since it made humans more wary in their interactions with the environment and therefore reduced the risk of unexpected encounters with predatory others. HADD hypothesises the existence of agency when it detects certain sorts of stimuli in the environment. Overdetection of agency seems a reasonable strategy for human minds because they are presumed to have evolved to maximise relevant information about their environments (Guthrie, 1993). But where no natural embodied agents can be discerned, invisible minimally counterintuitive supernatural agents become good candidates for explaining unusual events.

Thirdly, humans—with the help of another set of cognitive mechanisms, sometimes called *Theory of Mind*—represent religious entities as *minded agents* who, because of their counter-intuitive character, stand to benefit us in our attempt to maintain stable relationships in large interacting groups. It is proposed that events which trigger HADD are likely to serve as occasions to form beliefs of this sort about those agents which are thought to cause these unusual stimuli.

While none of these factors just on their own explain the cross cultural salience of religious belief, it is proposed that their combination adds up to a powerful explanation of the origin and prevalence of the diverse religious beliefs in the world and the easiness with which they transmit across cultures (for overviews, see Boyer, 2001; Barrett, 2004; Tremlin, 2006).

Evolutionary explanations. The theories and hypotheses of CSR tend to favor the idea that religious belief is a by-product or a "spandrel" of biological evolution: religious belief is not directly a product of natural selection, although natural selection has produced the underlying cognitive mechanisms. By contrast, some authors have argued that religious belief is a biological characteristic, that is, it has been produced by natural selection and has (or at least has had) adaptive value.

In current discussions, there are numerous and partly conflicting proposals with respect to the evolution of our capacity to form religious beliefs. We can distinguish two lines of argument in the contemporary discussion about the evolutionary function of religion.

Religious belief as a group-level adaptation that functions as a way to coordinate and create strategies for cooperation and shared goals. Religious groups are more likely to survive in competition with non-religious groups, because they are more integrated. Religion contributes to this integration by providing rituals, shared beliefs and values.

Religion as an individual-level adaptation that functions to maintain cooperation by minimizing defection and cheating. Individuals who are more likely to behave cooperatively will eventually survive better than those who do not.

Position (1), defended by David Sloan Wilson (2002), holds that group-level attributes might have significant effects on the transmission of genes. Although genes are the basic means of transmission of an organism's design, individuals and groups are vehicles for genes to act on. Natural selection, in Wilson's view, works on multiple levels: the fitness of groups can affect the selection of genes as well as genes affecting

the fitness of the group. The explanation of religion can be given in these terms in the following way. Religious beliefs enhance altruistic behavior in human groups, and when altruistic behavior increases, then groups become more cohesive and integrated. It follows, the argument continues, that religious groups have a selective advantage over non-religious groups. In the long run, this would result in religious groups outlasting the non-religious ones, because religious groups are the ones whose genes get transmitted. The result would be a religious tendency shared by almost all remaining humans.

Writers skeptical of group selection (see Lloyd, 2005 for an overview) argue (2) that religion could be an individual-level adaptation since human cooperation and grouping only make sense from a fitness point of view if the group can minimize cheaters and defectors. But policing and weeding out free riders can take a lot of time and effort, making it costly for the group as a whole.

Some have claimed that religious belief offers a neat device to solve this problem by providing mechanisms to minimize cheaters. According to Richard Sosis (2004; Sosis and Alcorta, 2003), religion might solve the problem of cooperation by providing ways to signal an individual's trustworthiness for other members in a group. Sosis's hypothesis is currently known as the "costly signalling theory." By participating in practices such as ritual and sacrifice that are highly costly for individuals, the individual signals to others his willingness to cooperate. The more costly the signals, the more unlikely it is that the individual is a potential cheater.

Joseph Bulbulia (Bulbulia, 2004, 2009) has claimed that individual displays of religious emotions and practices function as signals of genuine religious commitment. The more intense and costly the display is the more difficult it is to fake. Again, this provides a way of distinguishing genuine co-operators from cheaters.

Finally, Jesse Bering and others (Bering and Johnson, 2005; Johnson and Bering, 2006, 2009) have put forward a hypothesis known as "supernatural punishment theory." According to this theory, religion facilitates cooperation by removing the need for "external" policing by the group by positing supernatural agents. If individuals believe that there are moralizing supernatural and superpowerful agents around, they are much less likely to cheat or defect. Supernatural agents might, therefore, function as "internal" ways of discouraging cheaters. This, of course, frees the resources of the group for other tasks by removing the need for external policing and detection of defectors.

Recent responses. One would commit the genetic fallacy if one thought that naturalistic explanations of religious belief disproved theism. Thus, atheists have argued instead that, regardless of whether it is true or false, these naturalistic explanations render theism irrational (Dennett, 2006; Dawkins, 2006; and Bloom, 2005, 2007, 2009). Paul Bloom writes (2009, 125): "While it is true that nothing from empirical study of human psychology can refute religious belief, certain theories can challenge the rationality of those who hold such beliefs." If the mechanisms that produce theistic belief are unreliable, the rationality of theistic belief may be undermined.[3] Such arguments take the following forms:

1. The cognitive mechanisms that produce theistic beliefs were not selected to produce theistic belief but arose as by-products of natural selection. Therefore the cognitive mechanisms that produce theistic beliefs are unreliable sources of theistic belief.

2. Naturalistic explanations of theistic beliefs imply a lack of proper causal connection between theistic belief and its targets. Religious belief is not directly causally

connected to the reality (God) which it represents.

Paul Bloom implies something like (1): if religious beliefs are products of mechanisms not selected to produce beliefs about God, we might not be rational in trusting religious beliefs that they produce. The main premise of the argument is that if the mechanisms that produce religious belief are not selected by evolution to perform that task, their products should not be trusted. Theists have responded to this argument by refuting the major premise: we have no reason to think that beliefs that are evolutionary by-products, that is, products of mechanisms that have originally been selected to produce beliefs about other things, are unreliable (Barrett, 2007; Clark and Barrett, 2011). Moreover, many of our beliefs, including scientific and everyday beliefs, are also "accidental" by-products of our cognitive systems: natural selection did not favor individuals who were able to do quantum mechanics or calculus. We are able to form beliefs about God, quantum mechanics and calculus because our cognitive mechanisms, which originally evolved to do something else, are flexible enough to process different inputs.

Type (2) arguments are also mostly implied rather than clearly stated. These arguments hold that since we can now explain how religious belief emerges and persists without any reference to the supernatural objects of religious belief, religious beliefs are irrational. The underlying assumption of the argument is that religious belief must be causally connected to the reality which it represents, and if there is no connection, then the belief is irrational. The basic reply (e.g., van Inwagen, 2009; Barrett, Leech, and Visala, 2010; Thurow, 2014) holds that the argument identifies the origin of religious belief with its rationality in a questionable way: it implies that justified beliefs must be "directly caused" by the reality they represent. But in everyday religious life (and everyday life in general), our beliefs have multiple sources and causes: oral and written testimony, reasoning and memory, etc., are all among the direct causes of our beliefs (Clark and Rabinowitz, 2011). Since our beliefs are mediated through many different causal pathways, it does not make sense to require that God (or any other part of reality) must directly cause our beliefs. Some (Murray, 2009) have even claimed that it is enough for the theist that God enters into the causal chain of religious belief only in the beginning, that is, at the moment of creation when he sets up the physical world and its laws.

These responses assume that it is possible to incorporate a naturalistic account of the emergence of belief in God into a larger theistic framework (van Inwagen, 2009). The point can be exemplified by considering an argument of Alvin Plantinga against Freudian explanations of religion. Suppose Freud is right, and there is the psychological mechanism that Freud calls "wish-fulfilment"; if there is a God, he might use this very natural mechanism to produce belief in God (Plantinga, 2000, 139). Likewise, perhaps God might use cognitive and biological mechanisms to bring about various religious beliefs (Barrett, 2009; Clark and Barrett, 2011).

Leech and Visala (2011a) highlight the relevance of "big picture" background beliefs in assessing rationality given these naturalistic factors. For example, the metaphysical naturalist who holds that all socio-cultural phenomena can be reduced to cognitive or biological phenomena will see these factors as doing most of the heavy lifting in explaining religion. The theist might suppose that their causal importance is dwarfed by that of God's additionally making historical interventions to produce special revelations, cause religious experiences in people, etc. Naturalistic theories of religion are part of a larger causal nexus, and assumptions about what is *in* the larger causal nexus shape assessments about the significance of these naturalistic factors. If the undermining power of naturalistic explanations of religious belief depends on beliefs that constitute one's larger "big picture" of the world, then there seems to be no universal way of saying how explanations of religion might undermine theism.

In conclusion, CSR is a very new and developing science, so it is not clear what the scope of the new naturalistic explanations of religious belief are and what exactly they explain. Moreover, philosophical understanding of these new naturalistic explanations is still in its early stages, and the immediate task for philosophers of religion appears to be one of clarifying the basic philosophical stakes of the debate.

Notes

1. For an overview of earlier theories, see Preus 1987.

2. A corollary of this methodological choice is that most naturalistic explanations of religion are openly hostile, or at least very critical, towards more traditional hermeneutical (e.g., Geertz, 1973, 2000), and socio-cultural approaches (e.g., Durkheim, 1976) to religious belief that tend to make a strong distinction between explaining the natural world and understanding the "human" or the "social" world.

3. There is a body of literature on evolutionary debunking arguments of morality which is partly relevant to religious belief. For overviews, see Joyce, 2006 and Kahane, 2011.

References

Alcorta, Candace and Richard Sosis. "The Evolution of Religion as an Adaptive Complex." *Human Nature* 16 (2005): 323–59.

Atran, Scott. *In Gods We Trust: The Evolutionary Landscape of Religion.* New York: Oxford UP, 2002.

Aunger, Robert, ed. *Darwinizing Culture: The Status of Memetics as a Science.* New York: Oxford UP, 2002.

Barrett, Justin L. "Theological Correctness: Cognitive Constraints and the Study of Religion." *Method and Theory in the Study of Religion* 11 (1999): 325–39.

———. "Exploring the Natural Foundations of Religion." *Trends in Cognitive Sciences* 4 (2000): 29–34.

———. *Why Would Anyone Believe in God?* Walnut Creek, CA: AltaMira P, 2004.

———. "Is the Spell Really Broken? Bio-Psychological Explanations of Religion and Theistic Belief." *Theology and Science* 5:1 (2007): 57–72.

———. "Cognitive Science, Religion, and Theology." In *The Believing Primate: Scientific, Philosophical, and Theological Reflections on the Origin of Religion.* Ed. Jeffrey Schloss and Michael Murray. New York: Oxford UP, 2009. 76–99.

Barrett, Justin, David Leech, and Aku Visala. "Can Religious Belief Be Explained Away? Reasons and Causes of Religious Belief." In *The Nature of God—Evolution and Religion.* Vol 1. Ed. Ulrich Frey. Marburg: Tectum Verlag, 2010. 75–92.

Blackmore, Susan. *The Meme Machine.* Oxford: Oxford UP, 1999.

Bloom, Paul. *Descartes' Baby: How the Science of Child Development Explains What Makes Us Human.* New York: Basic Books, 2005.

———. "Religion Is Natural." *Developmental Science* 10 (2007): 147–51.

———. "Religious Belief as an Evolutionary Accident." In *The Believing Primate: Scientific, Philosophical and Theological Reflection on the Origin of Religion.* Ed. Jeffrey Schloss and Michael Murray. New York: Oxford UP, 2009. 118–27.

Boyd, Robert and Peter Richerson. *Culture and the Evolutionary Process.* Chicago: U of Chicago P, 1985.

———. *Not By Genes Alone: How Culture Transformed Human Evolution.* Chicago: U of Chicago P, 2005.

———. *The Origin and Evolution of Cultures.* New York: Oxford UP, 2005.

Boyer, Pascal. *The Naturalness of Religious Ideas: A Cognitive Theory of Religion.* Berkeley: U of California P, 1994.

———. *Religion Explained: The Evolutionary Origins of Religious Thought.* New York: Basic Books, 2001.

Bulbulia, Joseph. "The Cognitive and Evolutionary Psychology of Religion." *Biology and Philosophy* 19 (2004): 655–86.

———. "The Evolution of Religion." In *The Oxford Handbook of Evolutionary Psychology.* Ed. Louise Barrett and Robin Dunbar. New York: Oxford UP, 2007. 621–35.

———. "Religiosity as a Mental Time Travel: Cognitive Adaptations for Religious Behavior." In *The Believing Primate: Scientific, Philosophical, and Theological Reflections on the Origin of Religion.* Ed. Jeffrey Schloss and Michael Murray. New York: Oxford UP, 2009. 44–78.

Clark, Kelly James and Justin Barrett. "Reidian Religious Epistemology and the Cognitive Science of Religion." *Journal of the American Academy of Religion. Journal of the American Academy of Religion* 79(3) (2011): 639–75.

Clark, Kelly James and Dani Rabinowitz. "The Cognitive Science of Religion and the Rationality of Religious Belief." *European Journal of Philosophy of Religion* 3(1) (2011): 67–82.

Dawkins, Richard. *The God Delusion.* London: Bantam P, 2006.

Day, Michael. "Let's Be Realistic: Evolutionary Complexity, Epistemic Probabilism and the Cognitive Science of Religion." *Harvard Theological Review* 100 (2007): 47–64.

Dennett, Daniel. *Breaking the Spell: Religion as a Natural Phenomenon.* New York: Viking, 2006.

Durkheim, Emile. *Elementary Forms of Religious Life*. New York: Oxford UP, 2008.

Geertz, Clifford. *Interpretation of Cultures: Selected Essays*. New York: Basic Books, 1973.

Gregersen, Niels Henrik. "What Theology Might Learn (and Not Learn) from Evolutionary Psychology: A Postliberal Theologian in Conversation with Pascal Boyer." In *Evolution of Rationality: Interdisciplinary Essays in Honor of J. Wentzel Van Huyssteen*. Ed. F. LeRon Shults. Grand Rapids, MI: W.B. Eerdmans, 2006.

Guthrie, Stewart. *Faces in the Clouds: A New Theory of Religion*. New York: Oxford UP, 1993.

Haines, Valerie. "Evolutionary Explanations." In *Philosophy of Anthropology and Sociology*. Ed. Stephen Turner and Mark Risjord. Amsterdam: Elsevier, 2007. 249–309.

Kahane, Guy. "Evolutionary Debunking Arguments." *Nous* 45(1) (March 2011): 103–25.

Laidlaw, James. "Well Disposed Anthropologist's Problems with 'the Cognitive Science of Religion.'" In *Religion, Anthropology and Cognitive Science*. Ed. James Laidlaw and Harvey Whitehouse. Durham: Carolina Academic P, 2007. 211–46.

Laland, Kevin and Gillian Brown. *Sense and Nonsense: Evolutionary Perspectives on Human Behavior*. New York: Oxford UP, 2003.

Lawson, E. Thomas. "A New Look at the Science-and-Religion Dialogue." *Zygon: Journal of Religion and Science* 40 (2005): 555–63.

Lawson, E. Thomas and Robert McCauley. *Rethinking Religion: Connecting Cognition and Culture*. Cambridge: Cambridge UP, 1990.

——. *Bringing Ritual to Mind: Psychological Foundations of Cultural Forms*. Cambridge: Cambridge UP, 2002.

Leech, David and Aku Visala. "The Cognitive Science of Religion: A Modified Theist Response." *Religious Studies* 47 (2011a): 301–16.

——. "The Cognitive Science of Religion: Implications for Theism?" *Zygon: Journal of Religion and Science* 46(1) (March 2011): 47–64.

Murray, Michael J. "Four Arguments that the Cognitive Psychology of Religion Undermines the Justification of Religious Belief." In *The Evolution of Religion: Studies, Theories & Critiques*. Ed. Joseph Bulbulia, et al. Santa Margarita, CA: Collins Foundation P, 2007. 365–70.

——. "Scientific Explanations of Religion and the Justification of Religion Belief." In *The Believing Primate: Scientific, Philosophical, and Theological Reflections on the Origin of Religion*. Ed. Jeffrey Schloss and Michael Murray. New York: Oxford UP, 2009. 168–77.

Murray, Michael and Andrew Goldberg. "Evolutionary Accounts of Religion: Explaining and Explaining Away." In *The Believing Primate: Scientific, Philosophical, and Theological Reflections on the Origin of Religion*. Ed. Jeffrey Schloss and Michael Murray. New York: Oxford UP, 2009. 179–99.

Näreaho, Leo. "The Cognitive Science of Religion: Philosophical Observations." *Religious Studies* 44 (2008): 83–98.

Nielsen, Kai. *Naturalism and Religion*. New York: Prometheus Books, 2001.

Oviedo, Lluis. "Is a Complete Biocognitive Account of Religion Feasible?" *Zygon: Journal of Religion and Science* 43 (2008): 103–26.

Peterson, Gregory. R. "Theology and the Science Wars: Who Owns Human Nature?" *Zygon: Journal of Religion and Science* 41 (2006): 853–62.

——. "Are Evolutionary/Cognitive Theories of Religion Relevant for Philosophy of Religion?" *Zygon: Journal of Religion and Science* 45 (2010): 545–57.

Plantinga, Alvin. *Warranted Christian Belief*. New York: Oxford UP, 2000.

Preus, Samuel. *Explaining Religion: Criticism and Theory from Bodin to Freud*. New Haven: Yale UP, 1987.

Schloss, Jeffrey. "Introduction: Evolutionary Theories of Religion—Science Unfettered or Naturalism Run Wild?" In *The Believing Primate: Scientific, Philosophical, and Theological Reflections on the Origin of Religion*. Ed. Jeffrey Schloss and Michael Murray. New York: Oxford UP, 2009. 1–25.

Schloss, Jeffrey and Michael Murray, eds. *The Believing Primate: Scientific, Philosophical, and Theological Reflections on the Origin of Religion*. New York: Oxford UP, 2009.

Slingerland, Edward. "Who Is Afraid of Reductionism? The Study of Religion in the Age of Cognitive Science." *Journal of the AAR* 76 (2008): 375–411.

Sosis, Richard. "The Adaptive Value of Religion Ritual." *American Scientist* 92 (2004): 166–72.

Sosis, Richard and Candace Alcorta. "Signaling, Solidarity, and the Sacred: The Evolution of Religious Behaviour." *Evolutionary Anthropology* 12 (2003): 264–74.

Sperber, Dan. *Explaining Culture: A Naturalistic Approach*. Oxford: Blackwell, 1996.

——. "An Objection to the Memetic Approach to Culture." In *Darwinizing Culture: The Status of Memetics as a Science*. Ed. Robert Aunger. New York: Oxford UP, 2000. 163–74.

Thurow, Joshua. "Does the Scientific Study of Religion Cast Doubt on Theistic Beliefs?" In *The Roots of Religion*. Ed. Justin Barrett and Roger Trigg. New York: Oxford UP, 2014.

van Inwagen, Peter. "Explaining Belief in the Supernatural—Some Thoughts on Paul Bloom's 'Religious Belief as an Evolutionary Accident.'" In *The Believing Primate: Scientific, Philosophical and Theological Reflection on the Origin of Religion*. Ed. Jeffrey Schloss and Michael Murray. New York: Oxford UP, 2009. 128–38.

Wilson, David Sloan. *Darwin's Cathedral: Evolution, Religion and the Nature of Society*. Chicago, IL: U of Chicago P, 2002.

Whitehouse, Harvey. *Arguments and Icons: Divergent Modes of Religiosity*. Oxford: Oxford UP, 2000.

——. *Modes of Religiosity: A Cognitive Theory of Religious Transmission*. Walnut Creek, CA: AltaMira P, 2004.

Visala, Aku. "Religion and the Human Mind: Philosophical Perspectives on the Cognitive Science of Religion." *Neue Zeitschrift für Systematische Theologie und Religionsphilosophie* 50 (2008): 109–30.

Discussion

1. What are the components of the standard model of the cognitive science of religion (CSR)?

2. What does it mean to say that religious belief is a byproduct? What are some reasons for accepting this claim? For rejecting it?

3. How do some allege that CSR makes religious belief irrational? What is one response to this claim?

Chapter 14

Reflections on Reason and Belief in God

RECONCILING REASON AND RELIGIOUS BELIEF

RAYMOND J. VANARRAGON*

The problem stated. While some issues in philosophy can seem far removed from the concerns of ordinary people, the relationship between reason and religious belief is not one of them. Most people in the West hold reason in high regard, recognizing, for instance, impressive accomplishments in the sciences and in other domains of inquiry, all of which seem attributable to reason. At the same time, many people hold—and indeed, treasure—beliefs that can be called religious. Is there a tension here? Are these believers leading double lives? Is their religious believing a reflection of some sort of hypocrisy, where they praise reason and at the same time harbor irrationality at the very center of their lives? Is their religion the result of intellectual laziness or cowardice? Or, on the other hand, is religious belief rational and, if so, in what sense? Can it be rational to hold religious beliefs when many thoughtful people reject them?

In what follows I propose to explore these questions by considering the plight of a hypothetical young theist I'll call Sadie. (For simplicity I'll focus solely on her belief in God, though similar issues could also be raised with regard to her other religious beliefs.) Sadie, like many religious people, wants to use her rational faculties properly; she wants to believe in God without ignoring or contradicting the deliverances of reason or being in some other way irrational. But she is not sure that she can. I'll consider the options she has for reconciling reason with her belief in God and I'll argue that it can in fact be done, even though the reconciliation may not be as simple and decisive as she may have hoped it would be.

Why reason and religious belief appear at odds. While it is commonly thought that there is a tension between reason and religious belief, Sadie might first of all wonder why this is so. Many theists can't right away see how belief in God may run contrary to reason, and the same could be true of Sadie, especially if she has grown up in an environment where everyone believes as she does. It may take thinking in unfamiliar ways for her to see a problem. How could we help Sadie to do this? Well, it is often useful to have a person first consider the religious beliefs of *other* people, and when she notes the tension between reason and *their* beliefs, she might be brought around to noticing similar problems with her own beliefs. So perhaps we could start with that.

There are many religious beliefs that Sadie would likely find problematic, but suppose we introduce her to the beliefs of the infamous Heaven's Gate cult. As some readers may recall, these cultists believed that

---

* Raymond J. VanArragon teaches philosophy at Bethel University.

there was a spaceship flying behind the Hale-Bopp Comet and that if they would only free themselves from their earthly bodies (by committing suicide), they would be transported on that ship to a place of heavenly bliss. The story ended tragically when, in 1997, thirty-nine members of the cult demonstrated the courage of their misguided convictions by killing themselves. Some of them left behind family members, including children, in an act motivated by beliefs that will likely strike Sadie as hopelessly irrational.[1]

Why were those beliefs irrational? Well, Sadie might think, the cultists didn't have decent evidence that there really *was* such a spaceship or that killing themselves was the way to catch a ride on it. It wasn't proper for them to blindly accept the testimony of their leaders: most of the general populace considered those leaders to be deranged, and the cult members should have caught wind of this and established the sanity and reliability of those leaders before believing what they said. To believe rationally one must seek evidence, be open to possible reasons for doubting, and refrain from firm belief if evidence is lacking and reasons for doubting are significant. By all appearances the cultists didn't do any of this, and if they had then they wouldn't have continued holding those misguided beliefs and heading toward such a catastrophic end.

After reflecting on these things, Sadie might wonder whether *she* is any different from the cultists, whether her own theistic beliefs stand up to rational scrutiny any better than their beliefs did. She doesn't have to go far these days to find people who think they don't. Books, journal articles, internet sites, and college professors say of Sadie's beliefs almost exactly what she was inclined to say about the beliefs of the members of Heaven's Gate. She doesn't have decent evidence for them; she can't just accept the testimony of her parents, teachers, or pastor without checking their credentials or investigating the truth of the matter for herself; she needs to be sufficiently open to objections to her beliefs. If she does search out the evidence or look carefully at objections, these skeptics say, she would find reason to give up her theism. And if under those conditions she hangs on to it, perhaps because of stubbornness or a failure of nerve, then she believes irrationally; and she doesn't want that!

The need for evidence. So, what to do? Sadie wants to have a coherent and rational system of beliefs, where her belief in God isn't held off to one side, far from the penetrating light of reason. If the Heaven's Gate cultists had said that their beliefs were simply a matter of faith and therefore not properly the subject of rational scrutiny, Sadie would have scoffed. It's cheap to claim blanket immunity for religious beliefs, especially when they have such an impact on the behavior of those who hold them. But then the same applies to her. The perceived tension between reason and belief in God is not something that Sadie can just ignore; so let's accompany her on her quest to reconcile the two.

What does she need to do to ensure that her belief in God is rational? Suppose she turns to W.K. Clifford, that zealous guardian of rationality. According to Clifford, one can only ensure rationality by acquiring *evidence* for one's beliefs. In fact, this demand for evidence is not just a rational one, it's also a *moral* one. "It is wrong always, everywhere, and for any one, to believe anything upon insufficient evidence," as Clifford famously intones.[2] But here Sadie may be a bit puzzled: what exactly *is* sufficient evidence? What does reason (and morality) actually require here? Clifford himself doesn't really answer this question; instead, he simply gives some poignant examples—including the case of the shipowner who believes, with disastrous results, that his ship is seaworthy—where it's clear that the demand for evidence isn't met.

So under what conditions *is* it met? Perhaps the evidence required for rational belief must be sufficient to persuade an honest truth seeker who starts out agnostic (not believing one way or the other) or standing on the opposing side. Clifford's shipowner could have met this standard, say, by acquiring unanimous approval of recognized experts on ship seaworthiness, or by becoming an expert and inspecting the ship himself. Most of us would be persuaded by such evidence and would consider it sufficient. So let's suppose Sadie attempts to meet that standard. It would be a wonderful thing if she could find evidence for God's existence that would convince truth-seeking atheists (or agnostics) to switch sides. Surely *that* would straightforwardly establish the rationality of her belief in God.

But before she begins her quest for this sort of evidence, Sadie has another puzzle. She *already* believes in God—she has been a theist, let's say, for as long as she can remember. Her parents believed in God and told her that God exists. She was taught the same in Sunday school and church every week (or at her synagogue or mosque). And she simply believed what she was told, without really asking questions. Has she been flouting the demands of rationality—and, by Clifford's lights, doing wrong—all these years? Well, maybe not. The evidence requirement probably doesn't apply to children: a person must reach a certain level of intellectual development before those demands take effect. So she can rest easy in the knowledge that as a child she may have been doing nothing wrong by believing in God on the testimony of those others. But what about now? Now that she is able to understand the demand, it *does* apply to her. The time has come for her to put aside childish ways and become a full member of the rational community, believing only on sufficient evidence. And until she has it, presumably, she should set her belief in God aside.

But this raises more questions. No doubt her belief in God is not the only one that she has simply believed on the basis of testimony, without checking into the reliability of her sources. Should she set all those other beliefs aside as well? What about her beliefs about science, history, and politics? What about her moral beliefs? Temporarily abandoning all of those beliefs would leave her with something of a belief vacuum, a vacuum that may not be filled anytime soon since the quest for evidence is likely to be a long and drawn out affair. And Sadie has a life to live! Unfortunately, Clifford doesn't have much sympathy for this concern: If there's no time to find evidence, then there's no time to believe, he snaps.[3] But that seems uncharitable. We shall return to this issue shortly; but for now it's important to note just how stringent Clifford's demand for evidence has already turned out to be.

Invigorated by the challenge, Sadie turns to search for evidence for God's existence. What sort of evidence will she find? Well, she might first consult her own experience. She considers the proposition that God exists, and she just feels that it's true. Moreover, when she does something wrong, she often finds herself with the belief that God is unhappy with her; in times of trial she finds herself calling out to God for help; when taking in the beauty of nature she finds herself with the belief that God is wondrous. Even further, once or twice in her life she has enjoyed what she took to be a religious experience, an episode in which she felt a profound sense of God's presence and love for her. Do these experiences and inclinations constitute sufficient evidence for God's existence?

Sadly, it's pretty clear they wouldn't meet the standards that Clifford might accept. Few atheists would consider such evidence persuasive. Naturalistic explanations of religious experience have become all the rage in evolutionary psychology these days, and a well-informed atheist would likely be able to come up with an (admittedly sketchy) account of how Sadie had them that doesn't involve any appeal to God.[4] In response to this, Sadie could perhaps come up with some *argument* that those feelings and experiences of hers are reliable sources of truth; but it's hard to see how she might do so without acquiring independent evidence that God in fact exists. So, experiential evidence for God's existence is not going to meet our Cliffordian standards for rational belief.

Second, Sadie might appeal to the testimony of others. She could take note, for instance, of the many people of enormous intellectual power throughout the ages who have believed in God. In addition, she could point out that atheism is a minority view in human history, even if atheists may constitute a more significant minority now than they once did. But this too would not be sufficient. For one thing, there have been many sharp-minded atheists as well—some of the best known philosophers in the western world since the Enlightenment have been atheists. For another thing, not only have naturalistic explanations been provided for religious experiences, such explanations have been provided for the very fact that so many people are religious.[5] So it seems that the existence of so many others who testify that God exists will not constitute sufficient evidence for theism. If Sadie is to persuade a clear-headed atheist, she will have to take a look herself at the more direct evidence for God's existence.

And this means that poor Sadie must turn, finally, to the famous and historic arguments for God's existence. Now, there is no need to consider those arguments here; they are detailed in Part One of this book. But let me note three things about the arguments that together may diminish Sadie's hopes that she will find here the evidence she seeks.

First, it seems that there are obvious problems with the simpler versions of the arguments, and the more complicated versions are difficult even for professional philosophers to understand and assess. As Kelly James Clark puts it, "Adequate assessment of these arguments would require a lengthy and torturous tour through the history of philosophy and may require the honing of one's logical and metaphysical skills beyond the capacity of most of us."[6] So, if Sadie wants to be in the best position to assess the arguments, she is going to have to put forth enormous effort, and even that may not be enough.

Second, while each of the major arguments for God's existence has its share of important adherents, each also has its critics, even among theists. To take one example, the Kalaam Cosmological Argument, originally developed by Arabic philosophers, endorsed by Saint Bonaventure, and more recently championed by William Lane Craig,[7] was rejected by Saint Thomas Aquinas, himself a friend of such arguments, and by many other Christian philosophers besides. These arguments, or some of them anyway, may nonetheless be very powerful (and their opponents mistaken); but Sadie might think it unlikely that she could find one sufficient to persuade a well-informed atheist (and hence sufficient to meet our Clifforidian evidence test) when so many *theists* who are well acquainted with them find them unconvincing.

Third, even if Sadie were to decide after a great deal of study and contemplation that one of the arguments is compelling (and that it should be so for a rational atheist or agnostic), she may not yet have evidence sufficient for the level of *conviction* characteristic of belief in God. For one thing, many of these arguments—the fine-tuning argument, for example—don't directly prove the existence of the God of traditional theism. Instead they attempt to prove the existence of some powerful designer or some non-descript First Cause of the universe. For another, if her belief in God is to be fully justified by an argument, she cannot believe the conclusion any more firmly than she believes any of the premises. If she is uncertain about a premise, or uncertain about how strongly the premises support the conclusion, she should be similarly tentative about the conclusion.[8] And again, given the complexity of the arguments and the controversies surrounding them, it would be quite surprising if Sadie found an argument such that she was absolutely convinced of the truth of each premise and the strength of the inference. So there is reason for doubting that such arguments can vindicate the firm belief in God that many theists maintain.

Questioning the demand for evidence. Assuming that Sadie hasn't found one or more of the arguments for God's existence to be utterly convincing, she may be a tad disheartened at her failure to reconcile reason and belief in God in the most straightforward way—by proving that God exists. But she should take heart, for the very evidential demand that set the rationality standard for her is itself questionable, for a number of reasons.

We have already glanced at the first reason: fulfilling Clifford's demand seems well nigh impossible for ordinary and even extraordinary people. Part of the problem, as we saw, is that we simply don't have the time to investigate the evidence for everything that we believe, or for checking the veracity of our sources (and, for that matter, checking the sources we depend on in order to establish the veracity of the first sources). We have heard Clifford's impatient retort to this concern—Then you should have no time to believe!—but it's just not as easy as that. For a further problem which he doesn't mention is that our beliefs aren't usually under our direct control. It is unrealistic to expect someone like Sadie, upon recognizing her lack of evidence for all sorts of things that she believes, to be able simply to drop those beliefs until she is able to establish that they are true. Consider Descartes, who in his famous *Meditations* attempted to discard all those beliefs about which he could imagine himself being mistaken. My guess is that he failed, or that even if he momentarily succeeded, while he was writing, in giving up his belief that he had a body, that belief came rushing back the moment he got up to get a new pen or take a sudsy bath. And it could be the same way for Sadie and her beliefs. Perhaps she comes to think that she doesn't have sufficient evidence for her moral beliefs or for her belief that other people have minds, but we can hardly expect her on that account to cease believing that slavery is wrong or that her friends have feelings just like she does. And, like those beliefs, her belief in God may be central to her interpretation of reality. That is certainly true for many theists. They see the world as created, dependent; they see God's hand in daily events. If Sadie is like that, she simply won't be able to set aside her belief in God as Clifford seems to think she ought. But if she can't, then it's not the case that she ought to—not *morally*, at least. And if she *rationally* ought to do something she can't do, then maintaining her theism while recognizing that she is failing to believe on the basis of sufficient (Cliffordian) evidence may be irrational; but Sadie can take solace in the fact that she is joined in her irrationality by much of the human race.[9]

The second reason for thinking that Clifford's demand is illegitimate has been put forward by Alvin Plantinga and is explained in Clark's essay in this volume. We might get a grip on this problem by noting that reasoning has to start somewhere. Sadie can search for evidence for God's existence, and evidence for the evidence, and evidence for the evidence for the evidence . . . but she eventually has to start with claims that she simply accepts *without* evidence (without *propositional* evidence anyway). And what beliefs can she properly start with? Again, Clifford doesn't say; but Plantinga suggests that he may have in mind the sorts of beliefs commonly accepted as "properly basic" by modern philosophers, namely, beliefs that are incorrigible (such as my belief that I am in pain), self-evident (such obvious beliefs as that all bachelors are unmarried), and evident to the senses (for instance, that there is a water bottle in front of me). According to the theory Plantinga calls *Classical Foundationalism*, we may only start with beliefs of that sort, and all other beliefs must be suitably inferred from them. The problem with this theory is that it seems to have the result that *very* few of our beliefs are based on sufficient evidence. Moreover, as Clark makes clear, the *theory itself* turns out to be unjustified by its own standard (neither properly basic nor legitimately inferred from beliefs that are properly basic) and hence such that it is wrong to believe it. So a proponent of Clifford's evidence requirement will have to state more clearly (and plausibly) what can count as evidence, and do so in such a way that the requirement itself can be sufficiently supported by it.

A similar problem arises if we accept the looser criterion for sufficient evidence that we used to fill in Clifford's demand. According to that criterion, for belief in God to be rational it must be held on grounds sufficient to persuade a truth-seeking agnostic or atheist. But apply that standard to Clifford's assertion that "it is always wrong, everywhere, and for anyone to believe anything on insufficient evidence." That is a contentious assertion, and it is extraordinarily difficult to imagine a case that could be made for the assertion that would persuade those who disagree with it. Clifford's own argument for it seems to amount to a universal generalization derived from only a few examples (like that of the ship owner) together with some exaggerated claims about the supposedly inevitable consequences of failing to fulfill the demand. Perhaps a convincing case could be made for Clifford's demand, but until it is Sadie can surely be excused for not going out of her way to live by it.

The third reason for doubting the requirement is related to the previous two and has been ably developed by Peter van Inwagen.[10] If the evidence requirement rules out belief in God, van Inwagen argues, then it should also rule out belief on any matter of substance in such subjects as philosophy or politics. After all, in both those subject areas people of great intellectual power and accomplishment hold views that are firmly opposed by others with similar gifts. The very fact that they can't persuade those with whom they disagree obviously does not render their believing irrational. Neither does it mean that they have insufficient evidence for their beliefs; again, it depends on what counts as sufficient evidence. Perhaps evidence can be incommunicable, like an insight that a person can't convey to others, an insight that prompts him to accept a premise that his opponents reject. ("Can't they just *see* that this is true?" he may wonder.) But whatever the demand for evidence amounts to—if

there even *is* such a universal demand—it is clear that the Cliffordian standards for sufficient evidence and rational belief are too stringent and should be rejected.

Pondering defeaters. Earlier we mentioned Sadie's personal evidence for her belief in God, including the fact that it *seems* to her that God exists, the fact that when she does what is wrong she can feel God's displeasure, and the fact that she has had one or two religious experiences in which she took herself to be profoundly aware of God's presence and love for her. (In addition, she has the testimony of many of the intellectual giants of Western history and of people whom she knows and loves, such as her parents.) None of this evidence takes the form of an *argument* for God's existence. If it did, the argument would likely be pretty poor—certainly nothing to persuade anyone who doesn't already accept the conclusion. Instead, these experiences simply trigger in her the belief that God exists, or at least they trigger beliefs about God while at the same time firming up her belief that God exists. And maybe that's enough for rational belief, initially (or at least Sadie can justifiably think so, after learning of the problems facing Clifford's demand for evidence). Maybe her belief is, as we might say, innocent until proven guilty.

But when Sadie reflected on the epistemic failings of the members of the Heaven's Gate cult, she didn't note only their lack of positive evidence for their beliefs. She also noticed their failure to be open to reasons for doubting the testimony of their leaders. It seems characteristic of rational people to be open-minded, investigating and responding to objections to their beliefs, not shying away from doubt but dealing with it head-on, willing to alter their beliefs as new considerations dictate. (Clifford's readers may notice that he occasionally engages in hyperbole, but there is something to his concern about those who "nourish belief by suppressing doubts and avoiding investigation."[11]) If Sadie thinks badly of the cultists' failure to reflect on the religious beliefs they happen to hold, she should surely seek to model rationality in that area herself. In particular, she should investigate some of the reasons that have been offered for the conclusion that God does not exist.

This may inspire some anxiety in her, for what if she finds some of these reasons powerful? Well, then, perhaps she needs to seek out evidence for God's existence that offsets those reasons, or else give up her belief in God (or hold it less firmly). In other words, if she finds powerful evidence that God doesn't exist, she can no longer treat her belief in God as innocent; she should instead perceive it as guilty, and she'll need to develop a comprehensive case to exonerate it.

There are several potential defeaters that Sadie may encounter for her belief in God (and probably more that threaten her specific religious beliefs about God's dealings with the world). But suppose she considers the one that historically has been considered especially significant: the problem of evil (the subject of Part Four in this volume). Theists have struggled with the problem of evil for thousands of years—witness the biblical book of Job. Will the existence of evil constitute for Sadie a powerful defeater for her belief in God? Here again I just want to note three things in support of the contention that it need not do so.

First, it is well known that many people who encounter profound suffering in their own lives do not on that account lose their faith in God. In fact, many have their belief in God strengthened by the experience. They find themselves believing firmly, for instance, that a deceased loved one is now in heaven, or they feel what they take to be God's comforting presence in their time of trial.

Of course, the mere fact that many have their faith strengthened through suffering (and the same could happen to Sadie) does not solve whatever philosophical problems evil may pose for theism. So the second point is this. Sadie may learn that theists, while working within their particular religious traditions, have

come up with suggestions about *why* God might allow evil. Sadie may not find these explanations (known as "theodicies") to be comprehensive or completely satisfying, but she may find some of them plausible. They may give *part* of the answer for why God allows evil. At the same time, as many philosophers have pointed out, one could hardly expect to understand *all* of God's reasons, or God's reasons for allowing every evil that occurs. On traditional theism, after all, God is omniscient—somewhat better informed than the rest of us—and by anyone's lights the world is a complicated place. It would hardly be surprising, then, if we weren't able to understand everything about the world, including God's reasons for allowing particular evils. So Sadie might wonder how the fact that this is the way things are is supposed to provide evidence that God does not exist.[12]

Finally, Sadie might encounter the argument that evil disconfirms theism (and hence provides her a defeater) because the evils we see are more probable on atheism than on theism. But it seems that arguments of this sort will cause her trouble only if she considers atheism to be a live option. She could conceivably wonder whether atheism is even *possibly* true, whether it is even possible that this world has come to exist without the guidance of *something*. Of course, she may not have an argument for this intuition; but if she is not at all sure that atheism is even possible, perhaps she can legitimately ask for some reasons for thinking that it is before she is bothered by the supposed fact that the evil we see is more likely on atheism than on theism.

I don't mean for a moment to suggest that I have presented a conclusive response to all so-called arguments from evil. But here it is worth returning to van Inwagen's observation that rational people, even ones well apprised of the arguments surrounding particular issues in politics, philosophy, and religion, still end up disagreeing with each other. So if Sadie, after careful consideration, finds some responses to the problem of evil persuasive but notes that others find them wrong-headed, she need not be deterred. Or if she has doubts that atheism is even possible but realizes that many people believe it's true, she need not on that account change her mind or accept an atheist's terms of the debate.

There are, of course, many other potential defeaters for belief in God.[13] For example, increasingly sophisticated naturalistic explanations of religion contend that religious belief is produced by unreliable cognitive faculties and hence is irrational.[14] Philosophers pondering religious pluralism and the fact that God remains unknown ("hidden") to so many people argue that if God existed, neither phenomenon would be real, and that both are more easily explained on the assumption that God does not exist.[15] Others contend that the whole notion of God is incoherent: it doesn't make any sense. For Sadie, the principles just discussed could play an integral part in her responses to such problems. She may grant that the naturalistic explanations contain elements of truth, but she may doubt their sufficiency and suspect that God must have been involved somehow. And she may not be surprised at her inability to understand why God's existence isn't more obvious to everyone, or her failure to grasp some of the finer points about the divine essence (for example, God's relation to time). In short, it seems that she could be appropriately open-minded when it comes to potential defeaters and yet continue, rationally, to believe that God exists.

Rationality more broadly construed. But suppose Sadie finds herself filled with uncertainty as she investigates arguments surrounding God's existence. She ponders the pros and cons, and doesn't know quite what to think. This is a common occurrence today with controversial matters in politics. There is a veritable blizzard of arguments for different views, each with enthusiastic, high-profile proponents; and many people feel that they don't have the time or ability to follow the arguments and come to their own conclusions. So they find themselves withholding belief on some issues, uncertain and unwilling to commit. Suppose that something similar happens to Sadie with regard to belief in God. The way forward is cloudy, and she isn't sure which way the arguments would lead her if she pursued them. Is there any way for her to emerge from this predicament and become (perhaps again) a rational theist?

It seems to me that at this point the arguments of Blaise Pascal and William James become especially relevant. Both of them appear to recognize that Sadie's reasons for believing can be rational in a significant sense without being rational in the narrower sense that we have been implicitly discussing so far. That is, her reasons for believing (or trying to) need not be directly connected to the *truth* of the proposition that God exists in order for them to be good reasons. Something similar can apply to Sadie's reasons for doing anything at all. Consider, for instance, the activity of going to a movie with her friends. If Sadie were to sit down before choosing to engage in such an activity, and think very deeply about whether she had sufficient reasons to do that rather than some other thing, she would never do much of anything. Often we don't take the time to reason carefully about our specific options before deciding to act, because we could lose out on all sorts of goods if we were to delay. In those circumstances, we do not choose an option on the basis of careful calculation that yields the conclusion that *that* option is clearly the best among the options that we have. Neither do we sit and wait for evidence that will make the right choice clear to us. Instead, we simply choose. We have to do *something* in order to avoid missing out on all sorts of possible goods, and there is no obvious reason that we shouldn't do *that*; but then our choice to do *that*, though not rational in a narrow sense (not based on reasons for preferring that option to the others), is nonetheless rational in some broader sense.

Something similar may be true about belief in God. The arguments for and against God's existence may leave Sadie confused and dispirited, or she may lack the time and know-how to study them in the first place. And yet, she may think, she has got to make a decision. Either God exists or not. And there may be all sorts of reasons to commit one way or the other, in the absence of conclusive evidence about the truth of the matter. For instance, with Pascal, Sadie might consider the possible eternal benefits of belief in God (and the possible nasty consequences of disbelief). Or, more tangibly, she could consider the benefits she may gain in this life if she commits to theism. With theism (conjoined with some fuller account of God's relation to humankind) comes hope, hope about an afterlife, hope about the ultimate defeat of evil, and hope about being loved and cared for by one's Creator even when things are going badly. That seems like an attractive package. Surely Sadie, uncertain on the basis of evidence where the truth lies, could nonetheless choose rationally when she decides to become a theist.

We already know that Clifford has no patience for a choice like this. Indeed, he'd consider her decision, and her subsequent belief, to constitute one egregious sin against humanity. And of course if Sadie really does believe she has such duties to humanity, she should take those seriously. But this contention of Clifford's seems more than a little strained. There may be something noble about refraining from belief in God unless the evidence sweeps one in that direction (Pascal's consequences notwithstanding). But Sadie's decision is profound. What kind of person is she going to be? What kind of life will she try to lead? Is she going to remain skeptical? Non-committal? Is she going to commit to atheism? Or is she going to try to cultivate in herself the belief in God? Pascal certainly considers that the choice to make. "What harm will befall you if you take this side?" he asks.

You will be faithful, humble, grateful, generous, a sincere friend, truthful. Certainly you will not have those poisonous pleasures, glory and luxury [pleasures that may accrue to a non-believer]; but will you not have others? I will tell you that you will thereby gain in this life, and that, at each step you take on this road you will see so great certainty of gain . . . for which you have given nothing.[16]

So suppose that Sadie finds herself without definitive experiences to point her to God, puzzled by the arguments on both sides of the debate, and quite certain that further study is not going to settle the matter for her. And yet she has to choose what sort of life she wants to lead and what kind of person she wants to be. If she then considers the hoped-for consequences of committing to theism (and some associated religion) and decides to do so, why can't that be a perfectly rational thing for her to do?

Reconciling reason and religious belief. Many people, even after finding themselves with experiences that strongly incline them to believe that God exists, deciding that supposed defeaters lack any force, or recognizing other non-evidential reasons for belief, are nonetheless sometimes plagued by doubts, both about theism itself and about the rationality of believing it. Those latter doubts may emerge in part from subconscious clinging to overly stringent standards of evidence and rationality. But another concern goes back to movements like the Heaven's Gate cult: it appears possible that if Sadie's theistic beliefs could be rational in some of the ways mentioned above, a cultist's beliefs could be rational as well. And if so, it seems our standards of rationality have dropped too far and must be revisited so that the significance of rational belief might be recovered.

Or maybe not. One thing that seems clear from recent philosophical reflection on the notion of rationality is that what is rational for one person to believe may not be rational for another.[17] What is rational is determined, at least in part, by what a person already believes, and there is no set of foundational beliefs from which every rational person must start. All sorts of factors—for example, a person's upbringing, psychological constitution, experiences, the testimony of others—play a role in what a person actually believes and what it is rational for him to believe. This doesn't mean that anything goes, that there is no point in trying to change people's minds, that there is no truth on matters about which people disagree, or that some people's religious beliefs, even if quite properly inferred from the beliefs they start out with, are not in fact ultimately due to serious cognitive problems. It also doesn't mean that people are never morally blameworthy for believing as they do. Perhaps when a person's beliefs can be traced to selfish motives, to consciously setting aside moral concerns, or to character flaws for which he is culpable, he can be properly blamed for holding them. But we may have difficulty determining when a person's beliefs meet those conditions, and it appears quite possible that some people's beliefs that we consider off base actually *don't* meet them.

It seems, then, that Sadie's belief in God can be rational. And so can many other beliefs. Perhaps the moral of this story is that the issue of the rationality of religious belief, or of any belief whatever, is in the end not the most important issue we face. What may be more important is the question of how we ought to deal with people with whom we rationally disagree.

Notes

1. Information on Heaven's Gate can be found at https://en.wikipedia.org/wiki/Heaven's _Gate_(religious_group).

2. See Clifford's "The Ethics of Belief," Chapter 9 in this volume.

3. "The Ethics of Belief," Chapter 9 in this volume.

4. Thorough discussion of these issues can be found in Chapter 13.

5. For one such account, see David Sloan Wilson's book, *Darwin's Cathedral* (Chicago: U of Chicago P, 2002); see also Chapter 13 and the "critiques of God" in Part Three of this volume.

6. "Without Evidence or Argument," Chapter 10 in this volume.

7. See Chapter 2 in this volume.

8. So called "cumulative case" arguments may be an exception to this rule. It may be that while some of the arguments taken individually are subject to doubt, together they provide evidence sufficient for firm conviction. Readers are invited to pursue this possibility themselves (see Chapter 7 in this volume).

9. Maybe if Sadie is unable to discard immediately her belief in God, she ought to take steps to try to rid herself of the belief over the long haul. But (a) she may not have that sort of control either and (b) doing that would also take considerable effort and be disruptive of her life, especially if she tries to do the same with all the other beliefs she holds that aren't supported by Cliffordian evidence. (And if her moral beliefs aren't so supported, one wonders what sort of negative consequences the attempt to unload those might have on her.)

For more on the issue of control we have over our beliefs, see William Alston's important essay, "The Deontological Conception of Epistemic Justification," in his *Epistemic Justification: Essays in the Theory of Knowledge* (Ithaca, NY: Cornell UP, 1989), pp. 115–52.

10. See "Quam Dilecta" in *God and the Philosophers*, ed. Thomas V. Morris (New York: Oxford UP, 1994), pp. 31–60. See also his "Is it Wrong Everywhere, Always, and for Anyone to Believe Anything on Insufficient Evidence?" at http://comp.uark.edu/~senor /wrong.html. One of van Inwagen's concerns is that the objection that religious belief is held on insufficient evidence is hardly ever applied in turn to beliefs in politics or philosophy, a fact that he believes indicates bias on the part of many of the objection's more vocal proponents.

11. "The Ethics of Belief," Chapter 9 in this volume.

12. For much more detail, see the section in this volume on the problem of evil, Part Four. For arguments that apparently pointless evils do not constitute evidence that God does not exist, see also Stephen Wykstra, "The Humean Obstacle to Evidential Arguments from Suffering," in *The Problem of Evil*, ed. Marilyn McCord Adams and Robert Merrihew Adams (New York: Oxford, 1990), pp. 138–60, and Michael Bergmann and Daniel Howard-Snyder, "Evil Does Not Make Atheism More Reasonable than Theism," in *Contemporary Debates in Philosophy of Religion*, ed. Michael Peterson and Raymond VanArragon (Oxford: Blackwell Publishing, 2004), pp. 13–25.

13. For consideration of potential defeaters for belief in God and for specifically Christian belief, see Alvin Plantinga, *Warranted Christian Belief* (New York: Oxford UP, 2000), chapters 11 to 14.

14. See Chapter 13 in this volume.

15. See, for instance, J.L. Schellenberg, *The Hiddenness Argument: Philosophy's New Challenge to Belief in God* (New York: Oxford UP, 2015).

16. Blaise Pascal, "The Wager," in this volume, Chapter 12. For a defense of Pascal's Wager, see William Lycan and George Schlesinger, "You Bet Your Life," reprinted in R. Douglas Geivett and Brendan Sweetman, eds., *Contemporary Perspectives on Religious Epistemology* (New York: Oxford, 1993), pp. 270–82.

17. For an important discussion of the notion of rationality, and of different senses of that term, see Plantinga's *Warranted Christian Belief*, Chapter 4. Much of what I say here applies to what he calls "internal" rationality which involves, roughly, forming beliefs appropriately in response to experience, reasoning properly from those beliefs, and maintaining a more or less coherent belief system. As an extreme example, inspired by Descartes, Plantinga considers a person who due to psychosis believes that his head is made of earthenware (it just seems obvious to him) and then infers from this that he ought not to play football (p. 112). This unfortunate person's beliefs, given his experiences, are internally rational, even though they are false and result from serious cognitive malfunction.

Discussion

1. What reasons does VanArragon give for
    doubting Clifford's demand for evidence?
    What do you think of the demand? Is it *always*
    wrong to believe on insufficient evidence? Is it
    sometimes wrong? When do you need evidence
    for belief, and why?

2. Why does VanArragon think it may be
    rational to commit to theism on pragmatic
    grounds? What do you think? Might it be
    rational to commit to atheism for similar
    reasons?

3. Do you think a member of the Heaven's Gate
    cult could reconcile reason with his religious
    beliefs in the same way that Sadie could with
    hers? Why or why not?

Part Two

Suggestions for Further Study

Atran, Scott. *In Gods We Trust: The Evolutionary Landscape of Religion.* Oxford UP, 2002.

Barrett, Justin. *Why Would Anyone Believe in God?* Lanham: AltaMira P, 2004.

Bulbulia, Joseph, ed. *The Evolution of Religion: Studies, Theories, & Critiques.* Santa Margarita, CA: Collins Foundation P, 2008.

Chignell, Andrew, and Andrew Dole, eds. *God and the Ethics of Belief: New Essays in the Philosophy of Religion.* Cambridge: Cambridge UP, 2005.

Clark, Kelly James. *Return to Reason.* Grand Rapids, MI: Eerdmans, 1991.

Dougherty, Trent. *Evidentialism and Its Discontents.* Oxford UP, 2011.

Helm, Paul, ed. *Faith and Reason.* Oxford UP, 1999.

Kenny, Anthony. *What Is Faith?* Oxford: Oxford UP, 1992.

Morris, Thomas. *Making Sense of It All: Pascal and the Meaning of Life.* Grand Rapids, MI: Eerdmans, 1992.

Penelhum, Terence. *Reason and Religious Faith.* Boulder, CO: Westview P, 1995.

Penelhum, Terence, ed. *Faith.* New York: Macmillan, 1989.

Phillips, D.Z. *Faith after Foundationalism.* London: Routledge, 1988.

Plantinga, Alvin, and Nicholas Wolterstorff. *Faith and Rationality.* Notre Dame: U of Notre Dame P, 1983.

Sessions, William Lad. *The Concept of Faith: A Philosophical Investigation.* Ithaca: Cornell UP, 1994.

Sudduth, Michael. *The Reformed Objection to Natural Theology.* Burlington, VT: Ashgate, 2009.

Swinburne, Richard. *Faith and Reason.* Oxford: Oxford UP, 1981.

Wainwright, William. *Reasons and the Heart: A Prolegomenon to a Critique of Passional Reasons.* Ithaca: Cornell UP, 1995.

Critiques of God

Part Three

Introduction

Introduction. The title of this section is, of course, an exaggeration. If there is a God, a supremely perfect being, then he is beyond reproach. He is also, according to most Western religions, omnipotent, sovereign, and righteous. So God stands above us ordering and judging our lives. God as so conceived is, therefore, a threat. So there is a reason to revolt against the moral tyranny and domineering sovereignty of God. Within the Bible itself passionate rebels like Job have questioned God's character and authority: "What are human beings that you make so much of them, that you set your mind on them, visit them every morning, test them every moment? . . . Why have you made me your target?" (Job 7:17–20). God is a threat to human autonomy. In Friedrich Nietzsche's *Thus Spoke Zarathustra*, Zarathustra exclaims: "*If* there were gods, how could I endure not to be a god! Hence there are no gods."[1] And Jean-Paul Sartre seems to reject belief in God because of sovereignty's overpowering threat to human freedom.[2] So there is a rich tradition of critiques of God.

The essays in this section are critiques of a rather different sort. Each of the thinkers in this section assumes at the outset that God does not exist. Perhaps there is insufficient evidence to reasonably believe in God or perhaps there is evidence (say evil or science) but it is unfavourable to God's existence. In the nineteenth century, as science progressed, the explanatory need for God diminished. Natural processes were considered sufficient to account for the physical world. There was less and less need to call on God to explain natural phenomena. God was considered intellectually unnecessary. As belief in God declined among intellectuals, explanations of religious belief were increasingly naturalistic and suspicious. By "naturalistic" I mean without reference to any supernatural forces or entities. And by "suspicious" I mean skeptical of the noble or altruistic motives often (self-) attributed to religious believers.

If God is intellectually superfluous, these thinkers ask (at least) two questions: Given that God does not exist, how could belief in God have become so deeply entrenched in Western thought? What is the value or, better, disvalue of belief in God? Their criticism, therefore, is not so much of God as of belief in God.

The hermeneutics of suspicion. Marx was an ethnic Jew in a Christian family. He abandoned any religious beliefs and made atheism the foundation of his philosophy. Marx's starting point is the nineteenth-century working conditions of labourers. Due in part to the industrial revolution, workers were exploited with menial labour, low wages, and long hours. Children often worked fifteen to eighteen hours per day and were given just enough food to sustain their existence so that they could continue working. Workers were treated as a commodity, according to the law of supply and demand: easily replaced workers (i.e., economically unvaluable people) could be paid little. Behind this exploitation, Marx saw the ignoble forces of religion.

Through the influence of Feuerbach, Marx came to believe that human beings create religion. Religion is, Marx contends, the opium of the masses: it is a pain-killer which treats the symptoms while ignoring the disease—it dulls the pain of exploitation but it fails to redress the cause of pain and suffering. Religion arises because of legitimate needs but offers a false and illusory remedy. Marx also rejects religious belief because of the social atrocities that have been perpetrated in the name of God.

Friedrich Nietzsche was the son of a Lutheran pastor. He was educated in classics and, early on, theology. While studying at university, he moved decisively away from Christianity. Nietzsche's philosophy begins, first and foremost, with the death of God. Western society, nonetheless, continued to accept the trappings of Judeo-Christian morality without its metaphysical and theological underpinnings. With the foundation of theism dislodged, Nietzsche believed, Judeo-Christian morality would eventually crumble. If there is no God, then these questions arise: where do Christianity, morality, and guilt come from? What, if not God, is the source of good and evil? In answering these questions, Nietzsche not only looks at values themselves, but he wants to know the value behind the value. What weight, authority, or power do values have? Are they life-affirming or life-denying? Are they destructive of what is most fundamentally human or are they creative and satisfying?

Nietzsche's work is a *genealogy* of morals, what he sometimes calls a "history of morals"—how do moralities arise, become approved and maintain their power? How is the history forgotten when moralities are charged with an allegedly transhistorical or transcendental legitimation and power? Nietzsche believes that there are two basic moralities: the Herd and Master Moralities. The Herd or Slave Morality is that of the weak, the feeble, and the enslaved. Herd morality arose in the priestly cultures which denied desire

and endorsed the weaknesses of the priest. The priestly morality developed out of fear and hatred of the master class. The impotent, unable to conquer their more worthy and physically powerful foes, sought "spiritual revenge." They made everything that is opposed to the master class "good." Aligning God with their cause, they endorsed the eternal damnation of everyone who violated their moral standards. Eternal damnation, the ultimate revenge, shows that Judeo-Christian morality is rooted not in love but in hatred and vengefulness.

Freud, like Nietzsche, looks for the value behind religious belief. Standing behind every human action is our natural narcissism—the drive for pleasure. Since the unfettered satisfaction of desires would create a chaos for human beings, we all join together for a measure of peace and security. But even within civilization our peace and security are threatened, this time by nature. By projecting human qualities and person-like entities onto the forces of nature, we attempt to "civilize" nature; we entreat those various powers as we might entreat various persons who would seek to wreak havoc.

The ultimate projection of human properties onto nature is the belief that the ultimate power is like a father. We wish God into existence—religious belief as "wish-fulfillment"—and he hears our prayers: he can tame nature, help us accept our fate, and reward us for our sufferings. Narcissism creates gods: in God all of our desires are satisfied.

Reflections. Westphal's essay mines Marx, Nietzsche, and Freud for insights that these thinkers offer for religious believers. The atheism of Marx, Nietzsche, and Freud can be called "atheism of suspicion" in contrast to "evidential atheism." For while the latter focuses on the truth of religious beliefs, the former inquires into their function. It asks, in other words, what motives lead to belief and what practices are compatible with and authorized by religious belief. The primary response of religious philosophers should not be to refute these analyses, since they are all too often true and, moreover, very much of the same sort as found in the teachings of Jesus and the prophets. Rather, Westphal argues, our primary response should be to show the religious community how even the truth can become an instrument of self-interest. In this way the atheism of suspicion can provide helpful conceptual tools for personal and corporate self-examination.

Notes

1. *Thus Spoke Zarathustra*, Walter Kaufmann, ed. (New York: Penguin Books, 1954), p. 86.

2. I draw this inference from Sartre's play "The Flies," from *No Exit and Three Other Plays* (New York: Alfred A. Knopf, 1948).

Chapter 15
The Hermeneutics of Suspicion

THE OPIUM OF THE MASSES

KARL MARX*

Man makes religion. For Germany *the criticism of religion* is in the main complete, and criticism of religion is the premise of all criticism.

The *profane* existence of error is discredited after its heavenly *oratio pro aris et focis* [prayer for earth and home] has been disproved. Man, who looked for a superhuman being in the fantastic reality of heaven and found nothing there but the reflection of himself, will no longer be disposed to find but the semblance of himself, only an inhuman being, where he seeks and must seek his true reality.

The basis of irreligious criticism is: *Man makes religion*, religion does not make man. Religion is the self-consciousness and self-esteem of man who has either not yet found himself or has already lost himself again. But man is no abstract being encamped outside the world. Man is the world of man, the state, society. This state, this society, produce religion, an inverted world-consciousness, because they are an inverted world. Religion is the general theory of that world, its encyclopaedic compendium, its logic in a popular form, its spiritualistic *point d'honneur*, its enthusiasm, its moral sanction, its solemn complement, its universal source of consolation and justification. It is the *fantastic realisation* of the human essence because

the human essence has no true reality. The struggle against religion is therefore indirectly a fight against the world of which religion is the spiritual aroma.

The opium of the masses. Religious distress is at the same time the *expression* of real distress and also the *protest* against real distress. Religion is the sigh of the oppressed creature, the heart of a heartless world, just as it is the spirit of spiritless conditions. It is the *opium* of the people.

To abolish religion as the *illusory* happiness of the people is to demand their *real* happiness. The demand to give up illusions about the existing state of affairs is *the demand to give up a state of affairs which needs illusions*. The criticism of religion is therefore in *embryo the criticism of the vale of tears*, the halo of which is religion.

Criticism has torn up the imaginary flowers from the chain not so that man shall wear the unadorned, bleak chain but so that he will shake off the chain and pluck the living flower. The criticism of religion disillusions man to make him think and act and shape his reality like a man who has been disillusioned and has come to reason, so that he will revolve round himself and therefore round his true sun. Religion is only the illusory sun which revolves round man as long as he does not revolve round himself.

The task of history, therefore, once the *world beyond the truth* has disappeared, is to establish *the truth of this world*. The immediate task of philosophy, which is at the service of history, once the *holy form* of human self-estrangement has been unmasked, is to unmask self-estrangement in its unholy forms. Thus the criticism of heaven turns into the criticism of the earth, the

---

* Karl Marx (1818–83) was born in Prussia but did most of his writing in exile in England.

criticism of religion into the criticism of law and the criticism of theology into the criticism of politics.

Critique of Christian morality. The social principles of Christianity have now had eighteen hundred years to develop and need no further development by Prussian consistorial councillors.

The social principles of Christianity justified the slavery of Antiquity, glorified the serfdom of the Middle Ages and equally know, when necessary, how to defend the oppression of the proletariat, although they make a pitiful face over it.

The social principles of Christianity preach the necessity of a ruling and an oppressed class, and all they have for the latter is the pious wish the former will be charitable.

The social principles of Christianity transfer the consistorial councillors' adjustment of all infamies to heaven and thus justify the further existence of those infamies on earth.

The social principles of Christianity declare all vile acts of the oppressors against the oppressed to be either the just punishment of original sin and other sins or trials that the Lord in his infinite wisdom imposes on those redeemed.

The social principles of Christianity preach cowardice, self-contempt, abasement, submission, dejection, in a word all the qualities of the *canaille* [rabble]; and the proletariat, not wishing to be treated as *canaille*, needs its courage, its self-feeling, its pride and its sense of independence more than its bread.

The social principles of Christianity are sneakish and the proletariat is revolutionary.

So much for the social principles of Christianity.

Discussion

1. Has the net effect of religious belief on history been positive or negative? Defend your answer.

2. Is it possible for religions that are committed to the heavenly realm to provide a stimulus for this worldly social change?

RELIGION AS RESENTMENT

FRIEDRICH NIETZSCHE*

Preface, Section 3

Having a kind of scrupulousness peculiar to myself, which I do not readily acknowledge—inasmuch as it has reference to *morality*, to all that so far was known on earth, and celebrated as morality—a scrupulousness which arose in my life so prematurely, so uncalled-for, so irresistibly, so in contradiction to surroundings, age, precedent and ancestry, that I should almost be justified in calling it my *A priori*,—my curiosity as well as my suspicions had to be confronted, at an early date, by the question of *what origin* really are our Good and Evil? ...

Fortunately, I learned betimes to separate theological from moral prejudices and to seek no longer *behind* the world for the origin of evil. A little historical and philological schooling, together with an inborn and delicate sense regarding psychological questions, changed my problem in a very short time into that other one: under what circumstances and conditions did man invent those valuations Good and Evil? *and what is their own specific value?* Did they retard or further human progress so far? Are they a sign of need, of impoverishment, of degeneration of life? Or is the reverse the case, do they point to the fullness, the strength, the will of life, its courage, its confidence, its future? ...

Preface, Section 6

The problem of the *value* of sympathy and morality of sympathy (I am an opponent of shameful modern effeminacy of sentiment) seems, at first sight, to be something isolated,—a single interrogation mark; but he who will pause here and will *learn* to question

here, will fare even as I have fared: a vast, new prospect reveals itself to him, a possibility seizes upon him like some giddiness; every kind of distrust, suspicion, fear springs up; the faith in morality, in all morality, is shaken,—and finally, a new demand makes itself felt. Let us pronounce this *new demand*: we stand in need of a criticism of moral values; *the value of these values is first of all itself to be put in question*—and to this end a knowledge is necessary of the conditions and circumstances from which they grew and under which they developed and shifted in meaning (morality as effect, as symptom, as mask, as tartuffism [religious hypocrisy], as disease, as misunderstanding; but also, morality as cause, as remedy, as stimulant, as impediment, as poison),—a knowledge which hitherto was not existent, nay, not even desired. The *value* of these "values" was taken for granted, as a matter of fact, as being beyond all ... question. Never until now was there the least doubt or hesitation, to set down "the good man" as of higher value than "the evil man,"—of higher value in the sense of furtherance, utility, prosperity as regards *man* in general (the future of man included). What if the reverse were true? What if in the "good one" also a symptom of decline were contained, and a danger, a seduction, a poison, a narcotic by which the present might live *at the expense of the future*? Perhaps more comfortably, less dangerously, but also in humbler style,—more meanly?

So that just morality were to blame, if a *highest mightiness and splendour* of the type of man—possible in itself—were never attained? And that, therefore, morality itself would be the danger of dangers?

First Essay, Section 2

All due deference, therefore, to the good spirits who may hold sway in these historians of morality! But I am sorry to say that they are certainly lacking in the *historical spirit*, that they have been, in fact, deserted by all the good spirits of history itself. They think, each and every one, according to an old usage of philosophers,

---

* Friedrich Nietzsche (1844–1900), a German philosopher who was trained in classical philology, taught briefly at the University of Basel and then devoted his life to writing.

essentially unhistorically; no doubt whatever! The botchery of their genealogy of morals becomes manifest right at the outset in the determination of the origin, of the concept and judgment "good." "Unselfish actions"—such is their decree—, "were originally praised and denominated 'good' by those to whom they were manifested, i.e., those to whom they were *useful*; afterwards, this origin of praise was *forgotten*, and unselfish actions, since they were always *accustomed* to be praised as good, were as a matter of course also felt as such,—as if, in themselves, they were something good." We see at once that this first derivation contains all the typical traits of English psychological idiosyncrasy,— we have "utility," "forgetting," "custom," and last of all "error," and all this as the basis of a valuation which hitherto formed the pride of superior man as being a kind of prerogative of man in general. This pride *must* be humbled, this valuation—devalued. Did they succeed in this?

Now in the first place it is clear to me, that the true and primitive home of the concept "good" was sought for and posited at the wrong place: the judgment "good" was *not* invented by those to whom goodness was shown! On the contrary, the "good," i.e., the noble, the powerful, the higher-situated, the high-minded, felt and regarded themselves and their acting as of first rank, in contradistinction to everything low, low-minded, mean and vulgar. Out of this *pathos of distance* they took for themselves the right of creating values, of coining names for these values. What had they to do with utility! In the case of such a spontaneous manifestation and ardent ebullition of highest rank-regulating and rank-differentiating valuations, the point-of-view of utility is as distant and out of place as possible; for in such things the feelings have arrived at a point diametrically opposite to that low degree of heat which is presupposed by every kind of arithmetical prudence, every utilitarian calculation,—and not momentarily, not for a single, exceptional hour, but permanently. The pathos of nobility and distance, as I

said, the lasting and dominating, the integral and fundamental feeling of a higher dominating kind of man in contradistinction to a lower kind, to a "below"— *such* is the origin of the antithesis "good" and "bad." (The right of masters to confer names goes so far that we might venture to regard the origin of language itself as a manifestation of power on the part of rulers. They say: "This *is* such and such," they seal every thing and every happening with a sound, and by this act take it, as it were, into possession.) It follows from this derivation that the word "good" has *not* necessarily any connection with unselfish actions, as the superstition of these genealogists of morals would have it. On the contrary, it is only when a *decline* of aristocratic valuations sets in, that this antithesis "selfish" and "unselfish" forces itself with constantly increasing vividness upon the conscience of man,—it is, if I may express myself in my own way, the *herding instinct* which by means of this antithesis succeeds at last in finding expression (and in coining words). And even after this event, a long time elapses before this instinct prevails to such an extent that the moral valuation makes halt at and actually sticks to this antithesis. . . .

First Essay, Section 7
The reader will have conjectured by this time, how readily the priestly manner of valuation will branch off from that of the chivalric-aristocratic caste and *develop* into the antithesis of it; which is especially prone to happen whenever the priest and the warrior-caste jealously oppose each other and fail to come to an agreement as to the prize. The chivalric-aristocratic valuations presuppose a powerful corporality, a vigorous, exuberant, ever-extravagant health, and all that is necessary for its preservation,—war, adventure, hunting, dancing, sports, and in general, all that involves strong, free and cheerful activity. The priestly aristocratic valuation has—as we have seen—other presuppositions: so much the worse it fares in case of war! The priests are, as is well known, the *worst enemies*—and

why? Because they are the most impotent. From impotence in their case hatred grows into forms immense and dismal, the most spiritual and most poisonous forms. The greatest haters in history were, at all times, priests; and they were also the haters with the most *esprit*. Indeed, compared with the *esprit* of priestly vindictiveness, all the remaining intelligence is scarcely worth consideration. Human history would be an extremely stupid affair, but for the *esprit* brought into it by the impotent. Let us at once consider the greatest instance! All that has ever been accomplished on earth against the "noble," the "powerful," the "lords," the "mighty" is not worth speaking of, when compared with that which *the Jews* have done against them; the Jews, that priestly people, which finally succeeded in procuring satisfaction for itself from its enemies and conquerors only by a transvaluation of their values, i.e., an act of the keenest, *most spiritual vengeance*. Thus only it befitted a priestly people—the people of the most powerfully suppressed, priestly vindictiveness. It was the Jews who, with most frightfully consistent logic, dared to subvert the aristocratic equation of values (good = noble = powerful = beautiful = happy = beloved of God), and who, with the teeth of the profoundest hatred (the hatred of impotency), clung to their own valuation: "The wretched alone are the good; the poor, the impotent, the lowly alone are the good; only the sufferers, the needy, the sick, the ugly are pious; only they are godly; them alone blessedness awaits;—but ye, ye, the proud and potent, ye are for aye and evermore the wicked, the cruel, the lustful, the insatiable, the godless; ye will also be, to all eternity, the unblessed, the cursed and the damned!"

It is known *who* has been the inheritor of this Jewish transvaluation.

In regard to the enormous initiative fatal, beyond all measure, which the Jews gave by this most fundamental declaration of war, I refer to the proposition which elsewhere presented itself to me (*Beyond Good and Evil*, aph. 195)—namely, that with the Jews *the*

slave-revolt in morality begins: that revolt, which has a history of two thousand years behind it, and which today is only removed from our vision because it—has been victorious.

First Essay, Section 8

But this ye do not understand? Ye are blind to something which needed two thousand years ere it came to be triumphant? There is nothing in it surprising to me: all *long* things are hard to see, hard to survey. But *this* is the event: from the trunk of that tree of revenge and hatred, Jewish hatred—the deepest and sublimest hatred, i.e., a hatred which creates ideals and transforms values, and which never had its like upon earth—something equally incomparable grew up, a *new love*, the deepest and sublimest kind of love:—and, indeed, from what other trunk could it have grown?

Quite wrong it is, however, to suppose, that this love grew up as the true negation of that thirst of vengeance, as the antithesis of the Jewish hatred! No, the reverse is true! This love grew out of this trunk, as its crown,—as the crown of triumph, which spread its foliage ever farther and wider in clearest brightness and fullness of sunshine, and which with the same vitality strove upwards, as it were, in the realm of light and elevation and towards the goals of that hatred, towards victory, spoils, and seduction, with which the roots of that hatred penetrated ever more and more profoundly and eagerly into everything deep and evil. This Jesus of Nazareth, as the personified gospel of love, this saviour bringing blessedness and victory unto the poor, the sick, the sinners—did he not represent seduction in its most awful and irresistible form—the seduction and by-way to those same *Jewish* values and new ideals? Has not Israel, even by the round-about-way of this "redeemer," this seeming adversary and destroyer of Israel, attained the last goal of its sublime vindictiveness? Does it not belong to the secret black-art of truly *grand* politics of vengeance, of a vengeance far-seeing, underground, slowly-gripping and forereckoning, that Israel itself should deny and crucify before all the world the proper tool of its vengeance, as though it were something deadly inimical,—so that "all the world," namely all enemies of Israel, might quite unhesitatingly bite at this bait? And could, on the other hand, any still *more dangerous* bait be imagined, even with the utmost refinement of spirit? Could we conceive anything which, in influence seducing, intoxicating, narcotising, corrupting, might equal that symbol of the "sacred cross," that awful paradox of a "God on the cross," that mystery of an unfathomable, ultimate, extremest cruelty and self-crucifixion of God *for the salvation of man?*

Thus much is certain, that *sub hoc signo* [under this sign] Israel, with its vengeance and transvaluation of all values, has so far again and again triumphed over all other ideals, over all *nobler* ideals.

First Essay, Section 9

But, Sir, why still speak of *nobler* ideals? Let us submit to the facts: the folk have conquered—or the "slaves," or the "mob," or the "herd" or—call it what you will! If this has come about through the Jews, good! then never a people had a more world-historic mission. The "lords" are done away with; the morality of the common man has triumphed. This victory may at the same time be regarded as an act of blood-poisoning (it has jumbled the races together)—I shall not object. But, beyond a doubt, the intoxication *did succeed.* The redemption of mankind (from "the lords," to wit) is making excellent headway; everything judaïses, christianises or vulgarises in full view. . . .

First Essay, Section 10

The slave-revolt in morality begins by *resentment* itself becoming creative and giving birth to values—the *resentment* of such beings, as real reaction, the reaction of deeds, is impossible to, and as nothing but an imaginary vengeance will serve to indemnify. Whereas, on the one hand, all noble morality takes its rise from a

triumphant Yea-saying to one's self, slave-morality will, on the other hand, from the very beginning, say No to something "exterior," "different," "not—self "; *this* No being its creative deed. This reversion of the value-positing eye—this *necessary* glance outwards instead of backwards upon itself—is part of *resentment.* Slave-morality, in order to arise, needs, in the first place, an opposite and outer world; it needs, physiologically speaking, external irritants, in order to act at all;—its action is, throughout, reaction.

The reverse is true in the case of noble valuation. It acts and grows spontaneously. It only seeks for its antithesis in order to say, still more thankfully, still more rejoicingly, Yea to itself. Its negative concept "low," "mean," "bad," is merely a late-born and pale after-image in comparison with the positive fundamental concept of the noble valuation which is thoroughly saturated with life and passion, and says: "We, the noble, we, the good, we, the fair, we, the happy!". . .

First Essay, Section 13

But to revert to our theme: the problem of the *other* origin of "good," of "good" as conceived by the man of resentment, calls for its settlement.—That the lambs should bear a grudge to the big birds of prey, is nowise strange; but this is no reason for blaming the big birds of prey for picking up small lambs. And if the lambs say among themselves: "These rapacious birds are wicked; and he who is as little as possible of a bird of prey, but rather the opposite, i.e., a lamb—should not he be good?" we cannot find fault with the establishment of such an ideal, though the birds of prey may make rather mocking eyes and say: "*We* do not bear at all a grudge to them, these good lambs, we even love them. Nothing is more delicious than a tender lamb." To demand of strength, that it should *not* manifest itself as strength, that it should *not* be a will to overpower, to subdue, to become master of, that it should *not* be a thirst for enemies, resistance, and triumphs, is as absurd as to demand of weakness that it should manifest itself as strength. . . . No wonder, therefore, if the suppressed and secretly glowing emotions, hatred and revenge, avail themselves of this belief and, in fact, support no belief with so much zeal as this, that the *strong are free* to be weak, and that a rapacious bird can, if it will, be a lamb. For in this way they appropriate in their minds the right of *imputing* to the bird of prey the fact that it is rapacious.

If the suppressed, the down-trodden and the wronged, prompted by the craft of impotence, say to themselves: "Let us be different from the bad, let us be good! and good are all those who wrong no one, who never violate, who never attack, who never retaliate, who entrust revenge to God, who, like us, live aloof from the world, who avoid all contact with evil, and who, altogether, demand little of life, as we do, the patient, the humble, the just"—this means, viewed coolly and unprejudicially, no more than: "We, the weak, are,—it is a fact—weak; it is well for us not to do anything, *for which we are not strong enough*." But this stern matter of fact, this meanest kind of prudence, shared even by insects (which occasionally simulate death, in order not to do "too much" in case of great danger), has, thanks to the trickery and self-imposition of impotence, clothed itself in the apparel of renouncing, silent, abiding virtue, as if the weakness of the weak one itself, i.e., presumably his *being*, his action, his entire, unavoidable, inseparable reality— were a voluntary performance, a thing self-willed, self-chosen, a *deed*, a *desert*. To this kind of man, the *necessity* of the belief in an indifferent, free-willed "subject" is prompted by the instinct of self-preservation, self-assertion,—an instinct by which every falsehood uses to sanctify itself. The subject (or, speaking more popularly, the *soul*) has perhaps been, so far, the best religious tenet on earth, even for the reason that it made possible for the majority of mortals, the weak and oppressed of every description, that sublime self-defraudation of interpreting weakness itself as freedom, the fact of their being thus and thus as a *desert*.

First Essay, Section 14

Will someone look down and into the secret of the way in which *ideals are manufactured* on earth? Who has the courage to do so? Up! Here the view into this dark workshop is open. Yet a moment, my good Sir Pry and Break-neck! Your eye must first get accustomed to this false and fickle light.

So! Enough! Now speak! What is going on below? Speak out, what you see, man of most dangerous curiosity! Now I am the listener.—

"I see nothing, I hear the more. It is a cautious, knavish, suppressed mumbling and muttering together in every nook and corner. It seems to me they lie. A sugared mildness cleaves to every sound. Weakness is to be falsified into *desert*, no doubt whatever—it is as you said."—

Go on!

"And impotence which requiteth not is falsified into 'goodness'; timorous meanness into 'humility'; submission to those whom one hates into 'obedience' (namely to one who they say commands this obedience; they call him God). The inoffensiveness of the 'weak one,' cowardice itself, in which he is rich, his standing at the door, his unavoidable necessity of waiting comes here by good names, such as 'patience'; they even call it *the cardinal virtue*. Not-to-be-able-to-take-revenge is called not-to-will-revenge, perhaps even forgiveness ('for *they* know not what they do; we alone know what *they* do'). They also talk of 'love for their enemies'—and sweat in doing so."

On!

"They are wretched, no doubt, all these mumblers and underground forgers, though warmly seated together. But they tell me that their wretchedness is a selection and distinction from God, that the dogs which are liked most are whipped, that their misery may, perhaps, also be a preparation, a trial, a schooling perhaps even more—something which at some time to come will be requited and paid back with immense interest in gold, no! in happiness. This they call blessedness."

On!

"Now they will have me understand, that not only they are better than the mighty, the lords of the earth, whose spittle they must lick (*not* from fear, no, not at all from fear! but because God commands to have respect for all authority)—that not only they *are* better, but are also, or certainly will be, 'better off' one day. But enough! enough! I cannot stand it any longer. Bad air! Bad air! This work-shop in which *ideals are manufactured*—methinks, it stinks from lying all over."

No! Yet a moment! You have not yet said anything of the masterpiece of these necromancers, who from every black prepare white, milk and innocence. Did you notice what the very acme of their *raffinement* [refinement] is,—their keenest, finest, subtlest, falsest artist manipulation? Mark well! These cellar-animals filled with hatred and revenge—what is it they are making just out of hatred and revenge? Have you ever heard such words? Would you believe, if trusting merely their words, that you are all among beings of resentment?

"I perceive, once again I open my ears (ah! ah! ah! and *shut* my nose). Now only I hear, what they were saying so often: 'We, the good, *we are the just*.' What they ask for, they do not call retribution, but 'the triumph of *justice*'; what they hate, is not their enemy, no! they hate '*wrong-doing*,' and 'ungodliness.' What they believe in, and hope for, is not the hope of revenge, the drunkenness of sweet revenge (—sweeter than honey, already Homer called it), but 'the victory of God, the just God, over the godless.' What remains for them to love on earth, is not their brethren in hatred, but their 'brethren in love,' as they say,—all the good and the just on earth."

And how do they call that which serves them as consolation in all the sufferings of life—their phantasmagoria of an anticipated future blessedness?

"What? Hear I right? They call it 'the final judgment,' the coming of *their* kingdom, of the 'kingdom of God!' *Meanwhile* they live 'in faith, in love, in hope.'"

Enough! Enough!

Discussion

1. Nietzsche is searching for the value behind values. Consider your moral values: what motives could lead you to cherish them? How is it possible for unrecognized motives to encourage the sustenance of these values?

2. If morality is not God-given, then it must have come from somewhere else. What is Nietzsche's explanation of the origin of Christian values? How satisfying is his explanation?

3. Nietzsche is often criticized for being nihilistic (denying all values). But he endorses knightly-aristocratic values. What are these values and what is the value behind these values?

THE FUTURE OF AN ILLUSION

SIGMUND FREUD*

Wherein lies the special value of religious ideas?

We have discussed the hostility toward culture engendered by the pressure culture exerts and the renunciations of drives it demands. If one imagines its prohibitions lifted—thus one may now take any woman one wishes as sexual object; may without hesitation kill one's rival in love, or anyone else standing in the way; may take anything belonging to another person without asking permission—how marvelous, what a sequence of satisfactions life would be! But one soon discovers the first problem: all others have just the same wishes I do, and will treat me no more gently than I treat them. Essentially, then, if cultural restrictions are abolished, only one person can become unlimitedly happy: a tyrant, a dictator who has seized for himself all the means of power. And even he has every reason to hope others will at least observe the one cultural commandment: "Thou shalt not kill."

But how ungrateful, indeed how short-sighted, to aim to abolish culture! Only a state of nature would remain—harder by far to bear. True, nature would demand of us no restrictions of drives: she would let us do as we pleased. But she has her own highly effective means of constraining us. She kills us—coldly, cruelly, recklessly, it seems to us—and perhaps through the very sources of our satisfaction. Precisely because of these dangers with which we are threatened by nature, we joined together and created culture, which, among other things, is intended to make possible our communal life. Indeed, the chief task of culture, its actual *raison d'être*, is to defend us against nature.

Clearly, culture already does this well enough in many aspects, and will certainly do so much better

in the future. But no one is fooled into thinking that nature is already conquered; few dare hope she will ever be completely subject to humankind. There are the elements, which seem to mock all human force; the earth, which quakes and is torn asunder, burying all humanity and its works; water, which floods and drowns everything in a great cataclysm, and storms, which blow away the refuse; there are diseases, only recently recognized as the attacks of other organisms; and finally there is the painful riddle of death, against which no healing herb has yet been discovered nor probably ever will be. With these forces nature rises up against us, magnificent, cruel, inexorable, again showing us our weakness and helplessness, from which we planned to extricate ourselves through the work of culture. One of the few pleasant and uplifting impressions of humanity one can have is presented when, faced with a natural disaster, humanity forgets its cultural disunity—all the internal difficulties and hostilities—and remembers the great communal task: preserving itself against the overwhelming power of nature.

Just as is true for humanity in general, life is hard to bear for the individual. The culture of which one is a member imposes on one a certain degree of privation, and other people, too, create a measure of suffering—despite the precepts of the culture or as a consequence of its imperfection. There are also the injuries inflicted by untamed nature—the individual calls it fate. We would expect the consequence of this situation to be a continuing state of anxious expectation and a heavy blow to innate narcissism. We already know how the individual reacts to the injuries culture and others inflict: by developing a corresponding measure of resistance to the institutions of the culture—hostility toward it. But how does one defend oneself against the overwhelming forces of nature, of fate, which threaten the individual and all others?

Culture frees one from this task; it performs this task for everyone equally. It is also noteworthy that nearly all cultures do the same in this respect. Culture

---

* Sigmund Freud (1856–1939), considered the father of psychoanalysis, spent most of his life in Vienna.

never ceases to carry out its task of defending human-kind against nature, but perpetrates it by other means. The task here is multifaceted. Humankind's seriously threatened self-regard requires solace; the terrors of the world and of life must be eliminated. And human curiosity—albeit driven by the strongest practical interest—wants an answer too.

With the very first step—the humanization of nature—much is already attained. Impersonal forces and fates are unapproachable, eternally unfamiliar. But if passions rage in the elements as they do in the human soul; if death itself is nothing arbitrary, but the violent act of an evil will; if nature is filled with beings like those in one's own society, then one can breathe a sigh of relief, then one feels at home in the uncanny and can mentally work through one's senseless anxiety. One may still be defenseless, but is no longer helplessly paralyzed. At least one can react. And perhaps one is not defenseless after all. Against these violent super-men outside, one can apply the same methods used within society. One can try to conjure them up, pla-cate them, bribe them—and through such influence rob them of some of their power. Such a substitution of natural science by psychology not only produces immediate relief, but also shows the way to further mastery of the situation.

Indeed, this situation is nothing new. It has an infantile prototype—is, in fact, only the continuation of that prototype, for one has been in a similar state of helplessness once before: as a small child in relation to one's parents. There was reason to fear them, espe-cially the father, yet one could be sure of his protection against the dangers one knew at the time. Thus it was natural to regard the two situations as similar. Here, too, as in dream life, wishing came into its own. A pre-monition of death may come over the sleeper, may seek to place him in the grave. But the dreamwork knows how to choose the condition under which even that feared event becomes a wish fulfillment: the dreamer sees himself in an old Etruscan tomb he had climbed

down into, happy to satisfy his archaeological inter-ests. Similarly, one does not simply turn the forces of nature into human beings to be associated with as with equals: that would do no justice to the overpowering impression they create. Rather, one gives them the character of a father—turns them into gods. Here one follows not only an infantile prototype, but, as I have sought to demonstrate, a phylogenetic one as well.

As time progresses, humankind first observes the regularity and conformity to law of natural phe-nomena; thus, the forces of nature lose their human traits. Yet human helplessness remains, and with it the human longing for a father. The gods, too, remain, retaining their threefold task: warding off the terrors of nature, providing reconciliation with the cruelty of fate (particularly as it appears in death), and pro-viding compensation for the sufferings and privations imposed on humankind by cultural, communal life.

Gradually, though, there is a shift of accent in these functions. It is observed that natural forces develop on their own, based on internal necessities. Indeed, the gods are the lords of nature; they have established nature as it is, and can now leave it to its own devices. Only rarely, in so-called miracles, do they intervene, as if to provide assurance that they have given up nothing of their original sphere of power. As for the vicissitudes of fate, an uncomfortable foreboding remains that the perplexity and helplessness of the human race cannot be ameliorated. Here, above all, the gods fail; if they themselves create fate, then one must declare their determinations inscrutable. The most gifted nation of Antiquity begins to grasp that Moira [Fate] stands above the gods and that the gods themselves have their own fates. The more autonomous nature becomes, and the more the gods recede from it, the more earnestly all expectations concentrate on the third function assigned to them and the more morality becomes their actual domain. The task of the gods is now to provide compensation for the inadequacies and hurts of cul-ture, to fix their attention on the sufferings people inflict on one another in their communal life, and to watch over the execution of the precepts of culture, so inadequately observed by humankind. The precepts of culture themselves are ascribed divine origin; they are raised above human society and extended to nature and the universe.

Thus a store of ideas is created, born of the need to make human helplessness bearable, and constructed with the material of recollections of the helplessness of one's own childhood and that of the childhood of the human race. It is clear that these ideas protect humankind in two directions—against the dangers of nature and fate, and against the injuries originating from within human society itself. In summary: life in this world serves a higher purpose—one difficult to guess, but certainly signifying a perfecting of human nature. The spiritual part of humankind, the soul, which through time has so slowly and reluctantly separated itself from the body, is probably seen as the object of this elevation and exaltation. Thus, whatever happens in this world results from the intentions of an intelligence superior to us, which, albeit through ways and detours difficult to follow, ultimately steers everything toward the good—that is, toward a state of affairs pleasant for us. Over each one of us watches a kindly Providence, stern only in appearance, which will not allow us to become the ball played with by the super-strong and ruthless forces of nature. Death itself is no destruction, no return to an inorganic lifeless state, but the start of a new type of existence on the path of higher development. On the other hand, the same moral laws our cultures have established also govern all that occurs in the universe, but they are safeguarded by a supreme judicial authority with incomparably more might and consistency. All good is ultimately rewarded, and all evil punished—if not in this form of life, then in the later existences commencing after death. Thus all the terrors, sufferings, and hardships of life are destined for annihilation. Life after death, which adjoins our earthly life just as the invisible portion of the spectrum adjoins the visible portion, brings all the perfection we may have missed here. And the superior wisdom that governs this progression, the perfect goodness that expresses itself therein, the justice that asserts itself therein—these are the attributes of the divine beings who also created us and the whole universe, or rather, these are the attributes of the one divine being into whom, in our culture, all the ancient gods have been subsumed. . . .

Discussion

1. Is it surprising that the religious beliefs of most believers turn out to include just those things (powers or gods) that satisfy their deepest desires?

2. Suppose Freud was right in his understanding of the origin of religious belief. What is the relevance of Freud's claim to the truth of religious beliefs?

3. Try to use wish-fulfillment on Freud. Can you think of any deep desires that atheism would satisfy?

Chapter 16

Reflections on the Hermeneutics of Suspicion

TAKING SUSPICION SERIOUSLY: THE RELIGIOUS USES OF MODERN ATHEISM

MEROLD WESTPHAL*

Masters of suspicion. It is not every form of modern atheism that I have in mind. It is, in particular, the atheism of Marx, Nietzsche, and Freud, three of the most widely influential atheists of the modern era. For Marx, Nietzsche, and Freud are not representative of a specific type of atheism that we can call evidential atheism. Evidential atheism is nowhere better summarized than in Bertrand Russell's account of what he would say to God if the two were ever to meet and God were to ask him why he had not been a believer: "I'd say, 'Not enough evidence, God! Not enough evidence!'"[1]

Following Ricoeur, who has designated Marx, Nietzsche, and Freud as the "masters" of the "school of suspicion,"[2] we can speak of the atheism of suspicion in distinction from evidential atheism. Suspicion can be distinguished from Cartesian doubt and the epistemological tradition governed by it in that Cartesian doubt is directed toward the elusiveness and opacity of things or facts, while suspicion is directed toward the evasiveness and dishonesty of consciousness.[3] Its target is not the proposition but the person who affirms

it, not the belief but the believer. Its attack on the theory and practice of religion is an indirect one, whose immediate goal is to discredit the believing soul. In other words, suspicion assumes that the task of epistemological reflection is not completed until the problem of false consciousness is met head on.

Hume's analysis. The difference between these two types of reflection can be illustrated from David Hume's philosophy of religion. In his *Dialogues Concerning Natural Religion* and in Sections x and xi of *An Enquiry Concerning Human Understanding* he asks familiar questions about whether there is sufficient evidence to provide rational support for belief in God and miracles. But in the Introduction to *The Natural History of Religion* Hume distinguishes between such questions "concerning [religion's] foundation in reason" and those "concerning its origin in human nature."[4]

This question of origin, to which the *Natural History* is devoted, turns out in the first instance to be a question of motive. Belief in an "invisible intelligent power" to whom prayers and sacrifices could be directed does not arise from "speculative curiosity" or "the pure love of truth." To lead people's attention beyond the immediacy of the here and now, "they must be actuated by some passion, which prompts their thought and reflection; some motive, which urges their first inquiry." Such motives include "the anxious concern for happiness, the dread of future misery, the

---

* Merold Westphal is Distinguished Professor of Philosophy at Fordham University.

terror of death, the thirst of revenge, the appetite for food and other necessaries." In short, the originating motive for the religious life is the hopes and fears of ordinary life, especially the latter.[5]

The hopes and fears that come to our attention in this way are not, at least not primarily, those which have been fashioned in the school of moral ideals. They are rather the hopes and fears of more or less immediate self-interest, and Hume sees them as constituting a "selfish view." It is this standpoint of self-interest which Hume finds at the heart of "idolatry or polytheism." But since the negative effects which Hume sees as stemming from this "selfish view" belong to popular religion as such and are not limited to polytheism, it looks as if Hume is working toward a definition of idolatry or superstition—he uses the terms interchangeably—which depends more on the motivation of the believing soul than on the propositional content of belief.

Hume gives special attention to two such effects. Where our relation to someone of superior power is primarily based on our hopes and fears of what we can get out of the relationship, the temptation is all but unavoidable to resort to flattery. The believing soul will naturally speak of adoration, but the suspicion of Hume detects adulation. Just to the degree that this suspicion is well founded, the relationship between believer and deity shows itself to be dishonest, founded on falsehoods. Naturally, if the believer is not shameless and cynical, it will be necessary not only to hide this dishonesty from the deity but from the believing soul as well. Piety becomes inseparable from self-deception. When piety is grounded in self-interest there is a second consequence, however, which reveals that the self-deception and dishonesty just noted do not remain internal to the relation between believer and deity. Hume notes that idolatrous worship is "liable to this great inconvenience, that any practice or opinion, however barbarous or corrupted, may be authorized by it," and that "the greatest crimes

have been found, in many instances, compatible with a superstitious piety and devotion." He finds himself forced to ask, "What so pure as some of the morals, included in some theological systems? What so corrupt as some of the practices, to which these systems give rise?" And he immediately identifies such systems as "comfortable views."[6] Once again it looks as if he is giving a contextual definition of idolatry and superstition as the comfortable views which provide moral and religious legitimation for the barbarous and criminal behaviors which self-interest often generates.

Hume has intolerance and persecution particularly in mind, but the issue is obviously a general one. To ask about the *origin* of religion in human nature is not only to ask about the *motives* of the religious life, and thus about the inwardness of the believing soul; it is also to ask about the *function* of the religious life, and thus about the public behavior "compatible with" or "authorized by" it.

Hume's suspicion of religion culminates in this question about the function of faith. On his view reflection on religious beliefs can be neither serious nor complete until the question is posed: what practices (lifestyles, institutions) do these beliefs in fact (that is, in real life) serve to legitimate? This question of function does not replace the question of motive; for, as the later masters of the school of suspicion know full well, in a context where self-deception is all too possible, function is the best and sometimes the only key to motive. We find out what our real motives are only when we find out what role our beliefs actually play in our lives.

Taking suspicion seriously. Marx, Nietzsche, and Freud are the masters of the school of suspicion because they carry out this Humean project unrelentingly. Unlike Hume, they do so in the context of an unambiguous atheism. It seems to me, however, that it is not the aggressive and uncompromising nature of their atheism that should govern our response as

Christian philosophers to them but rather its foundation in suspicion. For I believe, and this is the major point I want to make, that our response to the atheism of suspicion should be entirely different from our response to evidential atheism.

Our primary response to evidential atheism, it seems to me, should be to seek to refute it. This can be done by trying to show that there is sufficient evidence to make religious beliefs (and the practices linked to them) rationally respectable. Or it can be done by challenging the way in which the evidentialist demands evidence. I shall not here discuss the relative merits of these strategies, though I will predict that the most recent challenge to evidentialism as such in the form of the so-called Calvinist epistemology is likely to be as central to the discussion of evidential atheism for the foreseeable future as discussion of invisible gardeners was a few decades ago.[7]

Our primary response to the atheism of suspicion, by contrast, should not be attempted refutation but the acknowledgment that its critique is all too true all too much of the time. Further, while the apologetic refutation of evidential atheism is addressed to the unbeliever (even if the believer is the primary consumer), the acknowledgment that Marx, Nietzsche, and Freud have described us all too accurately should be addressed to the community of believers. In short, I am calling upon Christian philosophers to be the prophetic voices which challenge the Christian community to take seriously the critique of religion generated by suspicion and which show the Christian community how to do so fruitfully. To that end I want a) to indicate why I think this should be our response, b) to address two objections or potential obstacles to accepting this responsibility, and c) to illustrate, if ever so briefly, how to go about taking suspicion seriously.

If the nasty things suspicion says about religion are indeed all too true all too much of the time, that would be sufficient reason to take suspicion seriously rather than to seek to refute it. The commitment of

philosophy to the truth should be, if anything, deepened by our identity as Christian philosophers. We, of all people, should be the last to be interested in refuting the truth.

But how can we be enabled to recognize in the diatribes of Marx, Nietzsche, and Freud the painful truth about ourselves? The best way, in my view, is to recognize the powerful parallel between their critique of religion and the biblical critique of religion. One has but to mention Jesus' critique of the Pharisees, Paul's critique of works righteousness, and James's critique of cheap grace to be reminded that the Christian faith has built into it a powerful polemic against certain kinds of religion, even if they are practiced in the name of the one true God.[8] These New Testament diatribes against false religion cannot be neutralized by appeals to either metaphysical orthodoxy or ritual rectitude and zeal, which is to say that the God of the New Testament transcends both metaphysics and ritual and cannot be captured by either or both.

But this is not new. The same kind of critique permeates the Old Testament, whose writers know, in the words of Buber, that "if there is nothing that can so hide the face of our fellow-man as morality can, religion can hide from us as nothing else can the face of God."[9] The kinds of religion which can do this are forms of instrumental religion, the religion in which the sacred power becomes a means to the achieving of human ends. Instrumental religion need not violate the first two of the Ten Commandments, for it can be practiced in the name of Yahweh and without the aid of graven images. But it violates the third commandment, "You shall not take the name of the Lord your God in vain." In historical context this is not so much a prohibition of what we think of as swearing as it is of magical practices and conjuring. Commenting on this meaning of the third commandment, von Rad gives in effect a helpful definition of instrumental religion. "Israel has been assailed at all periods by the temptation to use the divine power with the help of the divine name in an anti-social manner and to place it at the service of private and even sinister interests."[10]

The Old Testament critique of instrumental religion finds its clearest expression in the sustained polemic, not against Israel's tendency to go "whoring" after other gods, but against religious practices, especially sacrifice, performed in Yahweh's own name. Sacrifice is unacceptable, even detestable, when it is combined with disobedience to the revealed will of God. More specifically, when sacrifice is "compatible with" economic exploitation and indifference toward the poor, allowing people to think that these practices are "authorized by" the halo of sanctity which shines forth from such rites, the rites themselves become sinful acts which evoke God's wrath and lead to punishment.[11] As one theologian has put it, in such circumstances "what is in fact required by Yahweh has become blasphemy."[12]

Another way to put the same point would be to say that what is verbally the worship of the one true God has become idolatry. We might call it third commandment idolatry, for when we take God's name in vain by using religion to legitimate impious practices we worship in fact another god.

Martin Buber has described "the degenerate sacrificial cult, in which the offering is changed from being a sign of the extreme self-devotion and becomes a ransom from all true self-devotion" as "the baalisation of YHVH Himself."[13] Part of what it means to say that God is a jealous God is that he allows himself to be worshipped only in conformity with his character as it has been revealed to human understanding. Therefore, to seek to place the divine power at our disposal while freeing ourselves from responsibility to God's revealed will is to worship another god, no matter what name we use. In the ancient world magical practices were a primary way of doing this. In the modern world there are many creative variations on this theme of magical, instrumental religion; and it is precisely these that

Marx, Nietzsche, and Freud are so good at exposing. Eagerness to refute the masters of suspicion rather than to take them seriously may well be a way of putting ourselves in the company of those who rejected Jesus and the prophets in biblical times.

Self-deception. An example of the wide ranging contexts in which we encounter suspicion is from Augustine's *Confessions*. In the midst of the story of how the friends of Ponticianus were dramatically changed by reading the life of Antony, Augustine writes, "But you, Lord, while he was speaking, were turning me around so that I could see myself; you took me from behind my own back, which was where I had put myself during the time when I did not want to be observed by myself, and you set me in front of my own face so that I could see how foul a sight I was. . . . If I tried to look away from myself . . . you were setting me in front of myself, forcing me to look into my own face, so that I might see my sin and hate it. I did know it, but I pretended that I did not. I had been pushing the whole idea away from me and forgetting it."[14]

Along with Sartre's analysis of bad faith in *Being and Nothingness* this passage is the finest account I know of the nature of the self-deception which suspicion seeks to uncover. That of which we are fully aware we nevertheless manage not to notice because it is easier not to notice than to deal honestly with what is there to be noticed. Thus, to use a very apt figure of speech, we turn a blind eye to unwelcome facts.[15]

It was only as he was freed from this kind of bad faith that Augustine was able to discover the *origin*, in the Humean sense, of his Manichean faith, the pride which was its *motive* and the self-justification which was its *function*.[16] Not only was his religion "compatible" (Hume's term) with a lifestyle of which he himself did not approve, focused as it was on the pursuit of sexual pleasure, wealth, and social status; his religion "authorized" (Hume's term) his immoral behavior by providing a metaphysical theory which made him the innocent victim of an evil power outside himself. Augustine's primary complaint against the Manichean faith, once he had abandoned it, was not that it was false, but that it functioned to legitimate a life of sin.

One could multiply examples, but I think this is sufficient to raise doubts about the disinterestedness of thought to become suspicious that behind many, if not all, things bright and beautiful there lies motivated self-deception. Like Marx, Nietzsche, and Freud, Augustine is fully aware of both the ironical discrepancy between official meaning and actual use and the need of the ironist to hide this, not just from others but especially from himself or herself. Marx, Nietzsche, and Freud's critique of morals and politics is embedded in their critique of religion and their critique of religion is directed primarily toward the theory and practice of orthodox biblical religion. In both these respects their critique stands in the closest relation to that of Jesus and the prophets. As such it can become a powerful tool for personal and corporate self-examination if we will open ourselves to it in honesty and humility. Perhaps it would not be going too far to think of suspicion as the hermeneutics of Lent.

On knowing when not to refute suspicion. Some object to taking suspicion seriously because the atheism of suspicion involves the systematic practice of bad reasoning in the support of its unbelief. It combines the *ad hominem* and genetic fallacies and illegitimately infers the irrationality of religious belief and practice from the unfaithfulness of the believer. For the sake of truth and for the protection of the logically unsophisticated, it is important to point out the fallaciousness of these arguments.

There is a way to return the fire of suspicion's atheists. It derives from Dostoyevsky's insight that the psychological argument cuts both ways. We can call it the *et tu Brute* strategy. It is easy to play this game with, for example, Freud. He finds our belief in the

God of Judeo-Christian theism to be a wish-fulfilling illusion derived from our sense of helplessness before the impersonal indifference of nature. Under those circumstances he thinks we "tell ourselves that it would be very nice if there were a God who created the world and was a benevolent Providence, and if there were a moral order in the universe and an after-life; but it is a very striking fact that all this is exactly as we are bound to wish it to be."[17] This is the origin, in the Humean sense, of God the Father. But both Freud's biography and his theory of the Oedipal complex testify to the fact that we have at least as powerful an inclination to hate and resent paternal power and authority as to long for it. *Et tu Sigmunde.* The pot is calling the kettle black. If our belief is a childish wish-fulfillment, is not your unbelief an adolescent rebellion combined with an infantile wish-fulfillment?

It is unquestionably possible to score points against the atheism of suspicion using either of these two strategies. The problem is that one only wins Pyrrhic victories in this manner and ends up dead right, which is just as dead as dead wrong. One reason for this is that while the writings of Marx, Nietzsche, and Freud often encourage the reader to make the fallacious inferences in question, they never, or at least almost never, formally make the arguments themselves. In fact, they sometimes warn against confusing the questions of motive and function with the question of truth. For example, in *The Future of An Illusion* Freud is careful to note that while we have reason to be suspicious of illusions, which he defines as beliefs whose motivation includes wish-fulfillment as a "prominent factor," such beliefs may nevertheless be true.[18]

The reason why the atheists of suspicion need not formally rely on *ad hominem* or genetic arguments to establish their atheism is that if questioned about the grounds of their unbelief they would often reply in evidentialist terms. This is clearly the case in the instance just mentioned, Freud in *The Future of An Illusion.* There he gives a positivist, evidentialist rationale for his atheism. Whatever we cannot get from science in the way of justified belief simply cannot be justified.[19] In general I think the typical atheist of suspicion, if pressed for the grounds of that atheism, will give an evidentialist answer of some sort. The hermeneutics of suspicion is not so much an answer to the question, "How can we prove that religion is wrong?" as it is to the question, "Since we already know that it is wrong, how can we explain how it survives and has such influence?" To argue that atheistic conclusions do not follow from suspicion's descriptions, even if these are well founded, is to make a good point. But it is also to throw a knockout punch that doesn't land.

But there is a more profound reason why attempting to refute or discredit the atheism of suspicion by either of the strategies under consideration is not an appropriate first response. The story of the Good Samaritan is introduced by an exchange between Jesus and a lawyer of the Pharisees about eternal life. The Pharisee is able to give the same magnificent two-fold summary of the law which Jesus himself gives on another occasion. But when Jesus tells him simply to do this and he will live he gets defensive. We read, "But he, desiring to justify himself, said to Jesus, 'And who is my neighbor?'" In itself this is a perfectly legitimate question, and in fact anyone seriously interested in the command of neighbor love is bound to ask it. But in the four simple words "desiring to justify himself" the narrative levels a devastating critique at the Pharisee.[20]

We open ourselves to precisely this same critique when our first response to Marx, Nietzsche, and Freud is to try to score points against them by either of the strategies we've just noted. In either case the points we raise are worth raising in themselves. But in the circumstances we discredit ourselves more than our unbelieving brothers by raising them. For we stand accused by their critique of being Pharisees, of practicing a religion which by virtue of its instrumentalism of self-interest is idolatrous by our own standards.

If our first response is to defend ourselves by attacking them, we invite the impartial observer to say, "But they, willing to justify themselves, began to talk about *ad hominem* and genetic fallacies and to turn suspicion against the suspicious." Just as Jesus taught us to attend to the speck in our brother's eye only *after* removing the log from our own, so there will be plenty of time to make the points that need to be made against the atheism of suspicion *after* we have taken their critique seriously.[21]

There is a final reason why we should resist the immediate inclination to refute the atheism of suspicion. We have already noted that what presents itself as the love of liberty or justice can turn out under the cross examination of suspicion to be but greed or envy. Nietzsche is especially fond of making this point and finds an elegant German word play for doing so. He writes, "And when they say, 'I am just,' [*ich bin gerecht*] it always sounds like 'I am just-revenged' [*ich bin gercht*]."[22] The point is a general one about the irony of the moral life, that what presents itself as an altruistic virtue may be, in terms of motive and function, but an egoistic vice dressed up in its Sunday-go-to-meetin' clothes.

Atheism for Lent. The best, in fact only real, refutation of Nietzsche and company on this issue is a practical one and not a theoretical one. It is to practice the virtue (or proclaim the belief) even when it is manifestly not in one's interest (as usually understood) to do so. If, for example, the call for socio-economic justice is discredited as the envy and greed of the poor, then let the wealthy, whose possessions would be fewer in a more nearly just society, be the ones who preach justice and begin to practice it through the voluntary adoption of a less affluent lifestyle. This is just what Jesus taught with reference to the virtue of hospitality when he said, "But when you give a feast, invite the poor, the maimed, the lame, the blind, and you will be blessed, because they cannot repay you."[23]

There is an important point to note about this practical refutation of suspicion, and it has a bearing on the claim that our first response to suspicion should be to take it seriously. Unless we have already taken suspicion seriously and learned from its critique the pitfalls of ironical morality and instrumental religion, we will neither see the need for this response to suspicion nor know what sort of behavior would constitute such a response. According to the practical logic of the situation, the one truly unanswerable refutation of suspicion's critique cannot be our first response but can only be a subsequent response.

There is an understandable hesitancy about subjecting our faith to a secular critique. Subjecting piety to suspicion may seem too much like casting pearls before swine. But perhaps Balaam's ass would provide a better metaphor, reminding us that God does not always speak to us through official priestly voices.

Domesticating the divine. I would like to conclude this invitation for you to join me in your own way in the project I've been describing with a single example of the sort of thing I have in mind and a warning. The example comes from Freud's discussion of the taboo upon rulers in *Totem and Taboo*. In the theories of the ruler's sanctity and especially in the ceremonials in which it is celebrated in some cultures, Freud detects the same deep-seated ambivalence and compromise formation that he first encountered in his neurotic patients, where love and hate, duty and inclination often co-exist most ingeniously.

This phenomenon can be seen in the elaborate protection rituals of sacred rulers like the Mikado of Japan. "It must strike us as self-contradictory," writes Freud, "that persons of such unlimited power should need to be protected so carefully from the threat of danger; but that is not the only contradiction. . . . For these people also think it necessary to keep a watch on their king to see that he makes a proper use of his

powers." Freud then quotes Frazer about this proper use. In such societies the sovereign

"exists only for his subjects; his life is only valuable so long as he discharges the duties of his position by ordering the course of nature for his people's benefit. So as soon as he fails to do so, the care, the devotion, the religious homage which they had hitherto lavished on him cease and are changed into hatred and contempt; he is dismissed ignominiously, and may be thankful if he escapes with his life. Worshipped as a god one day, he is killed as a criminal the next. . . . A king of this sort lives hedged in by a ceremonious etiquette, a network of prohibitions and observances, of which the intention is not to contribute to his dignity, much less his comfort, but to restrain him from conduct which, by disturbing the harmony of nature, might involve himself, his people, and the universe in one common catastrophe." [24]

Another example Freud gives from Frazer concerns the Timmes people from Sierra Leone, "who elect their king, reserve to themselves the right of beating him on the eve of his coronation; and they avail themselves of this constitutional privilege with such hearty goodwill that sometimes the unhappy monarch does not long survive his elevation to the throne." To which Freud adds, "Even in glaring instances like this, however, the hostility is not admitted as such, but masquerades as a ceremonial." [25]

Needless to say, the official meaning of such ceremonials is veneration, affection, and homage, even when their motivation is envy and hostility and their function is to seize control of the sacred power embodied in the ruler. Here is the finest *coup d'état* one could imagine, for the effectiveness of the rebellion consists precisely in its being unacknowledged and unnoticed. Such a king is "hedged in" by rites which "restrain" him and "annihilate his freedom," even though they purport to "contribute to his dignity."[26] I am reminded of the Mother's Day celebrations of my childhood, in which the restriction of women to one particular role in society was reinforced and legitimated by rites of veneration in which Mother was placed on a pedestal as Queen for a Day.

Freud's question, of course, is not addressed to Japan or Sierra Leone but to his Jewish and Christian contemporaries and to us. To what degree does our worship, like that on the first Palm Sunday, honor in order to domesticate divine power, seeking to turn Aslan[27] into a watchdog, or a hunting dog, or even a lap dog? Theory is as much at issue as practice. For the metaphysical different functions. To discover the actual function of both our theology and our worship would be the task of the kind of self-examination the masters of suspicion lay before us.

Warning. Finally a word of warning. Suspicion easily turns sour. MacIntyre wisely warns against the aesthete, whose suspicion sees through everything and is deceived by nothing except its own cynicism. It is all too easy to become the Sunday School teacher who, at the end of a lesson on the Pharisee and publican who went up to the temple to pray, said, "And now, children, let us fold our hands and close our eyes and thank God that we are not like that Pharisee." We need to remind ourselves that our role is not to pass judgment on the sincerity of others, nor even to earn points with God by the purity of our own hearts; and so we will have to learn even to be suspicious of our suspicion. But we will first need to learn to be suspicious of our reluctance to learn the kind of self-examination that Marx, Nietzsche, and Freud can teach us.

Notes

1. Quoted in *Faith and Rationality: Reason and Belief in God*, ed. Alvin Plantinga and Nicholas Wolterstorff (Notre Dame: U of Notre Dame P, 1983), pp. 17–18.

2. Paul Ricoeur, *Freud and Philosophy: An Essay on Interpretation*, trans. Denis Savage (New Haven: Yale UP, 1970), p. 32.

3. David Hume, *The Natural History of Religion*, ed. H.E. Root (Stanford: Stanford UP, 1957), p. 21.

4. Hume, pp. 43, 65–67.

5. Hume, pp. 27–28, 31.

6. Hume, pp. 48, 72, 76.

7. See Plantinga and Wolterstorff, *Faith and Rationality*, for important discussions of the "Calvinist" challenge to evidentialist assumptions about religious knowledge.

8. See Juan Luis Segundo, *Faith and Ideologies*, trans. John Drury (Maryknoll, New York: Orbis, 1984), pp. 120–30 for a discussion of Paul and James which illustrates their compatibility by showing how each offers a religious critique of religion.

9. Martin Buber, *Between Man and Man* (New York: Macmillan, 1965), p. 18.

10. Gerhard von Rad, *Deuteronomy*, trans. Dorothea Barton (Philadelphia: Westminster, 1966), p. 57. On the sanctity of the divine name and God's unwillingness to be conjured, see Merold Westphal, *God, Guilt, and Death: An Existential Phenomenology of Religion* (Bloomington: Indiana UP, 1984), pp. 237–38, with notes.

11. Prov. 21:3, Isa. 1:10–17, Amos 5:21–24, and Micah 6:6–8. Cf. Isa. 58, where the same theme is developed in relation to fasting.

12. Otto Kaiser, *Isaiah 1–12*, 2nd ed., trans. John Bowden (Philadelphia: Westminster, 1983), p. 30 on Isa. 1:12.

13. Martin Buber, *The Prophetic Faith*, trans. Carlyle Witton-Davies (New York: Harper, 1960), p. 119.

14. Augustine, *Confessions*, VIII, 7 (Warner translation). Cf. Jean-Paul Sartre, *Being and Nothingness*, trans. Hazel Barnes (New York: Philosophical Library, 1956), I, 2, "Bad Faith."

15. Pine-Coffin uses just this figure in translating the passage just cited from the *Confessions*. "I had known it all along, but I had always pretended that it was something different. I had turned a blind eye and forgotten it."

16. *Confessions*, IV, 15; V, 10; VII, 3; VIII, 10; and IX, 4.

17. Sigmund Freud, *The Future of An Illusion* in The Standard Edition of the *Complete Psychological Works of Sigmund Freud* (henceforth S.E.), ed. and trans. James Strachey et al. (London: Hogarth P, 1953–74), XXI, 33 and 24.

18. Freud, XXI, 31.

19. Freud, XXI, 31–32, 51–56. Thus, when Freud writes in *Totem and Taboo* that "it would be another matter if demons really existed. But we know that, like gods, they are creations of the human mind . . ." this is a premise and not a conclusion of his psychoanalytic analysis. S.E., XIII, 24.

20. Luke 10:29 (RSV). In Matt. 22:35 the lawyer is identified as a Pharisee. 36.

21. Matt. 7:5 (RSV).

22. Friedrich Nietzsche, *Thus Spoke Zarathustra*, trans. Walter Kaufmann (New York: Viking P, 1966), p. 95 (Second Part, "On the Virtuous").

23. Luke 14:13 (RSV).

24. Freud, S.E., XIII, 43–44.

25. XIII, 49.

26. XIII, 44.

27. Quoted in *Faith and Rationality: Reason and Belief in God*, ed. Alvin Plantinga and Nicholas Wolterstorff (Notre Dame: U of Notre Dame P, 1983), pp. 17–18.

Discussion

1. Distinguish between the atheism of suspicion and evidential atheism. What is Hume's suspicion of religion? What do you think of Hume's suspicion?

2. What does Westphal think the response of Christians should be to the suspicion of religion? Why?

3. What, according to Westphal, is the only genuine response to the suspicion of religion? What would that involve?

Part Three

Suggestions for Further Study

de Lubac, Henry. *The Drama of Atheist Humanism.* Cleveland: World Publishing Company, 1963.

Dupré, Louis. *The Philosophical Foundations of Marxism.* New York: Harcourt, Brace and World, 1966.

Kaufmann, Walter. *Nietzsche: Philosopher, Psychologist, Antichrist.* 3rd ed. New York: Random House, 1968.

Ricoeur, Paul. *Freud and Philosophy.* Trans. Denis Savage. New Haven: Yale UP, 1970.

Rieff, Philip. *Freud: The Mind of a Moralist.* Garden City, NY: Doubleday, 1961.

Westphal, Merold. *Suspicion and Faith: The Religious Uses of Modern Atheism.* New York: Fordham UP, 1998.

God and Human Suffering

Part Four

Introduction

Introduction. The mournful cry "Why, God?" is as ancient as belief in God itself. Human suffering is often followed by spiritual suffering. When we need Him most God may seem to be angry, vindictive, hidden, wicked or even non-existent. And these accusations have come from believers! (See, for example, the book of Job.) Little wonder that evil has been taken by agnostics and atheists as evidence against the existence of God.

Evil is a problem for theism, which includes the claims that God is both omnipotent and perfectly good. Indeed, talk of "*the* problem of evil" is something of a misnomer. There are a number of problems here—arguments against theism based upon the existence of evil. The first readings in this section revolve around what is perhaps the most straightforward problem of evil—what has come to be known as "the Logical Problem of Evil." Here the basic claim is that the existence of any evil whatsoever is logically inconsistent with the existence of God. If God is omnipotent he would be able to eliminate all evil and if he were all good he would want to. If so, it would seem that the following three propositions are logically inconsistent:

1. God is Omnipotent

2. God is Wholly Good

3. Evil Exists

The Logical Problem of Evil is just the assertion that this is the case. If so, then logic requires giving up at least one of these three propositions.

The cost of giving up any one of these is quite severe. How could one, for example, deny the third proposition, the claim that evil exists? In considering this question a couple of clarifications are in order. First, "evil" here refers simply to bad things—evil may, but need not involve some sort of sinister moral agent as its cause. The characters in Hume's *Dialogues* catalogue at great length a host of example evils. It does not make for pleasant reading. Here is an illustrative passage:

> A perpetual war is kindled among all living creatures. Necessity, hunger, want, stimulate the strong and courageous; fear, anxiety, terror agitate the weak and infirm. The first entrance into life gives anguish to the new-born infant and to its wretched parent; weakness, impotence, distress attend each stage of that life, and it is, at last, finished in agony and horror. Man is the greatest enemy of man. Oppression, injustice contempt, contumely, violence, sedition, war, calumny, treachery, fraud—by these they mutually torment each other, and they would soon dissolve that society which they had formed were it not for the dread of still greater ills which must attend their separation.

Along these lines it is common to divide evils into two classes: natural and moral. Natural evils arise solely from nature: earthquakes, pestilence, famine, drought, flooding, mudslides, and hurricanes (to mention just a few). Moral evils are due to the free choices of human beings and include, for example, war, poverty, and racism.

The second clarification that needs to be made regarding evil is that to call something evil is not to deny that good can result from that thing. Clearly good often comes out of evil. For example, instances of suffering and death may give rise to incredible acts of compassion and courage. Saying *that* is not to deny that the suffering and death are bad things—it is merely to acknowledge that good consequences can result from such evils.

So, giving up the third proposition seems untenable. But to give up either of the first two is to give up theism. In the *Dialogues* Hume might be arguing that God is not good in any sense analogous to human goodness. Given God's sure and certain power and wisdom but also all of the immense human infelicity, God's goodness cannot be at all like human goodness. Some find refuge in this sort of mystery; however, God's moral attributes (more than God's power, surely) are central to his divinity. To call God good, if Hume is right, is tantamount to calling God "fobbertival" or any other nonsense term. One might, on the other hand, opt for giving up omnipotence. God is very powerful, on this view, but even God cannot eliminate all evil. By abandoning either of these divine attributes, God's existence might be maintained. But who would wish to worship a perverse bully or a well-intentioned wimp? Denying God's omnipotence or perfect goodness seems to denigrate divinity, and should, therefore, be a recourse of last resort for the theist.

Theists have at their disposal a powerful argument designed to show that evil is not inconsistent with the existence of an omnipotent, wholly good God—Alvin Plantinga's free will defense. Following the selection from Hume, Paul Tidman presents a simplified overview of the Free Will Defense written specifically for an undergraduate audience—indeed, written for this volume. Tidman presents the basic idea of the Defense without the technical details that accompany Plantinga's original argument. Tidman explains how the Free Will Defense has achieved something fairly rare in Philosophy: widespread consensus that it works.

The Free Will Defense assumes that it is possible for God to create human beings that are *free* in the sense that their actions are *uncaused*—no antecedent state of affairs can cause or coerce free actions. A "caused free action" is a contradiction in terms, no more possible than a square circle. If it is not possible for there to be caused free actions, then it is not possible for God to cause free actions. (I am assuming that God cannot do the logically impossible.) But, if God cannot cause free actions, then even God may not be able to create free creatures who always freely choose to refrain from doing evil. Thus, if God can create a free being, it must be possible for God to create such a being who chooses freely to bring about evil, which means it is possible for God and evil to co-exist. The Free Will Defense claims just this, namely that it is possible that God could not create free beings who never bring about evil.

Theodicy. The Free Will Defense makes a persuasive case that it is at least possible for God and evil to co-exist. What the Free Will Defense does not do (nor does it attempt to do) is explain why God, in fact, permits evil. That is the task of a theodicy. A theodicy, which Daniel Howard-Snyder assesses more generally, is an attempt to justify God given the facts of evil. God, after all, may very well be omnipotent and wholly good yet have a perfectly good reason (or two) for allowing evil. The most important suggestion of God's reason for allowing evil dates to Augustine—the free will theodicy. According to the free will theodicy, the possibility described by the free will defense is in fact actual. According to this theodicy the reason God permits evil is so that humans can exercise their free will.

John Hick's soul-making theodicy unites the free-will explanation of moral evil with a view of human nature as less than perfect. On the traditional, Augustinian view of human nature, humans were created perfect (but with free will) and placed in paradise. How, given these circumstances, humans could possibly fail is surely a mystery (or a contradiction). If human beings are less than perfect, however, and are not placed in paradise, then human failure seems almost inevitable. What could justify God's putting people a lot like us in harm's way? According to Hick, facing real dangers and challenges is the only way that God could accomplish the goal that he set for human beings—to (freely) become children of God. Hick's "soul-making theodicy" explains how natural evils assist in the development of such virtues as courage, patience, and generosity. Evil is justified because it is necessary for immature, incomplete people to become heirs of eternal life.

Appealing to distinctly religious (even Christian) goods, Marilyn McCord Adams focuses on the troubling "horrific evils"—evils which, if one suffered them, one would have good reason to doubt that one's life was a great good on the whole. Adams outlines the deficiencies of classical theodicies for explaining horrific evils. Her own solution appeals to a more adequate conception of divine goodness—God is good to created persons. Adams believes we are incapable of understanding—because of the vast intellectual distance between humans and God—God's reasons why people suffer horrifically. Nonetheless, she believes that God has shown us three ways that he can defeat horrific evil within the context of the sufferer's life: by identifying with Christ, divine gratitude, or vision into the inner life of God. By appealing to distinctively Christian beliefs, Adams contends that she can show that God and evil—including horrific evil—are not incompatible.

The evidential problem of evil. The focus of discussion of the problem of evil has shifted in the past twenty years. Virtually everyone, atheist and theist alike, concedes that Plantinga has demonstrated that God and evil are not logically incompatible. Nonetheless some philosophers contend that there is simply too much evil, or that some evil is too horrific, for God to exist or for a person reasonably to believe that God exists.

William Rowe contends that there is some evil, apparently pointless evil, which gives us reason to believe that God does not exist. Rowe does not believe that he has disproved God's existence but he does believe that he has given good reasons for believing that God does not exist. His argument may be stated, roughly, as follows:

1. If there is a God, there would be no pointless evil.

2. We have reason to believe that there is pointless evil.

3. Therefore, we have reason to believe that God does not exist.

Suppose we grant the truth of the first premise, how could Rowe demonstrate the truth of the second premise? He does so by offering the example of a fawn who suffers serious burns and dies days later. Because we can point to the fawn's suffering, Rowe contends that we have reason to believe that there is no point to the fawn's suffering. And if the fawn's suffering is indeed pointless then he has established the second premise of his argument. And from (1) and (2) it surely follows that it is unreasonable to believe that God exists.

Rowe's famous essay elicited a flurry of responses; Daniel Howard-Snyder brings together some of the most important of them. Howard-Snyder carefully outlines Rowe's argument, showing Rowe's explicit inferences as well as his hidden assumptions. The crucial assumption involves what have been called "Noseeum Inferences." One makes a Noseeum Inference when one assumes that because one can't see something it isn't there. Rowe makes such inferences when he argues that because we can't see the point to some suffering, it is reasonable to believe that there is no point to that suffering. Howard-Snyder takes Rowe to task, contending that, at least with respect to certain areas of human inquiry, Noseeum Inferences are not valid. This is true, Howard-Snyder contends, with respect to God. With our puny cognitive abilities we simply should not expect to see certain kinds of reasons even if they exist.

No doubt Rowe and other non-theists are at this very moment dreaming up powerful responses to the likes of Plantinga, Hick, Adams, and Howard-Snyder. The lively debate over God and evil is not likely to end soon.

Reflections. Nicholas Wolterstorff raises the problem of suffering from within a community of believers. In the Judeo-Christian tradition, there is attestation of God speaking of his intentions that people live long and well. But people's lives are cut short and are sometimes marked by pain and suffering so powerful they cannot flourish. And, in the midst of suffering, the God who speaks is painfully typically silent. So, for believers, suffering and pain raise both intellectual and existential problems from within their own systems of belief. Wolterstorff considers several prominent types of theodicy and finds them wanting often because they would turn God into a crass utilitarian (permitting the suffering of some for the good of the whole). He concludes with some passionate advice for living in the silence.

Chapter 17

The Problem of Evil

GOD AND EVIL

DAVID HUME*

Philo: On the contrary, it is here chiefly, cried Philo, that the uniform and equal maxims of Nature are most apparent. Man, it is true, can, by combination, surmount all his real enemies, and become master of the whole animal creation.... This very society, by which we surmount those wild beasts, our natural enemies; what new enemies does it not raise to us? What woe and misery does it not occasion? Man is the greatest enemy of man. Oppression, injustice, contempt, contumely, violence, sedition, war, calumny, treachery, fraud; by these they mutually torment each other; and they would soon dissolve that society which they had formed, were it not for the dread of still greater ills, which must attend their separation.

Demea: But though these external insults, said Demea, from animals, from men, from all the elements, which assault us, form a frightful catalogue of woes, they are nothing in comparison of those which arise within ourselves, from the distempered condition of our mind and body. How many lie under the lingering torment of diseases? Hear the pathetic enumeration of the great poet.

---

* David Hume (1711–76) was a Scottish philosopher best known for his skeptical views.

Intestine stone and ulcer, colic-pangs,
Demoniac frenzy, moping melancholy,
And moon-struck madness, pining atrophy,
Marasmus, and wide-wasting pestilence.
Dire was the tossing, deep the groans: *despair*
Tended the sick, busiest from couch to couch.
And over them triumphant *death* his dart
Shook: but delay'd to strike, though oft invok'd
With vows, as their chief good and final hope.
(Milton, *Paradise Lost* 11: 484–93)

The disorders of the mind, continued Demea, though more secret, are not perhaps less dismal and vexatious. Remorse, shame, anguish, rage, disappointment, anxiety, fear, dejection, despair; who has ever passed through life without cruel inroads from these tormentors? How many have scarcely ever felt any better sensations? Labour and poverty, so abhorred by every one, are the certain lot of the far greater number; and those few privileged persons, who enjoy ease and opulence, never reach contentment or true felicity. All the goods of life united would not make a very happy man; but all the ills united would make a wretch indeed; and any one of them almost (and who can be free from every one?) nay often the absence of one good (and who can possess all?) is sufficient to render life ineligible....

Philo: And is it possible... said Philo, that after all these reflections, and infinitely more, which might be suggested, you can still persevere in your Anthropomorphism, and assert the moral attributes of the

Deity, his justice, benevolence, mercy, and rectitude, to be of the same nature with these virtues in human creatures? His power we allow is infinite: whatever he wills is executed: but neither man nor any other animal is happy: therefore he does not will their happiness. His wisdom is infinite: He is never mistaken in choosing the means to any end: But the course of Nature tends not to human or animal felicity: therefore it is not established for that purpose. Through the whole compass of human knowledge, there are no inferences more certain and infallible than these. In what respect, then, do his benevolence and mercy resemble the benevolence and mercy of men?

Epicurus's old questions are yet unanswered.

Is he willing to prevent evil, but not able? then is he impotent. Is he able, but not willing? then is he malevolent. Is he both able and willing? whence then is evil?

Discussion

1. What are the different kinds of evils that Philo and Demea speak of? Are any of these easier to reconcile with God's goodness and power than any others?

2. If you don't know what anthropomorphism means, look it up. Is anthropomorphism, when applied to God, good or bad? Defend your answer.

3. What conclusion do you think Hume is drawing here? Support your position.

Chapter 18

Plantinga's Free Will Defense

THE FREE WILL DEFENSE

PAUL TIDMAN*

God and evil. It has long been maintained that the mere existence of evil is incompatible with theism, because theism includes the claim that God is both omnipotent and perfectly good. In Hume's classic *Dialogues Concerning Natural Religion* the character Philo asserts:

> Epicurus's old questions are yet unanswered. Is he willing to prevent evil, but not able? Then is he impotent. Is he able, but not willing? Then is he malevolent. Is he both able and willing? Whence then is evil?[1]

Today, Epicurus's old questions are just that—old. They have been answered decisively by Alvin Plantinga, who coined the term "Free Will Defense" as a label for his detailed and carefully constructed response to this line of attack.[2] Plantinga's Free Will Defense achieved something fairly rare in philosophy—widespread consensus that it works. As a consequence the objection that the mere existence of evil is problematic for theism has fallen into disuse in contemporary academic philosophy of religion. For example, one leading figure offers the following observation, "It used to be widely held that evil—which for present purposes we may

identify with undeserved pain and suffering—was incompatible with the existence of God: that no possible world contained both God and evil. So far as I am able to tell, this thesis is no longer defended."[3]

It is the Free Will Defense that has led to the disappearance of this line of objection to theism. However, Plantinga's presentation of the Free Will Defense can be rather daunting for the novice philosopher. It involves not only possible worlds, but essences, world indexed properties, and something called "transworld depravity." My purpose in this chapter is to try to present the basic idea of the Free Will Defense in a manner that is understandable to the beginning student in Philosophy.

In thinking about the Free Will Defense there are two important features to keep in mind. First, the defense is a response to a particular formulation of the problem of evil, what has come to be known as the "Logical Problem of Evil." The hallmark of the Logical Problem of Evil is that it charges the theist with believing propositions that are logically inconsistent. In other words, the logical problem of evil claims that theism is not even possibly true, given the undeniable truth that evil exists. The Free Will Defense defends the theist from this serious charge.

The second key feature of the Free Will Defense is a consequence of the first. To defend the theist (or anyone) from inconsistency all that is required is that one show that a particular state of affairs is possible—namely one in which all of the allegedly inconsistent propositions are true. Thus to successfully defend the Free Will Defense you do not need to say anything

---

* Paul Tidman is Associate Professor of Philosophy and Religious Studies at Mount Union College.

23

about what is actually the case. Indeed, the Free Will Defense might succeed even if, in fact, no one is free—it is enough that free choices merely be possible. The particular possibility at the heart of the Free Will Defense is one in which a good omnipotent God creates beings with free will who misuse their freedom to bring about evil. If this is possible theism is consistent with the existence of evil.

In what follows I will explore the Free Will Defense by focusing on these two features. I will describe more carefully the charge of inconsistency laid against the theist and how the Free Will Defense is a response to this charge. I will then explain more carefully the possibility claims that lie at the heart of the Free Will Defense. I will describe a simple version of the defense and then move on to explain the basic features of Plantinga's more sophisticated version. I will conclude by raising a problem common to any version of the Free Will Defense.

The charge of inconsistency. To be guilty of inconsistent beliefs is a very bad thing intellectually speaking. It is to be, not merely wrong, but necessarily wrong. It is to be guilty of a failure of logic. In his defense of the logical problem of evil, J.L. Mackie accuses the theist of just such a shortcoming:

> It can be shown, not merely that religious beliefs lack rational support, but that they are positively irrational, that the several parts of the essential theological doctrine are inconsistent with one another, so that the theologian . . . must be prepared to believe, not merely what cannot be proved, but what can be disproved from other beliefs that he also holds.[4]

Specifically, the logical problem of evil asserts that the following three propositions are inconsistent:

1.   God is omnipotent.

2.   God is wholly good.

3.   Evil exists.

Or, more simply one could pose the same problem using just two propositions

1.   An omnipotent and wholly good being exists.

2.   Evil exists.

Likewise, one could restate the logical problem of evil in the form of an argument as follows:

1.   Evil exists.

Therefore,

2.   It is not the case that an omnipotent and wholly good being exists.

All of these ways of putting the problem come to the same thing. If this argument is valid, or if the existence of God is inconsistent with the existence of evil, one must either give up theism or deny the reality of evil. The only alternative to either of these unpalatable options is to mount a defense. A defense purports to show the argument above is invalid; that the theist is not inconsistent in acknowledging the existence of evil, because it is possible for God and evil to co-exist.

It is important, therefore, to keep in mind that to mount a defense one need not explain why God *in fact* permits evil. All that is required to rebut the logical problem of evil is to show that it is *possible* for these two propositions both to be true.

1.   An omnipotent and wholly good being exists.

2.   Evil exists.

You can do this by producing a third proposition that is consistent with the claim that an omnipotent and perfectly good being exists, and which is such that when added to that claim entails the existence of evil. As Alvin Plantinga puts it, this proposition "need not be true or known to be true; it need not be so much as plausible."[5] The proposition in question only needs to be possible.

Another way to state the problem is in terms of possible worlds. There are a number of accounts of possible worlds. On Plantinga's account, possible worlds are states of affairs. A state of affairs is a way things could be. There is a possible world corresponding to each way things could be. So, there are possible worlds where you never read this paper. Indeed, there are possible worlds in which you were never born. There are possible worlds where the laws of physics are different, where, like Superman, you can leap tall buildings in a single bound!

One world, the actual world, is the way things are. For a proposition to be true is for it to be true in the actual world. For a proposition to be possible is for it to be true in at least one possible world. And for a proposition to be necessary is for it to be true in every possible world. Stated in terms of possible worlds, the logical problem of evil is the claim that there is no possible world in which the propositions God is omnipotent, God is perfectly good and evil exists are all true. The Free Will Defense, on the other hand, attempts to show that these propositions are consistent by describing such a possible world.

A simple version of the free will defense. The proposition at the heart of the Free Will Defense is the claim that it is possible for an omnipotent, perfectly good being to create someone who has "significant moral freedom" who then misuses the freedom and brings about evil. There are ways, of course, that an omnipotent being could insure evil free acts never happen. God could create beings with no free will whatsoever—automata who always do the right thing merely

because that is what they are programmed to do. Or, God could allow freedom only with respect to morally insignificant matters, such as whether to scratch one's ear or not. The problem is, such creatures could never do anything morally praiseworthy. Significant moral freedom is the freedom to make morally significant choices. To have significant moral freedom one must have the ability not only to do good, but also evil. According to the Free Will Defense there is something even an omnipotent God cannot do. God cannot causally determine someone to *freely* choose to do the right thing. If God were to causally determine the choice, it would not be free. Plantinga argues:

> A world containing creatures who are significantly free (and freely perform more good than evil actions) is more valuable, all else being equal, than a world containing no free creatures at all. Now God can create free creatures, but he can't *cause* or *determine* them to do only what is right *freely*. To create creatures capable of *moral good*, therefore, He must create creatures capable of moral evil, and He can't give these creatures the freedom to perform evil and at the same time prevent them from doing so.

If it is possible for God to create such creatures, it would seem that the logical problem of evil fails. For if God can create a being with morally significant freedom, it must be possible for God to create such a being who chooses to freely bring about evil. So, if it is possible for God to create creatures that make morally significant free choices, then it is possible for God and evil to co-exist.

The above argument can be stated in very precise terms as follows:

1. It is possible for an omnipotent, wholly good being to create a being that has morally significant freedom.

2. If it is possible for an omnipotent, wholly good being to create a being that has morally significant freedom, then it is possible for an omnipotent, wholly good being to create a being who then freely chooses to bring about evil.

Therefore,

3. It is possible for an omnipotent, wholly good being to create a being who then freely chooses to bring about evil.

Could God create a world with moral good, but no moral evil? There remains however, a puzzle. It is this puzzle that leads to the intricacies of Plantinga's formulation of the Free Will Defense. Since God is omnipotent, why couldn't he just create beings who only freely choose to do good? Here's how Mackie puts the point:

> If God has made men such that in their free choices they sometimes prefer what is good and sometimes what is evil, why could he not have made men such that they always freely choose the good? If there is no logical impossibility in a man's freely choosing the good on one, or on several occasions, there cannot be a logical impossibility in his freely choosing the good on every occasion. God was not, then, faced with a choice between making innocent automata and making beings who, in acting freely, would sometimes go wrong; there was open to him the obviously better possibility of making beings who would act freely but always go right. Clearly, his failure to avail himself of this possibility is *inconsistent* with his being both omnipotent and wholly good.[6]

It does seem possible that every moral agent could always freely choose to do good. If so, then there is a possible world where God has created free creatures and yet they never bring about evil. So, why didn't God create such a world? Mackie, in effect, argues that if there are such worlds, God's moral goodness would require him to bring that kind of world about, as opposed to any world where freedom is misused.

Plantinga's response to this question proceeds along two lines. First Plantinga argues that it is a mistake to think that God can bring about any possible world. There are possible worlds that even an omnipotent being cannot bring about. We will explore this line of argument in the remainder of this section. In the next section we will take up the second part of Plantinga's response. As we shall see, Plantinga constructs the Free Will Defense to show that it is possible that God could not have created free creatures who do no wrong.

Plantinga argues that Mackie's mistake is to assume that it follows from the fact that God is omnipotent that He can bring about any possible world He pleases. Plantinga labels this assumption "Leibniz's Lapse" and argues it is a mistake. Leibniz is famous for his claim that God must create the best of all possible worlds. What he failed to see is that there are many worlds that even an omnipotent being cannot bring about. To see the problem, imagine someone who is about to make a free choice. God, let us assume, can put someone in a set of circumstances to make the choice. But God cannot determine which choice will be made. In one possible world, the person makes one choice when placed in those circumstances. In another possible world, the person makes the other choice in the very same circumstances. One of those two worlds is one that even an omnipotent being could not bring about.

Plantinga offers the example of Maurice, who is deciding whether or not to have some oatmeal. Consider Maurice's free decision whether or not to eat the oatmeal, made at a particular moment of time, t. If the decision is a free one, then there is a possible world where Maurice eats the oatmeal at t, and there is also a possible world where, in exactly the same circumstances, Maurice chooses not to eat the oatmeal at *t*. One of these worlds even God could not have brought about. Which world is actual depends on the free choice of Maurice, not God. The other world, where Maurice chooses differently, is a possible world, but it was not within even God's power to bring it about.

Here is how Plantinga, with characteristic wit, summarizes the situation:

> Accordingly, there are any number of possible worlds such that it is partly up to Maurice whether or not God can actualize them. It is, of course, up to God whether or not to create Maurice and also up to God whether on not to make him free with respect to the action of taking oatmeal at time *t*. (God could, if He chose, cause him to succumb to the dreaded *equine obsession*, a condition shared by some people and most horses, whose victims find it *psychologically impossible* to refuse oats or oat products.) But if He creates Maurice and creates him free with respect to this action, then whether or not he actually performs that action is up to Maurice—not God.[7]

Where Leibniz, and Mackie, go wrong is to assume that because God is omnipotent He can bring about any possible world. If an omnipotent being brings about worlds where His creatures exercise free choice, there are some worlds even God cannot bring about.

Plantinga's possibilities. So it does not follow then from the fact that a being is omnipotent that he can bring about just any possible world. To assume that God can create a world with moral good but no moral evil, as Mackie does, is to make this mistake—the mistake Plantinga refers to as "Leibniz's Lapse." But that point is not quite the same as the Free Will Defense. The Free Will Defense purports to show that, indeed,

it is possible that God could not have created a world in which everyone freely chooses to do what is right.

According to the Free Will Defense it is possible that every free agent God might have created would suffer from what Plantinga dubs "Transworld Depravity." Moral agents suffer from transworld depravity if they are such that if they were created they would go wrong with respect to at least one moral choice. The core of the Free Will Defense is the claim that it is possible that no matter who God created it was true that they would have performed at least some wrong actions.

Plantinga's specific example of someone that suffers from transworld depravity is Curley, the mayor of Boston. Unlike Maurice, Curley is faced with a morally significant choice. Curley freely chooses to accept a bribe. Since Curley freely accepts the bribe, there must be a possible world where Curley meritoriously refuses. Unfortunately, it may not be within even God's power to actualize such a world. This is because prior to God's decision of which world to actualize there is already a truth to the matter regarding how Curley would choose. If God places Curly in the relevant circumstances, Curley chooses wrongly. As was the case with Maurice and his oatmeal above, because Curley's choice is free, there are worlds God cannot bring about. Because Curley would freely accept the bribe, God cannot bring about a world where in those same circumstances he freely turns it down.

Curley suffers from transworld depravity if it is true that for any world God might have actualized there is at least one free choice like this one where Curley would have gone wrong. The Free Will Defense is the claim it is possible that every person God might have created suffers from this kind of depravity, and thus that it might not have been possible for God to create a world with moral good but no moral evil.

What is important about the idea of transworld depravity is that if a person suffers from it, then it wasn't within God's power to actualize any world in which that person is significantly free but does no wrong—that is, a world in which he produces moral good but no moral evil. . . . Obviously it is possible that there be persons who suffer from transworld depravity. More generally, it is possible that *everybody* suffers from it. And if this possibility were actual, then God, though omnipotent, could not have created any of the possible worlds containing just the persons who do in fact exist, and containing moral good but no moral evil.[8]

Plantinga goes on to argue that it is possible that, not only the persons that do in fact exist, but anyone God could have created would suffer from transworld depravity. Therefore, it is possible that God could not have created a world with moral good, but no moral evil. It is this possibility that has led to the logical problem of evil's well-deserved demise.

Is the Free Will Defense successful? Despite its reputation, there is a problem with the Free Will Defense. At the heart of the Free Will Defense is a claim about what is possible—namely, the claim that it is possible that God could not have created a world with moral good, but no moral evil. But how do we know that this is possible?

An appealing answer is to say that this seems possible simply because it does not seem impossible. The situation described by the Free Will Defense seems perfectly conceivable, quite unlike the way it is when one attempts to conceive of impossible states of affairs like round squares, or married bachelors. When we attempt to conceive of states of affairs like these, the result is a distinctive kind of mental cramp, what is sometimes referred to as a modal intuition. It's not just that we cannot conceive of these states of affairs, it is that when we attempt to do so we can "just see" that they are impossible. The problem is that there are impossible states of affairs about which our intuitions

are silent. Merely *failing* to see that something is *impossible* is not the same as *seeing* that it *is possible*. There are some propositions about which our intuitions give us no clear, decisive guidance. Arguably the claim at the heart of the Free Will Defense, that it is possible that God could not have created a world with moral good but no moral evil, is just such a proposition.

Consider in this vein the question of whether God is a necessary being—i.e., a being that exists in every possible world. If God is a necessary being, then it is impossible for God not to exist. But it might seem that it is just obvious that God could fail to exist. After all, we can conceive of worlds without God. Indeed, it seems we can conceive of a world in which nothing at all exists. The problem is, we can also just as easily entertain the possibility that God is a necessary being. So we can imagine God not existing, but we can also imagine that it is impossible for God not to exist. One of these things we can easily imagine is impossible.[9]

The claim that it is possible for a necessary being to exist is at the center of another widely discussed issue in Philosophy of Religion, the Ontological argument. Plantinga has made his mark here as well. As Plantinga reconstructs the argument, the crucial premise is the claim that it is possible for there to be a being that possesses the property of maximal greatness. A being possesses that property only if it exists in every possible world. What is of interest to us is the epistemic status of this premise. Can we see that such a being is possible? Even Plantinga shies away from this claim.

> . . . We must ask whether this argument is a successful piece of natural theology, whether it *proves* the existence of God. And the answer must be, I think, that it does not. . . . It must be conceded that not everyone who understands and reflects on its central premise—that the existence of a maximally

great being is *possible*—will accept it. Still, it is evident, I think, that there is nothing *contrary to reason* or *irrational* in accepting this premise.[10]

A similar assessment would seem appropriate for the Free Will Defense. Though Plantinga talks at times as though he has *demonstrated* that it is possible that God could not create a world with moral good but no moral evil, he has not really done that. Like the Ontological Argument, the Free Will Defense could not stand up as a piece of natural theology.[11]

Fortunately, the Free Will Defense does not need to rise to such a high standard in order to effectively rebut the Logical Problem of Evil. It is a *defense*, not a proof. It is enough that a reasonable person could find the possibilities described by Plantinga to be possible. It is the Logical Problem of Evil that purports to be a proof (or, in this case, disproof), not the Free Will Defense. Recall that the logical problem of Evil accuses the theist of holding inconsistent beliefs. That is a very serious charge. The burden of proof is on those who would defend this claim. No one has come close to doing so. Given the evident reasonableness of the possibility claims at the heart of the Free Will Defense, it is not surprising that the Logical Problem of Evil has slipped into intellectual oblivion.

Notes

1. David Hume, *Dialogues Concerning Natural Religion*, Part x.

2. Plantinga's most accessible presentation of the Free Will Defense can be found in *God, Freedom, and Evil* (Grand Rapids, MI: Eerdmans, 1977), pp. 29–59. The Defense is presented with much greater technical detail in *The Nature of Necessity* (Clarendon: Oxford UP, 1974), pp. 165–95.

3. Peter van Inwagen, "The Problem of Evil, the Problem of Air, the Problem of Silence," in *The Evidential Problem of Evil*, ed. Daniel Howard-Snyder (Bloomington, Indiana: Indiana UP, 1996), p. 151.

4. J.L. Mackie, "Evil and Omnipotence," *Mind* 64 (1955): 200, reprinted in *The Problem of Evil*, ed. Marilyn McCord Adams and Robert Adams (Oxford: Oxford UP, 1991), p. 25 (subsequent page references are to Adams's volume).

5. Alvin Plantinga, *The Nature of Necessity* (Clarendon: Oxford UP, 1974), p. 165.

6. Mackie, p. 33.

7. *God, Freedom, and Evil*, p. 44.

8. *God, Freedom, and Evil*, p. 48. Plantinga's account of transworld depravity is developed in much greater technical detail. For the sake of simplicity, I am passing over his discussion of essences, world-indexed properties, etc. For these details, see *The Nature of Necessity*, pp. 184–89, and *God, Freedom, and Evil*, pp. 40–53.

9. For an argument that being able to conceive of worlds in which God does not exist does not give one good reason to think such worlds possible, see Paul Tidman, "The Epistemology of Evil Possibilities," *Faith and Philosophy* (10 April 1993): 181–97.

10. *God, Freedom, and Evil*, p. 112. See also *The Nature of Necessity*, ch. 10, sec. 8.

11. Criticisms of the Free Will Defense along these lines can be found in Keith DeRose,

"Plantinga, Presumption, Possibility and the Problem of Evil," *Canadian Journal of Philosophy* 21 (1990): 497–512, and Daniel Howard-Snyder and John O'Leary-Hawthorne, "Transworld Sanctity and Plantinga's Free Will Defense," *International Journal for the Philosophy of Religion* 44 (1998): 1–21.

Discussion

1. The Free Will Defense argues that God might have to permit moral evils in order to create beings that possess free will. But, what about natural evils? Is the existence of natural evil inconsistent with theism? Plantinga suggests the possibility that natural evil may result from, say, Satan's misuse of his free will. Does that solve the problem?

2. Some philosophers argue that free will is a myth and that all human actions are causally determined. This view is known as Hard Determinism. Another camp, Soft Determinism, holds that there are free actions, but that even free actions are causally determined. Does the Free Will Defense require rejecting either view?

3. Must God create the best possible world? If, as the Free Will Defense argues, it is possible God cannot create a perfect world, must he create the best one he possibly can?

Chapter 19

Theodicy

THE SOUL-MAKING THEODICY

JOHN HICK*

The Augustinian legacy. Within the Augustinian tradition, which has dominated the thought of Western Christendom since the fifth century, the doctrine of a fearful and calamitous fall of man long ago in the "dark backward and abysm of time," and of a subsequent participation by all men in the deadly entail of sin, is, as we have seen, deeply entrenched. According to this conception in its developed form, man was created finitely perfect, but in his freedom he rebelled against God and has existed ever since under the righteous wrath and just condemnation of his Maker. For the descendants of Adam and Eve stand in a corporate unity and continuity of life with the primal pair and have inherited both their guilt and a corrupted and sin-prone nature. We are accordingly born as sinners, and endowed with a nature that is bound to lead us daily into further sin; and it is only by God's free, and to us incomprehensible, grace that some (but not all) are eventually to be saved.

It is helpful to distinguish two separable elements within this tradition: namely, the assertion of an inherited *sinfulness* or tendency to sin, and the assertion of a universal human *guilt* in respect of Adam's crime, falling upon us on account of a physical or mystical presence of the whole race in its first forefather. As we shall

---

* John Hick (1922–2012) was a prominent philosopher of religion.

see, the former idea is common to all Christian traditions—whether in the form of a physiologically or of a socially transmitted moral distortion—while the latter idea is peculiar to Augustinian and Calvinist theology.

The Augustinian picture is so familiar that it is commonly thought of as *the* Christian view of man and his sinful plight. Nevertheless it is only *a* Christian view. . . .

The Irenaean tradition. Fortunately there is another and better way. As well as the "majority report" of the Augustinian tradition, which has dominated Western Christendom, both Catholic and Protestant, since the time of Augustine himself, there is the "minority report" of the Irenaean tradition. This latter is both older and newer than the other, for it goes back to St. Irenaeus and others of the early Hellenistic Fathers of the Church in the two centuries prior to St. Augustine, and it has flourished again in more developed forms during the last hundred years.

Instead of regarding man as having been created by God in a finished state, as a finitely perfect being fulfilling the divine intention for our human level of existence, and then falling disastrously away from this, the minority report sees man as still in process of creation. Irenaeus himself expressed the point in terms of the (exegetically dubious) distinction between the "image" and the "likeness" of God referred to in Genesis i. 26: "Then God said, Let us make man in our image, after our likeness." His view was that man as a personal and moral being already exists in the image, but has not yet been formed into the finite likeness

221

of God. By this "likeness" Irenaeus means something more than personal existence as such; he means a certain valuable quality of personal life which reflects finitely the divine life. This represents the perfecting of man, the fulfillment of God's purpose for humanity, the "bringing of many sons to glory" the creating of "children of God" who are "fellow heirs with Christ" of his glory.

And so man, created as a personal being in the image of God, is only the raw material for a further and more difficult stage of God's creative work. This is the leading of men as relatively free and autonomous persons, through their own dealings with life in the world in which He has placed them, towards that quality of personal existence that is the finite likeness of God. The features of this likeness are revealed in the person of Christ, and the process of man's creation into it is the work of the Holy Spirit. In St. Paul's words, "And we all, with unveiled faces, beholding the glory of the Lord, are being changed into his likeness ... from one degree of glory to another; for this comes from the Lord who is the Spirit"; or again, "For God knew his own before ever they were, and also ordained that they should be shaped to the likeness ... of his Son." In Johannine terms, the movement from the image to the likeness is a transition from one level of existence, that of animal life (*Bios*), to another and higher level, that of eternal life (*Zoe*), which includes but transcends the first. And the fall of man was seen by Irenaeus as a failure within the second phase of this creative process, a failure that has multiplied the perils and complicated the route of the journey in which God is seeking to lead mankind.

In the light of modern anthropological knowledge some form of two-stage conception of the creation of man has become an almost unavoidable Christian tenet. At the very least we must acknowledge as two distinguishable stages the fashioning of *homo sapiens* as a product of the long evolutionary process, and his sudden or gradual spiritualization as a child of God.

But we may well extend the first stage to include the development of man as a rational and responsible person capable of personal relationship with the personal Infinite who has created him. This first stage of the creative process was, to our anthropomorphic imaginations, easy for divine omnipotence. By an exercise of creative power God caused the physical universe to exist, and in the course of countless ages to bring forth within it organic life, and finally to produce out of organic life personal life; and when man had thus emerged out of the evolution of the forms of organic life, a creature had been made who has the possibility of existing in conscious fellowship with God. But the second stage of the creative process is of a different kind altogether. It cannot be performed by omnipotent power as such. For personal life is essentially free and self-directing. It cannot be perfected by divine fiat, but only through the uncompelled responses and willing cooperation of human individuals in their actions and reactions in the world in which God has placed them. Men may eventually become the perfected persons whom the New Testament calls "children of God," but they cannot be created ready-made as this.

The value-judgement that is implicitly being invoked here is that one who has attained to goodness by meeting and eventually mastering temptations, and thus by rightly making responsible choices in concrete situations, is good in a richer and more valuable sense than would be one created *ab initio* in a state either of innocence or of virtue. In the former case, which is that of the actual moral achievements of mankind, the individual's goodness has within it the strength of temptations overcome, a stability based upon an accumulation of right choices, and a positive and responsible character that comes from the investment of costly personal effort. I suggest, then, that it is an ethically reasonable judgement, even though in the nature of the case not one that is capable of demonstrative proof, that human goodness slowly built up through personal histories of moral effort has a value in the eyes of the

Creator which justifies even the long travail of the soul-making process.

The picture with which we are working is thus developmental and teleological. Man is in process of becoming the perfected being whom God is seeking to create. However, this is not taking place—it is important to add—by a natural and inevitable evolution, but through a hazardous adventure in individual freedom. Because this is a pilgrimage within the life of each individual, rather than a racial evolution, the progressive fulfillment of God's purpose does not entail any corresponding progressive improvement in the moral state of the world. There is no doubt a development in man's ethical situation from generation to generation through the building of individual choices into public institutions, but this involves an accumulation of evil as well as of good. It is thus probable that human life was lived on much the same moral plane two thousand years ago or four thousand years ago as it is today. But nevertheless during this period uncounted millions of souls have been through the experience of earthly life, and God's purpose has gradually moved towards its fulfillment within each one of them, rather than within a human aggregate composed of different units in different generations.

The soul-making theodicy. If, then, God's aim in making the world is "the bringing of many sons to glory," that aim will naturally determine the kind of world that He has created. Antitheistic writers almost invariably assume a conception of the divine purpose which is contrary to the Christian conception. They assume that the purpose of a loving God must be to create a hedonistic paradise; and therefore to the extent that the world is other than this, it proves to them that God is either not loving enough or not powerful enough to create such a world. They think of God's relation to the earth on the model of a human being building a cage for a pet animal to dwell in. If he is humane he will naturally make his pet's quarters as pleasant and

healthful as he can. Any respect in which the cage falls short of the veterinarian's ideal, and contains possibilities of accident or disease, is evidence of either limited benevolence or limited means, or both. Those who use the problem of evil as an argument against belief in God almost invariably think of the world in this kind of way. David Hume, for example, speaks of an architect who is trying to plan a house that is to be as comfortable and convenient as possible. If we find that "the windows, doors, fires, passages, stairs, and the whole economy of the building were the source of noise, confusion, fatigue, darkness, and the extremes of heat and cold" we should have no hesitation in blaming the architect. It would be in vain for him to prove that if this or that defect were corrected greater ills would result: "still you would assert in general, that, if the architect had had skill and good intentions, he might have formed such a plan of the whole, and might have adjusted the parts in such a manner, as would have remedied all or most of these inconveniences."

But if we are right in supposing that God's purpose for man is to lead him from human *Bios*, or the biological life of man, to that quality of *Zoe*, or the personal life of eternal worth, which we see in Christ, then the question that we have to ask is not, Is this the kind of world that an all-powerful and infinitely loving being would create as an environment for his human pets? or, Is the architecture of the world the most pleasant and convenient possible? The question that we have to ask is rather, Is this the kind of world that God might make as an environment in which moral beings may be fashioned, through their own free insights and responses, into "children of God"?

Such critics as Hume are confusing what heaven ought to be, as an environment for perfected finite beings, with what this world ought to be, as an environment for beings who are in process of becoming perfected. For if our general conception of God's purpose is correct the world is not intended to be a paradise, but rather the scene of a history in which human personality may be formed towards the pattern of Christ. Men are not to be thought of on the analogy of animal pets, whose life is to be made as agreeable as possible, but rather on the analogy of human children, who are to grow to adulthood in an environment whose primary and overriding purpose is not immediate pleasure but the realizing of the most valuable potentialities of human personality.

Needless to say, this characterization of God as the heavenly Father is not a merely random illustration but an analogy that lies at the heart of the Christian faith. Jesus treated the likeness between the attitude of God to man, and the attitude of human parents at their best towards their children, as providing the most adequate way for us to think about God. And so it is altogether relevant to a Christian understanding of this world to ask, How does the best parental love express itself in its influence upon the environment in which children are to grow up? I think it is clear that a parent who loves his children, and wants them to become the best human beings that they are capable of becoming, does not treat pleasure as the sole and supreme value. Certainly we seek pleasure for our children, and take great delight in obtaining it for them; but we do not desire for them unalloyed pleasure at the expense of their growth in such even greater values as moral integrity, unselfishness, compassion, courage, humour, reverence for the truth, and perhaps above all the capacity for love. We do not act on the premise that pleasure is the supreme end of life; and if the development of these other values sometimes clashes with the provision of pleasure, then we are willing to have our children miss a certain amount of this, rather than fail to come to possess and to be possessed by the finer and more precious qualities that are possible to the human personality. A child brought up on the principle that the only or the supreme value is pleasure would not be likely to become an ethically mature adult or an attractive or happy personality. And to most parents it seems more

important to try to foster quality and strength of character in their children than to fill their lives at all times with the utmost possible degree of pleasure. If, then, there is any true analogy between God's purpose for his human creatures, and the purpose of loving and wise parents for their children, we have to recognize that the presence of pleasure and the absence of pain cannot be the supreme and overriding end for which the world exists. Rather, this world must be a place of soul-making. And its value is to be judged, not primarily by the quantity of pleasure and pain occurring in it at any particular moment, but by its fitness for its primary purpose, the purpose of soul-making.[1] . . .

Conclusion. This, then, is the starting-point from which we propose to try to relate the realities of sin and suffering to the perfect love of an omnipotent Creator. And as will become increasingly apparent, a theodicy that starts in this way must be eschatological in its ultimate bearings. That is to say, instead of looking to the past for its clue to the mystery of evil, it looks to the future, and indeed to that ultimate future to which only faith can look. Given the conception of a divine intention working in and through human time towards a fulfillment that lies in its completeness beyond human time, our theodicy must find the meaning of evil in the part that it is made to play in the eventual outworking of that purpose; and must find the justification of the whole process in the magnitude of the good to which it leads. The good that outshines all ill is not a paradise long since lost but a kingdom which is yet to come in its full glory and permanence.

Note

1. The phrase "the vale of Soul-making" was coined by the poet John Keats in a letter written to his brother and sister in April 1819. He says, "The common cognomen of this world among the misguided and

superstitious is 'a vale of tears' from which we are to be redeemed by a certain arbitrary interposition of God and taken to Heaven— What a little circumscribed straightened notion! Call the world if you Please 'The vale of Soul-making.'" In this letter he sketches a teleological theodicy. "Do you not see," he asks "how necessary a World of Pains and troubles is to school an Intelligence and make it a Soul?" (*The Letters of John Keats*, 4th ed., ed. M.B. Forman [London: Oxford UP, 1952], pp. 334–35).

Discussion

1. Is the end of soul-making a great enough good to explain all of human suffering?

2. Can you think of evils which are so horrific that they couldn't possibly contribute to soul-making? How do you think Hick might explain these?

3. Could we become virtuous without facing real dangers? Show why this is or is not the case.

HORRENDOUS EVILS AND THE GOODNESS OF GOD

MARILYN MCCORD ADAMS*

Introduction. Over the past thirty years, analytic philosophers of religion have defined "the problem of evil" in terms of the *prima facie* difficulty in consistently maintaining

   (1) God exists, and is omnipotent, omniscient, and perfectly good.

and

   (2) Evil exists.

In a crisp and classic article, "Evil and Omnipotence,"[1] J.L. Mackie emphasized that the problem is not that (1) and (2) are logically inconsistent by themselves, but that they, together with quasi-logical rules formulating attribute-analyses—such as

   (P1) A perfectly good being would always eliminate evil so far as it could,

and

   (P2) There are no limits to what an omnipotent being can do—

constitute an inconsistent premise-set. . . .

   In debates about whether the argument from evil can establish the irrationality of religious belief, care must be taken, both by the atheologians who deploy it and the believers who defend against it, to insure that the operative attribute-analyses accurately reflect

that religion's understanding of Divine power and goodness. It does the atheologian no good to argue for the falsity of Christianity on the ground that the existence of an omnipotent, omniscient, pleasure-maximizer is incompossible with a world such as ours, because Christians never believed God was a pleasure-maximizer anyway. . . .

   The moral . . . might be summarized thus: where the internal coherence of a system of religious beliefs is at stake, successful arguments for its inconsistency must draw on premises (explicitly or implicitly) internal to that system or obviously acceptable to its adherents; likewise for successful rebuttals or explanations of consistency. The thrust of my argument is to push both sides of the debate towards more detailed attention to and subtle understanding of the religious system in question.

   As a Christian philosopher, I want to focus in this essay on the problem for the truth of Christianity raised by what I shall call "horrendous" evils. Although our world is riddled with them, the Biblical record punctuated by them, and one of them—viz., the passion of Christ, according to Christian belief, the judicial murder of God by the people of God—is memorialized by the Church on its most solemn holiday (Good Friday) and in its central sacrament (the Eucharist), the problem of horrendous evils is largely skirted by standard treatments for the good reason that they are intractable by them. After showing why, I will draw on other Christian materials to sketch ways of meeting this, the deepest of religious problems.

Defining the category. For present purposes, I define "horrendous evils" as "evils the participation in (the doing or suffering of) which gives one reason *prima facie* to doubt whether one's life could (given their inclusion in it) be a great good to one on the whole." Such reasonable doubt arises because it is so difficult humanly to conceive how such evils could be

---

* Marilyn McCord Adams is Regius Professor of Philosophy at Oxford University.

overcome.... [H]orrendous evils seem *prima facie*, not only to balance off but to engulf the positive value of a participant's life. Nevertheless, that very horrendous proportion, by which they threaten to rob a person's life of positive meaning, cries out not only to be engulfed, but to be made meaningful through positive and decisive defeat.

I understand this criterion to be objective, but relative to individuals. The example of habitual complainers, who know how to make the worst of a good situation, shows individuals not to be incorrigible experts on what ills would defeat the positive value of their lives. Nevertheless, nature and experience endow people with different strengths; one bears easily what crushes another. And a major consideration in determining whether an individual's life is/has been a great good to him/her on the whole, is invariably and appropriately how it has seemed to him/her.

I offer the following list of paradigmatic horrors: the rape of a woman and axing off of her arms, psychophysical torture whose ultimate goal is the disintegration of personality, betrayal of one's deepest loyalties, cannibalizing one's own offspring, child abuse of the sort described by Ivan Karamazov, child pornography, parental incest, slow death by starvation, participation in the Nazi death camps, the explosion of nuclear bombs over populated areas, having to choose which of one's children shall live and which shall be executed by terrorists, being the accidental and/or unwitting agent of the disfigurement or death of those one loves best. I regard these as *paradigmatic* because I believe most people would find in the doing or suffering of them *prima facie* reason to doubt the positive meaning of their lives.[2] ...

For better or worse, the by-now-standard strategies for "solving" the problem of evil are powerless in the face of horrendous evils.

Seeking the reason-why. In his model article "Hume on Evil,"[3] Pike takes up Mackie's challenge,

arguing that (P1) fails to reflect ordinary moral intuitions (more to the point, I would add, Christian beliefs), and traces the abiding sense of trouble to the hunch that an omnipotent, omniscient being could have no reason compatible with perfect goodness for permitting (bringing about) evils, because all legitimate excuses arise from ignorance or weakness. Solutions to the problem of evil have thus been sought in the form of counter-examples to this latter claim, i.e., logically possible reasons why that would excuse even an omnipotent, omniscient God! The putative logically possible reasons offered have tended to be *generic* and *global*: generic insofar as some *general* reason is sought to cover all sorts of evils; global insofar as they seize upon some feature of the world as a whole. For example, philosophers have alleged that the desire to make a world with one of the following properties—"the best of all possible worlds," "a world more perfect than which is impossible," "a world exhibiting a perfect balance of retributive justice,"[4] "a world with as favorable a balance of (created) moral good over moral evil as God can weakly actualize"—would constitute a reason compatible with perfect goodness for God's creating a world with evils in the amounts and of the kinds found in the actual world. Moreover, such general reasons are presented as so powerful as to do away with any need to catalogue types of evils one by one, and examine God's reason for permitting each in particular. Plantinga explicitly hopes that the problem of horrendous evils can thus be solved without being squarely confronted.[5]

The insufficiency of global defeat. A pair of distinctions is in order here: (i) between two dimensions of divine goodness in relation to creation—viz., "producer of global goods" and "goodness to" or "love of individual created persons"; and (ii) between the overbalance/defeat of evil by good on the global scale, and the overbalance/defeat of evil by good within the context of an individual person's life. Correspondingly, we may separate two problems of evil parallel to the two sorts of goodness mentioned in (i).

In effect, generic and global approaches are directed to the first problem: they defend divine goodness along the first (global) dimension by suggesting logically possible strategies for the global defeat of evils. But establishing God's excellence as a producer of global goods does not automatically solve the second problem, especially in a world containing horrendous evils. For God cannot be said to be good or loving to any created persons the positive meaning of whose lives He allows to be engulfed in and/or defeated by evils—that is, individuals within whose lives horrendous evils remain undefeated. Yet, the only way unsupplemented global and generic approaches could have to explain the latter, would be by applying their general reasons-why to particular cases of horrendous suffering.

Unfortunately, such an exercise fails to give satisfaction. Suppose for the sake of argument that horrendous evil could be included in maximally perfect world orders; its being partially constitutive of such an order would assign it that generic and global positive meaning. But would knowledge of such a fact, defeat for a mother the *prima facie* reason provided by her cannibalism of her own infant to wish that she had never been born? Again, the aim of perfect retributive balance confers meaning on evils imposed. But would knowledge that the torturer was being tortured give the victim who broke down and turned traitor under pressure any more reason to think his/her life worthwhile? Would it not merely multiply reasons for the torturer to doubt that his/her life could turn out to be a good to him/her on the whole? Could the truck-driver who accidentally runs over his beloved child find consolation in the idea that this middle-known[6] but unintended side-effect was part of the price God accepted for a world with the best balance of moral good over moral evil He could get?

Not only does the application to horrors of such generic and global reasons for divine permission of evils fail to solve the second problem of evil; it makes it worse by adding generic *prima facie* reasons to doubt whether human life would be a great good to individual human beings in possible worlds where such divine motives were operative. For, taken in isolation and made to bear the weight of the whole explanation, such reasons-why draw a picture of divine indifference or even hostility to the human plight. Would the fact that God permitted horrors because they were constitutive means to His end of global perfection, or that He tolerated them because He could obtain that global end anyway, make the participant's life more tolerable, more worth living for him/her? Given radical human vulnerability to horrendous evils, the ease with which humans participate in them, whether as victim or perpetrator, would not the thought that God visits horrors on anyone who caused them, simply because he/she deserves it, provide one more reason to expect human life to be a nightmare?

Those willing to split the two problems of evil apart might adopt a divide-and-conquer strategy, by simply denying divine goodness along the second dimension. For example, many Christians do not believe that God will insure an overwhelmingly good life to each and every person He creates. Some say the decisive defeat of evil with good is promised only within the lives of the obedient, who enter by the narrow gate. Some speculate that the elect may be few. Many recognize that the sufferings of this present life are as nothing compared to the hell of eternal torment, designed to defeat goodness with horrors within the lives of the damned.

Such a road can be consistently travelled only at the heavy toll of admitting that human life in worlds such as ours is a bad bet. Imagine (adapting Rawls's device) persons in a pre-original position, considering possible worlds containing managers of differing power, wisdom, and character, and subjects of varying fates. The question they are to answer about each world is whether they would willingly enter it as a human being, from behind a veil of ignorance as to which position they would occupy. Reason would, I submit, dictate a negative verdict for worlds whose omniscient and omnipotent manager permits *ante-mortem* horrors that remain undefeated within the context of the human participant's life; *a fortiori*, for worlds in which some or most humans suffer eternal torment. . . .

The how of God's victory. Up to now, my discussion has given the reader cause to wonder whose side I am on anyway? For I have insisted, with rebels like Ivan Karamazov and John Stuart Mill, on spot-lighting the problem horrendous evils pose. Yet, I have signalled my preference for a vision of Christianity that insists on both dimensions of Divine goodness, and maintains not only (a) that God will be good enough to created persons to make human life a good bet, but also (b) that each created person will have a life that is a great good to him/her on the whole. My critique of standard approaches to the problem of evil thus seems to reinforce atheologian Mackie's verdict of "positive irrationality" for such a religious position.

Whys versus hows. The inaccessibility of reasons-why seems especially decisive.[7] For surely an all-wise and all-powerful God, who loved each created person enough (a) to defeat any experienced horrors within the context of the participant's life, and (b) to give each created person a life that is a great good to him/her on the whole, would not permit such persons to suffer horrors for no reason. Does not our inability even to conceive of plausible candidate reasons suffice to make belief in such a God positively irrational in a world containing horrors? In my judgment, it does not.

To be sure, motivating reasons come in several varieties relative to our conceptual grasp: There are (i) reasons of the sort we can readily understand when we are informed of them (e.g., the mother who permits her child to undergo painful heart surgery because it is the only humanly possible way to save its life). Moreover, there are (ii) reasons we would be cognitively, emotionally, and spiritually equipped to grasp if only we had a larger memory or wider attention span (analogy: I may be able to memorize small town street plans; memorizing the road networks of the entire country is a task requiring more of the same, in the way that proving Gödel's theorem is not). Some generic and global approaches insinuate that Divine permission of evils has motivating reasons of this sort. Finally, (iii) there are reasons that we are cognitively, emotionally, and/or spiritually too immature to fathom (the way a two-year old child is incapable of understanding its mother's reasons for permitting the surgery). I agree with Plantinga that our ignorance of Divine reasons for permitting horrendous evils is not of types (i) or (ii), but of type (iii).

Nevertheless, if there are varieties of ignorance, there are also varieties of reassurance. The two-year old heart patient is convinced of its mother's love, not by her cognitively inaccessible reasons, but by her intimate care and presence through its painful experience. The story of Job suggests something similar is true with human participation in horrendous suffering. God does not give Job His reasons-why, and implies that Job isn't smart enough to grasp them; rather, Job is lectured on the extent of divine power, and sees God's goodness face to face! Likewise, I suggest, to exhibit the logical compossibility of both dimensions of divine goodness with horrendous suffering, it is not necessary to find logically possible reasons *why* God might permit them. It is enough to show *how* God can be good enough to created persons despite their participation in horrors—by defeating them within the context of the individual's life and by giving that individual a life that is a great good to him/her on the whole.

What sort of valuables? In my opinion, the reasonableness of Christianity can be maintained in the face of horrendous evils only by drawing on resources of religious value theory. For one way for God to be *good to* created persons is by relating them appropriately to relevant and great goods. But philosophical and religious theories differ importantly on what valuables they admit into their ontology. Some maintain that "what you see is what you get," but nevertheless admit a wide range of valuables, from sensory pleasures, the beauty of nature and cultural artifacts, the joys of creativity, to loving personal intimacy. Others posit a transcendent good (e.g., the Form of the Good in Platonism, or God, the Supremely Valuable Object, in Christianity). In the spirit of Ivan Karamazov, I am convinced that the depth of horrific evil cannot be accurately estimated without recognizing it to be incommensurate with any package of merely non-transcendent goods and so unable to be balanced off, much less defeated thereby.

Where the *internal* coherence of Christianity is the issue, however, it is fair to appeal to its own store of valuables. From a Christian point of view, God is a being a greater than which cannot be conceived, a good incommensurate with both created goods and temporal evils. Likewise, the good of beatific, face-to-face intimacy with God is simply incommensurate with any merely non-transcendent goods or ills a person might experience. Thus, the good of beatific face-to-face intimacy with God would *engulf* . . . even the horrendous evils humans experience in this present life here below, and overcome any *prima facie* reasons the individual had to doubt whether his/her life would or could be worth living.

Personal meaning, horrors defeated. *Engulfing* personal horrors within the context of the participant's life would vouchsafe to that individual a life that was a great good to him/her on the whole. I am still inclined to think it would guarantee that immeasurable divine goodness to any person thus benefitted. But there is good theological reason for Christians to believe that God would go further, beyond engulfment to defeat. For it is the nature of persons to look for meaning, both in their lives and in the world. Divine respect for

and commitment to created personhood would drive God to make all those sufferings which threaten to destroy the positive meaning of a person's life meaningful through positive defeat.

How could God do it? So far as I can see, only by integrating participation in horrendous evils into a person's relationship with God. Possible dimensions of integration are charted by Christian soteriology. I pause here to sketch three:

(i) First, because God in Christ participated in horrendous evil through His passion and death, human experience of horrors can be a means of *identifying* with Christ, either through *sympathetic* identification (in which each person suffers his/her own pains, but their similarity enables each to know what it is like for the other) or through *mystical* identification (in which the created person is supposed literally to experience a share of Christ's pain[8]).

(ii) Julian of Norwich's description of heavenly welcome suggests the possible defeat of horrendous evil through divine gratitude. According to Julian, before the elect have a chance to thank God for all He has done for them, God will say, "Thank you for all your suffering, the suffering of your youth." She says that the creature's experience of divine gratitude will bring such full and unending joy as could not be merited by the whole sea of human pain and suffering throughout the ages.[9]

(iii) A third idea identifies temporal suffering itself with a vision into the inner life of God, and can be developed several ways. Perhaps, contrary to medieval theology, God is not impassible, but rather has matched capacities for joy and for suffering. Perhaps, as the Heidelberg catechism suggests, God responds to human sin and the sufferings of Christ with an agony beyond human conception. Alternatively, the inner life of God may be, strictly speaking and in and of itself, beyond both joy and sorrow. . . . And if a face-to-face vision of God is a good for humans incommensurate with any non-transcendent goods or ills, so any vision of God (including horrendous suffering) would have a good aspect insofar as it is a vision of God (even if it has an evil aspect insofar as it is horrendous suffering). For the most part, horrors are not recognized as experiences of God (any more than the city slicker recognizes his visual image of a brown patch as a vision of Beulah the cow in the distance). But, Christian mysticism might claim, at least from the *post-mortem* perspective of the beatific vision, such sufferings will be seen for what they were, and retrospectively no one will wish away any intimate encounters with God from his/her life-history of this world. The created person's experience of the beatific vision together with his/her knowledge that intimate divine presence stretched back over his/her *ante-mortem* life and reached down into the depths of his/her worst suffering, would provide retrospective comfort independent of comprehension of the reasons-why akin to the two-year-old's assurance of its mother's love. Taking this third approach, Christians would not need to commit themselves about what in any event we do not know: viz., whether we will (like the two-year-old) ever grow up enough to understand the reasons why God permits our participation in horrendous evils. For by contrast with the best of earthly mothers, such divine intimacy is an incommensurate good and would cancel out for the creature any need to know why.

Conclusion. The worst evils demand to be defeated by the best goods. Horrendous evils can be overcome only by the goodness of God. Relative to human nature, participation in horrendous evils and loving intimacy with God are alike disproportionate: for the former threatens to engulf the good in an individual human life with evil, while the latter guarantees the reverse engulfment of evil by good. Relative to one another, there is also disproportion, because the good that God *is*, and intimate relationship with Him, is incommensurate with created goods and evils alike.

Because intimacy with God so outscales relations (good or bad) with any creatures, integration into the human person's relationship with God confers significant meaning and positive value even on horrendous suffering. This result coheres with basic Christian intuition: that the powers of darkness are stronger than humans, but they are no match for God!

Standard generic and global solutions have for the most part tried to operate within the territory common to believer and unbeliever, within the confines of religion-neutral value theory. Many discussions reflect the hope that substitute attribute-analyses, candidate reasons-why and/or defeaters could issue out of values shared by believers and unbelievers alike. And some virtually make this a requirement on an adequate solution.... But agreement on truth-value is not necessary to consensus on internal consistency. My contention has been that it is not only legitimate, but, given horrendous evils, necessary for Christians to dip into their richer store of valuables to exhibit the consistency of (1) and (2). I would go one step further: assuming the pragmatic and/or moral (I would prefer to say, broadly speaking, religious) importance of believing that (one's own) human life is worth living, the ability of Christianity to exhibit how this could be so despite human vulnerability to horrendous evil, constitutes a pragmatic/moral/religious consideration in its favor, relative to value schemes that do not....

Notes

1. J.L. Mackie, "Evil and Omnipotence," *Mind* 64 (1955).

2. Most people would agree that a person *p*'s doing or suffering of them constitutes *prima facie* reason to doubt whether *p*'s life can be, given such participation, a great good to *p* on the whole.

3. "Hume on Evil," *Philosophical Review* 72 (1963): 180–97.

4. Augustine, *On Free Choice of Will*, iii, pp. 93–102.

5. Alvin Plantinga, "Self-Profile," in James E. Tomberlin and Peter van Inwagen, eds., *Profiles: Alvin Plantinga* (Dordrecht, Boston: Reidel, 1985), p. 38.

6. Middle knowledge, or knowledge of what is "in between" the actual and the possible, is the sort of knowledge of what a free creature *would do* in every situation in which that creature could possibly find himself. . . .

7. Following Plantinga, where horrendous evils are concerned, not only do we not know God's *actual* reason for permitting them; we cannot even *conceive* of any plausible candidate sort of reason consistent with worthwhile lives for human participants in them.

8. For example, Julian of Norwich tells us that she prayed for and received the latter (*Revelations of Divine Love*, ch. 17). Mother Theresa of Calcutta seems to construe Matthew 25: 31–46 to mean that the poorest and the least *are* Christ, and that their sufferings *are* Christ's (Malcolm Muggeridge, *Something Beautiful for God* [New York: Harper & Row, 1960], pp. 72–75).

9. *Revelations of Divine Love*, ch. 14.

Discussion

1. Do you think "producer of global goods" is an adequate understanding of divine goodness? If not, what ramifications would adding "good to created persons" to divine goodness have for one's theodicy?

2. Why are non-transcendent goods inadequate to make up for horrific suffering?

3. Are the goods that Adams offers—identifying with Christ, divine gratitude, vision into the inner life of God—adequate consolations for victims of horrendous suffering? Do you think any of these reasons likely to be true?

THEODICY

DANIEL HOWARD-SNYDER*

Evil and suffering. Not long ago, an issue of my local paper reminded its readers of Susan Smith, the Carolinan mother who rolled her Mazda into a lake, drowning her two little sons strapped inside. It also reported the abduction and gang rape of an eleven-year old girl by eight teenage members of Angelitos Sur 13, and the indictment, on 68 counts of sexual abuse, of the "Frito Man," a forty-five year old man who handed out corn chips to neighborhood children in order to lure them to a secluded location. More recently, the headlines announced the untimely death of Ashley Jones, a twelve-year old girl from nearby Stanwood, Washington—she was raped and bludgeoned to death while babysitting her neighbor's kids.

These are particularly disgusting, appalling cases of evil, all the more so because children are the victims. One might think that such cases occur only very rarely. I wish that were so. ABC News recently reported that in the United States a child dies from abuse by a parent or guardian every six hours. One is left with the disturbing thought: if that is how frequently a child *dies* from abuse in the US, how frequently are children *merely* abused? A sinister side-effect of familial abuse is that abused children are much more likely to abuse their own children; and so the attitudes and habits of abuse pass from generation to generation, a cycle of evil and suffering from which it can be enormously difficult to extricate oneself.

Such suffering and evil is wrought by human hands. There are other sources, however. A visit to just about any major hospital reveals children born with grossly debilitating genetic abnormalities that impair them so severely one can't help but think that their lives are

---

*   Daniel Howard-Snyder is Professor of Philosophy at Western Washington University.

not worth living. Moreover, children are not exempt from the horrors resulting from earthquakes, tornadoes, hurricanes, famine and the like. Just last month, a colleague of mine took her little daughter on a walk at one of the local parks; a loose limb fell from one of the tall Douglas firs and struck her dead. Of course, adults suffer horribly as well. And the numbers of those who suffer—children and adults—are staggering: six million snuffed out in the Holocaust, thirty million in the slave trade, forty million in Stalin's purges, a third of Europe's population during the Plague, several million Africans starved just in my lifetime: the list goes on and on. And what about nonhuman animals? We in the enlightened West like to think we are more civilized than our predecessors in our relations to the beasts. We regard the once common practice of beating animals as barbaric, for example. Nevertheless, we don't think twice about hunting for sport, or how the livestock and poultry we don't need to eat got on our plates, or how the musk got into our perfumes. But that's nothing compared to the suffering doled out by Nature. It boggles the mind to consider the billions upon billions of animals stalked and killed or eaten alive by predators or who died slowly and painfully, decimated by disease, famine, or drought.

So it is that we must face a sobering fact: the history of our planet is a history stuffed with horrific evil, suffering, and pain.

Theodicy. According to traditional theism, there exists an unsurpassably powerful, knowledgeable, just and loving creator of the world ("God," for short); thus, according to theism, nothing happens that God does not permit, including the horrific evil and suffering that permeates our world. Theism can be quite perplexing in light of the facts about horrific evil and suffering. After all, it isn't just obvious why God (if there is a God) would permit horrific evil and suffering, or so much of it. And surely he must have a reason. To suppose otherwise is to suppose that, even though a perfectly good being could prevent it, he permits it for no reason whatsoever—which is absurd.

So what *are* God's reasons? What might His purposes be? Such questions naturally lead to a simple line of thought that many honest and reflective people—theists, atheists, and agnostics alike—find compelling. We can't think of any reason that would justify God, so there probably is none; but if there is none, then there is no God; so in all likelihood, God does not exist.

Let's express this line of thought neatly, in the form of an argument. We might do so like this:

1.   There is a lot of horrific evil and suffering.

2.   If God exists, then there is no horrific evil and suffering, or not so much of it—unless there is a reason that would justify Him in permitting it, and so much of it.

3.   There probably is no reason that would justify God in permitting horrific evil and suffering, or so much of it.

4.   So, there probably is no God.

4 follows from 1, 2 and 3, and 1 and 2 are true. That leaves premise 3. Is it true? Before we address that question directly, we should note two things about the argument.

First, the argument appeals to two facts about evil and suffering in our world; the fact that there is horrific evil and suffering, and the fact that there is so much of it. Both of these facts are important in assessing premise 3. For even if we can think of a reason that would justify God in permitting *evil and suffering*, it does not automatically follow that there is a reason that would justify God in permitting any *horrific* evil and suffering; and even if we can think of a reason that would justify God in permitting some horrific evil and suffering, it does not automatically follow that there is a reason

that would justify God in permitting *so much* of it. A military commander might have a justifying reason to permit thousands of troops to be shot in battle, say for national self-defense; it does not follow that she has a reason that would justify her in permitting them to be tortured by the enemy for decades, or to permit millions of them to be tortured for the rest of their lives.

Second, suppose that the conclusion is true. In that case, what should we believe? Should we believe that there is no God? It's quite natural to think that we should, but it is important to see why that doesn't follow. There are two reasons. (1) Even if horrific evil and suffering make it likely that there is no God, they might not make it likely enough. Perhaps the probability is only very slight, too slight for belief. (2) Even if horrific evil and suffering make it likely enough that there is no God, likely enough to believe, we need to take into account our total evidence before believing there is no God. If our total evidence included items that made it *about as likely* that there is a God as not, then perhaps we should withhold judgment on the matter. Alternatively, if our total evidence included items that made it *much more likely* that there is a God than that there isn't, then perhaps we should believe that there is a God.

Still, other considerations aside, it's an interesting question whether horrific evil and suffering make it likely that there is no God. Given the argument we are considering, the answer to that question boils down to whether premise 3 is true. Is it true? Is it true that there probably is no reason that would justify God in permitting horrific evil and suffering, and so much of it?

Some people have argued that not only is it probable that there is no such reason, it's *absolutely guaranteed*. It's impossible for there to be a reason that would justify God! After all, the only reason to permit evil is that one was unaware that it would occur or that one was powerless to prevent it. But neither of these reasons applies in the case of God, who is supposed to be unsurpassable in knowledge and power.[1]

As plausible as this line of thought might initially appear, it fails. It is not generally true that the only reason to permit evil is that one was unaware that it would occur or that one was powerless to prevent it. Sometimes it is neither wrong nor unloving to permit preventable evil one was aware of. For example, a mother might know that if she lets her sons wrestle together, they might well get hurt. Still, she lets them wrestle and thereby permits them to suffer injury. Is this wrong or unloving on her part? I wouldn't think so. There's a lot of good that attends rule-governed wrestling even if there is some chance of injury, and that good is worth the risk. (If you think less of the mother for letting her sons wrestle, then substitute some other activity. It's hard to think of one that's worthwhile that doesn't involve the risk of injury, at least hurt feelings.)

The same point applies to God and his creatures. If there's a lot of good that attends what He allows us to do, then, even if there is some chance of suffering and evil, the good might be worth it.

But, it might be replied, even if it is not *generally* true that the only reason to permit evil is that one was unaware that it would occur or that one was powerless to prevent it, it is true in the case of God. After all, while the mother can't arrange things so that the good that attends activities of various sorts can be had without risk of injury, God can. For God is supposed to be unsurpassably powerful and knowledgeable; surely He can figure out a way to bring about whatever greater goods He has in mind without permitting evil and suffering.

But what if there is no such way? What if the goods themselves cannot occur without the permission of evil? In that case, not even God could figure out a way to get the goods while preventing evil. To suppose otherwise would be like supposing that an unsurpassably knowledgeable and powerful being could figure out a way to make a married bachelor, or make a thing exist and not exist at the very same time. So *if* there is some good that absolutely could not occur without

the permission of horrific evil and suffering, and *if* it is worth the risk of evil, then it might well figure in God's reason to permit horrific evil and suffering, in which case He would do nothing wrong or unloving in permitting it.

Of course, those are big *ifs*. Can we think of such a reason? Can we think of an outweighing good that could not occur unless horrific evil and suffering were permitted, and so much of it? Attempts to state a reason are called *theodicies*. If we can think of one, then we can conclude that there is a reason that would justify God (if such there be) in permitting horrific evil and suffering, and so much of it. In what follows, I'll sketch the more popular theodicies and evaluate the standard objections.

Punishment theodicy. God would be justified in *punishing evildoers* and suffering is a result of His punishing them. You can think of the greater good involved in punishment in whatever way you like, e.g., balancing the scales of justice, or its deterrent effect, or preventing further suffering by the wrongdoer, or some combination of these.

While God would be justified in punishing wrongdoers for their wrongdoing, much of the suffering in the world is *undeserved*. And no one can sensibly say that God would be justified in punishing those who don't deserve it.

But might not *all* the suffering in the world be deserved? I doubt it. Nonhuman animals, very young children and severely impaired adults suffer immensely but do not deserve it since they are not morally responsible for their actions. They lack the requisite capacities for moral deliberation and awareness. Moreover, although many morally responsible persons suffer to a degree that is proportionate to their wrongdoing, many more do not.

So, while *some* suffering might be accounted for by divine punishment, the punishment theodicy cannot explain the overwhelming majority of it. Most importantly, however, it does not even begin to explain why God permitted wrongdoing in the first place. At best, the punishment theodicy is seriously incomplete.

Counterpart theodicy. Good and evil are like pairs of opposites or counterparts. If one exists so does the other. So, if there were no evil, its opposite—moral goodness—wouldn't exist. Likewise for pain and suffering. If there were no pain, there would be no pleasure; and if there were no suffering, there would be no happiness. Thus, God would be justified in permitting evil, pain, and suffering since that's the only way there can be moral goodness, pleasure, and happiness.

One difficulty here is that, according to theism, God is unsurpassably morally good. Moreover, *He* could have existed without there being any evil. After all, what if He had never created anything? Then He would have existed and there would have been good—but there would have been no evil. So, according to theism, it's *false* that if there were no evil there would be no good. Another difficulty is that, even if it is true that something good implies that there is something that is evil, it would only require a speck of evil, a smidgen of pain, and a modicum of suffering, not a world stuffed with them like ours is.

Perhaps those who use the counterpart theodicy mean something very different from what I have been discussing. Perhaps they mean that we couldn't *know* one of a pair of opposites without knowing the other of the pair. Thus, we couldn't *know* something was morally good without knowing evil; and we couldn't *know* evil without there *being* evil; so, to know something is morally good, there has to be evil. Likewise for pain and suffering. We couldn't know pleasure and happiness unless there was pain and suffering. Thus, God would be justified in permitting evil, pain, and suffering because without it we wouldn't know good, pleasure, and happiness.

In this case the underlying principle seems to be that

If we know something has a certain feature, F, then we know something has the opposite feature, not-F.

Call this the *Knowledge Version of the Principle.*

I have three misgivings. First, even if the Knowledge Version is true, it only implies that there be some evil, not as much as there in fact is. Second, the Knowledge Version of the Principle does not imply that if we know something that is morally good, then we know something that is evil, since evil is not the opposite of moral goodness; all that is needed to satisfy the requirement of the Knowledge Version is that we know something that is morally neutral. Third, the Knowledge Version of the Principle is false because it incorrectly implies that if I know you have the feature of being a non-unicorn, then I know something has the opposite feature, namely that feature of being a unicorn, which is to say that I know that at least one unicorn exists (which is false).

Let's now consider some theodicies that have a better chance of explaining evil.

Free will theodicy. God could have created us so that there was no chance of us going wrong or being bad. If He had done so the result would have been splendid, but we would have missed out on a very great good, namely, self-determination. For one to be *self-determined* is for one to be free to a significant degree with respect to the sort of person one becomes, the sort of character one has—and that requires that one have it within one's power to be both good and evil. Lacking such freedom, we could not be deeply responsible for who we are, who we will become and whether we will manifest and confirm our character through the choices we make. Since the capacity for self-determination is such a great good and it requires that we be given considerable latitude with respect to harming ourselves severely, it is a reason that would justify God in permitting evil.

But why not block harm to others? One might object that development of my character requires only that my choices affect me, that is, that they serve to develop my character in one way or another. But couldn't God have arranged things in such a way that while my choices have an effect on me and my character, they have no effect on anyone else (or at least none of the bad ones has an effect on anyone else). For example, suppose I choose freely to steal from you. My choice can contribute to my being untrustworthy without my ever actually stealing since God can arrange things in such a way that I believe I stole even though I didn't. In a nutshell, self-determination doesn't account for the bad consequences for others of evil free choices.[2]

There are several replies to this objection, foremost of which are two.

Reply 1. If God systematically prevents us from harming others yet permits us to have a significant say about the sorts of persons we become, then it will have to *look* to us as though we can harm others even though we can't. For if I know nothing I do can harm others, then I won't have the same opportunity to develop my character as I would if it seemed that I could harm others. But deception is incompatible with God's goodness, one might urge.

Unfortunately, this reply overlooks the fact that deception is not always wrong nor always unloving. (Just ask as any parent.) Perhaps preventing the horrific consequences for others of our free choices is as watertight a reason for deception as there can be. Then again, perhaps not. Let's look into the matter a little more closely.

If God were to arrange things so that none of the horrific consequences for others of our choices really occurred although they appeared to, then we—each of us—would be living a massive illusion. It would seem as though we were involved in genuine relationships with others, making choices that matter for each other, when in fact nothing of the sort really occurred. Our whole lives would be a charade, a sham, a farce; and we wouldn't have a clue. While such massive deception would not result in an utterly meaningless existence (we would still be self-determining creatures), it isn't obvious that such massive deception about matters so central to our lives would be permissible or loving.

Reply 2. A related reply agrees that self-determination does not justify God's permitting us to harm others, even if it does justify God's permitting us to harm ourselves. What other goods, then, would be lost if God were to give us the freedom only to affect ourselves? Well, as indicated in the last reply, we would have no responsibility for each other and we would not be able to enter into the most meaningful relationships; for we are deeply responsible for others and can enter into relationships of love only if we can both benefit and harm others.

This point deserves development. We are deeply responsible for others only if our choices actually make a big difference to their well-being, and that cannot happen unless we can benefit them as well as harm them. This seems obvious enough. Frequently missed, however, is the fact that a similar point applies to love *relationships*, as contrasted with loving attitudes and feelings. Two persons cannot share in the most significant relationships of love unless it is up to each of them that they are so related; this fact can be seen by considering what we want from those whose love we value most. Since those love relationships which we cherish most are those in which we are most deeply vested, in light of love's freedom they are also those from which we can suffer most. It simply is not possible, therefore, for us to be in relationships of love without (at some time) having it within our power to harm and be harmed in a serious fashion.

Something analogous might be said of our relationship with God as well. Suppose God wanted a relationship of love with some of His creatures, and so made some of them fit to be loved by Him and capable of reciprocating His love. Here He faces a choice: He could guarantee that they return His love, or He could leave it up to them. If He guaranteed it, they would never have a choice about whether they loved Him, in which case their love of Him would be a sham and He'd know it. Clearly, then, God cannot be in a relationship of love with His creatures unless He leaves it up to them whether they reciprocate His love. And that requires that they (at some time) have it within their power to withhold their love from Him. But, that cannot be unless they are able to be and do evil.[3]

Deep responsibility for others, relationships of love with our fellows and with God: if these were worthless or even meagerly good things, God would not be justified in permitting evil in order that we might be capable of them. But these are goods of tremendous—perhaps unsurpassable—value. And they are impossible in a world where our choices only have an effect on ourselves.[4]

Why not create persons who always freely choose the good? Another objection is that, since God knows before creating how each of His creatures will act, He can make a world in which everyone *always freely* chooses the good. He is omnipotent, after all, and so He can create any world He pleases.[5] It follows that God can create a world with the great goods of self-determination, deep responsibility for others, and love *without* there being any evil at all. Thus, these goods cannot justify God's permission of evil.

Reply. Note that this objection relies on the thought that *if God is omnipotent, then He can create any world He pleases.* This is false. For if God creates free creatures, He must leave it up to them what world results from their choices. Let's develop this point briefly.

Out of all of the possible creatures God could create, suppose He aims to create me, and suppose He considers whether to make me free with respect to planting roses along Walhout Way, a little section of my garden. If He did, He would have to place me in a situation in which it is *up to me* whether I plant roses or refrain from doing so. Now, if He placed me in such a situation, either I would freely plant or I wouldn't. For

the sake of illustration, suppose I would. Now imagine that God tries to make a world in which I freely *refrain* from planting. Can He? Not if He leaves it up to me whether I plant. For, given our supposition, if He left it up to me, I would *not* refrain; rather, I would plant. So, given that I would freely plant roses along Walhout Way if it were left up to me, God—even though omnipotent—cannot make a world in which I am in that situation and I freely refrain from planting roses. To make that world God would have to *make* me so that I refrain, in which case I would not *freely* refrain.

Therefore, the assumption made by this objection is false. If God creates free persons, He *cannot* create just any world He pleases, even though He is omnipotent. Which world results from His creative activity is, in no small part, up to His free creatures.

We can go further. For we can now see that, for all we know, it was not within God's power to create a world with persons who always freely choose the good. How could this be? Well, as we just saw, if God creates free creatures, then He can't create some worlds. In the example above, God cannot create a world in which I freely refrain from planting roses along Walhout Way. That's because I would freely plant if God left it up to me. Now, what if it were true that for *any* world that has at least as much good as ours and in which every person always freely chooses the good, no matter how God started things off, persons would freely go wrong at least as much as we (actual humans) go wrong? If that were true, then no matter how hard God tried, He simply could not create a world with persons who always freely choose good, at least not one with as much good in it as our world. And here's the rub: for all we know, maybe that's the way things are.[6]

This is a good place to observe that the free will theodicy is *not* to be confused with the cliché, "God doesn't *do* evil, we do. He just *allows* it. So He's not to blame, we are." This cliché, unlike the free will theodicy, assumes that if one does not *do* evil but only *allows* it, then one is not responsible for its happening. That's false. I may not cut off my son William's fingers but only allow his twin Peter to do it; still, if Peter does it and I could have prevented it, I am at least partially responsible.

What about evil resulting from natural disturbances? One might object that the free will theodicy doesn't explain why God would permit *natural evil*, that is, suffering resulting from natural disturbances like earthquakes, disease, and famine—sources of evil other than free persons.

Reply. We might try to extend the free will theodicy to explain natural evil. For example, we might say that, contrary to appearances, such evil really is a *direct* result of the activity of free *nonhuman* persons, powerful evil angels intent on destroying God's creation and harming His creatures. Satan and his cohorts crumple the earth's crust causing volcanoes and earthquakes, they twist strands of DNA into destructive forms, they get inside animals and make them eat each other, and so on. This explanation, however, has questionable apologetic value since it presupposes there are angels, a thesis not accepted by most nonbelievers. Moreover, it flies in the face of our understanding of the natural causes of volcanoes, earthquakes, genetic mutation, predation and other sources of natural evil. A more plausible explanation is that natural evil results *indirectly* from free *human* choices. This line of thought has been sketched most recently in the context of the "natural consequences theodicy," which is worth considering in its own right as well. Let's take a closer look.

Natural consequences theodicy. Suppose God created humans so He might love them and they might return His love. In giving our ancestors the power to love Him, God gave them the ability to withhold their love. And that's what they did. As a consequence, they ruined themselves. Having turned from God, they began to harm one another. Moreover, the potentially destructive forces of nature became their foe since a consequence of separating themselves from God was the loss of their special intellectual powers to predict where and when natural disturbances would occur and to protect themselves from disease and wild beasts, powers dependent upon their union with God. The result is natural evil. This condition—their wickedness and helplessness—has persisted through all the generations, being somehow hereditary.

But God has not left us to our misery. He has instituted the means for us to become reconciled with Him and to undo our ruin. Each of us, however, must cooperate in the venture since the sort of regeneration required involves reorienting our deepest passions and appetites away from our own power and pleasure and directing them toward Him. God could miraculously and immediately regenerate us but He doesn't because our love of Him would then be a sham. Unfortunately, our deepest inclinations so thoroughly turn us away from a proper love of Him that we will not fix ourselves without some sort of external impetus.

The problem God faces, then, is to get us to turn to Him for help while leaving us free in the matter. We will freely turn to Him, however, only if we see our wretched condition and become dissatisfied with it. There is no better way for us to come to see our condition and to grow dissatisfied with it than to permit its natural consequences, the pain and suffering and wrongdoing that our separation from Him has led to, and to make it "as difficult as possible for us to delude ourselves about the kind of world we live in: a hideous world, much of whose hideousness is quite plainly traceable to the inability of human beings to govern themselves or to order their own lives."[7]

An essential part of God's plan of reconciliation, therefore, is for us to perceive that a natural consequence of our attempting to order our lives on our own is a hideous world, a world with evil, including natural evil. Were God to intervene, He would deceive us about the hideousness of our living unto ourselves and He would seriously weaken our only motivation for turning to Him.

What about the suffering of nonhuman animals? While the natural consequence of theodicy may well account for God's permitting natural evil to befall human beings, it provides no reason for Him to permit natural evil to befall nonhuman animals.

Reply. To fill the gap, one might offer the "natural law theodicy."

Natural law theodicy. In order to have a world with creatures who can choose freely, the environment in which they are placed must be set up in certain well-defined ways. One of these environmental requirements is that the world be governed by regular and orderly laws of nature. Why is this a requirement? Well, imagine a world in which nature was not governed by such laws. What would it be like? Simply put, there would be no regular relationship between the occurrence of one sort of event and another. Let go of the ball and sometimes it drops, sometimes it flies straight up, sometimes it does a loop and crashes through the window. Things would happen haphazardly. The world would be quite chaotic.

But why would this disrupt our ability to choose freely? Because without a great deal of order and regularity in nature we could not predict the effects of our choices, even in the slightest; but we can choose freely only if we can predict the effects of our choices, specifically their most immediate effects. To see the point here, imagine a world in which, despite our best efforts, things just happened haphazardly. Suppose I chose to give you a flower and a big hug to express my affection, but my limbs behaved so erratically that it was as likely that my choice would result in what I intended as that I would poke you in the eye and crush your ribs. Or suppose you were very angry with me, but the air between us behaved so irregularly that any attempt on your part to give me a piece of your mind was about as likely to succeed as rolling a pair of sixes twice in a row. If that's how things worked, then our choices would be related to the world in the way they are related (in this world)

to the results of pulling a lever on a slot machine. How things came out would be completely out of our control. They wouldn't be up to us. So we cannot be free unless we are able to predict the (immediate) effects of our choices. And that requires an environment that allows our choices to have predictable effects, that is, an environment that behaves in a law-like, regular, constant fashion.

But now the downside. The very laws of momentum that enable you to give and receive flowers will also cause a falling boulder to crush you if you happen to be under it. The same laws of thermodynamics and fluid dynamics that allow me to talk via air causing my vocal chords to vibrate also cause hurricanes and tornadoes. In general, the sources of natural evil which afflict nonhuman animals, and us—disease, sickness, disasters, birth defects, and the like—"are all the outworking of the natural system of which we are a part. They are the byproducts made possible by that which is necessary for the greater good."[8]

What about worlds with different natural laws? The most wide-ranging objection to the natural law theodicy is that there are worlds God could have created which operate according to different laws of nature, laws which do not have sources of natural evil as a byproduct of their operation but which nevertheless provide a sufficiently stable environment in which we could reliably predict the effects of our free choices. Thus, God could have made free creatures without permitting natural evil, in which case we can't say that God might justifiably permit natural evil for the sake of freedom.

Reply. This objection presupposes that there are worlds with the requisite sort of natural laws, those that would provide a stable environment for freedom but which don't have natural evil as a side-effect. But no one has ever specified any such laws. Furthermore, the very possibility of life in our universe hangs on "a large number of physical parameters [that] have apparently arbitrary values such that if those values had been only slightly (very, very slightly different) the universe would contain no life," and hence no free human persons.[9] For all we know, the laws that govern our world are the only possible laws; alternatively, for all we know, there are very tight constraints on what sorts of adjustments in the laws can be permitted while retaining life-sustaining capabilities. Thus, for all we know, there *couldn't* be a world of the sort the objector appeals to: one suitable for free creatures to relate to each other but governed by laws which have no source of natural evil as a byproduct.

Couldn't God prevent a lot of natural evil without undermining freedom? Suppose we distinguish (i) cases of natural evil where God's interference would contribute to the weakening of our ability to predict the consequences of our choices from (ii) cases of natural evil where God's interference would have no such effect at all. Clearly enough, there is a lot of natural evil where God's interference would have no ramifications for our freedom—indeed, mind-boggling much when we take into account evolutionary history or predation. Thus, the only reason given in the natural law theodicy for God's permitting natural evil fails to justify His permitting (ii)-type natural evil, cases where His interference would have had no effect on our ability to predict the consequences of our choices.[10]

Reply. One might say that justice requires even-handedness. In that case, if God—who is perfectly just—intervenes to prevent the pain of this or that nonhuman animal in isolated circumstances, He would be obliged to act similarly in all cases of similar suffering. So, for example, if He were to prevent a squirrel deep in the Cascades from feeling pain as it hit a limb on its way down from the top of a towering fir, even-handedness would require Him to prevent me from feeling pain when the wind blew the car door shut on my thumb. But if God prevented the pain of *every* nonhuman animal in isolated circumstances, then even-handedness would require the same intervention for humans; such massive intervention would severely undermine the regularity of the laws of nature and hence eliminate our freedom.

While some people are happy with this reply, I am less sanguine. First, it seems that principles of justice do not require even-handedness—or that if they do, they can be trumped by other considerations in some cases.[11] Second, even-handedness requires treating like cases alike. But the cases at hand are not alike. God's systematic prevention of natural evil in the human domain would result in a loss of human freedom and all that such a loss entails. If God systematically prevents humans from harm when they collide with solid objects, their freedom will be undermined. Similar intervention in the animal kingdom would have no such effect, provided it didn't happen around us. If God regularly prevents nonhuman animals from harm when they collide with solid objects, nobody's freedom will be undermined. Certainly this is a relevant difference, a difference a just God would take into account.

One final, general observation. In my reply to the objection that God could have created another world with different laws, I expressed skepticism about our ability to tell whether any such laws would result in a world that was hospitable to life. This reply is a double-edged sword. For, just as we cannot confidently affirm that there are hospitable worlds with different laws that would have no source of natural evil as a byproduct, so we cannot confidently deny it. My sense is that we have no idea how God would be justified in permitting the suffering of nonhuman animals at Nature's hand, especially suffering unrelated to human society.

Higher-order goods theodicy. Certain goods require evil: "higher-order goods," they are called. These include showing sympathy, compassion and generosity to the sick, the poor, and the marginalized. It is not merely *having* these virtues that is good. Developing, exercising, and confirming them is of immense value, especially when it is difficult to do so since, in that case, a certain sort of courage, self-sacrifice, and fortitude is displayed. Likewise, forgiving wrong done to us, making compensation for having wronged others, showing gratitude for help received, and rewarding those who have done well through serious adversity all require evil. Unless there is evil, there cannot be such higher-order goods. Since these goods are of such tremendous value and they require evil, they justify God's permission of evil.[12]

Higher order goods don't require real evil. True enough, we cannot respond with compassion *to the poor* unless there *are* poor people. We cannot exercise fortitude *in the face of hardship* unless we *are* going through rough times. We cannot forgive *another* unless another *has* wronged us. However, we can develop, exercise, and confirm such character traits in response to *simulated* poverty, hardship, and wrongdoing, "illusory evil," we might call it. There doesn't have to be *real* evil for that to occur. To see how this is possible, imagine a world in which persons were, unbeknownst to them, plugged into "experience machines," complex devices programmed to simulate reality perfectly (as in the popular Hollywood flicks *Total Recall* or *The Matrix*). Even though the poverty, hardship, wrongdoing, etc. that they "experienced" while on the machine was only illusory evil, they would still be able to respond to it in a virtuous fashion. And we can imagine the machine's program being sensitive to their responses. In that way, they would be able to develop, exercise and confirm their characters without there being any *real* evil to which they are responding. In general, only illusory evil is required for there to be higher-order goods; real evil is unnecessary. So God could have created a world with higher-order goods but without (real) evil.

Reply. The objection correctly states that higher-order goods only require illusory evil. However, if God were to set up a world in which there was only illusory evil to which we could respond in the formation of our character, something of immense value would be missing. No one would in fact help anybody else; and no one would be helped. No one would in fact be compassionate and sympathetic to another; and no one would receive compassion and sympathy. No one would in fact forgive another; and no one would be forgiven. No one would in fact make compensation to another; and no one would receive compensation. No one would in fact praise or admire their fellows for pursuing noble ends in the face of adversity; and no one would receive such praise and admiration. No one would in fact satisfy their admirable aims and desires; and no one would be their recipient. No one would in fact generously give of their time, their talents or their money to the poor; and no one would receive generosity from another. In short, if every opportunity for a virtuous response were directed at illusory evils, each of us would live in our own little "world," worlds devoid of any genuine interaction and personal relationships.

It seems, then, that if God were to fit us with a capacity to develop, exercise, and confirm our characters *in the context of persons forming relationships with each other,* He must permit evil and suffering.

"The Big Reason." Let's take stock of where we have come so far. Some have argued that there probably is no reason that would justify God in permitting horrific evil and suffering, or so much of it. Our question was whether this was true. One way to answer this question is to try to think of a justifying reason, a theodicy. That's what we've been doing. It's now time to assess our efforts.

What we have seen so far, I submit, is this: each of the reasons sketched above helps us to see how God would be justified in permitting *some* evil and suffering, even a great deal of it. But at least two questions remain. For even if these reasons would justify God in permitting a great deal of evil and suffering, it doesn't follow that they would justify God in permitting any *horrific* evil and suffering. And even if they would justify God in permitting some horrific evil and suffering, even a good deal of it, it does not follow that any of them would justify God in permitting *as much* as there in fact is.[13] So, do these reasons help us see how God would be justified in permitting horrific evil and suffering, and so much of it?

In answering this question, we need to remember that even if none of these reasons by itself would justify God, taken together they would. Too often when people reflect on our question, they approach it in a piecemeal fashion, arguing that this reason doesn't work, that reason doesn't work, and so on, only considering each reason in isolation from all the others. We need to be alive to the possibility that these reasons might be *combined* into a single reason that would help us see how God would be justified.

So suppose we lump together all the different reasons sketched above, and let's add any we know of that have been left out, even those that are distinctive to a particular theological perspective, e.g., sympathetic identification with Christ's suffering, or the great goods of Incarnation and Atonement.[14] Call the result *The Big Reason*.[15] And let's focus on the really difficult part of our question, the part about the amount of horrific evil and suffering: Does The Big Reason allow us to see how God would be justified in permitting *so much* of it?

Suppose *one instance* of horrific evil or suffering had not occurred. Just to focus our reflections, note that hundreds of thousands of human beings have undergone extreme torture throughout human history. Suppose that just one of those cases had not occurred. Suppose that fourteen-year old Motholeli had lost consciousness after being gang-raped and beaten on March 25, 2004, and that her attackers had left her for dead, instead of burning and then dismembering her while she was fully conscious, which is in fact what happened. Could God have prevented the burning and dismemberment, and just allowed the rape and beating? Of course. Is it apparent to you that,

had He prevented the burning and dismemberment, and just allowed the rape and beating, the great goods involved in The Big Reason would either fail to obtain or be objectionably reduced? (Think through each of the goods carefully in this connection, and their combination.)

Some people say that we should not expect to be able to see how each particular instance of horrific evil and suffering must be permitted in order for the goods in question to be achieved. Rather, they say, we should expect to see how horrific evil and suffering in general must be permitted; and we should expect to see how the permission of so much rather than a lot less is required. Suppose they are right. What would count as a lot less? A world without extreme torture would do, I would think. Or how about a world in which genocide didn't occur? Or perhaps a world in which the ebola virus never evolved. Take your pick. God could have easily prevented any of them. Suppose He had. Then *a lot* less horrific evil and/or suffering would have occurred. In that case, is it apparent to you that the goods involved in The Big Reason would have been lost or objectionably reduced?

Suppose God had simply prevented us from ever having genocidal thoughts. Would we then have been unable to perceive the hideousness of living unto ourselves? Would we have lacked the requisite incentive to turn to God? Presumably not: our hideousness would still have been apparent in the vast panoply of non-genocidal activities we engage in.[16] What about self-determination, deep responsibility, relationships of love, higher-order goods, punishment, union with God, sympathetic identification with Christ, the Incarnation and Atonement, and so on, and their combination into one colossal good? Would any of them, by themselves or in combination, have been lost or significantly diminished if God had systematically prevented genocide or torture or the ebola virus? (Think through each of the goods carefully in this connection, and their combination.)

We each need to answer this question for ourselves, but for my own part, on careful reflection I can't see how any of them by themselves or in combination would have been lost or diminished if God had prevented Motholeli's burning and dismemberment. Nor can I see how any of them by themselves or in combination would have been lost or reduced if God had prevented genocide, or extreme torture or the ebola virus. Thus, I can't see how God would be justified in permitting so much horrific evil and suffering rather than a lot less.

If I'm right, does it follow that there probably is no reason that would justify God in permitting horrific evil and suffering (that is, that premise 3 is false), or so much of it? Not at all. That would follow only on the assumption that if there were a God-justifying reason, we would probably discern it and see how the goods it involved required the permission of so much horrific evil and suffering. And it is by no means clear that this assumption is true. Still, it seems that an important basis for thinking that it is false that there is no reason that would justify God in permitting evil and suffering—the way of theodicy—is not available to us.

Notes

1. See Nelson Pike, "Hume on Evil," in Pike, ed., *God and Evil* (Englewood Cliffs, NJ: Prentice-Hall, 1964), pp. 85–102.

2. See Steven Boer's "The Irrelevance of the Free Will Defense," *Analysis* (1975): 110–12.

3. A question arises: God enters into relationships of love, and yet He is not able to be or do evil; so why can't He make us capable of relationships of love while also making us unable to be and do evil? In response, some deny that God is unable to be or do evil. Others distinguish love at its best *for a divine*

being from love at its best *for a human*, and then argue that while the latter requires the ability to withhold love, the former does not. And there are other options as well.

4. These themes are developed by Richard Swinburne in *The Existence of God*, chapter 11, and "Some Major Strands of Theodicy," in Daniel Howard-Snyder, ed., *The Evidential Argument from Evil* (Bloomington: Indiana UP, 1996), pp. 36–42.

5. Mackie takes this line in *The Miracle of Theism* (Oxford, 1982), p. 164.

6. A more thorough presentation of this sort of reply is in Plantinga's *God, Freedom, and Evil* (Grand Rapids, MI: Eerdmans, 1974), pp. 32–44. Note that both the objection and the reply I gave presupposes that an omniscient being could know before creation what uncreated (merely possible) creatures would do if he created them and left it up to them how to behave. Many theists deny this. See, e.g., Robert Adams, "Middle Knowledge and the Problem of Evil," *American Philosophical Quarterly* (1977).

7. Peter van Inwagen, "The Magnitude, Duration and Distribution of Evil: A Theodicy," *Philosophical Topics* (1988), collected in his *God, Knowledge and Mystery* (Ithaca, NY: Cornell UP, 1995), p. 110. My presentation follows his closely. See also Eleonore Stump, "The Problem of Evil," *Faith and Philosophy* (1985).

8. Bruce Reichenbach, *Evil and a Good God* (New York: Fordham UP, 1982), p. 101. See also Richard Swinburne, "Natural Evil," *American*

Philosophical Quarterly (1978): 295–301, and *The Existence of God*, chapter 11. C.S. Lewis takes this line in *The Problem of Pain* (New York: Macmillan, 1978, 21st printing), p. 30ff.

9. The point here is Peter van Inwagen's. See his "The Problem of Evil, the Problem of Air, and the Problem of Silence," in *The Evidential Argument from Evil*, p. 160. For more on the physical parameters in question, see John Leslie, *Universes* (London: Routledge, 1989), chapters 1–3.

10. See William Rowe, "William Alston on the Problem of Evil," in Thomas Senor, ed., *The Rationality of Belief and the Plurality of Faith* (Ithaca, NY: Cornell UP, 1995), pp. 84–87; also see Quentin Smith, "An Atheological Argument from Evil Natural Laws," *International Journal for the Philosophy of Religion* (1991): 154–74.

11. Jesus arguably taught that God does not always treat us even-handedly. See the Parable of the Laborers in the Vineyard.

12. See Swinburne, "Some Major Strands of Theodicy," and *Providence* (Oxford: Oxford UP, 1998); also see John Hick, *Evil and the God of Love* (New York: Harper & Row, 1978, rev. ed.).

13. Furthermore, none of the reasons we've canvassed seem to do justice to the phenomenon of nonhuman animals undergoing pain and suffering at times (e.g., pre-human history) and in locations (e.g., the wilderness) far removed from human concern. In the latter connection, we might consider an argument from evil that appeals exclusively to this phenomenon. For a consideration of other theodicies about animal pain generally, and animal suffering throughout pre-human evolutionary history in particular, see Michael Murray, *Nature Red in Tooth and Claw: Theism and the Problem of Animal Suffering* (Oxford: Oxford UP, 2011).

14. On identification with the suffering of Christ, see, e.g., Marilyn McCord Adams, "Redemptive Suffering: A Christian Solution to the Problem of Evil," *Faith and Philosophy* 3 (1986), and "Horrendous Evils and the Goodness of God," *Proceedings of the Aristotelian Society* 63 (1989): 297–310. On the great goods of Incarnation and Atonement and their potential role in theodicy, see Alvin Plantinga, "Supralapsarianism, or 'O Felix Culpa,'" in Peter van Inwagen, ed., *Christian Faith and the Problem of Evil* (Grand Rapids, MI: Eerdmans, 2004), pp. 1–25.

15. For a defense of this approach to theodicy, see Kelly James Clark, "Evil and Christian Belief," *International Philosophical Quarterly*, Vol. XXIX, No. 2 Issue No. 114 (June 1989): 175–89.

16. But wouldn't God be deceiving us about the natural consequences of our ordering our lives on our own? Perhaps. But *some* deception may be worth it. Think of it like this: Suppose that unbeknownst to us, God would not allow an all-out global nuclear war even if a natural consequence of our miserable condition included an ability to do it. Should we accuse Him of wrongful deception upon learning this? Hardly. We should be grateful.

Discussion

1. Why does Howard-Snyder reject the punishment and counterpart theodicies?

2. What general sorts of problems face theodicies like the free will theodicy or the natural law theodicy?

3. What is the Big Reason theodicy and why does it fail?

Chapter 20

The Evidential Problem of Evil

THE PROBLEM OF EVIL AND SOME VARIETIES OF ATHEISM

WILLIAM ROWE*

Introduction. This essay is concerned with three inter-related questions. The first is: Is there an argument for atheism based on the existence of evil that may rationally justify someone in being an atheist? To this first question I give an affirmative answer and try to support that answer by setting forth a strong argument for atheism based on the existence of evil.[1] The second question is: How can the theist best defend his position against the argument for atheism based on the existence of evil? In response to this question I try to describe what may be an adequate rational defense for theism against any argument for atheism based on the existence of evil. The final question is: What position should the informed atheist take concerning the rationality of theistic belief? Three different answers an atheist may give to this question serve to distinguish three varieties of atheism: unfriendly atheism, indifferent atheism, and friendly atheism. In the final part of my essay I discuss and defend the position of friendly atheism. . . .

The argument stated. In developing the argument for atheism based on the existence of evil, it will be useful to focus on some particular evil that our world contains in considerable abundance. Intense human and animal suffering, for example, occurs daily and in a great plenitude in our world. Such intense suffering is a clear case of evil. Of course, if the intense suffering leads to some greater good, a good we could not have obtained without undergoing the suffering in question, we might conclude that the suffering is justified, but it remains an evil nevertheless. For we must not confuse the intense suffering in and of itself with the good things to which it sometimes leads or of which it may be a necessary part. Intense human or animal suffering is in itself bad, an evil, even though it may sometimes be justified by virtue of being a part of, or leading to, some good which is unobtainable without it. What is evil in itself may sometimes be good as a means because it leads to something that is good in itself. In such a case, while remaining an evil in itself, the intense human or animal suffering is, nevertheless, an evil which someone might be morally justified in permitting.

Taking human and animal suffering as a clear instance of evil which occurs with great frequency in our world, the argument for atheism based on evil can be stated as follows:

1. There exist instances of intense suffering which an omnipotent, omniscient being could have prevented without thereby losing some greater good or permitting some evil equally bad or worse.

2. An omniscient, wholly good being would prevent the occurrence of any intense

---

* William Rowe (1931–2015) was Professor of Philosophy at Purdue University.
* William Rowe (1931–2015) was Professor of Philosophy at Purdue University.

suffering it could, unless it could not do so without thereby losing some greater good or permitting some evil equally bad or worse.

3.   There does not exist an omnipotent, omniscient, wholly good being.

What are we to say about this argument for atheism, an argument based on the profusion of one sort of evil in our world? The argument is valid; therefore, if we have rational grounds for accepting its premises, to that extent we have rational grounds for accepting atheism. Do we, however, have rational grounds for accepting the premises of this argument?

Let's begin with the second premise. . . . Premise (2) says that an omniscient, wholly good being would prevent the occurrence of any intense suffering it could, unless it could not do so without thereby losing some greater good or permitting some evil equally bad or worse. This premise (or something not too distant from it) is, I think, held in common by many atheists and nontheists. Of course, there may be disagreement about whether something is good, and whether, if it is good, one would be morally justified in permitting some intense suffering to occur in order to obtain it. Someone might hold, for example, that no good is great enough to justify permitting an innocent child to suffer terribly. Again, someone might hold that the mere fact that a given good outweighs some suffering and would be lost if the suffering were prevented, is not a morally sufficient reason for permitting the suffering. But to hold either of these views is not to deny (2). For (2) claims only that *if* an omniscient, wholly good being permits intense suffering *then* either there is some greater good that would have been lost, or some equally bad or worse evil that would have occurred, had the intense suffering been prevented. (2) does not purport to describe what might be a *sufficient* condition for an omniscient, wholly good being to permit intense suffering, only what is a *necessary* condition. So

stated, (2) seems to express a belief that accords with our basic moral principles, principles shared by both theists and nontheists. If we are to fault the argument for atheism, therefore, it seems we must find some fault with its first premise.

Suppose in some distant forest lightning strikes a dead tree, resulting in a forest fire. In the fire a fawn is trapped, horribly burned, and lies in terrible agony for several days before death relieves its suffering. So far as we can see, the fawn's intense suffering is pointless. For there does not appear to be any greater good such that the prevention of the fawn's suffering would require either the loss of that good or the occurrence of an evil equally bad or worse. Nor does there seem to be any equally bad or worse evil so connected to the fawn's suffering that it would have had to occur had the fawn's suffering been prevented. Could an omnipotent, omniscient being have prevented the fawn's apparently pointless suffering? The answer is obvious, as even the theist will insist. An omnipotent, omniscient being could have easily prevented the fawn from being horribly burned, or, given the burning, could have spared the fawn the intense suffering by quickly ending its life, rather than allowing the fawn to lie in terrible agony for several days. Since the fawn's intense suffering was preventable and, so far as we can see, pointless, doesn't it appear that premise (1) of the argument is true, that there do exist instances of intense suffering which an omnipotent, omniscient being could have prevented without thereby losing some greater good or permitting some evil equally bad or worse?

It must be acknowledged that the case of the fawn's apparently pointless suffering does not *prove* that (1) is true. For even though we cannot see how the fawn's suffering is required to obtain some greater good (or to prevent some equally bad or worse evil), it hardly follows that it is not so required. After all, we are often surprised by how things we thought to be unconnected turn out to be intimately connected. Perhaps, for all we know, there is some familiar good outweighing the fawn's suffering to which that suffering is connected in a way we do not see. Furthermore, there may well be unfamiliar goods, goods we haven't dreamed of, to which the fawn's suffering is inextricably connected. Indeed, it would seem to require something like omniscience on our part before we could lay claim to *knowing* that there is no greater good connected to the fawn's suffering in such a manner that an omnipotent, omniscient being could not have achieved that good without permitting that suffering or some evil equally bad or worse. So the case of the fawn's suffering surely does not enable us to *establish* the truth of (1).

The truth is that we are not in a position to prove that (1) is true. We cannot know with certainty that instances of suffering of the sort described in (1) do occur in our world. But it is one thing to *know* or *prove* that (1) is true and quite another thing to have *rational grounds* for believing (1) to be true. We are often in the position where in the light of our experience and knowledge it is rational to believe that a certain statement is true, even though we are not in a position to prove or to know with certainty that the statement is true. In the light of our past experience and knowledge it is, for example, very reasonable to believe that neither Goldwater nor McGovern will ever be elected President, but we are scarcely in the position of knowing with certainty that neither will ever be elected President. So, too, with (1), although we cannot know with certainty that it is true, it perhaps can be rationally supported, shown to be a rational belief.

Consider again the case of the fawn's suffering. Is it reasonable to believe that there is some greater good so intimately connected to that suffering that even an omnipotent, omniscient being could not have obtained that good without permitting that suffering or some evil at least as bad? It certainly does not appear reasonable to believe this. Nor does it seem reasonable to believe that there is some evil at least as bad as the fawn's suffering such that an omnipotent being simply could not have prevented it without permitting the fawn's suffering. But even if it should somehow be reasonable to believe either of these things of the fawn's suffering, we must then ask whether it is reasonable to believe either of these things of *all* the instances of seemingly pointless human and animal suffering that occur daily in our world. And surely the answer to this more general question must be no. It seems quite unlikely that *all* the instances of intense suffering occurring daily in our world are intimately related to the occurrence of greater goods or the prevention of evils at least as bad; and even more unlikely, should they somehow all be so related, that an omnipotent, omniscient being could not have achieved at least some of those goods (or prevented some of those evils) without permitting the instances of intense suffering that are supposedly related to them. In the light of our experience and knowledge of the variety and scale of human and animal suffering in our world, the idea that none of this suffering could have been prevented by an omnipotent being without thereby losing a greater good or permitting an evil at least as bad seems an extraordinarily absurd idea, quite beyond our belief. It seems then that although we cannot *prove* that (1) is true, it is, nevertheless, altogether *reasonable* to believe that (1) is true, that (1) is a *rational* belief.

Returning now to our argument for atheism, we've seen that the second premise expresses a basic belief common to many theists and nontheists. We've also seen that our experience and knowledge of the variety and profusion of suffering in our world provides *rational support* for the first premise. Seeing that the conclusion, "There does not exist an omnipotent, omniscient, wholly good being" follows from these two premises, it does seem that we have *rational support* for atheism, that it is reasonable for us to believe that the theistic God does not exist.

The theist's defense. Can theism be rationally defended against the argument for atheism we have just examined? If it can, how might the theist best respond to that argument? Since the argument from (1) and (2) to (3) is valid, and since the theist, no less than the nontheist, is more than likely committed to (2), it's clear that the theist can reject this atheistic argument only by rejecting its first premise, the premise that states that there are instances of intense suffering which an omnipotent, omniscient being could have prevented without thereby losing some greater good or permitting some evil equally bad or worse. How, then, can the theist best respond to this premise and the considerations advanced in its support?

There are basically three responses a theist can make. First, he might argue not that (1) is false or probably false, but only that the reasoning given in support of it is in some way *defective*. He may do this either by arguing that the reasons given in support of (1) are in *themselves* insufficient to justify accepting (1), or by arguing that there are other things we know which, when taken in conjunction with these reasons, do not justify us in accepting (1). I suppose some theists would be content with this rather modest response to the basic argument for atheism. But given the validity of the basic argument and the theist's likely acceptance of (2), he is thereby committed to the view that (1) is false, not just that we have no good reason for accepting (1) as true. The second two responses are aimed at showing that it is reasonable to believe that (1) is false. Since the theist is committed to this view I shall focus the discussion on these two attempts, attempts which we can distinguish as "the direct attack" and "the indirect attack."

By a direct attack, I mean an attempt to reject (1) by pointing out goods, for example, to which suffering may well be connected, goods which an omnipotent, omniscient being could not achieve without permitting suffering. It is doubtful, however, that the direct attack can succeed. The theist may point out that some suffering leads to moral and spiritual development impossible without suffering. But it's reasonably clear that suffering often occurs in a degree far beyond what is required for character development. The theist may say that some suffering results from free choices of human beings and might be preventable only by preventing some measure of human freedom. But, again, it's clear that much intense suffering occurs not as a result of human free choices. The general difficulty with this direct attack on premise (1) is twofold. First, it cannot succeed, for the theist does not know what greater goods might be served, or evils prevented, by each instance of intense human or animal suffering. Second, the theist's own religious tradition usually maintains that in this life it is not given to us to know God's purpose in allowing particular instances of suffering. Hence, the direct attack against premise (1) cannot succeed and violates basic beliefs associated with theism.

The best procedure for the theist to follow in rejecting premise (1) is the indirect procedure. This procedure I shall call "the G.E. Moore shift," so-called in honor of the twentieth century philosopher, G.E. Moore, who used it to great effect in dealing with the arguments of the skeptics. Skeptical philosophers such as David Hume have advanced ingenious arguments to prove that no one can know of the existence of any material object. The premises of their arguments employ plausible principles, principles which many philosophers have tried to reject directly, but only with questionable success. Moore's procedure was altogether different. Instead of arguing directly against the premises of the skeptic's arguments, he simply noted that the premises implied, for example, that he [Moore] did not know of the existence of a pencil. Moore then proceeded indirectly against the skeptic's premises by arguing:

I do know that this pencil exists.

If the skeptic's principles are correct I cannot know of the existence of this pencil.

The skeptic's principles (at least one) must be incorrect.

Moore then noted that his argument is just as valid as the skeptic's, that both of their arguments contain the premise "If the skeptic's principles are correct Moore cannot know of the existence of this pencil," and concluded that the only way to choose between the two arguments (Moore's and the skeptic's) is by deciding which of the first premises it is more rational to believe—Moore's premise "I do know that this pencil exists" or the skeptic's premise asserting that his skeptical principles are correct. Moore concluded that his own first premise was the more rational of the two.[2]

Before we see how the theist may apply the G.E. Moore shift to the basic argument for atheism, we should note the general strategy of the shift. We're given an argument: *p, q,* therefore, *r.* Instead of arguing directly against *p,* another argument is constructed—not-*r, q,* therefore, not-*p*—which begins with the denial of the conclusion of the first argument, keeps its second premise, and ends with the denial of the first premise as its conclusion.

Compare, for example, these two:

I. *p*　　　II. not-*r*
　 q　　　　　 *q*
　 r　　　　　 not-*p*

It is a truth of logic that if I is valid II must be valid as well. Since the arguments are the same so far as the second premise is concerned, any choice between them must concern their respective first premises. To argue against the first premise (*p*) by constructing the counter argument II is to employ the G.E. Moore shift.

Applying the G.E. Moore shift against the first premise of the basic argument for atheism, the theist can argue as follows:

not-3. There exists an omnipotent, omniscient, wholly good being.

2. An omniscient, wholly good being would prevent the occurrence of any intense suffering it could, unless it could not do so without thereby losing some greater good or permitting some evil equally bad or worse.

therefore,

not-1. It is not the case that there exist instances of intense suffering which an omnipotent, omniscient being could have prevented without thereby losing some greater good or permitting some evil equally bad or worse.

We now have two arguments: the basic argument for atheism from (1) and (2) to (3), and the theist's best response, the argument from (not-3) and (2) to (not-1). What the theist then says about (1) is that he has rational grounds for believing in the existence of the theistic God (not-3), accepts (2) as true, and sees that (not-1) follows from (not-3) and (2). He concludes, therefore, that he has rational grounds for rejecting (1). Having rational grounds for rejecting (1), the theist concludes that the basic argument for atheism is mistaken.

Varieties of atheism. We've had a look at a forceful argument for atheism and what seems to be the theist's best response to that argument. If one is persuaded by the argument for atheism, as I find myself to be, how might one best view the position of the theist? Of course, he will view the theist as having a false belief, just as the theist will view the atheist as having a false belief. But what position should the atheist take concerning the *rationality* of the theist's belief? There are three major positions an atheist might take, positions which we may think of as some varieties of atheism. First, the atheist may believe that no one is rationally justified in believing that the theistic God exists. Let us call this position "unfriendly atheism." Second, the atheist may hold no belief concerning whether any theist is or isn't rationally justified in believing that the theistic God exists. Let us call this view "indifferent atheism." Finally, the atheist may believe that some theists are rationally justified in believing that the theistic God exists. This view we shall call "friendly atheism." In this final part of my essay I propose to discuss and defend the position of friendly atheism.

If no one can be rationally justified in believing a false proposition then friendly atheism is a paradoxical, if not incoherent position. But surely the truth of a belief is not a necessary condition of someone's being rationally justified in having that belief. So in holding that someone is rationally justified in believing that the theistic God exists, the friendly atheist is not committed to thinking that the theist has a true belief. What he is committed to is that the theist has rational grounds for his belief, a belief the atheist rejects and is convinced he is rationally justified in rejecting. But is this possible? Can someone, like our friendly atheist, hold a belief, be convinced that he is rationally justified in holding that belief, and yet believe that someone else is equally justified in believing the opposite? Surely this is possible. Suppose your friends see you off on a flight to Hawaii. Hours after take-off they learn that your plane has gone down at sea. After a twenty-four hour search, no survivors have been found. Under these circumstances they are rationally justified in believing that you have perished. But it is hardly rational for you to believe this, as you bob up and down in your life vest, wondering why the search planes have failed to spot you. Indeed, to amuse yourself while awaiting your fate, you might very well reflect on the fact that your friends are rationally justified in believing that you are now dead, a proposition you disbelieve and are rationally justified in disbelieving. So, too, perhaps an atheist may be rationally justified in his atheistic belief and yet hold that some theists are rationally justified in believing just the opposite of what he believes.

What sort of grounds might a theist have for believing that God exists? Well, he might endeavor to justify his belief by appealing to one or more of the traditional arguments: Ontological, Cosmological, Teleological, Moral, etc. Second, he might appeal to certain aspects of religious experience, perhaps even his own religious experience. Third, he might try to justify theism as a plausible theory in terms of which we can account for a variety of phenomena. Although an atheist must hold that the theistic God does not exist, can he not also believe, and be justified in so believing, that some of these "justifications of theism" do actually rationally justify some theists in their belief that there exists a supremely good, omnipotent, omniscient being? It seems to me that he can.

If we think of the long history of theistic belief and the special situations in which people are sometimes placed, it is perhaps as absurd to think that no one was ever rationally justified in believing that the theistic God exists as it is to think that no one was ever justified in believing that human beings would never walk on the moon. But in suggesting that friendly atheism is preferable to unfriendly atheism, I don't mean to rest the case on what some human beings might reasonably have believed in the eleventh or thirteenth century. The more interesting question is whether some people in modern society, people who are aware of the usual grounds for belief and disbelief and are acquainted to some degree with modern science, are yet rationally justified in accepting theism. Friendly atheism is a significant position only if it answers this question in the affirmative.

It is not difficult for an atheist to be friendly when he has reason to believe that the theist could not reasonably be expected to be acquainted with the grounds for disbelief that he (the atheist) possesses. For then the atheist may take the view that some theists are rationally justified in holding to theism, but would not be so were they to be acquainted with the grounds for disbelief—those grounds being sufficient to tip the scale in favor of atheism when balanced against the reasons the theist has in support of his belief.

Friendly atheism becomes paradoxical, however, when the atheist contemplates believing that the theist has all the grounds for atheism that he, the atheist, has, and yet is rationally justified in maintaining his theistic belief. But even so excessively friendly a view as this perhaps can be held by the atheist if he also has some reason to think that the grounds for theism are not as telling as the theist is justified in taking them to be.

Conclusion. I've presented what I take to be a strong argument for atheism, pointed out what I think is the theist's best response to that argument, distinguished three positions an atheist might take concerning the rationality of theistic belief, and made some remarks in defense of the position called "friendly atheism." I'm aware that the central points of my essay are not likely to be warmly received by many philosophers. Philosophers who are atheists tend to be tough-minded—holding that there are no good reasons for supposing that theism is true. And theists tend either to reject the view that the existence of evil provides rational grounds for atheism or to hold that religious belief has nothing to do with reason and evidence at all. But such is the way of philosophy.

Notes

1. Some philosophers have contended that the existence of evil is *logically inconsistent* with the existence of the theistic God. No one, I think, has succeeded in establishing such an extravagant claim. Indeed, granted incompatibilism, there is a fairly compelling argument for the view that the existence of evil is logically consistent with the existence of the theistic God. For a lucid statement of this argument see Alvin Plantinga, *God, Freedom, and Evil* (New York, 1974). There remains, however, what we may call the *evidential* form—as opposed to the *logical* form—of the problem of evil: the view that the variety and profusion of evil in our world, although perhaps not logically inconsistent with the existence of the theistic God, provides, nevertheless, *rational support* for atheism. In this essay I shall be concerned solely with the evidential form of the problem, the form of the problem which, I think, presents a rather severe difficulty for theism.

2. See, for example, the two chapters on Hume in G.E. Moore, *Some Main Problems of Philosophy* (London: Collier, 1953).

Discussion

1. Does the fawn's *apparently* pointless suffering give us reason to believe that the fawn's suffering *is* pointless? Why or why not?

2. Can you think of any goods which might result from the suffering of the fawn (which goods outweigh the badness of the fawn's pain)? If not, what follows?

3. Distinguish between the different varieties of atheism. Why does Rowe contend that "friendly atheism" is the only reasonable option? Do you agree with him? Why or why not?

ROWE'S ARGUMENT FROM PARTICULAR HORRORS

DANIEL HOWARD-SNYDER*

Introduction. It is commonly thought that the evil and suffering in our world constitutes strong evidence for *atheism*, the thesis that no omnipotent, omniscient and wholly good God exists. But exactly *how* is it strong evidence? And is it *strong enough* to make it rational to believe there is no God?

Suppose God and evil are incompatible; then, since there clearly is evil, we have enormously strong evidence for atheism. Very few philosophers today who study our topic would endorse this argument, however. Why? Because it seems that God and evil are, strictly speaking, compatible. We can think of various reasons God might have to permit a fair bit of evil; and to the extent that we cannot think of any reason for God to permit so much, we have no good grounds to think that there *could not* be a justifying reason we do not know of.

Nevertheless, even if God and evil are compatible, and even if we can see how God might be justified in permitting a good deal of evil and suffering, certain facts about evil and suffering may constitute strong evidence for atheism, so strong that it is rational to be an atheist—provided one has no equally good grounds to think there is a God. This is William Rowe's thesis in his justly famous essay "The Problem of Evil and Some Varieties of Atheism."

The argument stated. In what follows, let's suppose—just to see what follows, or perhaps because we really believe it's true—that there are no equally good grounds for theism. With this supposition in place, let's turn to our title question: does evil make it

rational to be an atheist? Rowe answers "yes," and he gives a powerful argument for it. In its official form, it can be put as follows:

1. There are instances of intense suffering which God could have prevented without thereby losing some greater good or permitting some evil equally bad or worse.

2. God would prevent the occurrence of any intense suffering He could, unless He could not do so without thereby losing some greater good or permitting some evil equally bad or worse.

3. So, God does not exist.

What should we make of this argument? It is logically valid, i.e., the premises cannot all be true while the conclusion is false. But are all the premises true?

For the purposes of this essay, let's grant the second premise, although I don't mean to give the impression that all is clear sailing here.[1] What about the first? It is equivalent to a claim that something of a certain sort does not exist, specifically this claim:

1. There is no greater good that would have been lost and no evil equally bad or worse that would have been permitted if God had prevented some instances of intense suffering.

In what follows, I will focus on this claim because it will allow us to see more easily what we must be committed to if we accept premise 1.

Rowe's argument for premise 1. Well, what should we make of premise 1? Rowe offers one particular instance of intense suffering that God could have prevented without thereby losing some greater good or permitting some equally bad or worse evil—the case of the

* Daniel Howard-Snyder is Professor of Philosophy at Western Washington University.

fawn who is horribly burned in a forest fire, lying in agony for days before she dies, doubtlessly one of millions of such cases throughout history. In other essays, he points to other occurrences of especially horrible suffering. So Rowe initially supports premise 1 by pointing to certain cases of suffering, saying of *each one* that there is no greater good that would have been lost nor any equally bad or worse evil that would have been permitted if God had prevented it, that very occurrence of suffering. In effect, then, he draws up a list that begins like this:

1a. There is no greater good that would have been lost nor any other equally bad or worse evil that would have been permitted if God had prevented that fawn from being burned in that forest fire, or if He had prevented the fawn from lying in terrible agony for several days after being burned.

1b. There is no greater good that would have been lost nor any other equally bad or worse evil that would have been permitted if God had prevented Ashley Jones from being brutally raped and bludgeoned to death last September in Stanwood, Washington.[2] . . .

So Rowe supports premise 1 initially by a list of propositions like 1a and 1b. It will make things easier if we pretend that you and I have one list, *Our List of Pointless Evils*. A moment's reflection reveals that if all of the propositions on our list are true, then premise 1 is certainly true; indeed, if *just one* of them is true, then premise 1 is true.

An important question arises: *are* any of them true? Rowe briefly sketches his answer to this question:

So far as we can see, the fawn's intense suffering is pointless. For there does not appear to be any greater good such that the prevention of the

fawn's suffering would require either the loss of that good or the occurrence of an evil equally bad or worse. Nor does there seem to be any equally bad or worse evil so connected to the fawn's suffering that it would have had to occur had the fawn's suffering been prevented. Could [God] have prevented the fawn's apparently pointless suffering? The answer is obvious, as even the theist will insist. [God] could have easily prevented the fawn from being horribly burned, or, given the burning, could have spared the fawn the intense suffering by quickly ending its life, rather than allowing the fawn to lie in terrible agony for several days. Since the fawn's intense suffering was preventable and, so far as we can see, pointless, doesn't it appear that premise (1) of the argument is true?

And similar things might be said of Ashley Jones. Consider the various candidates for greater goods that we know of, for example determining the sort of character one has, being of use to others, entering into and maintaining worthwhile relationships with our fellows and with God, seeing the hideousness that naturally follows from rejecting God and living on our own, sympathetically identifying with Christ's sufferings, and being punished for wrongdoing. (You may add any goods that you think should be listed here.) So far as we can see, none of these goods would have been lost or objectionably reduced if God had prevented Ashley's suffering and not permitted some other instance of comparable agony. On reflection, similar things can be said about the other goods mentioned above, and about their conjunction into one colossal good. Doesn't it seem, then, that Ashley's suffering was pointless, and therefore that premise 1 of Rowe's argument is true?

Here we have only considered the cases of Ashley Jones and the fawn. The other cases on our list must likewise be examined. Suppose we are able to say of each one what Rowe said of the fawn and what I suggested we should say about Ashley Jones: "So far as we can see, there is no greater good that would have been lost nor any other equally bad or worse evil that would have been permitted if God had prevented it." In that case, we can draw up a second list that exactly parallels our first list. It would start like this:

1a$_1$. So far as we can see, there is no greater good that would have been lost nor any other equally bad or worse evil that would have been permitted if God had prevented that fawn from being burned in that forest fire, or if He had prevented the fawn from lying in terrible agony for several days after being burned.

1b$_1$. So far as we can see, there is no greater good that would have been lost nor any other equally bad or worse evil that would have been permitted if God had prevented Ashley Jones from being brutally raped and bludgeoned to death last September in Stanwood, Washington. . . .

And so on. Let's call the second list *Our Noseeum List* (pronounced, noh-see-um). It will become apparent below why I give it this name.

Now we're in a position to sum up our characterization of Rowe's initial defense of premise 1. It goes like this: none of the propositions on Our Noseeum List are false.[3] At least some of them make it highly likely that the corresponding propositions on Our List of Pointless Evils are true. If this last claim is correct, then premise 1 is highly likely to be true, and thus it is "altogether reasonable to believe" it. But *do* any of the items on Our Noseeum List make it highly likely that any of the corresponding items on Our List of Pointless Evils are true? More generally, is it really reasonable to infer that there is no greater good that would be lost on the grounds that, so far as we can tell, there is none? These

are the questions that we must now answer. To get at them, let's pause to reflect on what *kind* of inference is involved here.

Rowe-style Noseeum Inferences. Suppose that, after rummaging around carefully in my fridge, I can't find a carton of milk. Naturally enough, I infer that there isn't one there. Or suppose that, on viewing a chess match between two novices, Kasparov says to himself, "So far as I can tell, there is no way for John to get out of check," and then infers that there is no way. These are what we might call *no-see-um inferences*: we don't see 'um, so they ain't there![4]

Notice four things about noseeum inferences. First, they have this basic shape: "So far as we can tell, there is no x; so, there is no x." Second, note that in each of the cases just mentioned, it is possible for the conclusion to be false even if the premise is true. Even though I rummaged through the fridge carefully and my vision is in tip-top shape, I could just simply miss the carton of milk. And even Kasparov can have an off day. Nevertheless—and this is the third point—in each case the argument is a strong one. Under certain conditions (about which I will say more shortly), our inability to see something makes it highly likely that there isn't anything of the sort we failed to see. Finally, it won't do to object to any particular noseeum inference that even if the premise is true the conclusion *might* be false. For *every* noseeum inference—even the strongest of them—is like that. When evaluating a particular noseeum inference, we can't just write it off with a casual, "Ah! But there *might* be an x we don't know of even if so far as we can tell there isn't one." That's true, but it's irrelevant to the strength of the inference.

Now, in effect, Rowe bids us to use at least some of the items on Our Noseeum List as a basis for believing some of the items on Our List of Pointless Evils, and this amounts to deploying some, perhaps several, noseeum inferences, like the inference from 1a$_1$ to 1a:

1a₁. So far as we can tell, there is no greater good that would have been lost if God had prevented that fawn from being burned in that forest fire, or from lying in terrible agony for several days afterwards.[5]

So, it is very likely that

1a. There is no such greater good.

Let us call this type of noseeum inference a *Rowe-style Noseeum Inference*. What should we make of this type of noseeum inference?

Obviously enough, many noseeum inferences are reasonable, like the ones mentioned at the beginning of this section. And just as obviously, many are not. For example, looking at my distant garden from my kitchen window, the fact that so far as I can tell, there are no slugs there hardly makes it likely that there are none. Likewise, a beginner viewing a chess match between Kasparov and Deep Blue would be ill-advised to reason: "I can't see any way for Deep Blue to get out of check; so, there is none." Or imagine us listening to the best physicists in the world discussing the mathematics used to describe quantum phenomena or the theory of general relativity. Presumably it would be unreasonable for us to infer that, since we can't comprehend or grasp what they are saying, there is nothing there to be grasped. The crucial question, then, is this: what distinguishes the reasonable noseeum inferences from the lousy ones?

Consider the cases already sketched. Notice that it is quite likely that I would see a milk jug in the fridge if one were there, and it is very likely that Kasparov would see a way out of check if there were one. That's because Kasparov and I have what it takes to discern the sorts of things in question. On the other hand, it is not very likely that I would see a slug in my garden even if there were one there, at least not from my kitchen window. Nor is it very likely that a beginner

would be able to see a way out of check for Deep Blue even if there were one since strategy at the grandmaster level can be very complex. And the same goes for our comprehending exceedingly complex mathematics: even if what the physicists were talking about did make sense, it isn't very likely that we would be able to understand it.

We can distill these reflections in the following principle, which marks an important difference between reasonable and unreasonable noseeum inferences:

A noseeum inference is reasonable only if it is reasonable to believe that we would very likely see (grasp, comprehend, understand) the item in question if it existed.

Applying this principle to Rowe-style Noseeum Inferences, we get the following result:

The move from "So far as we can tell, there is no greater good..." to it is very likely that "There is no such greater good" is reasonable only if it is reasonable to believe that *we would very likely see or comprehend a greater good, if there were one.*

Call the italicized portion *Rowe's Noseeum Assumption.*

Now we are in a position to raise a very important question: Is it reasonable to believe Rowe's Noseeum Assumption? Several arguments for Rowe's Noseeum Assumption have been given in the literature, and I have explained elsewhere why I think that those arguments fail.[6] Here I will simply offer reasons to think that it is not reasonable to believe Rowe's Noseeum Assumption.

Two strategies for assessing Rowe's Noseeum Assumption. I begin by distinguishing two strategies for assessing whether it is reasonable to believe Rowe's Noseeum Assumption. We can get at them by way of analogy, comparing two questions.

First: is it highly likely that I would see a slug in my garden from the kitchen window if one were there? Not at all. I know that slugs are relatively small and I know that the unaided human eye is not suited to see such small things at a hundred feet; moreover, my garden is over an acre large and, per usual, it's overgrown. So we have superb reason to think that it is false that I would very likely see a slug in my garden even if one were there. Now, another question: is it highly likely that extra-terrestrial life forms would contact us if they existed? The only answer suitable here is "How should I know?" If there were extra-terrestrial life forms, how likely is it that some of them would be intelligent enough to consider contact? And of those intelligent enough, how many would care about it? And of those with the smarts and the desire, how likely is it that they would have the means at their disposal to try? And of those with the means, how likely is it that they would succeed? I haven't the foggiest idea how to answer any of these questions. I can't even begin to say with even the most minimal degree of confidence that the likelihood is low or middling or high. I just don't have enough to go on. In that case, I should be *in doubt* about how likely it is that extra-terrestrial life forms would contact us if they existed. I should be of two minds, neither for it, nor against it. I should just shrug my shoulders and say "I don't know. I'm in the dark on that score."

There are two points to see here. First, in each case it is *not reasonable to believe* that the proposition in question is highly likely to be true, although for different reasons. In the first case, it is not reasonable to believe it is highly likely that I would see a slug in the garden even if there were one there because it is reasonable to believe that the proposition is positively *false*—indeed, because the garden is large and overgrown and I am viewing it from quite a distance, I have good reason to believe it is very, very likely that I would *not* see a slug. In the second case, however, it is *not* reasonable to believe that the proposition in

question is *false*. Rather, for the reasons mentioned, we have good reason to be *in doubt* about how likely it is that we would have been contacted by extra-terrestrials if there were any. Indeed, we don't even have enough to go on to make a rough guess. As a consequence—and here is the second, absolutely crucial point—*having good reason to be in doubt* about the matter is good enough reason all by itself to think that it is *not* reasonable to *believe* that we would probably have been contacted. For how could it be reasonable for us to believe something about which we have good reason to think we are utterly in the dark?

Now let's apply these points to Rowe's Noseeum Assumption. To assess the reasonableness of believing that we would very likely see a greater good if there were one, we might consider whether Rowe's Noseeum Assumption is *false*. In that case, we might try to think of reasons to believe that it is very likely that we would *not* see a greater good. We would then be treating Rowe's Noseeum Assumption as I treated the proposition that it is very likely that I would see a slug in my garden from the kitchen window. On the other hand, we might consider whether we should be *in doubt* about whether we would very likely see a greater good. This would be to treat Rowe's Noseeum Assumption as I treated the proposition that it is highly likely that extra-terrestrials would contact us if there were any. The crucial point to understand here is that even if *all* we have is good reason to be *in doubt* about whether it is highly likely that we would see a greater good, that is enough reason to deny that it is reasonable to believe Rowe's Noseeum Assumption.

Reasons to doubt Rowe's Noseeum Assumption. I suspect that it is not reasonable to believe Rowe's Noseeum Assumption. In what follows, I focus on reasons to be in doubt about it rather than reasons to think it is false. Why? Because the only reasons I can think of for believing that it is false presuppose that God has informed us that we should expect to be unable to discern His purposes in permitting particular horrors, which, of course, presupposes that there is a God. I don't want to presuppose that here. I want to show that even a *non*believer can have good reason to refrain from believing Rowe's Noseeum Assumption. So, what considerations might put us in doubt about whether it is reasonable to believe Rowe's Noseeum Assumption? Several have emerged in the literature. I have space for three.

Alston's analogies. The first consideration targets Rowe-style Noseeum Inferences directly. It says that such inferences involve two aspects which should make us wary of our ability to tell whether we would very likely see a greater good or a God-justifying reason if there were any.

First, a Rowe-style Noseeum Inference takes "the insights attainable by finite, fallible human beings as an adequate indication of what is available in the way of reasons to an omniscient, omnipotent being." But this is like supposing that when I am confronted with the activity or productions of a master in a field in which I have little expertise, it is reasonable for me to draw inferences about the quality of her work just because I "don't get it." I've taken a year of university physics. I'm faced with some theory about quantum phenomena and I can't make heads or tails of it. Certainly it is unreasonable for me to suppose it's likely that I'd be able to make sense of it. Similarly for other areas of expertise: painting, architectural design, chess, music, and so on.

Second, a Rowe-style Noseeum Inference "involves trying to determine whether there is a so-and-so in a territory the extent and composition of which is largely unknown to us." It is like someone who is culturally and geographically isolated supposing that if there were something on earth beyond their forest, they'd likely discern it. It is like a physicist supposing that if there were something beyond the temporal bounds of the universe, we'd probably know about it (where those bounds are the big bang and the final crunch).

All these analogies point in the same direction: we should be in doubt about whether we would very likely discern greater goods that would justify God's permission of particular horrors even if one were there.[7]

The progress argument. Knowledge has progressed in a variety of fields of enquiry, especially the physical sciences. The periodic discovery of previously unknown aspects of reality strongly suggests that there will be further progress of a similar sort. Since future progress implies present ignorance, it is very likely that there is much we are now ignorant of. Now, what we have to go on in charting the progress of the discovery of intrinsic goods by our ancestors is meager to say the least. Indeed, given the scant archaeological evidence we have, and given paleontological evidence regarding the evolutionary development of the brain in *homo sapiens*, it would not be surprising at all that humans discovered various intrinsic goods over tens of thousands of years dotted by several millennia-long gaps in which nothing was discovered. Hence, given what we have to go on, it would not be surprising if there has been the sort of periodic progress that strongly suggests that there remain goods to be discovered. Thus it would not be surprising if there are *goods* of which we are ignorant, goods of which God—in His omniscience—would not be ignorant.

The argument from complexity. One thing Mozart's Violin Concerto No. 4, Ste. Michelle's Cabernet Sauvignon (Reserve), and the best sorts of love have in common when compared to Chopsticks, cheap Gallo, and puppy love is that each illustrates the fact that the goodness of a state of affairs is sometimes greater, in part, because it is more complex. Now, since intense, undeserved suffering and horrific wickedness are so bad, it would take correspondingly greater goods to justify God's permitting such horrors. Hence, it would not be surprising if the greater goods involved in God's purposes possess a degree of complexity well beyond our grasp. It follows that it would not be surprising if there were *greater* goods outside our ken. Of course, while complexity does not always adversely affect our ability to recognize value, it can and sometimes does. To defend this claim, I cannot show you a complex state of affairs whose value we fully recognize but whose complexity hinders such recognition. I must resort to more general considerations.

First, there is the general phenomenon of the complexity of something hindering our view of some important feature it has, e.g., the complexity of an argument hindering our ability to discern its validity, or the complexity of your opponent's strategy hindering your ability to discern that unless you move your knight to queen's side bishop 5, her next move is checkmate. But, more to the point, why can a child discern the literary merits of a comic book but not *Henry V* or *The Brothers Karamazov*? Why can a child clearly discern the aesthetic value of toffee but have a difficult time with alder-smoked Copper River sockeye served with pesto, lightly buttered asparagus *al dente*, fresh greens in a ginger vinaigrette, and chilled chardonnay? Why can a child recognize the value of his friendship with his buddy next door but not the full value of his parents' mutual love? Surely because great works of literature, fine cuisine and adult love at its best involves much more than he is able to comprehend. And this is true of adults as well, as reflection on our progress in understanding the complexity of various things of value reveals. For example, periodically reflecting on the fabric of our relationships with those whom we love most and whose love we most cherish, we might well find strands and shades that when brought to full light permit us to see those love-relationships as more valuable than we had once thought. If the failure to grasp the more complicated aspects of our relationships can prevent a full appreciation of love's value, surely the failure to grasp the complexity of a state of affairs might well hinder us from discerning its goodness. Value is often veiled in complexity.

The three considerations presented here—Alston's Analogies, the Progress Argument, and the Argument from Complexity—*together* constitute good reasons to doubt whether it is highly likely that we would see a greater good if there were one. More specifically, they cumulatively constitute good reason to be in doubt about *each* of the instances of Rowe's Noseeum Assumption that we will have to believe reasonably if we are to move from *any* of the propositions on Our Noseeum List to any of the propositions on Our List of Pointless Evils. For example, here is one of the noseeum inferences that Rowe bids us to make in connecting Our Noseeum List to the corresponding items on Our List of Pointless Evils.

1a$_1$. So far as we can tell, there is no greater good that would have been lost if God had prevented that fawn from being burned in the forest fire, or from lying in terrible agony for several days afterwards.

So, it is very likely that

1a. There is no such greater good.

We [have seen] that the move from "So far as I can tell, there is no greater good that would have been lost if God had prevented that fawn from being burned in the forest fire, or from lying in terrible agony for several days afterwards" to it is very likely that "There is no such greater good" is reasonable only if it is reasonable to believe that *we would very likely see or comprehend a greater good that would have been lost if God had prevented that instance of suffering.* The italicized portion is an instance of Rowe's Noseeum Assumption. We now see that Alston's Analogies, the Progress Argument, and the Argument from Complexity together constitute good reason to be in doubt about whether this instance of Rowe's Noseeum Assumption is true.

And the same can be said for every other instance of Rowe's Noseeum Assumption that we would have to use if we were to move from *any* of the propositions on Our Noseeum List to the corresponding propositions on Our List of Pointless Evils.

So what? Three paragraphs before stating his argument, Rowe asks this question: "Is there an argument for atheism based on the existence of evil that may rationally justify someone in being an atheist?" He says the answer is "yes" and gives the argument we've been examining. As you might expect, Rowe's argument can rationally justify us in being atheists only if we are rationally justified in believing all of its premises. Unfortunately, his initial defense of premise 1 does *not* rationally justify us in believing premise 1. So if that's all we have to go on, we are *not* rationally justified in being atheists on the basis of Rowe's argument.

But what if some *other* defense of premise 1 works?[8] I suspect that any defense will not avoid the objections raised above. If all we have to go on is Rowe's initial defense, then we are not rationally justified in believing all of the premises of Rowe's argument; consequently, we are not rationally justified in being atheists on the basis of Rowe's argument. That strikes me as a point worth understanding, a point that fits snugly with our ignorance of whether there are any pointless evils. If the game is Let's Make An Argument That Rationally Justifies Us In Being Atheists, then doesn't this point seem like a winner?[9]

Notes

1. Michael Peterson and William Hasker deny premise 2 in *Evil and the Christian God* (Baker, 1982) and "The Necessity of Gratuitous Evil," *Faith and Philosophy* (1992), respectively. To see why their arguments fail, see my "Is

Theism Compatible with Gratuitous Evil?" *American Philosophical Quarterly* (1999), co-authored with Frances Howard-Snyder. Peter van Inwagen, on the other hand, has sketched a fascinating objection in "The Magnitude, Duration, and Distribution of Evil: A Theodicy," *Philosophical Topics* 16 (1988): 167–68, and "The Problem of Evil, the Problem of Air, and the Problem of Silence," *Philosophical Perspectives* 5 (1991): 164, note 11. Both are collected in *God, Knowledge and Mystery* (Ithaca: Cornell UP, 1995), where pp. 15–16 are particularly instructive. Also see "Reflections on the Chapters by Draper, Russell, and Gale," in Daniel Howard-Snyder, ed., *The Evidential Argument from Evil* (Indiana UP, 1996), 234–35.

2. It is a useful exercise to come up with your own list of specific horrors that you think God would be able to prevent without thereby losing a greater good or permitting an equally bad or worse evil.

3. Richard Swinburne would challenge this claim. See *Providence and the Problem of Evil* (Oxford, 1998).

4. The noseeum lingo is Stephen Wykstra's. See "Rowe's Noseeum Arguments from Evil," in *The Evidential Argument from Evil*, pp. 126–50.

5. I omit the phrase "nor any other equally bad or worse evil that would have been permitted" here and in what follows since it is not germane to my argument.

6. "The Argument from Inscrutable Evil," in *The Evidential Argument from Evil*, and

"The Argument from Divine Hiddenness," *Canadian Journal of Philosophy* (1996).

7. William Alston, "Some (Temporarily) Final Thoughts on Evidential Arguments from Evil," pp. 316–19, in *The Evidential Argument from Evil*.

8. Rowe initially defends premise 1 by identifying some *particular* horrible instances of suffering and asserting of at least some of them that *they* are pointless. In the penultimate paragraph of section I of his essay, he offers a different argument. Suppose it really is reasonable to believe that some greater good would have been lost if God had prevented the fawn's suffering, he says; indeed, we might suppose the same thing about the other horrors on our List of Pointless Evils. Of course, the particular horrors that we've identified are but a mere drop in the vast ocean of all the evil there is. And here an important point emerges: even if we cannot reasonably say of any *particular* horror on our list that *it* is pointless, it is reasonable to believe that no greater good would require God to permit *so much* evil—the vast quantity of horrific suffering and misery and wickedness that has stuffed terrestrial history and shows every sign of continuing unabated. Surely a being who is perfect in power and wisdom would not have to permit all of this enormous variety and profusion of intense human and animal suffering in order to achieve His purposes. Surely He could have prevented *some* of it without losing any greater good, *just some*. The idea that *none* of it could have been prevented by God without thereby losing a greater good seems an extraordinarily absurd idea, quite beyond our belief. In that case, at least *some instances of evil or other* are pointless, even if the instances on our List are not pointless and even if we can't say which instances are pointless.

The main thing to see about this second defense of premise 1 is that all of the worries about the initial defense arise for it as well. First, why suppose it is reasonable to believe that there is no greater good that would require God to permit so much horrible suffering in the world? Presumably because, so far as we can tell, there is no greater good that would require God to permit so much. So we have a new version of Rowe's Noseeum Assumption: we would very likely be able to see a greater good that would require God to permit *so much* horrible suffering, if there were one. Isn't it pretty clear that Alston's Analogies, the Progress Argument, and the Argument from Complexity jointly constitute just as good a reason to be in doubt about this new version of Rowe's Noseeum Assumption as they do its counterparts about particular horrors? If so, then the new defense of premise 1 is no better than the initial one. I leave it as homework to the reader to try to come up with a more promising option.

9. For useful reminders on an earlier draft of this essay, I thank William Rowe. I am indebted to William Alston and, especially, Stephen Wykstra for the main lines of thought I develop.

Discussion

1. What sort of initial plausibility would you apply to Rowe's Noseeum Inferences?

2. Consider Howard-Snyder's counter-examples to Rowe's Noseeum Inferences. Are they sufficiently powerful to overcome the initial plausibility of Rowe's Noseeum Inferences?

3. If Howard-Snyder's arguments are sound, what rational options are open with respect to belief in God? Are any closed off?

4. Can you come up with a defense of premise 1 that avoids Howard-Snyder's worries?

Chapter 21

Reflections on God and Human Suffering

THE SILENCE OF THE GOD WHO SPEAKS

NICHOLAS WOLTERSTORFF*

Silence. The silence of which I speak is the silence of the biblical God—the biblical God being a God who is not only capable of speaking but has on many occasions spoken. More specifically, I will be speaking of the *biblical* silence of the biblical God. The biblical silence of God is the nonanswering silence of God. It's like the silence of the parent who doesn't answer when the child asks "Why? Why did it happen? Where were you?" It's the silence which the poet of Psalm 83 pleads with God to break: "O God, do not keep silence; do not hold thy peace or be still, O God!"

The Bible—both the Hebrew Bible and the Christian Bible—represents God as having spoken. In addition, there's a long tradition within both Judaism and Christianity of regarding the Bible itself as a medium of divine speech. Nothing incoherent or impossible in the claim that God performs such actions as commanding, assuring, promising, asserting, and so forth. The silence of God is not an ontologically necessitated silence. It's not like the silence of the rocks and the hills, of which it is only metaphorically true that they speak. If God were impersonal—the "ground of being" or something of that sort—then God's silence

would be ontologically necessitated. The silence of the biblical God is the silence of a God who speaks.

Though the biblical God—by which I mean, God as represented in the Bible— though the biblical God does indeed speak, nonetheless, on most matters, God chooses not to say anything. Most matters God leaves it to us to find out about, by observation and inference. And that's wonderful. Who wants to be told everything? The silence of God—the *biblical* silence of God—does not consist in the fact that on many matters, God says nothing.

The biblical silence of God is the failure or refusal of God to answer a question put to Him. Though not the failure or refusal to answer any question you please, however. Some of the questions put to God are questions which, given what God has already said, are misguided questions. Questions that one wouldn't ask if one has heard and genuinely listened to what God has already said. The biblical silence of God is the nonanswering silence of God in the face of those questions which take into account what God has already said.

There are many such questions, and of many sorts. I shall focus all my attention on just one sort. The sort I have in mind are questions which we find ourselves incapable of answering on our own. At least, we have been unsuccessful thus far in answering them on our own. Yet they are questions to which the person who believes in the biblical God wants an answer with all one's soul. They are questions which, unanswered, put biblical faith at risk. The risk has proved too great for

* Nicholas Wolterstorff is Noah Porter Professor Emeritus of Philosophical Theology at Yale University.

many; faith has succumbed. Yet God does not answer the questions. Strange and disturbing. Though one poses the questions in the context of having listened to God, to ask them is to find oneself standing alongside the psalmist before the nonanswering silence of God.

Locating the silence. Let me begin by locating the sort of questions I have in mind, thus locating the silence. Strange forked creatures, we human beings: animalic persons, personic animals. Persons indeed, but also animals. Animals indeed, but also persons: creatures endowed with consciousness and free agency, reflective of God, meant to enjoy and tend the earth and to live in fellowship with other persons, both those of our own kind and God. Placed in a spatio-temporal physical world along with lots of other forms of life, including other kinds of animals.

Upon inspecting this curious forked creature which he had made, God pronounced the workmanship good; by which God no doubt meant, in part, that our design plan was a good one for our situation. Inspection completed and passed, God sent us on our way with various instructions for conduct, and a blessing: May you flourish, said God. May you flourish as a species. When one reads the report of God's blessing of humanity in the context of the other Genesis blessings, that's the natural interpretation. But as the Bible proceeds it becomes clear that the Genesis report of God's blessing of humanity had a latent meaning. What God had in mind was not just that we flourish as a species but that we flourish as individual members of the species. That we each live until "full of years"—the three score years and ten built into our design plan; and that during those years we flourish. Flourish *qua* the animalic persons, the personic animals, that we were created as being. And flourish in the earthly and social environment in which we have been placed. In Genesis, God was not pronouncing a blessing on disembodied souls about to enter an immaterial heaven.

But things have gone awry, terribly awry, with respect to God's creating and providential intent for these creatures. The divine experiment has not worked out: the experiment of creating this species of forked creatures, placing and maintaining the species in this physical universe along with other forms of life, giving the species instructions for conduct, and doing this creating and maintaining with the intent that each member of the species should flourish on earth in society until full of years. The blessing has not been fulfilled. Some do not flourish; some do not live until full of years; some neither flourish nor live until full of years.

Prominent among the things which have gone awry in human existence are life duration and suffering. The lives of many do not endure as they were meant to endure. And suffering does not serve the function it was meant to serve. Neither do affection and volition function as they were meant to function; they do not measure up to God's instructions. But on this occasion, I shall concentrate on the malfunctioning of suffering.

To see in what way suffering malfunctions, we must reflect on the nature of suffering and on its proper function. For it does indeed have a *proper* function. Let me take *joy*, or synonymously for my purposes, *delight*, as the opposite of suffering.

Being constituted as we are serves our flourishing as animalic persons in the world in which we are placed. That we need water, food, and intact flesh if we are to remain alive is a direct consequence of our animalic constitution. Accordingly, it's conducive to our endurance as animalic persons that we have feelings of thirst when in need of water, feelings of hunger when in need of food, feelings of pain when our flesh gets burned, and that we experience these sensations negatively. In some cases we experience them with such intense negativity that we *suffer* from parched throat sensations, *suffer* from hunger pang sensations, *suffer* from burn sensations. Our endurance as animalic persons would be vastly more precarious than it is if we didn't experience thirst, hunger, and the pain of burned flesh, or if we didn't experience them negatively.

The examples I have given, of the proper functioning of unpleasantness and suffering, were all taken from the animalic side of our existence; examples of the same point from the personal side of our existence—can also easily be given. Our dislike of loneliness leads us to establish families and communities. Our dislike of intellectual bewilderment leads us to pursue knowledge. Our dislike of disappointment over unachieved goals leads us to try harder. And our dislike of a wide range of things makes them candidates for functioning as means of appropriate punishment and chastisement.

The conclusion is unavoidable that suffering in particular, and negative evaluations in general, often serve our flourishing as the animalic persons that we are. Of course the person suffering doesn't *like* the suffering. But that's exactly the point. We draw back from the experiences we dislike, do what we can to alleviate and forestall them. It's the combination of our being so constituted as to feel pain upon being burned and our not liking that pain which makes it much easier for us to survive than would otherwise be the case; witness the precarious existence of those rare human beings who do not feel such pain. The suffering serves our flourishing. Dislike and suffering are existential No-saying to that from which and over which we suffer. But when a human being placed in this world has a constitution which includes such capacities for existential No-saying as ours typically does, we must pronounce a judgmental Yes on that aspect of our constitution itself. For we cannot imagine creatures such as ourselves flourishing, or even surviving, in environments such as ours without such capacities as we have for existential No-saying. Part of what God found good about the way God created us was surely that we were capable of suffering.

Yet, to say it once again, things have gone terribly awry with respect to the function of suffering in our lives—and with respect to life duration. It was and is the intent behind God's creation and maintenance that with the constitution God gave us we would each and all flourish until full of years in the environment in which God placed us. But with reference to that intent, things have gone terribly awry. Sometimes a person's constitution itself becomes disordered in such a way that the person doesn't flourish; one lives in severe depression or intractable pain. More often, the fit between our constitution and our environment does not serve our flourishing. The food I need to maintain my animal existence isn't available; so I die long before full of years, suffering intensely from starvation. You fall. If you merely break an arm, that doesn't significantly inhibit your flourishing, since the break soon heals and the suffering caused by the break nicely exemplifies the design plan functioning properly. Life would be far more precarious than it is if breaking bones produced no pain. But if your fall brings about your early death, I can expatiate as long as I have breath on the fact that this is just a natural consequence of your doing what you did with the animal body that you have in the physical universe which is ours; that doesn't address the fact that things have gone awry with reference to God's intent that you should live until full of years. Again, rather than flourishing in the company of your fellow human beings you may be subjected to indignity and even torture. Your human constitution operating in your social and physical environment does not bring about your flourishing until full of years.

The divine experiment has not worked out: the experiment of creating these forked creatures with the constitution that they have, placing them in this physical and social situation, and doing that, as well as maintaining and instructing them, with the intent that each and every one should flourish until full of years.

Suffering and life duration have gone agonizingly awry with reference to that intent.

Why have they gone awry? The very speech of God invites us to pose the question. Invites us to pose the question for this case and for that case; and for all the cases in general. Why was the life of this person snuffed out when young? Why did that person suffer years of intractable suffering that not only went beyond all proper functioning but from which nothing redemptive could any longer be extracted? Why all this brevity of life and why all such suffering? But no answer is forthcoming. Listen as we may, we hear no further speech. Only silence. Nonanswering silence.

Objection: the world has been misdescribed. Most philosophers and theologians in the Christian tradition would deny that I have rightly located the silence of God. My location of the silence is predicated on the claim that things have gone awry with reference to God's creating and maintaining intent—in particular, that suffering and life duration have gone awry. They would insist that that is not so.

Some would say that I have misdescribed the world. I said that in this world of ours we are confronted—not just now and then but over and over—with malfunctioning suffering and suffering which we prove incapable of making redemptive. The tradition of "soul making theodicy," initiated by Irenaeus, would deny this. Let me quote Calvin as an example. He says in one passage that "Whether poverty or exile, or prison, or insult, or disease, or bereavement, or anything like them torture us, we must think that none of these things happens except by the will and providence of God, that he does nothing except with a well-ordered justice" (*Institutes* III, viii, 11). Coming to the surface in this passage is Calvin's inclination toward radical occasionalism—toward the view that God is the only true causal agent in reality. As to the character of God's agency, Calvin was persuaded that

God acts always out of justice or love. Thus we get this other passage: "All the suffering to which human life is subject and liable are necessary exercises by which God partly invites us to repentance, partly instructs us in humility, and partly renders us more cautious and more attentive in guarding against the allurements of sin for the future" (*Commentary on Genesis* 3:19). The thought is clear: All suffering is sent by God. Partly out of retributive justice, but mainly *out of love*. Suffering is God's gift to us: God's medicine, God's surgery. We don't like the medicine and the surgery; who does like medicine and surgery? But suffering is for our moral and spiritual welfare. It prods us, provokes us, into reorienting and deepening our moral and spiritual selves. The experience of suffering may even, in mysterious ways, provide us with the material *necessary* for such deepening. As I put it in a passage in my *Lament for a Son*:

> Suffering is the shout of "No" by one's whole existence to that over which one suffers—the shout of "No" by nerves and gut and gland and heart to pain, to death, to injustice, to depression, to hunger, to humiliation, to bondage, to abandonment. And sometimes, when the cry is intense, there emerges a radiance which elsewhere seldom appears; a glow of courage, of love, of insight, of selflessness, of faith. In that radiance we see best what humanity was meant to be. In the valley of suffering, despair and bitterness are brewed. But there also character is made. The valley of suffering is the vale of soul-making. (96–97)

Soul-making theodicy points to something deep and true. Yet if we judge ourselves answerable to the biblical speech of God, then we cannot accept its claim that, with reference to God's creating and maintaining intent, suffering and life duration have not gone awry in our world—cannot accept its assumption that only our affections and volitions have gone awry. It may well be that the suffering of a parent over the death of a child provides opportunity for the spiritual growth of the parent, or that the wrong-doing of the parent merits some suffering. But what about the child? What about the benediction God pronounced over the child: May you flourish until full of years? Or to move to a totally different scale: It may well be that the suffering of the survivors of the Jewish Holocaust provided an opportunity for their spiritual growth, or that their wrong-doing merited suffering. But what about the victims? What about the benediction God pronounced over each and every one of them: May you flourish until full of years?

Soul-making theodicy speaks only of the survivors, not of the victims. Either that, or it links victims with survivors by saying that the chastisement or opportunity for spiritual growth provided to the survivors outweighs in its goodness the evil of the early death and suffering of the victims. In so speaking, it displays its obliviousness to that "each-and-every" note in the biblical speech of God. The biblical God is not a nineteenth-century English utilitarian concerned only with the greatest flourishing of *the greatest number*. The God who kills children for the sake of the chastisement or spiritual growth of parents, the God who kills millions of Jews for the sake of the chastisement for spiritual growth of the survivors, is a grotesque parody of the biblical God. And should someone suggest that the early death of the child represents the punishment of the child for the child's own sins, and that the early death of the victims of the Holocaust represents the punishment of the victims for the victims' own sins, we must, emboldened by God's own book of Job, reject this suggestion as blasphemy against the justice of God and grotesquely libelous of those we loved.

Objection: the divine intent misdescribed. To suggest that God trades off the suffering and early death of victims for the opportunity provided to survivors for chastisement or spiritual growth is to imply that I have not so much misdescribed the world as misdescribed the divine intent. Probably that is the more common objection to the picture I have drawn.

The most common form of the objection holds that it is essential to distinguish between, on the one hand, God's creating and maintaining intent, and on the other hand, God's desires. Nothing goes awry with reference to God's intent. Yet it would be profoundly mistaken to say that God is indifferent as between a life of seventy seconds and a life of seventy years, indifferent as between a life of malfunctioning and unredemptive suffering and a life absent of such. God desires, for each and every human being, that that human being flourish on earth in the community of persons until full of years.

From this point onward, the objection is developed along two distinct lines. Call the one, the *Leibnizian* position. The Leibnizian holds that what must be distinguished from God's creating and maintaining intent is God's *ceteris paribus* [all things being equal] desires. With reference to God's intent, everything happens exactly as God's plan: early death, unredemptive suffering, everything. Nonetheless it remains true that God desires, *other things being equal*, that each human being flourish on earth in the community of persons until full of years. But other things are not equal—so much so that it's not possible for God to bring about a world in which that *ceteris paribus* desire is satisfied for each and every human being. We can be assured that in choosing to create this actual world, from among all possible worlds, God was choosing the best possible— or if there isn't any best possible, that God was choosing as good a world as any. But the only reasonable conclusion, given the nature of God and the way the world is, is that any such world incorporates trade-offs; not even God can achieve everything that God desires, other things being equal. That's why we cannot equate what God desires *ceteris paribus* with God's creating intent. Though suffering and life duration certainly go awry with reference to the former, nothing goes awry with reference to the latter.

Call the other way of developing the objection, the *free will* position. The person who embraces this position holds that suffering and life duration, and other things as well, go awry with reference to God's *actual* desires, not just with respect to God's *ceteris paribus* desires. Not, though, with reference to God's creating and maintaining intent; on this central point he agrees with the Leibnizian. The root of the disagreement between the two lies in the fact that the person espousing the *free will* position holds—as the name suggests— that human beings are created capable of free agency. There are, in turn, two different ways of working out the free will position, depending on whether one holds that God can and does know in advance what agents will freely do in such-and-such situations, or denies that.

The *Molinist* holds that God does know this; and that God uses that knowledge to select, from among all the possible worlds, this actual world of ours to create and maintain. Everything happens according to the foreknowledge of God. But not everything happens because God brings it about; some of it happens because of the free agency of created persons. Though God knew in advance what Hitler would freely do, nonetheless it was not God who perpetrated the holocaust but Hitler, along with his henchmen and underlings. And God profoundly disapproved of Hitler's actions. With reference to God's desires and commands for those creatures capable of free agency, volitions and affections have gone profoundly awry; as the consequence of that, in turn, very much suffering and life duration have gone awry. Yet nothing has gone awry with reference to God's creating intent. For as on the Leibnizian position, the only reasonable conclusion, given the nature of God and the world, is said to be that God at creation was confronted with no option but to make trade-offs. Among the good-as-any worlds available to God for creating, there was none in which

it was both true that human beings were free to make significant choices between good and evil, and true that each and every human being flourished on earth in the community of persons until full of years. The course of the world makes clear that God regards free agency as something of enormous value. But the fact that God tolerates the evil of our choices for the sake of our freedom by no means implies that God approves of that evil. God disapproves of it: *actually* disapproves of it, not just *ceteris paribus* disapproves.

The *Banezian*, by contrast, denies that God could know in advance what a person capable of free agency would freely do in such-and-such a situation. Accordingly assuming that God does sometimes allow persons capable of free agency actually to act freely, we cannot think of this actual world of ours as selected by God from among all the possible worlds. Its realization does not represent the unfolding of a plan chosen by God before the foundations of the world. That's not to say that the world as it develops is constantly surprising God; though one cannot know what an agent *will* freely do in such-and-such a situation, often one can know what he or she is *likely* to do. Nonetheless, whereas providence on the Leibnizian and Molinist views consists basically of maintenance, on the Banezian view it requires a considerable degree of intervention if God is to bring about as good a world as any that God is capable of bringing about. The counterpart to God's creating intent in the Leibnizian and Molinist views is, in the Banezian view, the combination of God's creating and providential intents. By reference to that intent, nothing goes awry—even though very many of the actions of free agents and the consequences thereof go radically contrary to God's actual desire and command. Three ways of working out the same idea: Though things go awry with reference to God's desires and commands, nothing goes awry with reference to God's creating and maintaining intent. The history of the world simply exhibits the trade-offs already built into the divine intent.

But if we judge ourselves answerable to the biblical speech of God, we can no more accept this position than that of soul-making theodicy. Again it is especially the "each-and-every" note in God's self-characterizing speech which goes unheard—or perhaps in this case not so much unheard as consciously rejected. Let's be sure that we rightly hear that "each-and-every" note. There's no problem, as such, with trade-offs in the life of a single person: no problem as such with the fact, for example, that I suffer from the consequences of my own free agency. I say, "no problem as such"; as a matter of fact, the suffering caused by physical and mental disease in our world often goes far beyond what could possibly be redemptive. The problem inherent in the Irenaean position, as in the Leibnizian articulation of it, is that the divine intent is regarded as using the suffering and early death of *one* person as a means for the chastisement or spiritual growth of *another*; and the problem inherent in the free will position is that the divine intent is regarded as allowing the suffering and early death of *one* person as a means for the chastisement or spiritual growth of *another*; and the problem inherent in the free will position is that the divine intent is regarded as allowing the suffering and early death of *one* person for the sake of the unencumbered free agency of *another*. It is this using of one person for the good of another that the person who judges himself or herself answerable to the biblical speech of God cannot accept as belonging to the divine intent.

Or, given the working of laws of nature in our world and the consequences of free agency, must we concede that God doesn't really pronounce over each and every person the creational and providential benediction: May you flourish on earth in the community of persons until full of years? Must we concede that that's an unsustainable interpretation of the biblical speech of God—for the reason that that benediction could not possibly be fulfilled in a world with free agency and laws of nature such as ours, and that God would know that, and accordingly would not pronounce such

a benediction? I think we should not concede this. It's thinkable, indeed, that a lot more knowledge about laws of nature than we actually have might force us to make that concession, as would a lot more knowledge about the relation between divine and human agency. But in our current state of relative ignorance, there is, so far as I can see, no such rational compulsion. Though the point is certainly relevant: a fundamental principle for the interpretation of divine discourse is that God does not say what entails or presupposes falsehood.

The root of the difficulty, for the person who judges himself or herself answerable to the biblical speech of God, is that the God of the Bible has told us too much. If we hadn't been told that it was God's intent that we should live until full of years, then no problem. If we hadn't been told that it was God's intent that we should flourish, then no problem. If we hadn't been told that it was God's intent that we should flourish here on earth in the community of persons, then no problem. If we hadn't been told that it was God's intent that each and every one of us should flourish until full of years, then no problem. It's the speech of the biblical God that leads us to see that suffering and life-duration have gone awry with reference to God's creating and maintaining intent. If we could dispense with answering to that speech, it would be possible to devise a point of view which fits together such suffering and brevity of life as we find in our world with the divine intent; many have done exactly that.

Living in the silence. Suffering and life duration have gone awry with reference to God's creating and maintaining intent. To acknowledge that is to have the question well up irresistibly: Why? Why this untimely death? Why that unredemptive suffering? Why any untimely death and why any unredemptive suffering?

We cannot help but ask. Yet we get no answer. None that I can discern. We confront nonanswering silence. We confront the biblical silence of the biblical God. We shall have to live in the silence.

What will such living be like? If we have all this while judging ourselves answerable to the speech of God in determining the questions we put to God, then we shall likewise judge ourselves answerable to the speech of God as we live in the silence of God.

In the first place, we shall endure in holding on to God, and shall engage in the practices of devotion whereby such holding on is accomplished, expressed and nurtured. Secondly, we shall join with God himself in keeping alive the protest against early death and unredemptive suffering. Till breath dies within us we shall insist that this must not be. We shall reject all consolation that comes in the form of urging us to accept untimely death, all that comes in the form of urging us to be content with unredemptive suffering. We shall endure in our existential No to untimely death; we shall forever resist pronouncing No on our existential No to untimely death. We shall endure in our existential No to unredemptive suffering; we shall forever resist pronouncing No on our existential No to unredemptive suffering. In the stories we tell of humanity's dwelling on earth, we shall not forget untimely death and unredemptive suffering. We shall keep the memory alive so as to keep the protest alive. And in the stories we tell of our lives, we shall not disown our suffering but own it. There will be more to our stories than that; but there will be at least that.

Thirdly, we shall hope for the day, await the occasion, and seize the opportunity to own our own suffering redemptively. We shall struggle to wrest good from this evil—"to turn it to our profit"—while still saying No to untimely death and unredemptive suffering.

And lastly whenever and wherever we spot an opening, we shall join the divine battle against all that goes awry with reference to God's intent. We shall join God in doing battle against all that causes early death and all that leads to unredemptive suffering: disease, injustice, warfare, torture, enmity. The self-characterization of the biblical God is not that of a God who passively accepts things going awry with reference to his intent but that of a God who does battle; and is not that of a God who weakly struggles in a failing cause but that of a God whose cause will triumph. Is it really true that God will win? Can we trust the struggle's outcome when we don't know the struggle's cause? Or wouldn't it help to know the cause?

Discussion

1. What is the problem of suffering and silence?

2. Present one of Wolterstorff's rejections of traditional theodicies. What do you think of his argument?

3. Since he can't solve the problem of suffering and silence, how does Wolterstorff propose to live with it?

4. Wolterstorff is a Christian who is able to maintain his faith in the face of silence. How do you respond?

Part Four

Suggestions for Further Study

Adams, Marilyn McCord. *Horrendous Evils and the Goodness of God*. Ithaca: Cornell UP, 2000.

Adams, Marilyn McCord, and Robert Merrihew, eds. *The Problem of Evil*. New York: Oxford UP, 1990.

Davies, Brian. *The Reality of God and the Problem of Evil*. Bloomsbury Academic, 2006.

Gale, Richard. *On the Nature and Existence of God*. New York: Cambridge UP, 1991.

Hick, John. *Evil and the God of Love*. New York: Harper & Row, 1978.

Howard-Snyder, Daniel, ed. *The Evidential Argument from Evil*. Bloomington and Indianapolis: U of Indiana P, 1996.

Lewis, C.S. *The Problem of Pain*. New York: Macmillan, 1962.

Murray, Michael. *Nature Red in Tooth and Claw*. Oxford: Oxford UP, 2008.

Peterson, Michael, ed. *The Problem of Evil: Selected Readings*. Notre Dame: U of Notre Dame P, 1992.

Plantinga, Alvin. *God, Freedom and Evil*. Grand Rapids, MI: Eerdmans, 1977.

Stump, Eleonore. *Wandering in the Darkness: Narrative and the Problem of Suffering*. Oxford: Oxford UP, 2012.

van Inwagen, Peter. *The Problem of Evil*. Oxford: Oxford UP, 2008.

Wolterstorff, Nicholas. *Lament for a Son*. Grand Rapids, MI: Eerdmans, 1987.

Divine Language and Attributes

Part Five

Introduction

Introduction. Most textbooks in the philosophy of religion contain a section on what are considered the traditional divine attributes of omnipotence, omniscience, immutability, aseity, perfect goodness, and eternity; let us call the view that ascribes all of these properties to God *classical theism*. Omnipotence is the ability to do anything (with some qualifications as we shall see shortly). "Omniscience" means all-knowing and "immutability" means unchanging. God's aseity means that God does not depend on anything; this idea is usually attached to the doctrine of divine sovereignty— that everything depends upon God. Perfect goodness means that God is perfectly good but it is difficult to say just exactly what that means! And eternity means that God is outside of, and therefore not bound by, time.

Although these attributes are at the centre of a great many philosophical puzzles, there is no reason that these particular attributes should merit more attention than any other divine attributes. Unfortunately, most non-philosophers find these puzzles abstract, sterile, and unconnected with their own religious concerns. The essays in this section will raise some of the problems of classical theism but through the medium of more existentially pressing concerns: the problems of divine suffering, prayer, hell, and religious pluralism. These issues are not unrelated, as we shall see, to classical theism. We can, for example, raise the issue of divine immutability and eternity through a consideration of either divine suffering or prayer. We can approach God's omnipotence and omniscience through the problem of hell (or, as we have seen, through the problem of evil).

Many recent philosophers have seen fit to reject one or another of the divine attributes of classical theism. Arguments have been offered against divine eternity, immutability, omnipotence, foreknowledge, and even goodness. If all of the attributes the classical theist ascribes to God are rejected, one may wonder, of course, about just what is left that is distinctly *divine* in the nature of God. The essays in this section contain a cross-section of both classical theists and their critics.

Classical theism. Omniscience, omnipotence, immutability, and eternity are parts of a set of divine attributes that are considered necessary for a maximally perfect being. What is seen as necessary by some will be rejected by others as being too Greek. Early Judeo-Christian theology was more anthropomorphic, less abstruse and systematic than the subsequently developed theologies of Augustine, Anselm, and Aquinas (or Maimonides for Jewish theology and Averroes and Avicenna for Muslim theology). Finding inspiration in the ideas of Plato, Aristotle, and the neoplatonists, these thinkers wedded the philosophical systems of the Greeks with Biblical revelation. The resulting orthodoxy, classical theism, raised both problems and prospects for subsequent theorizing about the divine.

Omnipotence is, at first glance, a simple property: God can do anything. Many people have heard (and snickered at) the so-called paradox of omnipotence: can God create a stone so big that he cannot lift it? Various answers are "no" (a "stone that God cannot lift" is impossible and God can only do the logically possible) and "yes" (God *can* make a stone that he cannot lift and, being omnipotent, can lift it!). This paradox does raise a serious problem for omnipotence: can God do just anything? Is God limited by the logically impossible? And there are other concerns related to omnipotence: can God sin or change the past? The prospect of defining omnipotence is not nearly so simple as one might have at first thought.

Omniscience creates problems both in itself and in conjunction with other properties. If, for example, God is outside of time, can he know what time it is now? Since time is ever-changing, doesn't this sort of knowledge require that God be ever-changing (hence, creating a problem for immutability)? Omniscience of the foreknowledge variety generates a problem for belief in human freedom. Classical theism holds that God has exhaustive foreknowledge of the future. If God infallibly knows whatever one will do before one does it, could one possibly be free? Freedom seems to include the ability to do otherwise (to be able to accept or refuse, say, that tempting piece of chocolate). But if God infallibly knows that you are going to accept that piece of chocolate, then you must do so. For, if you were not to choose that piece of chocolate, God would have had a false belief. But this, surely, is impossible. So you must, of necessity, do whatever God has already foreseen that you will do. So no one's actions are free. The most famous solution to this problem was offered by Boethius, who appealed to divine eternity to solve the matter.[1]

As stated above, it is difficult to define divine goodness. Theists believe in God's paternal care but must reconcile such care with the evils faced by his children. We would call no earthly father good if he could have prevented his children from suffering in, say, the Holocaust, but did not. In what sense was God good to the Ukrainians who were forced to starve under Stalin? In reply, theists often claim that God's ways are not our ways, but then the doctrine of divine goodness becomes an utter mystery. If God's ways are totally unlike human ways, then we could not possibly understand what it might mean for God to be good. The problem of divine goodness is also important in connection with the problem of the eternal suffering of the damned. How could a perfectly good being permit or cause the eternal suffering of any of his creatures?

Since some of the properties of classical theism are entailed by other properties, there is a tight conceptual connection among all of the properties. For example, an immutable being must also be outside of time (for time, on some accounts, is the measure of change). Some thinkers contend that a perfectly good being must also be omniscient (to be good, one must know the good and how to maximize it); or perhaps it goes the other way around; an omniscient being is perforce a perfectly good being. So the rejection of a single property might have ramifications for an entire set of properties contained in classical theism.

Although classical theism is a rather abstract view about the metaphysics of God, it finds expression in a host of considerations that concern ordinary believers, such as prayer, God's attitude toward human suffering, God's love for God's creatures, God's activity in the salvation of his creatures, etc. So issues in classical theism can find expression in discussions of prayer, the problem of evil, the doctrine of hell, and issues of religious pluralism.

Religious language. As a preliminary to discussion of the nature of God, we must consider the language that we use to speak of God. After all, how can finite, human language be adequate to express transcendence?

One might expect a medieval theologian to favour minute precision in theological language. Thomas Aquinas, the pre-eminent medieval theologian, however, argues that this is impossible when it comes to language about God, rejecting the idea that any language about God can be univocal or literal; a term is univocal if it is used in exactly the same sense when applied to two perhaps quite different things. A univocal understanding of, for example, God as Father would mean that God was our biological progenitor; but, of course, God can't literally or univocally be a father. Does this mean that God-talk has no meaning, or, to use his language, is religious language "equivocal," as some mystics claimed? Equivocal language is language that changes completely when applied to two different things; so the term "father" when applied to God has no connection with the term "father" when applied to a human being. If all religious language were equivocal, then we could understand little or nothing about God. Some, like John Duns Scotus, claimed that these are the only two alternatives, univocal or equivocal, and we must choose between the two. Aquinas's creative answer was to propose a third way, the way of analogy; analogical terms are similar in some respects (but different in others) when applied to different things. So an analogical understanding of "father" might mean that God exercises something like paternal care for his creatures but is not our biological progenitor. Since the univocal approach seems to claim too much and the equivocal approach too little, much hangs on the cogency of Aquinas's alternative.

Stiver contends that a great deal of religious language, in fact a great deal of language in general, is metaphorical. Metaphor and symbolic language in general, while widely used, have been regarded with suspicion, if not outright hostility, in the Western tradition because they lack the clarity and precision of literal or univocal language. If metaphor were used, it was required to be translated into univocal language, a "substitution" approach that can be traced back to Aristotle. This prioritizing of more precise language is behind the distinction between the "hard" and "soft" sciences, or between the sciences in general and the humanities. With this background, language about God put enormous pressure on the capacity to convey cognitive meaning.

More recently, a radical transformation of the understanding has occurred that challenges whether metaphors must be—or can be—translated into univocal language. Moreover, metaphor may sometimes be more effective than literal language, with obvious significance for language about God, which is highly metaphorical. It has further been noticed that metaphors, in metaphorical models, are much more pervasive in the hard sciences than was previously thought, perhaps even indispensable. If metaphors have this irreducible nature that cannot be explicated by some explanatory and controlling calculus, then new meaning is given to Aristotle's ancient dictum, "the greatest thing by far is to be master of metaphor."

What Stiver discusses is how such linguistic and cognitive skill may shed light on a wider issue, namely, the universality of hermeneutics. For similar reasons as with metaphor, the "hermeneutical" disciplines such as the soft sciences and humanities have been often regarded with disdain because of the lack of precision. If Hans-Georg Gadamer is correct that all the sciences are based on hermeneutical insights, this tradition of privileging the hard sciences is completely overturned and points to the overriding importance of understanding the dynamics of hermeneutical thinking. Paul Ricoeur then suggests that the kind of ability that enables one to be a "master of metaphor" is a clue to the kind of cognition of hermeneutics. With the emergence of the significance of hermeneutics, grasping such ability may well be "the greatest thing by far," especially with respect to God-talk.

Analogical and metaphorical religious language, Elizabeth Burns argues, have theological implications. Consider the claim that God is a person. To claim that the divine is a person or personal is, according to Richard Swinburne, "the most elementary claim of theism" (1993, 101). Burns argues that, whether the classical theist's concept of the divine as a person or personal is construed as an analogy or a metaphor, or a combination of the two, analysis necessitates qualification of that concept such that any differences between the classical theist's concept of the divine as a person or personal and revisionary interpretations (for example, conceiving of God as an impersonal force or as Nature) of that concept are merely superficial. Thus, either the classical theist has more in common with revisionary theism than he/she might care to admit, or classical theism is a multi-faceted position which encompasses interpretations which some might regard as revisionist.

The suffering of God. The idea that God (the Father) could suffer was dismissed by the early Christian church as heresy. God, so it was believed, existed in a perfect state of uninterrupted, suffering-free bliss. God depends solely upon himself for his happiness and is sufficiently interesting and communal to satisfy himself. God need not, indeed could not, depend on his creatures for his well-being.

God's immutability, aseity, timelessness, and, some claim, perfect goodness are all connected with the issue of whether or not God can suffer. If God suffers with us, that is, upon the occasion of the suffering of his children, then God changes from a suffering-free condition (say prior to creation) to a suffering condition (say upon the fall of Adam or upon hearing the cries of his people in bondage in Egypt). If God were to change, then God would be in time. And if God were the kind of being whose well-being depended upon the well-being of his creatures, then God's aseity would be in jeopardy. On the other hand, how could God be loving, that is, care for the welfare of his creatures, and remain in a state of bliss?

Johannes Scotus Eriugena, John the Scot (who was Irish), defends the classical view of God and God's imperviousness to human woes. Eriugena raises a particular problem for classical theism and its relation to divine love. If God is neither moved nor mover, neither actor nor acted upon, in what sense does God love his creatures? Eriugena first makes a claim about language: we only speak of God's motion and action, and hence love, in metaphorical terms. Eriugena then tries to cash out the metaphors in a less metaphorical

manner which preserves both God's love and God's independence from his creatures. God loves his creatures not by acting upon them, nor by being affected by them, but by attracting them like a magnet attracts shards of iron.

Nicholas Wolterstorff locates the discussion of God's suffering within the broader context of happiness. The eudaemonistic ideal—that we are happiness seekers—finds expression in the desire to remove all suffering and grief from our lives. To do so we must attach our loves, our *eros*, only to that which both fully satisfies and cannot be lost. For human beings that means attaching our eros to God and, here's the crucial point, for God it means exactly the same thing. God's eros is a longing for that which is fully adequate and cannot be lost—God's eros is for God himself. That means that God loves us in a manner which does not requite; God wills good things for his creatures (God is benevolent) but God's well-being does not depend on any (positive or negative) responses of his creatures. Wolterstorff condemns this picture of the divine life as both unbliblical (many Jewish thinkers have made this point well) and as incoherent. God embraces the world in suffering love—he cares enough for his creation to suffer with it. And—here we step into a new arena—God's suffering grounds the demand to relieve the suffering of this world.

Prayer. Prayer is a simple matter on the surface. Many people acquire the practice of prayer as early as they acquire language, and for the rest of their lives, they pray as naturally and unconsciously as they employ their native tongue. Prayer becomes part of the fabric of their lives in the same way that language does; so, if someone were to ask "Why do you pray as you do?" she would get the same puzzled expression that the question "Why do you speak as you do?" would elicit. However, as soon as one begins to respond to the former question, she enters a large and complicated labyrinth of ideas that mingle in and around the core of theological thought. One's ideas about prayer have significant ramifications for one's beliefs about God's power, knowledge, goodness, and agency, the nature of causal relations, and human freedom. All of these ideas are interrelated; one's views on one of these ideas will significantly affect one's views on the others. Those who haven't thought much about prayer may find, upon reflection, that their spontaneous practice of prayer is inconsistent with their beliefs on these related ideas.

There have been at least two significant attempts to systematize these ideas into a coherent package. Classical theism, defended here by Thomas Aquinas, held that because it was impossible to move the will of an immutable God with requests, prayer was meant for the edification of human beings. There are many different modes of prayer, including thanksgiving, praise, worship, intercession, petition, and repentance, but they can all be summed up in the following way: prayer is a discipline which humans practice in order to develop appropriate attitudes towards God. When we bring praise to God in prayer we are acknowledging his awesome power and his tender love which naturally gives birth to joy and thanksgiving in us. When we bring a sin to God in prayer, we are acknowledging our depravity before God, which cultivates the appropriate feelings of guilt and repentance. When we bring a request to God in prayer, we are acknowledging our utter dependence on God, which enables us in turn to strive more diligently to perform his will with humility.

Recent thinkers have suggested that prayer is meant to establish a relation between God and humans, a relation that affects both members. Eleonore Stump, a classical theist, brings together the relational and the edificational views of prayer in her essay. Petitionary prayer, according to Stump, is precisely what is necessary for God to establish a good relationship with human beings. If God were to give us everything we need without asking, we would get spoiled and be ungrateful. And if God did not permit his creatures to communicate with him through prayer, we might despair. Prayer keeps human beings at the right distance from God, neither too close nor to distant, for a good relationship.

Is there a hell? The problem of evil as traditionally framed is minor in comparison to the eternal suffering of the damned. No finite, earthly suffering could create a problem as big as an eternity of suffering, especially if the suffering is as severe as indicated in most holy writ.

In "Universalism, Hell, and the Fate of the Ignorant," Stephen Davis takes on the formidable task of defending the doctrine of hell. After criticizing the doctrine of universalism (that all people will eventually end up in heaven), Davis defines and defends his understanding of the doctrine of separationism—that some people will be separated from divine grace forever. His defense is partly biblical—he is part of the Christian tradition that accepts the authority of scripture. And his defense is partly philosophical—paying heed to philosophical consequences of free will, justice and grace.

Marilyn McCord Adams finds the problems related to the traditional doctrine of hell insurmountable. Her critique of hell and corresponding defense of universalism trade on notions of divine goodness and finite human agency. Adams believes that God is good to people as individuals, wishing to create a life for each person that is good (to them) on the whole. Eternal suffering, of course, would prevent God from being good to persons. Adams also defends an Irenaean view of human persons: human beings are not created perfect (contra Augustine) but are finite in both moral and intellectual capacities. Our inability to conceive of the consequences of our actions diminishes our moral responsibility for those actions. Eternal punishment of such impaired creatures would be disproportionate to the "crime." Intriguingly, Adams defends a cognitive role for feelings in making judgments about the doctrine of hell.

Religious diversity. I live in the midwest of the United States of America. Many Dutch immigrants settled here, most of whom are in the Protestant tradition of John Calvin. There are many Latinos in my town, the vast majority of whom are Roman Catholics. In other places, there are different correlations between religious belief and socio-economic background, ethnicity, country of origin, and so on. If I were teaching philosophy of religion in Saudi Arabia, my students would just as certainly believe that Allah is God and Mohammed is his prophet as my predominantly Christian students believe that Jesus is God. The problems of religious diversity loom large: who's to say who's right and who's wrong in matters religious? Isn't a claim to exclusive truth on the part of religious practitioners arrogant and unjustifiable? Is religion simply a matter of socio-historical accident?

The leading defender of religious pluralism, the belief that there are many, equally valid paths to God, is John Hick. Hick divides the territory into three options: religious exclusivism: that there is only one path to God; religious inclusivism: that there is only one path to God but people can take it without knowing it (there might be "anonymous" Christians or Jews); and religious pluralism: the claim that there are many paths all leading to ... to what? This is difficult to say because each religion postulates a different goal for life: nirvana, God (in the Judeo-Christian-Muslim sense), Brahman, the ground of being, non-being, the Tao, etc. Hick claims that each religion is equally successful at salvation-transformation-fulfillment. So, at the level of practice, each religion is roughly equal. But it is at the cognitive level that Hick is revisionary. Following Kant, Hick believes that each religion is an expression of the ultimate *as humanly experienced* but not the ultimate *as it is in itself*. One's socio-cultural background shapes the experience of the divine or ultimate reality. The divine reality exceeds one's puny cognitive and linguistic grasp. But, since each religion is equally efficacious at salvation, the essence of religion is left unimpaired; the essence of religion, according to Hick, is to move us from self-centredness to "reality-centredness."

Peter van Inwagen is, to put it mildly, an enthusiastic critic of religious pluralism.[2] He paints a picture of the world as viewed by pluralists and seeks to erase it. Van Inwagen's critique is partly just a summary of his Christian beliefs, which entail that other religions are theologically and salvifically deficient. This so-called scandal of particularity may sound arrogant, so van Inwagen faces these charges straightaway. Suppose that, in fact, Christianity (or Islam or Judaism) *is* the only way to God; shouldn't its practitioners to the best of their ability both defend and propagate their beliefs? Van Inwagen also notes the similarities between political and religious beliefs. Political beliefs are often mutually exclusive and are seldom rejected simply because of their holders' socio-cultural backgrounds. And van Inwagen puts the shoe of arrogance on the pluralist's foot: pluralists are making a claim about reality and our abilities to grasp it; in so doing they are claiming that whoever disagrees with them—every Muslim, Buddhist, or Christian who makes a claim about divine reality—is wrong. Van Inwagen concludes with a defense of the role of the Church, which is salvifically generous.

Jeanine Diller looks at issues of religious diversity in an entirely novel way: within the context of an individual person's life. She asks how one can live out multiple religions at once. She explores eight answers to this question in the form of eight multiple religious orientations that form a continuum from lighter to more intense forms of participation, from merely seeking (without any religious commitments whatsoever) to various forms of belonging to religious traditions. This understanding of the possible religious orientations gives us names and a conceptual order for multiple religious participation. In so doing, she moves the discussion from more abstract questions of metaphysics, theology, and logic to concrete and personal questions of living one's life in a religiously ambiguous world.

Feminist theology. Patricia Altenbernd Johnson heeds Alvin Plantinga's advice to do philosophy from a Christian perspective. However, she takes her task as doing Christian philosophy without the patriarchy, which may be embedded in the very conceptual scheme of typical Christian philosophy. Drawing upon the work of Elizabeth Schussler-Fiorenza, Johnson begins with a biblical deconstruction of patriarchy. She also rejects the exclusive use of masculine names of God because names are symbols which the divine reality only partially participates in. Especially in patriarchal societies, negative associations of, for example, "Father" limit our conception of God. These misconceptions can be partly alleviated by expanding our symbols of the sacred to include feminine names and imagery. Johnson develops a philosophy of religion from the perspective of God as Mother.

Harriet Baber, who rejects the view that men and women have different duties by virtue of gender alone, likewise rejects the claim that various doctrines assumed to be sex-neutral are in fact male-biased. More specifically, she rejects the claim that there is any empirical support for so-called "women's ways of knowing," ways of knowing that are less objective and detached, on the one hand, and more empathetic and contextual, on the other. Baber goes on to ask why epistemologies so lacking in empirical support sell—why, given their intellectual and even social costs, do people continue to "buy" them? Although not directly aimed at philosophy of religion or philosophical theology, her arguments may have implications for attempts to reconstruct various theologies in order to accommodate a style of behavior, way of knowing, and moral "voice" thought (wrongly)
to be characteristic of women's experience. Indeed, such reconstructions may actually prove detrimental to women's interests.

Reflections. Stephen Davis offers three options for conceiving of the nature of God. The reader should by now be familiar with classical and open theism. The option that Davis defends is neo-classical theism, the view that God is the unique, omnipotent, omniscient, and perfectly good creator of the heavens and the earth; God is a necessary being; and God is temporal, weakly immutable, passible, and not metaphysically simple. Neo-classical theism accepts a great deal of open theism: for example, God can change (although not in respect to God's character) and God suffers with us. But it rejects open theism's rejection of exhaustive divine foreknowledge. That is, Davis's theory holds that God knows everything—past, present, future—including what free creatures will freely do in the future. Davis rejects classical theism's less than robust understanding of moral responsibility (compatibilism) in favour of open theism's commitment to libertarian freedom. The compatibilist holds that all human actions are caused and determined (ultimately by causes or agents outside of the individual who is acting) but that some are nonetheless free; theistic compatibilists reject the claim that humans could do otherwise than what God has pre-determined or foreknown. Davis rejects classical theism's determinism and embraces libertarianism—the view that humans are free in two senses: (a) their choices are (sometimes) their own choices, not caused by things outside of themselves and (b) when presented with a choice a person is (sometimes) able to accept or reject that choice (people have "the ability to do otherwise"). Davis rejects open theism's thin conception of omniscience and develops two views of God's omniscience that preserve God's foreknowledge of the future (including future free choices) without violating libertarian freedom.

Conclusion. Although this section has focused on differences among conceptions of divinity and the difficulties of resolving these differences, there is a rich tradition of agreement about the divine nature. Davis raises this point at the beginning of his essay; both classical and open theists, he points out, concur about the following divine attributes: God is ultimate reality; God necessarily exists; and as the unique, omnipotent, omniscient, and perfectly good creator of the heavens and the earth, God is worthy of our worship.

Disagreement on the disputed aspects of God's nature may be due to (a) a paucity of information on our part and (b) intuitions that are not entirely clear but at least appear to be in conflict.

We may not have adequate cognitive resources clearly to determine the truth of the matter. In addition, for those within a religious tradition, one's authoritative, sacred writings may likewise not offer adequate evidence to decide these matters one way or another. I suspect the Hebraic-Christian texts are ambiguous on those issues which divide classical and open theists in part because the early Hebrews simply didn't reflect on, for example, divine immutability or exhaustive foreknowledge of the future, or the precise nature of human freedom. They believed, in their best moments, that God is faithful, in control of the future, and that humans were morally responsible. This set of data, sparse as it is, is consistent with classical, open, and neo-classical theism; but the data does not rationally compel any of these competing views.

And our intuitions (initial intellectual commitments) on these matters may not be easy to reconcile. Theists may want a God who is in complete control of everything that happens with the hope that everything is part of a (perfectly good) divine plan. And they have intuitions about moral responsibility. Intuitions about God's complete control and moral responsibility are at least apparently in conflict, with no obvious means of resolution. Both classical and open theism offers resolutions by emphasizing, respectively, either God's control or human freedom. Davis's theory offers two ways of reconciling divine foreknowledge (God cannot control all events if God doesn't know the future) and human freedom, without betraying either one. But his resolution is not easy and, as he notes, raises important philosophical objections.

One might think that the only option, under these circumstances, is skepticism or agnosticism about the divine nature. With respect to the Transcendent, a healthy scepticism and agnosticism is surely in order. Perhaps one can reasonably embrace one alternative rather than the other but only with a healthy dose of intellectual humility. One wonders what the history of the world might have been like if people rallied around the important and relatively clear matters they believed in common rather than those often abstract and difficult matters they disagreed about.

Notes

1. Boethius, *The Consolation of Philosophy*, Book v.

2. For those inclined to believe that the character of philosophers plays a role in the development of their philosophies, there are curious asymmetries between Hick and van Inwagen. Hick was formerly an orthodox Christian who "converted" to an anti-incarnational Christianity (mostly due to the pressures of pluralism). Van Inwagen was not raised in a Christian home and was an adult convert to Christianity.

Chapter 22

Speaking of God

SPEAKING OF GOD

THOMAS AQUINAS*

Objections. 1. It seems that the things attributed to God and creatures are univocal. For every equivocal term is reduced to the univocal, as many are reduced to one; for if the name "dog" be said equivocally of the barking dog, and of the dog-fish, it must be said of some univocally—viz. of all barking dogs; otherwise we proceed to infinitude. Now there are some univocal agents which agree with their effects in name and definition, as man generates man; and there are some agents which are equivocal, as the sun which causes heat, although the sun is hot only in an equivocal sense. Therefore it seems that the first agent to which all other agents are reduced, is an univocal agent: and thus what is said of God and creatures, is predicated univocally.

2. Further, there is no similitude among equivocal things. Therefore as creatures have a certain likeness to God, according to the word of Genesis (Gn. 1:26), "Let us make man to our image and likeness," it seems that something can be said of God and creatures univocally.

3. Further, measure is homogeneous with the thing measured. But God is the first measure of all beings. Therefore God is homogeneous with creatures; and thus a word may be applied univocally to God and to creatures.

---

*   Thomas Aquinas (1225–74), Italian philosopher-theologian, taught at the University of Paris.

Aquinas's view. On the contrary, whatever is predicated of various things under the same name but not in the same sense, is predicated equivocally. But no name belongs to God in the same sense that it belongs to creatures; for instance, wisdom in creatures is a quality, but not in God. Now a different genus changes an essence, since the genus is part of the definition; and the same applies to other things. Therefore whatever is said of God and of creatures is predicated equivocally.

Further, God is more distant from creatures than any creatures are from each other. But the distance of some creatures makes any univocal predication of them impossible, as in the case of those things which are not in the same genus. Therefore much less can anything be predicated univocally of God and creatures; and so only equivocal predication can be applied to them.

Univocal predication is impossible between God and creatures. The reason for this is that every effect which is not an adequate result of the power of the efficient cause, receives the similitude of the agent not in its full degree, but in a measure that falls short, so that what is divided and multiplied in the effects resides in the agent simply, and in the same manner; as for example the sun by exercise of its one power produces manifold and various forms in all inferior things. In the same way, as said in the preceding article, all perfections existing in creatures divided and multiplied, pre-exist in God unitedly. Thus when any term expressing perfection is applied to a creature, it signifies that perfection distinct in idea from other perfections; as, for instance, by the term "wise" applied to man, we signify some perfection distinct from a man's essence, and distinct from his power and existence, and from all similar things; whereas when we apply to it God, we do not mean to signify anything distinct from His essence, or power, or existence. Thus also this term "wise" applied to man in some degree circumscribes and comprehends the thing signified; whereas this is not the case when it is applied to God; but it leaves the thing signified as incomprehended, and as exceeding the signification of the name. Hence it is evident that this term "wise" is not applied in the same way to God and to man. The same rule applies to other terms. Hence no name is predicated univocally of God and of creatures.

Neither, on the other hand, are names applied to God and creatures in a purely equivocal sense, as some have said. Because if that were so, it follows that from creatures nothing could be known or demonstrated about God at all; for the reasoning would always be exposed to the fallacy of equivocation. Such a view is against the philosophers, who proved many things about God, and also against what the Apostle says: "The invisible things of God are clearly seen being understood by the things that are made" (Rm. 1:20). Therefore it must be said that these names are said of God and creatures in an analogous sense, i.e., according to proportion.

Now names are thus used in two ways: either according as many things are proportionate to one, thus for example "healthy" predicated of medicine and urine in relation and in proportion to health of a body, of which the former is the sign and the latter the cause: or according as one thing is proportionate to another, thus "healthy" is said of medicine and animal, since medicine is the cause of health in the animal body. And in this way some things are said of God and creatures analogically, and not in a purely equivocal nor in a purely univocal sense. For we can name God only from creatures. Thus whatever is said of God and creatures, is said according to the relation of a creature to God as its principle and cause, wherein all perfections of things pre-exist excellently. Now this mode of community of idea is a mean between pure equivocation and simple univocation. For in analogies the idea is not, as it is in univocals, one and the same, yet it is not totally diverse as in equivocals; but a term which is thus used in a multiple sense signifies various proportions to some one thing; thus "healthy" applied to urine signifies the sign of animal health, and applied to medicine signifies the cause of the same health.

Replies. To Objection 1. Although equivocal predications must be reduced to univocal, still in actions, the non-univocal agent must precede the univocal agent. For the non-univocal agent is the universal cause of the whole species, as for instance the sun is the cause of the generation of all men; whereas the univocal agent is not the universal efficient cause of the whole species (otherwise it would be the cause of itself, since it is contained in the species), but is a particular cause of this individual which it places under the species by way of participation. Therefore the universal cause of the whole species is not an univocal agent; and the universal cause comes before the particular cause. But this universal agent, whilst it is not univocal, nevertheless is not altogether equivocal, otherwise it could not produce its own likeness, but rather it is to be called an analogical agent, as all univocal predications are reduced to one first non-univocal analogical predication, which is being.

To Objection 2. The likeness of the creature to God is imperfect, for it does not represent one and the same generic thing.

To Objection 3. God is not the measure proportioned to things measured; hence it is not necessary that God and creatures should be in the same genus.

Conclusion. The arguments adduced in the contrary sense prove indeed that these names are not predicated univocally of God and creatures; yet they do not prove that they are predicated equivocally.

Discussion

1. What is the problem that Aquinas sees with the univocal approach to language about God?

2. What is the problem with saying that religious language is equivocal?

3. Are Aquinas's explanations of analogy convincing?

4. Are his explanations of the transcendence of God univocal or analogical?

"THE GREATEST THING BY FAR": METAPHOR AS THE HERMENEUTICAL KEY TO HERMENEUTICS

DAN R. STIVER*

Introduction. In 1972, Paul Ricoeur published an essay entitled in English as "Metaphor and the Central Problem of Hermeneutics" (Ricoeur, 1981). In doing so, he was participating in a virtual revolution in the way both metaphor and hermeneutics were being understood. Several decades later I would like to revisit his subject and, in light of the developments that have occurred in the intervening years, suggest again that metaphor is a hermeneutical key, so to speak, to hermeneutics.

This is of more consequence today because the role of hermeneutics is more widely seen. Rather than hermeneutics being a way of understanding in the "soft" disciplines of history, literature, and religion, it is common among postmodern philosophers to affirm the earlier, prescient insight of Hans-Georg Gadamer, another hermeneutical philosopher like Ricoeur, into "the universality of hermeneutics," where hermeneutics is inextricably involved in the hard sciences and mathematics as well. In the process, important implications for language about God will also emerge because of the way Scripture and theology are inextricably linked both to metaphor and hermeneutics.

In his work on metaphor in the seventies, Ricoeur began with Aristotle. Although critical at many points of Aristotle, especially the way Aristotle has been traditionally appropriated, Ricoeur quoted approvingly Aristotle's observation in the *Poetics*, "But the greatest thing by far is to be a master of metaphor" (Section 22). What I would like to suggest is that Aristotle and Ricoeur are correct in that statement. Its import, however, goes far beyond metaphor and rare creative poets but pervades ordinary language and includes ordinary people. It also sheds light on the way language about God, notoriously indeterminate and imprecise, can be seen as cognitively significant.

Aristotle's dictum implies, despite the fluidity of metaphor, a positive connotation that has not always been seen. Figurative language was looked on with suspicion in much of the modern tradition as an untrustworthy way of conveying truth. Even after the linguistic turn of the twentieth century and a fresh appreciation of metaphor, the same suspicion of any linkage between metaphor and reality lingers. Graham Ward comments about the initial reception of Jacques Derrida, perhaps the most noted postmodern philosopher, who exhibits the close tie between his philosophy and language:

> Language pointed to itself, not to any realms or personages, revelations or hierarchies above, beyond or outside the secular world it constructed. Furthermore, this semiotic account of language pointed up the metaphoricity of all acts of communication. . . . a communicated message, like a letter, never simply arrived at the address to which it was posted. The world was a fable spun by words with an endless potential for being misread, misunderstood, and misinterpreted. (Ward, 2003, 78)

After that initial reception, Derrida himself as well as many others have questioned whether the immersion in language and metaphor necessarily derails truth and reality questions. In fact, it may be that following the cues given by reappraisal of metaphor provides a key to cognitivity. In other words, being a master of metaphor may indeed be "the greatest thing by far."

Ricoeur participated in a shift towards an "interaction theory" or a "semantic theory" of metaphor that stressed metaphor's cognitivity (Stiver, 1996, ch. 6;

---

* Dan R. Stiver is Professor of Theology at the Logsdon School of Theology at Hardin-Simmons University.

Johnson, 1981). After reviewing this familiar development, we will look at less-developed aspects of metaphor, namely, its role in ordinary language and its placement within community and tradition.

Interaction theory. As Ricoeur and others have pointed out, metaphor had long been understood as a novel use of a word whose meaning can in turn be found by substituting univocal words. Contrary to this approach, Ricoeur emphasized that metaphors involve at least the sentence, if not the entire work, and cannot be understood in terms of replacement of a metaphorical term by a literal term. Rather, the interaction between the clash of literal meanings produces a "semantic innovation" that is often irreducible to literal paraphrase, at least in terms of significant metaphors, which Ricoeur refers to as "living metaphors" (Ricoeur, 1977). Metaphor involves then a dynamic and elusive is/is not—it must be both affirmed and denied, which contributes to its exasperating capacity to elude demands for precision and determinateness. Sallie McFague keys in on this characteristic as the reason why metaphor is at the heart of theology because theologians have long recognized this tensive is/is not in language about God (McFague, 1982, 13). The capacity to erect from the clash of "the systems of associated commonplaces" of words a distinct new meaning is a mysterious, creative act not fully explicable—a reason for Aristotle's praise (Ricoeur, 1981, 172).

The new approach thus understands metaphorical meaning to be created and to be grasped without having to be explained in terms of univocal language or a method. In fact, the best explication of a metaphor may be another metaphor. Meaning is let loose, therefore, and escapes careful cognitive confines. The power of metaphor, as Janet Soskice suggests, perhaps lies in its very vagueness and fluidity (Soskice, 1985, 133). Her observation is all the more remarkable because she is talking here not so much about theology but about the hard sciences. Because metaphor cannot be pinned down, it cannot be exhausted either. Living metaphors have a way of erupting with fresh and surprising illumination. Their potency lies in part in the focused way in which they can frame an entire discourse, much like the proverb that a picture is worth a thousand words. One can say of a metaphor what Ricoeur says of a text: It "means all that it can mean" (Ricoeur, 1981, 176).

The extension of metaphors to metaphorical models has been seen as crucial to the understanding of scientific paradigms as well as theological approaches. As McFague points out:

> Systematic thought also tries to organize all the dominant models in a tradition into an overarching system with a key model of its own. For instance, for Paul it was justification by grace through faith; for Augustine, the radical dependence of all that is on God; for Aquinas, the analogy of being. . . .. Each of these is a radical model, which could be called a "root-metaphor." (McFague, 1982, 28–29)

In this sense, every discipline involves metaphorical judgments in its foundations. For example, the judgment of whether mathematics is primarily objective (Platonic) or subjective (psychologistic) is not something that itself can be proven by an equation. Such metaphorical judgments and, by implication, hermeneutical judgments thus go all the way down and are not optional. In some ways, they are more foundational, or central, than the literal language that is now seen as parasitic upon the metaphorical—which is quite a reversal of perspective and fortunes!

The worrisome problem, however, concerning this interaction approach to metaphors is the question of hermeneutical control. Is there any limit to the interpretation of a metaphor? Is such interpretation rule-governed at all? If not, how is it that people can use them meaningfully?

After his praise of metaphor, Aristotle went on to say, "It is the one thing that cannot be learnt from others; and it is also a sign of genius, since a good metaphor implies an intuitive perception of the similarity in dissimilars." What Aristotle apparently means by the unteachability of metaphor is something similar to what modern metaphorists mean by saying they are irreducible. He apparently assumes that teachability depends upon a repeatable, explicit operation, what Hans-Georg Gadamer would term "method." In his article on metaphor and hermeneutics, Ricoeur suggests that this irreducible nature of explanation in metaphor should be a guide to explanation in hermeneutics in general. Referring to the work of E.D. Hirsch, Ricoeur says that the construction of the sense of a metaphor (and of a text) is that of a wager or guess. "There are no rules for making good guesses, but there are methods for validating our guesses" (Ricoeur, 1981, 175). The logic of this kind of method is one of probability, of better or worse, rather than of empirical verification. Even then, it is "a logic of uncertain and qualitative probability" rather than quantitative probability (Ibid.). It is more like juridical interpretation than scientific analysis, like weighing the preponderant weight of evidence in the way a jury does than carefully controlling a scientific experiment. One can follow the clues of a text, but in the final analysis, personal hermeneutical judgment that cannot be conclusively demonstrated will determine the interpretation. As Ricoeur puts it in a later work in terms of what he termed "attestation":

> To my mind, attestation defines the sort of
> certainty that hermeneutics may claim, not
> only with respect to the epistemic exaltation
> of the cogito in Descartes, but also with
> respect to its humiliation in Nietzsche and
> its successors. Attestation may appear to
> require less than one and more than the other.
> (Ricoeur, 1992, 21)

Metaphors then may not be rule-governed in the sense that they are *rule-determined*, but they are not *rule-less* either. Ricoeur states in a related essay published in 1971:

> In conclusion, if it is true that there is always
> more than one way of construing a text [or a
> metaphor], it is not true that all interpretations
> are equal and may be assimilated to so-called
> "rules of thumb." The text is a limited field of
> possible constructions. The logic of validation
> allows us to move between the two limits of
> dogmatism and scepticism. It is always possible to
> argue for or against an interpretation, to confront
> interpretations, to arbitrate between them, and
> to seek for an agreement, even if this agreement
> remains beyond our reach. (Ricoeur, 1981, 213)

In his 1972 article, Ricoeur then turns to the peculiar way in which literary texts refer in order to find a basis for affirming the referential power of metaphor. Moving away from the Romantic emphasis on understanding the author's intent or a New Critical or structuralist emphasis on a self-enclosed, non-referential literary sphere, Ricoeur emphasizes that the reference, or "about what" of the text, is a configured "world." "Texts speak of possible worlds and of possible ways of orienting oneself in these worlds" (Ricoeur, 1981, 177). In different terminology, what is important is not the world behind the text but the world opened up in front of the text. This involves personal appropriation through what Gadamer called a "fusion of horizons" (Gadamer, 1991, 306). The referential power of texts, and by implication of metaphor, is thus the capacity to create or disclose a possible way of being in the world.

Neither metaphors nor texts are thus closed in upon themselves in a literary, non-cognitive universe, but refer to reality—albeit in an indirect way. Ricoeur speaks of this referential power as the "ontological vehemence" of metaphor (Ricoeur, 1977, 299). Metaphor then has clear philosophical significance, which it had not had since Aristotle.

The import of this reconfiguration in the understanding of metaphor was seen very quickly in being extended, for example, to parables in Gospel studies and to theology in general. In the former approach, they represent one of the most creative breakthroughs in parable interpretation, returning exegetes from allegorical or single meanings back to the explosive power of parables to shatter and create worlds. In the latter approach, metaphor becomes a model of how to think and speak of God in ways that avoid the limits of univocacy on the one hand and equivocacy on the other. It also offers a non-reductionist way of understanding analogies, symbols, and narratives, as we shall see below.

Despite these appropriations in other fields, the work by Aristotle and Ricoeur that we have seen thus far may suggest that metaphor is the province only of the most brilliant among us. Perhaps geniuses can use it responsibly, but what does it mean for the rest of us? Is a non-rule-governed yet reliable use of metaphor a part of ordinary language?

Metaphor and ordinary language. While Aristotle's praise is loved by the Romantics among us who prize the genius above all things, it causes alarm among the more positivist-minded since it suggests the lack of any hermeneutical restraints at all. In Mark Johnson's examination of the imagination, which includes a treatment of metaphor, he notes the oscillation between a Romantic approach that sees imagination as completely unfettered and the bailiwick of genius over against a more cautious approach that sees it as almost prosaic in its operation. As Johnson suggests, we need an approach somewhere in between (Johnson, 1987, ch. 6).

Despite the tenor of Aristotle's comments that have been cited, Aristotle implies that such creativity is not the whole picture. His ruminations on metaphor occur in the context of works on poetics and rhetoric that emphasize the importance of good and clear communication. For example, he says at the beginning of the section in which he discusses metaphor in the *Rhetoric*, "Style to be good must be clear, as is proved by the fact that speech which fails to convey a plain meaning will fail to do just what speech has to do. It must also be appropriate" (III.2). Aristotle says that metaphor "gives style clearness, charm, and distinction as nothing else can" but also that metaphors, "like epithets, must be fitting." Thus, metaphors must be "appropriate" to be effective and must be "fitting" to be understood—as judged by the hearer. It may take a genius to create a metaphor, but it surely does not take geniuses to understand one. Otherwise, the enterprise of poetics and persuasion would never get off the ground. Some hearers are better than others, to be sure, but Aristotle seems to assume that the populace of his day are able to grasp and judge the fittingness of metaphor. The point is that despite Aristotle's implication that metaphorical ability is rare and unusual, the capacity to use and understand metaphor is commonplace. It is something that almost all people do and, for the most part, do rather well. Perhaps the ability to make metaphors cannot be taught, but the capacity to understand metaphors is surely learned by virtually everyone just as they learn language.

What Aristotle is lacking in this context is the concept of something that can be taught without being totally explicit. Ironically, Aristotle himself had something like this idea in his ethics since he saw character as something that must be educated without it leading to a demonstrable activity, as we shall see below. Metaphors are thus perhaps not as mysterious and remote as Aristotle's words about genius suggest.

For both Aristotle and Ricoeur, therefore, metaphors cannot be exhaustively *explained*, but they can be *understood*. In other words, people use metaphors quite well without having a thorough explanation, method, or decision-procedure to determine their meanings. Metaphors are thus not common in the sense of being literal, but they are in terms of use.

The lack of tight hermeneutical control does not necessarily limit hermeneutical reliability. Metaphors are used to telling effect without being reducible to univocal language. For example, it was accurate to say of Michael Jordan that he "soared" through the air but not of Magic Johnson. It was accurate to speak of Ronald Reagan as the "Teflon" President but not of Jimmy Carter. Our discourse is laced with metaphors, and people use them, understand them, and appraise them with surprising ease without a lot of fanfare. The reliability of metaphors seems to emerge from their being part of common linguistic practices in which people develop competency as a part of general linguistic fluency. Again, most people develop expertise without necessarily being geniuses in Aristotle's sense. The lack of an algorithmic method does not undermine reliable usage.

Important support for the role of metaphor in ordinary language comes from George Lakoff and Mark Johnson in *Metaphors We Live By*. They argue that everyday language is shot-through with metaphor and that we commonly think in terms of metaphors. Metaphor is something we use often and well, yet without rigid hermeneutical constraints. Ricoeur notes that much discussion about metaphor uses familiar metaphors, which he sees only as "trivial metaphors" (Ricoeur, 1981, 172). He is more concerned with more powerful, "living" metaphors. Lakoff and Johnson, on the other hand, add a third category of common or conventional metaphors that frame much of our speech, realizing that these may be background assumptions rather than foreground assertions. For example, they analyze an "argument is war" metaphor and point out that apart from some such basic operative frame, it is difficult to connect otherwise unrelated propositions. To give their examples:

ARGUMENT IS WAR
Your claims are *indefensible*.
He *attacked very weak points* in my argument.

His criticisms were *right on target*.
I *demolished* his argument.
I've never *won* an argument with him.
You disagree? Okay, *shoot!*
If you use that *strategy*, he'll *wipe you out*.
He *shot down* all of my arguments.
(Lakoff and Johnson, 1980, 4)

Moreover, this approach helps us make new inferences. If argument is war, one can add newer permutations such "I nuked my opponent," or "We broke through their defenses." They emphasize also that the war root-metaphor not only shapes our talk but also structures our actions and practices as well. "We see the person we are arguing with as an opponent. We attack his positions and we defend our own. We gain and lose ground" (Lakoff and Johnson, 1980, 27). They explore numerous such metaphorical frames to reveal the dense metaphorical background even to our use of literal language. Greg Johnson, who studied with Mark Johnson, elaborates this approach in helping us see how the Christian language of grace functions over against an economy of exchange (Johnson, 2003). Rather than being an optional item in our linguistic repertoire, metaphors filter through all of our language, especially religious language.

The focus of Lakoff and Johnson on everyday metaphors is different from Ricoeur, but they make the same point that these follow a logic of their own different from an objectivist algorithm. They are not finely ruled, but they must still, in Aristotle's words, be fitting. The identification of a background metaphor helps us see the operative structure without eliminating the role of semantic innovation.

Support for the role of metaphor as a creative and yet rational common human activity can be seen in two other sources. The striking parallel in Aristotle himself is in ethics, as indicated before, which he does not see as a science but as a reliable activity that involves its own kind of thinking, "practical wisdom" (*phronesis*). Obviously, ethics is a common human activity, although not practiced well by everyone. Even though Aristotle cuts practical wisdom off from science since it does not allow for demonstration or proof, he clearly sees it as a rational activity that does not lack hermeneutical control. His honest and acute analysis, however, drove him to conclude that one cannot universalize in ethics. Each situation is different enough that responsible ethical judgment is put in play to judge the good in that situation. If asked what is the just thing to do in a given situation, one must ask what a just person with a developed character would do. This is not subjectivism or individualism since the just person has a sense both of ethical generalities and of cultural practice. It is clear for Aristotle in this area, as in the use of metaphor, that judgments can be fitting or unfitting, wise or unwise. There can be legitimate reflection, deliberation, and debate about an action without assuming a proof or demonstration. Gadamer in *Truth and Method* effectively turns Aristotle on his head by arguing that such "phronetic" thinking is the basis of all thinking, even scientific. The profound connection he makes is between phronesis in ethics to hermeneutics, art, and all other thinking. Ricoeur similarly extends "phronetic thinking" in his later use of the term "attestation." We can make a similar link between phronetic thinking and metaphorical thinking.

When we consider the emphasis of Aristotle and Ricoeur that the use of metaphor cannot be taught but can nevertheless be appraised in terms of suitability or fittingness with Lakoff and Johnson's emphasis that metaphors are commonplace, metaphorical usage begins to look more like a skill that is practiced than a demonstration that can be explicated. Like riding a bicycle, it is easier to show than to explain. Like character, it is easier to identify than to describe. The absence of a formal, theoretical explanation, however, does not hinder the ongoing, reliable use of metaphor.

Metaphor and community. Neither Aristotle nor Ricoeur in their works on metaphor underscore the role of a linguistic community or tradition in which metaphors come to have meaning. Lakoff and Johnson move in that direction, but do not develop the idea particularly. The reliable use of metaphors makes little sense, however, apart from such a presumption. When dealing with a criterion like being "fitting," context is crucial—just as in ethical judgments. In some traditions, argument is not war and such a metaphor is neither fitting nor felicitous. In a domestic dispute or in some religious traditions today, to say "I won the battle and you lost" is to miss the boat and "lose" in other, very significant ways.

The later Wittgenstein is helpful at this point in indicating that all of our words only have meaning "in the stream of thought and life" (Wittgenstein, 1963, par. 173). In other words, meaning depends on the form of life and language game in which words are used (Wittgenstein, 1958, pars. 3, 19, 23, 241, pp. 174, 226). George Lindbeck has drawn on Wittgenstein's work in his influential work *The Nature of Doctrine* to argue that doctrines and even experiences are shaped by the community of faith in which they are embedded. This "cultural-linguistic" model is opposed to the "experiential-expressive" model that supposes some uninterpreted, pristine experience that underlies all the different doctrines of different communities. To apply this insight to metaphor and models (as extended metaphors), we can see historically how different views of the atonement have prevailed in different epochs. The liberation or Christus Victor model dominated the early centuries of the church to be replaced by the satisfaction and then penal substitution models, all of which bear affinities with the cultures wherein they arose. Some communities of faith today find comfort in the understanding of God as the King in total control whereas others prefer to understand God as Lure and fellow-sufferer. The "fit" of God's power as dominative or donative depends in part on one's tradition and community (McGill, 1982). Believer's church preferences for images of the church as democratic and egalitarian versus hierarchical and sacerdotal images are rooted in the wider Western sociopolitical context and their own tradition, built up only over the last few centuries. Metaphors that relate to modern sports, computers, and space travel are obviously time- and culture-indexed. So adding to the imprecision of metaphor is the common hermeneutical factor of context. A metaphor may be meaningful or make sense in one time and tradition and not in another.

The fear of hermeneutical chaos. The most important issue for hermeneutics remains the question of rationality or hermeneutic control. Are there limits? If hermeneutics is not undergirded by a rigid method, a decision-making algorithm, or determining rules, is there any meaning left to rationality and cognitivity? In a time when foundationalism and objectivism and modernity are supposedly being left behind, is irrational relativism the only alternative? This is still the concern even of many who are hesitantly testing the waters of a "postmodern" age. In this context, the emergence of metaphor from the backwaters of cognitivity and philosophy to a position of prominence may offer a hermeneutical key. We will therefore consider the concern about lack of hermeneutical control first and then examine the possibility of creative but not chaotic hermeneutics.

The very drives that caused metaphor to be harnessed by being reduced to univocal language and then dismissed from cognitive significance altogether are behind the concern about "the universality of hermeneutics." Richard Bernstein perhaps expressed it best by linking this fear to that guide to so much of modernity, René Descartes, terming this fear "Cartesian anxiety" about objectivism. Bernstein says:

> By objectivism I mean the basic conviction that there is or must be some permanent, ahistorical matrix or framework to which we can ultimately appeal in determining the nature of rationality, knowledge, truth, reality, goodness, or rightness. An objectivist claims that there is (or must be) such a matrix and that the primary task of the philosopher is to discover what it is and to support his or her claims to have discovered such a matrix with the strongest possible reasons. Objectivism is closely related to foundationalism and the search for an Archimedean point. The objectivist maintains that unless we can ground philosophy, knowledge, or language in a rigorous manner we cannot avoid radical skepticism. (Bernstein, 1983, 8)

As we saw, this is the kind of reasoning behind the consternation about the fact that metaphor does not seem to be rule-governed. Eva Feder Kittay expresses this apprehension well:

> The reasoning goes as follows: if metaphor is semantically anomalous, then it cannot be subject to linguistic rules; hence we cannot speak of metaphorical meaning, for the production and interpretation of meaningful utterances is rule-governed; but if there is no distinctive metaphorical meaning, then there is no irreducible conceptual content which may have cognitive efficacy. (Kittay, 1987, 68)

Similarly, there are questions about many of the contemporary nonobjectivist movements: hermeneutical philosophy, neo-pragmatism, poststructuralism, neo-Reformed epistemology, narrative theology, communitarian ethics, and reader-response theory in literature, to name several. Whether it is the highly critical and nuanced appeal for a quasi-transcendental foundation by a Jürgen Habermas or the conservative appeal to a traditional rational framework by an evangelical, questions of relativism, fideism, even anarchy and nihilism are posed to these movements. The usual reason has to do with the lack of a determinative adjudication procedure. How can one determine the truth? How do we know, on these grounds, whether one is correct or not?

The specific problem in hermeneutics is the differing interpretations that cannot easily be settled, where supposedly competent interpreters or even experts proffer reasons and evidence that are convincing to them and their adherents but obviously are underdetermined in the opinions of others. Can such a situation be a rational one? Is there any room for critical evaluation at all?

In Christianity, for example, debates about the proper interpretation of the evidence for the historical Jesus proliferate more than ever. Traditional disputes continue about the nature and mode of baptism and about ecclesiology. Contemporary conflicts still hinge on biblical interpretation: on the ordination of women, on acceptance of homosexuals, on abortion, on capital punishment. Stephen Toulmin in *Cosmopolis* contends that in fact frustration over the toll of religious disputes is what created a climate in the seventeenth century for a turn to calm, objective, even certain, reason over the passions of religious authority (Toulmin, 1990).

Over against these religious debates, the constant temptation of Cartesian anxiety has been to say that if there is no determinative algorithm, there is no constraint, hence no science, no logic, and no reason. Hermeneutics has long struggled with these strictures and has as a consequence usually come off the worst in comparison to the "sciences," which did supposedly have such algorithms. God-talk has suffered a similar fate because it seems even further from the sciences than general hermeneutics. The contemporary breakdown, however, of the dichotomy between the hard sciences and other disciplines and the claims for the universality of hermeneutics ratchet the concern higher. At "the end of modernity," when reason turns out to be much like faith, some question whether there is any reason anywhere. After several centuries of attempting to carry out Descartes's quest, is it possible to have reason that is *not* clear and distinct, since it does not seem possible to have reason that *is* wholly clear and distinct? Is it possible to have *reason* without *Reason*?

Hermeneutical reliability. The movement of metaphor from the hinterlands of philosophy towards the center offers an affirmative response. Especially when one adds the reality of the commonality of metaphor, the significance of people judging fittingness for good if not determinative reason in common and reliable ways is underscored. In metaphor and the related figures of symbol and analogy, people have by and large realized that it is a futile quest to reduce them to literal language in order to understand or explain them.

In terms of analogy, older interpretations of Aquinas tended to emphasize his attempts to explain, or reduce, analogies to explanations in terms of causation or literal comparisons. More recent appropriations see Aquinas as not having an "algorithm," so to speak, for analogy but understand him as suggesting their irreducibility, much like metaphor (Burrell, 1973, 119–24; Johnson, 1992; Smith, 2004, ch. 5). Moreover, they understand him as not suggesting that such a reduction is necessary for analogy to be "rational."

In sorting out the contemporary linguistic landscape, one has to pay attention to context. Following Aquinas, recent Roman Catholic thinkers thus tend to stress the creative nature of analogy. Paul Tillich emphasized that symbols sometimes say what cannot be said in any other way (Tillich, 1957, ch. 3). Those influenced especially by literary theory tend to lay the emphasis upon the creative power of metaphor (McFague, 1982, 13–17; Soskice, 1985, 64). In this light, one can see how the cognitive significance of metaphor's dynamic can be widely extended beyond discussions merely of metaphor.

The burden of the interactionist approach to metaphor in the past few decades has thus been to affirm that metaphor has meaning despite not being able to be explained and despite not being wholly rule-governed. Likewise with hermeneutics in general (and analogy and symbol), the attempt to verify an interpretation by a knock-down argument is a futile quest. This sobering reality, however, should not lead to throwing in the towel or denigrating comparisons to "science," or to the "hard" sciences. Rather than seek for what cannot be found, one can return to the "rough ground" of practice to find that one is not left bereft of any kind of validation at all.

Some differences between metaphor and hermeneutical interpretation, however, are important. The basic question of metaphor often presupposed a common understanding of a metaphor; the question was, How to justify it? Is there a methodical explanation or a literal translation? In hermeneutics, the question of how one arrives at a decided conclusion is also important, but it is usually in the context of competent interpreters who differ greatly. Interpretation of texts may well be much more complicated and involve a wider range of clues.

There is, however, a similar dynamic between the two. First of all, the hermeneutic circle means that often a text's meaning is dependent on understanding the metaphors in the text, and conversely, understanding the metaphors involves the meaning of the text. Secondly, in both cases, the construction of meaning is a creative act not wholly reducible to explanation.

As Kittay claims, however, "To say a thing is not subject to a given set of rules is not to say that it is subject to no rules" (Kittay, 1987, 68). Similarly, Ricoeur wants to affirm a certain kind of "explanatory" dimension of metaphors, one which sees it as a "limited field of possible constructions." It follows a logic of better or worse rather than of either/or, to be sure, but it is a logic nonetheless. In hermeneutics in general, similarly, there are rarely "conversation stoppers"—as long

as brute force is not used (as it all too often has been; rigorous method fares no better in encounters with naked power). Evidence and reasons can be offered, better and worse interpretations can be judged, and some interpretations can be ruled out all together. Rarely does the conversation end because no more evidence is available and no more reasons are available.

When interpreters, however, arrive at deeply-held, contrary conclusions, what should happen? Think of a paedo-Baptist seeking to convince someone in a believer's church tradition of infant baptism or someone seeking to show the biblical grounds of a pro-choice position on abortion to someone with a pro-life position. They offer their arguments, they try to be open-minded, but in the final analysis, they end up as far apart as when they began. What should happen then? Rather than seek for a better method that will finally arbitrate for all time to come, rather than suggest that the other is irrational because he or she did not reach the same conclusion, rather than conclude that the issue is outside the range of reason because a determinative conclusion could not be reached, the approach to metaphor outlined above suggests other alternatives.

We can recognize that the other may be perfectly rational and competent, although he or she differs. We need not yield our convictions because someone else is not convinced; neither do we minimize the importance of the reasons and evidence that are convincing to us. The energy that is saved by not seeking a final method can be spent trying to understand why the other is differently convinced or coming up with new ways to help the other understand one's own point of view. We realize, moreover, that straightforward, prosaic argumentation may not be the key to convincing another. A metaphor may best be used to explicate a metaphor; a narrative may open the door to an expository text; and a parable may open the door to considering a new paradigm. It may even be that new life experiences or new experiences of community may be necessary to open up insights. Or it may be that new evidence can be found that can swing the tide. All of these, of course, can go both ways; the advocate may end up changing his or her mind. The temptation is wanting definitive proof, not only for oneself but for everyone else; it is wanting more than can be had.

The trick lies in not asking for more. As Wittgenstein put it, "If I have exhausted the justifications I have reached bedrock, and my spade is turned" (Wittgenstein, 1958, par. 217). This is not fideistic. If I can put it strongly, it is reality! It is not that there are no reasons, no arguments, and no evidence. It is that there are never enough (at least for many of the most important questions). What it calls for is a certain trust in human capacities that we cannot fully explicate. This again does not mean we simply accept what anyone says, much less what we say. In the final analysis, we realize that we can do no better than appeal to such judgments.

After all the arduous reflection on metaphor, the realization came that it was not something that could be reduced to univocal language or fully calculated. Metaphor is something people do. Aristotle had it better since he actually spoke of it as a verb, to "metaphorize." "Metaphorizing" is a human capacity that we see around us all of the time. Likewise, hermeneutical interpreting, or perhaps "hermeneuticizing" is also a human capacity that we see around us. If we take a cue from metaphor, we will realize that in hermeneutics, too, we will be able to make judgments that can be tested or validated without being demonstrated in the strong sense.

Narrative. The same goes for narrative, where narrative theology has been one of the most influential developments in contemporary theology (Stiver, 1996, ch. 7; Goldberg, 1982). The need for hermeneutical judgment is something that metaphor and narrative both have in common, which is part of the reason why narrative theology is as significant as metaphorical theology,

namely, both represent sharp moves away from the Cartesian paradigm that has heavily influenced modern theology. The changes in the understanding of story are similar and as far-reaching as those with metaphor, which we should be able to see more quickly. Just as Tillich said of symbols, many say of story that it discloses things that cannot be said in any other way. Now major philosophers such as Alasdair MacIntyre are prone to subordinate systematic exposition itself to a narrative context in order for it to be understood. Narrative is also not seen as reducible or translatable without remainder.

And while some took this to mean initially that we all simply live in our own relativistic stories, now the question is open to see that narratives also portray reality—just in a different way—and must be assessed in a different way. To return to MacIntyre, his position is well-known that traditions are arguments extended through time with an inherent narrative shape and cannot be reduced to traditional logical arguments. Interestingly, his first major work in this vein, *After Virtue*, was taken as relativistic, which his later work has taken pains to show is false and that he is actually attempting to overcome relativism. The way he does this is also instructive in that he does it in a narrative way. One may compare in this respect the emphasis of John Milbank, the central figure in the recently-emerged radical orthodoxy, that one cannot out-argue but must "out-narrate" one's opponents (Milbank, 1993, 330).

Conclusion. When we can to a great extent explain something so that it seems obvious or self-evident, we should value it as an intellectual feat, perhaps even as a work of genius. But we should also realize that any such explication presupposes a vast tacit background and that much of life, especially religion, is not amenable to such explication. In fact, trying to do so often distorts reality and leaves us "bewitched by language" as Wittgenstein would say (Wittgenstein, 1958, pars. 71, 109). What we should better realize is that short of such self-evidence, which is rather rare, is the capacity both to use metaphors and to make hermeneutical judgments. Unlike Aristotle, I would say that it does not take a rare genius to metaphorize or to interpret, even to be a master. Aristotle may well be right, however, that doing so is a kind of genius, but, like language in general, it is a genius that belongs more to the human race than to select individuals.

References

Ayer, A.J. "Editor's Introduction." In *Logical Positivism*. Ed. A.J. Ayer. Glencoe, IL: Free P, 1959. 3–10.

Bernstein, Richard J. *Beyond Objectivism and Relativism: Science, Hermeneutics, and Praxis*. Philadelphia: U of Philadelphia P, 1983.

Burrell, David. *Analogy and Philosophical Language*. New Haven, CT: Yale UP, 1973.

Gadamer, Hans-Georg. *Truth and Method*. Trans. Joel Weinsheimer and Donald G. Marshall. Rev. ed. New York: Crossroad, 1991.

Gill, Jerry. *On Knowing God: New Directions for the Future of Theology*. Philadelphia: Westminster P, 1981.

——. *Wittgenstein and Metaphor* (Dallas: UP of America, 1981).

Goldberg, Michael. *Theology and Narrative: A Critical Introduction*. Nashville: Abingdon, 1982.

Johnson, Elizabeth A. *She Who Is: The Mystery of God in Feminist Theological Discourse*. New York: Crossroads, 1992.

Johnson, Greg. "The Economies of Grace as Gift and Moral Accounting: Insights from Cognitive Linguistics." In *The Bible through Metaphor and Translation*. New York: Peter Lang, 2003. 87–111.

Johnson, Mark. *The Body in the Mind: The Bodily Basis of Meaning, Imagination, and Reason*. Chicago: U of Chicago P, 1987.

——. "Introduction: Metaphor in the Philosophical Tradition." In *Philosophical Perspectives on Metaphor*. Ed. Mark Johnson. Minneapolis: U of Minnesota P, 1981.

——. *Moral Imagination: Implications of Cognitive Science for Ethics*. Chicago: U of Chicago P, 1993.

Johnson, Mark, ed. *Philosophical Perspectives on Metaphor*. Minneapolis: U of Minnesota P, 1981.

Kittay, Eva Feder. *Metaphor: Its Cognitive Force and Linguistic Structure*. Oxford: Clarendon P, 1987.

Kuhn, Thomas. *The Structure of Scientific Revolutions*. 1962. 2nd ed. Chicago: U of Chicago P, 1970.

Lakoff, George, and Mark Johnson. *Metaphors We Live By*. Chicago: U of Chicago P, 1980.

McFague, Sallie. *Metaphorical Theology: Models of God in Religious Language*. Philadelphia: Fortress P, 1982.

McGill, Arthur C. *Suffering: A Test of Theological Method*. Philadelphia: Westminster John Knox P, 1982.

Milbank, John. *Theology and Social Theory: Beyond Secular Reason*. Cambridge: Blackwell, 1993.

Plantinga, Alvin. "Advice to Christian Philosophers." *Faith and Philosophy* 1, no. 3 (July 1984): 253–71.

Ricoeur, Paul. "Metaphor and the Central Problem of Hermeneutics." In *Hermeneutics and the Human Sciences: Essays on Language, Action, and Interpretation*. Ed. John B. Thompson. Cambridge: Cambridge UP, 1981. 165–81.

——. "The Model of the Text: Meaningful Action Considered as a Text." In *Hermeneutics and the Human Sciences: Essays on Language, Action, and Interpretation*. Ed. John B. Thompson. Cambridge: Cambridge UP, 1981. 131–44.

——. *Oneself as Another*. Trans. Kathleen Blamey. Chicago: U of Chicago P, 1992.

——. *The Rule of Metaphor: Multi-Disciplinary Studies of the Creation of Meaning in Language*. Trans. Robert Czerny, Kathleen McLaughlin and John Costello. Toronto: U of Toronto P, 1977.

Smith, James K.A. *Introducing Radical Orthodoxy: Mapping a Post-Secular Theology.* Grand Rapids, MI: Baker Book House, 2004.

Soskice, Janet Martin. *Metaphor and Religious Language.* Oxford: Clarendon P, 1985.

Stiver, Dan R. *The Philosophy of Religious Language: Sign, Symbol, and Story.* Cambridge: Blackwell, 1996.

Tillich, Paul. *Dynamics of Faith.* Harper and Row, 1957.

Toulmin, Stephen. *Cosmopolis: The Hidden Agenda of Modernity.* Chicago: U of Chicago P, 1990.

Tracy, David. *The Analogical Imagination: Christian Theology and the Culture of Pluralism.* New York: Crossroad, 1981.

Ward, Graham. "Deconstructive Theology." In *The Cambridge Companion to Postmodern Theology.* Ed. Kevin J. Vanhoozer. Cambridge: Cambridge UP, 2003. 76–91.

Wittgenstein, Ludwig. *Philosophical Investigations.* Trans. G.E.M. Anscombe. 3d ed. New York: Macmillan, 1958.

——. *Tractatus Logico-Philosophicus.* Trans. D.F. Pears and B.F. McGuinness. London: Routledge & Kegan Paul, 1981.

——. *Zettel.* Basil Blackwell, 1963.

Discussion

1. How does the newer "interaction" model of metaphor contrast with the more traditional "substitution" approach?

2. How does the interaction model of metaphor allow for a fresh approach to cognitive language, not only in theology but also in the hard sciences, and what are its limitations?

3. How does understanding the current philosophical significance of metaphor aid in dealing with the issue of hermeneutical control in relation to language about God?

4. How valid is the insight that a metaphor or a narrative may be more explanatory than recourse to univocal language?

CLASSICAL AND REVISIONARY THEISM ON THE DIVINE AS PERSONAL

ELIZABETH BURNS*

Introduction. To claim that the divine is a person seems, according to Richard Swinburne, "the most elementary claim of theism" (1993, 101). I argue that, whether the classical theist's concept of the divine as a person or personal is construed as an analogy or a metaphor, or a combination of the two, analysis necessitates qualification of that concept such that any differences between the classical theist's concept of the divine as a person or personal and revisionary interpretations of that concept (for example, understanding divine personhood as a manifestation of a non-personal transcendent reality or as a symbol for important spiritual values) are merely superficial. Thus, either the classical theist has more in common with revisionary theism than he/she might care to admit, or classical theism is a multi-faceted position which encompasses interpretations which some might regard as revisionist.

Classical theism: God as "a person," and God as "personal." By "classical theism" I mean belief in a God who, in Swinburne's often-quoted words, is "eternal, free, able to do anything, knows everything, is perfectly good, is the proper object of human worship and obedience, the creator and sustainer of the universe" (1993, 1). God may be construed either as "a person without a body (i.e., a spirit)" (Swinburne), or as personal.

Is God a person? In order to ascertain whether God may be described as "a person," it is necessary to define "person," which is notoriously difficult. Historically, the Latin *persona*, a development from some usages of

the Greek *prosopon* and *hypostasis*, was used to indicate distinctions within the triune God of Christianity, not to refer to an individual consciousness or will; it was not until the Enlightenment that "person" came to be applied in the latter sense, first to human beings, and then to God.[1]

If personhood entails embodiment, as Adrian Thatcher (1985, 61) and Brian Davies (2006, 61) think it must, it could be argued that we can claim that God is a person only if we adopt some version of pantheism or panentheism,[2] or regard divine embodiment as a metaphor.[3] But Swinburne suggests that it might be possible to define a person as an animate being who is normally, but not necessarily, described in terms of predicates which depict a material body (Swinburne, 1993, 102), and therefore that God is a person in an analogical sense which does not require embodiment.

Even if an analogical interpretation of divine personhood need not include embodiment, however, it would appear that there are other respects in which the divine person differs from human persons. First, God lacks some attributes which persons normally have. For example, it has been argued that God is not capable of abstract thought because divine knowledge is "complete and intuitive" (Ward, 1992, 261), and that Xe[4] cannot experience emotions, because to experience emotions is to be changed by something which is not oneself, and the creator of everything cannot be changed by something other than Godself (Davies, 2006, 209). Secondly, God has some attributes which persons do not normally have. For example, God is the creator of everything not Godself (Ward, 1992, 262). Indeed, Davies argues, if God were a person like us, Xe would be just another inhabitant of the universe whose existence would need an explanation; people are parts of creation and, if God is the creator, Xe cannot be a person (2006, 62–68). Ward notes that the person model fails to do justice to the idea that God is within us, or that we are one with God (264), while William

---

*   Elizabeth Burns is Senior Lecturer in Philosophy of
     Religion at Heythrop College, University of London.

J. Mander suggests that features of deity such as perfection, omniscience, infinitude and gender-neutrality are incompatible with personhood (1997, 411; see also Gary Legenhausen, 1986, 317).

Thus, if God is a person, God is a person without a body who lacks some of the attributes which persons normally have, and possesses other attributes which persons do not normally have. Swinburne argues that God is a person in an analogical sense if Xe resembles persons more than things which are not persons; it is not necessary for God to resemble persons in every respect. Swinburne claims that, although he has loosened the meanings of words such as "person," "thinks," "acts," and "brings about," he has not emptied them of meaning since "[t]here are still statable and precise rules for their use," which means that "information is still conveyed by the use of the words, although not as much as would have been conveyed if the words had been used in their normal senses" (1993, 287). For scholars such as Mander and Legenhausen, however, too many features of the divine are incompatible with personhood for the analogy to be meaningful.

Is God personal? Theists who are unwilling to think of God as a person sometimes suggest that God should, instead, be described as "personal"[5] or "supra-personal."[6] In other words, although God is not, in any sense, a person, we may still "truly speak of God while using terms . . . that we employ when talking of creatures" (Davies, 2006, 54)—i.e., we may say that God possesses "person-properties" (Ward, 1992, 262). Mander acknowledges that "God has many properties typically associated with persons" (411), while Legenhausen, noting that the claim "God is personal" is sometimes understood in a weak sense to mean that personal pronouns and predicates applicable to persons (e.g., "all-knowing," "all-wise," "aware," "merciful") may be attributed to God, observes that "[n]o one in the Judeo-Christian-Islamic tradition . . . would deny . . . [that God is personal] in this weak sense" (308).

Swinburne thinks that the distinction between "person" and "personal" is unnecessary, however, provided that the difference between divine and human persons is sufficiently emphasized (1993, 101), while John Hick claims that the distinction is meaningless, asking "what could a personal non-person be?" (2006, 162). Nevertheless, there does seem to be a distinction between those who think that God may be described as a person in an analogical sense, and those who think that God has some of the attributes we would normally expect a person to have—i.e., that God satisfies some of the necessary conditions for calling something a person—but not enough to warrant describing God as a person.

Classical theism: Divine personhood—analogy or metaphor? If the God of classical theism is at least personal insofar as God satisfies some of the necessary conditions for calling something a person, then perhaps the idea of God as a person may be plausibly characterized as a metaphor. Whereas analogical religious language might be broadly characterized as the use of human language "to speak about God, in such a way that we may make claims that are *literally* true of God, while yet respecting the fundamental difference between God and His creation" (White, 2010, 183), metaphorical religious language might be defined as speaking about God in terms which are normally applied to the world in such a way that we make claims which are not literally true but which are, nonetheless, in some sense "reality depicting" (Soskice, 1985, 145). Thus, "God is good" may be understood as an analogy because, although human beings cannot hope to comprehend the nature and extent of God's goodness, there is some sense in which God's goodness is related to human goodness, while "God is my rock" may be understood as a metaphor because, although the concept of "rock" may convey, for example, the notion of divine immutability, there is no sense in which the statement is literally true.

The distinction is less clear, however, when we try to categorize divine personhood. As we saw above, Swinburne thinks that "God is a person" may be understood in an analogical sense because, although he has loosened the meanings of terms such as "thinks" and "brings about," they are not meaningless, and we can still specify rules for their use. Vincent Brümmer, on the other hand, asserts that "[a]ll our thinking about God... [is] metaphorical in the sense that we think and speak about (our relations with) God in terms derived from our thinking and speaking about (our relations with) each other" (2005, 4), and that a central task of theological reflection is that of "sorting out critically what part of the penumbra of meaning can and what part cannot be transferred to our thinking and speaking about God" (4). Thus, while the notion of divine personhood "is so rich that it has been developed as the most fundamental and characteristic conceptual model in theistic godtalk" (5), like all theological metaphors, what it asserts "is always accompanied by the whisper 'and it is not.' The fruitfulness of personal models for talking about God should therefore never make us deaf to the whisper that God is not like other people!" (5). Failure to hear this can lead to "an unacceptable form of anthropomorphism in our understanding of God and his ways" (7). Brümmer cites Wittgenstein's explanation of the use of the picture: "God's eye sees everything." This means that "God is aware of all that happens, not only in the world but also in the hearts and minds of all people"; talk of eyebrows would be inappropriate because this would go beyond the logical limits of the picture (Brümmer, 2005, 9, referring to Wittgenstein, 1966, 71–72).

In support of the view that divine personhood is, indeed, a metaphor rather than an analogy, one might argue as follows: "God is good" may be understood as an analogy when it is agreed that there is a relationship of some kind between divine and human goodness; if, as Brian Davies argues (2006, ch. 4), there is no such relationship, then "God is good" is a metaphor—although it may be difficult to explain which aspects of goodness apply to God if God is not in some literal, albeit extended, sense good. Thus, "God is a person" is not an analogy because God is not a person in any extended sense; personhood is not magnified in the same way as goodness is magnified when predicated of the divine because God lacks some attributes of personhood and possesses other attributes which are incompatible with personhood. Whereas it might be difficult to determine the nature of the truth conveyed by "God is good" understood as a metaphor, on the grounds that only one facet of divinity is described and, if this is not understood to be true in any literal sense, little, if anything, remains but an appeal to apophatic theology, the metaphor of divine personhood is a much richer metaphor consisting of a range of attributes, each of which might be explained in terms of analogy, as Brümmer seems to suggest (2006, 163). For example, if the metaphor of divine personhood incorporates the notion that God thinks, unless this is regarded as, in some sense, an analogy, it is difficult for human beings to understand, even in part, the nature of the truth which is allegedly conveyed. As White notes, "if there were an entity X for which we could construct no literal propositions, and concerning which every sentence containing the name 'X' was to be interpreted metaphorically, we would lack the means for fixing the reference of the name 'X,' and so would not have any way of knowing what we were talking about" (2010, 184).

But perhaps it does not matter whether divine personhood is understood as analogy or metaphor—whether the meaning of personhood is stretched when applied to the divine, or whether it is not literally true, even in a stretched sense, but serves to communicate important truths about the nature of the divine. In either case, however, it can be argued that there is at least one attribute of personhood, possession of which is a necessary, if not a sufficient, condition for the God of classical theism—that of divine agency.

Classical theism: Divine personhood and divine agency. Roger Trigg claims that a personal God is an active God, and that a God who has no intentions or purposes cannot be distinguished from a non-existent God (1998, 210). For Trigg, loss of belief in an active God leads to loss of religious belief since, in the Judaeo-Christian tradition at least, religion is concerned with human relationships with a God who is able to have relationships with human beings (206). As David Pailin (1976) has noted, religious believers claim that God loves, calls, judges, punishes, and rewards, and all of these describe an action of some kind. If the idea of God acting is incoherent, then it would seem difficult to claim that God is, in any sense, personal.

As a minimum, then, it could be argued that a God who possesses person-properties or is a person in a metaphorical sense is a bodiless agent. But what account can we give of the actions of a bodiless agent? J.L. Gaskin (2000) considers the possibility that such an agent acts in a manner comparable to that in which an embodied agent performs psychokinetic acts—those which cause things to happen without any bodily act connecting the person and the event. Gaskin suggests that, if there are genuine psychokinetic acts which require no physical connection between the agent and the event, the connection must be between pure mind and the world. But there are two reasons why this does not help us to explain the actions of a bodiless divine agent. First, if we do have pure minds, we also have bodies which locate our pure minds in this space-time arena. If a psychokinetic act can be performed by a bodiless agent, the agent must be located in another world in which the agency of pure minds operates, but, Gaskin claims, the concept of agency has no application in relation to such a world. We cannot suppose that agents from that world operate in this one by a form of agency we know nothing of; this would be to pretend that, despite abandoning all the criteria for the application of the concept of "agent," we can think of God's agency as if

the criteria were still observed (78–79); "an entity that does not come under the concept of an agent cannot be used as if it were an agent in virtue of some unspecifiable, unknowable and other-worldly feature which no actual agent has" (79). Secondly, Gaskin asks, how can the acts of a pure mind or spirit reach into this world to operate any of the natural connections by means of which this world changes? He therefore concludes that "there is no point of similarity between the way in which a normal human person can be an agent and the supposed agency of God that would permit us to understand divine 'agency' in terms of human agency" (79).

One possible response to the kind of objections raised by Gaskin is offered by Hugh Rice. Rice argues that God may be described as "personal," first because the knowledge and will of persons bring about goodness in the world (2000, 88), and secondly because, although we cannot know the nature of God or the means by which God's knowledge and will bring about goodness, we can know that there is a link between God and God's effects (89). It could, however, be objected that Rice's arguments are of little help to the theist because Rice claims that God is an agent while largely—if not entirely—in Gaskin's words, "abandoning all the criteria for the application of the concept of 'agent.'" But the theist could, perhaps, claim that he or she has not, in fact, abandoned all the criteria for the application of the concept of "agent" since, for example, the actions of an agent may be postulated as the cause of an effect even when we do not understand the mechanism used to perform the actions, and the actions of a specified agent may be postulated as the cause of an effect when the nature of the effect is consistent with our—perhaps tentative—knowledge of the nature of that agent. Thus, whether God's agency is thought to consist in a single, timeless creative act which encompasses the temporal acts of all sub-agents, or, at the other extreme, in an infinite number of temporal responses to situations and the prayers of individuals, the theist might legitimately claim that it is not unreasonable to postulate a divine explanation for perceived effects.

Such an inference may be supported by divine revelation, which might include religious experience. Indeed, Clement C.J. Webb claims that "a satisfactory defence of Divine Personality can only be founded upon the facts of religious experience" (1919, 272). While it may not be unreasonable to argue that the actions of a specified agent are the cause of a given effect when the nature of the effect is consistent with our knowledge of the nature of the agent, however, if our knowledge of the nature of the agent is derived from knowledge of the actions of that agent, the argument is circular. Brümmer suggests that talk about the all-seeing eye of God implies "that God can see into our hearts and know all our thoughts and desires so that we cannot keep these secret from him" because this, unlike implications about eyebrows, "is relevant for our life and spirituality" (2005, 12). But does this mean that living as if there is an omniscient consciousness promotes moral behaviour? And that since, as Brümmer observes, the reality of God apart from the relationship between God and humanity remains mysterious, we cannot know whether such an omniscient consciousness exists independently of human thought and experience? Such an interpretation might be characterised as non-realist,[7] but Brümmer explicitly claims that "[i]t would be incoherent to live my life as a life in the presence of God if I were to deny that there really is a God in whose presence I live!" (2005, 6). Following Ronald W. Hepburn, he argues that feelings of exultation and an attitude of quiet confidence in response to the claim "The Lord is my Strength and Shield" are appropriate only if they are regarded as responses to the Being referred to in the sentence, and if that Being exists (Brümmer, 2005, 6–7; Hepburn, 1970). If, however, the existence of such a Being is confirmed only by means of experience which is commonly described in terms of metaphors and/or analogies the nature of which we are seeking to explain, we are appealing once more to a circular argument.

Revisionary theism: personhood without agency. One possible response to the difficulties associated with the notion of divine agency is to dispense with the concept altogether and to argue that divine personhood is one manifestation of a non-personal transcendent reality (e.g., Hick, 2006, 169), or, more specifically, that divine personhood is a symbol for important spiritual values (e.g., Robinson, 1967, 36). For example, John Robinson, following Paul Tillich, claims that "God is personal" means that God is the ground of everything personal, that personality is of ultimate significance (Robinson, 1963, 48–49; 1967, 36; Tillich, 1978, 245). Robinson suggests that the gods of the Greeks and Romans were personifications of religious convictions (1967, 36), although this seems somewhat surprising, given the morally dubious behavior which often features in the ancient myths. As an interpretation of the God described in the scriptures of the Abrahamic faiths it may be more promising—although parts of these texts, too, describe a deity who behaves in a manner which some would regard as morally reprehensible. It could, however, be argued that the personifications of God which we find in religious texts have been created by human beings in an attempt to understand the nature of what Hick calls "Ultimate Reality" (2006, 162) and what it requires of us and that, in some cases, and perhaps especially with regard to some of humanity's earlier attempts, some facets of the character of the deity described represent either a mistake, or a stage in the development of a personification of Ultimate Reality.

Pailin objects to such interpretations, however, because, in his view, to say that verbs which appear to describe divine actions simply "reify and personify what are really impersonal forces in the ultimate structure of reality is not to clarify their meaning but to hold that the religious faith expressed by them is basically wrong and must be replaced by a fundamentally different kind of understanding" (1976, 145). In a similar vein, Trigg argues that it is "not possible to undermine the basis of religion and simultaneously to retain its characteristic ethical claims about humanity" (1998, 212). For Trigg, God must make a difference; otherwise we will not be aware of God's existence. If God is the creator, God sustains and holds in being that which has created. But if God is merely the ultimate ground of everything, it is hard to see what more is claimed than "mere acknowledgement of and wonder at the existence of everything" (213).

Classical theism and the metaphor of divine agency.
We have seen that some scholars argue that God cannot be described as a person in an analogical sense because some aspects of persons do not apply to God. They therefore argue either that God must be described, instead, as "personal," or that God is a person in a metaphorical sense. In either case, God has some, but not all, of the characteristics of a person. Chief amongst these is the attribute of agency, but divine agency differs from human agency to such an extent that it is difficult to specify how it is to be understood. Others have therefore suggested that divine personhood must be understood as a manifestation of a non-personal transcendent reality or as a symbol for important spiritual values, but these interpretations are regarded by some as revisionist and thereby as undermining the basis of religious belief.

One possible solution might be to argue that it is not only divine personhood but also divine agency which should be understood in a metaphorical sense. We have seen that theists claim to know that God acts, but not how God acts; to borrow Brümmer's words, divine agency is not only quantitatively different from human agency, it is also qualitatively different (2005, 10). Gaskin's objections suggest that we cannot spell out the sense in which God is an agent clearly enough

for us to speak of divine agency. But this assumes that we are looking for some literal, if stretched, connection between our understanding of "agent" as applied to human beings and our definition of "agent" as applied to a divine person, metaphorically understood. If divine agency is also a metaphor, perhaps we can say that there are some respects in which the divine resembles a human agent, even if we struggle to articulate them. They might be insufficient to enable us to describe God as an agent in a literal or analogical sense, but sufficient for us to describe divine agency as a metaphor which enables us "to say that which can be said in no other way" (Soskice, 1985, 153).

In which respects, then, can we say that the divine resembles a human agent? In outline, an answer might go as follows: Human agents change the world by means of verbal communication—e.g., advice for someone experiencing a moral dilemma—and physical action—e.g., a medical intervention when someone is ill. Although the divine is rarely said to speak audibly, religious believers do say such things as "I feel that God is telling me to do x"—perhaps after reflection upon relevant passages from the scriptures of their religion and the teachings of their tradition, comparison with secular morality, consideration of the thoughts of other believers, and analysis of the application of these to their own circumstances. Similarly, although the divine is rarely said to perform physical actions in the manner of a human agent, believers do say that they see the hand of God in the way in which events unfold. In the case of a person suffering from an illness, for example, God might be said to work through the actions of the medical staff.

But how does this differ from God not acting at all? The problem becomes more acute, of course, if the advice turns out to have been mistaken, or the medical treatment is unsuccessful. Attempts to respond to such a difficulty led Antony Flew to conclude that religious belief has suffered death by a thousand qualifications (1990, 368),[8] but one might, instead, suggest that the qualifications point not to the death of belief but to something important about the nature of belief. They might, for example, enable us to gain a clearer idea of the forms in which divine action can be manifested. Thus, just as one might say that it is, at least in many religious cultures, no longer appropriate to pray for great wealth, so one might say that it is no longer appropriate to pray for a cure from illness—i.e., that it is no longer appropriate to expect divine action to manifest itself in this form. Divine action might, however, be manifested in, for example, a solution to a problem, the strength to cope with a difficult situation, or the help and support of others.

Classical and revisionary interpretations of the metaphor of God as personal. I have argued that the classical theist can retain the metaphor of God as personal if she or he also understands divine agency as a metaphor. But, if divine agency is manifested in such things as a solution to a problem, the strength to cope with a difficult situation, or the help and support of others, how does this differ from a revisionist interpretation of personhood and divine agency? Are we not left with feelings and attitudes which are unrelated to any state of affairs (Brümmer/Hepburn), a personification of impersonal forces (Pailin), and/or an ultimate ground of our being which makes no identifiable difference to our existence (Trigg)?

Brümmer argues that religious faith entails "some form of critical realism," and that religious metaphors are, as Janet Soskice has claimed, "reality depicting" (2005, 7; Soskice, 1985, 145). Since, for Brümmer, a religious metaphor can be explained, at least to some extent, in terms of analogy (7), at least some of that metaphor (the part whose meaning we can explain) expresses a literal truth, albeit in a stretched sense— but how far can it be stretched before the interpretation becomes revisionary? If divine personhood includes the metaphor of divine parenthood, explained at least partly in terms of God's care for me, if I suffer

an untimely death through disaster or disease, in what sense is God's care meaningfully expressed? The classical theist could reiterate the view that divine omnipotence is not to be construed in such a way that human suffering is always prevented, and that divine care is expressed by means of the human beings who help me. But the revisionist theist could say this, too.

Similarly, even if "The Lord is my Strength and Shield" refers to an objectively-existing state of affairs, it clearly does not mean that I will never suffer. Brümmer suggests that "God is my rock," which may be taken to have a similar meaning, refers to our dependence on God (2005, 6), but this does not entail the belief that God intervenes to prevent my suffering. Does Brümmer, perhaps, mean that God is whatever it is which brought about the existence of the universe, or even that God is to be identified with the material world on which we depend? The former might be construed as a version of the cosmological argument which a revisionist could accept, while the latter is a form of pantheism or panentheism. Brümmer notes that religious doctrines must not be seen as explanations of the same kind as scientific explanations; rather, we must note their importance for life (8). On the other hand, while we must be agnostic and apophatic about what God is like independently of our relationship with God, if we were entirely unable to describe in human terms the nature of God and our relationship with God, "our spirituality and fellowship with God would collapse into an incomprehensible something we know not what" (12). Brümmer argues that God has many faces and "reveals himself in manifold ways in his dealings with us"; believers therefore "claim that God is ever present to us in ways that are relevant to the demands we have to face in the specific circumstances or times in which we live" (11). But is "God reveals himself in ways which are relevant to believers' circumstances" equivalent to "believers interpret the divine in ways which are relevant to their circumstances"? In other words, is Brümmer really appealing to a form of Hick's concept of "experiencing-as," developed from Wittgenstein's idea of "seeing-as"? Wittgenstein noted that we may see an ambiguous figure as either a duck or a rabbit (1968, II:xi), but Hick argues that all our seeing is "seeing-as," and all our experiencing is "experiencing-as" (2004, 140). For Hick, faith is the interpretation through which we are conscious of the Real (160) or the "supra-natural" (2006, 145). This enables us to say that some believers experience God as a Being with whom they can interact, while others experience God as personal in a more limited sense, or as an impersonal standard which enlightens our human endeavours. This characterisation of belief may be employed to explain not only the existence of different religions, which are said to be different phenomenal manifestations of the same noumenal Real, but also different interpretations within the same religion (cf. Harrison, 2006, 147–52). Thus, within the same community of believers, "God is my friend" might have meaning for one member but not another, while the same noumenal Reality underlies the experience of both.

It could be argued that this interpretation of a classical understanding of the divine as personal is compatible with revisionist views of the nature of the divine. Thus, if God is whatever it is which brought about the existence of the universe, or may be identified with the material world upon which we depend, then Robinson's claim that the attribute of divine personality conveys the belief that "personality is of ultimate importance" entails that "God is whatever it is which makes the personal so important." The notion of divine personhood thereby includes the idea that the personal can, at its best, manifest the divine.

The characterisation of divine personhood for which I have argued is compatible even with the views of scholars such as D.Z. Phillips and Don Cupitt, the former of whom has often been described as a "non-realist" (although he himself denies this), while the latter has claimed that "all religions, philosophies of life and visions of the world are human imaginative

constructions... The truth in a religious or philosophical text is no longer seen as corresponding to ... a great Objective Truth out there" (1998, 4). Phillips suggests, however, that someone looking for realism in the philosophy of religion might begin by considering the way in which words which are not literally true and pictures which are neither portraits nor diagrams nonetheless manage to convey "something real" about the world (2002, 7). And even Cupitt talks about "Being" as "the extra-linguistic stuff out there that our descriptive uses of language are trying to refer to, or be about" (1998, 73), and suggests that we need Being for ethical and religious reasons; it is our "complementary Other" (74). Indeed, Being is "the religious object" (74); we "attend to it, have an attitude to it, and respond to it" (73). In *Reforming Christianity*, he claims that "the only basis for ethics" is "our newly realised full co-humanity" (2001, 103), which seems to imply that it is the "given" physical nature of human beings which determines what makes life worth living—i.e., that only a form of moral realism can explain genuine altruism. Thus, even when the divine is construed in the manner of Phillips and Cupitt, religious feelings and attitudes do refer to a state of affairs, and this state of affairs may be conceived of as personal and active in a metaphorical sense which is not dissimilar from that of the interpretation of the classical theist.

This means that Trigg's objection to religious beliefs which make no identifiable difference to human life need not apply to either classical or revisionist interpretations of theism. For either version of theism, "God" is the name for whatever it was which brought the universe into existence, and perhaps also for the totality of that which exists. God requires a certain form of life, and provides a standard against which we measure our behaviour. The task of human life is to try to understand and to communicate, both to our contemporaries and to future generations, the nature of the divine and what it requires of us, in order that we might "have life, and have it abundantly"

(John 10:10). This is achieved by contemplating the stories about God, God's actions, and the behaviour which God expects of humankind which are found in the scriptures and traditions of the world's religions. The task is difficult, and human beings are sometimes mistaken, but the divine can nonetheless guide us towards solutions to moral problems, offer a source of strength to cope with difficult situations, and manifest Godself in the help and support of others. Thus, the divine makes a difference to human beings because goodness makes a difference to human beings, both in the way in which it affects our lives and in the conduct it requires of us.

It is, perhaps, more difficult to avoid Pailin's charge that such a view personifies impersonal forces. Whether or not we think that, ultimately, this classical/ revisionist interpretation of the divine as personal agent succumbs to this objection depends upon the extent to which we think that the concepts of personhood and agency can be stretched before the links with those concepts as applied to human persons and agents are entirely broken. Nevertheless, if the divine can be understood as a guide, a source of strength, and an inspiration for human altruism, this supports an argument that, for both the classical and the revisionist theist, the links are sufficiently strong to enable the continued use of these metaphors in our conceptions of the divine.

Conclusion. On any interpretation of the divine, there are clearly many respects in which God is not like a human person, and, where there do appear to be similarities, the resemblance is always heavily qualified, either by means of analogy, or through the use of metaphor, the meaning of which may be at least partially explained in terms of analogy. I have argued that the metaphor of God as personal entails a metaphorical interpretation of divine agency, the latter of which may be explained by means of analogy. On such a view, "I feel that God is telling me to do *x*" might mean "In the light of my reading of scripture, study of my religious tradition, participation in religious ceremonies, and/or conversations with other believers, and my reflection on the application of these to my own circumstances, I feel that I am required to do *x*." Similarly, "God is my Strength and Shield" might mean "The divine, being the totality of the universe, including its optimal moral values, along with the scriptures and traditions by means of which human beings have attempted to capture its requirements and the support of fellow travellers on the religious path, gives me the strength to attempt to live a moral and meaningful life, even—and perhaps especially—in difficult circumstances."

I have also suggested that even the most "non-realist" of revisionist theists ultimately make a commitment to some form of realism, and thus that both classical and revisionist theists can explain the nature of divine personality and agency in a similar manner. I have argued that, for theists of both kinds, their commitment to a form of realism enables them to avoid the objection that they are simply attempting to generate feelings and attitudes which are unrelated to any state of affairs, and, secondly, that the functionality of their beliefs ensures that in neither case can they be reduced to belief in an ultimate ground of our being which makes no identifiable difference to our existence. Finally, I have argued that since, for both versions of theism, the links between the meanings of "personal" and "agent" when applied to the divine and the meanings of these terms when applied to human beings are stretched but not broken, neither the classical theist nor the revisionist simply personalises impersonal forces.

Thus, analysis of the nature of divine personhood and divine agency, understood as metaphors which may be at least partially explained by means of analogy, leads to an interpretation of these attributes which is compatible with both classical and revisionist versions of theism. This could imply that classical interpretations of theism are closer to revisionist views than it might, at first, be thought, or that classical theism is a multi-faceted position which encompasses interpretations which some might regard as revisionist. It could also imply that the views of scholars such as Phillips and Cupitt, insofar as they may be construed as realist, are closer to the classical end of the religious spectrum than perhaps they would care to acknowledge. This enables them to avoid the reductionist charge which is often levelled against them— i.e., the claim that they offer a watered-down, inferior version of theism for those incapable of genuine belief. It also offers support for Phillips's claim that he, like Wittgenstein, "leaves everything as it is" (Wittgenstein, 1968, 124; Phillips, 1993, 242). Thus, classical and revisionist theism meet in the middle, and the differences between them are largely—at least with respect to divine personhood and agency—superficial.

Notes

1. Herbert C. Wolf (1964, 28) notes that some of the earliest uses of the phrase "the personality of God" may be found in William Paley (1850), and the first edition of Schleiermacher (1958) (Wolf, 1964, 28).

2. Pantheism is the view that all of reality (the entire universe) is God. Panentheism is the view that all of reality is contained within God, but that there are also some respects in which God is more than the entirety of the universe.

3. For example, the teaching that Allah has two hands has been commonly interpreted by Muslim scholars as a symbol for divine power.

4. Since few would argue that the divine is literally masculine, I sometimes adopt the gender-neutral pronoun "Xe" (pronounced "Zee"). While some languages already employ gender-neutral pronouns, there is no generally-accepted English term. From those which have been suggested, I have chosen "Xe" to refer to divinity conceived of as a person, or personal, on the grounds that the "X" which replaces the first two letters of the gendered pronouns seems particularly appropriate in the context of an apophatic theology.

5. Thatcher claims that belief that God is a person is an impediment to Christian faith, but that belief in a personal God is essential to it (1985, 61), while Davies argues that God is personal on the grounds that God has knowledge and will and is active (2000, 561–63).

6. David Pailin uses this word to describe the position of Karl Jaspers (Jaspers, 1967, 141ff; Pailin, 1976, 149). See also Hans Küng (1980, 633), quoted in Thatcher (2006, 72) and Ward (1992, 265).

7. I use "non-realism" to refer to agnosticism about a God who exists independently of human thought—as opposed to "anti-realism" which claims that there is no God existing independently of human thought.

8. Flew seems to have changed his mind about this at the end of his life (Flew, 2007).

References

Armstrong, David. *A Materialist Theory of Mind.* New York: Humanities P, 1968.

Brümmer, Vincent. *Atonement, Christology and the Trinity: Making Sense of Christian Doctrine.* Basingstoke: Ashgate, 2005.

——. *Brümmer on Meaning and the Christian Faith: Collected Writings of Vincent Brümmer.* Basingstoke: Ashgate, 2006.

Cupitt, Don. *The Revelation of Being.* London: SCM P, 1998.

——. *Reforming Christianity.* London: SCM P, 2001.

Davies, Brian. "A Modern Defence of Divine Simplicity." In *Philosophy of Religion: A Guide and Anthology.* Ed. Brian Davies. Oxford: Oxford UP, 2000. 549–64.

——. *The Reality of God and the Problem of Evil.* London: Continuum, 2006.

Flew, Antony. "Theology and Falsification." In *Classical and Contemporary Readings in the Philosophy of Religion.* Ed. John Hick. Englewood Cliffs, New Jersey: Prentice-Hall, 1990. 367–90.

——. *There Is a God: How the World's Most Notorious Atheist Changed His Mind.* New York: HarperCollins, 2007.

Gaskin, John. "Gods, Ghosts and Curious Persons." *Philosophical Writing* 13 (2000): 71–80.

Harrison, Victoria. "Metaphor, Religious Language and Religious Experience." *Sophia: International Journal for Philosophy of Religion* 46.2 (2007): 127–45.

Hepburn, Ronald. W. "Poetry and Religious Belief." In *Metaphysical Beliefs.* Stephen Toulmin, Ronald W. Hepburn, and Alasdair MacIntyre. London: SCM P, 1970. 73–156.

Hick, John. *An Interpretation of Religion: Human Responses to the Transcendent.* Basingstoke: Palgrave Macmillan, 2004.

——. *The New Frontier of Religion and Science: Religious Experience, Neuroscience and the Transcendent.* Basingstoke: Palgrave Macmillan, 2006.

Jantzen, Grace M. *God's World, God's Body.* London: Darton, Longman and Todd, 1984.

Jaspers, Karl. *Philosophical Faith and Revelation.* London: Collins, 1967.

Küng, Hans. *Does God Exist?* London: Collins, 1980.

Lakoff, George and Mark Johnson. *Metaphors We Live By.* Chicago: U of Chicago P, 1980.

Legenhausen, Gary. "Is God a Person?" *Religious Studies* 22 (1986): 307–23.

Levine, Michael J. *Pantheism: A Non-Theist Concept of Deity.* Abingdon: Routledge, 1994.

Mander, William J. "God and Personality." *Heythrop Journal* 38 (1997): 401–12.

McFague, Sallie. *Metaphorical Theology.* London: Fortress P, 1982.

Pailin, David. "The Humanity of the Theologian and the Personal Nature of God." *Religious Studies* 12 (1976): 141–58.

Paley, William. *Natural Theology.* Boston: Gould, Kendall and Lincoln, 1850.

Pei, Mario. *Weasel Words: The Art of Saying What You Don't Mean.* New York: Harper and Row, 1978.

Phillips, D.Z. "Religion in Wittgenstein's Mirror." In *Wittgenstein and Religion.* New York: St Martins P, 1993. 237–55.

——. "Propositions, Pictures and Practices." In *Ars Disputandi* 2 (2002). At www.tandfonline.com/doi/abs/10.1080/15665399.2002.10819746#.U99vgZUg_IU. Accessed 4 August 2014.

Rice, Hugh. *God and Goodness.* Oxford: Oxford UP, 2000.

Robinson, John A.T. *Honest to God.* London: SCM P, 1963.

——. *Exploration into God.* London: SCM P, 1967.

Schliermacher, Friedrich. *On Religion: Speeches to Its Cultured Despisers.* Trans. J. Oman. New York: Harper, 1958.

Smart, J.J.C. "Sensations and Brain Processes." *Philosophical Review* 68 (1959): 141–56.

Soskice, Janet. *Metaphor and Religious Language.* Oxford: Clarendon, 1985.

Stiver, Dan R. *The Philosophy of Religious Language: Sign, Symbol and Story.* Oxford: Blackwell, 1996.

Swinburne, Richard. *The Coherence of Theism.* Oxford: Oxford UP, 1993.

Thatcher, Adrian. "The Personal God and the God Who Is a Person." *Religious Studies* 21 (1985): 61–73.

Tillich, Paul. *Systematic Theology Volume I: Reason and Revelation, Being and God.* London: SCM P, 1978.

Trigg, Roger. *Rationality and Religion: Does Faith Need Reason?* Oxford: Blackwell, 1998.

Ward, Keith. "Is God a Person?" In *Christian Faith and Philosophical Theology: Essays in Honour of Vincent Brümmer.* Ed. Gijsbert van den Brink, Luco J. van den Bron, and Marcel Sarot. Kampen: Kok Pharos, 1992. 258–66.

Webb, Clement C.J. *God and Personality.* London: George Allen and Unwin, 1919.

White, Roger M. *Talking about God: The Concept of Analogy and the Problem of Religious Language.* Farnham: Ashgate, 2010.

Wikipedia. "Gender-Specific and Gender-Neutral Pronouns." http://en.wikipedia.org/wiki /Gender-specific_and_gender-neutral_pronouns. Accessed 4 August 2014.

Wiktionary. Xe. http://en.wiktionary.org/wiki/xe. Accessed 4 August 2014.

Wittgenstein, Ludwig. *Lectures and Conversations on Aesthetics, Psychology and Religious Belief.* Oxford: Blackwell, 1966.

——. *Philosophical Investigations.* Oxford: Basil Blackwell, 1968.

Wolf, Herbert C. "An Introduction to the Idea of God as Person." *Journal of Bible and Religion* 32 (1968): 26–33.

Discussion

1. God is widely believed to be a person. What are the distinctive attributes of persons? How does Burns argue that such attributes cannot be literally true of God? In what sense are such attributions true?

2. What are some plausible alternatives to thinking of God as (literally) a person?

3. Although Burns is concerned with God as personal, she is also concerned about literal attributions of gender, usually male, to God. How does she address the metaphorical nature of gendered language for God?

Chapter 23
Does God Suffer?

DIVINE IMPASSIBILITY

JOHANNES SCOTUS ERIUGENA*

The problem raised. If action and reception of action, as we have said, are predicated of God not truly, i.e., not properly, it follows that He neither moves nor is moved; for to move is to act and to be moved is to be acted upon. Then, too, if He neither acts nor is acted upon, how can He be said to love everything and to be loved by everything made by Him? Love is a certain motion of one acting, and being loved is a motion of one being acted upon.... If God loves what He has made, He surely is seen to be moved, for He is moved by His own love. Also, if He is loved by whatever can love, whether or not they know what they love, isn't it obvious that He moves? Of course, the love of His beauty moves them. I cannot see by myself, therefore, how, in order to prevent His appearing to act and be acted upon, He can be said neither to move nor to be moved. I therefore beg you to solve this knotty problem....

Expressing the inexpressible. If the names of essences, substances, or accidents are attributed to God not truly, but by a certain necessity of expressing the Ineffable Nature, doesn't it necessarily follow that neither can the verbs which signify the motions

of essences, substances, and accidents be predicated properly of God who, by the incomprehensible and ineffable excellence of His nature, surpasses all essence, substance, accident, motion (both active and passive), and whatever is said and understood, or not said and understood about such things, and yet is present in them? For example, if God is metaphorically called Love, although He is More Than Love and surpasses all love, why would He not similarly be said to love, although He surpasses all motion of love since He aspires to nothing besides Himself, since He alone is all in all? Similarly, if He is described as acting and Actor, doing and Doer, not properly but by a kind of metaphor, why should the same kind of figure of speech not predicate that He acts and does, is acted upon and has something done to Him? I believe that we must have a similar understanding about the other verbs which signify the motions of all changeable creation, whether those motions are natural, unnatural, intellectual, rational, irrational, corporeal, incorporeal, local, temporal, straight, oblique, angular, circular, or spherical....

God cannot be acted upon. There is no question about reception of action, for I both believe and understand that God is wholly impassive. By *passivity* I mean being acted upon, "the opposite of action." Who would dare to say or believe, much less understand, that God is subject to being acted upon when He is Creator, not creature? A long time ago we concluded that when God is said to be acted upon, the expression is obviously figurative....

---

* Johannes Scotus Eriugena (810–?) was perhaps the greatest Christian philosopher from the time of Augustine (fifth century) to the time of Anselm (eleventh century).

The problem of divine impassibility and love. I wish that you would tell me more plainly, though, to make me see clearly that when I hear that God loves or is loved, I should understand simply His nature without any motion of lover or beloved. When I am convinced on this point, I won't have any hesitation when I read or hear that He wishes or desires and is desired, cherishes and is cherished, sees and is seen, longs and is longed for, and also moves and is moved. All of these must be grasped by one and the same concept. Just as will, love, affection, vision, longing, and motion, when predicated of Him, implant one and the same idea within us; so the verbs, whether active, passive, or intransitive and whatever their mood have no difference of meaning, in my opinion.

The solution. You are quite right. First, then, hear this definition of love: "Love is the connection and bond by which the whole universe is joined together with ineffable friendship and insoluble unity." It can also be defined as "the natural motion of all things in motion, and the end and resting place beyond which no motion of created things advances." St. Dionysius openly assents to these definitions in his "Amatory Hymns" when he says: "Let us understand love, whether we are speaking of the divine, angelic, intellectual, spiritual, or natural kind, as a unifying and blending power which moves higher things to forethought for the lower, joins equals in a reciprocal bond of communion, and turns the lowest and subordinate toward their betters, placed above them." In the same work he says: "Since we have arranged in order the many loves from the one, let us now join them all together again and gather them from the many into a single, combined love, the father of them all. First let us draw them together into the two universal powers of love, over which complete dominion and primacy are held by the immeasurable Cause of all love, which transcends all things. Toward It universal love reaches out in accordance with the nature of each and every existing thing." … God is deservedly called "Love," therefore, since He is the use of all love and is diffused through everything and gathers everything together, and revolves toward Himself with an ineffable motion of return, and limits the motions of love in all creation in Himself. The very diffusion of Divine Nature into everything in and from It is said to love everything, not that It really is diffused in any way (for It lacks all motion and fills everything at the same time), but that It diffuses and moves the sight of the rational mind through everything (since It is the cause of the mind's diffusion and motion) to search out and find It and, insofar as possible, to understand that It fills all things in order that they may have being; and that, as though by a pacifying bond of universal love, It collects and inseparably comprehends everything in an inseparable unity which is Itself. God is likewise said to be loved by all things that are from Him, not because He is acted upon by them in any way (for He alone is incapable of being acted upon), but because they all long for Him, and His beauty attracts all things to itself. He alone is truly lovable, because He alone is the highest and the true Goodness and Beauty. Indeed, everything in creatures which is understood as truly good, beautiful, and lovable is Himself. As there is nothing essentially good besides Him alone, so there is nothing essentially beautiful or lovable besides Him.

Just as a magnet by its natural power attracts iron near it without moving itself to do so, and without being acted upon by the iron which it attracts, so the Cause of all things leads everything from It back to Itself without any motion of Its own, but by the sole power of Its beauty.

Discussion

1. Describe the God of Johannes Scotus Eriugena. Is this being worthy of worship? Why or why not?

2. What problems does Eriugena's view of God raise for God's relationship with his creatures?

3. What is Eriugena's view of divine love? Do you think it covers all of the essential aspects of love?

SUFFERING LOVE

NICHOLAS WOLTERSTORFF*

My heart grew sombre with grief, and wherever I
looked I saw only death. My own country became
a torment and my own home a grotesque abode
of misery. All that we had done together was
now a grim ordeal without him. My eyes watched
everywhere for him, but he was not there to
be seen. I hated all the places we had known
together, because he was not in them and they
could no longer whisper to me, "Here he comes!"
as they would have done had he been alive but
absent for a while.... My soul was a burden,
bruised and bleeding. It was tired of the man who
carried it, but I found no place to set it down to
rest. (Augustine, *Confessions* IV, 4; IV, 7)[1]

Confessions. It is in passages such as this, where he
exposes to full view the grief which overwhelmed him
upon the death of his dear friend from Tagaste, that
Augustine is at his most appealing to us in the twentieth century. We are attracted both by the intensity of
his love and grief, and by his willingness to expose that
grief to his friends and the readers of his *Confessions*.
To any who may have experienced torments similar to
those Augustine here describes, the passage also has
the mysteriously balming quality of expressing with
delicate precision the grief they themselves have felt.
All the places and all the objects that once whispered
"Here he comes" or "Here she comes" have lost their
voice and fallen achingly mute.

It is a rough jolt, to discover that at those very points
in his life where we find Augustine most appealing, he,
from the time of his conversion onward, found himself thoroughly disgusting. His reason for exposing

his grief was to share with his readers his confession
to God of the senselessness and sinfulness of a love so
intense for a being so fragile that its destruction could
cause such grief. "Why do I talk of these things?" he
asks. And he answers, "It is time to confess, not to
question!" (*Confessions* IV, 6).

In the years between the death of his friend and the
death of his mother Augustine embraced the Christian
faith. That embrace made his response to his mother's
death very different from that to his friend's. "I closed
her eyes," he says, "and a great wave of sorrow surged
into my heart. It would have overflowed in tears if I had
not made a strong effort of will and stemmed the flow, so
that the tears dried in my eyes...." (*Confessions* IX, 12).
On that earlier occasion, tears and "tears alone were
sweet to him, for in his heart's desire they had taken
the place of his friend" (*Confessions* IV, 4). In his rem-
iniscences he asked why that was so, "why tears are
sweet to the sorrowful." "How ... can it be that there is
sweetness in the fruit we pluck from the bitter crop of
life, in the mourning and the tears, the wailing and the
sighs?" (*Confessions* IV, 5) But now, on the occasion of
his mother's death, he "fought against the wave of sorrow" (*Confessions* IX, 12).

His struggle for self-control was not successful. He
reports that after the burial, as he lay in bed thinking of
his devoted mother, "the tears which I had been holding back streamed down, and I let them flow as freely
as they would, making of them a pillow for my heart.
On them it rested...." (*Confessions* IX, 12) So now, he
says to God, "I make you my confession.... Let any
man read it who will.... And if he finds that I sinned by
weeping for my mother, even if only for a fraction of an
hour, let him not mock at me ... but weep himself, if his
charity is great. Let him weep for my sins to you...."
(*Confessions* X, 12). The sin for which Augustine wants
the person of charity to weep, however, is not so much
the sin of weeping over the death of his mother as
the sin of which that weeping was a sign. I was, says
Augustine, "guilty of too much worldly affection."

---

* Nicholas Wolterstorff is Noah Porter Professor Emeritus
of Philosophical Theology at Yale University.

Obviously there is a mentality coming to expression here which is profoundly foreign to us. In our own day there are still those who hold back tears—usually because they think it unbecoming to cry, seldom because they think it sinful. But rare is the person who believes that even to feel grief upon the death of a friend or one's mother is to have been guilty of too much worldly affection. The mentality expressed not only shapes Augustine's view of the proper place of sorrow and suffering in human life; it also contributes to his conviction that in God there is no sorrow or suffering. God's life is a life free of sorrow—indeed, a life free of upsetting emotions in general, a life free of passions, a life of apathy, untouched by suffering, characterized only by steady bliss. . . .

The eudaemonistic ideal. But why would anyone who placed himself in the Christian tradition think of God's life as that of non-suffering apathy? The identity of that tradition is determined (in part) by the adherence of its members, in one way or another, to the scriptures of the Old and New Testaments. And even those who read while running cannot fail to notice that God is there pictured as one who sufferingly experiences his world and therefore grieves. What was it, then, that led the tradition to "bracket" this dimension of the biblical picture of God? . . .

We cannot do better than begin with Augustine. But we would be ill-advised to move at once to what Augustine said about emotions and suffering in the life of God. For it was true of Augustine, as it was of most others in the tradition, that his reflections on the place of emotions and suffering in God's life were merely a component within his more comprehensive reflections on the place of emotions and suffering in the ideal life of persons generally—divine and human together. We must try, then, to grasp that totality. Let us begin with what Augustine says about the proper place of emotions and suffering in human experience.

Augustine frames his thought within the eudaemonistic [happiness] tradition of antiquity. We are all in search of happiness—by which Augustine and the other ancients did not mean a life in which happiness outweighs grief and ennui but a life from which grief and ennui have been cast out—a life of uninterrupted bliss. Furthermore, Augustine aligns himself with the Platonic tradition in his conviction that one's love, one's *eros*, is the fundamental determinant of one's happiness. Augustine never imagined that a human being could root out *eros* from his existence. Incomplete beings that we are, we inescapably long for fulfillment. The challenge, accordingly, is to choose objects for one's love such that happiness ensues.

Now it was as obvious to Augustine as it is to all of us that grief ensues when that which we love is destroyed or dies, or is altered in such a way that we no longer find it lovable. Says he, in reflecting on his grief upon the death of his friend, "I lived in misery like every man whose soul is tethered by the love of things that cannot last and then is agonized to lose them. . . . The grief I felt for the loss of my friend had struck so easily into my inmost heart simply because I had poured out my soul upon him, like water upon sand, loving a man who was mortal as though he were never to die" (*Confessions* IV, 6; IV, 8). The cure is to detach one's love from such objects and to attach it to something immutable and indestructible. For Augustine, the only candidate was God. "Blessed are those who love you, O God. . . . No one can lose you . . . unless he forsakes you" (*Confessions* IV, 9). . . . If it is happiness and rest for your soul that you desire—and who does not?—then fix your love on the eternal immutable God. . . .

Stoicism. Prominent in the ethical philosophy of middle and late antiquity were discussions over the proper place of emotions in life. In those discussions, the Stoic view was famous. Augustine, in *The City of God*,[2] participates in those discussions by staking out his own position on the proper place of emotions in the life of the godly person in opposition to the Stoic position.

Now the Stoics did not say that in the ideal life there would be no emotional coloring to one's experience. They insisted, on the contrary, that in such a life there would be various non-perturbing emotions which they called *eupatheidi*. They regularly cited three of these: Joy, wishfulness, and caution. Their thought was that the ideal life, the happy life, is the life of the wise person—of the person who, by virtue of directing his life by reason, is a person whose character and intentions are morally virtuous. To make it clear that, in their judgment, the only thing good in itself is moral good, they typically refused even to *call* anything else "good." Certain other things are, at best, *preferable*. The wise person, then, *will* rejoice over the moral status he has attained, will wish for the continuation of that status, and will be watchful for what threatens it.

The Stoics went on to say, though, that the sage would be without pathos, without passion. He would be *apathés*, apathetic. His condition would be that of *apatheia*—apathy, impassibility, passionlessness. What did they mean? . . .

It is clear that the classic Stoics thought [all emotional disturbances—with fear, grief, and ecstasy as prime examples—are passions]. One grieves, they would have said, only over what one evaluates as evil; but the sage, finding no trace of moral evil in himself, has nothing over which to grieve. So too, one fears what one evaluates as an evil threatening; but for the sage, who is steady in virtue, there are no threatening evils. And one goes into ecstasy over something that happens to come one's way which one evaluates as good. But for the sage, there are no goods which just happen to come his way; that which is the only thing good for him, namely, his own moral character, is entirely of his own making. It was, thus, the contention of the classic Stoics that as a matter of fact the upsetting emotions are all passions, and will, on that account, have no

place in the life of the wise person. The true sage experiences no emotional disturbances. . . .

We have been speaking of the place of the passions in the life of the imperfectly godly person in this imperfect world of ours. But, we must be reminded that Augustine also points us away from life in this world to a perfected life in a perfected world—a life not earned or achieved but granted. In that life there will be no such emotional disturbances as grief and fear. For that will be a life of uninterrupted bliss; and "who that is affected by fear or grief can be called absolutely blessed?" Even "when these affections are well regulated, and according to God's will, they are peculiar to this life, not to that future life we look for" (*City of God* XIV, 9). Augustine's argument, as we have seen, is not the Stoic argument that the passions are always based on false evaluations; they are not. His argument is that having emotions always involves *being overcome*, and that the pain embedded within such emotions as grief and fear is incompatible with full happiness. Grief and fear are not as such incompatible with *reason*. They are as such incompatible with *eudaemonia*. Hence the abolition of those passions from our lives will not occur by way of illumination as to the true nature of things. It will occur by way of removal from our existence of that which it is appropriate to fear or grieve over.

So our perfected existence will exhibit not only *eros* attached entirely to God, but apathy. For attachment to God and detachment from world, we struggle here and now. For *apathy*, we merely long, in the meanwhile fearing and grieving over the evil worth fearing and grieving over. Struggle and longing, aiming and hoping, pull apart in the Augustinian universe. It is not, though. . . . a feelingless apathy for which we long. We long for a life of joy and bliss. . . .

Divine impassibility. And now the eternal life of God, as understood by Augustine, can be very simply described: God's life satisfies the eudaemonistic ideal implicit in all that has preceded. God's life is through and through blissful. Thus God too is free of negative *pathe*. Of *Mitleiden* [sympathy] with those who are suffering, God feels nothing, as also he feels no pain over the shortfall of godliness in his errant creatures. His state is *apatheia*—an *apatheia* characterized positively by the steady non-perturbing state of joy. God dwells eternally in blissful non-suffering *apatheia*. Nothing that happens in the world alters his blissful unperturbed serenity. Certainly God is not oblivious to the world. There is in him a steady disposition of benevolence toward his human creatures. But this disposition to act benevolently proceeds on its uninterrupted successful course whatever transpires in the world.

In sum, the Augustinian God turns out to be remarkably like the Stoic sage: devoid of passions, unfamiliar with longing, foreign to suffering, dwelling in steady bliss, exhibiting to others only benevolence. . . .

Augustine does indeed make clear that in one important respect God's life is not to be identified with our eudaemonistic ideal. In humanity's perfected existence *eros* is fixed steadily on God. God, in contrast, has no *eros*. Since there is in him no lack, he does not reach out to what would fulfill him. God reaches out exclusively in the mode of benevolence, not in the mode of *eros*. . . .

Are we to say, then, that in his picture of God as dwelling in blissful non-suffering apathy Augustine shows that, whatever be the qualifications he wishes to make for human beings, he still embraces the late antique, Stoic notion of what constitutes perfect existence? Is that the bottom line? Yes, I think we must indeed say this—not only for Augustine but for the tradition in general. Shaped as they were by the philosophical traditions of late antiquity, it was inconceivable to the church fathers that God's existence should be anything other than perfect and that ideal existence should be anything other than blissful. . . .

It is possible, however, to be struck by quite a different aspect of the picture; namely, God remains blissfully unperturbed while humanity drowns in misery.

When looked at in this way the picture's look is startlingly reversed, from the compelling to the grotesque. It is this grotesque look of the picture which has forcefully been called to our attention by various contemporary thinkers as they have launched an attack on the traditional picture of the apathetic God. . . .

Suffering love. Does God sufferingly experience what transpires in the world? The tradition said that he does not. The moderns say that he does—specifically, that he sufferingly experiences our suffering. Both parties agree that God loves the world. But the tradition held that God loves only in the mode of benevolence; it proposed construing all the biblical passages in the light of that conviction. The moderns insist that God's love includes love in the mode of sympathy. The moderns paint in attractive colors a moral ideal which is an alternative to that of the tradition, and point to various biblical passages speaking of God's suffering love—passages which the tradition, for centuries, has construed in its own way. The tradition, for its part, offered essentially two lines of defense. It argued that the attribution of emotions and suffering to God was incompatible with God's unconditionedness[3]. . . . And second, it offered a pair of what it took to be obvious truths: that suffering is incompatible with ideal existence, and that God's existence is immutably ideal. . . .

How can we advance from here? Perhaps by looking more intently than we have thus far at that claim of the tradition that God's love consists exclusively of benevolence. Benevolence in God was understood as his steady disposition to do good to his creatures. And since as long as there are creatures—no matter what their condition—there is scope for God's exercise of that disposition, and since his exercise of that disposition is never frustrated, God endlessly takes joy in this dimension of himself. He does not take joy—let us carefully note—in his awareness of the condition of his creatures. He does not delight in beholding the creaturely good that he has brought about. If that were the case, his joy would be conditional on the state of things other than himself. What God joyfully experiences is simply his own exercise of benevolence. God's awareness of our plunge into sin and suffering causes him no disturbance; his awareness of the arrival of his perfected kingdom will likewise give him no joy. For no matter what the state of the world, there is room for God's successful exercise of his steady disposition to do good; and it is in *that* exercise that he finds delight.

An analogue which comes to mind is that of a professional healthcare specialist. Perhaps when first she entered her profession she was disturbed by the pain and limping and death she saw. But that is now over. Now she is neither perturbed nor delighted by the condition of the people that she sees. What gives her delight is just her inner awareness of her own well-doing. And always she finds scope for well-doing—so long, of course, as she has clients. To those who are healthy she gives reassuring advice on health maintenance. To those who are ill she dispenses medicine and surgery. But it makes no difference to her whether or not her advice maintains the health of the healthy and whether or not her proffered concoctions and cuttings cure the illness of the ill. What makes a difference is just her steadiness in well-doing; in this and in this alone she finds her delight. If it falls within her competence she will, of course, cooperate in pursuing the elimination of small-pox; that is doing good. But should the news arrive of its elimination, she will not join the party; she has all along been celebrating the only thing she finds worth celebrating—namely, her own well-doing. She is a Stoic sage in the modern world.

I dare say that most of us find such a person thoroughly repugnant; that shows how far we are from the mentality of many of the intellectuals in the world of late antiquity. But beyond giving vent to our feelings of repugnance, let us consider whether the picture I have drawn is even coherent. Though this person neither rejoices nor suffers over anything in the condition of her patients, nonetheless she rejoices in her own doing of good. But what then does she take as *good*? What does she *value*? The health of her patients, one would suppose. Why otherwise would she give advice to the one on how to maintain his health, and chemicals to the other to recover his, and all the while rejoice, on account of thus acting, in her own doing of good? But if she does indeed value the health of her patients, then perforce she will also be glad over its presence and disturbed by its absence (when she knows about these). Yet we have pictured her as neither happy nor disturbed by anything other than her own well-doing. Have we not described what cannot be?

Perhaps in his description of moral action that great Stoic philosopher of the modern world, Immanuel Kant, can be of help to us here. In the moral dimension of our existence, the only thing good in itself is a good will, said Kant. Yet, of course, the moral person will do such things as act to advance the health of others. Insofar as she acts morally, however, she does not do so because her awareness of health in people gives her delight and her awareness of illness proves disturbing. She may indeed be so constituted that she does thus value health and sickness in others and acts thereon. But that is no moral credit to her. To be moral she must act not out of delight over health nor out of disturbance over illness but out of duty. She must act on some rule specifying what one ought to do in her sort of situation—a rule to which, by following, she accords "respect." That is what it is to value good will: to act out of respect for the moral law rather than out of one's natural likings and dislikings, rejoicings and grievings. And the moral person is the person who, wherever relevant, thus values the goodness of her will. Her valuing of that will mean, when her will is in fact good, that she will delight therein. But if she acts out of a desire to delight in having a good will, that too is not moral action; she must act out of respect for the moral law.

Suppose then that our health-care specialist values the goodness of her will and acts thereon by dutifully seeking to advance the health of her patients—delighting in thus acting. She may or may not also value the health of her patients, being disturbed by its absence and delighted by its presence. But if she does not in that way value her patients' health, that does not in any way militate against her delighting in her own well-doing.

We have here, then, a way of understanding how it can be that God delights in his doing good to human beings without either delighting in, or being disturbed by, the human condition. God acts out of duty. Thus acting, he values his own good will without valuing anything in his creation. If we interpret God's benevolence as his acting out of duty, then the traditional picture becomes coherent.

But of course it buys this coherence at great price. For to think thus of God is to produce conflict at a very deep level indeed with the Christian scriptures. These tell us that it is not out of duty but out of love that God blesses us, not out of obligation but out of grace that he delivers us. To construe God's love as purely benevolence and to construe his benevolence along Kantian-Stoic lines as his acting out of duty, is to be left without God's love.

So we are back with the model in which God values things other than his own good will—values positively some of the events and conditions in his creation, and values negatively others. To act out of love toward something other than oneself is to value that thing and certain states of that thing. And on this point it matters not whether the love be erotic or agapic. If one rejects the duty-model of God's action, then the biblical speech about God's prizing of justice and shalom in his creation will have to be taken at face value and not construed as meaning that God has a duty to work for justice and shalom....

I come then to this conclusion: The fact that the biblical writers speak of God as rejoicing and suffering over the state of the creation is not a superficial eliminable feature of their speech. It expresses themes deeply embedded in the biblical vision. God's love for his world is a rejoicing and suffering love. The picture of God as a Stoic sage, ever blissful and nonsuffering, is in deep conflict with the biblical picture.

But are we entitled to say that it is a *suffering* love, someone may ask—a love prompted by a *suffering* awareness of what goes on in the world. An unhappy awareness, Yes; but does it reach all the way to suffering?

What the Christian story says is that God the Father, out of love for humanity, delivered his only begotten Son to the suffering and abandonment and death on the cross. In the light of that, I think it grotesque to suggest that God's valuing of our human predicament was so mildly negative as to cause him no suffering....

Conclusion. In closing let me observe that if we agree that God both sufferingly and joyfully experiences this world of ours and of his, then at once there comes to mind a question which the tradition never asked; namely what in it causes him joy? And then at once there also comes to mind a vision of the relation between *our* suffering and joy and *God's* suffering and joy.... What comes to mind now is the vision of *aligning ourselves* with God's suffering and with his joy: of delighting over that which is such that his awareness of our delight gives him delight and of suffering over that which is such that his awareness of our suffering causes him suffering.... To some of the things of this world one can pay the tribute of recognizing in them worth sufficient to merit a love which plunges into suffering upon their destruction. In one's love one can say a "Yes" to the worth of persons or things and in one's suffering a "No" to their destruction. To friends and relatives one can pay the tribute of loving them enough to suffer upon their death. To justice among one's people one can pay the tribute of loving it enough to suffer upon its tyrannical denial. To the delights of music and voice and birdsong one can pay the tribute of loving them enough to suffer upon going deaf. One can pay to persons and things the existential triumph of suffering love. . . . Suffering is an essential element in that mode of life which says not only "No" to the misery of our world but "Yes" to its glories.

[This] is a better way [to go]. For it is in line with God's sufferings and God's joys. Instead of loving only God we will love what God loves, including God. For it is in the presence of justice and shalom among his human creatures that God delights, as it is for the full realization of justice and shalom in his perfected Kingdom that he works. . . .

Notes

1. Translated by R.S. Pine-Coffin (Harmondsworth, Middlesex: Penguin Books, 1961). All my citations from the *Confessions* are from this translation.

2. Augustine, *The City of God*, trans. Marcus Dods (New York: Random House, 1950). My citations are from this edition.

3. In an omitted section, Wolterstorff rejects this argument.

Discussion

1. Which view of God—suffering or impassible—is more useful when one is suffering? Defend your view.

2. The Bible speaks of a suffering God. But it also speaks of a jealous God and a God who forgets. Where does one draw the line in attributing human properties to God?

3. Wolterstorff suggests that there are practical advantages (i.e., the pursuit of justice and shalom) that result from his conception of God. How could classical theism ground such a pursuit?

Chapter 24

Prayer

WHETHER IT IS BECOMING TO PRAY

THOMAS AQUINAS*

Objections to Aquinas's view. *Objection* 1. It would seem that it is unbecoming to pray. Prayer seems to be necessary in order that we may make our needs known to the person to whom we pray. But according to Matth. vi. 32, *Your Father knoweth that you have need of all these things.* Therefore it is not becoming to pray to God.

Obj. 2. Further, by prayer we bend the mind of the person to whom we pray, so that he may do what is asked of him. But God's mind is unchangeable and inflexible, according to 1 Kings xv. 29, *But the Triumpher in Israel will not spare, and will not be moved to repentance.* Therefore it is not fitting that we should pray to God.

Obj. 3. Further, it is more liberal to give to one that asks not, than to one who asks, because, according to Seneca (*De Benefic.* ii. 1), *nothing is bought more dearly than what is bought with prayers.* But God is supremely liberal. Therefore it would seem unbecoming to pray to God.

Aquinas's view. *On the contrary*, It is written (Luke xviii.1): *We ought always to pray, and not to faint.*

I answer that, Among the ancients there was a three-fold error concerning prayer. Some held that human

affairs are not ruled by Divine providence; whence it would follow that it is useless to pray and to worship God at all: of these it is written (Malach. iii. 14): *You have said: He laboreth in vain that serveth God.* Another opinion held that all things, even in human affairs, happen of necessity, whether by reason of the unchangeableness of Divine providence, or through the compelling influence of the stars, or on account of the connection of causes: and this opinion also excluded the utility of prayer. There was a third opinion of those who held that human affairs are indeed ruled by Divine providence, and that they do not happen of necessity; yet they deemed the disposition of Divine providence to be changeable, and that it is changed by prayers and other things pertaining to the worship of God. All these opinions were disproved in the First Part [of this work]. Wherefore it behooves us so to account for the utility of prayer as neither to impose necessity on human affairs subject to Divine providence, nor to imply changeableness on the part of the Divine disposition.

In order to throw light on this question we must consider that Divine providence disposes not only what effects shall take place, but also from what causes and in what order these effects shall proceed. Now among other causes human acts are the causes of certain effects. Wherefore it must be that men do certain actions, not that thereby they may change the Divine disposition, but that by those actions they may achieve certain effects according to the order of the Divine disposition: and the same is to be said of natural causes. And so is it with regard to prayer. For we pray not that

---

* Thomas Aquinas (1224–74) was a monk who taught at the University of Paris.

we may change the Divine disposition, but that we may impetrate that which God has disposed to be fulfilled by our prayers, in other words *that by asking, men may deserve to receive what Almighty God from eternity has disposed to give* as Gregory says (*Dial.* i. 8).

Aquinas answers the objections. *Reply Obj.* 1. We need to pray to God, not in order to make known to Him our needs or desires but that we ourselves may be reminded of the necessity of having recourse to God's help in these matters.

Reply Obj. 2. As stated above, our motive in praying is, not that we may change the Divine disposition, but that, by our prayers we may obtain what God has appointed.

Reply Obj. 3. God bestows many things on us out of His liberality, even without our asking for them: but that He wishes to bestow certain things on us at our asking, is for the sake of our good, namely, that we may acquire confidence in having recourse to God, and that we may recognize in Him the Author of our goods. Hence Chrysostom says: *Think what happiness is granted thee, what honor bestowed on thee, when thou conversest with God in prayer, when thou talkest with Christ, when thou askest what thou wilt, whatever thou desirest.*

Discussion

1. From this brief selection, what can be learned about Aquinas's view of God?

2. What problems do divine immutability, providence, and goodness create for prayer?

3. Since it is impossible for humans to have any effect upon God, prayer must affect the person praying. How, according to Aquinas, does prayer affect the person praying? Are these benefits adequate?

PETITIONARY PRAYER

ELEONORE STUMP*

Introduction. Ordinary Christian believers of every period have in general taken prayer to be fundamentally a request made of God for something specific believed to be good by the one praying. The technical name for such prayer is "impetration"; I am going to refer to it by the more familiar designation "petitionary prayer." There are, of course, many important kinds of prayer which are not requests; for example, most of what is sometimes called "the higher sort of prayer"—praise, adoration, thanksgiving—does not consist in requests and is not included under petitionary prayer. But basic, common petitionary prayer poses problems that do not arise in connection with the more contemplative varieties of prayer, and it is petitionary prayer with its special problems that I want to examine in this essay.

. . . I want to . . . concentrate on just one problem. It is, I think, the problem stemming from petitionary prayer which has most often occurred to ordinary Christian believers from the Patristic period to the present. . . .

Put roughly and succinctly, the problem comes to this: is a belief in the efficacy and usefulness of petitionary prayer consistent with a belief in an omniscient, omnipotent, perfectly good God? It is, therefore, a problem only on certain assumptions drawn from an ordinary, orthodox, traditional view of God and of petitionary prayer. If one thinks, for example, as D.Z. Phillips does,[1] that all "real" petitionary prayer is reducible to the petition "Thy will be done," then the problem I want to discuss evaporates. And if one thinks of God as the unknowable, non-denumerable, ultimate reality, which is not an entity at all, the problem I am interested in does not even

arise. The cases which concern me in this essay are those in which someone praying a petitionary prayer makes a specific request freely (at least in his own view) of an omniscient, omnipotent, perfectly good God, conceived of in the traditional orthodox way. I am specifying that the prayers are made freely because I want to discuss this problem on the assumption that man has free will and that not everything is predetermined. I am making this assumption, first because I want to examine the problem of petitionary prayer as it arises for ordinary Christian believers, and I think their understanding of the problem typically includes the assumption that man has free will, and secondly because adopting the opposite view enormously complicates the attempt to understand and justify petitionary prayer. If all things are predetermined—and worse, if they are all predetermined by the omnipotent and omniscient God to whom one is praying—it is much harder to conceive of a satisfactory justification for petitionary prayer. One consequence of my making this assumption is that I will not be drawing on important traditional Protestant accounts of prayer such as those given by Calvin and Luther, for instance, since while they may be thoughtful, interesting accounts, they assume God's complete determination of everything. . . .

The general problem. We can, I think, generalize these arguments to all petitionary prayer by means of a variation on the argument from evil against God's existence. (The argument that follows does not seem to me to be an acceptable one, but it is the sort of argument that underlies the objections to petitionary prayer which I have been presenting. I will say something about what I think are the flaws in this argument later in the essay.)

(1) A perfectly good being never makes the world worse than it would otherwise be if he can avoid doing so.

---

* Eleonore Stump is the Robert J. Henle Professor of Philosophy at St. Louis University.

The phrase "than it would otherwise be" here should be construed as "than the world would have been had he not brought about or omitted to bring about some state of affairs." In other words, a perfectly good being never makes the world, in virtue of what he himself does or omits to do, worse than it would have been had he not done or omitted to do something or other. *Mutatis mutandis* [changing equals for equals], the same remarks apply to "than it would otherwise be" in (4) and (7) below.

(2) An omniscient and omnipotent being can avoid doing anything which it is not logically necessary for him to do.

∴ (3) An omniscient, omnipotent, perfectly good being never makes the world worse than it would otherwise be unless it is logically necessary for him to do so. (1, 2)

(4) A perfectly good being always makes the world better than it would otherwise be if he can do so.

(5) An omniscient and omnipotent being can do anything which it is not logically impossible for him to do.

∴ (6) An omniscient, omnipotent, perfectly good being always makes the world better than it would otherwise be unless it is logically impossible for him to do so. (4, 5)

(7) It is never logically necessary for an omniscient, omnipotent, perfectly good being to make the world worse than it would otherwise be; it is never logically impossible for an omniscient, omnipotent, perfectly good being to make the world better than it would otherwise be.

∴ (8) An omniscient, omnipotent, perfectly good being never makes the world worse than it would otherwise be and always makes the world better than it would otherwise be. (3, 6, 7)

This subconclusion implies that unless the world is infinitely improvable, either the world is or will be absolutely perfect or there is no omniscient, omnipotent, perfectly good being. In other words, (8) with the addition of a pair of premises—

i. The world is not infinitely improvable

and

ii. It is not the case that the world is or will be absolutely perfect (i.e., there is and always will be evil in the world)—

implies the conclusion of the argument from evil. That is not a surprising result since this argument is dependent on the argument from evil.

(9) What is requested in every petitionary prayer is or results in a state of affairs the realization of which would make the world either worse or better than it would otherwise be (that is, than it would have been had that state of affairs not been realized). . . .

∴ (10) If what is requested in a petitionary prayer is or results in a state of affairs the realization of which would make the world worse than it would otherwise be, an omniscient, omnipotent, perfectly good being will not fulfill that request. (8)

∴ (11) If what is requested in a petitionary prayer is or results in a state of affairs the realization of which would make the world better than it would otherwise be, an omniscient, omnipotent, perfectly good being will bring about that state of affairs even if no prayer for its realization has been made (8)....

∴ (12) Petitionary prayer effects no change. (9, 10, 11)

There is, of course, a sense in which the offering of a prayer is itself a new state of affairs and accompanies or results in natural, psychological changes in the one praying, but step (12) ought to be understood as saying that no prayer is itself efficacious in causing a change of the sort it was designed to cause. An argument which might be thought to apply here, invalidating the inference to the conclusion (13), is that prayer need not effect any change in order to be considered efficacious, provided the offering of the prayer itself is a sufficient reason in God's view for God's fulfillment of the prayer. In other words, if, for certain reasons apart from consideration of a prayer for a state of affairs *S*, God has determined to bring about *S*, a prayer for *S* may still be considered to be efficacious if and only if God would have brought about *S* just in response to the prayer for *S*. But I think that even if this view is correct, it does not in fact invalidate the inference to (13)....

∴ (13) Petitionary prayer is pointless. (12)

The basic strategy of this argument is an attempt to show that there is an inconsistency between God's goodness and the efficacy of petitionary prayer; but it is possible to begin with other divine attributes and make a case for a similar inconsistency, so that we can have other, very different arguments to the same conclusion, namely, that petitionary prayer is pointless. Perhaps the most formidable of such alternative arguments is the one based on God's immutability,

an argument the strategy of which can be roughly summarized in this way. Before a certain petitionary prayer is made, it is the case either that God will bring about the state of affairs requested in the prayer or that he will not bring it about. He cannot have left the matter open since doing so would imply a subsequent change in him and he is immutable. Either way, since he is immutable, the prayer itself can effect no change in the state of affairs and hence is pointless. Even leaving aside problems of foreknowledge and free will to which this argument (or attempted objections to it) may give rise, I think that orthodox theology will find no real threat in the argument because of the doctrine of God's eternality. However problematic that doctrine may be in itself, it undercuts arguments such as this one because it maintains God's atemporality. My thirteen-step argument against petitionary prayer is, then, not the only argument rejecting petitionary prayer on theistic principles, but it (or some argument along the same lines) does, I think, make the strongest case against petitionary prayer, given Christian doctrine....

Friendship and prayer. Judaeo-Christian concepts of God commonly represent God as loving mankind and wanting to be loved by men in return. Such anthropomorphic talk is in sharp contrast to the more sophisticated-sounding language of the Hellenized and scholastic arguments considered so far. But a certain sort of anthropomorphism is as much a part of Christianity as is Thomas's "perfect being theology," and it, too, builds on intricate philosophical analysis, beginning perhaps with Boethuis's attempt in *Contra Eutychen et Nestorium* to explain what it means to say of something that it is a person. So to say that God loves men and wants to be loved in return is to say something that has a place in philosophical theology and is indispensable to Christian doctrine. Throughout the Old and New Testaments, the type of loving relationship wanted between man and God is represented by various images, for example, sometimes as the relationship between husband and wife, sometimes as that between father and child. And sometimes (in the Gospel of John, for instance) it is also represented as the relationship between true friends.[2] But if the relationship between God and human beings is to be one which at least sometimes can be accurately represented as the love of true friendship, then there is a problem for both parties to the relationship, because plainly it will not be easy for there to be friendship between an omniscient, omnipotent, perfectly good person and a fallible, finite, imperfect person. The troubles of generating and maintaining friendship in such a case are surely the perfect paradigms of which the troubles of friendship between a Rockefeller child and a slum child are just pale copies. Whatever other troubles there are for friendship in these cases, there are at least two dangers for the disadvantaged or inferior member of the pair. First, he can be so overcome by the advantages or superiority of his "friend" that he becomes simply a shadowy reflection of the other's personality, a slavish follower who slowly loses all sense of his own tastes and desires and will. Some people, of course, believe that just this sort of attitude towards God is what Christianity wants and gets from the best of its adherents; but I think that such a belief goes counter to the spirit of the Gospels, for example, and I don't think that it can be found even in such intense mystics as St. Teresa and St. John of the Cross. Secondly, in addition to the danger of becoming completely dominated, there is the danger of becoming spoiled in the way that members of a royal family in a ruling house are subject to. Because of the power at their disposal in virtue of their connections, they often become tyrannical, willful, indolent, self-indulgent, and the like. The greater the discrepancy in status and condition between the two friends, the greater the danger of even inadvertently overwhelming and oppressing or overwhelming and spoiling the lesser member of the pair; and if he is overwhelmed in either of these ways, the result will be replacement of whatever kind of friendship there might have been with one or another sort of using. Either the superior member of the pair will use the lesser as his lackey, or the lesser will use the superior as his personal power source. To put it succinctly, then, if God wants some kind of true friendship with men, he will have to find a way of guarding against both kinds of overwhelming.

It might occur to someone to think that even if we assume the view that God wants friendship between himself and human beings, it does not follow that he will have any of the problems just sketched, because he is omnipotent. If he wants friendship of this sort with men, one might suppose, let him just will it and it will be his. I do not want to stop here to argue against this view in detail, but I do want just to suggest that there is reason for thinking it to be incoherent, at least on the assumption of free will adopted at the beginning of this essay, because it is hard to see how God could bring about such a friendship magically, by means of his omnipotence, and yet permit the people involved to have free will. If he could do so, he could make a person freely love him in the right sort of way, and it does not seem reasonable to think he could do so. On the face of it, then, omnipotence alone does not do away with the two dangers for friendship that I sketched above. But the institution of petitionary prayer, I think, can be understood as a safeguard against these dangers.

It is easiest to argue that petitionary prayer serves such a function in the case of a man who prays for himself. In praying for himself, he makes an explicit request for help, and thereby he acknowledges a need or a desire and his dependence on God for satisfying that need or desire. If he gets what he prayed for, he will be in a position to attribute his good fortune to God's doing and to be grateful to God for what God has given him. If we add the undeniable uncertainty of his getting what he prays for, then we will have safeguards against what I will call (for lack of a better phrase) overwhelming spoiling. These conditions make the act of asking a safeguard against tyrannical and self-indulgent pride, even if the one praying thinks of himself grandly as having God on his side.

We can see how the asking guards against the second danger, of oppressive overwhelming, if we look for a moment at the function of roughly similar asking for help when both the one asking and the one asked are human beings. Suppose a teacher sees that one of his students is avoiding writing a paper and is thereby storing up trouble for himself at the end of the term. And suppose the student *asks* the teacher for extra help in organizing working time and scheduling the various parts of the work. In that case I think the teacher can without any problem give the student what he needs, provided, of course, that the teacher is willing to do as much for any other student, and so on. But suppose, on the other hand, that the student does not ask the teacher for help and that the teacher instead calls the student at home and simply presents him with the help he needs in scheduling and discipline. The teacher's proposals in that case are more than likely to strike the student as meddling interference, and he is likely to respond with more or less polite variations on "Who asked you?" and "Mind your own business." Those responses, I think, are healthy and just. If the student were having ordinary difficulties getting his work done and yet docilely and submissively accepted the teacher's unrequested scheduling of his time, he would have taken the first step in the direction of unhealthy passivity towards his teacher. And if he and his teacher developed that sort of relationship, he could end by becoming a lackey-like reflection of his teacher. Bestowing at least some benefits only in response to requests for them is a safeguard against such an outcome when the members of the relationship are not equally balanced.

It becomes much harder to argue for this defense of prayer as soon as the complexity of the case is increased even just a little. Take, for example, Monica's praying for her son Augustine. There is nothing in Monica's praying for Augustine which shows that *Augustine* recognizes that *he* has a need for God's help or that he will be grateful if God gives him what *Monica* prays for. Nor is it plain that *Monica's* asking shields Augustine from oppressive overwhelming by God. So it seems as if the previous arguments fail in this case. But consider again the case in which a teacher sees that a student of his could use help but does not feel that he can legitimately volunteer his help unasked. Suppose that John, a friend of that student, comes to see the teacher and says, "I don't know if you've noticed, but Jim is having trouble getting to his term paper. And unless he gets help, I think he won't do it at all and will be in danger of flunking the course." If the teacher now goes to help Jim and is rudely or politely asked "What right have you got to interfere?" he'll say, "Well, in fact, your friend came to me and *asked* me to help." And if John is asked the same question, he will probably reply, "But I'm your friend; I had to do *something*." I think, then, that because John asks the teacher, the teacher is in a position to help with less risk of oppressive meddling than before. Obviously, he cannot go very far without incurring that risk as fully as before; and perhaps the most he can do if he wants to avoid oppressive meddling is to try to elicit from *Jim* in genuinely uncoercive ways a request for help. And, of course, I chose Monica and Augustine to introduce this case because, as Augustine tells it in the *Confessions*, God responded to Monica's fervent and continued prayers for Augustine's salvation by arranging the circumstances of Augustine's life in such a way that finally Augustine himself freely asked God for salvation.

One might perhaps think that there is something superfluous and absurd in God's working through the intermediary of prayer in this way. If Jim's friend can justify his interference on the grounds that he is Jim's friend and has to do *something*, God can dispense with this sort of petitionary prayer, too. He can give aid unasked on the grounds that he is the *creator* and has to do something. But suppose that Jim and John are only acquaintances who have discussed nothing more than their schoolwork; and suppose that John, by overhearing Jim's phone conversations, has come to believe that all Jim's academic troubles are just symptoms of problems he is having with his parents. If John asks the teacher to help Jim with his personal problems, and if the teacher begins even a delicate attempt to do so by saying that John asked him to do so, he and John could both properly be told to mind their own business. It is not the *status* of his relationship or even the depth of his care and compassion for Jim which puts John in a position to defend himself by saying "But I'm your friend." What protects John against the charge of oppressive meddling is rather the degree to which Jim has freely, willingly, shared his life and thoughts and feelings with John. So John's line of defense against the charge of oppressive meddling can be attributed to God only if the person God is to aid has willingly shared his thoughts and feelings and the like with God. But it is hard to imagine anyone putting himself in such a relation to a person he believes to be omnipotent and good without his also *asking* for whatever help he needs.

Even if the argument can be made out so far, one might be inclined to think that it will not be sufficient to show the compatibility of God's goodness with the practice of petitionary prayer. If one supposes that God brought Augustine to Christianity in response to Monica's prayers, what is one to say about Augustine's fate if Monica had not prayed for him? And what does this view commit one to maintain about people who neither pray for themselves nor are prayed for? It looks as if an orthodox Christian who accepts the argument about petitionary prayer so far will be committed to a picture of this sort. God is analogous to a human father with two very different children. Both Old and New Testaments depict God as doing many good things for men without being asked to do so, and this human father, too, does unrequested good things for both his children. But one child, who is healthy and normal, with healthy normal relations to his father, makes frequent requests of the father which the father responds to and in virtue of which he bestows benefits on the child. The other child is selectively blind, deaf, dumb, and suffering from whatever other maladies are necessary to make it plausible that he does not even know he has a father. Now either there are some benefits that the father will never bestow unless and until he is asked; and in that case he will do less for his defective child, who surely has more need of his help than does the healthy child. Or, on the other hand, he will bestow all his benefits unasked on the defective child, and then he seems to make a mockery of his practice with the normal child of bestowing some benefits only in response to requests—he is, after all, willing to bestow the same benefits without being asked. So it seems that we are still left with the problem we started with: either God is not perfectly good or the practice of petitionary prayer is pointless. But suppose the father always meets the defective child's needs and desires even though the child never comes to know of the existence of his father. The child knows only that he is always taken care of, and when he needs something, he gets what he needs. It seems to me intuitively clear that such a practice runs a great risk, at least, of making the defective child willful and tyrannical. But even if the defective child is not in danger of being made worse in some respects in this situation, still it seems plain that he would be better off if the father could manage to put the child in a position to know his father and to frame a request for what he wants. So I think a good father will fulfill the child's needs unasked; but I think that he can do so without making a mockery of his practice of bestowing benefits in response to requests only if putting the child in a position to make requests is among his first concerns.

And as for the question whether God would have saved Augustine without Monica's prayers, I think that there is intermediate ground between the assertion that Monica's prayers are necessary to Augustine's salvation, which seems to impugn God's goodness, and the claim that they are altogether without effect, which undercuts petitionary prayer. It is possible, for example, to argue that God would have saved Augustine without Monica's prayers but not in the same amount of time or not by the same process or not with the same effect. Augustine, for instance, might have been converted to Christianity but not in such a way as to become one of its most powerful authorities for centuries.

With all this, I have still looked only at cases that are easy for my position; when we turn to something like a prayer for, say, victims of an earthquake in Guatemala . . . it is much harder to know what to say. And perhaps it is simply too hard to come up with a reasonable solution here because we need more work on the problem of evil. Why would a good God permit the occurrence of earthquakes in the first place? Do the reasons for his permitting the earthquake affect his afterwards helping the country involved? Our inclination is surely to say that a good God must *in any case* help the earthquake victims, so that in this instance at any rate it is pointless to pray. But plainly we also have strong inclinations to say that a good God must in any case prevent earthquakes in populated areas. And since orthodox Christianity is committed to distrusting these latter inclinations, it is at least at sea about the former ones. Without more work on the problem of evil, it is hard to know what to say about the difference prayer might make in this sort of case.

. . . Now suppose it is true that God would bring about his kingdom on earth even if an individual Christian such as Jimmy Carter did not pray for it. It does not follow in this case, however, that the prayer in question is pointless and makes no difference. Suppose no one prayed for the advent of God's kingdom on earth or felt a need or desire for those millennial times strongly enough to pray for them. It seems unreasonable to think that God could bring about his earthly kingdom under those conditions, or if he could, that

it would be the state of affairs just described, in which earth is populated by people who *freely* love God. And if so, then making [such] requests . . . resembles other, more ordinary activities in which only the effort of a whole group is sufficient to achieve the desired result. One man can't put out a forest fire, but if everyone in the vicinity of a forest fire realized that fact and on that basis decided not to try, the fire would rage out of control. So . . . too, it seems possible to justify petitionary prayer without impugning God's goodness.

Summary, review and conclusion. Obviously, the account I have given is just a preliminary sketch for the full development of this solution, and a good deal more work needs to be done on the problem. Nonetheless, I think that this account is on the right track and that there is a workable solution to the problem of petitionary prayer which can be summarized in this way. God must work through the intermediary of prayer, rather than doing everything on his own initiative, for man's sake. Prayer acts as a kind of buffer between man and God. By safeguarding the weaker member of the relation from the dangers of overwhelming domination and overwhelming spoiling, it helps to promote and preserve a close relationship between an omniscient, omnipotent, perfectly good person and a fallible, finite, imperfect person. There is, of course, something counter-intuitive in this notion that prayer acts as a buffer; prayer of all sorts is commonly and I think correctly said to have as one of its main functions the production of closeness between man and God. But not just any sort of closeness will result in friendship, and promoting the appropriate sort of closeness will require inhibiting or preventing inappropriate sorts of closeness, so that a relationship of friendship depends on the maintenance of both closeness and distance between the two friends. And while I do not mean to denigrate the importance of prayer in producing and preserving the appropriate sort of closeness, I think the problem of petitionary prayer at issue here is best solved by focusing on the distance necessary for friendship and the function of petitionary prayer in maintaining that distance.

As for the argument against prayer which I laid out at the start of the essay, it seems to me that the flaw lies in step (7), that it is never logically necessary for God to make the world worse than it would otherwise be and never logically impossible for him to make the world better than it would otherwise be. To take a specific example from among those discussed so far, orthodox Christianity is committed to claiming that the advent of God's kingdom on earth, in which all people freely love God, would make the world better than it would otherwise be. But I think that it is not possible for God to *make* the world better in this way, because I think it is not possible for him to *make* men *freely* do anything. And in general, if it is arguable that God's doing good things just in virtue of men's requests protects men from the dangers described and preserves them in the right relationship to God, then it is not the case that it is always logically possible for God to make the world better and never logically necessary for him to make the world worse than it would otherwise be. If men do not always pray for all the good things they might and ought to pray for, then in some cases either God will not bring about some good thing or he will do so but at the expense of the good wrought and preserved by petitionary prayer.

It should be plain that there is nothing in this analysis of prayer which *requires* that God fulfil every prayer; asking God for something is not in itself a sufficient condition for God's doing what he is asked. Christian writings are full of examples of prayers which are not answered, and there are painful cases of unanswered prayer in which the one praying must be tempted more to the belief that God is his implacable enemy than to the sentimental-seeming belief that God is his friend. This essay proposes no answer for these difficulties. They require a long, hard, careful look at the problem of evil, and that falls just outside the scope of this essay. . . .

Notes

1. D.Z. Phillips, *The Concept of Prayer* (New York, 1966), pp. 112 ff.

2. See especially John 15: 12–15.

Discussion

1. Show how the traditional doctrine of immutability or omniscience might raise a similar problem for petitionary prayer as does divine goodness.

2. Stump's defense of petitionary prayer relies on our intuitions concerning friendship, particularly friendship among non-equals. How does prayer affect the proper relationship between God and humans? Does Stump's account square with your intuitions about friendship?

3. Stump's defense of petitionary prayer focuses more (but not exclusively) on the proper relationship between humans and God than on the effect of prayer on future states of affairs. Does this adequately separate her view from a view that she intends to criticize—that the effect of prayer is solely on the one praying and not on future states of affairs?

Chapter 25

Is There a Hell?

UNIVERSALISM, HELL, AND THE FATE OF THE IGNORANT

STEPHEN T. DAVIS*

Introduction. Christianity traditionally teaches that at least some people, after death, live eternally apart from God. Let us call those who believe this doctrine *separationists*, because they hold that these people are eternally separated both from God and from the people who are with God. Some Christians, on the other hand, espouse the quite different doctrine known as *universalism*. Universalists believe that all human beings will ultimately live eternally with God, i.e., that no one will be eternally condemned.

. . . Though I am sympathetic with the intentions of those who espouse universalism, I am not a universalist myself, and will argue against the doctrine in this essay. What I will do here is: (1) state the strongest doctrine of universalism . . .; (2) present the strongest arguments in favor of it . . .; (3) reply to these arguments from a separationist standpoint; and (4) make a case for separationism. . . .

Universalism. Let me now sketch what I take to be a strong doctrine of universalism: God does indeed hate sin and does indeed judge sinners. But God's judgment is always therapeutic; it is designed to bring people to repentance. Thus God's wrath is an integral

part of God's loving strategy for reconciling people to God. Some are reconciled to God in this life; some die unreconciled. But God continues to love even those who die apart from God, and to work for their reconciliation. If there is a hell, it exists only for a time, i.e., until the last recalcitrant sinner decides to say yes to God. It is *possible* that hell will exist forever because it is possible some will deny God forever. But after death, God has unlimited time, arguments, and resources to convince people to repent. God will not force anyone into the kingdom; the freedom of God's creatures is always respected. But because of the winsomeness of God's love, we can be sure that God will emerge victorious and that all persons will eventually be reconciled to God. We are all sinners and deserve punishment, but God's love is so great and God's grace so attractive that eventually all persons will be reconciled to God. This, then, is what I take to be a strong version of universalism. Now, what about the arguments in favor? Let me mention five of them.

(1) *The Bible implies that universalism is true.* Many universalists are quite prepared to admit that their doctrine is not taught in the Bible and indeed that separationism seems much more clearly taught. Nevertheless, they do typically argue that universalism is at least implied or suggested in various texts. First, it can be pointed out that many texts show that it is God's intention that everyone be reconciled to God. Second, it can be shown that the work of God's grace in Christ was designed for the salvation of everyone. Third, texts can be cited in which God's total victory is proclaimed and in which it is said that everything

---

* Stephen T. Davis is Professor of Philosophy Emeritus at Claremont McKenna College.

will ultimately be reconciled to God. Finally, there are texts which seem to the universalists explicitly to predict that *all* will eventually be reconciled to God, that *every* knee shall bow at Christ's feet, that God so loves the world.[1] . . .

(2) *How can God's purposes be frustrated?* Universalists sometimes argue as follows: eternal sin and eternal punishment would obviously frustrate God's intention that no one be eternally lost. But if God is truly sovereign, how can any divine intention be frustrated? If separationism is true, some will eternally resist God and it follows that God is at least a partial failure. Surely if God is omnipotent nothing can eternally frustrate the divine aims; if it is God's aim that all be rescued, all *will* be rescued.

(3) *How can a just God condemn people to eternal torment?* Universalists frequently argue that no one deserves *eternal* punishment. Perhaps terrible sinners deserve to suffer terribly for a terribly long time. But surely sin should be punished according to its gravity; why do they deserve to suffer for an *infinitely* long time? They certainly do not cause anyone else (or even God) *eternal* sorrow or pain. Suppose we decide that some tyrant, say Nero, deserves to suffer a year in hell for every person he ever killed, injured, treated unfairly, insulted, or even inconvenienced. Suppose further that on this criterion he deserves to suffer for 20,000 years. The problem, however, is that once he has served this sentence he will not have made even the slightest dent in eternity. According to separationism, he must suffer forever. Is this just? It does not seem so. (And this is not even to speak of more run-of-the-mill sinners who perhaps never cause anyone serious harm.)

(4) *How can the Blessed experience joy in heaven if friends and loved ones are in hell?* Obviously (so universalists will argue), they can't. People can only know joy and happiness in heaven if everyone else is or eventually will be there too. If the Blessed are to experience joy in heaven, as Christian tradition says they are, universalism must be true.

(5) *What about the fate of those who die in ignorance of Christ?* Christianity has traditionally taught that salvation is to be found only in Christ. Jesus is reported as having claimed this very thing: "I am the way, and the truth, and the life; No one comes to the Father but by me" (John 14:6). And this claim seems to dovetail well with standard Christian notions about sin and salvation: there is nothing we can do to save ourselves; all our efforts at self-improvement fail; all we can do is trust in God as revealed in Christ; those who do not know God as revealed in Christ are condemned. And surely—so universalists argue—the traditional notion is unfair. It is not right to condemn to hell those who die in ignorance of Christ.

Suppose there was a woman named Oohku who lived from 370 to 320 BCE in the interior of Borneo. Obviously, she never heard of Jesus Christ or the Judeo-Christian God; she was never baptized, nor did she ever make any institutional or psychological commitment to Christ or to the Christian church. She *couldn't* have done these things; she was simply born in the wrong place and at the wrong time. Is it right for God to condemn this woman to eternal hell just because she was never able to come to God through Christ? Of course not. The only way Oohku can be treated fairly by God is if universalism is true. God is just and loving; thus, universalism is true.

Critique of universalism. These are the best arguments for universalism that I can think of. We now need to see how separationists will handle them and defend their own doctrine.

Let us begin with the biblical argument of the universalist. The first thing to notice is that separationists like me do not deny that God desires the salvation of all persons and that Christ's atoning work was designed to rescue everyone. Accordingly, the texts cited under these headings . . . do not tell against separationism. As to the texts that emphasize God's total victory and which seem to universalists to predict universal salvation, the separationist replies that this is not their proper interpretation. To affirm that God is ultimately victorious over all enemies and that God's authority will one day be universally recognized is one thing, and will be agreed on by all Christians. But to say that every person will eventually be reconciled to God is quite another, and can only be based on a surprisingly literalistic interpretation of such terms as "all," "all things," "every knee," and "the world" in the passages cited. It is odd that universalists, who typically protest against literalistic interpretations of the many texts that seem to teach separationism (see below), appear themselves to adopt a kind of literalism here. They need to approach the passages cited with a bit more hermeneutical subtlety; they need to ask (especially in the light of other texts—again, see below) whether this is what these passages really mean.

Furthermore, the fact that these "universalistic passages" appear in many of the same texts in which separationism seems clearly taught ought to make us doubt that universalists interpret them correctly. . . .

Furthermore, separationists can produce a biblical argument of their own, one which is much more compelling. For the reality of hell—and even of eternal hell[2]—is spoken of often in the New Testament, and seems inextricably tied to such major themes in New Testament theology as God, sin, judgment, atonement, and reconciliation. Thus it would seem that the introduction of universalism would require severe changes at various other points in the traditional Christian scheme of salvation. . . . In fact, if there is no hell it is hard to see, in New Testament terms, why there would be any need for atonement or a savior from sin. . . . Furthermore, it seems methodologically odd for a person both to deny the reality of eternal hell and (because of biblical teaching and Christian tradition) affirm the reality of heaven. For both seem to stand on an equally firm exegetical and traditional foundation. It is clear that for most universalists, exegetical considerations are outweighed by philosophical ones.

My reply to the biblical argument of the universalist, then, is as follows. It is true that when read in a certain way, a few New Testament and especially Pauline texts might lead one toward universalism. But a careful look shows that not even those texts actually imply universalism. Furthermore, biblically oriented Christians believe that problematical passages on any topic are to be interpreted in the light of the testimony of the whole of scripture, and universalism—so I have argued—is inconsistent with that testimony.

Let me confess that I would deeply like universalism to be true. Like all Christians, I would find it wonderfully comforting to believe that all people will be citizens of the kingdom of God, and certain thorny intellectual problems, especially the problem of evil, might be easier to solve if universalism were true. But as a matter of theological method, we cannot affirm a doctrine just because we would like it to be true. The fact is that separationism is taught in the Bible and that the so-called "universalistic passages" do not imply universalism. That is enough for me; that is why I am a separationist. Philosophical and theological arguments over what God should do are outweighed by the teaching of Scripture. God has revealed to us a doctrine of eternal judgment; we had best accept it. That God has not also revealed to us how to reconcile this doctrine with our understanding of God's love creates a theological problem which we must do our best to solve.

Separationism. I will now briefly sketch the separationist doctrine I believe in and am prepared to defend. It differs from some traditional theological accounts at two points: (1) For exegetical reasons I do not believe people in hell suffer horrible fiery agony; and (2) while I believe hell in some sense can be spoken of as punishment, I do not believe it is a place where God, so to speak, gets even with those who deny God. It is not primarily a place of retribution.

We know little about hell. Much of what the New Testament says is clearly metaphorical or symbolic. For example, the New Testament uses the metaphor of fire to convey the suffering of people in hell. But this need not mean that condemned people actually suffer the pain of burns. Mark 9:48 describes hell as a place where "the worm does not die" and "the fire is not quenched." Why take the second literally and not the first? I would say both are metaphors of the eternality of hell. The parable of the rich man and Lazarus in Luke 16:19–31 has been taken by some interpreters as a picture of the after-life, but this does not seem sensible. It is a parable, i.e., a made-up story designed to convey a certain religious message. Furthermore, it is difficult to imagine that heaven and hell could be separated by a "great chasm" which cannot be crossed but across which communication can take place. There are many biblical metaphors for hell, e.g., everlasting fire, bottomless pit, outer darkness, place of weeping and gnashing of teeth, place of no rest, place where the uttermost farthing must be paid.[3] None, I would argue, is a literal description.

Hell is a place of separation from God. Not total separation, of course—that would mean hell would not exist. Furthermore, the biblical tradition denies that anything or anyone can ever be totally separated from God.... But hell is separation from God as the source of true love, joy, peace, and light. It is not a place of agony, torment, torture, and utter horror (here I am opposing the lurid and even sadistic pictures of hell envisioned by some Christian thinkers). But there is no deep or ultimate joy there and I believe its citizens are largely miserable. To be apart from the source of love, joy, peace, and light is to live miserably.

A defense of separationism. *Why are the damned in hell?* I have already ruled out retribution or any notion of God's "getting even" with them.[4] To put it radically, I believe they are in hell because they choose to be in hell; no one is sent to hell against his or her will. Sadly, some people choose to live their lives apart from God, harden their hearts, and will continue to do so after death; some will doubtless do so forever. For such people, living in God's presence might well seem worse than living in God's absence. Allowing them to live forever in hell is simply God's continuing to grant them the freedom that they enjoyed in this life to say yes or no to God. I nevertheless suspect that people in hell are deeply remorseful. Can people both freely choose hell over heaven, knowing they would be unable to endure heaven, but still be full of remorse that they cannot happily choose heaven? I believe this is quite possible.

Is the existence of hell consistent with God's love and power? Yes, it is. Some Christians try to justify the existence of hell by speaking of it as the "natural consequence" of a life of sin. I accept the notion that hell is the natural consequence of a life of sin (and it is in this sense that hell is a punishment). But this in itself does not justify God in sending people to hell, for it does not justify the divinely-ordained laws of natural necessity that make hell sin's natural consequence. I claim, then, that the people who are in hell are there because they freely choose it, i.e., freely choose not to live in God's presence. If so, then hell can be an expression not only of divine justice but of divine love.

Response to philosophical objections to separationism. I have been replying to the biblical argument of the universalist. Now I must comment on the others.

How can God's purposes be frustrated? I agree that God desires the salvation of everyone; thus separationism implies that at least one of God's desires is not satisfied: some people will be lost. How can this be, if God is sovereign? The answer is that God created us as free agents; God gave us the ability to say yes or no to God. One of the risks God ran in so doing was precisely that God's purposes *would* be frustrated, and this, sadly, is exactly what has happened. God's will is flaunted whenever anyone sins. It is just not true that

"God's will is always done." . . . Furthermore, it seems that sovereignty entails only *the power* to impose one's will, not the actual imposition of it.

How can a just God condemn someone to eternal torment? In the first place, as already noted, I believe the citizens of hell are there because they freely choose to be there; they have hardened their hearts and would be unable to endure heaven. Unless one bows to God and makes the divine will one's own, heaven is too much to bear and one chooses hell. Thus, as I noted, it is not only just but loving that God allows them to live forever in hell. Second, hell may have the effect on many of strengthening their resolve never to repent; sin may voluntarily continue; and if it is right for evil-doers to experience the consequences of the evil deeds they do here and now, this will be true of the evil deeds they do after death. Third, Christians believe their salvation is a matter of grace alone; we deserve to be condemned, but out of love rather than sheer justice God forgives us and reconciles us to God. The notion of grace, then, is at the heart of the Christian good news. God loves us though we are unlovable; God accepts us though we are unacceptable. But the thing to notice here is that if separationism is inconsistent with God's love, i.e., if a loving God cannot condemn anyone to hell, then our salvation (i.e., our rescue from hell) is no longer a matter of grace; it becomes a matter of our justly being freed from a penalty we don't really deserve. In the end, universalism overturns the Christian notion of grace.

How can the Blessed be joyous if friends and loved ones are in hell? I do not know an adequate answer to this question. I expect that if I knew enough about heaven I would know the answer, but I know little about heaven. The problem is perhaps less acute for me than for those separationists who believe hell is a place of permanent torture. If I am right, the Blessed need not worry that loved ones are in agony and are allowed to hope (see below) that God's love can even yet achieve a reconciliation. But there is still the question how, say, a wife can experience joy and happiness in heaven while her beloved husband is in hell. And that is the question I am unable to answer satisfactorily. It would seem to be unjust for God to allow the wrong choices of the damned—i.e., their rejection of God—to ruin the joy of the Blessed, who have chosen to love God. But how God brings it about that the Blessed experience the joy of the presence of God despite the absence of others, I do not know.

The fate of the ignorant. What about the fate of those who die in ignorance of Christ? The main point to note here is that the Bible does not speak in any connected or clear way on this question. Biblical Christians must take seriously those exclusivistic sayings of Jesus and the New Testament writers . . . that create for us this problem. As an orthodox Christian, then, I do believe that salvation is to be found only in Christ. If any person at any time in this life or the next is ever reconciled to God, it is because of the saving work of Jesus Christ. His life, death, and resurrection made it possible. If I am somehow to be reconciled to God, if our imaginary friend Oohku is somehow to be reconciled to God, it is only through Christ that it happens.[5]

Some Christians have taken to heart the Bible's exclusivistic sayings and have concluded that people like Oohku must be lost, that their eternal destiny is hell. But this is to confuse the claim that the Bible is authoritative on matters of faith and practice with the claim that the Bible authoritatively tells us everything we might want to know about Christian faith and practice. It doesn't; I believe the Bible tells us enough so that we can read it, be convicted of sin, and learn how to come to God through Christ. But it does not answer all the questions we might want to ask it and it certainly does not say or imply that those who die in ignorance of Christ are lost. The Bible simply does not in any direct or thorough way address itself to the precise issue of the fate of people like Oohku. The Bible tells us what we *need* to know, not all that we might *want* to know.

What then must the separationist say about the fate of those who die in ignorance of Christ? Again, there is no clear or connected teaching in the Bible on this question; what we find are some vague and unformulated hints which can perhaps guide us but which cannot be used to justify a dogmatic position. . . . I am quite convinced that this much is true—God can indeed make us in any way God pleases and we have no authority over God to challenge this decision. But this by itself does not answer the question of the fate of those who die in ignorance of Christ. . . .

[Let me make] a theological conjecture: that there are ways those who are ignorant of Christ can be reconciled to God through Christ. In other words, if redemption is to be found only in Christ, and if the atoning work of Christ was intended for all people, and if God is loving and just, then it seems sensible to suppose that it must be causally possible for all people, wherever or whenever they live or however ignorant they are, to come to God through Christ. (I would like to stress that this is a conjecture, not a dogma or a teaching or even a firm belief.) . . . As long as it is recognized that these are conjectures without systematic or clear biblical warrant, we might even suggest that Christ has the power to save human beings *wherever* they are, even in hell. I recognize some will resist this suggestion. It is one thing—they will say—to suggest that the ignorant after death receive a chance (their first) to respond positively to the gospel. But it is quite another to suggest that those who have been condemned receive *other* chances to respond positively. But a question must be asked here: Is it possible that there are persons who would respond positively to God's love after death even though they have not responded positively to it before death? I believe this is possible. In fact, one reason for this latest conjecture is the observation that some who hear the gospel, hear it in such a way that they are psychologically unable to respond positively. Perhaps they heard the gospel for the first and only time from a fool or a bigot or a

scoundrel. Or perhaps they were caused to be prejudiced against Christianity by skeptical parents or teachers. Whatever the reason, I believe it would be unjust of God to condemn those who did indeed hear the good news but were unable to respond positively. This is why I suggest that even in hell, people can be rescued.

Conclusion. Does this bring in universalism by the back door? Certainly not. I have little doubt some will say no to God eternally (the Bible predicts this, in fact), nor do I see any need for a "second chance" for those who have freely and knowingly chosen in this life to live apart from God. Perhaps God never gives up on people, but some folk seem to have hardened their heart to such a degree that they will never repent. For such people, hell as separation from God exists forever, just as it exists for them now. But perhaps some who die in ignorance of Christ will hear the good news, repent, and be rescued. Perhaps even some citizens of hell will do so too. Again, the key word is *perhaps*. We have no ground to dogmatize here. I do not think we know the fate of those who die in ignorance of Christ. All I am sure of is that God's scheme for the salvation of human beings will turn out to have been just, perhaps in ways we cannot now understand.

Notes

1. First point: see Romans 11:32; I Timothy 2:4–6; II Peter 3:9. Second point: see II Corinthians 5:14, 15; Titus 2:11; Hebrews 2:9; I John 2.2. Third point: see I Corinthians 15:22; cf. 23–28; II Corinthians 5:19; Colossians 1:19. Fourth point: see Romans 5:18; Philippians 2:9–11; John 1:29; 3:17; 12:32, 47.

2. See Mark 9:43–50; Matthew 25:41, 46; II Thessalonians 1:7–9; Jude 6; Revelation 14:11; 19:3; 20:10.

3. Respectively: Matthew 25:41, Revelation 9:2, Matthew 8:12, Matthew 8:12, Revelation 14:11, Matthew 5:26.

4. It must be admitted that there are New Testament texts that can be taken to imply that hell is an act of vengeance or retribution on sinners. See Matthew 5:22, 29; 8:12; 10. 15; II Thessalonians 1:6–9; Hebrews 2:2–3; 10:28–31; II Peter 2:4–9; 12–13. Some even seem to suggest degrees of punishment corresponding to degrees of guilt. See Matthew 11:22–24; Luke 12:47–48; 20:47.

5. A suggestion also perhaps made (in literary form) by C.S. Lewis in *The Great Divorce* (New York: Macmillan, 1957), 120–24.

Discussion

1. Distinguish separationism from universalism. List some reasons in favour of each view. Now list some reasons in opposition to each view.

2. Davis theorizes about the doctrine of hell from within the Christian tradition. Has he adequately defended separationism, given the constraints of his tradition?

3. In the previous question, "constraints" suggests "unfair limitations"—how could the boundaries set by one's religious tradition be understood positively?

THE PROBLEM OF HELL: A PROBLEM OF EVIL FOR CHRISTIANS

MARILYN MCCORD ADAMS*

The problem. Since the 1950s, syllabi in analytic philosophy of religion have given the problem of evil pride of place. So-called atheologians have advanced as an argument against the existence of God the alleged logical incompossibility of the statements

    (I)   God exists, and is essentially omnipotent, omniscient, and perfectly good

and

    (II)   Evil exists. . . .

My own view is that hell. . . .

    (III)   Some created persons will be consigned to hell forever. . . .

poses the principal problem of evil for Christians. . . .

My purpose here is to engage the problem of hell at two levels: a theoretical level, concerning the logical compossibility of (I) and (III); and a pragmatic level, concerning whether or not a God who condemned some of His creatures to hell could be a logically appropriate object of standard Christian worship. My own verdict is no secret: statement (III) should be rejected in favor of a doctrine of universal salvation.

Theoretical dimension. The argument for the logical incompossibility of (I) with (III), mimics that for (I) with (II):

---

* Marilyn McCord Adams is Regius Professor of Divinity, Emeritus, Oxford University.

    (1)   If God existed and were omnipotent, He would be able to avoid (III).

    (2)   If God existed and were omniscient, He would know how to avoid (III).

    (3)   If God existed and were perfectly good, He would want to avoid (III).

    (4)   Therefore, if (I), not (III).

Obviously, the soundness of this argument depends on the construals given to the attribute terms and to "hell". . . . For example, the Gospel according to Matthew speaks in vivid imagery of the disobedient and unfaithful being "cast into outer darkness" where there is "weeping and gnashing of teeth" (Matt. 13:42, 50; 22:13) or being thrown into the "unquenchable fire" "prepared for the devil and all his angels" (Matt. 13:42, 50; 18:8–9; 22:13; cf. 3:10). Cashing the metaphors, it says of Judas that it would have been better for him never to have been born (Matt. 26:24). . . .

Premise (1) is true because an omnipotent creator could altogether refrain from making any persons or could annihilate created persons any time He chose; either way, He could falsify (III). Again, many traditional theologians (e.g., Augustine, Duns Scotus, Ockham, Calvin) have understood divine sovereignty over creation—both nature and soteriology [doctrine of salvation]—to mean that nothing (certainly not creatures' rights) binds God as to what soteriological scheme (if any) He establishes. For example, God could have had a policy of not preserving human persons in existence after death, or He could have legislated temporary reform school followed by life in a utopian environment for all sinners. In these, and many other ways, God could avoid (III), and such was within His power.

Likewise, (3) would be true if "perfectly good" is construed along the lines of person-relative goodness:

MARILYN MCCORD ADAMS | THE PROBLEM OF HELL: A PROBLEM OF EVIL FOR CHRISTIANS   **337**

"God is good to a created person p" if "God guarantees to p a life that is a great good to p on the whole, and one in which p's participation in deep and horrendous evils (if any) is defeated within the context of p's life,"

where

"Evil is horrendous" if "Participation in e by p (either as a victim or a perpetrator) gives everyone *prima facie* reason to believe that p's life cannot—given its inclusion of e—be a great good to p on the whole."

The traditional hell is a paradigm horror, one which offers not merely prima facie but conclusive reason to believe that the life of the damned cannot be a great good to them on the whole. Any person who suffers eternal punishment in the traditional hell will, on the contrary, be one within whose life good is engulfed and/or defeated by evils.

For all we know, however, (3) may be false if divine goodness is evaluated in relation to God's role as producer of global goods. It is at least epistemically possible that (III) be true of a world that exhibits maximum variety with maximum unity or of a very good world that displays the best balance of moral good over moral evil.... And in general, it is epistemically possible that the world have a maximally good overall order and still include the horrors of damnation for some created persons. Aquinas rationalizes this conclusion when he explains that since the purpose of creation is to show forth God's goodness, some must be damned to manifest his justice and others saved to advertise His mercy.[1]

Pragmatic implications. The pragmatic consequences of reconciling (1) with (III) by restricting divine goodness to its global dimension are severe.... [T]his assumption makes human life a bad bet. Consider persons in a preoriginal position, surveying possible worlds containing managers of varying power, wisdom, and character, and subjects with diverse fates. The subjects are to answer, from behind a veil of ignorance as to which position they would occupy, the question whether they would willingly enter a given world as a human being. Reason would, I submit, render a negative verdict already for worlds whose omniscient and omnipotent manager permits antemortem horrors that remain undefeated within the context of the human participant's life and a fortiori for worlds some or most of whose human occupants suffer eternal torment....

Free will and the problem of hell. Many Christians... [mount] a kind of free-will defense; they claim that God has done a good thing in making incompatibilist free creatures. Like any good governor or parent, He has established a set of general conditional decrees, specifying sanctions and rewards for various sorts of free actions. His preference ("antecedent" or "perfect" will) is that everyone should be saved, but He has given us scope to work out our own destinies. Damnation would never happen but for the errant action of incompatibilist free creatures within the framework of divine regulations. It is not something God *does*, but rather allows; it is neither God's means, nor His end, but a middle-known but unintended side effect of the order He has created. Thus, (3) is true only regarding God's antecedent but not His all-things-considered preferences, and the incompossibility argument ... fails....

Divine justice and the ontological gap. I merely join the consensus of the great medieval and reformation theologians in recognizing that God and creatures are *ontologically incommensurate*. God is a being a greater than which cannot be conceived, the infinite being in relation to which finite creatures are "almost nothing." Drawing on social analogies, Anselm contends that God is so far above, so different in kind from us, as not to be enmeshed in merely human networks of mutual rights and obligations; God is not the kind of thing that could be obligated to creatures in any way. Duns Scotus concurs, reasoning that God has no obligation to love creatures, because although the finite *goodness* of each provides *a* reason to love it, the fact of its *finitude* means that this reason is always defeasible, indeed negligible, almost nothing in comparison with the reason divine goodness has to love itself. Their conclusion from this ontological disproportion is that God will not be *unjust to* created persons no matter what He does.

Finite temporal agency versus eternal destiny. . . . More recently, I have concentrated on the incommensuration between horrendous evils and human life and agency. For, on the one hand, *horrors have a power to defeat positive meaning disproportionate to their extension in the space-time worm of an individual's life.* And, on the other, *horrors are incommensurate with human cognitive capacities.* For (i) the human capacity to cause horrors unavoidably exceeds our ability to experience them. Many examples make this clear as to quantity: for example, on the traditional doctrine of the fall, Adam experiences one individual's worth of ignorance and difficulty, but his sin brought it on his many descendants; Hitler organized a holocaust of millions; small numbers of government leaders, scientists, and military personnel brought about the atomic explosions over Hiroshima and Nagasaki. Likewise for quality, it is probably true that, for example, a childless male soldier cannot experience anything like enough to the suffering of a mother whose child is murdered before her eyes. But (ii) where suffering is concerned, conceivability follows capacity to experience, in such a way that we cannot adequately conceive of what we cannot experience. Just as a blind person's color concepts are deficient because lack of acquaintance deprives him or her of the capacity for imaginative representation of colors despite lots of abstract descriptive

knowledge about them, so lack of experience deprives an agent of the capacity empathetically to enter in to what it would be like to suffer this or that harm, despite more or less detailed abstract descriptive knowledge about such suffering. To these observations, I add the claim (iii) that agent responsibility is diminished in proportion to his or her unavoidable inability to conceive of the relevant dimensions of the action and its consequences, and I draw the conclusion that human agents cannot be fully responsible for the horrendous consequences of their actions.

Returning to the problem of hell, I maintain that damnation is a horror that exceeds our conceptual powers. For even if we could experience for a finite period of time some aspect of hell's torments (e.g., the burning of the fire, deep depression, or consuming hatred) or heaven's bliss (e.g., St. Teresa's joyful glimpse of the Godhead), we are unavoidably unable to experience their cumulative effect in advance and so unable more than superficially to appreciate what is involved in either. It follows that human agents are unavoidably unable to exercise their free choice with fully open eyes. . . .

Finite agency in the region of the divine. It may be objected that the ontological incommensuration between God and creatures redounds another way, however. For Anselm pointed out that the badness of sin is to be measured not simply in terms of what the creature is or does but in terms of the creature's relation to God, a being a greater/more worthy of honor, respect, and esteem than which cannot be conceived. Since God is infinitely worthy of honor, any offense against God is immeasurably indecent and hence infinitely culpable. Even if every created *harm* we caused were finite, at the very worst the ruin of finite created lives, Anselm's principle shows how we have the capacity to cause infinite *offense*. Any and every sin would turn out to be a horrendous evil. And if eternal torment for the creature is incommensurate with human agency taken in itself, it does not adequately measure the offensiveness of one small look contrary to God's will. Eternal torment is merely the closest approximation that creatures can make to experiencing the just punishment.

My reply is that it is not "fair" . . . to put created agency (even if we think of its starting in utopian Eden with ideal competence of its kind) into a position where the consequences of its exercise are so disproportionate to its acts. Suppose the powers that be threaten a nuclear holocaust if I do not always put my pencil down no more than one inch from the paper on which I am writing. Although it is within my power to meet such a demand, such disproportionate consequences put my pencil-placing actions under unnatural strain. Although in some sense I *can* comply, I am also in some sense *bound* to "slip up" sooner or later. Hence, the demand is unreasonable, the responsibility too hard for me to bear. . . .

I do not say that were God to create persons with the intention of condemning to hell any who fail to honor him appropriately, he would be unjust in the sense (a) of violating his (nonexistent) obligations to them (us). I do claim that such punishment would be *unusual*, because acting in the region of the divine levels out the differences among created act types (e.g., between peeking out at prayers and torturing babies). Moreover, God would be "unfair" . . . and hence cruel in setting created persons conditions relative to which not only were they (we) unlikely to succeed, but also their (our) lives were as a consequence more apt than not to have all positive meaning swallowed up by horrendous evil.

The idol of human agency. Where soteriology is concerned, Christians have traditionally disagreed about human nature along two parameters. First, some hold that human nature was created in ideal conditions and placed in a utopian environment: i.e., that *ab initio* humans had enough cognitive and emotional maturity to grasp and accurately apply relevant normative principles, while (on the occasion of their choice) their exercise of these abilities was unobstructed by unruly passions or external determinants of any kind. Others maintain, on the contrary, that humans are created immature and grow to adult competence through a messy developmental process. Second, where salvation is concerned, some take the human race collectively while others consider humans individualistically. According to the Augustinian doctrine of the fall, Adam and Eve began as ideal agents in utopian Eden. The consequence of their sin is not only individual but collective: agency impaired by "ignorance" (clouded moral judgment) and "difficulty" (undisciplined emotions), which passes from the first parents to the whole family of their descendants. In his earlier works, Augustine insists that despite such inherited handicaps, the reprobate still bring damnation on themselves, because God has offered help sufficient to win the difficult struggle through faith in Christ. In later anti-Pelagian works, Augustine abandons the idea that God confers on each fallen human grace sufficient for salvation; he concedes that damnation is the consequence of such divine omissions and Adam's original free choice to sin. Nevertheless, the damned deserve no pity, because the family collectively brought it on themselves through Adam's free choice of will.[2] . . .

In my judgment, the arguments from incommensuration . . . hold even where ideal human nature is concerned. For my own part, I reject the notion of a historical fall and read Genesis 2–3 the Irenaean way, as about the childhood of the human race. I deny not only that we human beings do have, but also that we ever had, ideal agency. . . .

By contrast, a realistic picture of human agency should recognize the following: (a) We human beings start life ignorant, weak and helpless, psychologically so lacking in a self-concept as to be incapable of choice. (b) We learn to "construct" a picture of the world, ourselves, and other people only with difficulty over a long period of time and under the extensive influence of other non-ideal choosers. (c) Human development is the interactive product of human nature and its environment, and from early on we humans are confronted with problems that we cannot adequately grasp or cope with, and in response to which we mount (without fully conscious calculation) inefficient adaptational strategies. (d) Yet, the human psyche forms habits in such a way that these reactive patterns, based as they are on a child's inaccurate view of the world and its strategic options, become entrenched in the individual's personality. (e) Typically, the habits are unconsciously "acted out" for years, causing much suffering to self and others before (if ever) they are recognized and undone through a difficult and painful process of therapy and/or spiritual formation. (f) Having thus begun *immature*, we arrive at adulthood in a state of *impaired freedom*, as our childhood adaptational strategies continue to distort our perceptions and behavior. (g) We adults with impaired freedom are responsible for our choices, actions, and even the character molded by our unconscious adaptational strategies, in the sense that we are the *agent causes* of them. (h) Our assessments of moral responsibility, praise, and blame cannot afford to take this impairment into account, because we are not as humans capable of organizing and regulating ourselves in that fine-tuned a way. And so, except for the most severe cases of impairment, we continue to hold ourselves *responsible to one another*.

Taking these estimates of human nature to heart, I draw two conclusions: first, that such impaired adult human agency is no more competent to be entrusted with its (individual or collective) eternal destiny than two-year-old agency is to be allowed choices that could result in its death or physical impairment; and second, that the fact that the choices of such impaired agents come between the divine creator of the environment and their infernal outcome no more reduces divine responsibility for the damnation than two-year-old agency reduces the responsibility of the adult caretaker. Suppose, for example, that a parent introduces a two-year-old child into a room filled with gas that is safe to breathe but will explode if ignited. Assume further that the room contains a stove with brightly colored knobs, which if turned will light the burners and ignite the gas. If the parent warns the child not to turn the knobs and leaves, whereupon the child turns the knobs and blows itself up, surely the child is at most marginally to blame, even if it knew enough to obey the parent, while the parent is both primarily responsible and highly culpable....

Once again, my further conclusion is not that God would (like the parent...) be culpable if He were to insert humans into a situation in which their eternal destiny depended on their exercise of impaired agency, for I deny that God has any obligations to creatures. Rather, God (like the parent...) would bear primary responsibility for any tragic outcomes, and God would be cruel to create human beings in a world with combinations of obstacles and opportunities such as are found in the actual world and govern us under a scheme according to which whether or not we go to the traditional hell depends on how we exercise our impaired adult agency in this life—cruel, by virtue of imposing horrendous consequences on our all-too-likely failures....

The hermeneutics of charity. When authorities seem to say things that are inconsistent or unreasonable, our first move is, not to cut off, but to twist the wax nose a bit, so that without crediting the troublesome pronouncements taken literally, we can "make something" of them by finding some deeper and more palatable truths which (we may claim) they were attempting to express. In this spirit, some agree that the notion of hell as an eternal torture chamber, as a punitive consequence for not accepting Christ, is not compatible with any tolerable understanding of divine goodness. That is, if "hell" is understood the traditional way, then they construe "perfectly good" in such a way as to render true the statement:

3. If God existed and were perfectly good, he would want to avoid (III).

Rather than abandon the doctrine of hell altogether, they modify or reinterpret it as some other fate involving permanent exclusion from heaven.

Hell as leaving people to the natural consequences of their choices. On [a] politico-legal model, the relation between a person's sinning to the end and his or her suffering eternal punishment is extrinsic and contingent (as is that between speeding and paying a monetary fine). Other philosophers think there is a better chance of construing (III) in such a way as to be compatible with (I) if one discovers an intrinsic connection between the created persons' choices and their postmortem punishments or deprivations. Thus, Richard Swinburne maintains that "heaven is not a reward for good behavior" but "a home for good people."[3] He insists on the high value not only of created free agency but also of the autonomy of created persons to determine their own destinies. Noting psychological commonplaces about how patterns of choice build habits of thinking, wanting, valuing, and doing, and the more entrenched the habit, the harder it is to break, Swinburne reckons such habits may become so entrenched as to be unbreakable. For a person may so thoroughly blind himself or herself to what is really worth going for, that she or he can no longer see or rationally choose it. Since heaven is a society organized around the things that are really worth wanting, being, and doing, people locked into their vices could not enjoy it there.

Swinburne is less interested in (III) than in

(III′) Some persons that God creates are permanently excluded from heaven.

He is willing to recognize "various possible fates for those who have finally rejected the good": (i) "they might cease to exist after death"; (ii) "they might cease to exist after suffering some limited amount of physical pain as part of the punishment for their wickedness"; or (iii) "they might continue to exist forever pursuing trivial pursuits." In Swinburne's estimation, "the crucial point is that it is compatible with the goodness of God that he should allow a man to put himself beyond possibility of salvation, because it is indeed compatible with the goodness of God that he should allow a man to choose the sort of person he will be," even where these decisions have eternal consequences.

Likewise, dismissing literal construals of Matthew 25:41–46 and Luke 16:19–26 as "a crude and simplistic account of the doctrine of hell,"[4] Eleonore Stump turns to Dante, who understands the fundamental awfulness of hell in terms of eternal deprivation of union with God. Stump takes Dante's "graphic images" at theological face value and suggests that the latter is fully compatible with a Limbo of beautiful physical surroundings "in which the noblest and wisest of the ancients discuss philosophy." Moreover, in the more punitive regions of hell, external tortures are not suffered the way they would be in this world but serve rather as outward and visible signs of inner psychological states—afflictions which are nevertheless compatible with long and leisurely intellectual discussions. So far as the problem of hell is concerned, Stump maintains, "Everlasting life in hell is the ultimate evil which can befall a person in this world; but the torments of hell are *the natural* conditions of some persons, and God can spare such persons those pains only by depriving them of their nature or their existence. And it is arguable that, of the alternatives open to God, maintaining such persons in existence and as human is the best." In other words, when "hell" in (III) is thus reinterpreted, Stump finds the logical compossibility of (I) with (III) defensible.

Once again, my principal complaint about these approaches centers on their understanding of human nature. Swinburne and Stump/Dante begin by taking human psychology very seriously: that entrenched habits of character, established tastes, and concomitant states of inner conflict are *naturally* consequent upon sinful patterns of choice is supposed to explain the *intrinsic* connection between the sinner's earthly behavior and his or her exclusion from heaven and/or consignment to hell. By contrast, their estimates of the *natural* effects of vice over the very (i.e., eternally) long run leave human psychology far behind. For vice is a psychospiritual disorder. Just as running a machine contrary to its design leads, sooner rather than later, to premature breakdown, so also persistent psychological disorders caricature and produce breakdowns even in the medium run of twenty to seventy years. My own view resonates with C.S. Lewis's suggestion in *The Problem of Pain*,[5] that vice in the soul preserved beyond three score and ten brings about a total dismantling of personality, to the torment of which this-worldly schizophrenia and depression are but the faintest approximations. A fortiori excluded is the notion that persons with characters unfit for heaven might continue forever philosophizing, delivering eloquent speeches, or engaging in trivial pursuits. Likewise, either union with God is the natural human telos, in which case we cannot both eternally lack it and yet continue to enjoy this-worldly pleasures forever; or it is not, because we are personal animals and unending life is not a natural but a supernatural endowment. For God to prolong life eternally while denying access to the only good that could keep us eternally interested would likewise eventually produce unbearable misery. In short, I think that the Swinburne/Stump/Dante suggestion that God might keep created persons in existence forever but abandon them to the consequences of their sinful choices collapses into the more traditional doctrine of hell, when such consequences are calculated from a realistic appraisal of human psychology.

Annihilation by the creator? Among others, Swinburne mentions the option of replacing (III) with

(III") Some created persons who die with characters unfit for heaven will be annihilated, either at death or after the Judgment.

Nor is this suggestion without ancient precedent: the non-canonical apocalyptic work, I Enoch, predicts that after the Judgment, the wicked will suffer for a while until they wither away.... [T]his move has the advantage of avoiding the claim that God has subjected created persons to cruel and/or unusual punishment by extending their life span into an eternity of horrendous suffering.

True to my Suarezian bias, I reject it, on the ground that it involves an uncharitable estimate of divine wisdom, goodness, and power. St. Anselm reasons that omnipotent, all-wise goodness would do the hard as well as the easy. For God, it is easy to make good from the good; what is more remarkable, it is no effort for Him to make good out of nothing. For Him, the real challenge would be to make good out of evil; so He must be able to do that. Moreover, St. Anselm argued that it is unfitting to omnipotent wisdom either to change its mind or to fail in what it attempts.[6] I agree both ways. To me, it is a better theological bargain to hold the mystery that God will not give up on the wicked, will eventually somehow be able to turn them to good, than to swallow the tragic idea that created persons, finite and dependent though we are, are able ultimately and finally to defeat our Creator's purpose, the mystery of transworld final impenitence ending in the Creator's destroying His own creation....

The pragmatics of universalism. Surprisingly many religiously serious people reject the doctrine of universal salvation, on the pragmatic ground that it leads to moral and religious laxity. Withdraw the threat, and they doubt whether others—perhaps even they themselves—would sustain the motivation for moral diligence and religious observance.

My pastoral experience suggests, on the contrary, that the disproportionate threat of hell ... produces despair that masquerades as skepticism, rebellion, and unbelief. If your father threatens to kill you if you disobey him, you may cower in terrorized submission, but you may also (reasonably) run away from home. My brand of universalism offers all the advantages of Augustine's and Calvin's *sola gratia* approaches (like them, it makes our salvation utterly gratuitous and dependent on God's surprising and loving interest in us) and then some (because it gives everyone reason to hope and to be sincerely thankful for his or her life).

The relevance of feelings. [Defenders of hell often] do not enter at any length into how bad horrendous sufferings are. ... [They] imply that those who are offended [by the doctrine of eternal torment] will be motivated by understandable feelings, which are nevertheless not relevant to a rational consideration of the subject.

I want to close with a contrary methodological contention ...: namely, that feelings are highly relevant to the problem of evil and to the problem of hell, because they are one source of information about how bad something is for a person. To be sure, they are not an infallible source. Certainly they are not always an articulate source. But they are *a* source. Where questions of value are concerned, reason is not an infallible source either. That is why so-called value calculations in abstraction from feelings can strike us as "cold" or "callous." I do not believe we have any infallible faculties at all. But our best shot at valuations will come from the collaboration of feelings and reason, the latter articulating the former, the former giving data to the latter.

Personally, I am appalled at [the] valuations of defenders of eternal torment, at levels too deep for words (although I have already said many). I invite anyone who agrees with [them]—that the saved can in good conscience let their happiness be unaffected by the plight of the damned because the destruction of the latter is self-willed—to spend a week visiting patients who are dying of emphysema or of the advanced effects of alcoholism, to listen with sympathetic presence, to enter into their point of view on their lives, to face their pain and despair. Then ask whether one could in good conscience dismiss their suffering with, "Oh well, they brought it on themselves!"[7]

I do not think this is sentimental. Other than experiencing such sufferings in our own persons, such sympathetic entering into the position of another is the best way we have to tell what it would be like to be that person and suffer as they do, the best data we can get on how bad it would be to suffer that way. Nor is my thesis especially new. It is but an extension of the old Augustinian-Platonist point, that where values are concerned, what and how well you see depends not simply on how well you think, but on what and how well you love (a point to which Swinburne seems otherwise sympathetic). I borrow a point from Charles Hartshorne[8] when I suggest that sensitivity, sympathetic interaction, is an aspect of such loving, one that rightfully affects our judgment in ways we should not ignore.

Notes

1. Thomas Aquinas, *Summa Theologica* I, q. 23, a. 5, ad 3.

2. These views are presented in Augustine, *De libero arbitrio*. Corpus Scriptorum Ecclesiasticorum Latinorum, vol. 74. (Vindobonae: Hoelder-Pichler-Tempsky, 1956), passim. And Augustine, *De gratia et libero arbitrio* (AD 426), and Augustine, *De correptione et gratia* (426 or 427 CE).

3. All quotations from Swinburne in this section are from Richard Swinburne, "A Theodicy of Heaven and Hell," in *The Existence and Nature of God*, ed. Alfred Freddoso (Notre Dame, IN: U of Notre Dame P, 1983), pp. 37–54.

4. All of the Stump quotations in this section are from Eleonore Stump, "The Problem of Evil," *Faith and Philosophy* 4 (1985): 392–423.

5. C.S. Lewis, *The Problem of Pain* (New York: Macmillan, 1979), pp. 124–26.

6. St. Anselm, *Proslogion*, chap. ix; *Sancti Anselmi: Opera Omnia*: 6 vols., ed. F.S. Schmitt (Edinburgh: Thomas Nelson, 1946–61); Schmitt I, p. 108. St. Anselm *Cur Deus homo* II, chap. IV; Schmitt II, 99; cf. *Proslogion*, chap. vii; Schmitt I, pp. 105–06.

7. William Lane Craig, "No Other Name," *Faith and Philosophy* 6 (1989): 183–85.

8. Charles Hartshorne, *The Divine Relativity* (New Haven: Yale UP, 1948, 1964), chap. 3, pp. 116–58.

Discussion

1. Consider Adams's definition of God's goodness. Do you think divine goodness entails such consideration for his (human) creatures? Why or why not? What do you think is a more adequate conception of divine goodness?

2. Defend either the Augustinian or the Irenaean view of human nature. Relate your view of human beings to your view of divine goodness (keeping the traditional doctrine of hell in mind).

3. Suppose you accept the Augustinian view of human nature and the traditional doctrine of hell but also reject the belief that God will ensure that the lives of his creatures will be a great good on the whole. If you had been consulted, would you have consented to being created under such circumstances? That is, does this combination of views make life a bad bet?

4. What role, if any, should feelings play in our understanding of God and his relations with his creatures?

Chapter 26

Religious Pluralism

THE PHILOSOPHY OF RELIGIOUS PLURALISM

JOHN HICK*

The lamps are different,
but the Light is the same.

—JALALU'L-DIN RUMI (THIRTEENTH CENTURY)

The need for such a hypothesis. I have argued that it is rational on the part of those who experience religiously to believe and to live on this basis. And I have further argued that, in so believing, they are making an affirmation about the nature of reality which will, if it is substantially true, be developed, corrected and enlarged in the course of future experience. They are thus making genuine assertions and are making them on appropriate and acceptable grounds. If there were only one religious tradition, so that all religious experience and belief had the same intentional object, an epistemology of religion could come to rest at this point. But in fact there are a number of different such traditions and families of traditions witnessing to many different personal deities and nonpersonal ultimates.

To recall the theistic range first, the history of religions sets before us innumerable gods, differently named and often with different characteristics.... What are we to say, from a religious point of view,

about all these gods? Do we say that they exist? And what would it be for a named god, say Balder, with his distinctive characteristics, to exist? In any straightforward sense it would at least seem to involve there being a consciousness, answering to this name, in addition to all the millions of human consciousnesses. Are we then to say that for each name in our directory of gods there is an additional consciousness, with the further attributes specified in the description of that particular deity? In most cases this would be theoretically possible since in most cases the gods are explicitly or implicitly finite beings whose powers and spheres of operation are at least approximately known; and many of them could coexist without contradiction. On the other hand the gods of the monotheistic faiths are thought of in each case as the one and only God, so that it is impossible for there to be more than one instantiation of this concept. It is thus not feasible to say that all the named gods, and particularly not all the most important ones, exist—at any rate not in any simple and straightforward sense.

Further, in addition to the witness of theistic religion to this multiplicity of personal deities there are yet other major forms of thought and experience which point to non-personal ultimates: Brahman, the Dharmakaya, Nirvana, Sunyata, the Tao.... But if the ultimate Reality is the blissful, universal consciousness of Brahman, which at the core of our own being we all are, how can it also be the emptiness, non-being, void of Sunyata? And again, how could it also be the Tao, as the principle of cosmic order, and again, the Dharmakaya or the eternal Buddha-nature? And if it

---

* John Hick (1922–2012) was Professor Emeritus of Philosophy at Claremont Graduate University.

is any of these, how can it be a personal deity? Surely these reported ultimates, personal and non-personal, are mutually exclusive. Must not any final reality either be personal, with the nonpersonal aspect of divinity being secondary, or be impersonal, with the worship of personal deities representing a lower level of religious consciousness, destined to be left behind in the state of final enlightenment?

The naturalistic response is to see all these systems of belief as factually false although perhaps as expressing the archetypal daydreams of the human mind whereby it has distracted itself from the harsh problems of life. From this point of view the luxuriant variety and the mutual incompatibility of these conceptions of the ultimate, and of the modes of experience which they inform, demonstrates that they are "such stuff as dreams are made on." However . . . it is entirely reasonable for the religious person, experiencing life in relation to the transcendent—whether encountered beyond oneself or in the depths of one's own being—to believe in the reality of that which is thus, apparently, experienced. Having reached that conclusion one cannot dismiss the realm of religious experience and belief as illusory, even though its internal plurality and diversity must preclude any simple and straightforward account of it.

Nor can we reasonably claim that our own form of religious experience, together with that of the tradition of which we are a part, is veridical while the others are not. We can of course claim this; and indeed virtually every religious tradition has done so, regarding alternative forms of religion either as false or as confused and inferior versions of itself. But the kind of rational justification . . . for treating one's own form of religious experience as a cognitive response—though always a complexly conditioned one—to a divine reality must (as we have already noted) apply equally to the religious experience of others. In acknowledging this we are obeying the intellectual Golden Rule of granting to others a premise on which we rely ourselves. Persons living within other traditions, then, are equally justified in trusting their own distinctive religious experience and in forming their beliefs on the basis of it. For the only reason for treating one's tradition differently from others is the very human, but not very cogent, reason that it is one's own! . . .

Having, then, rejected . . . the sceptical view that religious experience is *in toto* delusory, and the dogmatic view that it is all delusory except that of one's own tradition, I propose to explore the third possibility that the great post-axial faiths constitute different ways of experiencing, conceiving and living in relation to an ultimate divine Reality which transcends all our varied visions of it.

The real in itself and as humanly experienced. In discussing . . . problems of terminology I opted— partly as a matter of personal linguistic taste—for "the Real" (in preference to "the Ultimate," "Ultimate Reality," "the One" or whatever) as a term by which to refer to the postulated ground of the different forms of religious experience. We now have to distinguish between the Real *an sich* [in itself] and the Real as variously experienced-and-thought by different human communities. In each of the great traditions a distinction has been drawn, though with varying degrees of emphasis, between the Real (thought of as God, Brahman, the Dharmakaya . . .) in itself and the Real as manifested within the intellectual and experiential purview of that tradition. . . .

In one form or another such a distinction is required by the thought that God, Brahman, the Dharmakaya, is unlimited and therefore may not be equated without remainder with anything that can be humanly experienced and defined. Unlimitedness, or infinity, is a negative concept, the denial of limitation. That this denial must be made of the Ultimate is a basic assumption of all the great traditions. It is a natural and reasonable assumption: for an ultimate that is limited in some mode would be limited by something other than itself, and this would entail its non-ultimacy. And with the assumption of the unlimitedness of God, Brahman, the Dharmakaya, goes the equally natural and reasonable assumption that the Ultimate, in its unlimitedness exceeds all positive characterisations in human thought and language. . . .

Using this distinction between the Real *an sich* and the Real as humanly thought-and-experienced I want to explore the pluralistic hypothesis that the great world faiths embody different perceptions and conceptions of, and correspondingly different responses to, the Real from within the major variant ways of being human; and that within each of them the transformation of human existence from self-centredness to Reality-centredness is taking place. These traditions are accordingly to be regarded as alternative soteriological "spaces" within which, or "ways" along which, men and women can find salvation/liberation/ultimate fulfilment.

Kant's epistemological model. In developing this thesis our chief philosophical resource will be one of Kant's most basic epistemological insights, namely that the mind actively interprets sensory information in terms of concepts, so that the environment as we consciously perceive and inhabit it is our familiar three-dimensional world of objects interacting in space.

. . . Kant's later much more detailed development of the theme is particularly helpful because he went on to distinguish explicitly between an entity as it is in itself and as it appears in perception. For the realisation that the world, as we consciously perceive it, is partly our own construction leads directly to a differentiation between the world *an sich* unperceived by anyone, and the world as it appears to, that is as it is perceived by, us.[1] The distinction plays a major part in Kant's thought. He points out that since the properties of something as experienced "depend upon the mode of intuition of the subject, this object as appearance is to be distinguished from itself as object in itself"

(*Crit. Pure Reason*, B69 1958, 88). And so Kant distinguished between noumenon and phenomenon, or between a *Ding an sich* [thing in itself] and that thing as it appears to human consciousness. . . . In this strand of Kant's thought—not the only strand, but the one which I am seeking to press into service in the epistemology of religion—the noumenal world exists independently of our perception of it and the phenomenal world is that same world as it appears to our human consciousness. The world as it appears is thus entirely real. . . . Analogously, I want to say that the noumenal Real is experienced and thought by different human mentalities, forming and formed by different religious traditions, as the range of gods and absolutes which the phenomenology of religion reports. And these divine *personae* and metaphysical *impersonae*, as I shall call them, are not illusory but are empirically, that is experientially, real as authentic manifestations of the Real.

. . . In the religious case there are two fundamental circumstances: first, the postulated presence of the Real to the human life of which it is the ground; and second, the cognitive structure of our consciousness, with its capacity to respond to the meaning or character of our environment, including its religious meaning or character. In terms of information theory, we are speaking of the transmission of information from a transcendent source to the human mind/brain and its transformation by the mind/brain into conscious experience. . . . The "presence" of the Real consists in the availability, from a transcendent source, of information that the human mind/brain is capable of transforming into what we call religious experience. And, as in the case of our awareness of the physical world, the environing divine reality is brought to consciousness in terms of certain basic concepts or categories. These are, first, the concept of God, or of the Real as personal, which presides over the various theistic forms of religious experience; and second, the concept of the Absolute, or of the Real as non-personal, which presides over its various non-theistic forms.[2]

. . . On this view our various religious languages—Buddhist, Christian, Muslim, Hindu . . .—each refer to a divine phenomenon or configuration of divine phenomena. When we speak of a personal God, with moral attributes and purposes, or when we speak of the non-personal Absolute, Brahman, or of the Dharmakaya, we are speaking of the Real as humanly experienced: that is, as phenomenon.

The Relation between the Real *an sich* and its *personae* and *impersonae*. It follows from this distinction between the Real as it is in itself and as it is thought and experienced through our religious concepts that we cannot apply to the Real *an sich* the characteristics encountered in its *personae* and *impersonae*. Thus it cannot be said to be one or many, person or thing, substance or process, good or evil, purposive or non-purposive. None of the concrete descriptions that apply within the realm of human experience can apply literally to the unexperiencable ground of that realm. For whereas the phenomenal world is structured by our own conceptual frameworks, its noumenal ground is not. We cannot even speak of this as a thing or an entity. . . . However we can make certain purely formal statements about the postulated Real in itself. The most famous instance in western religious discourse of such a formal statement is Anselm's definition of God as that than which no greater can be conceived. This formula refers to the ultimate divine reality without attributing to it any concrete characteristics. And in this purely formal mode we can say of the postulated Real *an sich* that it is the noumenal ground of the encountered gods and experienced absolutes witnessed to by the religious traditions.

There are at least two thought-models in terms of which we can conceive of the relationship between the Real *an sich* and its *personae* and *impersonae*. One is that of noumenon and phenomena, which enables us to say that the noumenal Real is such as to be authentically experienced as a range of both theistic and non-theistic phenomena. On this basis we cannot, as we have seen, say that the Real *an sich* has the characteristics displayed by its manifestations, such as (in the case of the heavenly Father) love and justice or (in the case of Brahman) consciousness and bliss. But it is nevertheless the noumenal ground of these characteristics. Insofar as the heavenly Father and Brahman are two authentic manifestations of the Real, the love and justice of the one and the consciousness and bliss of the other are aspects of the Real as manifested within human experience. As the noumenal ground of these and other modes of experience, and yet transcending all of them, the Real is so rich in content that it can only be finitely experienced in the various partial and inadequate ways which the history of religions describes.

The other model is the more familiar one in western thought of analogical predication, classically expounded by Aquinas. According to him we can say that God is, for example, good—not in the sense in which we say of a human being that he or she is good, nor on the other hand in a totally unrelated sense, but in the sense that there is in the divine nature a quality that is limitlessly superior and yet at the same time analogous to human goodness. But Aquinas was emphatic that we cannot know what the divine super-analogue of goodness is like: "we cannot grasp what God is, but only what He is not and how other things are related to Him" (*Summa contra Gentiles*, 1:30:4—Pegis 1955, 141). Further, the divine attributes which are distinguished in human thought and given such names as love, justice, knowledge, power, are identical in God. For "God . . . as considered in Himself, is altogether one and simple, yet our intellect knows Him according to diverse conceptions because it cannot see Him as He is in Himself."[3] When we take these two doctrines together and apply them to the Real we see that, while there is a noumenal ground for the phenomenal divine attributes, this does not enable us to trace each attribute separately upwards into the

Godhead or the Real. They represent the Real as both reflected and refracted within human thought and experience. But nevertheless the Real is the ultimate ground or source of those qualities which characterise each divine *personae* and *impersonae* insofar as these are authentic phenomenal manifestations of the Real.

This relationship between the ultimate noumenon and its multiple phenomenal appearances, or between the limitless transcendent reality and our many partial human images of it, makes possible mythological speech about the Real. I define a myth as a story or statement which is not literally true but which tends to evoke an appropriate dispositional attitude to its subject-matter. Thus the truth of a myth is a practical truthfulness: a true myth is one which rightly relates us to a reality about which we cannot speak in non-mythological terms. For we exist inescapably in relation to the Real, and in all that we do and undergo we are inevitably having to do with it in and through our neighbours and our world. Our attitudes and actions are accordingly appropriate or inappropriate not only in relation to our physical and social environments but also in relation to our ultimate environment. And true religious myths are accordingly those that evoke in us attitudes and modes of behaviour which are appropriate to our situation in relation to the Real. . . .

But what is it for human attitudes, behaviours, patterns of life to be appropriate or inappropriate within this ultimate situation? It is for the *persona* or *impersona* in relation to which we live to be an authentic manifestation of the Real and for our practical response to be appropriate to that manifestation. To the extent that a *persona* or *impersona* is in soteriological alignment with the Real, an appropriate response to that deity or absolute is an appropriate response to the Real. It need not however be the only such response, for other phenomenal manifestations of the Real within other human traditions evoke other responses which may be equally appropriate. . . .

[T]he "truthfulness" of each tradition is shown by its soteriological effectiveness. But what the traditions severally regard as ultimates are different and therefore cannot be all truly ultimate. They can however be different manifestations of the truly Ultimate within different streams of human thought-and-experience—hence the postulation of the Real *an sich* as the simplest way of accounting for the data. . . .

But if the Real in itself is experienced, why postulate such an unknown and unknowable *Ding an sich*? The answer is that the divine noumenon is a necessary postulate of the pluralistic religious life of humanity. For within each tradition we regard as real the object of our worship or contemplation. If, as I have already argued, it is also proper to regard as real the objects of worship or contemplation within the other traditions, we are led to postulate the Real *an sich* as the presupposition of the veridical character of this range of forms of religious experience. Without this postulate we should be left with a plurality of *personae* and *impersonae* each of which is claimed to be the Ultimate, but no one of which alone can be. We should have either to regard all the reported experiences as illusory or else return to the confessional position in which we affirm the authenticity of our own stream of religious experience while dismissing as illusory those occurring within other traditions. But for those to whom neither of these options seems realistic the pluralistic affirmation becomes inevitable, and with it the postulation of the Real *an sich* which is variously experienced and thought as the range of divine phenomena described by the history of religion. . . .

Notes

1. And also as it may appear to creatures with different cognitive equipment from our own. Kant was conscious that he was investigating the specifically *human* forms and categories of perception (*Critique of Pure Reason*, B59).

2. The term "Absolute" seems to be the best that we have, even though it is not ideal for the purpose, being more naturally applied to some non-personal manifestations of the Real than to others. It is more naturally applicable, e.g., to Brahman than to Nirvana . . .

3. *Summa Theologica*, part I, Q. 13, art. 12—Pegis, Anton C., ed., *Basic Writings of St. Thomas Aquinas* (New York: Random House, 1955), 1:133.

Discussion

1. There is a rather dizzying array of religious beliefs on offer. What is your attitude toward the various religions?

2. Hick sympathetically accepts the religious experience of religious believers of virtually every tradition. On what grounds is this acceptance justified? Is Hick justified in his affirmation of all of these religious experiences?

3. What is the difference between the Real *an sich* and the Real as humanly experienced? If you (as a religious believer) were to accept that you had no knowledge of the Real *an sich*, what affect would that have on your religious beliefs and practices?

NON EST HICK

PETER VAN INWAGEN*

Religious pluralism. There is a currently very popular picture of what are called "the World Religions" that looks to me a lot like those puzzle pictures from my childhood. The picture is done in prose, rather than in pen and ink outline. I shall have to provide you with a copy of it if I am to proceed with this essay, . . .

There are a number of entities called "religions"; the most important among them are called the "World Religions," with or without capitals. The world religions are the religions that appear in the history books, and appear not merely as footnotes or as clues to "what the Assyrians were like" or evidences of "the beginnings of cosmological speculation." The world religions are important topics of historical inquiry in their own right. Each of them, in fact, has a history of its own; the majority of them have founders and can be said to have begun at fairly definite dates. The list of world religions must include at least the following: Buddhism, Christianity, Confucianism, Hinduism, Islam, Judaism, and Taoism. But other religions are plausible candidates for inclusion in the list. . . . It is the division of humanity into the adherents of the various world religions (of course, many people practice a tribal religion or belong to some syncretistic [the often uncritical attempt to unite diverse religious traditions] cult or have no religion at all) that is the primary datum of all responsible thinking about religion. Comparative studies of the world religions have shown that each of these religions is a species of a genus and that they have important common characteristics that belong to no other human social institutions. There are, of course, differences as well as similarities among the world religions, and some might think that there

were grave differences, or even outright inconsistencies. . . . It might be thought, moreover, that these apparent inconsistencies among the world religions were not matters of the surface. It might be thought that each of them pertained to the very root and essence of the religions involved.

It cannot be denied that the apparent inconsistencies exist. What can be denied is that they have anything to do with "the root and essence" of the world religions. Each of the world religions is a response to a single divine reality. The responses are *different*, of course; no one could dispute that. The world religions are different because they arose and developed under different climatic, geographical, cultural, economic, historical, and social circumstances. . . .

The divine reality that each of the world religions responds to is in an important sense beyond the reach of human thought and language. Therefore, any attempt to conceptualize this reality, to describe it in words, to reduce it to formulas, must be woefully inadequate. And when we reflect on the fact that all our religious conceptualizations, descriptions, and formulations are reflections of local and temporary conditions of human social and economic organization, we are led irresistibly to the conclusion that the letter of the creed of any particular religion cannot possibly be an expression of the essence of the divine reality toward which that religion is directed. What we can hope to see over the next couple of hundred years—as each of the great world religions becomes more and more separated from the conditions and the geographical area in which it arose, and as the earth becomes more and more a single "global village"—is a sloughing off of many of the inessential elements of the world religions. And we may hope that among these discarded inessentials will be those particular elements that at present divide the world religions. It may be that each will retain much of its own characteristic language and sacred narrative and imagery. Indeed, one hopes that this will happen, for diversity that does not

---

*   Peter van Inwagen is the John Cardinal O'Hara Professor of Philosophy at the University of Notre Dame.

produce division is a good thing. But it is to be hoped that the great religions will "converge" to the point at which the differences between them are not incompatibilities—not even apparent incompatibilities. We may look forward to the day when a sincere seeker after the divine may (depending on the momentary circumstances of his or her life) move back and forth among the world religions as easily and consistently as the late-twentieth-century American Protestant who attends a Presbyterian church in California and a Methodist church after moving to North Carolina.

. . . There is a lot more that I might have included. I might, for example, have said something more about the sense in which each of the great world religions is supposed to be a response to the divine. (I might have included the idea that the aim of each of the world religions is to lead humanity to salvation, and that the real essence of salvation is a move from self-centeredness to "reality-centeredness.") I might have said something about the "credentials" that each of the world religions can produce to support its claim to be a response to the divine reality. (I might have included the idea that the hallmark of a religion that is truly a response to a divine reality is its capacity for "saint production," its capacity to produce people who have left self-centeredness behind and become reality-centered.) But one must make an end somewhere.

Christian belief. Now what am I to do with this picture? . . . I will present a sort of model or theory of "religion" that is intended to provide a perspective from which the traditional, orthodox Christian can view such topics as "the world religions," "the scandal of particularity," and "religious pluralism." I do not expect this theory to recommend itself to anyone who is not a traditional, orthodox Christian.

There is, to begin with, a God. That is, there is an infinite, perfect, self-existent person, a unique and necessarily unique bearer of these attributes. It may be, as many great Christians have said, that the

language of personality can be applied to this being only analogically. . . . But even if the language of personality can be applied to God only analogically, it is the only language we Christians have been given and the only language we have. It is not open to us to talk of God only in the impersonal terms appropriate to a discussion of Brahman or the Dialectic of History or the Absolute Idea or Being-as-Such or the *Elan vital* or the Force. . . . This is the meaning of Genesis 11:26–17—it is because we are made in the image of God and after His likeness that we can properly apply to Him terms that apply to human beings.

This God, although He is the only thing that is self-existent, is not the only thing that exists. But all other things that exist exist only because He has made them. . . . Moreover, He did not produce the world of created things and then allow it to go its own way. Even He could not do that, for it is intrinsically impossible for anything to exist apart from Him . . . even for the briefest moment. He sustains all other things in existence, and if He were to withdraw His sustaining power from any being—a soap bubble or a cosmos or an archangel—it would, of absolute, metaphysical necessity, immediately cease to exist. And He does not confine His interactions with the created beings to sustaining them in existence. He is, as we learn from St. John, love; He loves His creatures and, because of this love, governs the world they inhabit providentially.

Among His creatures are human beings, who were, as we have said, made in His image. They were made for a purpose. They have, as the Shorter Catechism of the Church of Scotland says, a "chief end": to glorify God and to enjoy Him forever. This end or purpose implies both free will and the ability to know God. . . .

Unfortunately, the first human beings, having tasted and enjoyed God, did not persist in their original felicity. . . . They turned away from God . . . and ruined themselves. In fact, they ruined not only themselves but their posterity, for the separation from God that they achieved was somehow hereditary. This turning away from God and its consequences are known as the Fall. . . .

Each of us is at birth the product of two factors: the original plan of a wise and providential Creator and the changes that chance—different in the case of every individual—has introduced into the original perfection that came from the Creator's hand. The effects of these changes are . . . moral and intellectual and aesthetic and spiritual. . . .

What is more relevant to our present concerns is our "spiritual endowments"—that is, the degree to which the spiritual endowment that was a part of the Creator's plan for each individual has managed to survive the Fall. We have said that human beings were made to be intimately aware of God. . . . I expect that this awareness was somehow connected with the subject's ordinary sensory awareness of physical objects (which endure and move and have their being in God). I expect that the way in which I am aware of the "invisible" thoughts and emotions of others through their faces and voices provides some sort of analogy. I expect that the way the natural world looked to unfallen humanity and the way it looks to me are as similar and as different as the way a page of Chinese calligraphy looks to a literate Chinese and to me. But whatever the nature of our primordial awareness of God, we have largely lost it. Perhaps, however, none of us has lost it entirely, or only a very few of us have. And it may be that this awareness is present in various people in varying degrees. . . .

It is because a capacity to be aware of God is present in people in varying degrees that people are more religious or less religious—or at any rate this is one reason among others for the varying degrees of engagement with religion exhibited by various people. It is because there are people in whom the capacity to be aware of God is relatively intact . . . that there are great religious leaders and doctors and saints—or, again, this is one reason among others. And these people are not confined to any particular geographical area or to any

historical period. This statement is, of course, consistent with the statement that it is only in certain social and cultural milieux that they will flourish spiritually or have any effect upon history. . . .

The world religions, insofar as they have any reality at all . . . are human creations. That is, they are the work of human beings, and their existence and properties are not a part of God's plan for the world. Other examples of human creations that are similar to religions in that they are in some sense composed of human beings would include the Roman Empire, Scotland, the Children's Crusade, Aunt Lillian's sewing circle, the Comintern, the Vienna Circle, the Gestapo, the American Academy of Religion, Tokyo, fauvism, the Palestine Liberation Organization, the *New York Times*, and the National Aeronautics and Space Administration.

The existence and properties of the institutions in this list are due to chance and to the interplay of a wide variety of "climatic, geographical, cultural, economic, historical, and social circumstances" that it is the business of the social sciences to identify and map. When I say that they are "not a part of God's plan for the world," I am assuming that there *are* things in the world that are not a part of God's plan for the world. As to the individual items in the list, I am assuming that given that there is anything that is not a part of God's plan for the world—it is fairly evident that none of these things is. Perhaps some will disagree with me about particular cases. And even if no one disagrees, it may be that we are all wrong. God's ways are mysterious, and I do not claim to be privy to them. I am proceeding only by such dim lights as I have. Nothing in the sequel really depends on whether the *New York Times* or the Vienna Circle is a part of God's plan for the world: the items listed are meant only to be suggestive examples. But I should make it clear that in saying that these institutions are not parts of God's plan for the world, I do not mean to deny that God may make use of them in carrying out His plan—as I may make pedagogical use of various physical objects that happen, independently of my plans and my will, to be among the fixtures of a lecture room in which I am giving a lecture on perception. Indeed, I would suppose that God makes *constant* use of human institutions, human individuals, animals, inanimate objects, and transient psychological phenomena in His moment-to-moment shepherding of His creatures toward the fulfilment of His plan.

Like the *New York Times* and the Vienna Circle, the world religions have arisen amid the turmoil of the fallen world by chance and have developed and grown and acquired their peculiar characteristics partly by chance and partly by the interplay of the factors that a completed social science would understand. In the case of the world religions, however, a third factor is present, one that can hardly be supposed to have been involved in the development of the *Times* and the Vienna Circle: their growth and properties are affected by the innate awareness of God (both within their "ordinary" members and within their founders and great teachers) that is still present, in varying degrees, throughout fallen humanity. It is also possible—and we might make the same point about any things that exist in this present darkness—that the world religions have been partly shaped by God so that they may be instruments of His purpose. (If this is so, it does not follow that there is some *common* purpose that they serve. For all I know, God may have shaped Islam partly to be a reproach to a complacent Christendom, and it may be that no other religion has this purpose.) . . .

There are, I suggest, two and only two things that are in any sense composed of human beings and are both God's creations and a part of His plan for the world. These are His people Israel and the Catholic Church.

By Israel I mean a *people*. I mean those descendants of Jacob who are the heirs of the promises made to Abraham. It was to this people, and not to a religion called Judaism, that the Law was given. . . . It was

not "Judaism" whom David ruled and who heard the prophets, but a people.

By the Catholic Church I mean a certain *thing*. . . . It was this thing that was created by the Holy Spirit on the day of Pentecost, of which Jesus Christ is the head and cornerstone, which has charge of the good news about Jesus Christ and the sacraments of Baptism and the Eucharist, which is specifically mentioned in the Creeds. There are, we believe, both a visible and an invisible Church. . . .

It will be noted that my characterization of Israel and the Catholic Church has been in terms of God's action in history. If God has not acted in history, these things do not exist. If God has not spoken of old by the prophets, then Israel does not exist. If He has not spoken in these last days by a Son, then the Catholic Church does not exist. . . .

May it not be that all the world's religions are instruments of God's salvation? May it not be that Islam and Buddhism are not merely accidental instruments of salvation, as literally anything under the sun may be, but intended instruments, spiritual equals of the Catholic Church?

I have no way to prove that this is false. If I had, I should be living not by faith but by sight. I can say only this: if that suggestion were true, then the Bible and the Creeds and all of Jewish and Christian history (as Jews and Christians tell the story) are illusions. The teachings of the Church are quite plain on the point that the Church is a unique instrument by which Christ and the Holy Spirit are working (and the Father is working through them) to bring us to the Father. And the teachings of the Church are quite plain on a second point: While the genesis and purpose of the Church belong to eternity, it has been given to us temporal creatures in time. (How else could it be given to us?) It was given to us through events that happened in Palestine in the first century of our era, and all possibility of our salvation depends on those events and on the Church's bringing us into the right relation with them. . . .

The scandal of particularity. I will devote the remainder of this essay to an investigation of a difficulty that people sometimes feel in connection with the idea of the uniqueness of the Church. If I understand the phrase, this difficulty is what is sometimes referred to as "the scandal of particularity." Is there not something arrogant about the Church's claim to be unique? The odd thing is, the idea of there being such a scandal seems to make no sense at all.

Most of us have probably heard the old anti-Semitic quatrain, "How odd / Of God / To choose / The Jews." In addition to being morally rather nasty, this verse makes no sense at all. It presupposes that the Jews are "the chosen people" in the following sense: They were *about* somewhere, and God examined the various peoples of the world and, from among them, chose the Jews. But that is not how things went. The only thing that God chose in that sense was Abraham and his household—who were not yet "the Jews." God's people are a *product* of that choice. In a very straightforward sense, God did not choose, but made, or, one might even say, *forged*, Israel. The Hebrew scriptures are the story of that terrible forging ("for it is a terrible thing I will do with you").

If the Jews claim the distinction of being the one people among all the peoples of the world that God has made, do they call down a charge of scandal upon themselves? No, indeed. One can understand why it would be scandalous if the Jews claimed that God had chosen them from among all the peoples of the earth because of their excellent qualities, if they claimed to have bested all the other peoples of the earth in a contest for God's favor. . . . But that is not the story the Jews tell.

In a similar way, if the Catholic Church claims to be the unique instrument of salvation, there is no scandal. The United States and the Soviet Union and many other things have invented themselves, but the Church did not invent herself. The Church is God's creation, and what makes her the unique instrument of His salvation

is no more the achievement of her members than the splendor and bounty of the earth are the achievements of her inhabitants. Those features of the Church that are the work of human beings (like those features of the earth that are the work of human beings) are mere details added to God's design. And those details, like all the other works of human hands, contain good, bad, and indifferent things, hopelessly intermingled.

"Well, isn't it fortunate for you that you just happen to be a member of this 'unique instrument of salvation.' I suppose you realize that if you had been raised among Muslims, you would make similar claims for Islam?" Yes, it is fortunate for me, very fortunate indeed. And I concede that if I and some child born in Cairo or Mecca had been exchanged in our cradles, very likely I should be a devout Muslim. (I'm not so sure about the other child, however. I was not raised a Christian.) But what is supposed to follow from this observation? If certain people claim to be the members of a body that is the unique instrument of God's salvation, who is supposed to defend their claim? Those who are not members of that body? It should be noted, moreover, that this style of argument (whatever its merits) can hardly be confined to religion. Consider politics. As is the case with religious options, a multitude of political options faces the citizens of any modern nation. . . . Tell the Marxist or the liberal or the Burkean conservative that if only he had been raised in Nazi Germany he would probably have belonged to the Hitler Youth, and he will answer that he is well aware of this elementary fact, and ask what your point is. No one I know of supposes that the undoubted fact that one's adherence to a system of political thought and action is conditioned by one's upbringing is a reason for doubting that the political system one favors is—if not the uniquely "correct" one—clearly and markedly superior to its available rivals. And yet any argument to show that the Church's belief in her own uniqueness was arrogant would apply a fortiori to this almost universally held belief about politics. The members of the

Church can, as I have remarked, take no pride in her unique relation to God, for that relation is His doing and not theirs. But the superiority of one's own political party to all others must be due to the superiority of the knowledge, intelligence, wisdom, courage, and goodness of one and one's colleagues to the knowledge, intelligence, wisdom, courage, and goodness collectively embodied in any other political party.

While we are on the topic of arrogance, I must say that if I am to be charged with arrogance, it had better not be by the authors of the picture of the world religions that I outlined at the beginning of this essay. Any of *them* that flings a charge of arrogance at me is going to find himself surrounded by a lot of broken domestic glass. I may believe that everything that the Muslim believes that is inconsistent with what I believe is false. But then so does everyone who accepts the law of the excluded middle or the principle of noncontradiction. What I do *not* do is to inform the Muslim that every tenet of Islam that is inconsistent with Buddhism is not really essential to Islam. (Nor do I believe in my heart of hearts that every tenet of Islam that is inconsistent with the beliefs of late twentieth-century middle-class Anglo-American professors is not really essential to Islam.) Despite the fact that I reserve the right to believe things that are not believed by Muslims, I leave it to the Muslims to decide what is and what is not essential to Islam.

"But why should membership in the unique instrument of God's salvation depend upon accidents of birth? Isn't that rather unfair to those born at the wrong time and place to belong to it? Wouldn't God's unique instrument of salvation, if there were one, be universally available?"

This is a serious question. Before I answer it, let me remove a red herring. It is not necessary for Christians to believe that there is no salvation outside the *visible* Church. I do not know how widespread this belief has been in the past, but it is certainly not widespread today.... Nor do very many Christians believe that those who died before the creation of the Church are denied salvation.... The medieval legend of the Harrowing of Hell may be without any actual basis in the Apostles' Creed, but it testifies to the popularity of the belief that Christ's salvation is offered to those who died before His Incarnation.

So much for the red herring. Now for the serious question.... I take the only sure condition of damnation in which Christian belief is involved to be the following: Anyone who has accepted Christian belief and rejects it and rejects it still at the moment of his death—and rejects it with a clear mind, and not when maddened by pain or grief or terror—is damned.... What provision God makes for those who have never heard the Christian message, or who have heard it only in some distorted and falsifying form, I do not know. That is God's business and not ours. Our business is to see that as many as possible do hear the Christian message, and do not hear it in a distorted and falsifying form. (But I do know that one of the things that may keep a person from hearing the Good News in its right form is the presuppositions of his native culture and religion. A Christian of our culture may know the words that a missionary has spoken to, say, a Buddhist who thereafter remains a Buddhist; he will not necessarily know what the Buddhist has heard. I do not know, but I suspect, that many people in our own culture who are, formally, apostate Christians may never have heard the Christian message in its right form. I certainly hope so, and the statements that many apostate Christians make about the content of the Christian message encourage me in this hope.)

The way for a Christian to look at the saving power of the Church is, I believe, like this: The Church is like an invading army that, having established a bridgehead in occupied territory, moves on into the interior, consolidating its gains as it goes. All those who do not consciously and deliberately cast in their lot with the retreating enemy and flee with him to his final refuge will be liberated—even those who, misled by enemy propaganda, fear and mistrust the advancing army of liberation.

If an army establishes a bridgehead, it must establish it at some particular place. "And why in Palestine?" Because that's where Israel was. "And why did God choose to locate His people there rather than in India or China?" Well, it would have to be *somewhere*. Why *not* there? The question borders on the absurd, although it has been pointed out that Palestine is approximately at the center of the great Euro-Afro-Asian supercontinent. Why did the Allied armies land in Normandy? No doubt Eisenhower and Montgomery had their reasons. But if a skeptical Norman farmer or Resistance fighter had heard rumors of the Allied landing, and had asked "Why *here*?" you wouldn't have to know the reasons the Allied commanders had for choosing the Normandy beaches to answer him. It would suffice to point out that the same question could be raised about any reported landing site by those who happened to be in its vicinity, and that the question therefore raised no doubts about the veracity of the rumor.

"But why should our salvation be accomplished by the institution of something that can be compared to an invading army?" I have no idea, although I am glad that God has chosen a method that allows some of His servants the inestimable (and entirely unearned) honor of being His co-workers in bringing salvation to others. Perhaps there was no other way. Perhaps there were lots of other ways, but this one recommended itself to the divine wisdom for reasons that surpass human understanding. Or perhaps the reasons are ones we could understand but that it would not, at present, be profitable for us to know ("What is that to thee? Follow thou Me."). But I am sure of one thing. Anyone who believes in God, in a being of literally infinite knowledge and power and wisdom, and who believes that human beings require salvation, and who thinks he can see that God would not have used such a method to procure our salvation, has a very high opinion of his own powers of *a priori* reason.

Conclusion. If we are Christians we must believe that salvation has not come to humanity through Confucius or Gautama or Mohammed. We must believe that the salvation of humanity began with events that were quite unrelated to the lives and teachings of these men. We must believe that it began when some women standing outside a tomb were told, "He is not here." Perhaps there is some authority who has discovered good reasons for thinking that these central Christian beliefs are false. If so, it is not John Hick.

Discussion

1. Van Inwagen defends his particularist beliefs from the perspective of his Christian commitments. How might a Buddhist, Hindu, Taoist, Jew, or Muslim approach this topic?

2. Particularists are often accused of arrogance. How would you define "arrogance"? Does it apply to particularists? Has van Inwagen adequately rebutted the accusation?

MULTIPLE RELIGIOUS ORIENTATION

JEANINE DILLER*

Introduction. I want to explore how people are living out an openness to multiple religions, not in a social, political or communal context so much, but rather in one's own personal plan of life, as part of what one intends, consciously or not, to do in one's life. This question arises *after* one has found a way to muscle through the theoretical issues about being involved with more than one religion—including for example the apparent contradiction between their central beliefs—some of which may be resolved by adopting a view such as John Hick's or Mark Heim's (see Hick; Heim). Suppose I am convinced that multiple religiosity can make sense, and I want to adopt it in some way. How then can I live?

This issue has been on my mind ever since I met my friend, whom I'll call "Nan," twenty years ago in graduate school. She was born to a Hindu mother and a Christian father and was dating a Jew whom she eventually married. On top of all this, she was an anthropology major—open to and relaxed with diversity and ready to engage it. As her roommate, I watched her go off to Diwali and then a couple months later prepare for Christmas and then Easter, and eventually Shabbat on Friday nights and more.

As a pure-bred Christian, I was bowled over. I'd never seen anyone engage in anything except one religion at a time, and I was both attracted and repelled. Attracted, because of experiences I'd had while traveling: I had seen Jews at the Western wall deep in prayer, and remembered thinking they looked holier than me, seemed in closer touch with God than I felt myself. I had also traveled to India by this time and had had

the great fortune of being on the ghats, the stairs that border the Ganges River, at a holy city for the Hindus, Varanasi, early one morning near dawn. I remember seeing a man, maybe about twenty years old, submerge into the river and resurface with an expression on his face so full of relief and connection that I could not help but think something spiritually real had happened to him in that moment. These experiences made me think that there was some path through Judaism and Hinduism in addition to Christianity to genuine religious experience and to God, and I suspected it was probably wider than just these three—that God would find a way to meet people, sincere people really searching for God, where they were. So when I saw Nan engaging in Jewish, Hindu and Christian practice, I was for it. It demonstrated an even-handed approach to the many paths to God that seem extant in the world's religious traditions. Also, Nan was experiencing more of a good thing; if one path is good, could three paths be better?

On the other hand, I was thrown by how religiously busy Nan was; it looked frenetic. Moreover, I experienced spiritual recoil. I was about as Christian as they come: my parents were Christian missionaries in Africa before I was born; I had been praying to God as far back as I could remember; I had been saved, baptized, and kept the faith: I even attended Wheaton College (Billy Graham's alma mater). So when Nan asked me to go to Diwali with her, I demurred, thinking, "This isn't my path. This could be a good path for someone else, but it's not my path."

Issues about multiple religiosity have been in my belly ever since. Here, I want to tackle what has bothered me about this issue recently: the concrete options for participating in multiple religions. That is, Nan showed me one way to be multiply religious—to practice the major holidays of three traditions, without delving deeply into their value and belief claims. What are other ways people participate in multiple religions; what is, really, the full slate of options for multiple religiosity?

---

* Jeanine Diller is Director, Center for Religious Understanding and Assistant Professor of Philosophy and Religion at the University of Toledo.

Multiple religious participation: what, why, who. To prepare to explore the "how" of multiple religious participation later, let's turn in this section to what multiple religious participation is, why people do it, and who they are. John Berthrong's wonderfully titled book *The Divine Deli*—as in "I'll take a Christian hamburger on a Jewish Kaiser bun with a bit of Hindu mango chutney on top"—provides a good start at a definition of multiple religious participation:

> ... the conscious (and sometimes even unconscious) use of religious ideas, practices, symbols, meditations, prayers, chants and sensibilities derived from one tradition by a member of another ... for their own purposes. (Berthrong, 35)

So "multiple religious participation" is borrowing something from another tradition to use in one's own tradition or—to make an addendum to Berthrong—to use even if one stands in no tradition or in multiple traditions, as we will see.

Why might someone be motivated to participate in multiple religions? I take the motivations to break into two types: situational and intentional. The situational reasons come from forces in one's life present for some reason other than one's religiosity; for example, by dint of love or marriage or one's family's practice or culture. Nan is a great example: she was born into a family that was already participating in two traditions and then, by covenant of marriage, she was thrown into a third. So, to borrow a line from Shakespeare, some are born multiply religious, and some have multiple religiosity thrust upon them. But some *achieve* multiple religiosity—that is, they consciously aim for it and get it into their lives, voluntarily.

Sometimes, I find myself envying people who have a situational reason for multiple religiosity because I am attracted to it and there is a certain naturalness about situational reasons. If someone says: "why are you trying to practice all these religions?" Nan for instance has the ready reply that she was born and married into this life. No question of artifice there. I don't have that. I'm from a Mennonite bloodline on both sides, to the point that after my Irish-Catholic husband and I married and he came to the first family reunion for my side, he said, "I bet you're thanking me for diversifying the gene pool around here." And, although marrying a Catholic husband has brought some intrareligious diversity in my life, that bond alone does not explain my forays into religious practices outside Christianity. Someone like me actually needs a reason to be interested in multiple religious participation; I don't have one built in, as it were.

Possible reasons are manifold. My stories about Israel and India already suggest that one might have an experiential basis for being interested. One doesn't have to cross seas to meet people of other faiths; there is plenty of religious diversity in America to provide an experiential basis for interest. Even if one does not encounter religious others directly, one might find wisdom in the writings or speech of people from other religious traditions. Or one might find techniques that enhance one's spirituality—such as ways of purifying the ego or calming the mind that enable deeper forms of prayer than one had before, or more truthful interactions in one's day-to-day life. If one finds such enhancements important enough, they might, as an anonymous commentator indicated, develop a "hunger" for multiple religious forms—a hunger that arises from the realization that one tradition is not sufficient to nourish one's spiritual life. Sheer curiosity is also a driving force. As with physical travel, one might be simply curious—what is it like over there, in that religion?

Finally, those whose spiritual journey is at least partly intellectual might be attracted to multiple religiosity as a means to know God or—said more broadly to attempt to refer to the object of religious concern in more traditions—to know ultimate reality. Saying that it takes participation in more than one religion to come to know ultimate reality implies a stance on the three customary theologies of religious pluralism. One might think there is just one path to knowledge of the ultimate, a position generally called "exclusivism" but which I call "loyalism" to make it habitable (it is generally motivated by a desire to stay true to claims in one's scriptures, and that is too beautiful a thing to give an ugly name). Or one might think there are many paths to get to the ultimate, called pluralism. Or one might think something in between—the "inclusivist" view that there is only one effective path all the way to the ultimate, but there are many paths that get one part of the way there, or that the sincerity or intensity with which one follows a "not-as-effective" path puts one on the effective path without one's knowing it.

If one takes the pluralist or inclusivist view, one might be drawn to multiple religious participation as a necessary means of getting a fuller picture of what ultimate reality is truly like. Think of ultimate reality in this picture as a diamond which one can see from one's viewpoint, on one side. In order to see all its facets, one actually has to move around it to grasp it from other viewpoints. If one stays just in one's position, one can find out important truths about it but will miss out on other truths of what it is like from over there, and there. On this understanding one actually *requires* the other viewpoint in order to get a fuller grasp of what it is one knows from one's own. So that is another motivation for voluntarily taking on multiple religious participation.

Whatever the reasons, there seems to be an increasing number of people participating in multiple religions. As Francis X. Clooney, S.J., says, there are signs we are now riding a "new inter-religious wave":

> The phenomenon of "multiple religious belonging" is now deeply engrained in American culture. We can no longer imagine simply the prospect of well-established religions and their members deciding whether to dialogue or not. People, younger people in particular, find

themselves having multiple religious attractions, experiences and commitments which cannot easily be fit into any given religious system. (Clooney 2013, paragraph 3)

It is this range of "multiple religious attractions, experiences and commitments" that Clooney says people "find themselves having" which we will track next.

Multiple religious orientation: how. How would one order up a multiply religious life if one wanted to? We are about to delve into a plethora of options available for doing this, a smorgasbord of ways of being multiply religious. Why are there so many? My hypothesis: because of the inherently complex nature of religion itself.

I was a bio/pre-med major for the first couple years of college. When I switched to philosophy and religion, everything felt extremely abstract. I kept craving my fetal pig and my vial of liquids because I knew what it was that I was trying to understand; it was there, right in front of my eyes. I wondered, "*Where is religion? What is it I am trying to understand?*" and finally got an answer when I read Ninian Smart. His seven dimensions of religion are the seven different places where religion can be found: (1) rituals, such as taking communion; (2) narratives, or stories that ground traditions, such as the cosmic story of creation or Jesus' last supper story which underlies the ritual of the mass; (3) religious experiences and emotions, such as awe; (4) people—everyone who's part of a tradition—are actually part of the stuff of the tradition, as well as the institutional structures that people create and inhabit together, such as the church; (5) ethics, meaning norms about the right thing to do by people; (6) beliefs, such as that Jesus is the Son of God; and (7) material religion, such as sacred spaces, candles, icons, prayer beads, music and more, which are tangible traces of the other six dimensions or are conducive to creating them.

These seven dimensions create the many ways one can participate in religion: one can dip into one or more of the dimensions. One can pray or meditate or attend a service, retell a religious story, be inspired by a religious exemplar, discipline one's actions around a religious code, believe a religious tenet, take solace in a religious sanctuary, and much more. Once we grasp the number of ways one might be involved in a religion, and then think of the number of religions, we can see that the logically possible number of combinations for multiple religious participation is incredibly vast.

Two continua. Furthermore—and I say this with a little trepidation since it semi-quantifies an utterly qualitative phenomenon—the many options for participating in a religion or religions run on a continuum. Working with Smart's stuff of religion, we can order forms of religious participation from light to more intense forms of participation in this way:

1. *Conceptual openness.* One is not yet doing anything, believing anything, or putting one's body anywhere. But one is open to the possibility that some of the beliefs of this religion are true, or that some of its practices are useful for spiritual growth, or that some of its ethics are morally right, etc. Many of my non-religious students, for instance, are open in this way. This is a very slight form of participation, but I take it to be one because it is so markedly different from conceptual closure.

2. *Material contact.* I have another friend who is not very religious, but she does enter sacred spaces and takes comfort and solace from just being in them. This is fairly low-stakes participation, in the sense that one is not believing or practicing anything, but one is still participating just a little by being in the

space. The same is true when I visited the ghats at Varanasi; I participated just a little that morning in Hinduism by being there that morning by watching and in that case also by sensing the religious emotions of the moment that Smart mentioned, maybe even co-feeling or vicariously feeling them in the way we do at the movies. The same can be true of holding prayer or meditation beads, or seeing an icon, or hearing chants, or visiting a congregational service when one is not using them ritualistically oneself but taking in the materiality in still form or as actively used by others.

3. *Interfaith collaboration.* A paradigmatic example of this is the Better Together Campaign that Interfaith Youth Core out of Chicago is advancing: it brings college students together across religious divides to do something good in the name of religious difference, whether it be advocating for people without a voice, housing people who are homeless, feeding people who are hungry or working for sustainable energy solutions. These multifaith activities rely on a shared ethics of compassion and being a force for the good implicit in so many religious and secular perspectives. Working shoulder to shoulder with people who think differently about religion builds relationships and understanding of shared values. It can also be a form of multiple religious participation depending on the way participants see it, e.g., it is if one takes oneself to be living out the ethical branches of various religions together.

4. *Dialogue* with someone whose perspective on religion is different from one's own is another form of participating in another religion

lightly. One talks with people of different religious perspectives about their perspectives firsthand. In so doing, one steps into how that religion gets embodied, and thus learns about its practices, beliefs, experiences, emotions, etc., encounters one of the myriad of people who themselves help make up the social stuff of the religion itself, and in deep forms of dialogue comes away grasping one's own perspective and life anew in transformative ways. As Leonard Swidler explains: "The goal of dialogue is to learn, and to change accordingly" (see Swidler). Such dialogues are happening worldwide.

Note that these last two categories—interfaith collaboration and dialogue—are necessarily forms of multiple religious participation, whereas the first two—conceptual openness and material contact—could be done for one or multiple religions.

All four categories constitute relatively low-stakes ways of participating in a religion. They are all ways of learning about it from the outside, watching or hearing about or working alongside others who are doing it. The remaining categories go progressively deeper because in them one engages in the tradition *oneself*, from the inside. These represent a new level of intensity of participation, different not just in degree but in kind.

5. *Comparative theology.* Francis Clooney founded a method called "comparative theology" that aims at "small, useful engagements in diversity" (Clooney, 2010, 68) by selecting just two texts across a religious divide of which one is on one side; e.g., Clooney as a Christian pairs a Christian text with a non-Christian one. One studies first the text from the other tradition—slowly and carefully, owning and watching the bias

of one's perspective—then takes what one learns from it *back* to the text from one's own tradition, looking for fresh insights about one's own view from the other view (Clooney, 2010, 60).

At first comparative theology sounds like an approach from the outside, as with the first four, this time by way of study. However, this last step of letting the other tradition inform one's own means that comparative theologians are actually *trying on for themselves* the other religion's ways of thinking. It goes beyond conceptual openness or listening to a conceptual participation in another tradition—even if just temporarily in one's imagination or conceptualization, for the sake of one's grasp of one's own.

6. *Adopting belief(s).* This form of participation goes beyond temporary or imaginative conceptual participation to actual adoption of one or more of a religion's beliefs in an isolated way that does not rise to the level of identity or belonging. Perhaps comparative theologians sometimes arrive here, when a belief that they have imagined fits.

Adopting selected beliefs from a single religion is, I think, relatively common and unproblematic, e.g., someone might say that they believe in what Jesus said during the Sermon on the Mount but not the further claim that Jesus is God. Adopting selected beliefs from multiple religions, though, can be trickier because in some cases—for some traditions, and for some beliefs—they *contradict* one another. Take beliefs about the status of Jesus in Judaism, Christianity, and Islam. These contradict each other. In Judaism, Jesus is not seen as God or a prophet. In Christianity, he is seen as God and not just a prophet, and in Islam he is seen as a prophet but not as God. One cannot adopt all three of these beliefs simultaneously without being incoherent.

How then does one believe across these traditions without being incoherent? Be careful not to adopt the beliefs that conflict. Adopt *other, supplementary* beliefs that *are* consistent. For example, beliefs that one religion proclaims but about which the other remains silent are formally consistent. So a reformed Jew without a specific idea of life after death could adopt a Muslim idea of Paradise. Similarly, Jews, Christians and Muslims could adopt Buddhism's Four Noble Truths since all three traditions are basically silent about them.

7. *Adopting practices.* This is a very visible form of religious participation—people engaging in one or more practices from a tradition such as attending public services, being involved in other communal events, adopting forms of prayer or meditation, etc.

As was the case with adopting selected beliefs, adopting selected practices from a single religion is at least conceptually unproblematic, e.g., someone might adopt Buddhist vipassana meditation without also proclaiming the Triple Gem. Adopting selected practices from multiple religions, though, can be difficult since practices might conflict in the same way beliefs do; in some cases this is because contradictory beliefs underlie the practices in question. For instance a Jew or Muslim could not consistently take the Christian Eucharist given its connections with Christian beliefs about Jesus' death and resurrection. But, as with beliefs, people can still adopt *other* practices that *complement* or *supplement* one another. Among the many available examples, Thomas Merton (*Seven Storey*), Robert Kennedy (*Zen Gifts*), and Paul Knitter (*Without Buddha*) have each added Buddhist practices to their Christian ones; Thich Nhat Hanh (*Living Buddha*) has done the reverse; the memorably-titled class of "Jew-Bu's" combine Jewish and Buddhist forms. There are

also Christians taking up Jewish Sabbath and Passover rituals, to name a few.

8. *Identity.* Identity is calling oneself a participant in a particular tradition ("I am a Buddhist")—a deep form of participation that might happen suddenly or gradually, sometimes after sufficient belief or practice to warrant self-identifying. Identity is, I am sure, subject to a host of psychological and sociological pressures. Such identity, as I am using the term, is decided by the *individual*. Though most religious identities at least in the United States are single-religious identities, it is in principle possible to identify with multiple religions. As in the belief and practice cases, though, one will need to be judicious about which ones (more on this soon).

9. *Belonging.* In contrast, belonging is decided by the *community* of the religion in question in some way. This might be by way of a leader in the tradition, as when a rabbi confers the status of being a convert to Judaism, or by way of an initiation rite, such as saying and earnestly meaning the *shahadah* for Islam (no leader required), or by both, such as when a Catholic priest takes a candidate through the rites of Christian baptism and confirmation or a Zen priest takes a candidate through Jukai. Again, single belonging is the norm at least in the United States, but multiple belonging is theoretically possible and actually done, as we shall see soon.

Identity and belonging are both deep forms of participation. I place identity before belonging here since, in adult conversion anyway, it is precisely the fact that someone self-identifies with a religion that makes him or her seek belonging to make that identity official. But this may run the other way 'round, too: for example, in cases where one belongs as an infant, one may self-identify only later, and in that case identity will be the deeper form.

This is then a continuum of ways of participating in religion. The farther one goes on this continuum, the *deeper* one participates in religion. At the same time, there is a second continuum: one can participate in these ways for one or two or a number of religions. The more traditions one practices, the *broader* one participates in religion.

How would one order up a multiply religious life if one wanted to?

Religious orientations. Understanding the variety of ways one can participate in religion as we just did can heighten self-understanding: it enables one to see one's own tree in the forest of possibilities for religious participation. It is interesting for me to see, for example, that I have been participating in dialogues and interfaith community action that have put me into contact with an indefinite number of religious perspectives at a relatively low-stakes level, and that simultaneously I have limited my higher-stakes participation to a limited, definite set of traditions. The reader can explore where her or his own profile lies.

There are common *patterns* of religious participation, which I will call "religious orientations." Understanding them allows us to talk carefully about radically different kinds of religious orientations that run the gamut from no participation in any religion to multiple ways of participating in multiple religions. Some of these patterns are engaged in frequently enough that they have been given names in the literature; I will suggest a couple other patterns that do not as yet have names as we proceed.

The first pattern, which I will call *non-religiosity*, refers to those who have no religious activity at all. Non-religious people may be pro-religious or anti-religious or neutral about religion; their essential feature is that they do not engage in religion. Some of the sharply increasing number of Americans who are religiously "unaffiliated" probably follow this pattern. The Pew report "'Nones' on the Rise" (2012) suggests some of the unaffiliated do not believe or practice in major ways, e.g., 49% of this group never attend a religious service (Pew, 11), and 32% do not believe in God (Pew, 9). Moreover, 88% say they are "not looking for a religion that would be right" for them (Pew, 10), which probably means they are not dialoguing or studying or collaborating with religious traditions either.

So some of the religiously unaffiliated are probably non-religious altogether.

Some of the unaffiliated display what I would call *light religiosity*—with some religious activity but lacking in identity and belonging that comprise affiliation. Eight per cent are attending religious services at least annually, and an interesting 18% are doing enough with religion to count themselves as religious but unaffiliated, though why they say this and thus what they may be up to religiously is unreported by Pew (Pew, 22). The unaffiliated also report strikingly high degrees of spirituality: 68% believe in God (30% are indeed "absolutely certain" there is a God), and 41% pray at least monthly (21% in fact daily). Some of these forms of spirituality may surface occasionally in a religious form unreported by Pew, e.g., occasional use of a Hail Mary or prayer beads, etc. I assume that light religiosity typically occurs in a single religion.

There are other patterns of unaffiliated behavior I'll call *seeking* and *multiple religious curiosity*. The seekers are the 10% of the unaffiliated that Pew says *are* looking for a religion that is right for them and who thus are probably engaging multiple religions in various ways as part of their search. Those with multiple religious curiosity behave like seekers but have a different intention. They are *not* actively looking for a "right" religion but have as Clooney says "multiple religious attractions and experiences" for an indefinite number of religions.

These then are the major religious orientations short of identity and belonging: non-religiosity, light religiosity, seeking and multiple religious curiosity. The first pattern that rises to the level of identity is *single identity without belonging* which is (as the name indicates) participation in *one* religious tradition to the point of identity, but without taking the steps to belong formally (such as baptism or jukai; about which more below). *Hybrid identity without belonging* is (1) participation in *multiple* traditions to the point of identity but without formal belonging, and (2) the melding of these identities into one. So think of Nan: instead of saying "I'm a Hindu and a Christian and a Jew," she would say "I'm a Jewish-Christian-Hindu," where the hyphens are a verbal trace of her combining the religions in her identity.

The phenomenon of religious hybridity is nicely elaborated by two thinkers, Jeannine Hill Fletcher and Michelle Voss Roberts. Hill Fletcher, in a wonderful piece called "Shifting Identity," writes: "When aspects of identity are forged into a singular individual in such a way that they cannot easily be compartmentalized, one cannot ask what it means to be a Christian without recognizing that the answer is also conditioned by other identity categories.... [In] lived experience... our identity features are mutually informing..." (Hill Fletcher, 17).

The fact that our identities "mutually inform" each other seems powerfully right. I am both a professor and a mother. But one can't really understand the kind of professor I am until one understands that I am a mother; I am the kind of professor who will not answer emails between 5 and 9 pm. One also can't understand the kind of mother I am until one understands that I am a professor; I am the kind of mother who is not going to be able to go on all the field trips.

Thus, although it is accurate to say I am a professor and accurate to say I am a mother, it is even more accurate to say that I am a professor-mother, the hybrid which explains how these two identities inform one another.

Nan's religious hybridity seems to go deeper than my professor-motherhood, though, since I am comfortable claiming either identity solo, but she would not say she is a Jew full stop, or a Christian full stop, or a Hindu full stop. Her identity is only with the hybrid. As Voss Roberts says: "Hybrid identity is both double and partial. Hybrid identity is double because it affirms multiple realities; it is partial because it is never completely at home in any of them.... [given] the necessity of everyday life (Voss Roberts, 51).

I suspect Nan is "never completely at home" in her religious identities because of two colliding facts: (1) "holding [these identities] loosely" means avoiding holding a belief from one of these religions that contradicts a belief in another, and (2) for her particular triad, Nan might reasonably take some of the beliefs that contradict each other to be essential to these traditions—for example, she may take the contradictory beliefs about Jesus' divinity in Christianity and Judaism to be essential to those faiths, or she might take beliefs about God's being one in Judaism and Christianity but many or all in Hinduism to be essential to all three faiths. To hold the triad together, then, she might avoid believing *any* of these things, which would make her *lack* beliefs essential to being a full-blown Jew, Christian, or Hindu. So the most she could do is identify with the hybrid "Jewish-Christian-Hindu" and adopt the remaining non-conflicting beliefs and practices. Since these are legion, Nan can still be very religiously occupied, but there will be silences about the conflicts even in the midst of the activity.

Now let's move from religious identity to religious *belonging*, beginning with *single belonging* in which one participates in a single religion to the point of formally belonging to it, by whatever leader or rite of initiation makes it official. Single belonging is a common form of religiosity. Moreover, some of the greatest saints and mystics of all time are single-belongers. To use Christian examples, St. Theresa of Avila, St. John of the Cross, St. Thomas Aquinas—all were engaged completely and only in the Christian tradition. Obviously, single belonging to any major religious tradition is rich enough to command our attention for a lifetime and still leave us with more to know and experience.

Open single belonging, as I am calling it, parallels the conceptual openness which sits between non-religiosity and the lower-stakes forms of religious participation. It is a conceptual openness to another tradition while sitting in one's home tradition. Another friend of mine is an open single-belonger. She practices, identifies and belongs as a Christian. Though she doesn't engage other traditions actively, she takes her identity as a Christian to be historically contingent on her being born into her family and culture, and she is probably right about this given the statistics showing that, had she been born somewhere else in the world, she probably would have had a *different* home tradition. She knows she could switch to some other path but takes her path to work equally well and really better for her: it is no accident that the symbols and the practices and the beliefs on this path are efficacious for her because it's her tradition. So she is open to the truth or efficacy of another tradition, but content belonging where she is.

Single belonging with crossing over applies to people who belong in one tradition but "cross over" by adopting beliefs or practices from other traditions as a way to inform their own tradition. Thomas Merton is a good example. Although he travelled, dialogued, studied, and wrote eloquently and with insight about Buddhism and Daoism, and though he engaged in Buddhist meditation, he never identified with or belonged to either Buddhism or Daoism. He was a Catholic monk, a single-belonger, who crossed over by using practices and taking inspiration from the texts of other traditions (see Merton).

Another orientation is *hybrid identity with belonging*. This is similar to hybrid identity without belonging, since it involves participation to the point of identity in multiple traditions and identity with a "dash," but in the context of *belonging* to one of them. In this regard, Francis Clooney is interesting because he seems to maintain a primary allegiance and belonging to Christianity but in a form that imbues Christianity with Hinduism. Peter Feldmeier writes of Clooney: "If asked, 'Are you a Hindu or a Christian-Hindu?' Clooney would say that he is not, that he is a Christian, particularly a Roman Catholic Jesuit. Then he might say, as he has in public conferences, something like: 'But, in a way, I am a kind of Hindu-Christian. It has become a part of me'" (Feldmeier, 272). For Clooney, Hinduism is enhancing Christianity, not the other way around. The order matters. Clooney has gone through all of the rites of initiation to become a Hindu (indeed can administer them all) but as a Christian.

The logic of Clooney's single-belonging with hybridity may mirror Nan's non-belonging hybridity in at least one way: for his particular diad, Clooney might reasonably take some of the Hindu and Christian beliefs that contradict each other to be essential to these traditions—for example, beliefs about Jesus' status or God's nature. But, unlike Nan who stays agnostic about beliefs that conflict in her traditions which makes her unable to belong to any of them, Clooney can drop the Hindu beliefs that conflict with Christian ones to honor his full belonging in Christianity—certainly at least until further dialogue indicates otherwise.

Double belonging is comparatively neat and clean: one formally belongs to the two traditions of interest by going through the rites of initiation for both. Take as a good example Robert Kennedy, S.J., who is an American Jesuit priest and also a Zen Roshi master in the White Plume lineage. He says that Christians come to Zen for a deeper prayer life—that "Zen gives us a method to put (Christian) contemplation into practice" (2004). Or consider Paul Knitter, author of *Without Buddha, I Could Not Be a Christian* and both a Catholic and a Buddhist, who writes toward the end of his memoir: "In 1939 I was baptized. In 2008 I took refuge. I can truly call myself what I think I've been over these past decades: a Buddhist Christian" (216). Notice the two formal markers of his double belonging, and the lack of a hyphen between the identities.

Double belonging takes judgment. As in the hybrid cases, one tries to avoid holding beliefs in one tradition that conflict with the other. Combining that norm here with the call also to belong to both traditions entails that one must identify traditions whose essential beliefs do not contradict. It is generally assumed that the essential beliefs of Buddhism and Christianity do not contradict, at least regarding fundamentals, and hence we see Buddhist Christians and Christian Buddhists. This is not so for other pairings. For example, many Christian and Muslim denominations take the beliefs about the divinity of Jesus in their faiths both to conflict and to be essential, making double belonging to these faiths difficult if not impossible, at least within these denominations. For example, the Episcopal Church in 2009 deposed Ann Holmes Redding as an Episcopal priest after she proclaimed in 2007 that she had become "both Muslim and Christian," and in early 2016 Wheaton College (IL) terminated Associate Professor Larycia Hawkins for saying that Muslims and Christians worshipped the same God.

The final category of *beyond belonging* typically involves those who single-belonged but who by their own report moved beyond belonging to an embrace of every religious form. The category of "beyond belonging" is thus interestingly similar to multiple religious curiosity in its interest in an indefinite number of religious forms, but instead of being embodied without ever having belonged to a religion, this interest is typically embodied after religious belonging.

We can see beyond belonging in both Rumi and Ibn Arabi. Rumi says, "I am neither Muslim, nor Christian, Jew nor Zoroastrian; I am neither of the earth nor of the heavens; I am neither body nor soul" ("Poems," 11). Similarly, Ibn Arabi, roughly at the same time, writes: "My heart has become capable of every form: it is a pasture for gazelles and a convent for Christian monks, a temple for idols and the pilgrim's Ka'ba and the tables of the Torah and the book of the Qur'an. I follow the religion of Love: whatever way Love's camels take, that is my religion and my faith" (Al-Arabi, *Tarjuman*, verses 13–15).

Rumi's quotation makes beyond belonging sound like no-belonging; Ibn Arabi's makes it sound like all-belonging. But the point of both seems the same: the categories of belonging fail because the Reality that they take themselves to be "experiencing in two different traditions is [, they think,] both within and beyond all traditions." It is as the Buddha and Wittgenstein said: both have kicked the raft or ladder of belonging away because they have no need of it now.

Conclusion. I began this essay with the question of how one can live out multiple religions at once. We now have eight answers to this question in the form of eight multiple religious orientations—seeking, multiple religious curiosity, hybrid identity without belonging, open single belonging, single belonging with crossing over, hybrid identity with belonging, double belonging, and beyond belonging. We also have four other religious orientations that naturally arose on our way through the continuum—non-religiosity, light religiosity, single identity without belonging, and single belonging.

What does this understanding of religious orientations in general and multiple religious orientations in particular yield? For one thing, it gives us names and a conceptual order for states of multiple religious participation which together may allow us to ask old questions more carefully and ask some new questions, too. One new question that haunted me as I wrote is whether multiple religiosity is an acquired taste, and more specifically whether, for some people at least, the lighter forms of it such as seeking and multiple religious curiosity give way to the more intense forms of it.

Old questions about multiple religiosity that we can understand anew include a fidelity question: Is participating in multiple religions unfaithful? The work on orientations allows us to see that this question arises more urgently for the *more* intense forms of participation, since those without identity or belonging have little or no religion to be unfaithful *to*. The reverse is true of an ethical question about multiple religiosity: is participating in other religions plundering them for one's own gain? Vincent Miller argues in *Consuming Religion* that we are not plundering if, when we participate in another religion, we do so within this religion's fuller theoretical and practical context. Assuming that Miller is right, it turns out that the ethical question is more pressing for the *less* intense forms of participation since they take in less of the context Miller recommends.

Finally, this work on religious orientations leaves us with a wider personal perspective on the field: it creates self-understanding to know where our tree stands in the forest of options. It also may make us aware of new possibilities for living out religiosity that we had not yet considered—a result that could prove useful in these religiously transforming times.

References

Al-Arabi, Ibn. *The Tarjuman al-Ashwaq.* Tr. Reynold A. Nicholson. 1911. The Internet Sacred Texts Archive. www.sacred-texts.com/isl /taa/taa14.htm. Accessed 21 January 2016.

Berthrong, John. *Divine Deli: Religious Identity in the North American Cultural Mosaic.* Maryknoll, NY: Orbis, 1999.

Clooney, Francis X., S.J. *Comparative Theology: Deep Learning across Religious Borders.* Malden, MA: Wiley-Blackwell, 2010.

Clooney, Francis X., S.J. "New Wave Interreligious Thinking." *America.* In All Things Blog. June 7, 2013. Vol. 210, no. 5053. Accessed 7 June 2015 at www.americamagazine.org/content/all-things /new-wave-interreligious-thinking.

Cornille, Catherine. "Introduction: The Dynamics of Multiple Belonging." In Cornille, *Many Mansions?: Multiple Religious Belonging and Christian Identity.* Maryknoll, NY: Orbis, 2002. 1–6.

Hanh, Thich Nhat. *Living Buddha, Living Christ.* New York: Berkley Publishing, 2007.

Heim, S. Mark. *Salvations: Truth and Difference in Religion.* Maryknoll, NY: Orbis, 1995.

Hick, John. *An Interpretation of Religion: Human Responses to the Transcendent.* 2nd ed. New Haven, CT: Yale UP. 2004.

Hill Fletcher, Jeannine. "Shifting Identity." *Journal of Feminist Studies in Religion* 19.2 (2003): 5–24.

Kennedy, Robert, S.J., and Roshi. *Zen Gifts to Christians.* New York: Bloomsbury Academic, 2004.

Knitter, Paul. *Without Buddha I Could Not Be a Christian.* Croydon, UK: Oneworld Publications, 2009.

Merton, Thomas. *Mystics and Zen Masters.* New York: Douglas & McIntyre, 1967.

Merton, Thomas. *Seven Storey Mountain.* Fiftieth anniversary ed. New York: Harcourt Brace and Company, 1998.

Miller, Vincent. *Consuming Religion.* New York: Bloomsbury Academic, 2013.

Pew Forum on Religion and Public Life. "'Nones' on the Rise: One-in-Five Adults Have No Religious Affiliation." Luis Logo, Director. 2012. Accessed at http://www.pewforum.org/2012/10/09/nones -on-the-rise/.

Rumi, Jalal ad-Din. "Poems from the Divan-I Shams-I Tabriz" [1270]. The Internet History Sourcebooks Project of Fordham University: The Jesuit University of New York. https://legacy.fordham .edu/halsall/source/1270rumi-poems1.asp. Accessed 1/21/2016.

Swidler, Leonard. "What Is Dialogue?" under "Dialogue Resources" on the website of the Dialogue Institute/Journal of Ecumenical Studies, http://dialogueinstitute.org/what-is-dialogue/.

Voss Roberts, Michelle. "Religious Belonging and the Multiple." *Journal of Feminist Studies in Religion* 26.1 (2010): 43–62.

Discussion

1. Where on Diller's continuum would you locate yourself?

2. What are the benefits of your diverse religious beliefs/commitments?

3. What are some tensions you feel with respect to your religious beliefs/commitments?

Chapter 27

Feminist Theology

FEMINIST CHRISTIAN PHILOSOPHY?

PATRICIA ALTENBERND JOHNSON*

Advice to Christian philosophers. In 1984, Alvin Plantinga offered some Advice to Christian Philosophers.[1] He suggested that, within the philosophical community in which we, as Christians, find ourselves, we need to display more autonomy, more integrity, and more boldness. My aim is to offer some further, but related advice. Christian philosophers would do well to heed the voices of feminist philosophers both within and outside of the Christian community. If our philosophy is an "expression of deep and fundamental perspectives, ways of viewing ourselves and the world and God" (Plantinga, p. 271), then we must constantly examine those perspectives in order better to articulate them and to understand how those perspectives relate to our thought and our action. In this essay, I will set out the hermeneutical structure of the task that Plantinga recommends for Christian philosophers and show how the voices of feminism contribute to this task. . . .

The hermeneutical stance of the Christian philosopher. Plantinga's advice helps us understand our stance as Christian philosophers in relation to the wider philosophical community. He tells us the story of a young woman (Christian in her religious commitments)

---

* Patricia Altenbernd Johnson is Professor of Philosophy, Emerita at the University of Dayton.

who goes to college and discovers that "philosophy is the subject for her" (p. 254). As an undergraduate she learns how philosophy is currently practiced. She goes to grad school and learns even more fully the standards and assumptions that guide contemporary philosophical thought. She learns these parameters well. She respects her mentors, and she is inclined to think that departure from these parameters is "at best marginally respectable" (p. 255). Plantinga suggests that as time goes on this young philosopher—now a professional—may "note certain tensions between her Christian belief and her way of practicing philosophy" (p. 256). She may become so concerned about these tensions that she tries to put the two together, "to harmonize them" (p. 256). Plantinga's advice to her is that she is misdirected in doing this. What she should do instead is allow her sense of tension to help her critique the presuppositions of current philosophy. Moreover, she should listen to her own voice and be emboldened to set aside the philosophical parameters of her mentors, to reject their presuppositions and begin from within her own context. She must recognize that all philosophy is engaged, is committed to a definite presuppositional stance, and she must have the Christian courage to follow through on her own engagement.

I find this story compelling for a number of reasons. It describes the hermeneutical process of my own philosophical development in a simple and direct manner. It speaks to me as a religious person who loves philosophy and who is schooled within contemporary philosophical parameters. Moreover, it recognizes the philosophical voice of women.

The hermeneutical process depicted by this story is one that can be called a "hermeneutic of transformation".... It is a [hermeneutical] process that uncovers and critiques the presuppositions of our fundamental interpretive stances. It then provides us with a transformed framework for further interpreting our basic experiences and texts. This hermeneutical process involves four steps or stages.

(1) Contemporary philosophical hermeneutics has shown us that all understanding is engaged and has a presuppositional structure. Entering into any specific discipline or role requires that we take on certain presuppositions, that we become engaged in certain ways.

Usually we do not reflect on those presuppositions. We learn them as part of standing within a particular role or discipline. We do this from at least the time we begin to learn language. We learn to speak and conceptualize in a particular language long before we ever reflect on the implications of the structure of that language. Indeed, a person can speak a language for all of her or his life and never reflect on the structure of the language.

(2) Sometimes, as was the case with the young philosopher in Plantinga's account, something from our experience leads us to sense a tension between the commitments in one area of our life and those in another area, ... for example in our religious life, make us suspicious of our commitments in another area, for example in our philosophical activity. Often it is the experience of exclusion or of trivialization of something that our experience tells us is important that leads us to our suspicions.... This has certainly been the case for the Christian in contemporary philosophy. The experience of the importance of spiritual life or religious community has led us to be suspicious of any philosophy that excludes these.

(3) The first response to our suspicions is usually to try to harmonize the commitments that we experience in tension. Our understanding changes and we ask for changes in the discipline or role, but we try not to abandon the presuppositions, the engagements, of the areas that are in tension. ...

(4) While in some cases it may be possible to retain two sets of presuppositions, harmonizing them to eliminate the tensions, in many cases the suspicion raised leads us to reject certain presuppositions and so to transform a discipline or role. Plantinga advises us to listen to our experience as Christians and to be bold enough to philosophize out of that experience rather than to try to accommodate our thought to the parameters of others. Indeed, he advises us that we need not be concerned with trying to convince these others of the legitimacy or importance of our presuppositional structure. We are to do philosophy as Christians. We might say that he suggests that transformation takes place through action. ...

If we recognize this hermeneutical process as one that we have gone through in our experience as Christians and as philosophers, then we must also recognize the importance of examining the presuppositional structure of our present philosophical engagement. We must listen to the voices of those who, while sharing our Christian commitments, raise suspicions about the nature of our presuppositional structure. It is the voices of women I would urge us to hear today: women who stand committedly within the Christian community and within the philosophical community, women who raise suspicions out of the experience of lack of agency (exclusion) and silencing (trivialization), and women who speak out of their own experiences of what it means to be bold.

Their suspicion is that patriarchy is deeply embedded in the presuppositional structure of Christianity and so also of any philosophy that accepts unquestioningly this presuppositional structure. Their task, if they are to take Plantinga seriously, is to do Christian philosophy while rejecting patriarchy—to do feminist Christian philosophy. Those who make this attempt are cautioned as to its impossibility by two groups, both claiming that Christianity cannot abandon the presupposition of patriarchy. One group shares the experience of being a woman in a Christian society. They say: Abandon the Christian community. As long as you stay within it you are subject to tyranny and will succumb to patriarchy. This is like the advice that most of us have probably received that we should abandon philosophy so as not to destroy our faith. Others, who share the commitment to Christianity, say that God has ordained patriarchal presuppositions. To be Christian requires the acceptance of those presuppositions. This is not unlike the advice to leave our faith behind when we do philosophy. I would like to repeat Plantinga's advice and suggest that we have integrity and be bold. Let us do feminist Christian philosophy.

I want to suggest some of what this may mean for how we, as Christians, are to view ourselves, name and symbolize the sacred, and conceptualize the work of God in the world.

Visibility, voice, and the discipleship of equals. We are aware of gendered language and the way that such language has served to render women invisible. Since experience is so important to the hermeneutic process that I am following, it is still important to remind us of that experience. I grew up speaking the language "properly" using "man" and "he" as generic words. Like most women in our society, I became quite competent at hermeneutics, the art of interpretation, before I had any idea as to what the art was. I learned when these words meant male only and when they included me, and I became quite skilled in these interpretive moves. Like the young philosopher, I was so involved in the joy of what I was learning that I did not experience tensions. An awareness of those tensions came upon me slowly. But I still remember the day that I really understood how this language rendered women invisible. I was with colleagues (all male—and all reasonable people) and we were discussing our curriculum in relation to students' future needs. The pronouns were all male, and the word "guy" occurred frequently. As I listened to my colleagues, it hit me that even though half of their students were women, they really saw only the men. Their language revealed women as invisible.

Women also experience themselves as silenced. In the history of the Christian church, women have been told that their role is to be silent, at least about issues of any theological or social importance. If they do have something to say, it is better to have it spoken by a man. The male voice lends authority. While we may dismiss these ideas as part of the distant past, the experience of women today is often one of being silenced. Recent studies still indicate that women are often not heard. When an idea, already voiced by a woman, is put forward by a male voice, it becomes viewed as significant.

Other studies confirm this experience.[2] They show that children learn parameters from the language of their culture. Girls quickly come to exclude certain possibilities from their futures when the words and images they have for these possibilities are male.... Women [often] experience themselves as silent beings. And so I would urge you to listen to the voices of women who reflect on their experience of invisibility and silence and who develop in their Christian faith a critique of patriarchy that challenges us to rethink our anthropology. Elizabeth Schüssler Fiorenza is one of these voices.[3]

Fiorenza recognizes that women experience invisibility and silence within Christianity, but she also maintains that women find positive experiences within biblical religion; there is a source of strength and boldness.... In order to do the reconceptualization necessary to address this oppression, she sets out a feminist critical hermeneutics that stresses the importance of identifying, acknowledging, and taking responsibility for our theoretical presuppositions. This activity is particularly important as we reflect on the Jesus tradition and scriptures. While her work is primarily theological, it is important to our work as philosophers because it examines and critiques the biblical and theological presuppositions that often go unexamined in our work....

One presupposition that many readings of the Jesus movement perpetuate is that women were excluded from the new community that Jesus formed. The image of the disciples is of a band of itinerant men who had left family (including wives) and home behind them to live a radical ethos ... that those left at home did not live. This radical ethos is identified especially by the abandonment of traditional family relations. ... Fiorenza concludes that it is clear that Jesus did not respect patriarchal family bonds. Moreover, it would be a misreading "to claim that such a radical a-familial ethos is asked only of the male wandering charismatics" (p. 146) and not also of female disciples.

Fiorenza takes a further step in the interpretation that Jesus advocated a community of equal discipleship by looking at those texts where Jesus discusses the constitution of his true family. These texts (Mark 10:29–30 and 3:31–35) mention brothers, sisters, and mothers, but no fathers.... She concludes: "The discipleship community abolishes the claims of the patriarchal family and constitutes a new familial community, one that does not include fathers in its circle" (p. 147).

Certainly this does not mean that men who participated in the procreation of children were not part of the community. But that the word "father" is not used is significant.... The term "father" is not to be used to justify patriarchal relationships in the community. Reserving the term for God is intended "precisely to reject all such claims, powers, and structures" (p. 150). "Thus liberation from patriarchal structures is not only explicitly articulated by Jesus but is in fact at the heart of proclamation" (p. 151).

From her work Fiorenza proposes to draw strength for women in overcoming sexism and prejudice, especially that encountered within religion. But there are equally important implications to be drawn for Christian philosophy. If we acknowledge our roots in biblical tradition as important presuppositions to our work, then we must also acknowledge as part of our anthropological and political commitments the community of equality and the overcoming of patriarchy. More particularly, we must be committed to the visibility of women as women and be bold enough to follow out the implications of that commitment. If the name "Father" was to be reserved for God, but has been usurped by men within the family and within the church to perpetuate patriarchal structure, then how do we name God?

Naming the sacred. In his insightful and formative work on symbols, Paul Tillich shows why we must be wary of identifying our symbols of the sacred, the ultimate, with the fullness of such a reality.[4] Symbols point beyond themselves to the reality that they symbolize. But they also participate in that reality. It becomes easy for us to mistake that participation for the fullness of the reality. Our symbol may limit that which is symbolized and may even lead us to understand that which is symbolized in a fundamentally incorrect manner. This incorrect understanding can have destructive consequences for the religious community.

In a patriarchal society, it is very easy to slip into such problems when we use the word "Father" as a primary symbol for the sacred. While some fathers in our society take on work that has traditionally been the task of mothers, it is still the case that the title "Father" is used only of men and connotes patriarchal authority. Our concept of Father may include love, but it also includes a sense of distance and ultimate control. If we call the sacred "Father," then our image of the sacred includes these characteristics. If we limit the symbols we use of the sacred to the point that this is one of the few allowable symbols and we combine that symbol with those of Lord and Master, we define the sacred in a very limited and potentially destructive manner. The symbol serves to limit the possibility of other aspects of the sacred being present to us.

Religious feminists have addressed this problem by suggesting that we need a wide range of names for the sacred. Many do not totally reject "Father" as a way of naming the sacred, but suggest that also making use of other names will better enable us to experience the fullness of the sacred. Rosemary Ruether suggests that using the name "God/ess" would help us overcome the dualism of nature and spirit....

Letty Russell reminds us that we need not go outside of the Christian biblical and ecclesiastical traditions to find other names for God.[5] She points to the image of God as servant.... God is described as analogous to a female bird protecting her young.... And finally, she reminds us that there is biblical precedent for naming God "mother" and "wife" (Ps. 51; Deut. 32:18; Isa. 46:3, 51:1, 49:14–15; Ps. 131:2). The name "mother" seems particularly important for helping in overcoming the continued power of patriarchal structures in Christian society....

Certainly, as Tillich has cautioned, every symbol for the sacred has its limitations. The limitations of the image of father have clearly been to reinforce patriarchy and thus to alienate at least some humans from the divine. The symbol of mother will also have its limitations. But anticipation of these limitations should not prevent us from incorporating the power of this symbol into our Christian imagery.

Maternal work, maternal thinking, and Mother-God. In the context of this essay, I can neither set out nor develop all of the implications of incorporating the image of Mother-God into Christian symbolism and thus into the presuppositions of Christian philosophy arising out of the image of Mother-God. Since most of those working in Christian philosophy are men, many of whom identify with the name "father," I wish to stress that these suggestions are not intended to set mother against father. They are intended to lead to further reflection on the implications of including the image of mother.

There are many feminist philosophers who are reflecting on the epistemological and ethical implications of the work of mothering. These reflections come from a wide range of feminist perspectives. Sara Ruddick's recent book, *Maternal Thinking*,[6] is not particularly aimed at the Christian community and does not discuss the issue of God language. I will, however, present aspects of her work showing how these contribute to the discussion of what it means to speak of Mother-God.

Ruddick begins her analysis from the perspective that she terms "practicalism." She explains: "From the practicalist view, thinking arises from and is tested against practices. Practices are collective human activities distinguished by the aims that identify them and by the consequent demands made on practitioners committed to those aims" (pp. 13–14). It is from within the context of our practice that we raise questions, judge these questions to be sensible, determine criteria of truth and falsity, and determine what will count as evidence. In other words, practice and thinking are radically interconnected. Her contention is that the maternal practice gives rise to maternal thinking. She acknowledges that mothers as individuals are diverse and shaped by many practices. She focuses on the demands that all mothers must face and the disciplined reflection that arises out of the attempts to meet those demands. She ... does not restrict the activity of mothering to women. Men also perform maternal labor. She does think that mothering is far more often the work of women than of men [and] that we should be careful not to gloss over the labor of carrying and giving birth which only women do. In order not to conceal women's role she emphasizes the importance of retaining the word "maternal" rather than using "parental."

I find her work helpful to the task of thinking about the image of Mother-God. If God is our mother, then we are imaging Mother-God as carrying out certain practices and as thinking in ways similar to humans who carry out these practices.

She suggests that maternal practice is founded on giving birth.... Ruddick identifies three demands that all mothers face that are correlated with three sorts of maternal practice. The demands are for preservation, growth, and social acceptability. The work required is that of preservative love, nurturance, and training. Ruddick does not idealize the role of mother in her analysis. She uses stories that emphasize that the practice of mothering is a struggle, sometimes even a struggle against our own violence. Yet, she believes that out of this practice and struggle certain cognitive capacities can and do arise. Reflecting on these helps us better to understand what it means to be a mother.

The first demand, for preservation, requires the mother to develop "cognitive capacities and virtues of protective control" (p. 71). One capacity that mothers often develop is what Ruddick calls the scrutinizing gaze. Children must be watched, but not watched too closely. It is not that mothers relinquish control. They come to think about it differently. Often because of desire to resort either to domination or passivity, mothers can come to recognize the patience required in order to exhibit appropriate control. If children are to survive they must be protected, and yet they must learn to deal with their world, both social and natural. The practice of mothering tends to lead to the development of an ability to identify danger and to deal with it, not always by eliminating that danger, but by helping the child to deal with the danger. Sometimes that means helping the child to die.

Christian philosophers may be able to use this notion of the scrutinizing gaze of Mother-God in reflections on theodicy. If the preservative love of Mother-God is of this sort, then we should not be expected to be protected from all evil. On the other hand, we should expect a hopeful and supportive presence to help us face and cope with our lives. If God's power is not so much that of total control as of helping us deal with the real dangers of our existence, then the concern of theodicy may be to show how a caring Mother-God helps us to confront and cope with the real dangers and griefs of our lives. The expectation is

not that Mother-God will prevent all evil. Rather, the power of Mother-God is to help us preserve ourselves so that we may grow and flourish. I am not suggesting that this image will solve the problems of reconciling a good God with the existence of evil. Like human mothers, Mother-God may be experienced as destructive rather than preservative. That the image contributes to the complexity of the issue should not count against its significance.

The second demand that Ruddick identifies is for growth. This demand results in the development of ways of thinking that help the mother and child grow and change. Ruddick identifies storytelling as one of these cognitive practices.... To tell a child a story is to help that child incorporate change into an ongoing unity. It is to help the child and the mother to share a history.

Thinking of Mother-God as storyteller seems very compatible with the image of God as presented in Christian scriptures and traditions. The stories presented there tell of a *Heilsgeschichte*, a history of the presence and activity of the divine in and with human history. The notion of Mother-God can augment this tradition. The contribution of this aspect of maternal work to Christian philosophy may be to direct us to focus more on narrative and the use of narrative in legitimating philosophical as well as religious presuppositions.

The third demand, for social acceptance, requires the work of training. Ruddick describes training as a work of conscience. The work of training is to help "a child to be the kind of person whom others can accept and whom the mothers themselves can actively appreciate" (p. 104). Again, mothers must struggle against the tendency to dominate. There are many pressures placed on mothers, many of whom are quite young, to have well-behaved children. I remember well the pressure on me to toilet train my son. One person claimed that all of her children were trained by nine months— so mine should be too. A mother is pushed to examine her own conscience as she tries to give guidance to her children. Perhaps the child could be trained at nine months, but what sort of power would that require and what sort of relation would it establish? The work of training requires the mother to trust herself and to be sensitive to the spirit of her child. Ruddick suggests that when this practice is developed at its best, mother becomes more trustworthy so that the child can be trustworthy. Moreover, the child comes to recognize that when trust breaks down, as it inevitably does, it is proper to protest.

If Mother-God is our trainer, our guide in coming to conscience, then she is one who is our help in the ongoing struggle to develop our human goodness and trust. We look to her not as a source of all answers or as a dominating rule to be obeyed. She is a help, a guide, a refuge. She recognizes that the work of conscience is a struggle, ongoing and often difficult. For Christian philosophy, this image might contribute to discussions of a soul-making theodicy. For example, this image of God supports John Hick's claim that it would be contradictory to conceive of a God as creating human beings such "that they could be guaranteed freely to respond" to God "in authentic faith and love and worship."[7]

The image of Mother-God as part of the ongoing development of conscience may also contribute to process theology. Reflecting on how human parents change when they both trust and are trusted by their children could contribute to the process claim that God is, at least in one respect, changing. Such reflection could also provide a way of understanding God as both changing and unchanging. The mothering person may be very trustworthy to begin with, but in concretely exhibiting that characteristic, by being self-reflective about trustworthiness, and by being trusted by a child, may be said to be more trustworthy. So also, Mother-God might be said to be trustworthy and yet to become more trustworthy in the process of divine-human relationships. Indeed, the image of Mother-God may be better received by process theology than by other forms of Christian theology because process thought is already inclined to be open to changing images of God as well as to a changing God.

Conclusion. There is much more work going on in feminist religious and philosophical thought. Most of it remains to be incorporated into the work of Christian philosophy. What I have touched on in this essay only gives some suggestions for a beginning. In Alvin Plantinga's advice, with which I began, he warned us to be "wary about assimilating or accepting presently popular philosophical ideas and procedures" (p. 271). Some of you may be wary of developing feminist Christian philosophy, thinking that you are assimilating that which comes from outside the tradition. I have chosen to look primarily at thinkers who show us the basis of feminist work from within the Christian tradition. Reflecting on their work leads me to conclude that the autonomy, integrity, and boldness that Plantinga called for is advanced by the work of feminists. In particular, the integration of the name "Mother" for the sacred may help us relate to God in ways that enable us to develop these very virtues and thereby strengthen Christian philosophy.

Notes

1. Plantinga, Alvin. "Advice to Christian Philosophers," *Faith and Philosophy* 1.3 (1984): 253–71.

2. Vetterling-Braggin, Mary. *Sexist Language* (New York: Littlefield, Adams, 1981); and Baron, Dennis, *Grammar and Gender* (New Haven: Yale UP, 1986).

3. Fiorenza, Elizabeth Schüssler. *In Memory of Her. A Feminist Theological Reconstruction of Christian Origins* (New York: Crossroad, 1989).

4. Tillich, Paul. *Dynamics of Faith* (New York: Harper and Row, 1957).

5. Russell, Letty M. *Human Liberation in a Feminist Perspective—A Theology* (Philadelphia: Westminster, 1974).

6. Ruddick, Sara. *Maternal Thinking: Toward a Politics of Peace* (Boston: Beacon, 1989).

7. Hick, John. *Evil and the God of Love* (London: Collins, 1970), p. 311.

Discussion

1. Reflect on Johnson's affirmation of Plantinga's contention that philosophy is a reflection of one's deep and fundamental commitments about the world and God. Does Plantinga's contention seem right or does philosophy seem more like a purely rational, unprejudiced search for the truth?

2. Do the writings of the world's religions have the flexibility to accommodate feminist theorizing? Why or why not? (You might try to look at this from Johnson's own Christian tradition.)

3. Suppose you hold a traditional, patriarchal view of God. How would it change if you followed Johnson's advice? Would that change be positive or negative?

WHY FEMINIST EPISTEMOLOGY SELLS

HARRIET BABER*

Is "feminist epistemology" feminist? At first blush, the notion of a "feminist epistemology" appears peculiar: it is hard to see how an epistemology, a philosophical theory of knowledge, can be either feminist or anti-feminist since it is not clear how such a theory might benefit or harm women. Advocates of feminist epistemologies however suggest that traditional theories of knowledge are male-biased insofar as they fail to account for features of women's experience that are different from the characteristic experience of males.

While epistemology, the theory of knowledge, indeed has knowledge as its principal focus, it is more interested in *how* one knows not *what* one knows; epistemology asks what justifies one in holding one's beliefs.

Advocates of feminist epistemology have rejected this paradigm of epistemology on the grounds that the norms it embodies are male norms and hence that their acceptance sets standards which women find it difficult, or impossible, to meet. In particular they hold that the traditional epistemic ideal of an objective, detached observer, conducting "his" investigations in isolation from any historical or social context, is alien to women's engaged, concrete, contextual way of knowing:

> The female construction of self in relation to others, leads ... toward opposition to dualisms of any sort, valuation of concrete, everyday life, sense of variety of connectedness and continuities both with other women's relationally defined existence, bodily experience of boundary challenges, and activity of transforming both physical objects and human beings must

---

* Harriet Baber is Professor of Philosophy at University of San Diego.

be expected to result in a world view to which dichotomies are foreign. (Harding, 47)

Traditional epistemological views, according to which the female mode of reasoning is defective, they suggest, are bad for women insofar as they result in their denigration as knowers. Epistemologies which recognize the legitimacy of women's way of knowing are good for women because they result in women being more highly valued. To this extent, such epistemologies are "feminist."

Advocates of feminist epistemology make two assumptions, both of which are highly questionable.

First, many advocates of feminist epistemology assume that there are deeply entrenched differences in the ways in which men and women see the world which arise either from biological differences or from early developmental history and so are, at best, difficult to alter. Thus Allison Jaggar claims,

> Growing empirical evidence shows that women tend to conceive the world differently from men and have different attitudes towards it. The discovery of the precise nature and causes of these differences is a task for feminist psychologists and sociologists of knowledge. The task for feminist scientists and political theorists is to build on women's experience and insights in order to develop a systematic account of the world, together with its potentialities for change, as it appears from the standpoint of women. (Jaggar, 376)

However, "growing empirical evidence" does not support Jaggar's claim. Consider the thesis of gender differences in moral reasoning hypothesized by Carol Gilligan. According to Jaggar, Gilligan "demonstrated that the categories used to describe the moral development of children in fact fit the development only of boys" (Jaggar, 372). Yet this claim has been shown to be false—such categories seem to apply equally well to girls and boys (see Thoma). Nevertheless, like a number of other "scientific fictions," including the myth of mother-infant bonding to be considered presently, the myth of a woman's way of knowing took on a life of its own, in which feminist theoreticians cited other feminist theoreticians and the highly speculative work of feminist psychoanalysts in support of claims about gender differences, which have little or no empirical basis.[1]

Secondly, many advocates of feminist epistemology make a number of questionable normative assumptions which stand in need of explication since they are largely tacit. Arguably, even if all of the assumptions about women's distinctive way of viewing the world were correct, it would still not follow that we ought to reject traditional "androcentric" theories of knowledge, according to which women are considered intellectually defective, in favor of theories which legitimate and value women's way of knowing.

On the face of it, it seems reasonable that the acceptance of feminist accounts of epistemology would benefit women. Presumably, if a trait which women possess is valued, women benefit. This seems plausible because, more generally, we are inclined to accept the following argument:

(1) Members of Group G have trait X

(2) People benefit when traits that they possess are highly valued

(3) Therefore, members of group G benefit when trait X is highly valued

(2) and (3) are, however, ambiguous since it is not clear whether the suggestion is that people benefit *all other things being equal* when traits they possess are highly valued or whether the claim is that people actually benefit *on net* when traits they possess are highly valued. The former claim is plausible but is not adequate for the feminist epistemologist's purposes; the latter claim is, however, false—it is not the case that people invariably benefit on net when traits they possess are highly valued. Consider the following argument:

(1) Epileptics have fits

(2) People benefit on net when traits they possess are highly valued

(3) Epileptics benefit on net when having fits is highly valued

Some societies have valued having fits along with other manifestations of altered states of consciousness as signs of divine favor; presumably, in such societies epileptics gained a certain amount of prestige from their condition. However, the prestige they gain in such circumstances is outweighed by the costs and epileptics are, on net, better off in circumstances where fits are not valued and where, as a consequence, researchers successfully find ways to control seizures.

Assuming (falsely) that women really do think "differently" from men and speak in a different moral voice, to make the case that women would benefit by the acceptance of theories that value these modes of reasoning, we would have to show that the benefits of being recognized as intellectually and morally competent outweigh any costs associated with women's intellectual strategies and modes of moral reasoning. After all, it might turn out, when the costs are weighed against the benefits, that it is better for women to cure themselves of their "non-linear" thinking and proclivity for "caring," by psychotherapy, neurosurgery or, best of all, a solid course in logic, than to exalt the "women's way" of knowing.

Empirical considerations: flawed data and bogus explanations. Even if their empirical assumptions about gender differences were correct, advocates of feminist epistemology would still need to make a case for the benefit to women of their theories of knowledge. However, this case is difficult to make because many of their empirical claims about gender differences are false and the explanations given for those differences which do exist are implausible.

Consider again Carol Gilligan's highly influential study of moral reasoning in boys and girls which Jaggar cites as both having demonstrated that boys and girls follow radically different courses of moral development and as having shown that "basic categories of western moral philosophy such as rationality, autonomy and justice, are drawn from and reflect the moral experience of men rather than that of women" (Jaggar, 372). While these results would be astonishing, Gilligan's research methods were flawed and her results were disconfirmed by subsequent research.

Carol Tavris, citing an extensive body of empirical studies, notes that

> Research in recent years casts considerable doubt on the notion that men and women differ appreciably in their moral reasoning, or that women have a permanently different voice because of their early closeness to their mothers. . . .
>
> When subsequent research directly compared men's and women's reasoning about moral dilemmas, Gilligan's ideas have rarely been supported. In study after study, men and women use both care-based reasoning . . . and justice-based reasoning. In study after study, researchers report no average differences in the kind of moral reasoning that men and women apply. . . . [R]esults confirm Gilligan's argument that people make moral decisions not only according to abstract principles of justice, but also according to principles of compassion and care. But they fail to support her notion that women have any special corner on that compassion.

Two other psychologists in the field of moral development, Anne Colby and William Damon, likewise found little scientific support for Gilligan's claims. "While her portrayal of general, sex-linked life-orientations is intuitively appealing," they concluded, "the research evidence at this point does not support such a generalized distinction." (Tavris, 83–86)

If the task of feminist theorists in sociology, psychology, political science and the hard sciences is, as Jaggar suggests, "to build on women's experience and insights in order to develop a systematic account of the world, together with its potentialities for change, as it appears from the standpoint of women," these feminists are out of a job.

Similarly, Tavris cites additional empirical data which undermines what have become commonplace assumptions about gender differences as regards attachment/connection, cognitive abilities, dependency, emotions, empathy, moods and "moodiness," need for achievement, need for love and attachment, need for power, nurturance, pacifism/belligerence, sexual capacity, verbal aggressiveness and hostility.[2] At the very least, the theses about psychological differences between men and women which Jaggar and others believe to have been "demonstrated" and which have become commonplaces in pop psychology and self-help literature, have not been established.

To explain male-female differences, which she thought she had discovered, Gilligan invoked speculative (that is, empirically unfounded) theories of development espoused by feminist psychoanalysts including Nancy Chodorow and Jean Baker Miller.

Gilligan's work was, at first, an important correction of bias in the study of psychological development, which had been based almost entirely on studies of men's lives. She showed that earlier psychologists, finding that women did not seem to reason like men in evaluating moral dilemmas, concluded that women were somehow morally deficient, lacking in moral reasoning skills, and developmentally retarded. "I cannot evade the notion," Freud had written, "that for women the level of what is ethically normal is different from what it is in men."

Gilligan agreed with Freud that women and men differ in what they regard as "ethically normal," but she maintained that women's ways are just as moral.

The origin of women's "different voice," according to feminist psychoanalysts such as Nancy Chodorow and Jean Baker Miller, lies in the psychodynamic consequences of being raised primarily by mothers. Girls may continue to stay attached to their mothers as they form their identities, but boys, in order to develop a male identity, must separate themselves psychologically at an early age. The result, according to this view, is that adult women find comfort and solace in connection and are frightened of separation; adult men, on the other hand, find security in independence and are frightened of attachments, which they fear will swallow them up and obliterate their identity as males. "Since masculinity is defined through separation while femininity is defined through attachment," Gilligan summarized, "male gender identity is threatened by intimacy while female gender identity is threatened by separation."

As Chodorow put it, "The basic feminine sense of self is connected to the world, the basic masculine sense of self is separate" (Tavris, 80–81).

Such theories, however, are both highly speculative and unconfirmed by empirical data. Indeed, the empirical data suggest that those psychological and behavioral differences which do exist are explained more by one's current situation in life than by early development and relations with one's primary caretaker—and that, far from being deeply entrenched and virtually ineradicable, they can be changed.

New studies find that the behavior that we link to gender depends more on what an individual is doing and needs to do than on his or her biological sex. For example, sociologist Barbara Risman compared the personality traits of single fathers, single mothers, and married parents. If biological predispositions or childhood socialization create stable personality differences between men and women, she reasoned, then fathers should differ from mothers in their babycare skills and nurturing talents in general, regardless of marital status. Instead, Risman found that having responsibility for child care was strongly related to "feminine" traits, such as nurturance and sympathy, as being female was. The single men who were caring for children were more like mothers than like married fathers. These men were not an atypical group of especially nurturant men, either. They had custody of their children through circumstances beyond their control—widowhood, the wife's desertion, or the wife's disinterest in shared custody.

Similarly, a study of 150 men who were spending up to sixty hours a week caring for their ailing parents or spouses found that the men provided just as much emotional support as women traditionally do.

In the 1970s, sociologist and business consultant Rosabeth Moss Kanter, in studies of men and women in corporations, showed conclusively that conditions of employment, not qualities of the individual, determine what most people value about their work . . . When men and women hold the same prestigious jobs, their values and behavior are similar (Tavris, 63, 88–89).[3]

In addition to doctrines about psychological differences between men and women which allegedly make it difficult for women to meet the requirements of traditional theories of knowledge, and psychoanalytic accounts of their origin, most advocates of feminist epistemology hold also that such epistemologies are male-biased to the extent that they assume a mind-body dualism which denigrates the body in favor of the mind.

According to this view, women are "associated with nature . . . and the body" in such a way that what Jaggar calls "normative dualism, the excessive value placed on the 'mind' at the expense of the body," is detrimental to women's interests. She writes:

> Of course, both men and women have both minds and bodies but, through the western philosophical tradition, women have been seen consistently as being connected with (or entangled in) their bodies in a more intimate way than men are with theirs ... The traditional view, in short, is that women are more closely associated with nature and men with culture; women with the body and men with the mind.
>
> The association of women with body and men with mind has been reinforced if not generated by a sexual division of labor in which (some) men have dominated the "intellectual" fields of politics, science, culture and religion while women have been assigned the primary responsibility for many day-to-day tasks necessary for physical survival. (Jaggar, 46)

The suggestion that women are archetypally and universally associated with the body is simply implausible. The association of women with the body does indeed seem to be a feature of Greek culture which, as a consequence, found its way into the writings of philosophers.[4] The Victorians, however, whose attitudes are far more influential on the general public than the opinions of Greek philosophers, associated men with the body as brute nature and regarded "culture" as the domain of ladies. And while men monopolized prestigious leadership roles in religious, literary, and artistic activities, such men were regarded as effeminate, not truly "men's men." Religion and culture then, as now, were regarded as feminine domains.

The suggestion that women by and large do "physical labor" while men ("at least men of a certain class") monopolize "mental" work is false—unless we blur the distinction between "mental" and "physical" work in such a way that all low-prestige jobs typically done by women count as "physical." Otherwise it is hard to see how, e.g., clerical work, which occupies many women who work outside the home, counts as "physical labor." Indeed, arguably, one of the most egregious injustices against women which feminists ought to work to rectify is women's de facto exclusion from most jobs which are ordinarily understood as "physical work"— from carpentry, plumbing, and other construction work, from house painting, mining, auto mechanics and other skilled trades, from ditch-digging and the operation of heavy machinery, and generally from work that is mobile, involves physical exertion or is done outdoors.[5]

In addition to questionable claims about the association of women with the body, Jaggar suggests that women fare better in societies where the importance of the body and of natural, mutualistic relationships are recognized, than in those which embody ideologies that trivialize or denigrate the body and conceive of society as an "atomistic" association of rational egoists. "Women," writes Jaggar, "would be unlikely to have developed ideologies like the liberal theory of human nature which regard 'mental' activity more highly than physical work, embody an atomistic conception of society and place the highest value on individual autonomy." She continues:

> It is easy to see how certain features of the liberal theory of human nature are far more likely to have been produced by men than by women. For instance, it is easy to see how men, at least men of a certain class, would be likely to place supreme value on "mental" activity and to ignore the fact that such activity would be impossible without the daily physical labor necessary for survival, especially the physical labor of women. It is even harder to imagine women developing a political theory that presupposed political solipsism, ignoring

human interdependence and especially the long dependence of human young. Nor would women be likely to formulate a conception of rationality that stressed individual autonomy and contained such a strong element of egoism as the liberal conception. (Jaggar, 46)

As a matter of fact, despite highly speculative accounts of primitive matriarchy, historically women appear to have done better in communities where the body, the family, and the material world were regarded as suspect or positively evil.[6] In his account of sexual practices and sex roles in the ancient world, Richard Posner suggests that women were better off in early Christian communities, whose members were more distrustful of the body and material nature than their pagan neighbors, than in Greek society generally.

> Companionate marriage ... signified marriage between at least approximate equals, based on mutual respect and affection, and involving close and continuous association in child rearing, household management, and other activities, rather than merely the occasional copulation that was the principal contact between spouses in the typical Greek marriage....
>
> Despite its fulminations against woman the temptress and the devil's helper, Christianity seems to have been, on balance, more solicitous of women's interests than the pagan religions had been. By praising celibacy, the Church gave women other options besides marriage....
> In forbidding divorce, the Church protected married women from being cast off by husbands who had tired of them—and losing their children in the process, since, under both Greek and Roman law, in the event of divorce the children remained with their father. And by insisting that marriage should be consensual—that a man or woman should be free to reject the family's

choice of mate—the Church not only promoted companionate marriage but made indissoluble marriage more tolerable. (Posner, 45, 47)

Women did still better in communities that were even more hostile to the body and to natural, mutualistic relationships than the Church at large, such as monastic movements within the church and gnostic communities without. Thus Ross Shepard Kraemer, in her history of women's religious practice in the ancient world, notes grudgingly that dualistic cosmologies benefited women:

> The specific belief systems that provided women in antiquity with autonomy and alternatives are enormously problematic. Ascetic and monastic women from the Therapeutics to Thecla to the desert mothers found it necessary to repudiate the body and its female associations, becoming male both in theory and in aspects of appearance in order to achieve self-determination. Splitting the body from the soul, dualist cosmologies such as those advocated by gnostics frequently provided women with alternatives denied them by those (men) who insisted on the integral connection of body and spirit. Conversely, cosmologies that value embodiment seem then to need to constrain and confine women as a necessary corollary. The notion that self-determination for women is only available at the cost of psychic self-destruction, at the cost of the repudiation of the feminine, is hardly comforting. (Kraemer, 208)[7]

In general, women have been attracted to movements that have been antinomian, gnostic, individualistic and distrustful of both sexuality and of the body. In *The Pursuit of the Millennium*, a history of "revolutionary millenarians and mystical anarchists of the Middle Ages," for example, Norman Cohn documents the participation of women in such movements as the highly individualistic, anarchistic and dualistic heresy of the Free Spirit. More recent religious movements founded by women have rejected sexuality and denigrated materiality, e.g., the Shakers, who were celibate, and Christian Science and Theosophy, based on the assumption that material reality is, in some sense, "unreal." More generally it has been in just those religious groups that were the most distrustful of materiality, the Quakers for example, where women first exercised leadership roles; by contrast, within Christianity, it has been those traditions which are the most sacramental and "incarnational," and to that extent, the most "materialistic"—the Roman Catholic, Eastern Orthodox and Anglican Churches—which have been slowest to accept women in leadership roles.

There is good reason for this. To the extent that disabilities and constraints attach to being female, ideologies which denigrate the body trivialize gender differences and so liberate women from the disadvantages that have traditionally attached to the condition of being female, as Kraemer suggests. It is hard to see, however, why this "repudiation of the feminine" represents an act of "psychic self-destruction" for women. It may be that for some, if not most women, femininity itself, quite apart from any social, economic or political disabilities attached to it, is itself oppressive, is something which women happily repudiate. In any case, whether the repudiation of "femininity is intrinsically beneficial or costly to women, dualistic ideologies which enable women to detach themselves from it appear to benefit women."

In short, although the thesis that women are "connected with (or entangled in) their bodies in a more intimate way than men are with theirs" is too woolly to be conclusively refuted, and unless one relies quite heavily on sociological data about the ancient Greeks (mediated through the philosophical tradition), there is little reason to believe that this connection—whatever it may come to—holds universally. Moreover, an historical survey of the position of women in the West beginning with the Greeks of antiquity strongly suggests that dualism is good for women. Is it any wonder that Descartes, the villain of the feminist epistemologists' story, was sponsored by Queen Christina?

On the face of it, it may be puzzling how a large body of academic work could be built around claims—such as Gilligan's thesis of women's "different voice" or Jaggar's suggestion that "women have been seen consistently as being connected with (or entangled in) their bodies in a more intimate way than men are with theirs"—which were simply false. And yet books and articles in support of the views considered above boast extensive bibliographies of academic work by like-minded authors. Surely, one wishes to object, where there is so much smoke there must be some fire.

This is however to underestimate the power of scientific fictions which can be put to service in support of entrenched ideologies and institutional policies. Consider, for example, research during the latter half of the twentieth century on the supposed phenomenon of mother-infant bonding among humans. "By the early 1980s," writes Diane Eyer in her recent study *Mother-Infant Bonding: A Scientific Fiction*, "research on the bonding of mothers and their newborns had been dismissed by much of the scientific community as having been poorly conceived and executed" (Eyer, 3). Yet in the decade prior to this an extensive academic literature had been generated in an attempt to examine and explain this bogus phenomenon. Even when the scientific community had largely dismissed this body of research, at the popular level, doctors, nurses and social workers continued to accept it as factually accurate. In materials given to pregnant women, by doctors and Lamaze educators, bonding was described as if it were an uncontroversial, plain fact like the dilation of the cervix during labor. Bonding, in spite of its lack of empirical support, became widely accepted because it had been "pulled into the maelstrom of popular belief and the institutional goals that inspire science."

> The research on bonding was inspired by the popular belief that women, one and all, are inherently suited for motherhood. This belief coincided with a number of institutional goals, including the needs of the psychological and medical professions. . . . New mothers, whether feminist or traditional, also embraced the ideology of motherhood at a time when their sex role was being challenged. Bonding promised insurance against the psychological damage that might be caused by women's increasing involvement in work outside the home. . . .
> Bonding appeared to give women more control over their birth experience, and it supported their wish to have their newborn infants and other family members with them in what had previously been a lonely and often demeaning experience. (Eyer, 1–2)

The myth of mother-infant bonding is by no means the only scientific fiction that has enjoyed undeserved success in virtue of its apparent confirmation of popular assumptions about gender and gender differences. Relatively shoddy research which purported to demonstrate a neurological basis for psychological differences between the sexes has also been given undue favorable attention. Why?

Because the study of sex differences is not like the rest of psychology. Under pressure from the gathering momentum of feminism, and perhaps in backlash to it, many investigators seem determined to discover that men and women "really" are different. It seems that if sex differences (e.g., lateralization) do not exist, then they have to be invented.[8]

The costs of feminist epistemology. In spite of a lack of empirical support, Gilligan's book and other works which constructed and elaborated scientific fictions about psychological differences between men and women became popular among both academics and the general public. Tavris suggests that their appeal was due to their apparent confirmation of folk wisdom about gender differences: they embodied claims which many people found "intuitive." Nevertheless, she notes,

> One problem with intuitions, of course, is that what feels right to one person may feel entirely wrong to another. A friend of mine, a professor in a law school, was discussing Gilligan's theory with her class and met vociferous resistance from the students, male and female. Many of the males felt resentful that their very real affections and attachments were being overlooked or disparaged. Many of the females felt resentful that their professional abilities were being compromised or questioned. "These women are planning to be litigators," said my friend, "and they don't consider themselves 'naturally' soft or pliable, or less capable of a justice-based form of moral reasoning." (Tavris, 83)

In addition to being unintuitive and offensive to men and women who have, to a great extent, broken free from traditional sex roles, giving the academic seal of approval to folk wisdom about male-female differences seems to provide justification for policies which reinforce traditional sex roles.

The idea that women operate on a different moral wavelength and speak in a different voice has made its way into many fields and into common consciousness. In business, many employers and managers use Gilligan's theory to account for sex differences they "observe" in the workplace. Clinical psychologist Harriet Goldhor Lerner, describing her experiences as a consultant to organizations, says, "I frequently hear Gilligan's research interpreted as demonstrating that women on the job care primarily about people's feelings and personalities, whereas men, in contrast, think in rational, logical, and abstract terms and are primarily oriented toward the task at hand" (Tavris, 81–82).

The popular acceptance of such doctrines, particularly by management consultants and managers involved in personnel decisions, may be highly detrimental to women's interests. So, for example, the author of a popular journalistic account of the achievements of female executives in her introduction cautions readers aspiring to emulate them to "beware of 'experts' on working women." According to White:

> The legitimization of the notion of the schizophrenic working woman, torn between career and kids—"safe sexism" practiced by so-called experts on the workplace—has probably done more to sully the positive image of women in business than any backward attitude manifested by a male manager.
>
> The practitioners of "safe sexism" whether in the form of management consultants or advice-book authors, also defame women by legitimizing the notion of women as the second sex; that they have a distinct "management style" that emphasizes "nurturing," "building consensus," and "empowerment" while men are better at being leaders.
>
> Not surprisingly, it's this very simple-minded stereotyping of women that has relegated them to the soft, fluffy pink ghettos of human resources and public relations instead of being put in charge of running factories, leading sales teams, and heading up mergers and acquisitions departments. (White, 26)

While the myth of women's peculiarly feminine "management styles" may, to some extent, have benefitted women in business—to the extent that it provided some women with a way out of the typing pool and into what were at least nominally management positions—the overall result of myth was harmful to women in business.

Similarly, during a period when women were entering the sciences, while myths about women's "unique skills" and "special talents" opened doors, as Margaret Rossiter suggests in her study of women scientists in America, the creation of "women's work" within the sciences, the justification of which was grounded in such myths, was ultimately detrimental to the interests of women in the sciences.

> Even though women could claim by 1920 that they had 'opened the doors' of science, it was quite clear that they would be limited to positions just inside the entryway....
>
> Henceforth when better-educated and more qualified women tried to move beyond this territorial demarcation or up the hierarchy, they were met with strong resistance ... In their attempts to get around these artificial barriers and inconsistencies early women scientists developed a great many strategies. These tended to be of two sorts. One was the idealistic, liberal-to-radical, and often confrontational strategy of demanding that society reject all stereotypes and work for the feminist goal of full equality....
>
> The alternative strategy was the less strident and more conservative and "realistic" tactic of accepting the prevailing inequality and sexual stereotypes but using them for short-term gains such as establishing areas of "women's work" for women. Strategists for this approach emphasized that women had "unique skills" and "special talents" that justified reserving certain kinds of work for them....
>
> If success can be judged in numbers, women scientists had done very well indeed, for by 1940 there were thousands of such women working in a variety of fields and institutions.... This great

growth, however, had occurred at the price of accepting a pattern of segregated employment and underrecognition, which, try as they might, most women could not escape.
(Rossiter, xvii–xviii)

If this is correct, then the doctrine that there are profound and deeply entrenched psychological differences along the lines suggested by advocates of feminist epistemology is neither true nor beneficial to women. It is therefore, on the face of it, puzzling why a great many feminists eagerly accepted and promoted this view.

The market for scientific fictions. The answer, I think, is that while in the long run the doctrine of La Différence was detrimental to the interests of women as a group, in the short run invoking the doctrine (thus entrenching it all the more deeply in the popular imagination) was beneficial to individual women. Thus, for example, women having babies could invoke the myth of "bonding" and other dogmas of the natural childbirth movement to secure more humane treatment in hospitals and a greater measure of autonomy during the birth process and immediately afterward. Most women who bought into these views did not recognize their role in promoting traditional views about the nature and duties of women which were detrimental to women's interests.

Similarly, women in business and in the sciences stood to gain by promoting the idea that there were uniquely feminine talents and "management styles" since these were an entrée into management and the professions that they would not otherwise have had: better to be a manager in a "fluffy pink ghetto" (where "feminine management styles" were deemed appropriate) than a secretary; better "women's work" in a scientific area in which one had been trained than no work at all. The suggestion that women had "special talents" to offer businesses which would benefit their

employers opened doors for women that appeals to fairness could not budge. Rhetorically, it was effective to promote the idea that hiring women was "good business."

The difficulty with such a strategy however is that in many cases using gender stereotypes for short-term gains generates vicious circles which lock in policies that are detrimental to women's interests. Arguably, the promotion of feminist epistemology is pernicious because it helps to generate such vicious circles. To make this out, however, we need first to provide a brief account of how vicious circles are generated.

A vicious circle of the sort with which we are concerned arises when the following state of affairs obtains:

(1) Conditions C actually obtain.

(2) Under conditions C the best policy for members of group G, is P.

(3) Under conditions C' the best policy for members of group G, is P'.

(4) Pursuing P' under C' is preferable to pursuing P under C.

(5) Pursuing P contributes to the persistence of C.

Currently, myths about gender differences are deeply entrenched, and men and women as a rule play different roles in social and economic transactions. Under these conditions women benefit if the traits they are thought to possess and the roles they play are valued as equal to, or even superior to, what are perceived as characteristics and roles appropriate to men. So, Tavris notes,

In generating public reaction, Gilligan clearly struck a nerve: Thousands of women have seen themselves in her book. . . . One reason for this enthusiasm, I believe, is that Gilligan and others finally recognized and validated the long disparaged, unpaid work that women do: the work of day-to-day caring for children, the work of keeping extended families together with calls, letters and gifts, the work of worrying about everyone's feelings, the work of monitoring relationships to make sure they are going well. It was encouraging and life-affirming to read that intimacy and an ethic of care are as valuable as, indeed more valuable than, typical male aloofness and men's ethic of justice. (Tavris, 82)

Where most people believe that "men and women think differently," in particular that women are "intuitive" and prone to "non-linear thinking" that defies the canons of conventional logic, it is "encouraging and life-affirming" for women to be told, by feminist epistemologists, that this special women's way of knowing is equal or superior to men's way of knowing and so there is a market for feminist epistemology.

Nevertheless the market for feminist epistemology is inefficient since it creates a vicious circle.

1) It is generally believed that women "think differently" from men.

2) Under conditions in which it is believed that women think differently from men the best policy for women is to promote the idea that women's way of thinking is equal or superior to men's way of thinking, that is, to promote feminist epistemology.

3) Under conditions in which it is not believed that women think differently from men the best policy for women is not to promote this idea: feminist epistemology is at best pointless and potentially harmful.

4) A state of affairs in which people reject the view that women think differently from men is preferable to one in which people accept this view. For one thing, all other things being equal perhaps, a state of affairs in which people hold true beliefs is better than one in which they accept superstitions, myths and falsehoods.

5) Promoting feminist epistemology contributes to the persistence of the myth that men and women "think differently."

Thus women gain some benefits from the popularity of feminist epistemology, given prevailing myths about gender differences. Ultimately, however, the widespread acceptance of feminist epistemology is detrimental to women's interests since women suffer when myths of gender difference are rehearsed and given the academic imprimatur.

Academic women in particular lose insofar as the growing industry of "feminist scholarship" facilitates the construction of academic pink-collar ghettos. To see how and why academic pink-collar ghettos are constructed it may be instructive to compare the rise of feminist scholarship during the past two decades with the invention and development of home economics, perhaps the quintessential academic pink-collar ghetto, a hundred years earlier.

The founder of "home economics," and one whose leadership and character touched her contemporaries deeply, was Ellen Swallow Richards, Vassar 1870 and MIT 1873. . . . As a student at MIT she had learned how to make a place for herself (and other women) by capitalizing on woman's traditional role or, as she put it in 1871, "Perhaps the fact that I am not a Radical or a believer in the all powerful ballot for women to right her wrongs and that I do not scorn womanly duties, but claim it as a privilege to clean up and sort of supervise the room and sew things, etc., is winning me stronger allies than anything else.". . . .

By 1911 many [agricultural colleges of the Midwest and West] . . . had already formed programs and even departments of home economics and others were eager to do so. . . . Yet the very success of this kind of "women's work" on major campuses helped to harden the sexual segregation for future generations still further. Rather than being accepted for other scientific employment once the pioneers had shown women could handle this employment, the women found themselves more restricted to "women's work" than ever. Since women were finding such good opportunities in this field, many persons (including the first vocational guidance counselors, a new specialty around 1910) urged ambitious young women interested in science to head for home economics. It was the only field where a woman scientist could hope to be a full professor, department chairman or even a dean in the 1920s and 1930s. (Rossiter, 70)

Unlike many contemporary feminist philosophers, Ellen Swallow Richards never claimed that her acceptance of traditional views about gender differences on her creation of a separate sphere within Academe for women was "Radical." Nevertheless, as the above considerations suggest, the popularity of home economics in the early part of the century benefited academic women in the sciences in much the way that the current popularity of feminist philosophy benefits women in philosophy. And, of course, in light of these benefits it has not been unknown for graduate school faculty to advise female grad students in philosophy to "do feminism" so that they can put it on their vitae. Arguably, however, the association of women in philosophy with "feminism" thus understood is harmful to all women in the profession, including those who do "do feminism."

Conclusion. Shortly after I had successfully defended my dissertation on highly abstract metaphysics, I attended a national philosophy gathering wearing a tee shirt I had made in honor of the occasion which proclaimed, "Repeal Leibniz's Law." An earnest male philosopher approached me and asked whether that motto "had something to do with feminism." When I expressed bewilderment he explained that he assumed that it had something to do with feminists' rejection of "Western male logic." Mercifully, once I began expounding on my dissertation he walked away.

Granted that, even if "doing feminism" is merely a temptation for women in the profession and no woman is forced into the academic pink-collar ghetto, the visibility of "feminist philosophy," including "feminist epistemology," makes it difficult for women in the profession to avoid guilt by association unless they actively distance themselves from this enterprise by ignoring issues that concern women, remaining aloof from women's organizations in the profession and even by denying that they are feminists. These seem to me to be some of the worst consequences of the rise of "feminist philosophy." Even if "doing feminist philosophy" is, at best, a questionable business, doing philosophy as a feminist, in particular bringing analytic expertise to bear in the discussion of ethical and political issues that concern women, and exposing misconceptions about women, is extremely important. Worst of all, "feminist philosophy" has provided grist for the mill of conservatives in the profession—including some who claim to be feminists—who lampoon it in order to exploit anti-feminist backlash.

For these reasons I suggest that, on balance, quite apart from the intrinsic intellectual merits of what are currently understood as "feminist epistemologies," the identification of these theories as "feminist" motivated by unsubstantiated assumptions about psychological differences between men and women, is detrimental to women' interests.

Notes

1. For an empirically based summary of gender differences see Tavris, p. 296.

2. Tavris, 296 is Tavris's list of "where the differences aren't."

3. Numerous studies by Arrow, Blau, Bergmann and other economists confirm Kanter's result. In general, labor-force attachment and behavior on the job, including most notably absenteeism and quit behavior, are a function of the nature of the job and not the sex or race of the worker. Although women in the aggregate behave differently from men in the labor force, the differences are accounted for by the differences in the work that men and women in the aggregate do.

4. See Posner, esp. pp. 38–45, for a discussion of sexual mores and sex roles in the Mediterranean world during the period.

5. For a discussion of the characteristics of women's work, see, e.g., Game and Pringle, esp. ch. 1, "Masculinity and Machines." Taking as representative the sexual division of labor in the whiteware (appliance) industry, the authors suggest that, at least in manufacturing, women's work is characteristically unskilled, "light," perceived as "less dangerous" than men's work, "clean" rather than dirty, boring, and immobile. Although women's work within this context is less prestigious than men's work, it is also insofar as it is light, clean and immobile, less "physical."

6. See Tavris's account of "the search for the feminist Eden," pp. 71–79.

7. It should be noted that neither Posner nor Kraemer is sympathetic to Christianity.

8. Marcel Kinsbourne. "If Sex Differences in Brain Lateralization Exist, They Have Yet to Be Discovered," in *The Behavioral and Brain Sciences*, 3, p. 242, cited by Tavris, 53.

References

Bergman, Barbara. "Does the Market for Women's Labor Need Fixing?" in *Journal of Economic Perspectives*, vol. 3, no. 1 (Winter 1989): 43–60.

Cohn, Norman. *The Pursuit of the Millennium*. New York: Oxford UP, 1961.

Eyer, Diane E. *Mother-Infant Bonding: A Scientific Fiction*. New Haven, CT: Yale UP, 1992.

Game, A. and R. Pringle. *Gender at Work*. Boston: George Allen & Unwin, 1983.

Jaggar, Alison M. *Feminist Politics and Human Nature*. Totowa, NJ: Rowman & Allanheld, 1983.

Kraemer, Ross Shepard. *Her Share of the Blessings*. Oxford UP, 1992.

Posner, Richard. *Sex and Reason*. Cambridge, MA: Harvard UP, 1992.

Rossiter, Margaret W. *Women Scientists in America*. Baltimore, MD: Johns Hopkins UP, 1982.

Tavris, Carol. *The Mismeasure of Woman*. New York: Touchstone, 1992.

Thoma, Stephen J. "Estimating Gender Differences in the Comprehension and Preference of Moral Issues." *Developmental Review* 6, (1986): 165–80.

White, Jane. *A Few Good Women*. Englewood Cliffs, NJ: Prentice-Hall, 1992.

Discussion

1. How does Baber's feminism differ from Johnson's feminism of the previous essay?

2. Why does Baber reject major gender differences between men and women, and why does she think affirming such differences is detrimental to women?

3. Are there implications for Baber's rejection of feminist epistemology for philosophical discussions of religion?

Chapter 28

Reflections on Divine Language and Attributes

THREE CONCEPTIONS OF GOD IN CONTEMPORARY CHRISTIAN PHILOSOPHY

STEPHEN T. DAVIS*

Introduction. Nothing is more important in Christian philosophy than the concept of God. Christianity is essentially based on the notion of a God who creates and redeems us. But what is God like? What are God's attributes or properties? There is, among Christian philosophers, a great deal of agreement or overlap in their explanations of God's nature, but serious disagreement too. On the question of God's attributes, Christian philosophers have written a great deal.

There is a core concept of God that the vast majority of Christian philosophers and theologians affirm. They accept it because they believe that it is taught in scripture and in the Christian theological and confessional tradition.[1]

Core Concept: God is ultimate reality; God necessarily exists;[2] and as the unique, omnipotent, omniscient, and perfectly good creator of the heavens and the earth, God is worthy of our worship.

* Stephen T. Davis is Professor of Philosophy, Emeritus at Claremont McKenna College.

Obviously, the meanings of many of these terms can be and have been disputed, and there are Christian philosophers who deny some of them. But I believe that this core concept of God can be said to be common ground among most Christian philosophers today.[3]

But beyond this core concept, there are sharp differences among Christian philosophers on the concept of God. Those differences emerge mainly as a result of two factors. There are, for example, disagreements about how to interpret those passages in the Christian scriptures that talk about God. There are also different intuitions about the meaning and implications of such concepts as "ultimate reality," "perfect being," "worthy of worship," etc. In this essay I will focus on three views of God that are alive and well among Christian philosophers today.

Three views of God. Here, then, are the three views of God that I want to discuss. We'll call them, respectively, the Classical Theism (CT), the Neo-classical Theism (NCT) and the Openness Theism (OT). My descriptions of them will be rough and incomplete but, I hope, reasonably accurate.

CT has been held by very many great Christian philosophers and theologians, notably Augustine, Aquinas, and Calvin. It is ably defended these days by Christian philosophers such as David Burrell, Brian Davies, Paul Helm, Brian Leftow, Ralph McInerny, and Eleonore Stump. CT can be defined roughly as follows:

CT: God is the unique, omnipotent, omniscient, and perfectly good creator of the heavens and the earth; God is a necessary being; and God is timeless, strongly immutable, impassible, and metaphysically simple.

Very roughly, let us say that a being is *timeless* if it is "outside of time," if it has no temporal location or temporal extension. On CT, it makes no sense to say, for example, that "God existed in AD 1529" or that "God existed during the entire time of the Cold War." Temporal terms such as these have no application to God. A being is *strongly immutable* if it is never true to say that at one point in time it has a certain property and at another point in time does not have it, except for purely relational changes like, "Is believed in by Augustine or by Charles Colson" (to pick examples of two famous people who were adult converts to Christianity). On CT, it makes no sense to say, for example, that God's attitude toward me after I repent is different from what it was before. A being is *impassible* if it never suffers pain or is changed in attitude, emotion, or behavior by causes external to it. On CT, it makes no sense to say, for example, that God suffers with us when we suffer. And a being is *metaphysically simple* if it consists of no composite parts, i.e., has no complexity of any kind, and is accordingly indivisible. It has no spatial parts, nor even a set of distinct properties or attributes. Of course believers in divine simplicity can say things like, "God is good and wise." But they deny that that means that God has two properties (goodness and wisdom). They say that God "just is" God's properties, which is a slightly paradoxical way of expressing the doctrine. They even sometimes say that God's goodness "just is" God's wisdom, and vice-versa.

NCT is the view of God that is held, I believe, by the majority of Christian philosophers who write about God today, including David Brown, William L. Craig, Alan Padgett, Alvin Plantinga, and Nicholas Wolterstorff. (The fact that a majority hold the theory does not make it true, of course.)

NCT: God is the unique, omnipotent, omniscient, and perfectly good creator of the heavens and the earth; God is a necessary being; and God is temporal, weakly immutable, passible, and not metaphysically simple.

Again very roughly, let us say that a being is *temporal* if there is a real past, present, and future for it, if it has both temporal location and temporal duration. This is not to say, of course, that the being is temporally finite; defenders of NCT always insist that God is everlasting, has no beginning and no end. A being is *weakly immutable* if it changes in some ways but always retains its essential nature and character, is true to its word, keeps its promises, never wavers in its purposes, can always be relied upon, and is not fickle, mercurial, or moody. A being is *not metaphysically simple*, i.e., is metaphysically complex, if it consists of composite parts.

And OT is a view of God that has received considerable attention in Christian philosophical and theological circles in recent decades. Its hallmark is a denial of comprehensive divine foreknowledge; what God does not know about the future—so the most common version of the theory says—is the result of human free choices. What is called "Openness Theology" or the "Open View of God" is associated with people like David Basinger, Greg Boyd, William Hasker, Clark Pinnock, and John Sanders. OT can be briefly defined in this way:

OT: God is the unique, omnipotent, omniscient (in the sense of knowing everything that can possibly be known), and perfectly good creator of the heavens and the earth; God is a necessary being; God is temporal, weakly immutable, passible, and not metaphysically simple; and God does not know the results of future human free decisions.

Accordingly, OT holds that God does not know the entire future.

Now there are two ways that defenders of OT can develop their theory.[4] The less radical version (call it RFOT for "Real Future Open Theology") affirms that there is a real future to be known but denies that God knows all of it. God certainly knows, on this view, what will happen in the future as a result of God's own firm intentions about what to do, but God does not know future contingents, i.e., events that may or may not occur in the future, especially what will or will not occur due to free human choices. Accordingly, God can be said to take risks and to be surprised. The future is open, not fixed by divine foreknowledge or by anything else. If I will be free tomorrow morning to put on my left shoe either before or after my right shoe, God does not know, and has never known, which I will do.

The more radical version of OT (call it POT for "Presentist Open Theology") is based primarily on a metaphysical conviction, viz., that the future is not real. What we call "the future" does not exist, and so logically cannot be known by God or anyone else, since there is literally nothing to know. What is real is the present, and that is all. But I will discuss this version of OT no further in the present paper, and for two reasons. The metaphysical reason is that Presentism (since it holds that the past is not real either) reduces reality ("the present") to nothing but an infinitely thin boundary line between the past and the future. And that cannot be the right way of looking at reality; what is real must amount to more than that. The biblical reason is that if there is now no fact of the matter about future events, then there is no fact of the matter about whether Jesus will return or whether God will win in the end. And that seems a hard conclusion for Christians to accept.

How to think about God? So which of these theories is true or closest to the truth? Although abstruse debates about God are rarely easy to settle, this will be the question that I will try to answer in the present essay. My own views will become clear as I progress, but let me announce here that I am deeply attracted to CT but in the end cannot make sense of it; I reject OT; and so NCT is the theory that I embrace.

Christian thinking about God—so it seems to me—must be done in tension, so to speak, between two opposite poles. God is *transcendent* and God is *immanent*. Christians must hold that both claims are true, and the neglect of one over the other leads to error. The claim that God is transcendent entails that God is infinitely greater than and superior to the whole of creation; we are quite unable to understand God or God's ways; God is not like a powerful and grand human being.[5] The claim that God is immanent follows from Christian notions like these: we were created in God's image, so that in some ways we are like God (and since "being similar to" is a symmetrical relation, if we are in some ways like God then God is in some ways like us); God reveals himself to us and acts in the created order; and in the incarnation of Christ God became one of us. Indeed, God is a *person*—not, of course, in the same way in which we are persons, but at least in the sense of having a mental life that includes knowledge, desires, and intentions, as well as being an agent, as having the ability to bring those intentions to fruition.

Some theories of God go too far in one direction or the other. The danger of going too far in the immanence direction is *anthropomorphism*. This is the tendency to suppose that non-human things—in this case, God—are very much like human beings. The ancient Greek pantheon, for example, was anthropomorphic; gods like Zeus, Ares, and Athena were indeed far more powerful than human beings and did not have to die, but in most other ways they were similar to human beings. But it is possible to go too far in the transcendence direction too. The gods of the ancient Epicureans, for example, were ideal exemplars of *ataraxia* (calm, serenity, imperturbability), but they lived far away from the earth and had nothing to do with human affairs. The God of seventeenth-century Deism, who creates the heavens and the earth and its natural laws and processes but never interferes thereafter, also seems too transcendent. So the danger of going too far in the transcendence direction is that we arrive at a God who has little to do with us and about whom we can know little.

Problems with classical theism. As noted, the two theories that I wish to criticize are CT and OT. In approaching CT, I think a good way to proceed is for me to list five reasons why I think many Christian philosophers today reject it. They are: scripture, human freedom, the origin of sin, apologetic concerns, and pastoral considerations.

Scripture. Many Christian philosophers have a hard time—as I do—reconciling the God depicted in the Bible with a God who is timeless, immutable, simple, and impassible. It seems that God does temporally interact with people, issuing commands that they must obey in the future, judging them for things that they have done in the past, and forgiving them because of their acts of repentance. It also seems that God has different attributes that are not the same as each other, e.g., (as before) goodness and wisdom; moreover, Christians believe that in at least some sense of the word "part" (not physical parts like arms and legs), God has three parts, i.e., the Trinitarian persons. We know, of course, that there is anthropomorphism in the Bible, as well as very many literary genres. Moreover, we are aware of the exceedingly clever and nuanced attempts by medieval philosophers (especially Aquinas) and some of our contemporaries to achieve such a reconciliation between CT and the God of the Bible. Still, many of us are dubious that it can sensibly be done. This point constitutes a major impediment to accepting CT.

Human freedom. Those who accept CT are inevitably drawn to compatibilism vis-à-vis human freedom,

and this is a theory that is unacceptable to many contemporary philosophers of religion, including me. (Compatibilism is the philosophical theory which says that human moral responsibility is compatible with determinism. In theology, compatibilism says that human moral responsibility is compatible with divine foreordination of all things.) That human beings are sometimes free in a libertarian sense is one of our deepest phenomenological convictions; that is, we think it is sometimes possible for a human being, under the same set of antecedent causes, to do a given act or not do it. Moreover, we do not find plausible the various efforts that have been made by defenders of CT and others to reconcile compatibilist freedom with moral responsibility. And the assertion that human beings are morally responsible for their sins is one of the most important principles of biblical religion. Again, we are aware of the thoughtful attempts in the tradition to reconcile compatibilist freedom and human moral responsibility, but we are unconvinced.

The origin of evil. Those who defend CT always insist that the reason that God perfectly foreknows the future is that the future will be what it will be because, in some sense, God wills or foreordains what it will be.[6] It is crucial to CT that all of God's aims or purposes will be accomplished. And the obvious problem here is that this seems to make God the author of evil, both natural and moral. How can God, who is perfectly morally good, foreordain people to sin? How can God, who is perfectly just, condemn foreordained sinners to hell? Defenders of CT of course respond to this charge. But despite the subtle distinctions that defenders of CT make at this point, many contemporary Christian philosophers see nothing but paradox in affirming both divine foreordination of all events and human responsibility for their sins.[7]

Apologetic issues. People who are committed to CT often insist that it makes no sense for Christians to try to argue that God is "morally good," in some sense similar to the way in which respected and honored human beings are morally good. Now I too wish strongly to affirm that God's goodness far transcends even the best of human goodness. Still, apologetic issues come into play here whenever we try to reply to Mackie-like objections to the problem of evil.[8] Atheists certainly do pose questions about God's moral integrity. I once met a man—a veteran of World War II—who said to me, "I have seen things with my own eyes that God would never permit if God existed." In order to answer people who say things like that (more frequent, perhaps, are comments like, "I will not believe in a God who allows x, y, and z"), Christian philosophers have felt constrained to argue that God can still be perfectly morally good despite the occurrence of events like x, y, and z. I regard that as a perfectly understandable and acceptable reaction. Does God need our apologetic interventions? Of course not. But some people apparently need them. Such folk need to be told where their thinking has led them astray. So this point constitutes a reason to question CT as an adequate view of God if CT holds—as it normally does—that all human attempts to show that God is "morally good" cannot get off the ground.

Pastoral considerations. A closely related point: when I was a young assistant pastor just out of theological seminary, a member of my parish was diagnosed with lupus, a disease of which there was then (and so far as I know, still is) no known cure. I spoke with him, and with his wife, on several occasions. A metal worker without much education, he in effect asked me the question, "Why did this happen to me?" His wife was even more deeply troubled. I was faced with a pastoral situation where a believer, i.e., the wife, was calling into question God's moral integrity. I saw it as my pastoral responsibility to let her express her pain and anger, to suffer with her (usually in silence), and occasionally to try to get her to see that God was good and could be praised for his goodness despite what had happened to her husband. Had I been a strict defender of CT, I would not have been able to comfort either

the husband or the wife, unless they found it comforting to be told, "Get used to it: God causes every event that occurs, and we must love and honor God nevertheless."[9]

What about CT's doctrine of divine impassibility? The classical theorist's objection to passibility is this: If God were to feel sorrow when we suffer, that would make God's emotional state depend on us, and so God would not be wholly independent of us in God's existence and nature. Now despite this argument, in the past one hundred years, not just most philosophers of religion, but virtually the entire Christian theological world (with the exception of those who embrace CT), has moved to the notion that God *qua* God suffers.[10] It is now a virtual commonplace. (Again, that does not make it true.) The point that defenders of NCT or OT often make is this: Once God creates human beings, reveals himself to them, and makes covenants with them, God gives up being *wholly* independent of the creatures. Of course God does not depend in any sense on us for God's existence and essential nature. But God does respond to what we do, as literally hundreds of biblical passages imply.

In various ways, the defenders of CT want to increase the distance between God and human beings. For example, defenders of CT sometimes deny that God is a moral agent.[11] And I agree that God is not a moral agent in the same sense in which we are moral agents (i.e., morally responsible to a higher agent). But I would have thought that God becomes a moral agent of a sort the moment God issues moral commands to human beings or makes covenants with them. Indeed, the moment God does that, God makes us part of God's moral community.

What about the notion of divine simplicity? This is a part of CT that I confess I only dimly understand. One obvious problem is this: two attributes are obviously distinct from each other if it is logically possible for a substance to possess one of them but not the other. Thus *red* is not the same attribute as *tall* because it is possible for something to have one but not the other. So anything that is both red and tall is not metaphysically simple. But surely it is logically possible for a being to be *the creator of the heavens and the earth* without being *perfectly good*. Some religions have suggested this very thing. Thus if God possesses both these properties—as Christianity insists—God is not metaphysically simple.[12]

I do not think the arguments usually advanced in favor of divine simplicity are convincing. For example, it is sometimes said that whatever has parts that are distinct from it depends on them for its existence and nature.[13] But I would reply that if God is a necessary being and if God's parts are essential to God, this does not follow. No necessary being depends on *anything* for its existence. Another argument: Paul Helm claims that composite things must be caused to exist. Everything composite, he says, "is subsequent to its components and depends on them."[14] But I am unsure what "subsequent to" means in this context. Am I "subsequent to" my left foot? I certainly in some sense depend on it, but if God is composite, God cannot be separated from his parts, as I can, and so is not dependent on them in any theologically untoward way. A similar argument: James Ross claims that denying divine simplicity entails "God's incompleteness and dependence on things *ad extra*."[15] But I do not think this notion entails God's incompleteness at all since God's parts are obviously going to be essential parts of God, who is a necessary being. God's parts are related to each other and to God because they cannot not be so related. Accordingly, it does not entail God's dependence on anything external to God. Nor, if God is a necessary being, is any explanation required of why the parts of God are related to each other as they are. It is simply an essential aspect of reality that God's parts are related to each other as they are.

Some defenders of CT strongly deny that God is "an item in the universe."[16] In my view, the answer to the question whether that is true depends on what is meant by "the universe." Perhaps the term refers to the huge aggregate of all creatures, i.e., to all the contingent things that have ever existed, now exist, or will ever exist. On that understanding of the term, God is not an item in the universe. God is not a contingent thing. But if by the term "the universe" we mean the set of all real or existing things, then—or so I would hold—God is indeed an item in the universe. Does it necessarily demean God's transcendence and sovereignty to affirm as much? I do not see why. One can still be quite clear about all the ways in which God differs from the creatures.

Some theologians and philosophers of religion have denied that God is a "being." But I have always thought that the English term "being" is almost infinite in what it ranges over. A "being" is just anything whose name or referring term can appear in the subject position of a coherent sentence, is a property bearer, and has an identity apart from other things. Is God a being *like* other beings? Of course not. Is God a being *among* others beings? Of course (or so I would say).

What clinches God's membership in the set of existing beings, in my opinion, is the fact of revelation. Apart from God's revealing himself to us, we would know nothing of God. Thus Psalm 28:1: "To you, O Lord, I call; my rock, do not refuse to hear me, for if you are silent to me, I shall be like those who go down to the pit." If God were silent, some sort of Epicureanism or Deism would be believable. But, as the prophet Amos affirms, God does speak to us: "For lo, the one who forms the mountains, creates the wind, *reveals his thoughts to mortals*, makes the morning darkness, and treads on the heights of the earth—The Lord, the God of hosts is his name!" (Amos 4:13, italics added). If God reveals himself to us, and even becomes one of us in the incarnation, it is hard for me to see how sensibly to deny the claim that God is an item in the universe. Certainly, as just noted, God is not an item *like all the other items*, but that is another matter.

Problems with open theism. It is time to turn to OT. It is important to note that one central issue in relation to OT is philosophical in nature. Defenders of OT are convinced that: (1) the future is open (reality is such that much of the future is not settled), (2) human beings are sometimes free in a libertarian sense in the decisions that they make and the things that they do, and (3) complete divine foreknowledge is logically incompatible with human libertarian freedom. So God always knows everything that logically can be known, and as noted knows his own intentions about what to do in the future, as well as future events that can be inferred from past and present events. But results of future free decisions simply cannot be known. (Defenders of NCT, on the other hand, accept (1) and (2) but not (3).) According to OT, much of what God knows about the future is limited to possibilities. So God is in a sense vulnerable in that God must take risks in order to accomplish things that involve human beings and their free decisions; God will occasionally be surprised, and so must be flexible and tactically astute. God's will is going to be frustrated on occasion, and God will experience regret and disappointment; God must adapt and change in order to accomplish God's goals.

Despite the fact that I reject OT, it must be admitted that the theory has two strong points. First, it is indeed difficult to see how divine foreknowledge and human libertarian freedom can be consistent. (I will address that issue below.) Second, OT seems to have ready answers to questions like: Why would God create and bestow libertarian freedom on those human beings who would become moral monsters like Hitler or Charles Manson? and Why would God create and bestow freedom on those human beings whom he foreknew would end up condemned in hell? Their obvious answer is that God was not able to foreknow those sorts of outcomes.

Although one central issue here is philosophical, there is no denying that there are important biblical and theological ramifications of OT. Biblically,

defenders of OT tend to emphasize and interpret literally those biblical texts that have God ignorant of the future, changing his mind, or reworking his plans in response to human decisions and actions. For example, at the outset of the story of the great flood, Genesis 6:5–6 says: "The Lord saw that the wickedness of humankind was great in the earth, and that every inclination of the thoughts of their hearts was only evil continually. And the Lord was sorry that he had made humankind on the earth, and it grieved him to his heart." Open theologians will interpret these words as implying that when God originally made human beings, God did not know how rampant evil would become, and that God caused the great flood to occur as a way of dealing with his regret for having created human beings, and as an effort to find a new way to achieve his ends for humankind. Whether this is the correct way to interpret this text, and others like it, is a matter of considerable dispute, but it is a debate that we can enter into here only briefly.

Suffice it to say that opponents of OT argue that the Bible is largely a collection of texts about God's actions in human history as seen from a human perspective; that it is not a textbook in theology or the philosophy of religion; and that an understandable degree of anthropomorphism affects many such biblical texts. Accordingly, the fact that God is sometimes depicted as being ignorant of how things will turn out and as later regretful when they turn out badly is a function of how God's actions appeared to human observers of the events in question or how they seemed to the biblical writers at the time that they wrote. Such texts do not describe God's inner life, nor (in my opinion) are they meant to do so.[17] Since they describe God's actions in the world, they describe not God as he is in himself but God as seen in his work.[18]

Let me raise three objections to OT (again, we are speaking here only of RFOT). *What did God know at creation?* I would personally find it repugnant to admit, as Open theists must, that at the moment of creation, God did not know whether even a single human being would ever freely respond positively to God's call and thus eventually enter heaven.[19] Of course defenders of OT can insist that God could have made probability judgments about how many people would decide freely to love and obey God and how many would refuse to do so. Still, it is hard to resist the feeling that we are now dealing with a God who, so far as knowledge is concerned, has been *demoted*. I would suggest that even if (contrary to what I will argue below) we cannot adequately solve the problem of reconciling divine foreknowledge with human libertarian freedom, it would be better to affirm them both, and admit the paradox, than to embrace OT.[20]

Is anything left of omniscience? As we saw above, the claim that God is all-knowing is part of Christianity's core concept of God. Defenders of OT insist that the God they envision is omniscient because at all times God knows everything that can possibly be known; future contingents—so they say—logically *cannot* be known. Now this claim must mean that Open theists hold that propositions about future contingent states of affairs do not now have a truth value, i.e., are (for now) neither true nor false. It does not seem possible that there could be truths that are not knowable. Take the statement, "Tomorrow Stephen Davis will freely decide to wear a blue shirt." If that statement now has a truth value, surely an omniscient being must know it, i.e., must know whether it is true or false. So the defenders of OT must hold that such propositions are now neither true nor false (as philosophers say, they must deny the principle of bivalence).[21]

This is fair enough: although I am not prepared to grant that future contingent propositions have no truth value, I agree that, *if* they are neither true nor false, they cannot be known, and so it is no problem for omniscience if God does not know them. But there remains a thorny problem for defenders of OT. Let's think further about how defenders of OT analyze those stories in the Bible where God appears to be surprised or disappointed by what people do. In such cases, it appears that, before the event actually occurred, God held a false belief (e.g., that the people would respond as God desired). For example, it appears that (at least on the literalist hermeneutic that defenders of OT deploy in such cases) before the flood, God held the erroneous belief that the people would not descend into evil to the degree that they in fact did. But certainly anyone who holds a false belief is not omniscient, does not "know everything that can be known." It surely seems that mental states like surprise and disappointment could have been present in God only if prior to the surprising or disappointing event, God had an expectation that in the end was not met. Now beliefs are not the same things as expectations, but it is hard to see how someone can have an expectation that an event will occur without having some sort of belief (however strongly held) that it will occur. Accordingly, if God was surprised and disappointed at what eventually occurred, then before the event occurred, God had a false belief.[22] It will hardly do for defenders of OT to insist that the surprise and disappointment that God exhibits in these texts do not really represent God's mental states; that would violate the literalist hermeneutic that defenders of OT typically deploy in such cases.

If we consistently follow that hermeneutic, it seems that we will be led to hold that God has spatial location (he walked in the Garden of Eden at the time of the evening breeze—Genesis 3:8), is forgetful (he "remembered" Noah in his ark—Genesis 8:1; and he needed a reminder for himself [the rainbow] of his promise not to destroy all flesh again by flood—Genesis 9:11–17), is impatient (Exodus 32:7–14), and is sardonic, vengeful, and full of rage (Deuteronomy 29:28). Now defenders of CT and NCT have hermeneutically powerful ways of understanding these texts, but there appears to be little room for anthropomorphism or even accommodation among the defenders of OT. So it would be interesting to see what exegesis they would provide for such texts.

Does God's knowledge grow as time passes? Defenders of OT will want to argue that God's knowledge grows as time passes, and that eventually, in the eschaton, there will be no more future contingents for God to be ignorant of. At that point, God will know everything. But there is a problem with this picture. It seems that God's degree of ignorance about the future must grow as time passes. God must be unaware not only of the result of future human free decisions but of all the multitudes of effects resulting from them.

Note also that as more and more time passes, human knowledge also grows, as does human technology. We are now able to do things (fly airplanes, communicate instantly with people thousands of miles away, send space ships to Mars) that earlier generations could only dream of. And in one sense, this might mean that God knows *less and less* as time passes. In other words, in comparing the twenty-first century with, say, the Pleistocene Age, far more of what occurs in the world now depends on free human choices than previously. Perhaps one day human beings will possess the technical ability to destroy the entire solar system, just as we now have the ability to destroy human life on earth. Does God now know that human life will survive the twenty-second century? Of course, the God of OT always knows what people are presently doing, and so could presumably interfere—at the last moment, so to speak—to prevent the manufacture or use of a bomb that could destroy the solar system. Still, the point is that as long as God does not intervene, perhaps God knows less and less about the future rather than more and more. Maybe some day virtually every future event in the solar system will be unknown to God because virtually all of them will depend on human free choices.

Accordingly, my own view is that OT proposes a view of God that errs too much on the immanence side. Its God is insufficiently transcendent and insufficiently sovereign. In the end, I reject OT because (1) I believe that divine foreknowledge and human freedom are compatible and (2) because I believe that the Bible teaches both that human beings are free and morally responsible before God and that God has complete foreknowledge of all future events.

Neo-classical theism. Therefore, since I reject both CT and OT, I accept NCT almost by default. But one important point remains to be considered: both defenders of CT and defenders of OT agree that complete divine foreknowledge is incompatible with human libertarian freedom. If I am to defend NCT, I must try to refute that claim. So I will try to show, in two quite distinct ways, that divine foreknowledge and human freedom are compatible. My first argument will concern what is called "simple foreknowledge." The second will concern what is called "middle knowledge."

Simple foreknowledge is the claim that God knows or "sees" the future just as we experience or see the present. No defender of this theory claims to know *how* God foresees future events, but of course there is much that Christians believe God does or has done that we do not understand—how God created the heavens and the earth, for example, or how he raised Jesus from the dead. But the essential claim is that God has complete and infallible knowledge of everything that will occur in the future, including future contingents.

While it is clear that divine fore*ordination* of all future events (causing them to occur) would be incompatible with human libertarian freedom, defenders of simple foreknowledge argue that the same need not be true of divine fore*knowledge* of all future events. They point out that foreknowledge is not a species of causation. Suppose that today I know, of a certain person, that she will wear shoes tomorrow. Surely, my knowing today that she will wear shoes tomorrow does not *cause* her to wear shoes tomorrow (although it is logically incompatible with her not wearing shoes tomorrow). I am unable to argue the point fully here,[23] but the basic idea is this: while no one can change the past, it is perfectly possible that what God knew a million years ago about what I will freely (via libertarian freedom) decide to eat for lunch tomorrow logically depends on what I will freely decide to eat for lunch tomorrow. People often argue that if God knows that event E is going to happen at some time in the future, then since no one can know something that is not true, it follows that E will necessarily happen. And if E necessarily happens, I am not libertarianly free.

But this argument, in my opinion, rests on a fallacy. All that follows is something about which there is no dispute whatsoever, viz. that E *will* occur. But of course the fact that E will occur does not rule out the possibility that I will, at the relevant moment, have it fully within my power not to do E. Now we know that that power or ability is a power that I will not in fact exercise, but at virtually every moment we have powers that we do not exercise, and that fact does not rule out our freedom. It is within my power to insert a line of gibberish into the text at this point in the essay, but I will not do it. From God's knowledge that I will do E, what follows is not that I *must* do E but only that I *will* do E. Moreover, it seems perfectly possible that this statement is true:

A: What God knew yesterday is contingent upon what I will freely decide to do tomorrow.

Suppose it is true, say, that I am free to decide whether or not to wear a blue shirt tomorrow; if so, then both my wearing a blue shirt and my not wearing a blue shirt are (as we might say) real options for me. That is, both are within my power; it is up to me which I will do. Then whichever option I choose, God will have known yesterday (and indeed from all eternity) which I will do.

But three objections lie close at hand. First, suppose God believed yesterday that I will not in fact choose to wear a blue shirt tomorrow, and suppose it will be within my power to wear a blue shirt tomorrow. Then (so the objection goes) it will be within my power to make it such that God had a false belief yesterday (and so is not omniscient).[24] And that surely is an unacceptable consequence. But this is too hasty. What follows is not that God held a false belief, but that it will be within my power tomorrow to do something such that if I exercise that power, then a belief that God did in fact have would have been false. But, obviously, the defender of simple foreknowledge will insist that if I will in fact exercise my power tomorrow to choose to wear a blue shirt, *that* will be what God will have believed yesterday.[25] Since God is omniscient, we can be sure, on these assumptions, that "Davis will wear a blue shirt tomorrow" is what God will have believed yesterday.

The crucial point here is this: it is obvious that "Davis *will not* wear a blue shirt tomorrow" and "Davis *cannot* wear a blue shirt tomorrow" are quite different statements. But it is the first statement, not the second, that is entailed by *God knew yesterday that Davis will not wear a blue shirt tomorrow*. Accordingly, even if God knew yesterday or a million years ago that I will not wear a blue shirt tomorrow, I might still have it within my power tomorrow either to wear a blue shirt or not wear a blue shirt. Of course, if God knows that I will not wear a blue shirt tomorrow, then I will not do so (as noted, there is no dispute about that). But I might still be free to decide to wear a blue shirt (although I will not in fact exercise that power).

The second objection to the line of argument that I have been pursuing has to do with causality. It seems to some that this argument allows or even entails that an event can be caused by something that happens after it. That is, it seems to imply that *what God knew yesterday* can be caused by *what I will freely do tomorrow*. But this notion is incoherent; as Hume claimed and as all our intuitions confirm, a cause must be temporally prior to its effect.

But the objection does not succeed. The argument that I have been pursuing does not claim or entail that what I will freely do tomorrow causes God to know something yesterday. The claim is that it is God's ability to foreknow, exercised yesterday, that caused God yesterday to know what I will do tomorrow. But even if this is so, the critic will change the criticism slightly and claim that my argument must hold that *God's exercising yesterday his ability to foreknow* is caused by *what I will freely do tomorrow*. And that looks like a violation of the principle that causes must antedate their effects.

But the answer to this is that my argument is that what God foreknew yesterday *is contingent upon* (not is caused by) what I will freely decide to do tomorrow. (I have in mind here a purely logical notion of contingency, the sort involved in saying that in the famous syllogism, the truth of "Socrates is mortal" is contingent upon the truth of "All men are mortal" and "Socrates is a man.") And Hume's principle that causes must come before their effects does not apply to the logical relation "is contingent upon." Earlier events or states of affairs certainly can be logically contingent upon later ones. Take the state of affairs of "Stephen Davis being a great-grandfather" or rather the statement, "Stephen Davis will be, during his lifetime, a great-grandfather." I believe this statement is now either true or false. It might be true and it might be false, but its truth value is now unknown to me and, I believe, all non-omniscient knowers. But whichever truth value it now has is clearly contingent upon certain events that will or will not occur in the future.[26]

The third objection is this: "If in fact I will eat the cookie tomorrow, it follows (given comprehensive divine foreknowledge) that God knew a million years ago that I will eat the cookie tomorrow. But then my eating the cookie tomorrow is and always was inevitable in a really strong sense—it is logically entailed by things (either past or eternal facts) that neither I nor anyone else had any control over; ergo, I will not be free in choosing to eat the cookie." But this does not follow:

on my view when tomorrow arrives I will, in my free decision, have control over what will have been true, and thus known by God, a million years ago. What was then known to be then will have been logically dependent upon what I will freely decide tomorrow.

So it seems that simple foreknowledge is a coherent notion. Divine foreknowledge can be compatible with human libertarian freedom.

Molinism. But there is another, quite different, way of arguing that divine foreknowledge and human libertarian freedom are logically compatible. Molinism[27] is the doctrine that God possesses and uses "middle knowledge." Molina's view was that at the moment of creation, God knew three sorts of things. First, God's natural knowledge consists of everything that God knew prior to creating: all of the pure possibilities (knowledge of what *could possibly* be) like "It is possible that the world will have no people" or "It is possible for Steve Davis to be eight feet tall," and all necessary truths (knowledge of what *must* be) like "All triangles are three sided" and "No rocks are rational." Second, God's free knowledge obtained (knowledge of what *will* be). Accordingly, via his foreknowledge, God also knew all future actualities like "Stephen Davis will be a professor in Claremont" and "There will never exist any unicorns." Third, Molina reasoned that between God's natural knowledge (of the possible and the necessary) and his free knowledge (of the actual) lies God's middle knowledge (knowledge of what *would* be under various conditions and circumstances). Indeed, God had this knowledge logically prior to creating or issuing decrees.

Middle knowledge is also called counterfactual knowledge. It is knowledge of what would be the case if certain things that are not true were in fact true. Counterfactuals are quite common in human conversation: "If O'Neal had not been injured, the Lakers would have won the game"; "If you had offered Davis a chocolate chip cookie, he would have accepted."

Applied to persons, middle-knowledge is knowledge of *what they would do* in various non-actual situations.[28]

Counterfactuals can be true or false.[29] According to the standard theories we test a counterfactual like "If O'Neal had not been injured, the Lakers would have won the game" by asking whether the Lakers do win the game in the closest possible world to the actual world in which O'Neal is not injured. This analysis is somewhat controversial among logicians, and matters very quickly get more complex than this. But the point is that there are procedures for deciding the truth value of counterfactual statements.

Suppose we use the word *character* to mean the sum total of all the attributes or properties that make persons who they are and what they do in various circumstances. God then presumably foreknows the characters of all soon-to-be-actual persons even before they are born. Indeed, God knows the characters of all (what I will call) *possible persons*, which are simply coherent combinations of attributes of persons that may or may not ever actually exist. (Those possible persons that do at some time exist are also *actual persons*.) Presumably, then, God's middle knowledge allows God to know precisely what any possible person would do (would, in the various possible cases, freely decide to do) in any possible circumstance in which that person could be placed.

The point then is that human beings can be libertarianly free and God can nevertheless know, via middle knowledge, what any possible person would freely decide to do in any possible situation. Accordingly, again, divine foreknowledge and human free will are logically compatible. One advantage that middle knowledge has over simple foreknowledge is that defenders of it do not have to plead ignorance when asked how God achieves it. We have no idea how God could foresee the future, but we can understand how an omniscient being can know the character of each possible being so intimately as to be sure what he or she would do in any possible circumstance.

But it might be objected that middle knowledge after all ends up denying human libertarian freedom. Suppose there were a true counterfactual that involves libertarian freedom to the effect that

(J) *If Steve Davis is offered a chocolate chip cookie in situation S* [where S is suitably spelled out], *Davis will accept.*

Now why is this statement true (instead of, *"If Steve Davis is offered a chocolate chip cookie in situation S, Davis will refuse"*)? The answer is that (J) is true because in every possible world in which Davis is offered the cookie and everything else is as much as possible like the actual world, Davis accepts the cookie.

But—so it might be argued—this is inconsistent with Davis being free in a libertarian sense. Davis would only be libertarianly free in this case if the conclusion were that in situation S it is causally open to Davis to reject the cookie. Or to make the point more theologically, if God via middle knowledge knows precisely what Davis would do in any given circumstance, the very fact that God knows that Davis will exist, will exist in situation S, and will accept the cookie compromises Davis's libertarian freedom. He *will* accept the cookie.

But this argument is surely confused. Even if there logically can be no such thing as middle knowledge, it is still the case that any human being who is libertarianly free in a certain situation will, in the end, make a choice. So even if God has no middle knowledge, Davis, exercising his libertarian freedom, will choose either to accept or reject the cookie. Suppose he freely chooses to accept it. Then it could be argued with equal cogency (equally cogent, that is, to the objection that we are considering) that Davis is no longer libertarianly free because, tautologically, he *will* accept the cookie. I believe the two arguments are exactly analogous. So the objection to middle knowledge that we are considering goes nowhere. It reduces to the triviality that Davis *will* make a choice.

Conclusion. It appears, then, that NCT can be defended. Both simple foreknowledge and middle knowledge are possible and allow us to answer the most important objection to NCT. But since CT and OT are open to damaging criticisms, NCT is the view of God that ought to be recommended to theists.[30]

Notes

1. For a good introduction to the Christian understanding of God, see Colin E. Gunton, *The Triune Creator: A Historical and Systematic Study* (Edinburgh: U of Edinburgh P, 1998).

2. Let us define a "necessary being" as a being that (a) cannot not exist and (b) depends for its existence on no other being. This entails, of course, that it is also (c) everlasting (there is no time when it does not exist). Some people hold that (b) is considered a separate attribute called "aseity" and that (a) alone defines a necessary being. But I prefer to say that a necessary being has both (a) and (b).

3. Process philosophers, who deny omnipotence (as least as standardly understood in the tradition), are an exception to this point. I will not discuss Process views of God in the present essay.

4. See Dale Tuggy, "Three Roads to Open Theism," forthcoming in *Faith and Philosophy*.

5. Cf. Isaiah 45:15: "Truly, you are a God who hides himself." On God's incomprehensibility and unlikeness to human beings, see Numbers 23:19; I Samuel 15:29; Isaiah 46:5; 55:8–9; and Hosea 11:9.

6. Thus the Westminster Confession declares: "God from all eternity did by the most wise and holy council of his own will freely and unchangeably ordain whatsoever comes to pass."

7. Some defenders of CT are prepared to admit the paradoxical nature of their position at this point. See Paul Helm, "The Augustinian-Calvinist View," in James K. Beilby and Paul R. Eddy, eds., *Divine Foreknowledge: Four Views* (Downers Grove, IL: InterVarsity P, 2001), pp. 165–66, 169, 177.

8. See J.L Mackie, "Evil and Omnipotence," in *God and Evil*, ed. Nelson Pike (Englewood Cliffs, NJ: Prentice-Hall, 1964). Mackie argued that theists hold to a logically inconsistent position because three of their core beliefs—God is all-powerful; God is perfectly good; and Evil exists—form an inconsistent triad. That is, for purely logical reasons, any two of the three may be true, but not all three.

9. I recognize that my point about pastoral considerations does not amount to a refutation of CT. It is at best a reason why I find the theory rationally indefensible.

10. The expression "God *qua* God" here simply means "God apart from the incarnation." It is important to add this phrase because everybody—even the strictest defenders of CT—is prepared to admit that the Son of God suffered in his humiliation, e.g., in the Garden of Gethsemane.

11. Cf. Brian Davies, "Is God a Moral Agent?" in D.Z. Phillips (ed.), *Whose God? Which Tradition? The Nature of Belief in God* (Ashgate: Aldershot and Burlington, 2008).

12. A defender of divine simplicity might reply that all I have shown is that our *concepts* of goodness and wisdom are distinct, but not that the *properties* themselves are distinct; that is, our human limitations prevent us from seeing reality as God does; if we were to see things correctly we would see that it is logically impossible for God to possess one and lack the other. But my question would then be whether there is any good reason to hold such an obscure view.

13. See Brian Leftow, "God, concepts of," in *Routledge Encyclopedia of Philosophy*, 6.

14..See Paul Helm in *op. cit.*

15. See James Ross in *ibid.*

16. Cf. David Burrell in *ibid.*

17. Moreover, the Bible itself seems to me rather clearly to deny that God changes his mind. See Numbers 23:19 and 1 Samuel 15:29.

18. Moreover, there are texts in the Bible whose plain sense seems to imply divine foreknowledge of what look to be free human decisions. See, for example, Exodus 3:19; Deuteronomy 31:16; Psalms 139:16; Isaiah 44:28; John 6:70–71; and Acts 2:23. It would be interesting to know how defenders of OT would exegete these texts; perhaps they will say that the Bible only reports beliefs that God had about future human decisions that were, before those decisions were made, not true beliefs but only very probably true beliefs.

19. This especially in the light of texts like Revelation 13:8, which seem to imply that God knew in advance precisely who would be saved and who would not, and indeed wrote the names of the blessed in the Lamb's Book of Life. See also Ephesians 1:4, where the text affirms that God "chose us in Christ before the foundation of the world."

20. As is the position of J.L. Packer in his *Evangelism and the Sovereignty of God* (Downers Grove, IL: InterVarsity P, 1961), pp. 21–23.

21. In the following two paragraphs, I am largely following William L. Craig. See Beilby, pp. 55–57.

22. Note such texts as Jeremiah 3:7, 19–20 and especially Jeremiah 19:5, where God complains that the children of Israel built altars to Baal and burned their children on them "which I did not command or decree, nor did it enter my mind." If at a certain point in time the thought that the children of Israel would do these terrible deeds had not entered God's mind, it surely seems that at that time God had a false belief. Moreover, if some of God's plans backfire and fail to come to fruition because of God's ignorance of future contingents, that calls into question God's perfect wisdom as well as God's omniscience.

23. I have tried to do so in my "Divine Omniscience and Human Freedom," *Religious Studies*, Vol. 15, No. 3 (September, 1979).

24. This is the argument (on the assumption that God is essentially omniscient) of Nelson Pike. See his, "Divine Omniscience and Voluntary

Action," *Philosophy of Religion*, ed. by Steven Cahn (New York: Harper and Row, 1970), pp. 68–88.

25. This argument essentially follows Alvin Plantinga, *God, Freedom, and Evil* (New York: Harper and Row, 1974), pp. 69–73.

26. It is true that one event being contingent upon another is not a purely logical relationship. But I am not talking about events, because I believe that "God knowing what I will freely do tomorrow" is everlasting and so is not an "event." What God foreknew yesterday is not an event in the mind of God.

27. Molinism is named after the Spanish Jesuit philosopher Luis Molina (1535–1600). Alvin Plantinga introduced middle knowledge into the contemporary discussion among philosophers of religion. See his *God, Freedom, and Evil*, pp. 34–57. The foremost contemporary defenders of Molinism are Thomas P. Flint and William Lane Craig. See Flint's *Divine Providence: The Molinist Account* (Ithaca, NY: Cornell UP, 1998). In his various writings to date, Craig has fruitfully applied middle knowledge to several different problems in theology and the philosophy of religion.

28. I should mention that a certain philosophical objection to the very idea of middle knowledge has been much discussed of late. It is called "the grounding objection." I do not myself find the objection convincing, and so will not consider it here. For a brief discussion of it by Craig, see James K. Beilby and Paul Eddy, eds., *Divine Foreknowledge: Four Views* (Downers Grove, IL: InterVarsity

P, 2001), pp. 140–43. For a sensible assessment of the arguments, see Edward Wierenga, "Providence, Middle Knowledge, and the Grounding Objection," *Philosophia Christi*, Series 2, Volume 3, No. 2 (2001), pp. 447–54.

29. See David Lewis, *Counterfactuals* (Cambridge, MA: Harvard UP, 1973) and Robert Stalnaker, *Inquiry* (Cambridge, MA: MIT P, 1984).

30. I would like to thank Kelly James Clark, David Hunt, Alan Padgett, Susan Peppers-Bates, and Dale Tuggy for their helpful comments on an earlier draft of this essay. They do not agree with everything I've said here.

Discussion

1. What does NCT borrow from CT and from OT?

2. Why does Davis reject OT's view of omniscience?

3. What is Davis's basic defense of simple foreknowledge?

4. Put Molinism (middle knowledge) in your own words.

Suggestions for Further Study

Byrne, Peter. *Prolegomena to Religious Pluralism: Reference and Realism in Religion.* New York: St. Martin's P, 1995.

Creel, Richard. *Divine Impassibility.* Cambridge: Cambridge UP, 1986.

Crisp, Oliver. *A Reader in Contemporary Philosophical Theology.* London: T&T Clark, 2009.

Crisp, Oliver, and Michael Rea, eds. *Analytic Theology: New Essays in the Philosophy of Theology.* Oxford: Oxford UP, 2009.

Davis, Stephen. *Christian Philosophical Theology.* Oxford UP, 2006.

Flint, Thomas, and Michael Rea. *The Oxford Handbook of Philosophical Theology.* Oxford: Oxford UP, 2009.

Hamnett, Ian, ed. *Religious Pluralism and Unbelief.* New York: Routledge, 1990.

Kenny, Anthony. *The God of the Philosophers.* Oxford: Clarendon P, 1979.

Kvanvig, Jonathan. *The Problem of Hell.* New York: Oxford UP, 1993.

Morris, Thomas, ed. *The Concept of God.* Oxford: Oxford UP, 1987.

Pinnock, Clark et al. *The Openness of God.* Downers Grove: InterVarsity P, 1994.

Quinn, Philip, and Charles Taliaferro, eds. *A Companion to Philosophy of Religion.* Oxford: Basil Blackwell, 1997.

Stiver, Dan. *The Philosophy of Religious Language: Sign, Symbol, and Story.* Cambridge: Blackwell, 1996.

Swinburne, Richard. *The Coherence of Theism.* Oxford: Clarendon P, 1977.

Wolterstorff, Nicholas. *Divine Discourse: Philosophical Reflections on the Claim That God Speaks.* Cambridge: Cambridge UP, 1995.

Chinese Philosophy of Religion

Part Six

Introduction

Introduction. Adding a section on Asian philosophy of religion is complicated. Most Westerners don't know enough about Asian religions—Buddhism, Hinduism, or Daoism, for example—to meaningfully reflect on them philosophically. We will rectify this unfortunate situation by focusing. Our first focus is *geographical*: we focus on China (Asia is just too big with too many religions over too vast a period of time). Our second focus is *temporal*: we focus on early China (roughly 200 BCE and earlier). Our third focus is *textual*: we focus on just a few, formative primary texts to help develop a basic understanding of early Chinese religion (as represented in those few texts). Finally, I have selected a few fairly representative contemporary texts that offer varied reflections on the meanings of the selected ancient texts.

As an aid to understanding, I offer a lengthier introduction to these texts, which should help the reader travelling into an otherwise unfamiliar world. The introductions offer, I hope, adequate information for the reader to wrestle with the texts to determine their religious import.

Contemporary Chinese philosophy of religion is in its infancy partly because scholars are relatively new to Chinese studies and partly because there is widespread disagreement about the religious import of key texts. While throughout Chinese history Chinese scholars have countenanced divinities (lesser and greater), ancestor worship, and religious rituals, post-Enlightenment and post-Marxist scholarship has declared China to be more rationalistic, pragmatic, and naturalistic than religious. To put my cards on the table, I side with the more traditional, religious interpretations of early China. I believe Chinese thought includes deeply religious elements, which require wider and deeper understanding as well as more and better philosophical reflection.

Since text understanding is a matter of current debate, this section of the book will focus more on text understanding than on philosophical reflection. We focus on just a few texts from a long time ago. By focussing on texts, we resist the temptation to make sweeping conclusions about "the East," "the Chinese," or "Confucianism" (often thought to reflect "the Chinese mind"). It is just as meaningless to talk about "the Chinese mind" as it is "the Native American mind," as though people over such vast geographical and temporal distances are somehow united in thought.

Let us work our way into early Chinese religion by way of Confucius as represented in the *Analects*.

Confucius and the Analects. The world idealized by Confucius in the *Analects* was a harmonious society directed by humane scholar-rulers, held together by elaborate rituals. This social ideal hearkens back to an ancient, idyllic, and golden (but likely mythic) age of wise and virtuous Kings and a self-sacrificial Duke who ruled by the power of their own goodness. They ushered in an age of peace and harmony due to their wise, generous, and just rule. These rulers met their citizen's needs without having to be asked: they were, like a mother for her baby, so keenly attuned to the needs of their people they instantly sensed any lack or loss; and then they devoted themselves to meeting that need.

In the early Zhou Dynasty (commencing roughly 1100 BCE), we find the apogee of this golden age. Moreover, we find two moral exemplars in the dynasty's first king and most influential duke. King Wen, the honorific founder of the Zhou dynasty, was a living model of culture, benevolence, and wisdom. His son, the Duke of Zhou, set aside ambition and pride to serve his God-given role as advisor to the king (his much younger and less qualified nephew who had the God-given role of king). Together, King Wen and the Duke of Zhou exercised benevolence and justice and everyone lived in harmony.

The world at the time of Confucius (551–479 BCE) was a chaotic state of fragmentation and disharmony. Rulers failed to meet the demands of justice and retained power through arbitrary laws and harsh punishments.

Any discussion of what Confucius himself did or did not believe must overcome substantial historical obstacles. Confucius (in China, "Master Kong" or "Kongzi") died without leaving a written record of his life or thought. The extant text of the *Analects*, compiled and edited in the early Han era (the Han Dynasty was from 206 BCE to 220 CE), is an amalgamation of sayings from a wide variety of sources over perhaps a three-hundred-year period. The traditional view—that most if not all of the *Analects* are records of the voice of the Master—is untenable. The problem is compounded. There were thousands of "sayings of Confucius" circulating prior to the compilation of a relative few into the *Analects*, most of which are not contained in and are even contrary to ideas or sayings in the extant text; indeed, the text itself seems to contain contradictory ideas and sayings. We have little reason, then, to think that the extant text contains authentic sayings (analects) of Confucius. The *Analects* is an accretional, multi-authored, ideologically composite document, compiled/edited more than 300 years after Confucius.

Insofar as we know anything about Confucius, we know this and little more: Confucius was an itinerant teacher who offered counsel to various rulers; his advice was mostly ignored.

Confucius, as represented in the *Analects*, aligned himself with a tradition of cultured scholars who held that embracing various ancient rituals and culture could reshape personal character and society: that is, the rituals of the golden age of the Zhou dynasty, if precisely followed, could issue forth in a revival of righteousness, justice, harmony, and peace. In *Analects* 7.18 we read: "Topics which the Teacher regularly discussed were the *Book of Odes*, the *Book of Documents*, and the maintenance of propriety (rites). These were the topics which he regularly discussed." Confucius, as represented, assumes the authority of a set of canonical texts in which wisdom uniquely resides, including, according to this analect, the *Books of Odes*, *Ritual*, and *Documents*.

These texts were alleged to have been compiled, edited, and in some cases authored by the Master (Confucius) and as such endowed with a special sort of authority. While we today treat the *Analects* as uniquely authoritative for the Confucian tradition, the early Chinese did not. They assigned special authority to the so-called Five Classics (the number and content varied), which, in addition to the *Odes*, *Ritual*, and *Documents*, included the *I Ching* and *Spring and Autumn Annals*. The *Analects* would not achieve an elevated status for another 1,000 years.

Like the Confucius of the *Analects*, we look to these texts for our earliest understandings of the sort of religious beliefs that influenced the views in the *Analects*. These texts countenance a High God who grants the right to rule to various righteous men, usually after withdrawing the right to rule from a king who had fallen into dissolution and injustice. The high god is variously named *Di*, *Shangdi*, or *Tian* (Heaven). This divine right to rule—the Mandate of Heaven (*Tianming*)—is the most foundational political doctrine in Chinese thought.

"The Announcement to the Prince of Kang." The announcement to Kang is from *The Documents* (*Shujing*), which purports to be historical or court documents from the Zhou dynasty. This announcement is allegedly the charge given by the Duke of Zhou (1042–1036 BCE) to his younger brother, Feng, the Prince of Kang. King Wen, the "culture king," was the founder of the Zhou Dynasty, the greatest golden age to which Confucius avers. The Duke of Zhou, the wise and virtuous son of King Wen, is speaking to Feng, who is being sent out to the newly conquered eastern regions to govern them in the name of the king. As the homelands of the previous and conquered dynasty, the Shang, it was an important task.

We find in this announcement a very early reference to "the Mandate of Heaven" (*Tianming*), which claims divine authority for the king (kings and emperors were referred to as Sons of Heaven). In section two we learn that because of his selfishness and injustice the last king of the Shang dynasty relinquished his right to rule, so God removed his mandate from the Shang and transferred it to King Wen (in recognition of his goodness) and the dynasty to the Zhou. Feng is commanded to follow the example of his virtuous father—to care for and protect his people—thus assisting the king in strengthening the appointment of heaven (*Tianming*) for the Zhou dynasty.

The Book of Rites (Liji). These passages, selected from a much larger text, give the reader a sense of the deeply religious nature of early Chinese rituals. Ritually prescribed activity (*li*) extended into every area of life, from sweeping a room to bowing to superiors. In *Analects* 12:1, we read: "Do not look in a way which is not *li*, do not listen in a way that is not *li*, do not speak in a way that is not *li*, do not move in a way that is not *li*." Ritual is, in the *Book of Rites*, first and foremost religious. Of all of the ritual activities, none is more important than sacrifice and, in the *Book of Rites*,

sacrifices to God (again, alternately named *Tian*, *Di*, or *Shangdi*) and to ancestors.

Sacrifice to the High God took place at ritually specified times in a temple on the outskirts of the city. To be sure, the common people did not sacrifice to the High God and had, as far as we know, no direct or personal interactions with the High God. We read in the *Book of Rites* that "only the sage can sacrifice to God."

The people's most profound religiously informed and informing rituals centred on ancestral sacrifices, often at special ancestral temples or at gravesites (and at funerals). Ancestral sacrifice in early China was not merely to enliven one's memories of a virtuous parent or model grandparent; ancestors were thought to continue existing after biological death and to meddle in human affairs (and so to require ritual appeasement).

Failure to sacrifice to the High God and to ancestors was believed to be both morally and socially destabilizing. In the *Documents*, the downfall of the Shang dynasty is attributed to King Shou's lack of reverence to the High God and ignoring his ancestors. Most early Chinese texts concern themselves with the attainment of harmony in society, a harmony with everyone from king to farmer in their proper places, working together for the good of the whole. According to the *Book of Rites*, rituals engender this desired harmony by getting everyone into their proper places. In ritual sacrifices, the goal was "to bring down the spirits from above, even their ancestors; serving (also) to rectify the relations between ruler and ministers; to maintain the generous feeling between father and son, and the harmony between elder and younger brother; to adjust the relations between high and low; and to give their proper places to husband and wife. The whole may be said to secure the blessing of Heaven."

It is noteworthy that sacrifice would, in all of the key human relationships (ruler-minister, father-son, elder brother-younger brother, husband-wife), create a hierarchy between the proper superiors and their inferiors, one marked by harmony, generosity, and reconciliation. This well-ordered human world would be in consonance with the harmony of the cosmos, thereby securing the blessing of heaven (where "the things of the world are nurtured thereby").

Ritual propriety in both the *Rites* and the *Analects* is offered as an antidote to human pride; the diminishing of pride creates space for one's cultivation of benevolence or humaneness (*Rites* 2; *Analects* 12:1). It is, therefore, foundational both for personal moral transformation and for societal harmony.

Kelly James Clark and Justin Winslett find representations of a providential high God not only in the *Documents*, the *Odes*, and the *Ritual* but also in nearly every early Chinese text.

The Book of Odes (Shijing). This collection of roughly 300 odes, songs, or poetry is the oldest in China (c. 1000–600 BCE). As one of the revered Five Classics it was memorized and studied for two millennia. Allegedly compiled and edited by Confucius, it is referred to regularly in the *Analects* as a source of inspiration; "Be aroused by *Poetry*," Confucius exclaimed. I have selected two odes for this section, "King Wen Is on High" and "Mighty Is God on High."

In the former, we catch a glimpse of King Wen's postmortem existence in Heaven. Heaven is portrayed here both as a place and as an anthropomorphic deity. In the first case, it is the place where the deceased King Wen now resides (and shines). In the second, Heaven both gives and takes away his mandate, exercising a kind of moral providence. King Wen takes his rightful place in Heaven at the side of Heaven (the High God). The ode ends with a warning to subsequent rulers to cling in righteousness to Heaven above (or bring ruin upon their kingdom as Heaven did to previous dynasties).

While *Tian* can mean sky or heaven, in these early Zhou texts, it often refers to God (*Di*) or the High God (*Shangdi*). Indeed, these terms are often used as synonyms, often within the same context. In "Mighty Is God on High," we find *Di*, *Shangdi*, and *Tian* referring to the same being in the very first stanza. God is represented as above his people, ruler of his people, creator of the people, and source of the right to rule (and, likely, the source of morality). Though Heaven sends down blessings and curses alike, Heaven did not make the last rulers of the Shang dynasty drunkards ("Heaven did not flush you with wine"); the rulers themselves are responsible for their dissolution and for ignoring the cries of justice in their kingdom. The fallen rulers did not lack divine blessing; they simply failed to follow the old ways. Failing to hear and heed, they have upset and lost the Mandate of Heaven.

The Analects (Lunyu). As noted, the *Analects* is a collection of sayings (analects), many of which are attributed to the Master, Confucius (died 479 BCE). The current text of the *Analects* was compiled and circulated in the early Han dynasty, around 150 BCE. Again, it is a matter of debate how the current text is related to the historical Confucius. We shall prescind from that debate and simply refer to the text and what it teaches. We shall introduce the *Analects* through key themes and terms.

Moral exemplars. As noted, the *Analects* harkens back to various golden ages of exemplary rulers and kingdoms as moral models. The exemplary rulers include the legendary sage-kings Yao, Shun, and Yu (8.19) and, most importantly, the formative rulers in the early Zhou dynasty, King Wen and the Duke of Zhou. The exemplary kingdoms include those ruled by the sage-kings and the early Zhou dynasty (3.14). In the Zhou, the ideal was, in some sense, real. And although only Heaven is ultimately good (8.19), we can see goodness exemplified in the sage kings and King Wen and the Duke of Zhou. Here, Confucius points, is goodness.

Humaneness/benevolence (ren). The most important, all-encompassing virtue in the *Analects* is *ren*, which is translated variously as humaneness, benevolence, human-heartedness, humanity, compassion, and love. One can find textual support for each translation, thus rendering a simple definition impossible. The Chinese character is constructed from the character for person along with the character for the number two. So the literal meaning is "two-peopleness." Therefore, being truly humane implies at least a person's being in harmonious relationship with other people (along with the attitudes or actions necessary for peaceful coexistence).

Noble person (junzi). The term *junzi*, translated here as noble person, literally means "prince" ("son of the ruler"). Confucius, however, holds that anyone (through great effort) can become a *junzi*. A *junzi* is a morally and culturally perfected person. What makes one an excellent person, a person worthy of ruling, is not being born to royalty but attaining through great effort to the highest moral and cultural status.

Ritual (li 禮*).* The world of ancient China was a world of ritually prescribed ceremonies, attitudes, and manners. These ceremonies encompassed, as noted in the section on the *Book of Rites*, sacrifices to the High God and to ancestors. They also extended into every aspect of human life such as ceremonies of bowing and toasting that inculcate the sort of respect and deference necessary for an effective social hierarchy. Every aspect of human life was directed by ritual towards a harmoniously functioning hierarchical society—thus generating both attitudes and obligations (assuming superior-inferior relationships). While many claim that Confucius did not believe in an afterlife, the background texts certainly do represent an afterlife for deceased ancestors, which seems assumed in Confucius' ritual directives on the treatment of ancestors.

Filial piety (xiao). Respect for parents (*xiao*) is, in the *Analects*, the ground of a harmonious, hierarchical society. In the home one learns one's role-specific duties and attitudes. For example, the eldest son would cultivate obedience to and respect for parents, on the

one hand, and kindness towards younger siblings, on the other. It is precisely this sort of home-generated respect for parents (*xiao*) that grounds the sort of ritually-directed respect necessary for a harmonious society (1.2).

Heaven (Tian). Since this is a reader in philosophy of religion, let us consider, in more detail Confucius' views on *Tian* (Heaven) (remember, we are speaking of Confucius the character represented in the *Analects*, not the historical Confucius). It has become commonplace in contemporary scholarship to deny that Confucius believed in a deity or the afterlife. Yet Confucius aligns himself with a tradition which affirmed an anthropomorphic Heavenly Supreme Emperor who exercises moral providence. Given Confucius' self-confession as a transmitter of the Zhou tradition, we have prima facie reason to believe that Confucius aligns his religious beliefs with those of the Zhou. Heaven, instead of being a natural order or impersonal force, is repeatedly depicted in the *Analects* as an active and good will (that is, a divine person).

Confucius affirmed Heaven's cunning and power to intervene when humans have lost the Way (3.24). Heaven, we read, is working through Confucius to call for a return to the ancient glorious days of civilization. Confucius is portrayed not simply as a moral teacher, but also as a Heavenly commissioned emissary. In Heaven's exercise of providence, we find Heaven's concern for the condition of his people; Heaven is an intervening supernatural being who both calls and equips people like Confucius as emissaries to communicate Heaven's mandate for the renewal of the society.

Heaven is both the source and model of goodness. Although the great Yao is a human moral model, his goodness is derivative; ultimately only Heaven is great (8.19). The leaders of the Xia, Shang, and Zhou produced a harmoniously functioning society because they embodied the fixed patterns of Heaven. The superior or great person, then, stands in awe of the decrees or imperatives of heaven, while the inferior or small person ignores them (16.8). Confucius, in spite of his belief in the transformative powers of ritual (*li*), attributed his own goodness to Heaven (7.23).

Confucius thought it possible to incur Heaven's disapproval (6.28). This is consonant with Confucius' general view that Heaven exercises a kind of moral providence (9.5). Heaven is also portrayed as widely knowing, even of our inner thoughts and motives. For example, humans cannot deceive Heaven (9.12; 14.37).

Heaven is represented in the texts that inform the *Analects* and in the *Analects* itself, as a person—that is as a moral being with an intellect and a will. Robert Louden, in "What Does Heaven Say?", demurs, contending that "Confucius . . . is religious but not theistic." He claims that the ascriptions of intention and understanding to *Tian* are metaphorical. Ronnie Littlejohn, in "Confucius on Religious Experience," argues that the relevant analects, when understood within the tradition that informs the *Analects*, are robustly religious in terms of both practices and beliefs.

Daode Jing. There is little reason to affirm the traditional view that the *Daode Jing* was written by or is traceable to a wise scholar named Laozi who taught in Warring States China (475–221 BCE) and founded the school of Daoism. Laozi, which means "old master," very likely never existed at all. Moreover, like most early Chinese texts, the *Daode Jing* is an accretional, multi-source, and loose compilation of various thoughts and ideas. And while some allege that such thoughts are consistent and comprise the foundation of the school of Daoism, there is little reason to believe that either. The text is deeply enigmatic, elusive and inconsistent, and there was no identifiable school of Daoism in early China. Indeed, dividing early Chinese texts into schools falsifies history (there were no such schools in the Warring States period) and encourages one to emphasize differences and ignore similarities between texts and "schools."

"Daode Jing" means the classic of the way (*dao*) and its power (*de*). The first portion of the *Daode Jing* mostly explicates the notion of the *dao*, while the second portion explicates the notion of *de* (power or virtue). *Dao*, depending on context, can mean path or road, (moral) way of life, or ultimate reality. Conceptions of the *dao* as the (moral) Way were not limited to what we call "Daoism." Many thinkers in early China, including Confucius, offered their own conception of the Way (of life). The *Daode Jing*, likewise, offers its conception of the Way (of life).

Much of the text is a criticism of and reaction to the rigid rituals and social hierarchies of early China. Such rituals were perceived as forms of domination which hindered and distorted both human nature and our relationships with other people (and the natural world). Elaborate rituals were expensive—so the people are overtaxed to satisfy the excessive desires of their rulers. Wars, likewise, cost lots of money and, more importantly, lives and time (that could be spent, for example, raising crops or fishing or simply enjoying life). And so we read: "Whenever armies are stationed, briars and thorns become rampant. Great wars are inevitably followed by famines." Finally, rituals created, reinforced, and perpetuated unhealthy and unnatural social hierarchies.

The Way to live, then, is in accord with the dao (as Ultimate Reality). In the earliest chapters of the *Daode Jing*, the *dao* (as Ultimate Reality) is represented as a replacement for *Tian*. Whereas *Tian* is personal, moral, and providential, *dao*, in the *Daode Jing*, is impersonal, natural, and unconcerned with human affairs. While the *dao* is not a thing, it is not nothing—it is the undifferentiated reality/force/source beyond things, including Heaven (*tian*) and Earth (40). Lying beyond the world of things, it cannot be grasped by our senses or intellect (and so cannot be named—that is, grasped in language (1)). The *dao* is a natural force that flows through all of life. It is neither personal nor good (nor bad). It produces the universe through yin and yang—the pair of opposites that are, respectively, evil and good, dark and light, female and male, submissive and dominant (42). All change in the universe is mediated through the opposition of yin and yang. The *dao*, as understood in the opening chapters, is so thoroughly naturalistic, many deny that it constitutes a religion at all.

As noted, the *dao* does not providentially care for human beings. With respect to the *dao*, human beings are just one of the ten-thousand things—they have no privileged ontological status in the universe. Heaven and earth are not humane (*ren*: the chief Confucian virtue)—to ultimate reality people are as straw dogs (5). Straw dogs were used in sacrificial rituals and then tossed aside.

Sages are not humane (*ren*) either. I suspect the text means that sages refuse to participate in a hierarchical system in which some are superior people (*junzi*) and others are inferior people ("little people," Confucius called them); inferiors most characteristically respect their "superiors" while superior people are condescendingly "humane" to their "inferiors." Instead, the sage recognizes that there is nothing special about human beings in general (they are like straw dogs) and there is nothing special about any human being in particular. Thus, human hierarchies of superiority-inferiority are lies that hurt people. Recognizing that humans are not special, the sage refuses to lead from above (from pride) but instead leads from below (in humility). Thus, *dao* as Ultimately Reality generates *dao* as a Way of Life.

The second portion of the *Daode Jing* is the *de* (power or virtue), which describes how life is lived when ordered according to the *dao*, or the flow of nature. While human beings are inclined to value judgments and deliberative actions, both are distortions of Reality (*dao*). To tap into the power of the *dao*, one must act *wu wei*. While *wu wei* literally means "inaction," in the *Daode Jing* it means that actions should be done spontaneously and naturally, with little expense of energy or excessive striving or mental effort. Go with the stream of *dao*, don't resist it, and let the *dao* do the work. As such, the book is as much about spiritual freedom as it is about our knowledge of ultimate reality.

Given its naturalistic bent, the *Daode Jing* offers a way of being religious without God. Its supreme values—quiescence and tranquility—require a turning away from our ordinary ways of thinking and living. Followers developed a variety of spiritual exercises to attain to the spirit of emptiness (modelling the *dao*, out of which things come and into which things return). Grasping the equality of everything with respect to the *dao* permits one in humility to embrace all things gladly. And the cultivation of *wu wei* can release us from our endless obsession with our self and our own selfish interests.

It is very hard, given the amoral and indifferent nature of the *dao*, to reconcile its enthusiastic endorsement of compassion on the part of either humanity or Heaven. And yet the former is required (67) and the latter is affirmed (81). As Franklin Perkins points out, the final chapters of the *Daode Jing* are remarkably out of step with the first 2/3 of the text. The *Daode Jing* is, like the *Analects*, an accretional, multi-authored, ideologically composite document, compiled/edited over a long period of time. The later chapters, then, are more redolent of the benevolent and providential *Tian* we find in the *Analects* and pre-analects texts.

Xunzi. We know little about Xunzi except that he lived roughly in the third century BCE. He is regarded, along with Confucius and Mencius, as a founder and shaper of Confucianism. The text that bears his name was likely started by him and then edited and completed by others. Xunzi is known first and foremost for his claim that human nature is evil. He is known, second, for his claim that highly articulated, historically specific, and remarkably elaborate rituals (the way of the ancient sage kings) are required to transform evil people into superior, civilized persons (*junzi*).

Xunzi's understanding of personal transformation undergirds his social philosophy. People whose (evil) lives are transformed by ritual will not give in to their selfish desires in ways that lead to societal disorder. In short, personal, moral transformation undergirds the harmony one finds in civil society. Xunzi's ideal society is inherently hierarchical, with each person in his or her ritually prescribed place, ruled by the Confucian noble person (*junzi*) who is both wise and just.

I include Xunzi in this section because many contemporary philosophers find his views, among all of the early Chinese thinkers, most conducive to their own naturalistic views. I also include Xunzi because religion, for most people, concerns ritual, not simply belief in God. While philosophers are obsessed with belief, and so philosophical reflection on religion often focuses on religious beliefs, religion for most folks essentially and often primarily involves rituals such as prayer, worship, or sacrifice. Our study of early Chinese thought has already danced around ritual. It is fitting to conclude with a more sustained discussion of ritual and its philosophical underpinnings.

Although Xunzi rejected a providentially active Heaven or High God (one who intervenes to reward the good and to punish the bad) and superstitious beliefs in malevolent ghosts (*gui*), he endorsed the sacrificial rituals aimed at gods and spirits (*shen*). While it is fashionable these days to claim that Xunzi is, therefore, a secularist and a naturalist, Machle displays the flaws in that "argument." Being a religious critic and rejecting superstition is not tantamount to affirming atheism. According to Machle, Xunzi's text precludes taking Xunzi as a skeptic about spirits and Heaven, on the one hand, and a rationalist about the foundation of morality, on the other. Indeed, Machle argues that, for Xunzi, funeral rituals ensure that the spirits of deceased ancestors are respected, thus one takes one's proper place in both the cosmos and society. Xunzi, Machle argues, assumes belief in the continued, spiritual existence of one's ancestors: "But effectively to

produce the described results, the ritual, and its ritual references, must be *believed in*. Otherwise, one cannot be sincere about the whole transaction, and for Xunzi, as for any Confucian, sincerity is fundamental."

One might wonder, after all, if skepticism about, say, the spirits and the afterlife could sustain such elaborate and expensive sacrificial rituals. After all, to our modern ear the rituals of the Sage Kings seem arcane and excessive, and Xunzi's hierarchical society seems inegalitarian, undemocratic, and elitist. Release the rituals of the ancient way from their metaphysical grounding and they lose their power to motivate. They seem, at best, quaint, arbitrary, and optional—anything but obligatory.

Sor-Hoon Tan, on the other hand, argues that the Confucian rituals can be efficacious without being grounded in the metaphysics of divine persons and post-mortem spirits. Tan's extensive discussion of Xunzi's conception of ritual (*li*) offers an excellent textually-based sense of the relationship of ritual to ethics. She also explicates how the various role-specific rituals, always with someone in a superior and someone in an inferior position, undergird the social divisions of a harmonious, hierarchical society. We can bring together both themes in her analysis of elaborate funeral rituals: "Xunzi maintained that elaborate ritual practices served important functions of providing appropriate channels for emotions that people felt on such occasions, as well as displayed the appropriate distinctions that sustain social order." Ritually-specified activities, which facilitate well-ordered emotions, rightly-oriented desires, and a respectful sense of one's place (in relation to one's deceased ancestors), have morally and socially transforming power.

Mozi, a post-Confucius philosopher and critic, rejected elaborate and expensive rituals, especially funeral rituals and their associated three-year mourning period. Funds and time could be better spent if they benefitted everyone (alive) equally. Xunzi, on the other hand, defended these remarkably elaborate and expensive rituals of the ancient way as essential for human moral transformation and social harmony and stability.

One typical way of philosophically justifying elaborate rituals (or the ethics they engender) is to claim that they reflect the Way (*dao*) of Heaven or Heaven and Earth (Ultimate Reality) and that by acting in conformity to the Way, one is tapping into the transformative powers of Reality itself. In the West, from Plato's Good to Aristotle's *telos* to God's will, we find various versions of this pattern of thinking. In early China, we find similar appeals to the Mandate of Heaven and the *dao*. People walked many paths (*daos*) but early Chinese philosophers developed and defended versions of the ultimate Way of life (*dao*) that they contend correspond to ultimate Reality (*Tian, Di, Shangdi*, Heaven and Earth, or the *dao*).

Tan, on the other hand, argues that Xunzi's ritual way (the dao of the ancient sage kings) requires no such metaphysical grounding. She endorses ritual ethics but seeks to ground it pragmatically. It is acceptable, first and foremost, because it effects moral and social transformation. Its metaphysics, shorn of belief in the afterlife and the gods, is justified as a useful posit/guess that helps us achieve our desired ends (not as the sober truth about the nature of Reality). Her rationally reconstructed Xunzi is entirely practice-driven with metaphysics very lightly dragged along for the ride.

Conclusion. We have provided the reader with snapshots of a few texts from a long time ago in ancient China. From such a small sampling, one is precluded from thinking that one understands China or the Chinese mind or Chinese thought. Moreover, understanding these texts is disputed. Some of the texts, so I've claimed, represent an anthropomorphic High God (*Di, Shangdi, Tian*) who rewards the righteous and punishes the wicked (sometimes in the afterlife). Others, I've noted, reject this interpretation, arguing that the early Chinese were not religious and did not

believe in an afterlife. Yet even in the text that most explicitly rejects a providential Heaven (the *Daode Jing*), we find passages that seem redolent of a compassionate and providential deity. Early China included an amalgam of ideas, idioms, arguments, tropes, and assumptions—with many and inconsistent ones sometimes contained within a single text itself.

Some of the texts present and defend (or assume) ritual sacrifices both to the High God and to deceased ancestors (who exist post mortem in some spiritual form). These rituals are designed to eliminate pride and inculcate place (one's place in the cosmic and within the social hierarchy). While portions of the *Daode Jing* reject these rituals as unnatural and even dehumanizing, most of the texts endorse them. The text that affirms the most elaborate rituals, the *Xunzi*, does so in a context that some claim rejects the role of gods and spirits. While Machle argues that this view is wrong, we can certainly agree that the *Xunzi* does not endorse a providential High God (though it may assume the existence of a morally important yet spiritually distant High God).

Finally, it would be a mistake to think there is some sort of dialectic or historical progression in our assemblage of texts. While it is often alleged that in early China we find the depersonalization of *Tian*—from an anthropomorphic, providential deity to a moral force to Nature—the texts resist this simplistic narrative. While the *dao* in the early chapters of the *Daode Jing* is certainly non-anthropomorphic and is arguably non-moral, in the later chapters Heaven seems morally good and to care for people. And, if Machle is right, the *Xunzi* is not naturalistic in any conventional sense—while it does not endorse a providential high God, it does affirm a good god and an afterlife.

Even if we take the *Xunzi* as naturalistic, naturalism is not the culmination of early Chinese thought. We have omitted texts of thinkers who were arguably more influential and were decidedly theistic. Moreover, we have selected only pre-Han texts. The

Han dynasty, the second imperial dynasty in China, enshrined Confucianism as the official ideology of the empire. In roughly 150 BCE, Han Emperor Wu endorsed the ideas of Dong Zhongshu, whose texts defended an anthropomorphic *Tian* as the ground of morality, government, and humanity. Much later, Zhu Xi (1126–71), second only to Confucius in his influence on Chinese thought (but Confucius' superior in philosophical acumen), would pray daily to his ancestor, Confucius. Claiming to be a faithful transmitter and reinvigorator of the Confucian way, Zhu Xi's

thought is full of gods (high and lesser), ghosts, and spirits (of deceased ancestors) and the ritual activities appropriate to keeping them all at their proper distances.

Chinese religion is a relatively unexplored intellectual frontier. New texts are being unearthed almost daily, texts which shed light on Chinese religious beliefs and practices. We are just beginning to develop a deep and wide understanding of Chinese religion. And, as we better understand, we can begin to explore a philosophy of Chinese religion.

Chapter 29

The Ancient Texts

THE ANNOUNCEMENT TO THE PRINCE OF KANG

TRANSLATION BY JAMES LEGGE
(WITH MODIFICATIONS)

FROM THE *DOCUMENTS*

1. In the third month, when the moon began to wane, the Duke of Zhou commenced the foundations and proceeded to build the new great city at Luo of the eastern states. The people from every quarter assembled in great harmony. From the Hou, Dian, Nan, Cai, and Wei domains, the various officers stimulated this harmony of the people, and introduced them to the tasks there were to be done for Zhou. The Duke of Zhou encouraged all to diligence, and made a great announcement about the performance of the works.

2. The king speaks to this effect: "Head of the princes, my younger brother, little one, Feng. It was your greatly distinguished father, King Wen, who was able to make bright his Virtue and be careful in the use of punishments. He did not dare to show any contempt to the widower and widows. He employed the employable, and revered the reverend; he was terrible to those who needed to be awed: so getting distinction among the people. It was thus he laid the first beginnings of the sway of our small portion of the Empire, and the one or two neighboring countries were brought under his improving influence, until throughout our western regions all placed in him their reliance. The fame of him ascended up to the High God (*Di*), and God approved. Heaven (*Tian*) gave a great charge (*ming*) to King Wen, to exterminate the great dynasty of the Shang, and receive its great mandate, so that the various states belonging to it and their peoples were brought to an orderly condition. Then your unworthy elder brother [i.e., the Duke of Zhou] exerted himself, and so it is that you, Feng, the little one, are here in this eastern region."

3. The king says, "Oh, Feng, bear these things in mind. Now your management of the people will depend on your reverently following your father Wen: do you carry out his virtuous words which you have heard, and clothe yourself with them. Moreover, where you go, seek out extensively among the traces of the former wise kings of the Shang what you may use in protecting and regulating their people. Again, you must more remotely study the old accomplished men of the Shang, that you may establish your heart, and know how to instruct the people. Further, still, you must seek out besides what is to be learned of the wise kings of antiquity, and employ it in the tranquilizing and protecting of the people. Finally, enlarge your thoughts to the comprehension of all Heavenly principles, and Virtue will be richly displayed in your person, so that you will not render nugatory the king's mandate."

4. The king says, "Oh, Feng, the little one, it is as if some disease were in your person; be respectfully careful. Heaven (*Tian*) in its awfulness yet helps the sincere. The feelings of the people can for the most part be discerned, but it is difficult to calculate on the attachment of the lower classes. Where you go, employ all your heart. Do not seek repose, not be fond of

idleness or pleasure: so may you regulate the people. I have heard the saying, 'Dissatisfaction is caused not so much by great things or by small things, as by a ruler's observance of principle or the reverse, and by his energy of conduct or the reverse.'"

Yes it is yours, O little one, it is your business to enlarge the royal influence, and harmoniously to protect this people of the Shang. Thus also shall you assist the king, consolidating the appointment of Heaven (*Tianming*), and renovating this people.

Discussion

1. In what ways was King Wen, the founder of the Zhou Dynasty, considered virtuous?

2. What does Heaven (*Tian*) do in recognition of King Wen's virtue?

3. What attributes/properties/actions are ascribed to God (*Di*) and Heaven (*Tian*)?

THE BOOK OF RITES

TRANSLATED BY JAMES LEGGE

1. The Summary of the Rules of Propriety (*li*) says: Always and in everything let there be reverence; with the deportment grave as when one is thinking (deeply), and with speech composed and definite. This will make the people tranquil.

2. Pride should not be allowed to grow; the desires should not be indulged; the will should not be gratified to the full; pleasure should not be carried to excess.

3. The course (of duty), virtue, benevolence (*ren*), and righteousness cannot be fully carried out without the rules of propriety; nor are training and oral lessons for the rectification of manners complete; nor can the clearing up of quarrels and discriminating in disputes be accomplished; nor can (the duties between) ruler and minister, high and low, father and son, elder brother and younger, be determined; nor can there be the (proper) sincerity and gravity in presenting the offerings to spiritual Beings on occasions of supplication, thanksgiving, and the various sacrifices. Therefore the noble man (*junzi*) is respectful and reverent, assiduous in his duties and not going beyond them, retiring and yielding—thus illustrating (the principle of) propriety (*li*).

4. The parrot can speak, and yet is nothing more than a bird; the ape can speak, and yet is nothing more than a beast. Here now is a man who observes no rules of propriety; is not his heart that of a beast? But if (men were as) beasts, and without (the principle of) propriety, father and son might have the same mate. Therefore, when the sages arose, they framed the rules of propriety in order to teach men, and cause them, by their possession of them, to make a distinction between themselves and brutes.

5. Propriety (*li*) is seen in humbling one's self and giving honor to others.

6. When we speak of "a noble man" (*junzi*) we intend chiefly his virtue. The virtue perfect and his instructions honored; his instructions honored and the (various) officers correct; the officers correct and order maintained in the state: these things give the ideal of a ruler.

7. Yan Yan again asked, "Are the rules of Propriety indeed of such urgent importance?" Confucius said, "It was by those rules that the ancient kings sought to represent the ways of Heaven (*Tian*), and to regulate the feelings of men. Therefore he who neglects or violates them may be (spoken of) as dead, and he who observes them, as alive. It is said in the *Book of Poetry*, 'Look at a rat—how small its limbs and fine! Then mark the course that scorns the proper line. Propriety's neglect may well provoke a wish that the man would quickly court death's stroke.' Therefore those rules are rooted in heaven, have their correspondences in earth, and are applicable to spiritual beings. They extend to funeral rites, sacrifices, archery, chariot-driving, capping, marriage, audiences, and friendly missions. Thus the sages made known these rules, and it became possible for the kingdom, with its states and clans, to reach its correct condition."

8. Of all the methods for the good ordering of men, there is none more urgent than the use of ceremonies (*li*). Ceremonies are of five kinds, and there is none of them more important than sacrifices.

9. Thus it was that the ancient kings were troubled lest the ceremonial usages should not be generally understood by all below them. They therefore sacrificed to God (*Di*) in the suburb (of the capital), and thus the place of heaven (*tian*) was established. They sacrificed at the altar of the earth inside the capital, and thus

they intimated the benefits derived from the earth. Their sacrifices in the ancestral temple gave their fundamental place to the sentiments of humanity. Those at the altars of the hills and streams served to mark their intercourse with the spirits breathing (in nature). Their five sacrifices (of the house) were a recognition of the various business which was to be done. He himself was in the center. His mind had nothing to do, but to maintain what was entirely correct.

10. By means of the ceremonies (*li*) performed in the suburb, all the spirits receive their offices. By means of those performed at the altar of the earth, all the things yielded (by the earth) receive their fullest development. By means of those in the ancestral temple, the services of filial duty and of kindly affection come to be discharged. By means of those at the five sacrifices of the house, the laws and rules of life are correctly exhibited. Hence when the ideas in these sacrifices in the suburb, at the altar of the earth, in the ancestral temple, at the altars of the hills and streams, and of the five sacrifices of the house are fully apprehended, the ceremonies used are found to be lodged in them.

11. The object of all the ceremonies (*li*) is to bring down the spirits from above, even their ancestors; serving (also) to rectify the relations between ruler and ministers; to maintain the generous feeling between father and son, and the harmony between elder and younger brother; to adjust the relations between high and low; and to give their proper places to husband and wife. The whole may be said to secure the blessing of Heaven.

12. The noble man (*junzi*) observes these rules of propriety, so that all in a wider circle are harmonious with him, and those in his narrower circle have no dissatisfactions with him. Men acknowledge and are affected by his goodness, and spirits enjoy his virtue.

13. Yen Yen again asked, "Are the rules of Propriety indeed of such urgent importance?"

Confucius said, "It was by those rules that the ancient kings sought to represent the ways of Heaven (*Tian*), and to regulate the feelings of men.... Therefore those rules are rooted in heaven."

14. Below (in the courtyard), the flute-players played the tune of the Hsiang, while the Tâ-wei was danced, all uniting in the grand concert according to their parts, giving full development to the spirit (of the music), and stimulating the sense of virtue. The positions of ruler and minister, and the gradations of noble and mean were correctly exhibited, and the respective duties of high and low took their proper course. The officers having announced that the music was over, the king then charged the dukes, marquises, earls, counts, and barons, with all the officers, saying, "Return, and nourish the aged and the young in your eastern schools." Thus did he end (the ceremony) with (the manifestation of) benevolence.

15. When the Grand course was pursued, a public and common spirit ruled all under the sky; they chose men of talents, virtue, and ability; their words were sincere, and what they cultivated was harmony. Thus men did not love their parents only, nor treat as children only their own sons. A competent provision was secured for the aged till their death, employment for the able-bodied, and the means of growing up to the young. They showed kindness and compassion to widows, orphans, childless men, and those who were disabled by disease, so that they were all sufficiently maintained. Males had their proper work, and females had their homes.

16. The course (of duty), virtue, benevolence (*ren*), and righteousness *cannot be achieved without the rules of propriety* (*li*); nor can (the duties between) ruler and minister, high and low, father and son, elder brother

and younger, be determined; nor can students and (other) learners, in serving their masters, have an attachment for them; nor can majesty and dignity be shown in assigning the different places at court, in the government of the armies, and in discharging the duties of office so as to secure the operation of the laws; nor can there be the (proper) sincerity and gravity in presenting the offerings to spiritual Beings on occasions of supplication, thanksgiving, and the various sacrifices. Therefore the noble man (*junzi*) is respectful and reverent, retiring and yielding—thus illustrating (the principle of) propriety.

17. In the sacrifice to God (*Di*) in the suburb, we have the utmost expression of reverence. In the sacrifices of the ancestral temple, we have the utmost expression of humanity. In the rites of mourning, we have the utmost expression of faithfulness. In the preparation of the robes and vessels for the dead, we have the utmost expression of affection. Therefore, the *noble man* finds the ways of *benevolence* (*ren*) and *righteousness* rooted in these ceremonial usages.

Discussion

1. What are the most important sacrifices and how are they described?

2. Describe the relationships between ritual, reverence, and pride.

3. How do the rituals ensure order or harmony in society?

THE BOOK OF ODES

TRANSLATED BY JAMES LEGGE

King Wen Is on High

King Wen is on high;
Oh! bright is he in heaven (*tian*).
Although Zhou was an old country,
The [favoring] appointment lighted on it recently.
Illustrious was the House of Zhou,
And the appointment (*ming*) of God (*Di*) came at
    the proper season.
King Wen ascends and descends,
On the left and the right of God.

Full of earnest activity was king Wen,
And his fame is without end.
The gifts [of God] to Zhou,
Extend to the descendants of king Wen;—
To the descendants of king Wen,
In the direct line and the collateral branches for a
    hundred generations.
All the officers of Zhou,
Shall [also] be illustrious from age to age.

They shall be illustrious from age to age,
Zealously and reverently pursuing their plans.
Admirable are the many officers,
Born in this royal kingdom.
The royal kingdom is able to produce them,—
The supporters of [the House of] Zhou.
Numerous is the array of officers,
And by them king Wen enjoys his repose.

Profound was king Wen;
Oh! continuous and bright was his feeling of
    reverence.
Great is the appointment of Heaven (*Tian*)!

There were the descendants of [the sovereigns]
    of Shang;—
The descendants of the sovereigns of Shang,
Were in number more than hundreds of
    thousands;
But when God (*Di*) gave the command,
They became subject to Zhou.

The appointment is not easily [preserved],
Do not cause your own extinction.
Display and make bright your righteousness
    and name,
And look at [the fate of] Yin in the light of Heaven.
The doings of High Heaven,
Have neither sound nor smell.
Take your pattern from king Wen,
And the myriad regions will repose confidence
    in you.

Mighty Is God on High

Mighty is God on high (*Shangdi*),
Ruler of His people below;
Swift and terrible is God on high,
His mandate has many statutes.
Heaven (*Tian*) gives birth to the multitudes of
    the people,
But its mandate cannot be counted upon.
To begin well is common;
To end well is rare indeed.

King Wen said, "Come!
Come, you Yin and Shang!
Why these violent men?
Why these slaughterers?
Why are they in office? Why are they in power?
Heaven has sent down to you an arrogant spirit;
What you exalt is violence!"

King Wen said, "Come!
Come, you Yin and Shang,
And hold fast to what is seemly and fitting;
Your violence leads to much resentment.
You support slanders and also,
To thieves and bandits you give entry,
Who curse, who use evil imprecations,
Without limit or end."

King Wen said, "Come!
Come, you Yin and Shang!
You rage and seethe in Chung Kuo
You count the heaping up of resentment as
     inward power;
You do not make bright your power,
So that none backs you, none is at your side.
No, your merit does not shine bright,
So that none cleaves to you nor comes to you."

King Wen said, "Come!
Come, you Yin and Shang!
Heaven did not flush you with wine.
Not good are the ways you follow;
Most disorderly are your manners.
Not heeding whether it is dawn or dusk
You shout and scream,
Turning Day into night."

King Wen said, "Come!
Come, you Yin and Shang!
You are like grasshoppers, like cicadas,
Like frizzling water, like boiling soup;
Little and great you draw near to ruin.
Men long to walk in right ways,
But you rage in the Middle Kingdom,
And as far as the land of Kuei."

King Wen said, "Come!
Come, you Yin and Shang!
It is not that God on high did not bless you;
It is that Yin does not follow the old ways.
Even if you have no old men ripe in judgment,
At least you have your statutes and laws.
Why is it that you do not hear,
But upset the Mandate of Heaven (*Tianming*)?"

King Wen said, "Come!
Come, you Yin and Shang!
There is a saying among men:
'When a towering tree crashes,
The branches and leaves are still unharmed;
It is the trunk that first decays.'
A mirror for Yin is not far off;
It is the times of the Lord of the Xia."

Discussion

1. What are the various meanings of "Heaven" (*Tian*) in the two Odes?

2. How is Tian's appointment (*Tianming*) understood?

3. What attributes/properties/actions are ascribed to God (*Di*) and Heaven (*Tian*)? Are they attributes of persons or impersonal forces? In what ways is *Tian* creator?

THE ANALECTS

CONFUCIUS

TRANSLATED BY A. CHARLES MULLER

1.1 The Master said: "Isn't it a pleasure to study and practice what you have learned? Isn't it also great when friends visit from distant places? If people do not recognize me and it doesn't bother me, am I not a noble man (*junzi*)?"

1.2 You Zi said: "There are few who have developed themselves filially and fraternally who enjoy offending their superiors. Those who do not enjoy offending superiors are never troublemakers. The noble man (*junzi*) concerns himself with the fundamentals. Once the fundamentals are established, the proper way appears. Are not filial piety (*xiao*) and obedience to elders fundamental to the actualization of fundamental human goodness?"

1.13 You Zi said: "When your own trustworthiness is close to *fairness*, your words can be followed. When your show of respect is according to propriety (*li*), you will be far from shame and disgrace. If you have genuine affection within your family, you can become an ancestor."

2.4 The Master said: "At fifteen my heart was set on learning; at thirty I stood firm; at forty I had no more doubts; at fifty I knew the mandate of heaven (*tianming*); at sixty my ear was obedient; at seventy I could follow my heart's desire without transgressing the norm."

2.5 Mengyi Zi asked about the meaning of filial piety (*xiao*). Confucius said, "It means 'not diverging (from your parents).'" Later, when Fan Chi was driving him, Confucius told Fan Chi, "Mengsun asked me about the meaning of filial piety, and I told him 'not diverging.'" Fan Chi said, "What did you mean by that?" Confucius said, "When your parents are alive, serve them with propriety (*li*); when they die, bury them with propriety, and then worship them with propriety."

2.24 The Master said: "To worship to other than one's own ancestral spirits is flattery. If you see what is right and fail to act on it, you lack courage."

3.11 Someone asked for an explanation of the Great Sacrifice. Confucius said, "I don't know. If there were someone who knew this, he could see the whole world as if it were this": He pointed to the palm of his hand.

3.12 "Sacrificing as if present" means sacrificing to the spirits as if they were present. Confucius said, "If I do not personally offer the sacrifice, it is the same as not having sacrificed at all."

3.13 Wang Sun Jia asked: "What do you think about the saying 'It is better to sacrifice to the god of the stove than to the god of the family shrine.'?" Confucius said, "Not so. If you offend Heaven (*Tian*), there is no one you can pray to."

3.14 The Master said: "The people of the Zhou were able to observe the prior two dynasties and thus their culture flourished. I now follow the Zhou."

3.24 The border guard at Yi requested an audience with the Master, saying: "Whenever a noble man comes here, I never miss the opportunity to see him." The disciples sent him in. When he came out, he said, "Friends, don't have any doubts about your master failing. The world has certainly lacked the Way for a long time now, but Heaven (*Tian*) will use your master to awaken everyone."

3.26 The Master said: "Men of high office who are narrow-minded; propriety without respect and funerals without grief: how can I bear to look at such things?!"

4.13 The Master said: "If you can govern the country by putting propriety (*li*) first, what else will you need to do? If you can't govern your country by putting propriety first, how could you even call it propriety?"

5:13 Zi Gong said: "What our Master has to say about the classics can be heard and also embodied. Our Master's words on the essence and the Heavenly Way, though not attainable, can be heard."

6.20 The Master said: "Knowing it is not as good as loving it; loving it is not as good as delighting in it."

6.28 The Master visited Nan Zi (a woman known for her sexual excesses) and Zi Lu was displeased. The Master dealt with this, saying: "Whatever I have done wrong, may Heaven (*Tian*) punish me! May Heaven punish me!"

7:1 The Master said: "I am a transmitter, rather than an original thinker. I trust and enjoy the teachings of the ancients. In my heart I compare myself to old Peng."

7:8 The Master said: "If a student is not eager, I won't teach him; if he is not struggling with the truth, I won't reveal it to him. If I lift up one corner and he can't come back with the other three, I won't do it again."

7:18 Topics which the Teacher regularly discussed were the *Book of Odes*, the *Book of History*, and the maintenance of propriety. These were the topics which he regularly discussed.

7:21 The master never discussed strange phenomena, physical exploits, disorder or ghost stories.

7:23 The Master said: "Heaven (*Tian*) gave birth to the virtue within me. What can Huan Tui do to me?"

7:35 The Master was very sick, and Zi Lu said that he would pray for him.

Confucius said, "Is there such a thing?"

Zi Lu said, "There is. The *Eulogies* say: 'I pray for you to the spirits of the upper and lower realm.'"

Confucius said, "Then I have been praying for a long time already."

8:19 The Master said: "The rulership of Yao was so magnificent! He was so sublime that even though there is nothing as great as Heaven (*Tian*), he could accord with it. His greatness was so boundless it is beyond description. His efficacy was amazing, his writings were enlightening."

9:12 The Master was extremely ill, and Zi Lu wanted the disciples to become Confucius' "ministers."

Confucius, during a remission in his illness, said, "Ah, You has been deceitful for a long time. Though I don't have ministers, you would make it appear that I have them? Who would I be fooling? Heaven (*Tian*)? I would much rather die in the hands of my disciples than in the hands of ministers. And I would prefer dying in the streets to a pompous funeral!"

11:9 When Yanyuan died, the master cried: "How cruel! Heaven (*Tian*) is killing me! Heaven is killing me!"

11:12 Chi Lu asked about serving the spirits. Confucius said, "If you can't yet serve men, how can you serve the spirits?"

Lu said, "May I ask about death?" Confucius said, "If you don't understand what life is, how will you understand death?"

12:1 Yanyuan asked about the meaning of humaneness (*ren*). The Master said, "To completely overcome selfishness and keep to propriety (*li*) is humaneness. If for a full day you can overcome selfishness and keep to propriety, everyone in the world will return to humaneness. Does humaneness come from oneself, or from others?"

12:5 Sima Niu, upset, said: "Everyone has brothers, I alone have none."

Zi Xia said, "I have heard this proverb":

Life and death are up to Fate.
Wealth and honor are held by Heaven.

"If the noble man (*junzi*) is reverent without lapse, and courteous to everyone within the frame of propriety, everything within the four seas will be his brother. Why should a noble man be concerned about not having brothers?"

12:11 Duke Jing of Qi asked Confucius about government. Confucius replied: "Let the ruler be a ruler, minister be a minister, father be a father, son be a son." The Duke said, "Excellent! Indeed, if the ruler is not a ruler, the ministers not ministers, fathers not fathers and sons not sons, even if I have food, how can I eat it?"

14:35 The Master said: "Aah! No one understands me!"

Zi Gong said, "What do you mean, 'No one understands you'?"

Confucius said, "I have no resentment against Heaven (*Tian*), no quarrel with men. I study from the bottom and penetrate to the top. Who understands me? Heaven does!"

16:8 The Master said: "The noble man stands in awe of three things":

(1) He is in awe of the decree of Heaven (*Tian*).

(2) He is in awe of great men.

(3) He is in awe of the words of the sages.

The inferior man does not know the decree of Heaven; he takes great men lightly, and laughs at the words of the sages.

17:17 The Master said: "I wish I could avoid talking."

Zi Gong said, "Master, if you didn't speak, what would we disciples have to pass on?"

Confucius said, "Does Heaven (*Tian*) speak? Yet the four seasons continue to change, and all things are born. Does Heaven speak?"

Discussion

1. Search all of the references to *Tian* and develop a sense of the *Analects'* understanding of *Tian*.

2. Religion does not simply concern belief in God. What does Confucius say about rituals relating to deceased ancestors?

3. How is ritually-regulated ancestor veneration related to filial piety (*xiao*)?

THE DAODE JING OF LAOZI

TRANSLATED BY A. CHARLES MULLER

1. The Way (*Dao*) that can be followed (*Dao*) is not
   the eternal Way (*Dao*).
The name that can be named is not the eternal name.
The nameless is the origin of heaven and earth
While naming is the origin of the myriad things.
Therefore, always desireless, you see the mystery
Ever desiring, you see the manifestations.
These two are the same—
When they appear they are named differently.

This sameness is the mystery,
Mystery within mystery;

The door to all marvels.

4. The Way is so vast that when you use it, something
   is always left.
How deep it is!
It seems to be the ancestor of the myriad things.
It blunts sharpness
Untangles knots
Softens the glare
Unifies with the mundane.
It is so full!
It seems to have remainder.

It is the child of I-don't-know-who.
And prior to the primeval Lord-on-high.

5. Heaven and Earth are not humane,
And regard the people as straw dogs.
The sage is not humane,
And regards all things as straw dogs.
The space between Heaven and Earth is just like
   a bellows:

Empty it, it is not exhausted.
Squeeze it and more comes out.

Investigating it with a lot of talk
Is not like holding to the center.

6. The valley spirit never dies.
It is called "the mysterious female."
The opening of the mysterious female
Is called "the root of Heaven and Earth."
Continuous, seeming to remain.

Use it without exertion.

8. The Dao is like water.
Water easily benefits all things without struggle.
Yet it abides in places that men hate.
Therefore it is like the Way.

For dwelling, the Earth is good.
For the mind, depth is good.
The goodness of giving is in the timing.
The goodness of speech is in honesty.
In government, self-mastery is good.
In handling affairs, ability is good.

If you do not wrangle, you will not be blamed.

11. Thirty spokes join together in the hub.
It is because of what is not there that the cart
   is useful.
Clay is formed into a vessel.
It is because of its emptiness that the vessel is useful.
Cut doors and windows to make a room.
It is because of its emptiness that the room is useful.
Therefore, what is present is used for profit.

But it is in absence that there is usefulness.

14. Look for it, it cannot be seen.
It is called the distant.
Listen for it, it cannot be heard.
It is called the rare.
Reach for it, it cannot be gotten.
It is called the subtle.
These three ultimately cannot be fathomed.
Therefore they join to become one.

Its top is not bright;
Its bottom is not dark;
Existing continuously, it cannot be named and it
    returns to no-thingness.

Thus, it is called the formless form,
The image of no-thing.
This is called the most obscure.

Go to meet it, you cannot see its face.
Follow it, you cannot see its back.

By holding to the ancient Way
You can manage present existence
And know the primordial beginning.

This is called the very beginning thread of the Way.

25. There is something that is perfect in its disorder
Which is born before Heaven and Earth.

So silent and desolate! It establishes itself
    without renewal.
Functions universally without lapse.
We can regard it as the Mother of Everything.

I don't know its name.

Hence, when forced to name it, I call it "Way."
When forced to categorize it, I call it "great."

Greatness entails transcendence.
Transcendence entails going-far.
Going-far entails return.

Hence, the Way is great, Heaven is great, the Earth
    is great
And the human is also great.

Within our realm there are four greatnesses and the
    human being is one of them.

Human beings follow the Earth.
Earth follows Heaven
Heaven follows the Way
The Way follows the way things are.

40. Return is the motion of the Way.
Softening is its function.
All things in the cosmos arise from being.
Being arises from non-being.

42. The Way produces one, one produces two.
The two produce the three and the three produce
    all things.
All things submit to *yin* and embrace *yang*.
They soften their energy to achieve harmony.

People hate to think of themselves as "orphan,"
    "lowly," and "unworthy"
Yet the kings call themselves by these names.

Some lose and yet gain,
Others gain and yet lose.
That which is taught by the people
I also teach:
"The forceful do not choose their place of death."
I regard this as the father of all teachings.

63. Do without "doing."
Get involved without manipulating.
Taste without tasting.
Make the great small,
The many, few.
Respond to anger with virtue.
Deal with difficulties while they are still easy.
Handle the great while it is still small.

The difficult problems in life
Always start off being simple.
Great affairs always start off being small.
Therefore the sage never deals with the great
And is able to actualize his greatness.

Now light words generate little belief,
Much ease turns into much difficulty.
Therefore the sage treats things as though they
    were difficult,

And hence, never has difficulty.

67. The reason everybody calls my Way great
Is because there is nothing quite like it.
It is exactly because it *is* great
That there is nothing quite like it.
If there were something that were consistently like it

How could it be small?

I have three treasures that I hold and cherish.
The first is compassion,
The second is frugality,
The third is not daring to put myself ahead
    of everybody.

Having compassion, I can be brave.
Having frugality, I can be generous.
Not daring to put myself ahead of everybody
I can take the time to perfect my abilities.

Now if I am brave without compassion
Generous without frugality, or
Go to the fore without putting my own concerns last,
I might as well be dead.

If you wage war with compassion you will win.
If you protect yourself with compassion you will
    be impervious.
Heaven will take care of you,

Protecting you with compassion.

68. The best warrior is never aggressive.
The best fighter is never angry.
The best tactician does not engage the enemy.
The best utilizer of people's talents places himself
    below them.

This is called the virtue of non-contention.
It is called the ability to engage people's talents.
It is called the ultimate in merging with Heaven.

76. When people are born they are gentle and soft.
At death they are hard and stiff.
When plants are alive they are soft and delicate.
When they die, they wither and dry up.
Therefore the hard and stiff are followers of death.
The gentle and soft are the followers of life.

Thus, if you are aggressive and stiff, you won't win.
When a tree is hard enough, it is cut. Therefore
The hard and big are lesser,
The gentle and soft are greater.

77. The Way of Heaven
Is like stretching a bow.
The top is pulled down,
The bottom is pulled up.
Excess string is removed
Where more is needed, it is added.

It is the Way of Heaven
To remove where there is excess
And add where there is lack.
The way of people is different:
They take away where there is need
And add where there is surplus.

Who can take his surplus and give it to the people?
Only one who possesses the Way.

Therefore the sage acts without expectation.
Does not abide in his accomplishments.
Does not want to show his virtue.

79. After calming great anger
There are always resentments left over.
How can this be considered as goodness?
Therefore the sage keeps her part of the deal,
And doesn't check up on the other person.

The virtuous ascertain the content of the
    contract itself;
Those without virtue are concerned about it's
    being exacted.

The Heavenly Way has no favorites:
It raises up the Good.

81. True words are not fancy.
Fancy words are not true.
The good do not debate.
Debaters are not good.
The one who really knows is not broadly learned,
The extensively learned do not really know.
The sage does not hoard,
She gives people her surplus.
Giving her surplus to others she is enriched.

The way of Heaven is to help and not harm.
The way of the Sage is to act without wrangling.

Discussion

1. What are some of the (admittedly enigmatic) ways that the Way is described?

2. What does it mean to say that "Heaven and Earth are not humane / And regard the people as straw dogs"? How is that different from the *Odes*, *Documents*, and *Analects*?

3. How is Heaven (*Tian*) described in the final three sections? How is that different from how the Way is described in the first parts?

4. The *Daode Jing* affirms some spiritual disciplines, which if followed would create a certain kind of person. What are some of those disciplines and what kind of person does the text commend?

Chapter 30

"Confucian" Religion

THE EVOLUTIONARY PSYCHOLOGY OF CHINESE RELIGION

KELLY JAMES CLARK AND
JUSTIN WINSLETT*

Chinese atheism? It is widely asserted that the ancient Chinese were non-theistic. Unlike most other religions, Chün-Fang Yü writes of Chinese religions that "there is no God transcendent and separate from the world" (Yü, 2007, 1243–45). Jacques Gernet holds that the ancient Chinese had no notion of transcendence whatsoever; theirs was a world of radical immanence; the Chinese, he claims, never imagined a spiritual substance distinct from the material (Gernet, 1985). Marcel Granet claimed that the Chinese had no notion of a transcendent Law or God (Granet, 1985, 476). Even those who concede China's gods contend that they are either unique to a single non-representative thinker (usually Mozi) or inconsequential to Chinese moral/political thought and life. And so, the gods are irrelevant in the writings of mainstream Chinese thinkers (usually called "the Confucians") who directly channeled "the Chinese mind." China, so it is claimed, is the great cultural exception to otherwise highly pervasive god beliefs.

However, recent scholarship on religious topics in Early China (pre-220 CE) has helped to push forward new understandings in this field (summarized in Kalinowski and Lagerwey, 2009). This scholarship has shown that religious life in Early China was not one of atheistic humanism but rather was a diverse panoply of various paradigms, idioms and practices held by diverse communities separated both geographically and temporally (Clark, 2005, 109–36 and Clark, 2009). Though research has identified many of these ancient and diverse ritual practices, prescriptive paradigms and religious prescriptions, other topics that fall under the scope of religion, such as deities, remain poorly understood. This is an interesting turn of events when one considers that anthropologists such as Pascal Boyer and Stewart Guthrie point out that deities, or simply extrahumans, are a primary and nearly universal feature of religion (Boyer, 2001; see also Barrett, 2004). Claims to Chinese exceptionalism notwithstanding, anthropology and careful consideration of the ancient texts are converging on a new and richer understanding of China's divinities.

Empirical support for Chinese deities can be found in the newly emerging cognitive science of religion. Cognitive science rejects the assumption that cultural groups are radically different. Studies show that our common biological heritage and relatively similar environments produce both relatively similar minds and relatively similar beliefs. Evolutionary processes have shaped human cognitive faculties and, when those faculties are applied to their specific challenges (which are fairly similar across cultures), produce roughly similar beliefs. These common cognitive faculties include relatively specialized "subsystems" that structure, inform, enhance, and limit our view of the

---

* Justin Winslett received his PhD from Oxford University in 2009 and is an independent scholar.

world. Rejecting the empiricist assumption of the mind as a blank slate on which experience writes, cognitive scientists hold that our minds come equipped with a set of cognitive faculties that actively processes our perceptions and shapes our conceptions of the world. Some of these faculties, in turn, have a direct influence upon the origin and development of religious beliefs. According to this model, *humans have a natural tendency to believe in gods*. Belief in gods naturally arises when certain common cognitive faculties are stimulated. A culture without gods is as much to be expected as a culture without beliefs in other persons or the external world.

In this chapter, we will use the cognitive science of religion to direct an examination of ancient Chinese texts for specific conceptions of divinity and their relation to humanity. While the cognitive science of religion in general would lead us to expect to find various sorts of disembodied agents in China, supernatural punishment theory in particular would lead us to expect to find a high, moralizing god with strategic knowledge who exercises a kind of moral providence (Johnson and Bering, 2005, 2006; Johnson et al., 2005).

In order to better understand China's High Deities—*Di* 帝, *Shangdi* 上帝 and *Tian* 天—we constructed a database of instances of these three terms in texts from the Pre-Qin (pre-221 BCE) period.[1] This database was composed of intuitively coded, representative passages from these texts where extrahuman agents appear. By employing this database in these capacities, this essay, guided by supernatural punishment theory, will highlight one of the common ways with which these High Deities are represented in Pre-Qin texts, as punishers and rewarders. We then show how the representation of these agents as punishers and rewarders is pervasive throughout the texts of the Pre-Qin period.

Though these are too diverse to be fully explained in a single essay, by taking a general survey of these representations, common idioms emerge that continue to present themselves in the passages where these agents are punishers and rewarders. Most commonly, this manifests as a moral dimension with these agents being cast as moralizing agents that punish and reward according to moral criteria, something argued for by cognitive theories of religion. This essay will hence present and analyze some of the most salient and representative passages that show agents under such representations and idioms, showing them to be both pervasive and fundamental to Pre-Qin understanding of the High Deities.

Supernatural punishment theory. Cognitive science has converged on a general picture of how our common cognitive faculties produce belief in gods. Human beings are equipped with a cognitive faculty—*an agency-detecting device* (ADD)—that generates beliefs about agency. When stimulated, ADD immediately produces beliefs in an agent. The evolutionary advantages of agency detection are obvious: without such immediate beliefs/responses to certain motions (rustling bushes) or sounds (things going bump in the night), we might end up as food for a predator or the victim of an enemy. So ADD is highly sensitive, prompting us to instantly respond to slight provocation. Justin Barrett has named the disposition to form beliefs about agents given minimal stimulation the *hypersensitive agency detection device* (HADD).

Upon the detection of agency, another cognitive faculty that cognitive scientists call the *Theory of Mind* (TOM) begins operating and attributes beliefs, desires, and purposes to the postulated agent. How do HADD and TOM produce belief in gods? If ordinary agents—animals and enemies—are unsuited to account for one's experiences, one might find oneself immediately believing in extraordinary, supernatural personal beings, including ghosts, angels, or gods. And then HADD quickly gives way to TOM: these agents have reasons for the things they do. Surely only a very powerful, minded agent could cause such extraordinary events (and for extraordinary reasons), so we attribute super qualities—super powers and super knowledge, for example—to the causes of super events.

Supernatural punishment theory leads us to expect that ancestral groups with high moralizing gods will be more successful than groups without them. Supernatural punishment theory helps explain the puzzling evolution of larger and larger human groups that depend on high levels of cooperation. As group size increases, the ability to detect cheaters, who are a threat to the stability of the group, decreases. Because of the threat of such norm-violations to the group, detection of cheaters and their punishment is paramount but very costly. But the enforcement of moral norms, while costly, enhances cooperation and the benefits that cooperation make possible. Belief in a supernatural punisher would transfer the "costs" of detection and punishment to (a) non-human agent(s), thereby reducing the human costs.

If belief in "High Gods" that are active in human affairs and supportive of human morality can be inculcated in a group, moral defection can be diminished (and at a fairly low cost). In order to prevent cheaters, such agents must have access to strategic information—they must be superknowing about defections or cooperations that are hidden from merely human agents. And they must be believed to efficaciously exercise a kind of moral providence—to reward virtue and to punish vice. So supernatural punishment theory leads to the expectation of high moralizing gods with strategic information who exercise moral providence. The bottom line: groups of god-fearing individuals will outcompete groups of non-believers (assuming roughly equal size and complexity).

Evidence supporting supernatural punishment theories is wide ranging. We can only here give the briefest sense of its empirical support. Studies show increased voluntary payment (when no one is watching) when the collection can has eyes drawn on it, and

less cheating on computer-assisted exams when virtual eyeballs float on the screen (Bateson, Nettle, and Roberts, 2006). When children are prompted with ghost-beliefs, they are less likely to give in to temptation when no one else is in the room. Religious groups with costly religious rituals show remarkably higher levels of cooperation and last vastly longer than secular groups (Sosis and Ruffle, 2003). Finally, Dominic Johnson's survey of 186 people groups showed an extremely high correlation between cooperation and belief in moralizing high gods (Johnson, 2005).

The cognitive science of religion holds that religious belief is natural and will routinely take characteristic shapes and forms. The evolutionary psychology of religion suggests that religious beliefs that have been channeled into moralizing high gods can effectively overcome human selfishness necessary for the gain of cooperative benefits. Taken together, they suggest that successful human groups, including those in ancient China, will likely and repeatedly develop beliefs in high, moralizing, providential gods who exercise moral providence. Armed with this insight, what do we find when we carefully consider the ancient texts?

The High Deities of Pre-Qin texts. From the ritual functional agents of *shen* 神 and the ephemeral *gui* 鬼 to the diverse angry spirits, forces, and malevolencies, many texts from this time reveal a rich and diverse lexicon and discourse on the extrahuman. Within this pantheon of figures sit two extrahuman agents who in many texts are assigned paramount or privileged roles in sacrificial rituals and discourses on the extra-human—the High Deities of *Di* 帝 and *Shangdi* 上帝, which are understood as two different terms referring to the same agent, and *Tian* 天; these "High Deities" rule above this panoply of lesser deities. Their status as High Deities, something that transcends other deities, and their strong socio-political associations resonate with the arguments of supernatural punishment theory. However, for these arguments to hold, these extrahuman agents must be shown to be represented as moralizing agents possessing specialized knowledge who reward virtue and punish vice.

High Deities as punishers and rewarders. The texts we examine contain a vast quantity of information produced by many different hands throughout the entire Pre-Qin period (these texts are seldom single-authored, and they are compiled from earlier and often inconsistent extant texts). When looking through the database of these passages, one sees a great diversity in terms of how these agents are represented and the capacities in which they are used in the texts. While often not provided detailed physical descriptions, in some passages these extrahuman agents are described in highly anthropomorphic form, often taking on the characteristics of rulers or sovereigns. In some passages, these agents are recipients of sacrifices while in others they are used in common curses. Hence, these texts reflect a spectrum of representations of the High Deities that were clearly of concern to these authors.

However, though there is great diversity, patterns and similarities present themselves, suggesting representations shared by authors divided in space and time (as cognitive science of religion would expect). One of the most prominent ways in which these High Deities are represented is in the capacity of providing punishments or rewards to human recipients. These punishments and rewards are quite numerous, and when compared to other categories of representations seen in the database have proven to be the most variable. These agents issue forth generic punishments or calamities upon individuals or groups. Likewise, the rewards can also be generic, usually described as simply good fortune *fu* 福 or assistance *zhu* 助. More specific rewards range from these agents bestowing material rewards, fecundity, internal powers and strengths, portents and omens, alleviating problems and even sagehood or transcendent states. These

agents also inflict specific punishments, including famines, droughts and plagues, disruptions to the natural world, psychological problems, abandonment, and murder.

One of the most common forms of punishment and reward is that of socio-political power. Given the nature of these texts as advocating good governance (Lewis, 1999, 287–89), it is not surprising that such power and authority is granted and removed by these agents, as circumstances require. The sovereign is often both the intended audience of many of these texts and the subject who suffers these punishments or gains these rewards. Passages commonly show the sovereign's house or state collapsing through either unspecified means or invasion. The reward of rulers with socio-political power is also common, and resonates well with previous studies on *Di*, *Shangdi*, and *Tian* that point to their association with the legitimization of the ruling houses of the Shang and the Zhou.

Why, then, do these agents bestow these things to these subjects, most often the sovereign? In some of the passages seen, that these extrahuman agents engage in punishment and reward is simply passively stated as having occurred, with no explicit explanation as to why. In several passages, however, these extrahuman agents explicitly give punishments or rewards because of reasons explained in the passage. These reasons are often of a moral dimension wherein the subjects are rewarded for proper behavior, usually for displaying virtue, righteousness, and sincerity. Consequently, subjects who do not possess these qualities or are said to have transgressions are punished.

Statistical data on the over four hundred passages in Pre-Qin texts show that punishments and rewards figure in more than a third of all passages featuring *Di* and *Tian* (and in a little more than a quarter of those featuring *Shangdi*). Additionally, in almost two-thirds of the passages where *Tian* is represented as punisher or rewarder, *Tian* is also represented in some capacity as moral providence. This is seen to be so in forty-seven per cent of the cases with *Di* and in sixty per cent of the passages with *Shangdi*.

This statistical information strongly supports the presence of idioms and paradigms related to supernatural punishment theory in Pre-Qin texts. As cognitive science would hold, these representations seem to be relatively widespread throughout the corpus of Pre-Qin texts. These High Deities are clearly being represented as higher agents possessed of some moralizing characteristic who engage in issuing punishments and rewards. However, these quantitative data can only provide some clues and highlight the larger trends as to how these idioms actually function in these texts, particularly if, as supernatural punishment theory holds, these High Deities punish vice and reward virtue. Furthermore, though it seems Gernet and Yü are wrong in asserting a paradigm of non-theism to religion in Pre-Qin China, can it be argued that these idioms and paradigms are isolated to specific periods or thinkers in Pre-Qin China, or, as cognitive science would hold, that they are universal?

The case of the Mozi. Scholars of Chinese philosophy have long claimed the *Mozi* as an "uncharacteristic" text for its highly anthropomorphized, extrahuman agents. A.C. Graham has noted that these extrahuman agents, *Tian* among them, can be understood as punishers and rewarders. Graham points to the Understanding Ghosts, Will of Heaven, and Anti-fatalism sections as best exemplifying this view, stating that the *Mozi* argues "that men will act morally only if they cease to regard changes of fortune as their destiny, and come to recognize that Heaven [*Tian*] and the spirits reward the good and punish the wicked" (Graham, 1978, 13–14).

Graham's interest in extrahuman agents in the *Mozi* is motivated by his constant contrasting of the ideas of the text to those found in the "Confucian" texts. "Confucian" texts, he claims, question whether these extrahuman agents exist and adhere to a more secular philosophy in line with Gernet and Yü. The *Mozi*, then, is unique in its assertion of extrahuman agents like *Tian* as divine punishers and rewarders. However, such a dichotomy between "the Confucians" and "the Mohists" is problematic if, as seems likely, no such cohesive group as "Confucians" existed in the Pre-Qin period, and no people from that time would identify themselves as such (Nylan, 2001, 2–5; Schaberg, 2001, 9, 308–09).

Graham is not operating entirely from misconceptions about the philosophical discourse of this time; the *Mozi* itself is full of criticisms of ideas put forward by characters identified with the philosophical figure of Confucius such as Mencius. For example, in a dialogue between he and Mozi, Mencius raises ideas about the lack of deities in ritual only to be refuted by Mozi (*Mozi*, 2006, 48.690). But to assume that this is a discourse against all things "Confucian" is misleading—no such distinction is present in this specific passage, nor are texts labeled as "Confucian" bereft of extrahumans.

Indeed, the representation of *Tian* as punisher is found in the texts considered paramount in understanding Confucius, such as in *Analects* 6.28, wherein Confucius asks Heaven to punish him if he has committed any wrongdoing:

> The master had an audience with Nanzi, and Zilu was not pleased. The Master swore an oath, saying, "If I have done anything wrong, may Heaven [*Tian*] punish me! May Heaven [*Tian*] punish me!" (Slingerland, 2003, 62)[2]

And in *Mencius* VA.5, where Wan Zhang asks Mencius how it was that the king Shun came to be given the throne. Expecting that the answer is to be that Yao, bestowed it upon him, Mencius asserts that such is not the case, and rather it was bestowed by Heaven who, along with the people, were to have accepted Shun because,

When he was put in charge of sacrifices, the hundred gods enjoyed them. This showed that Heaven accepted him. When he was put in charge of affairs, they were kept in order and the people were content. This showed that the people accepted him. Heaven gave it to him, and the people gave it to him. Hence I said, "The Emperor cannot give the Empire to another." Shun assisted Yao for twenty-eight years. This is something which could not be brought about by man, but by Heaven alone. (Lau, 1970, 143–44)

Or consider the *Xunzi's Youzuo*, where the disciple of Confucius, Zilu, asks Confucius why he and his followers must endure hardship when *Tian* is meant to reward the good:

Zilu went before him and asked, "From what I have heard, as for those who do good, Heaven [*Tian*] repays them with good fortune. As for those who do bad, Heaven [*Tian*] repays them with calamities. Now, you have accumulated virtue, gathered righteousness and held close the beautiful, yet we have been walking for many days. Why do we dwell like hermits?" (*Xunzi*, 1988, 28.516)

Zilu's claim assumes a certain and expected relationship between *Tian* and the good. Furthermore, Robert Eno, in his study of the *Tian* in the *Mengzi* and *Xunzi*, has noted numerous, what he claims to be rhetorical rather than theoretical, uses of *Tian*, among which punishment and moral qualities are found (Eno, 1990, 102–04, 167–68).

It is clear, then, that an understanding of the High Deities as punishers and rewarders is not peculiar to the *Mozi*, nor does it seem to accord to any "Mohist"– "Confucian" difference. Indeed cognitive science would argue that such idioms are quite common, and representations of the High Deities have already been

shown to be statistically present in a variety of texts. The representations in these three passages certainly accord well with the ideas of supernatural punishment theory; but are these idioms of punishment for the wicked and reward for the good as widespread through the time of Pre-Qin China as they seem to be philosophically?

Earliest writings. The understanding of extrahuman agents as punishers and rewarders originating in the *Mozi* can easily be overturned by the wide distribution of these representations in Pre-Qin texts and in texts that pre-date the *Mozi*. Indeed, these representations are found in the earliest strata of Pre-Qin texts, the *Documents* where they are widely articulated. Both of these texts are composed of material, probably both orally and textually transmitted, that originates over a large span of time from the Western Zhou (eleventh century–771 BCE) and Spring and Autumn (770– 475 BCE) periods, though the *Documents* contains some material composed after this and into the Han (Shaugnessy, 1993, 377–80).

Of the sections of the *Documents* composed prior to the Qin, one sees High Deities issuing punishments and rewards in all strata of the text—all three of these terms appear in terms of punishment and rewards is temporally well-distributed, even appearing in the passages dated to the Warring States and the Han. Let us examine some of the typical ways in which this representation of the gods as punisher is articulated in the passages in the *Documents*:

The duke of Zhou said, "The king speaks to the following effect: 'Ho! I make an announcement to you of the four states, and the numerous (other) regions. Ye who were the officers and people of the prince of Yin, I have dealt very leniently as regards your lives, as ye all know. You kept reckoning greatly on (some) decree of Heaven [*Tian*], and did not keep with perpetual awe before your thoughts (the preservation of) your sacrifices.

"'God [*Di*] sent down correction on Xia, but the sovereign (only) increased his luxury and sloth, and would not speak kindly to the people. He showed himself dissolute and dark, and would not yield for a single day to the leadings of God [*Di*]—this is what you have heard. He kept reckoning on the decree of God [*Di*] (in his favor), and did not cultivate the means for the people's support. By great inflictions of punishment also he increased the disorder of the states of Xia. The first cause (of his evil course) was the internal misrule, which made him unfit to deal well with the multitudes. Nor did he endeavor to find and employ men whom he could respect, and who might display a generous kindness to the people; but where any of the people of Xia were covetous and fierce, he daily honored them, and they practiced cruel tortures in the cities. Heaven [*Tian*] on this sought a (true) lord for the people, and made its distinguished and favoring decree light on Tang the Successful, who punished and destroyed the sovereign of Xia.'" (Legge, 2000 reprint, 214–15)

Betraying the *Documents'* constant concern with socio-political authority, this passage is an excerpt from a speech purportedly given by the Duke of Zhou, a legendary culture-hero who served as regent to his young nephew, King Cheng, early in the Zhou dynasty. In the above excerpt, he is expounding to the defeated vassals of the state of Shang and explaining how their defeat by the hands of the Zhou mirrors the defeat of the Xia by the Shang centuries before. His explanation for the causes of this are couched in the metaphysical and assigned as the actions of *Tian* and *Di*, the latter of whom is said to have "sent correction on Xia." The last king of the Xia ignored this correction and continued to behave wantonly and cruelly. The duke explains

then that this internal misrule translated to misrule throughout the land, until his transgressions were such that *Tian* is said to have "sought a (true) lord for the people" and chose Tang, the first ruler of the Shang, to punish and destroy the Xia.

On a rhetorical level, this story serves as an explication of what has happened to the Shang and justification of the overthrow of them by the Zhou. The earlier Shang overthrow of the Xia in the same manner was due to the choice of the extrahuman agents *Di* and *Tian*. The highly moralistic language of the passage couched the last king of Xia as morally bankrupt while Tang, the first king of Shang, is morally superior. This moral behavior prompts both *Di* and *Tian* to take action. In this first instance by sending down a correction, meant to be a warning, to the last king of the Xia who instead of mending his licentious ways continues them. This prompts the second action, the searching for a virtuous ruler by *Tian* who upon finding him is said to have favored him to overthrow the Tang.

In this passage one sees that these extrahuman agents are identified with proper moral behavior and also search for it in others. Furthermore, they are observed to operate as agents, of their own accord, and to select rulers that show proper moral conduct and to attempt to rectify the behavior of those of ill repute by issuing them warnings. Should these rulers not heed these warnings, they are punished with the loss of socio-political power and its transference to the one whom the extrahuman agent selects.

This idiom of an extrahuman agent identifying the moral and rewarding them with socio-political power, while punishing the wicked by taking that power away, often through invasion by those who have been rewarded, is typical in the *Documents* and consistent with supernatural punishment theory. From the perspective of extrahuman agents, it shows how the high deities are understood in the texts. In keeping with what has been statistically argued, and what Graham has noted as a common idiom in the *Mozi*, *Di* and *Tian*, the High Deities, are clearly portrayed in this passage as punishers and rewarders who do so in accordance with the respective moral character of those being punished or rewarded.

These representations and idioms are common in the other passages of the *Documents* and can be found in one of the other earliest texts of the Pre-Qin period—the *Books of Songs*:

> Heaven [*Tian*] protects and establishes thee,
> With the greatest security;
> Makes thee entirely virtuous,
> That thou mayest enjoy every happiness;
> Grants thee much increase,
> So that thou hast all in abundance.
> Heaven [*Tian*] protects and establishes thee,
> It grants thee all excellence,
> So that thine every matter is right,
> And thou receivest every Heavenly [*Tian*] favour.
> It sends down to thee long-during happiness,
> Which the days are not sufficient to enjoy.
> Heaven [*Tian*] protects and establishes thee,
> So that in every thing thou dost prosper,
> Like the high hills, and the mountain masses,
> Like the topmost ridges, and the greatest bulks;
> That, as the stream ever coming on,
> Such is thine increase.
> (Legge, 2000 reprint[b], 255–56)

The *Books of Songs* is a collection of about three hundred poems that are believed to have emerged in the Western and Eastern Zhou and have come to serve various intellectual, ritual and socio-political purposes. *Tian*, in the passage above, blesses the one with virtue and excellence, and is ultimately responsible for one's prosperity (through *Tian*'s protection and establishment of the individual). Using poetic rhetoric of verse repetition and organic imagery to reinforce this point regarding *Tian*, it also elucidates some of the more common modes of representation of *Tian* and shows how these agents can be understood as punishers and rewarders in much the same way as was observed in the *Documents*. *Tian* bestows moral qualities upon those under its protection, and this protection evokes an air of the socio-political observed in the *Documents* (although the idiom of morally good behavior being rewarded with socio-political power is not present, nor is there any explanation as to why *Tian* is rewarding the individual in this poem).

However, in other poems of the *Books of Songs*, we see how *Shangdi* and *Tian* are "sending down calamities," "exercising oppression," and "displaying anger," among others (*Shijing*, 2007, 9.338; Loewe, 1993, 415; Legge, 2000 reprint[b], 499). These stanzas then proceed to describe how and why these agents are doing such things. This is mainly explained as due to the moral impropriety of the people and the nation. The people are then encouraged to amend their ways by engaging in unspecified proper behavior and supporting a just state. A closing stanza of a passage, quoted below, provides explicit representations of *Tian*, pointing to it having mental and emotional capacities, something that the last, warning line explains as allowing it to understand the behavior of individuals.

> Revere the anger of Heaven [*Tian*],
> And presume not to make sport or be idle.
> Revere the changing moods of Heaven [*Tian*],
> And presume not to drive about
>   [at your pleasure].
> Great Heaven [*Tian*] is intelligent,
> And is with you in all your goings.
> Great Heaven [*Tian*] is clear-seeing,
> And is with you in your wandering
>   and indulgences.
> (Legge, 2000 reprint[b], 499–503)

As expected from supernatural punishment theory, *Tian* is portrayed as possessing strategic information—

an awareness of morally significant behaviors (which may or may not be visible to human agents). Based on the gathering of this strategic information, punishment and reward are justly distributed.

Representations of *Tian* and *Shangdi* as punishers and rewarders can be observed throughout texts from the entire Warring States, including a text dated to the very close of the Warring States, the *Spring and Autumn Annals*. A compendium of a diverse array of topics and subjects, this text is representative of world-building texts, what Mark Edward Lewis points out as the start of an "encyclopedic epoch" of writing, wherein a prescriptive microcosm of the world is constructed within the text, a genre that becomes dominant in the early Han (Lewis, 1999, 303–08). As such, extrahuman agents, such as the High Deities, are also represented in this microcosm constructed by the text and tend to appear often in sections devoted to socio-political and religious discourse. Consider the dialogue between King Wen and his ministers:

King Wen asked, "What steps do you suggest that I take to avert it?"

They replied, "Initiate projects and encourage the multitude to enlarge the city walls. Surely this could avert it!"

King Wen said, "No, I cannot permit that. Heaven [*Tian*] exhibits inauspicious signs when it intends to punish the guilty. I must certainly be guilty of something, and that is why Heaven [*Tian*] has done this—to punish me. Now were I to initiate projects and encourage the multitude to enlarge the city walls, that would simply multiply my guilt. No, I cannot permit it!"

They replied, "Alter your conduct and multiply your good deeds in order to avert it. Surely this could evade such consequences."

King Wen replied, "I, Chang, am requested to alter my conduct and multiply my good

deeds in order to avert it." (Knoblock and Riegel, 2000, 164–65)

This passage explains proper socio-political behavior through the use of historical parables, a common trope in Warring States texts. The dialogue was prompted by the occurrence of several earthquakes after the King fell ill for five days. The ministers inform him that these are negative signs and urge him to "avert disaster."

This passage marks a change, in contrast to the *Documents*, from the expository speeches given by culture-heroes to a narrative in which culture-heroes ask the advice of their ministers, a trope seen in other Warring States texts like the *Mencius* and *Xunzi*. In terms of extrahuman representation, the idea that *Tian* is a punisher and punishes for moral and socio-political reasons is still very much apparent in this passage. The King Wen argues that his illness and the earthquake, inauspicious signs, are punishments from *Tian*, something given only to the guilty. Although his ministers at first encourage him to urge on the masses, he states that as the faults are his, they are not the responsibility of the masses. The ministers then advise him to cultivate his own moral behavior to avert disaster, which the remainder of the passage states the King Wen did. By according to proper moral behavior, which is associated with ritual, the reader is told the inauspicious signs disappeared and the king reigned for fifty-one years.[3]

That inauspicious signs and calamities are punishment inflicted by *Tian* and *Shangdi* is emphasized elsewhere in this section, in a list of ill omens, often revolving around natural disasters, strange signs in the sky or oddities appearing in the countryside. The *Spring and Autumn Annals'* argument as to why this happens is again explicitly stated as follows:

If these anomalies appear in a state, but the ruler is not sufficiently alarmed to change his ways quickly, then the Supreme Sovereign [*Shangdi*] will send down misfortune, with catastrophes and disasters quickly following. The lord will cruelly perish and there will be no reprieve. The populace will flee, overwhelmed by starvation in less than a day. (Knoblock and Riegel, 2000, 170)

Furthermore, the idiom of extrahuman reward of the morally good is argued in other sections of the text. Consider *Spring and Autumn Annals* 9.2 below, which depicts another didactic historical episode of another culture-hero, Tang 湯, the founder of the Shang, and whose rise to power over the Xia, as rewarded by *Tian*, was also recounted in the *Documents*.

In the past, when Tang conquered the Xia and put the world aright, there had been great drought with no harvest for five years. Tang thereupon offered a prayer at Singling in which he offered his own body as the pledge, beseeching: "If I, the One Man, am guilty, let the punishment not reach the myriad peoples. If the myriad peoples are guilty, let it rest on me, the One Man. Do not let the One Man's lack of diligence cause the Supreme Sovereign [*Shangdi*] and the ghosts and spirits to harm the lives of the people." Thereupon, he cut his hair, put his hands in manacles, and had himself prepared in lieu of the usual animals as the offering in a sacrifice to beseech the blessings of the Supreme Sovereign [*Shangdi*]. The people were overjoyed, and the rains came as in a deluge. Thus, Tang influenced the transforming powers of the ghosts and spirits and the course of human events. (Knoblock and Riegel, 2000, 210)

Conclusion. These few examples vindicate supernatural punishment theory's expectation, even in China, of high deities as punishers and rewarders. This is not an understanding isolated to specific texts, or portions of texts, that represent a particular genre of literature (say, "Confucian") or period of time within the Pre-Qin corpus, but rather representations that can be found throughout numerous different texts from the beginnings of Chinese literature, as seen in the *Documents* to the end of the Warring States and the dawn of Imperial China in the *Spring and Autumn Annals*. These representations manifest themselves in the earlier works of historiography and even in the intellectual discourses of the *Analects* (*Lunyu*), *Mozi* and the *Zhuangzi*.

These examples are but a handful, though, of the more than four hundred other instances throughout other texts where these extrahuman agents are observed to engage in punishing or rewarding others and should only be taken to be the most representative of what is clearly a dominant understanding of these agents in Pre-Qin texts. The representation as punishers and rewarders is often coupled into an idiom where these extra-human agents are also represented in moral terms in various capacities. In some instances they are the source of moral providence while in others they are its guardian or defender. Whatever the case, they have strategic information about the morality or the lack thereof in humans, and, based on this information, provide proper punishments and rewards—wherein they punish vice and reward virtue as would be expected from the understanding of High Deities in a large population as described by supernatural punishment theory.

Contrary to claims of a lack of theism in Early China and Graham's assertion that idioms of moralizing High Deities who are punishers and rewarders are common only in certain works like the *Mozi*, it is clear that such ideas were surprisingly common throughout texts produced at this time, often forming cautionary tales and moralizing advice to these texts' intended readers.

It is clear, then, that rather than being some small, ancillary realm dealt with by unpopular thinkers, or a vague enigmatic mess that cannot be understood, the realm of the extrahuman was an active area of engagement for many writers and thinkers in the Pre-Qin who felt no compunctions in evoking it when need be, and no problems in engaging in discourse on it when they felt such was necessary. That modern scholarship has ignored it for so long is unfortunate. But thanks to new understandings of this period from a diverse range of fields, this lack of scholarship is beginning to be addressed and the realm of the extrahuman in Pre-Qin thought is being explored.[4]

Notes

1. Twenty-five transmitted texts identified from the Pre-Qin period are included in the database as of August 2010: the *Chuci* 楚辭, *Gongyang zhuan* 公羊傳, *Guanzi* 管子, *Guliang zhuan* 穀梁傳, *Erya* 爾邪, *Hanfeizi* 韓非子, *Laozi* 老子, *Analects (Lunyu)* 論語, *Lüshi chunqiu* 呂氏春秋, *Mengzi* 孟子, *Mozi* 墨子, *Shangshu* 尚書, *Shangjun shu* 商君書, *Shenzi* 慎子, *Shijing* 詩經, *Sunzi bingfa* 孫子兵法, *Wuzi* 吳子, *Xiaojing* 孝經, *Xunzi* 苟子, *Yanzi chunqiu* 晏子春秋, *Yijing* 易經, *Yinwenzi* 尹文子, *Zhouli* 周禮, *Zhuangzi* 莊子, and *Zuozhuan* 左傳. Searches were performed on all of these, with only the *Shangjun shu* and *Shenzi* not yielding any results.

2. The theistic aspects of the *Analects* are further discussed in Slingerland, 2003 and Clark, 2005.

3. Extrahuman agents are often represented as being a part of ritual in Pre-Qin texts. See Winslett, 2009.

4. We'd like to express our gratitude to Edward Slingerland for both inspiring and advising this project.

References

Barrett, Justin L. *Why Would Anyone Believe in God?* Lanham: Altamira P, 2004.

Bateson, M., D. Nettle, and G. Roberts. "Cues of Being Watched Enhance Cooperation in a Real-World Setting." *Biology Letters* 2 (2006): 412–14.

Bering, Jesse M., and D.D.P. Johnson. "Hand of God, Mind of Man: Punishment and Cognition in the Evolution of Cooperation." *Evolutionary Psychology* 4 (2006): 219–33.

——. "'O Lord . . . You Perceive My Thoughts from Afar': Recursiveness and the Evolution of Supernatural Agency." *Journal of Cognition and Culture* 5.1–2 (2005): 118–42.

Boyer, Pascal. *Religion Explained: The Human Instincts that Fashion Gods, Spirits and Ancestors.* London: Vintage, 2001.

Chang, K.C. *Art, Myth, and Ritual: The Path to Political Authority in Ancient China.* Cambridge, MA: Harvard UP, 1983.

Clark, Kelly James. "The Gods of Abraham, Isaiah and Confucius." *Dao: A Journal of Comparative Philosophy* 5.1 (Winter 2005): 109–36.

——. "Tradition and Transcendence in Masters Kong and Rorty." In *Rorty, Pragmatism, and Confucianism.* Ed. Yong Huang. Albany: State U of New York P, 2009.

Eno, Robert. *The Confucian Creation of Heaven.* Albany: State U of New York P, 1990.

Gernet, Jacques. *China and the Christian Impact.* Trans. Janet Lloyd. Cambridge: Cambridge UP, 1985.

Graham, A.C. *Disputers of the Tao: Philosophical Argumentation in Ancient China.* Chicago: Open Court, 1989.

——. *Later Mohist Logic, Ethics and Science.* Hong Kong: Chinese UP, 1978.

Granet, Marcel. *La Pensée Chinoise.* Paris: Albin Michel, 1950.

Guthrie, Stewart. *Faces in the Clouds*. Oxford: Oxford UP, 1993.

Johnson, D.D.P. "God's Punishment and Public Goods: A Test of the Supernatural Punishment Hypothesis in 186 World Cultures." *Human Nature* 16 (2005): 410–46.

Kalinowski, Marc, and John Lagerwey, eds. *Early Chinese Religion, Part One: Shang through Han (1250 BC–220 AD)*. Leiden: Brill, 2009.

Knoblock, John, and Jeffery Riegal. *The Annals of Lü Buwei*. Stanford: Stanford UP, 2000.

Lau, D.C., trans. *Mencius*. London: Penguin Books, 1970.

Legge, James. *The Chinese Classics*, vol. IV. Reprint [b]. Taibei: SMC Publishing, 2000.

——. *The Sacred Books of the East*. Vol. III. Reprint. Oxford: Clarendon P, 2000.

Lewis, Mark Edward. *Writing and Authority in Early China*. Albany: State U of New York P, 1999.

Loewe, Michael. "*Shih Ching* 詩 經." In *Early Chinese Texts: A Bibliographic Guide*. Ed. Michael Loewe. Berkeley: The Society for the Study of Early China, 1993. 415–23.

Nylan, Michael. *The Five "Confucian" Classics*. New Haven: Yale UP, 2001.

Schaberg, David. *A Patterned Past: Form and Thought in Early Chinese Historiography*. Cambridge, MA: Harvard Asia Center, 2001.

Shaugnessy, Edward L. "*Shang shu* 尚書 (*Shu ching* 書經)." In *Early Chinese Texts: A Bibliographic Guide*. Ed. Michael Loewe. Berkeley: The Society for the Study of Early China, 1993. 376–89.

Slingerland, Edward, trans. *Confucius: Analects: With Selections from Traditional Commentaries*. Indianapolis: Hackett, 2003.

Sosis, Richard, and Bradley Ruffle. "Religious Ritual and Cooperation: Testing for a Relationship on Israeli Religious and Secular Kibbutzim." *Current Anthropology* 44 (2003): 713–22.

Winslett, Justin. "Form or Function: The Representation of Deities in Early Chinese Texts." Doctoral thesis, University of Oxford, 2009.

Yü, Chün-Fang. "Eye on Religion: Miracles in the Chinese Buddhist Tradition." *Southern Medical Journal* 100.12 (December 2007): 1243–45.

Discussion

1. What are the basic tenets of the cognitive science of religion and supernatural punishment theory?

2. Why is Mozi not unique in his assertion of supernatural punishment theory?

3. How do the Pre-Qin texts represent the attributes and actions of *Tian-Di-Shangdi*?

"WHAT DOES HEAVEN SAY?": TIAN 天 IN THE ANALECTS[1]

ROBERT B. LOUDEN*

> The Master said, "I would prefer not to speak."
> Tzu-Kung said, "If you did not speak, what would there be for us, your disciples, to transmit?"
> The Master said, "What does Heaven ever say? Yet there are the four seasons going round and there are the hundred things coming into being. What does Heaven ever say?"
> (Confucius, Analects, 17:19)[2]

Introduction. The passages in the Analects that are most relevant to the religion question are those in which the term tian (天, also romanized as t'ien, and normally translated as "Heaven") plays a prominent role. H.G. Creel, for instance, writes: "If we look for a firm and frankly stated conviction on the part of Confucius as to things religious, we shall find it most clearly in connection with t'ien, Heaven."[3] More recently, Benjamin Schwartz, in his discussion of the religious dimension in Confucius' thought, echoes Creel's familiar assertion: "If there is any central religious term in the Analects, it is the term 'Heaven.'"[4] The tian passages form a frequently debated topic among interpreters of Confucius, and in the following brief discussion I cannot cover all aspects of it. Rather, my aim is simply to examine the main passages in the Analects in which the term tian occurs, asking: (1) whether they support consistently the claim that Confucius espoused, in a noncontroversial sense, a fundamentally religious outlook; and (2), if so, how and to what extent this religious outlook affects his moral theory.

* Robert B. Louden is Professor of Philosophy, University of Southern Maine.

The tian topic is also an extremely old one, and has plagued Western interpretations of Confucian texts since the time of Matteo Ricci (1552–1610), founder of the first Jesuit mission in China. Cook and Rosemont write:

> Theologically there were two burning questions which divided the missionaries to China, and the divisions quickly spread back to Europe. The first of these was whether the Chinese language did or did not contain a close lexical equivalent for the Christian "God." If not, it must follow that the Chinese were all atheists. The Jesuit founder of the mission in China, Matteo Ricci, allowed two terms from the Chinese: Shang Di [上帝]—"Supreme Ancestor"—and Tian—"Heaven"—as equivalents for "God."[5]

There are additional complications on the Chinese side. As a term within the Chinese language, tian has multiple meanings—"a range of uses running from the most to the least anthropomorphic," with more anthropomorphic meanings dominating in the time before Confucius, and less anthropomorphic ones later.[6] And within the text of the Analects itself, many critics claim that the tian passages contradict one another. Some of them are allegedly antireligious, portraying Confucius as "insincere, having no faith in anything extra-human, but following an opportunist's policy of conformity for the sake of attaining his objects"; others are religious, revealing a man who is "inspired by a profound sense of mission," that is, a mission to help human beings live in accord with "the guiding intelligence of the cosmos."[7]

Despite these and other problems, the tian passages in the Analects are not the mystery that many critics have made them out to be. In what follows I shall argue against the view of Herbert Fingarette and others, who hold that although Confucius "did speak of Heaven, its role is not too clear and is unelaborated in the *Analects*."[8] On my view, the *tian* passages do form a consistent whole, one from which we can reliably infer both that Confucius was a strong religious believer in a noncontroversial sense, and that his moral orientation was itself dependent upon his religious outlook.

Tian 天 in the Analects. Let me start with the "easy" passages: that is, those in which almost all commentators agree that a religious dimension is present. First are what might be called the "divine mission" passages—texts where Confucius asserts that Heaven is the source of the moral power within him and that Heaven has entrusted him with a sacred mission. For instance, when informed that Huan Tui, the Minister of War in Song, was attempting to kill him, Confucius replied: "*T'ien* is author of the virtue [*de* 德] that is in me. What can Huan T'ui do to me?" (7:23). And when Confucius was surrounded in Kuang after being mistaken for Yang Huo, a scoundrel who had caused trouble there earlier, he repeated his conviction of a divine mission by stating that Heaven had now selected him as the champion and carrier of China's culture: "With King Wen dead, is not culture [*wen* 文] invested here in me? If Heaven intends culture to be destroyed, those who come after me will not be able to have any part of it. If Heaven does not intend this culture to be destroyed, then what can the men of K'uang do to me?" (9:5).

Similarly, Confucius' student Zigong reports that *tian* "set him [Confucius] on the path to sagehood" (9:6). Finally, a border official at Yi also expressed a similar view of Confucius' vocation to a group of the master's students: "The Empire has long been without the Way [*dao* 道]. Heaven is about to use your Master as the wooden tongue for a bell" (3:24)—that is, to rouse the Empire by "ringing out truth and justice."

Related to the divine mission passages are a group of darker statements in which Confucius despairs of achieving his goals of moral reform, but in which the overriding intention to follow Heaven is nevertheless present. For instance, at one point he complains to Zigong, "There is no one who understands me"—and then takes comfort in the thought that although human beings do not understand him, Heaven (perhaps) does: "I do not complain against Heaven, nor do I blame man. In my studies, I start from below[9] and see through to what is up above. If I am understood at all, it is, perhaps, by Heaven" (14:35). And when his favorite disciple Yan Yuan died, Confucius declared, "Alas! Heaven has bereft me! Heaven has bereft me!" (11:9). Similarly, on returning from a visit to Nanzi, "the notorious wife of Duke Ling of Wei," and hearing that his disciple Zilu was displeased, the "Master swore, 'If I have done anything improper, may Heaven's curse be on me, may Heaven's curse be on me!'" (6:28).

A third group of *tian* passages, although not as dark in tone as the second group, repeat Confucius' underlying conviction that a good man must always try to model himself on, and seek moral guidance from, Heaven. On being asked by Wangsun Jia, commander in chief in the state of Wei, to explain a remark, Confucius replied, "The saying has got it wrong. When you have offended against Heaven there is nowhere you can turn to in your prayers" (3:13). Elsewhere Confucius eulogizes the legendary ruler Yao with the remark: "Great indeed was Yao as a ruler! How lofty! It is only Heaven that is great and it was only Yao who modeled himself upon it" (8:19). (That is, only Heaven is unqualifiedly great: it alone must therefore be our primary moral teacher.)

Confucius also criticizes his disciple Zilu for ordering other followers to act as retainers for him when he was sick, out of office, and not in position to have retainers, by chiding: "In pretending that I had retainers when I had none, who would we be deceiving? Would we be deceiving Heaven?" (9:12). (That is, ultimately it is Heaven's judgment alone that counts—not that of mere mortals.) Similarly, Confucius opens his litany of three things the gentleman (*junzi* 君子) fears by proclaiming: "He is in awe of the Decree of Heaven [*tian ming* 天命].... The small man, being ignorant of the Decree of Heaven, does not stand in awe of it" (16:8). A second well-known passage in which the important phrase *tian ming* occurs is 2:4, where Confucius states: "at fifty I understood the Decree of Heaven." Here the difficulty of attaining such understanding is obviously stressed, but in both 16:8 and 2:4 the underlying message is that *tian ming* is a fundamental moral imperative to which individuals are subject.[10]

It may still be the case, as Creel noted back in 1932, "that if a poll of Western scholars must decide the matter, Confucius was beyond all doubt agnostic, or at least very, very skeptical."[11] However, if this is so it tells us more about the state of Western sinological scholarship (and/or the relevance of polls for deciding matters of textual interpretation) than it does about what Confucius meant.[12]

The fundamental message that I see expressed in each of the above passages is a very strong conviction on the part of Confucius that *tian* is the most important moral force in the universe and that human beings who wish to be morally good must therefore seek to discern and follow it. I believe that this faith in a more-than-human power that is believed to give moral values and obligations a deep grounding entitles us to call Confucius "religious" in a garden variety, noncontroversial sense.

At the same time, I do not see any evidence that Confucius' *tian* is anything like the "personal God" of the Western religions. I am thus essentially in agreement with Heiner Raetz, who writes that for Confucius "*t'ien* is clearly not a naturalistic concept but a religious one, ... though it is not very much thought of anthropomorphically."[13] Confucius, we may say, is thus religious but not theistic.[14]

But the obligation to seek to discern *tian* creates a special problem for Confucius, one that is highlighted in the passage chosen as an epigram for this essay, 17:19. Because *tian* is not a personal being (much less an anthropomorphic personal being who commands us from on high), it does not speak. Consequently, it is extremely difficult for those of us who are verbally fixated to discern accurately the moral message of *tian*. Still, despite Heaven's nonverbal modes of communication, the wise are able to discern *tian* by examining "the four seasons going round and ... the hundred things coming into being" (17:19). Confucius' point here is not simply that *tian* is "the source of all phenomena and of the processes of natural change,"[15] or even that the "spirit of Heaven is still very much present in the regularities, routines, and generative processes of nature, even though Heaven does not speak."[16] Rather, he is implying that through the harmony, beauty, and sublimity of its natural processes Heaven communicates a great deal about how human beings ought to live and act,[17] at least to those who have learned to listen carefully to it.

Counter-evidence? What then of the allegedly antireligious *tian* passages in the *Analects*? What do they tell us about Confucius' moral outlook? Given all the interpretive weight they have been asked to carry, they are surprisingly few in number. At 5:13 disciple Zigong complains: "One can get to hear about the Master's accomplishments, but one cannot get to hear his views on human nature and the Way of Heaven (*tian dao* 天道)." In Waley's note on this passage we are informed that what Zigong is getting at is that the "Tao taught by Confucius only concerned human behavior ('the ways of man'): he did not expound a corresponding Heavenly Tao, governing the conduct of unseen powers and divinities." But because 5:13 also states that Confucius allegedly declined to talk about his views "on human nature," it is not at all clear, based on this passage alone, how much teaching concerning "the ways of man" one could reasonably expect from him! Waley tries to finesse this conundrum by claiming that a distinction between human nature before and after "it has been embellished with 'culture'" is at work here, but it is extremely unlikely that Confucius could have believed that "the ways of man" were shaped completely by the embellishment of culture and not at all by natural forces.[18]

A more sensible reading of 5:13, I suggest, is simply that Confucius was reticent to expound on speculative matters—human or divine—when he was not sure he knew exactly what he was talking about, and when he felt that such speculative chatter would only detract people's attention away from the more fundamental moral task of deciding how to live and act.[19]

A second passage often cited to show Confucius' supposedly strictly secular orientation is 6:22. When his student Fan Chi asked what constituted wisdom, Confucius replied: "To work for the things the common people have a right to and to keep one's distance from the gods and spirits while showing them reverence can be called wisdom." According to Creel, this passage, "more than any other, [has] given rise to the belief that Confucius was agnostic."[20]

But why is a counsel of "keeping one's distance" from god and spirits necessarily an indication of religious skepticism? A more likely scenario (as both Creel and Schwartz emphasize) is simply that Confucius is reminding his audience that distance is a proper factor in the relationship between human beings and gods: indeed, not to respect this distance would itself be a sign of blasphemy. (Compare the story in Exodus that, when God spoke to Moses from the burning bush, he warned him, "Come no closer! . . . And Moses hid his face, for he was afraid to look at God" [NRSV 3:5–6].)

A similar passage is 7:21: "The topics the Master did not speak of were prodigies, force, disorder and gods." Here too, from the report that Confucius "did not speak of" certain things we should not infer either that he did or did not believe in the existence of those things of which he did not speak. Rather, the point is that he was not given to speculation about such matters.

The last of the allegedly antireligious passages, *Analects* 11:12, runs as follows:

Chi-lu asked how the spirits of the dead and the gods should be served. The Master said, "You are not able even to serve man. How can you serve the spirits?"

"May I ask about death?"

"You do not even understand life. How can you understand death?"

Here, too, I read this passage as evidence of Confucius' fundamentally practical (as opposed to speculative or metaphysical) orientation. His reluctance to engage in the latter tendency is not a sign of an antireligious attitude, but rather a reflection of his determination to adhere to what he feels is most important in human life.

Conclusion. When philosophers argue for or against "the autonomy of morality," they normally have in mind the thesis that moral principles are not dependent on religious belief—that we can attain accurate knowledge of correct moral norms without the assistance of any religious belief. A classic Enlightenment statement in defense of the thesis is the following, from Baron d'Holbach:

> To learn the true principles of morality, men
> have no need of theology, of revelation, or gods:
> They have need only of reason. They have only to
> enter into themselves, to reflect upon their own
> nature, consult their sensible interests, consider
> the object of society, and of the individuals, who
> compose it; and they will easily perceive, that
> virtue is the interest, and vice the unhappiness of
> beings of their kind.[21]

I do not see evidence of this outlook in the *Analects* of Confucius. Confucius does not advise human beings who wish to learn the true principles of morality "only to enter into themselves, to reflect upon their own nature." (Compare 5:13, where, as we have seen, Confucius declines even to present his views on human nature.) Nor does he console us by saying we "have need only of reason."[22]

Rather, Confucius urges us to look outward and upward to Heaven if we wish to find our true moral bearings. Confucius' moral outlook is religious (though again, not theistic) in the straightforward sense that he holds that moral standards are dependent on something outside of us, something bigger than human nature—or culture—that is much more than a human or even a rational construction. Additionally, to count as religious this source of value that is outside of us must be felt to be holy or sacred.[23] The sense of awe that Confucius experiences in contemplating *tian* (compare 16:8) meets this basic description of religious experience.

Notes

1. This is a shortened and lightly edited version of Robert B. Louden's original essay. All changes have been made with the permission of the author.

2. In citing from the *Analects*, I use D.C. Lau's translation and chapter divisions in *Confucius: The Analects* (New York: Penguin Books, 1979).

3. H.G. Creel, *Confucius: The Man and the Myth* (New York: John Day, 1949), p. 116.

4. Benjamin I. Schwartz, *The World of Thought in Ancient China* (Cambridge: Harvard UP, 1985), p. 122.

5. Gottfried Wilhelm Leibniz, *Writings on China*, trans. Daniel J. Cook and Henry Rosemont, Jr. (Chicago: Open Court, 1994), p. 3. As Cook and Rosemont also note,

many later missionaries objected to Ricci's translations, claiming that both *shangdi* and *tian* had "connotations inconsistent with the Christian concept of deity" (p. 3). Albrecht, in his introduction to the Oratio, points out that Noel translated tian as "heaven," whereas Couplet rendered it as "God" (in Christian Wolff, *Oratio de Sinarum philosphia practica. Re über die praktische philosophie der Chinesen*, ed. Michael Albert [Hamburg: Felix Meiner, 1985], p. XXVII). Unfortunately, the underlying assumption in this debate (viz., that in order to have a concept of God one needs one or another specific word for God) seems clearly false. The same concept can be referred to by means of many different combinations of many different words.

6. Bryan W. Van Norden, s.v. "*t'ien*," *The Cambridge Dictionary of Philosophy*. See also Arthur Waley's and D.C. Lau's discussions of *t'ien* in their respective translations of the *Analects* (Arthur Waley, *The Analects of Confucius* [New York: Vintage Books, 1989; originally published 1938], pp. 41–43, and D.C. Lau, pp. 17–30) and David L. Hall and Roger T. Ames, *Thinking through Confucius* (Albany, NY: SUNY P, 1987), pp. 201–16. For brief discussions of pre- and post-Confucius meanings of *tian*, see H.G. Creel, *Chinese Thought: From Confucius to Mao Tse-Tung* (New York: New American Library, 1960), pp. 21–23; C.K. Yang, "The Functional Relationship between Confucian Thought and Chinese Religion," in John K. Fairbank, ed., *Chinese Thought and Institutions* (Chicago: U of Chicago P, 1957), p. 273; and Hans Kung and Julia Ching, *Christianity and Chinese Religions* (New York: Doubleday, 1989), pp. 16–17. See also Robert Eno's book-length study,

The Confucian Creation of Heaven: Philosophy and the Defense of Ritual Mastery (Albany, NY: SUNY P, 1990), esp. his discussion, "The Origins of the Term 'T'ien,'" pp. 181–89. For a critical discussion of Eno's approach, see Kwong-loi Shun's review in the *Harvard Journal of Asiatic Studies* 52 (1992), pp. 739–56.

7. Creel, "Was Confucius Agnostic?" *T'ung pao* 29 (1932), p. 64. Yet another complication concerns much-debated issues regarding the composition of the *Analects*, and how these might relate to determining Confucius' own views on *tian*. (Eno, for instance, draws a very strong distinction between the historical Confucius' views of *tian* and those we find in the text of the *Analects*. See "Confucius' Doctrinal Silence," in Robert Eno, *The Confucian Creation of Heaven: Philosophy and the Defense of Ritual Mastery* [Albany, NY: SUNY P, 1990], pp. 94–98.)

8. Herbert Fingarette, *Confucius—The Secular as Sacred* (New York: Harper and Row, 1972), p. 62. Similarly, Hall and Ames contend that "the *Analects* itself does not provide us with an altogether clear statement on t'ien" (*Thinking through Confucius*, p. 208). On the other hand, Eno holds that "the portrait of t'ien that emerges (in the *Analects*) is remarkably consistent" (*The Confucian Creation of Heaven*, p. 84, cf 94).

9. Even this passage has been interpreted by some as implying a secular outlook on the part of Confucius. James Legge, for instance, translates the flagged sentence as "My studies lie low, and my penetration rises high," and then comments: "the meaning appears to be that he [Confucius] contented himself with

the study of men and things, common matters as more ambitious spirits would deem them" (James Legge, trans., *Confucian Analects, The Great Learning and The Doctrine of the Mean* [New York: Dover, 1971], p. 289. But Lau's choice of "start" (which I follow) suggests merely that Confucius begins with "common matters"—not that "he contented himself with the study of men and things."

10. Compare Lau, "Introduction," *Analects*, p. 28.

11. Creel, "Was Confucius Agnostic?" p. 66. Certainly the opinion of Legge, "the formidable Scottish missionary-scholar" who published "what can be considered the archetype of all later scholarly editions of the Analects" (and who also "coined the title 'Analects'") would carry considerable weight in such a poll (Jonathan Spence, "What Confucius Said," *New York Review of Books*, April 10, 1997, p. 8). Legge's towering influence indicates a basic flaw in the poll scenario: some scholars' votes always count for more than others. In his discussion of Confucius' "Influence and Opinions," Legge notes: "Not once throughout the *Analects* does he use the personal name [God]. I would say that he was unreligious rather than irreligious; yet by the coldness of his temperament and intellect in this matter, his influence is unfavorable to the development of ardent religious feeling among the Chinese people generally" (*Confucian Analects*, p. 99).

12. A different kind of agnostic reading is present in the following remark: "T'ien is wholly immanent, having no existence independent of the calculus of phenomena that constitute it. . . . The meaning and value of t'ien is a

function of the meaning and value of its many phenomena, and the order of t'ien is expressed in the harmony that obtains among its correlative parts" (Hall and Ames, *Thinking through Confucius*, p. 207). When it is a question of the moral meaning and value of *tian*, this assertion is false. Confucius looks to *tian* for moral guidance, not vice versa. Confucius qua natural creature is one of the many phenomena that collectively constitute nature and physical reality, but Confucius nowhere suggests that human beings should get together and collectively calculate what their moral norms ought to be. Rather, the value and status of *tian* as a moral norm is independent of such phenomena. *Tian* qua moral norm is not simply a function of the value of its constituent parts.

13. Heiner Roetz, *Mensch und Natur im alten China* (New York: Peter Lang, 1984), p. 203, n. 3. My one doubt here concerns Roetz's dualism between naturalism and religion. Why couldn't *tian* for Confucius be *both* a naturalistic and religious concept? *Tian* is not transcendent in the sense of being above or outside of nature, in the way that Western religions construe God. Rather, *tian* is part of the cosmos itself and thus naturalistic. But *tian* also serves as the ground of moral norms, and the wise feel a sense of awe in contemplating it. In this latter sense, *tian* is both transcendent and religious.

14. I would like to thank Philip J. Ivanhoe for conversation on this point. It is true that in several of the passages cited above *tian* is said to have intentions (9:5, perhaps 3:24); and in others to possess understanding (14:35, 9:12). These uses of language seem to me to

be metaphorical. However, even if one thinks they are not, they do not add up to anything close to the "God-as-personal-being" that most mainstream believers within the major Western religions regard as being essential to their faith.

15. Contra Hall and Ames, *Thinking through Confucius*, p. 206. Later, on p. 277, they offer a second reading of 17:19, stating that the point of the passage concerns the "harmony and meaning effected in the absence of the spoken word." On my reading, the point of 17:19 is not the romantic notion that language destroys meaning or that nonverbal communication is always to be preferred over verbal, but simply that Heaven does in fact communicate a great deal of moral meaning to the wise, albeit nonverbally.

16. Schwartz, *The World of Thought in Ancient China*, pp. 124–25. Schwartz's assertion that "the spirit of Heaven is still very much present" in the unspoken processes of nature heads in the right direction, but the normative content of this spirit needs to be articulated. What do the wise learn about how to live and act from the spirit of Heaven when they observe these processes of nature?

17. Compare Mencius: "Heaven does not speak but reveals itself through its acts and deeds" (D.C. Lau, trans., *Mencius* [New York: Penguin Books, 1970], 5A5, p. 143). The vexing question of *how* exactly Heaven reveals its intentions is unfortunately not explored in detail in either the *Analects* or *Mencius*, and the hints that one finds in these two texts do not appear to be entirely compatible. (In the

latter text, the idea seems to be that Heaven reveals its intentions through the happiness of the people under virtuous rule. However, both texts agree that Heaven communicates nonverbally, and that its messages carry strong moral import.) The hypothesis I am proposing, based in part on *Analects* 17:19, is that the wise can discern moral norms in the regular patterns and interrelations of the natural world. At 2:1, for instance, we are told that the relationship between the Polestar and other stars provides us with a paradigm of "the rule of virtue [*de* 德]." The idea of reading moral norms in nature is admittedly not elaborated on in great detail in the *Analects*, but I do believe it can be correctly attributed to Confucius. It is also a common thought that one finds expressed in many different cultural traditions.

18. Waley, *The Analects of Confucius*, p. 110, notes 4 and 3 (respectively).

19. Compare Schwartz, *The World of Thought in Ancient China*, pp. 118–20. Here we find what is often referred to as Confucius' "pragmatic" orientation. On my view, his orientation is "pragmatic" only in the popular sense that it is fundamentally concerned with human practice rather than speculation. But Confucius' outlook is not what most philosophers mean by "pragmatic," because he does not espouse a doctrine of efficacy in practical application. Confucius does not argue that that which works out most effectively provides a standard of moral rightness. Rather, *tian* itself provides us with this standard—regardless of whether it is or is not efficacious.

20. Creel, "Was Confucius Agnostic?" p. 82. Creel cites Legge's translation of this passage, in which wisdom is said to consist in keeping "aloof from" spiritual beings while also "respecting" them (cf. Legge, *Confucian Analects*, p. 191—in Legge's version this passage is numbered 6:20). Creel then suggests the following revision: "to respect spiritual beings, maintaining the proper distance in *relations* with them" (pp. 87–88).

21. Baron d'Holbach, *Common Sense, or Natural Ideas Opposed to Supernatural* (1772), in Isaac Kramnick, ed., *The Portable Enlightenment Reader* (New York: Penguin Books, 1995), p. 144.

22. I do not mean here that Confucius disavows reason. On the contrary, the goal is to *understand* the Decree of Heaven (cf. 2:4). However, I do not see evidence in the *Analects* for the strong rationalism that . . . others attribute to Confucius. Max Weber exaggerates when he claims that "Confucianism is more rationalist and sober, in the sense of the absence and the rejection of all non-utilitarian yardsticks, than any other ethical system, with the possible exception of J. Bentham's" ("The Social Psychology of the World Religions," *From Max Weber: Essays in Sociology*, ed. H.H. Gerth and C. Wright Mills [New York: Oxford UP, 1946], p. 293).

23. For a classic discussion see Rudolf Otto, *The Idea of the Holy*, trans. John W. Harvey (London: Oxford UP, 1923).

Discussion

1. How do the cited texts show that *tian* in the *Analects* is religious?

2. Why does Louden think *tian* is religious but not theistic? How well do the texts support his claim?

3. What is the relationship of morality to *tian* in the *Analects*?

CONFUCIUS ON RELIGIOUS EXPERIENCE

RONNIE LITTLEJOHN*

Confucius as secular humanist? The dominant contemporary view is that Confucius was, if not a secular humanist philosopher, at least a teacher who treated religious experience as tangential to his project of cultivating *junzi* (morally perfected person).[1] This view of Confucius' religious experience may rest on a neglect of some very strategic analects. In this essay, I offer a brief study of these important analects in order to see what they can contribute to an understanding of Confucius on religious experience.[2]

While my focus will principally be on *Analects* (*Lunyu* 論語) Books Three and Ten, these passages have deep connections to the picture we get of Confucius' role not only as a participant in ritual, but also as a master who instructs students in ritual performance and its meaning as understood in other classical texts including most formatively, the *Book of Rites* (*Liji* 禮己). Knowing that the *Analects* is a redaction of earlier written and oral materials, it may be that the analects in Books Three and Ten having to do with Confucius' ritual practices orbited in the same community that created and collected the *Book of Rites* materials.[3] So, I will frequently consult the *Book of Rites* for interpretive clues about Confucius' religious experiences. Another classical text from which I will seek guidance is the *Book of Odes* (*Shijing* 詩經). According to the *Analects*, Confucius loved to discuss the *Odes* (1.15; 3.8; 7.15), and he found inspiration by singing them (8.8).[4] Indeed, some analects under study in this paper cite the *Odes*, and even for those that do not specifically cite this text, its materials do often shed light on religious practices in which Confucius

likely participated. I will also make use of some passages from *Zhongyong* and the *Mencius* in order to illumine our understanding of Confucius' experiences.

Respect for spirits. Let us begin with *Analects* 6.22: "Fan Chi asked about wisdom. The Master said, 'Devote yourself to what is appropriate *yi* 義 for the people, and show reverence (*jing* 敬) for the ghosts and spirits while keeping them at a distance, this can be called wisdom.'" This passage has been taken to mean that Confucius thinks that wisdom lies in keeping one's distance from any religious beliefs about spirits, perhaps suggesting an agnosticism on Confucius' part. But it seems another interpretation is possible. We may understand Confucius as saying that a wise person approaches numinal entities always giving careful attention to the appropriate decorum *li* 禮, for relating to them. This reading is consistent with Confucius' view that there is always an appropriate decorum *li* for our behavior toward those of greater authority (e.g., the ruler or even one's father).

Some help in interpreting what Confucius means in 6.22 comes from 16.13 in which the same character for "distance" *yuan* 遠 is used for how a son should not be overly familiar with his father, or approach him without proper deference. In the case before us, my view is that Confucius is extending the requirements of ritual propriety toward those in authority to cover our relationship with numinal entities.[5] In taking this position he is following the lead of the *Odes*. Ode 209 (楚茨 *Chu Ci*) teaches that the spirits admired sacrificers who were respectful, circumspect, and appropriate in relating to them. It says,

> For offerings and sacrifice;
> We seat the representatives of the dead, and
> urge them to eat:
> Thus seeking to increase our bright happiness, . . .
> Only with correct and reverent deportment
> [toward the spirits] . . .

* Ronnie Littlejohn is Professor of Philosophy and Director of Asian Studies at Belmont University.

The able priest announces [the will of the Spirits],
And the Spirits enjoy your wines and viands.
They will ever confer upon you the choicest
favours (Legge, *Shijing*)

Ode 240 (思齊 *Si Qi*) says King Wen impressed spirits by following the *li* for approaching them set down from antiquity (Legge, *Shijing*). In the *Book of Rites*, there are extensive rules for how to approach spirits, some of which almost certainly predate Confucius, and others of which are attributed to him (*Liji* 1.5.8, Legge). The *Book of Rites*' "ten most important human relationships" places the normative *li* for relating to spirits at the head of its list (28, 245, Legge).

According to the *Mencius*, the first thing Confucius did upon coming to hold office in Lu was to lay down the correct rituals governing sacred vessels and sacrifices (5B4). So, it seems in Analects 6.22 that instead of teaching his students that there are no numinal entities and that to be wise is to recognize this, Confucius is teaching them to be respectful toward spirits and to honor their power, and I take this same line of interpretation to be a defensible reading of *Analects* 7.21, which says, "The Master had nothing to say about strange happenings, the use of force, disorder, or the spirits (*shen* 神)." Following this reading, Confucius would be taken to mean that the *li* about describing one's experiences with numinal entities required circumspection and discretion when speaking about the spirits and not that he refused to speak of them because he thought that belief in them was superstitious or only for the common and uneducated.

Rituals of sacrifice. The appropriate decorum (*li*) toward spirits is especially significant when they are approached through rituals such as sacrifice. *Analects* 3.12 says,

The expression "sacrifice as though present" is taken to mean "sacrifice to the spirits as though

the spirits are present." But the Master said: "If I myself do not participate in the sacrifice, it is as though I have not sacrificed at all."

In this passage, Confucius is endorsing the statement, "sacrifice as though the spirits are present." However, in spite of the use of "as though," he does not seem to be counseling his students to go through the motions of doing the rituals while actually believing himself that there are no such things as spirits. Confucius never advises his students to do anything with duplicity, insincerity, or sham. In fact, he makes a sharp distinction between acting sincerely and pretending, and warns sternly against the latter (11.21).[6]

Confucius' comment to his students in the remaining part of 3.12 is important to a well-rounded interpretation. In it, he says, "If I myself do not participate in the sacrifice, it is as though I have not sacrificed at all." On one level, this comment tells us that Confucius felt he should be physically present at a sacrifice rather than sending a specialist to perform the ritual on his behalf. The practice of using a ritual specialist was widely done in the time of Confucius, and this analect reveals his distaste for such an approach to religious life (Puett, 98).[7] But there is more to *Analects* 3.12 than rejecting the employment of ritual specialists. The text helps us notice that Confucius is also affirming that something significant *does* take place in his religious activity. The text implies that when Confucius practiced religious acts, he had meaningful religious experiences, consequently, he would not dream of having someone else perform the rituals for him.

The evidence for Confucius' participation in religious sacrifices and rituals is both adequate and clear. For example, *Analects* 3.17 bears testimony to his involvement at the beginning of the month sacrifice: "Zigong wanted to do away with the practice of sacrificing a sheep to announce the beginning of the month. The Master said, Zigong! You love the sheep; I love the ritual." This passage is often taken to mean that Zigong does not see the point of continuing the ritual when a sheep is such a valuable commodity, whereas Confucius endorses ritual propriety over such pragmatic financial considerations (Slingerland, 24).

Such a reading accords with Richard Wollheim's claim in his "The Sheep and the Ceremony." Wollheim stresses how important the rites were to Confucius for instantiating a particular form of life. All this seems right so far as it goes. It is undoubtedly true that Confucius did treasure the religious form of life. However, if we follow the guiding principle of internal hermeneutics not to take one analect as atomistically discrete from another, then our previous discussion of 3.12 authorizes a more robust interpretation of 3.17 and helps us understand *why* Confucius valued this form of life. Confucius wanted to retain the practice of the sacrifice Zigong wanted to discontinue because he valued what happened when he participated in it, and not merely because he supported the preservation of rituals as forms of life along with others such as archery, music, and charioteering.

Confucius as ritual master. The fact that Confucius' love of rituals was directly related to the experiences he had when he participated in them is made all the more manifest when we note his leadership in ritual performance. That is, he was a ritual master.[8] Yet some think this an odd thing to say. Perhaps we are so conditioned to see Confucius only as a moral philosopher, that the appellation of ritual master seems immediately wrong. However, in early China the fusion of the philosopher and the ritual master in the same person was not uncommon, and the *Analects* represents Confucius as playing this role. *Analects* 10.9 is one description of Confucius as a ritual master:

> After assisting his Duke at a sacrifice, he would not keep the portion of the sacrificial meat bestowed upon him overnight. When sacrificing at home he would not let the meat sit for more

than three days. If it had sat for more than three days, he would not eat it.

According to Zhousheng Lie's commentary in the Three Kingdoms period, there was no hygienic reason for eating the meat from the Duke's sacrifice on the same day, but the religious belief was that the spiritual benefit of the sacrifice would dissipate if not consumed promptly. Confucius' behavior suggests that he shared this belief.

In contrast, there was no such belief about the family sacrifice, and so the period of delay in eating it was subject only to the normal three-day demand of hygiene (Slingerland, 104). Mencius reports that, while holding office in Lu, Confucius led a sacrifice but was not given a share of the meat of the sacrificial animal. The result was that Confucius left the state without so much as removing his ritual garments (6B6). There is, of course, the insult offered to him in the host's not doing sharing the meat. But I hold that the omission is an affront precisely because Confucius believed the meat was imbued with spiritual power as a result of his ritual action.

When Confucius conducted rituals, not only was he careful with the sacrificial remains, but also *Analects* 7.18 reports that he would use only the proper pronunciations in the rites. It is not entirely clear what this means.[9] Liu Baonan thinks that this reference to proper ritual speech means simply that Confucius used the dialect spoken in the Western Zhou capital (Slingerland, 70). However, since we know that masters performing rituals employed formulas as performative transformations, invocations, affirmations, and confessions, it is also possible that this analect refers directly to the use of appropriate performative formulas. Such formulas were often in a special language that may not have been known by those observing.

Confucius at home. With respect to his private religious practices, *Analects* 10.11 tells us that at home

Confucius always took a small portion of each type of his food and placed it in the sacrificial vessels as an offering to his ancestors. Confucius' practice of giving a little food to his ancestors provides a background for understanding *Analects* 3.13, which begins with a question from Wang-sun Jia about ancestral offerings made in the home. He asks Confucius, "What do you think about the saying, 'It is better to pay homage to the kitchen stove than to the corner shrine'?" In his interpretation of 3.13, Arthur Waley says that Jia's question represents the rather cynical view that it would be much better to be well fed from the products of the kitchen stove, than to waste food by giving it to the ancestors by placing it on their shrine (97). This reading makes Confucius' answer all the more interesting. He replies: "Not so. Once you have incurred the wrath of Heaven, there is no one to whom you can pray for help." Confucius' answer implies his belief in the efficacy of such small rituals and in the communion with spirits they were meant to establish.

There are some analects that describe Confucius' participation in rituals which he did not lead or help conduct. One of the most interesting is 10.14: "When the villagers were performing the end of the year exorcism (*nuo* 儺), he would stand on the Eastern steps dressed in full court regalia." The ritual referred to in this analect is probably the New Year's exorcism in which the entire populace participated and which is described in the *Zhouli* 周禮, Chs. 48 and 54. Its purpose was to drive away evil spirits and bad influences from the previous year. During the ritual, Confucius stood solemnly in the position of the host of the house (the East steps), but also facing the direction to which the spirits of the dead return to their proper place. What Confucius experienced in participating in the ritual is unknown to us. However, his Han dynasty descendant, Kong Anguo (156–74 BCE), commenting on this analect, wrote that Confucius stood on the steps of his ancestral temple (rather than his home) in order to comfort his own ancestral spirits during

the exorcism and keep them from fleeing along with the hungry ghosts and evil spirits (Slingerland, 105). If we follow Kong Anguo's interpretation, we get some look into the inner intentions and experiences of Confucius.

Not only did Confucius perform and participate in rituals, but virtually the entire section entitled *Questions of Zang-Dze* of the *Book of Rites* is devoted to a report of his role as an instructor in ritual action (Book v, Legge). He tells his students how to perform rituals, when to stop a ritual, where to stand, what to say and chant, and how to judge the ceremony's auspiciousness.

Confucius is also pictured as seeking instruction in the performance of ritual or the significance of ritual objects and space. For example, in *Analects* 3.15, he asks many questions about the Great Ancestral Temple, and the *Book of Rites* reports that Confucius sought instruction about mourning rituals from Laozi.

Conclusion. The reader may feel that up to now I have made very few comments about Confucius' actual internal religious experiences. As a partial explanation for this deficiency, I think it is well to remember that even the explicitly ritual texts of this period such as the *Book of Rites* are virtually silent on what a practitioner actually experienced. Deborah Sommer writes, "Whereas one can learn that the priests, for example, were responsible for dancing at prayers for rain and exorcising baneful influences with peach wands, . . . yet one cannot determine their emotional or spiritual state when conducting rituals" (214). This silence is certainly attributable in part to the appropriate decorum (*li*) directing one's discussion of encounters with the spirits and it may also be evidence of the ineffability of the experiences themselves.

All of this notwithstanding, we can add one more observation about Confucius' religious experiences. He definitely believed that a religious experience could provide one with illumination and power. An evidence of such belief is in *Analects* 3.11, which is mirrored with only slight changes in *Zhongyong* 19. When Confucius is asked for an explanation of the *di* sacrifice, he answers in 3.11: "'I do not understand it. One who understood it could handle the world as if he had it right here,'" and he pointed to the palm of his hand. What interests me here is not whether Confucius understood *how* to perform the *di* ritual, because I do not take him to be referring to the method of the ritual. Rather it is his sense of the power that a practitioner could gain through a religious experience that is important. He believes that a person who has such an experience would obtain the knowledge and virtue necessary to handle the world, suggesting that he believed something transpired in ritual that was empowering and cognitively illuminating.

Noticing the close connection between *Zhongyong* 19 and *Analects* 3.11 opens the door for us to comment on *Zhongyong* 16. Although there is no parallel passage for *Zhongyong* 16 in the *Analects* as we find with *Zhongyong* 19, nevertheless, it is relevant to an understanding of Confucius' religious experiences. This text is attributed to Confucius. In it, he offers us a fitting end to our brief study saying,

> The *de* 德 (power, virtue) of the gods and spirits is profound. Looking, we do not see them; listening, we do not hear them. And yet they inform events to the extent that nothing can be what it is without them. Because of them, the people of the world fast, purify themselves, and put on their finest clothes in carrying out the sacrifices to them. It is as though the air above our heads is suffused with them, and as though they are all around. The *Odes* says: "The descent of the gods cannot be fathomed. How much less can it be ignored."

Notes

1. Scholars who have held and continue to hold such a view are a veritable who's who of our intellectual lineage: James Legge (1880); Herbert Giles (1906, Ch. 2); Wing-tsit Chan (1969); Bruce and Taeko Brooks (1998, 304, 06), and even many of the authors in *Confucian Spirituality* (Tu and Tucker).

2. I wish to express my appreciation to a number of colleagues who have given me guidance and correction in collecting these notes and thoughts: Robin Wang, Eric Hutton and Erin Cline. I want to give special thanks to Li Qingjun, Roger Ames, and P.J. Ivanhoe for their important suggestions for revisions. In all cases, the remaining deficiencies lie at my feet and are not attributable to these fine scholars from whom I have learned so much.

3. The work of Bruce Brooks and Taeko Brooks helps us appreciate how the formation and/or collection of these materials for the *Analects* and *Book of Rites* may derive from the same source community, even if some of their reconstructions are arguable (Brooks and Brooks, "The Kung Transition" in their *Original Analects*).

4. I am indebted to Deborah Sommer for helping me notice many of these connections and to P.J. Ivanhoe, who has reminded me that he has stressed in his own work that the *Odes* is the only text later recognized as a classic that clearly was used in Confucius' school.

5. See Louden for a similar argument.

6. Robin Wang has encouraged me to notice the way in which Kang Youwei (1858–1927) employs the Confucian concept of sincerity (*cheng* 诚) when interpreting 3.12. According to Kang, Confucius' point is that if one has sincerity there will be a spirit, if one does not have sincerity, there will be no spirit (Kang, 37). While I value the effort of Kang in this interpretation, nevertheless, as I show in the text, I think the force of this passage lies in Confucius' point about the necessity of his own personal participation in the ritual to his sense that a religious experience has occurred. On the other hand, while agreeing with me that Confucius probably did believe in spirits, Eric Hutton has reminded me that as the case of Xunzi shows, it is possible to believe that one can practice the rituals, even while knowing that they do not communicate with spirits, and still not regard the rituals as empty. So, Hutton does not think my appeal to Confucius' aversion to duplicity rules out reading the comment "sacrifice as though the spirits are present" as implying that one should go through the motions even though there are no spirits. But in spite of what we take Xunzi to be saying, I think we must remember Confucius' caution against "pretending" in *Analects* 11.21. Putting all of this aside, I want to stress again that I think the major thrust of this passage is to be found in Confucius' insistence that religious gain comes only by direct participation, it cannot come vicariously by having someone else perform religious acts for you.

7. Both the *Zhouli* and the *Guanzi* mention ritual specialists who function at levels from the court to the common villages. The *Guanzi* says, "People made their own offerings, and each family had a ritual specialist (*wu*) and a scribe. . . . The people exhausted themselves in sacrifices and yet knew no good fortune. They made offerings without proper moderation. The people and the spirits occupied the same position. . . . There was neither respect nor reverence" (*Guoyu*, the *Chu Yu, Xia* chapter, 18.22).

8. Even more shocking than calling Confucius a ritual master is the tradition that he was a master of the reading of omens, a seer and physiognomer who could predict the future. In *Analects* 9.9 Confucius says, "The Yellow River has not yielded its chart. The Luo River does not produce its writings. I am finished!" The omen-reading tradition about Confucius was so well entrenched that Liu Xiang's favorite protagonist providing interpretations of omens in his "Discriminating Things" (c. 77 BCE) Wang Chong (27–100 CE) felt the need to refute it (Wang, 94).

9. In a personal note to me, Deborah Sommer mentions that there were special terms for the sacrificial victims. Sheep were called "fuzzy ones" and cattle "big footed ones."

References

Brooks, E. Bruce, and A. Taeko Brooks. *The Original Analects: Sayings of Confucius and His Successors.* New York. Columbia UP, 1998.

Chan, Wing-tsit, trans. *A Sourcebook in Chinese Philosophy.* Princeton, NJ: Princeton UP, 1969.

Giles, Herbert. *Religions of Ancient China.* London: Constable and Co., 1906.

Ivanhoe, Philip J. "Death and Dying in the *Analects.*" *Confucian Spirituality.*

Ed. Tu Weiming and Mary Evelyn Tucker. New York: New Crossroads, 2002. 222–35.

Kang Youwei. *Commentary to Analects*. Beijing: Chinese Press [Zhonghua Shuju], 1984.

Lau, D.C., trans. *Mencius*. London: Penguin Books, 1970.

Legge, James, trans. *The Chinese Classics, Shijing The Book of Odes*. 1997. University of Virginia Library Chinese Text Initiative. 21 September 2006 <http://etext.lib.virginia.edu/chinese/shijing /AnoShih.html>.

——, trans. *The Li Ki (The Book of Rites)*. 2006. Internet Sacred Texts Archive. 18 September 2006 <http://www.sacred-texts.com/cfu/liki/liki01 .htm>.

——. *The Religions of China: Confucianism and Taoism Described and Compared with Christianity 1880*. Whitefish, MT: Kessinger, 2004.

Liu Xiang. "Discriminating Things 辨物." *Readings in Han Chinese Thought*. Ed. and trans. Mark Csikszentmihalyi. Indianapolis: Hackett, 2006. 127–37.

Louden, Robert. "'What Does Heaven Say?': Christian Wolff and Western Interpretations of Confucian Ethics." *Confucius and the Analects: New Essays*. Ed. Bryan W. Van Norden. New York: Oxford UP, 2002. 73–93.

Puett, Michael. *To Become a God: Cosmology, Sacrifice, and Self-Divinization in Early China*. Cambridge: Harvard UP, 2002.

Slingerland, Edward, trans. *Confucius: Analects, with Selections from Traditional Commentaries*. Indianapolis: Hackett, 2003.

Sommer, Deborah. "Ritual and Sacrifice in Early Confucianism: Contacts with the Spirit World." *Confucian Spirituality*. Ed. Tu Weiming and Mary Evelyn Tucker. New York: New Crossroads, 2002. 197–220.

Tu, Weiming and Mary Evelyn Tucker, eds. *Confucian Spirituality*. New York: New Crossroads, 2002.

Waley, Arthur, trans. *The Analects of Confucius*. New York: Vintage Books, 1989.

Wollheim, Richard. "The Sheep and the Ceremony." *The Mind and Its Depths*. Cambridge, MA: Harvard UP, 1993. 1–21.

Wang Chong. "Asking Questions about Confucius 問孔." *Readings in Han Chinese Thought*. Ed. and trans. Mark Csikszentmihalyi. Indianapolis: Hackett, 2006. 93–95.

Discussion

1. What were Confucius' attitudes towards the spirits?

2. Describe Confucius' relationship towards rituals and what it says about his *beliefs* in spirits.

3. What, overall, does Littlejohn think of Confucius' religious beliefs and practices?

Chapter 31

Religion in the *Daode Jing*

DIVERGENCES WITHIN THE *LǍOZǏ*

FRANKLIN PERKINS*

Introduction. The *Lǎozǐ* 老子 is one of the most influential texts in the Chinese tradition, having a profound effect not only on Daoist religion but also on Chinese philosophy, art, and poetry. Based on the sheer number of translations, the *Lǎozǐ* has spread globally more than any religious text aside from the Bible. According to the traditional view, the origins of the text and of Daoism are quite simple. There was a great sage named "Lǎozǐ" who lived in the sixth century BCE and was a senior contemporary of Confucius (Kongzi). Due to the corruption of the times, he decided to leave the declining Zhou dynasty and headed northwest. As he left, the official in charge of the border asked him to make a record of the wisdom and he composed the 81 chapters of the *Lǎozǐ*, also known as the *Daodejing* 道德經. That text became the founding document of Daoism as both a religion and a philosophy. Most scholars now believe the story is much more complex. A series of major archeological discoveries in China have revealed two things. First in the fourth century BCE, there was a great diversity of cosmogonic views that were similar to but distinct from the *Lǎozǐ*, which shows the *Lǎozǐ* was not as unique or dominant as it now seems. Second, several manuscript versions of the *Lǎozǐ* itself have been found. These reveal the degree

to which the text varied and changed over time. In particular, bamboo texts discovered at Guodian and originally buried around 300 BCE include versions of 31 chapters of the received text. Some of these chapters are partial and shorter, though, and their wording frequently differs from later versions. The fact that the other 50 chapters are missing in those bamboo strips suggests that the *Lǎozǐ* as a whole may not have existed at that time. In any case, we now know that the *Lǎozǐ* that has been passed down to us differs considerably from its original form.

In this article, I focus on divergences within the *Lǎozǐ*, arguing that the last 15 chapters of the text (none of which were found in the Guodian bamboo strips) represent a view that differs from the remainder of the text. I begin with the traditional reading of the *Lǎozǐ* and then turn to the divergent views that appear in the last part of the text. In the conclusion, I consider the implications of this divergence for interpreting the *Lǎozǐ* as a whole.

The philosophy of the *Lǎozǐ* (chapters 1–66). The *Lǎozǐ* can be approached from many directions, but here I focus on its views of the divine. In that context, the *Lǎozǐ* can be seen as reacting against a traditional view that centered on *tiān* 天, which is conventionally translated as "heaven." In early texts, *tiān* is a vaguely anthropomorphic deity that supports good rulers and punishes bad ones. This influence of heaven was known as *tiānmìng* 天命, usually translated as the "Mandate of Heaven." The Mohists explicitly extended this belief into a general doctrine in which heaven

* Franklin Perkins is Associate Professor at Nanyang Technological University, Singapore.

supports the good of the people, rewarding those who care inclusively for others and punishing those who do not, but such views were probably widespread at the time. Heaven is not a place and is neither a transcendent being (like the Christian God) nor a fully individuated deity (like the Greek Zeus). Heaven rather was seen as an immanent aspect of the world. As Chinese philosophy developed, *tiān* more and more came to refer to something like the order or basic patterns of nature.

The central philosophical concept in the *Lǎozǐ* (in chapters 1–66) is the *dào* 道, which marks a radical break from the anthropomorphism and anthropocentrism associated with *tiān*. While *tiān* acts deliberately to enforce certain values, *dào* happens spontaneously and without deliberation, following what is so of itself (*zìrán* 自然). Chapter 37 holds that *dào* has no actions, and that if rulers can maintain it, things will transform of themselves (A: 13). Chapter 40 connects *dào* to the state of no-being: "Returning is the movement of *dào*, weakness is the function of *dào*. The things of the world are born from beings, born from no-being."[1] This shift from *tiān* to *dào* replaces a moralistic and anthropomorphic conception of the ultimate with a conception of the way as a spontaneous process.

Many passages explicitly reject a heaven-centered cosmos. The most important passage is chapter 25:

There is a shape that took form in the undifferentiated, generated before heaven and earth.
Soundless, shapeless, standing alone, unaltered, it can be considered the mother of the world.
Its name is unknown, but it is styled "*dào*"; if forced to make a name for it, one says "great."
Great is called [passing, passing] is called distant, distant is called return.
Heaven is great, earth is great, *dào* is great, the king also is great.
In the state there are four greats, and the king occupies one of them.

People follow earth, earth follows heaven, heaven follows *dào*, *dào* follows what is so of itself. (A: 21–23)[2]

"*Dào*" is here given as a tentative name for the ultimate origin, which existed before heaven and earth. The final lines explicitly subordinate heaven to *dào*—heaven follows *dào* as its model or law (*fǎ* 法). Chapter 32 says that heaven and earth do not dare make *dào* into their subordinates (天地弗敢臣) (A: 18). Six passages explicitly subordinate *tiān* to something higher, as chapter 6 says the "valley spirit" is the root of heaven and earth, or chapter 39 says that heaven is able to remain clear and earth is able to remain stable only because they attain oneness, or "the one."[3]

Tiān is further displaced in being paired with earth (*dì* 地) (5, 25, 32). While heaven is still given priority, only heaven-and-earth (sky-and-land) together constitute the world as a whole. Of the first 66 chapters of the received text of the *Lǎozǐ*, only three mention heaven without pairing it with earth or subordinating it to *dào* (9, 47, 59).[4] Many passages are concerned with the ultimate source of things, often but not always labeled *dào*. These passages either leave out *tiān* entirely or else present *tiān* as a secondary product of something more fundamental. For example, chapter 51 explains the origin of the myriad things: "*Dào* generates them, *dé* 德 (virtue/potency) raises them, things form them, and utensils complete them." For this reason, the myriad things spontaneously honor *dào* and *dé*. Heaven does not appear at all in the passage.

The most striking passage opposing an anthropomorphic conception of heaven is chapter 5, which begins:

Heaven and earth are not benevolent, they take the myriad things as straw dogs.
Sagely people are not benevolent, they take the people as straw dogs.

The term translated here as "benevolent," *rén* 仁, was one the most central ethical concepts in early China and it was a key virtue for both the Confucians (Ru) and the Mohists. The point in this passage is not that heaven and earth are actively bad but that they are amoral and unbiased, simply letting the spontaneity of nature continue.

In this passage, though, it is not just that heaven and earth are not benevolent: sages also are not benevolent. The *Lǎozǐ* goes beyond just giving up the idea of a conscious being that guides the universe. It also questions the underlying view of actions based on absolute standards enforced through rewards and punishments.

The *Lǎozǐ* also criticizes moralizing and moral categories. For example, chapter 2 says:

> When all the world knows beauty as beauty, this
>   is already repulsive.
> When they all know good, this is its already not
>   being good. (A: 15)

Chapter 20 says that the beautiful and the ugly are not far apart (B: 4). The point is that once people have to strive for the good as a conscious ideal, that is already bad. Other passages present moralizing as damaging. So chapter 18 says:

> Thus when the great *dào* is abandoned, then
>   there is benevolence and rightness.
> When the six relations are not in harmony, then
>   there is filial piety and kindness.
> When the state is in chaos, then there are
>   correct ministers. (C: 1–3)

As seen in chapter 5, this rejection of moralizing in favor of spontaneity and non-coercion has parallels on the metaphysical level in the rejection of *tiān* in favor of *dào*.

The skepticism of normative categories is closely connected to an awareness of the limits of human language. The critique of language is grounded most of all in the impossibility of naming the indefinite generative power of nature, tentatively called *dào*. The difficulty of naming *dào* has already been seen in chapter 25 above. Chapter 32 links this to the problem of naming in general:

> *Dào* is constantly without name. Although in its
>   unhewn simplicity it is minute, heaven and earth
>   do not dare subordinate it.[5] If princes and kings
>   can preserve it, the ten thousand things will make
>   themselves guests.
> Heaven and earth will combine together to bring
>   down sweet dew, and the people, without being
>   commanded, will distribute it evenly on their own.
> In beginning regulations one has names; once
>   names are had one must still know where to stop.
>   Knowing where to stop is that by which there is
>   no disaster.
> *Dào* in relation to the world is like the rivers
>   and oceans in relation to small streams. (A: 18–20)

Concerns with the fundamental adequacy of language run throughout the rest of the *Lǎozǐ*, appearing in ten chapters.[6]

Dào can be seen as good in that it generates and nurtures life, but its indeterminacy and lack of concrete form make it impossible to derive absolute moral rules. Unsurprisingly, in chapter 17 the discussion of punishments offers a criticism aimed at governments that rely on power or fear:

> The greatest in being a ruler is those below
>   knowing he exists.
> The next is them cherishing and praising him.
> The next is them fearing him.
> The next is them reviling him. (C: 17)

Using awe or fear (*wèi* 畏) is admitted as a way of governing, but it is the third best, which is to say, second to worst. In contrast to a heaven that is exclusively with the good, chapter 62 says of the *dào*:

> Dào is the leader of the ten thousand things,
>   the treasure of good people,
>   and what people who are not good protect.

It then concludes:

> Why did the ancients honor this *dào*?
> Isn't it said that:
>   with it, those who seek attain,
>   with it, those who are guilty avoid trouble!
> Thus it is honored by the world.

The fact that the *dào* protects both the good and the bad naturally shapes human attitudes toward justice. Thus chapter 49 says that sagely people are good to those who are good *and* good to those who are not good.

It is not that the *Lǎozǐ* gives no guidance for how to act or that it would see all actions as equally good. This is best seen in chapter 19:

> Cut off wisdom and abandon arguments and the
>   people will benefit a hundredfold.
> Cut off craftiness and abandon benefit and
>   thieves and robbers will not be had.
> Cut off striving and abandon deliberation and
>   the people will return to being like children.
> If these three are considered insufficient
>   for managing, you might make them have
>   something on which to rely:
>   Manifest plainness and embrace the unhewn;
>   Reduce selfish concerns and make
>   desires few. (A: 1–2)

In this passage, explicit goals and norms are harmful because they lead to disruptive and artificial behavior. The recommended way has two sides. On the one side, the *Lǎozǐ* focuses on internal cultivation, employing a set of terms connected to a properly cultivated state of mind: knowing satisfaction, stillness or quietude, emptiness, and unhewn simplicity. Roughly one quarter of chapters 1–66 can be plausibly connected to concerns about cultivating the right state of mind. Fundamental to this self-cultivation is the reduction or elimination of desires. Chapter 19 says that one should reduce desires (*yù* 欲) (19/A: 2), and chapter 46 says that the greatest disaster is having deep desires. On the other side, one should harmonize with *dào* by minimizing interference and coercion. This way of acting is called *wúwéi* 無為, non-action. These two sides are interdependent: we can only engage in non-action when we have freed ourselves of selfish desires.

The philosophy of the *Lǎozǐ* chapters 67–81. The view given in the previous section is the standard interpretation of the *Lǎozǐ* as a whole, but one finds other views in the text as well. The final fifteen chapters in particular seem to offer a different view of the divine. None of these chapters were found in the Guodian bamboo strips, suggesting they may have come from a different source. The most consistent and fundamental difference between these final fifteen chapters and the materials in the rest of the *Lǎozǐ* is the role of heaven. Heaven is central in six of the fifteen passages. We can begin with chapter 73:

> Those brave in daring are killed;
> Those brave in not daring live.
> Of these two, some benefit and some are harmed.
> What heaven hates—who knows its reason?
> The way of heaven is
>   to not go to battle but be good at conquering,
>   to not speak but be good at responding,
>   to not summon but have things come
>   of themselves,
>   to be at ease but good at plotting.
> Heaven's net is cast far and wide, loose-meshed
>   but losing nothing.

While there are some difficulties in interpreting this passage, the initial and final lines emphasize the way in which our own actions determine results. The middle line, on what heaven hates, is more difficult to interpret, but it must be that heaven hates being brave in daring. The passage presents heaven in anthropomorphic terms, linking what heaven *hates*, *wù* 惡, to enforcing correct actions through punishments.

Heaven's supportive role appears in chapter 67, which lays out the three treasures (*sānbǎo* 三寶)— "nurturing care" (*cí* 慈), "frugality" (*jiǎn* 儉), and "not daring to be first"—and then claims that these treasures always bring success. That might be hardest to justify in relation to nurturing care, so the passage ends with heaven's intervention:

> Now, with nurturing care,
>   if they go to battle, they are victorious;
>   if they undertake protective measures,
>   they are secure.
> Heaven will establish them, as if using nurturing
>   care to fortify them.

The claim that heaven recognizes those who have care and assists them implies awareness, deliberateness, and judgment. Other passages fill in more information about what heaven supports. The final lines of chapter 81 use the term benefit, *lì* 利, saying that the way of heaven is "to benefit and not harm"; benefit appears also in chapter 73, quoted above. Chapter 79 adds that heaven supports the good impartially, with no familial attachments or biases (*wúqīn* 无親). The fact that good people are singled out implies that bad people do not get the same treatment, something equally implicit in the claim above that heaven supports those with nurturing care. This impartiality appears in a different way as the theme of chapter 77, which says:

> The way of heaven is like pulling a bow:
>   what is high it restrains, what is low it lifts up;

> what has extra it reduces, what is lacking it aids.
> Thus the way of heaven is to reduce what has
>   extra and increase what is lacking.

The passage then contrasts the way of heaven with the way of human beings, who take from those with little in order to give to those who already have a surplus.

The final appeal to heaven in these chapters also concerns aligning with heaven, as stated in chapter 68:

> Thus:
>   those good at being commanders do not fight,
>   those good in battle do not get angry,
>   those good at conquering enemies do not
>   meet them,
>   those good at making use of people put
>   themselves below them.
> This refers to the virtue [*dé* 德] of not contending.
> This refers to making use of people.
> This refers to pairing with heaven, the ultimate of
>   the ancients.

Heaven is described as the ultimate (*jí* 極) of the ancients, and one is told to pair with or match (*pèi* 配) heaven.[7] This leads to success by avoiding conflict.

Taken together, the six chapters 67, 68, 73, 77, 79, and 81 present a clear and coherent view. Heaven is the ultimate guide and force. It has awareness and enforces its values. It benefits without harming, it distributes things equally, and it impartially rewards the good. It does these, though, without contention or struggle. Such a view appears explicitly in just over a third of the last fifteen chapters, and *dào* as an element of the cosmos plays no role in any of those fifteen chapters. Aside from the one passage quoted above that mentions *dào* as a way of acting, the character *dào* appears only as subordinated to *tiān* in the phrases *tiāndào* or *tiānzhīdào*, or to human beings in the phrase *rénzhīdào*. Similarly, there is no mention of emptiness or non-being. In fact, there is absolutely no mention of anything higher than heaven in any of the last fifteen chapters.[8]

As we have seen, the belief in a divine being that rewards and punishes requires that there be clear categories of right and wrong. Normative categories go unquestioned in the last fifteen chapters, which also have no critical discussions of morality. Without a conception of the *dào* as an unnamable generative force, it follows that the last fifteen chapters would also lack the worry about the adequacy of language. One line criticizes fine words (81), and another says that correct words seem like the reverse (78). The latter phrase comments on the claim that what makes a great ruler is the opposite of what one would expect—taking on insults and ill-omens. Chapter 73 says that the way of heaven is to not speak yet be good at responding, but that claim appears in a list of phrases describing achieving results with little effort. While the latter views are shared with the rest of the *Lǎozǐ*, they do not imply a concern with the fundamental adequacy of language. The last fifteen chapters even affirm the use of punishments. The strongest statement advocating the use of punishments is in chapter 74:

> If the people are constant in not fearing death, how can one use killing to frighten them?
> If the people are constant in fearing death, and I then take and kill those who act wrongly, who will dare?
> If the people must be constant in fearing death, then there is a regular executioner.
> Now, to kill in place of the executioner is to cut in the place of the master carpenter.
> Now, few who cut in place of the master carpenter avoid harming their hands.

One can use the threat of death to keep people from engaging in aberrant behavior, but only if the people fear death. Chapter 72 makes the same point: "If the people do not fear terrible might, then something more terrible will appear." Chapter 80 explains how a ruler can get the people to take death seriously by keeping their lives simple but pleasant. Chapter 75 explains why the people would instead take death lightly: if those above take so much that the people are left starving, then the people will take death lightly.

The last point to note is that while the last fifteen chapters advocate certain virtues and ways of acting, they show no concern with internal cultivation. They do not mention knowing satisfaction, stillness, emptiness, or simplicity and they never discuss reducing or controlling desires. If there is a core set of values in the last chapters of the *Lǎozǐ*, it would be the "three treasures" that are explained in chapter 67 and referred to again in chapter 69. They are presented as involving action in the world and as having the support of heaven. There is no evidence of these values as a set anywhere else in the *Lǎozǐ*, and of the three, only "not daring to be first" can be taken as a central theme in the *Lǎozǐ* as a whole. It is not just that the "three treasures" are ignored. While they are consistent with the rest of the text, no one would pick them out as a summary of its values. A much better summary would be the concluding lines we have seen from chapter 19:

> Manifest plainness and embrace the unhewn;
> Reduce selfish concerns and make desires few.
> (A: 2)

Ultimately, it seems that the final chapters and the rest of the *Lǎozǐ* work on different sets of values. The three treasures represent values for interacting with the world, while the rest of the text focuses more on values of internal cultivation.

Commonalities across the *Lǎozǐ*. So far, my goal has been to show that the last fifteen chapters present a set of positions that differs significantly from and even contradicts the viewpoint of the remainder of the

Lǎozǐ. There are, of course, significant points of overlap as well, which explains why these materials might have ultimately ended up forming one text. Even within these commonalities, though, one finds differences in emphasis. One of the most prominent themes in the final chapters is the problem of war. We have already seen chapter 68, which advocates avoiding war but implies that sometimes war is inevitable, in which case it should be done without anger and by avoiding direct confrontation. The subsequent chapter deals with strategy, saying that one should play the host rather than the guest. It adds that if battle is necessary, the one who does it with mournful sorrow (āi 哀) will be victorious (69). Chapter 67 says that one with nurturing care will win in battle. These passages are quite close to others in the *Lǎozǐ*, particularly chapter 31, which says that weapons of war are ill omens and that one should mourn (āibēi 哀悲) even in victory (C: 10). Chapter 30 (A: 6–7) also provides an explicit criticism of war.[9]

A second central concern is a critique of the oppression of the people. Chapter 75 is most explicit:

> That people are hungry is because those [above]
> consume too much in taxes. Thus they are hungry.
> That the common people are not well ordered is
> because those above act for a purpose.
> Thus they are not well ordered.
> That the people take death lightly is because
> those [above] seek to live so richly. Thus they
> take death lightly.
> Now, just having no actions for the sake of life—this
> is more worthy than esteeming life.

We have already seen chapter 77, which says that human beings take from those who do not have enough and give to those who have extra, which is contrary to the way of heaven. Chapter 72 says simply "do not constrict the places in which they dwell, do not oppress that by which they live." Chapter 79 portrays the people as indebted to those who lead them, but says that sagely people never collect on this debt. This approach is better than causing resentment and then trying to ease it. In the first 66 chapters of *Lǎozǐ*, a few passages present the sagely king as taking care of the people (3, 9), and two warn that accumulating too much will bring harm on oneself (9, 44), but only one chapter explicitly criticizes inequality and the oppression of the people (53).

While opposition to war and to inequality and oppression aligns with the rest of the *Lǎozǐ*, these concerns are more explicit and more central in the last fifteen chapters than in the text as a whole—one third of the last fifteen chapters discuss war, compared to only 6 per cent of chapters 1–66; criticisms of oppression appear in 27 per cent of the last fifteen chapters, but in 2 per cent of chapters 1–66. This suggests that the last chapters may be more concretely concerned with alleviating the suffering of the common people and are perhaps more activist in orientation. That difference would fit with the different emphasis in values as well, between those relating to action in the world rather than internal cultivation.

The most distinctive point of overlap between the last fifteen chapters and the rest of the *Lǎozǐ* can be generalized under the third "treasure" of chapter 67: not daring to go first. One theme of the last fifteen chapters is the power of softness and yielding. Chapter 76 puts the point directly, saying that the soft and weak are followers of life while the hard and strong are followers of death. Chapters 66 and 32 use the same metaphor of water in positive ways. Chapter 78 begins by saying that water is the softest but for that reason also most able to conquer what is hard and strong. Chapters 68 and 69 apply the power of non-contention to military strategy, and chapter 81 ends by saying that sagely people act but do not contend. Chapter 68 calls this "the virtue of not contending" (*bùzhēng zhī dé* 不爭之德). Similar language appears in chapter 66, which concludes, "it is by their not contending that none in the world are able to contend with them."

This focus on yielding connects to claims that one is benefitted by not seeking benefit. Consider the middle lines of the final chapter 81:

The good do not have much;
Those who have much are not good.
Sagely people do not accumulate —
    in being for other people, they themselves gain;
    in giving to other people, they themselves have more.

The paradox in this passage is that although sagely people do not seek their own interest, they are benefitted. Similar claims are made throughout the *Lǎozǐ*, most clearly in chapter 66. This criticism of seeking one's own benefit is coupled with another of the most central themes of the final chapters, which is opposition to making oneself too prominent. Such concerns appear in six of the fifteen chapters (67, 68, 70, 72, 77, 78). In most cases, this is an extension of the previous point— seeking fame and honor is just another form of selfishness. For example, chapter 72 concludes:

Thus sagely people—
    know themselves but do not show themselves,
    care for themselves but do not value themselves.

Chapter 77 says directly that sagely people do not desire to be seen as worthies. Such comments help explain the third treasure, not daring to go first.

In the context of the whole *Lǎozǐ*, we naturally take such statements as manifestations of *wúwéi* 無爲 (non-action), expressing a view of *dào* as spontaneously supportive of human life. The final chapters certainly share an appreciation of softness and yielding, a concern that does seem to be distinctive of the *Lǎozǐ*. It is striking, though, that they never use the term *wúwéi*. In fact, two chapters advocate action (*wéi*): chapter 81 says the way of human beings is to act but not struggle; chapter 77 says sagely people act but do not possess.

Similarly, none of the last fifteen chapters mention spontaneity, *zìrán*.

Interpreting the *Lǎozǐ*. The claim that the *Lǎozǐ* is a heterogeneous collection of materials is not new.[10] The analysis of the final fifteen chapters shows, though, not just that the *Lǎozǐ* includes different perspectives but that it reflects internal disagreements, bringing together different positions in a shared debate. This shifts the import of many passages; for example, the demotion of heaven in earlier passages may not be directed against other groups like the Mohists, but may rather reflect internal debates within the *Lǎozǐ* itself. On a broader level, the principle of charity may lead us to read the *Lǎozǐ* with the question of how to interpret this passage to make it fit with the rest of the text. This attempt to read the *Lǎozǐ* as a coherent whole skews our readings of particular passages, something best seen in the fact that the differences between the last fifteen chapters and the Guodian materials have gone almost entirely unnoticed. Instead of just looking for consistency, we should also read with the question of whether or not the differences between these passages express different positions on a common issue. While I have attempted to apply such an approach to the relationship between chapters 67–81 and the rest of the *Lǎozǐ*, this should not be taken to imply that either the Guodian materials or the first 66 chapters represent one coherent viewpoint. Rather, this particular contrast should encourage us to look for others.

The contrast drawn here has particularly significant consequences for how we understand the split between what is commonly called "philosophical" and "religious" Daoism. If the *Lǎozǐ* incorporated two different views of the ultimate—one an anthropomorphic divine heaven and the other a spontaneously generative *dào*—then both approaches can be taken as right (for one part of the text) and wrong (for the other part). Consider the obvious incompatibility between the start of chapter 5 and the end of chapter 67:

> Heaven and earth are not benevolent, they take the myriad things as straw dogs.
> Sagely people are not benevolent, they take the people as straw dogs. (5)

But in chapter 67 heaven operates with nurturing care:

> if they go to battle, they are victorious;
> if they undertake protective measures, they are secure.
> Heaven will establish them, as if using nurturing care to fortify them. (67)

Neither statement is ambiguous, creating a problem for anyone who wants to read them as consistent. If we take chapter 67 more seriously, we are led to something like the explanation of chapter 5 found in the *Xiǎng'ěr* 想爾 commentary:

> Heaven and earth imitate *dào*, being benevolent to those who are good and not benevolent to those who are evil. Thus when they destroy the myriad things, it is the evil that they do not care for, seeing them like straw and grass or dogs and livestock. [. . .] Sagely people model themselves after heaven and earth, being benevolent to good people and not benevolent to evil people. When kings govern and destroy evil, they also see it like straw and dogs.[11] Thus people should accumulate good deeds, and then their refined essence and spirit will commune with heaven. If someone wants to bully and harm them, then heaven will save them.[12]

We might at first be astonished that anyone could interpret the passage in a way that so clearly contradicts the surface meaning. The final line of the commentary, though, refers specifically to chapter 67 (which in the received versions uses *jiù* 救, "to save," rather than *jiàn* 建, "to establish"). If heaven really is always with the good, it is difficult to read chapter 5 in any other way.

As we would expect, "philosophical" readings run into the same problem in reverse. They easily explain chapter 5 but struggle with many of the last fifteen chapters. The difficulty is often obscured in translation, as Ames and Hall translate the lines from chapter 67 as "When nature sets anything up, it is as if it fortifies it with a wall of compassion."[13] Chén Gǔyìng translates the phrase "match heaven" (*pèitiān*) into modern Chinese as "this is called fitting with natural principles."[14] Michael LaFargue expresses a common view behind such readings:

> Traditional religious beliefs like this [appealing to heaven as a divine being] play no *central* role in the thought of Laoists (or that of most other contemporary *shih*, who in this respect resemble modern secular "intellectuals"). At times, some traditional ideas associated with Heaven are indirectly alluded to or invoked in the *Tao Te Ching*, but this is always to make some other point, not to teach some Laoist doctrines about Heaven. [. . .] The phrase "Heaven's Tao/Way" is a conventional designation of the "the right way," which Laoists sometimes use to describe the Laoist way.[15]

The evidence LaFargue gives is the obvious way in which the statements about heaven contradict earlier passages, citing the contradictions between chapter 5 and chapters 79 and 81 in particular. If one insists on a consistent reading, though, the contradictions can be used just as well to argue the opposite direction, taking the whole text as theistic. Ultimately, "philosophical" and "religious" readings of the *Lǎozǐ* appear to be equally legitimate, or equally illegitimate. I hope in this paper to have established another alternative, which is simply to recognize that the current *Lǎozǐ* combines together (at least) two distinct perspectives on the ultimate, one of which could be called more "religious," the other more "philosophical." Such an approach becomes available once we give up an *a priori* commitment to the unity of the text.[16]

Notes

1. Unless otherwise noted, quotations from the *Lǎozǐ* are based on the Mǎwángduī B manuscript, as published in Gāo Míng 高明, *Bóshū Lǎozǐ jiàozhù* 帛書老子校註 (Beijing: Zhonghua shuju, 1996). Where that manuscript has been damaged, I have followed Gāo Míng in placing the corresponding characters from the A manuscript in brackets. This particular line is damaged in the B manuscript, and I have followed the A version instead. Translations are my own, but I have regularly consulted the following others: Roger T. Ames and David L. Hall, *Laozi—Making This Life Significant—A Philosophical Translation* (New York: Ballantine Books, 2003); Robert G. Henricks, *Lao Tzu's Tao Te Ching: A Translation of the Startling New Documents Found at Guodian* (New York: Columbia UP, 2000); D.C. Lau, *Tao Te Ching: Translation of the Ma Wang Tui Manuscripts* (New York: Alfred A. Knopf, 1994); Hans-Georg Moeller, *Dao De Jing* (Chicago: Open Court, 2007); Moss Roberts, *Dao De Jing: The Book of the Way* (Berkeley: U of California P, 2001). I have inevitably incorporated some phrases from these translators.

2. For the Guodian manuscript, I have followed the text in Liú Xiàogǎn, *Lǎozǐ gǔjīn*, unless otherwise noted. Quotations are cited by the corresponding chapter number in the received text and by bundle (A, B, or C) and strip number. In this passage, I follow Henricks in reading *duó* 敓 as *jì* 寂, "silent" (Henricks, *Lao Tzu's Tao Te Ching*, 208 n. 41). The character in place of *shì* 逝 ("passing," "departing") in the Guodian manuscript is still undetermined. Rather than venture a guess, I have inserted *shì* 逝, which appears in the Mǎwángduī manuscripts and all versions of the received text. For discussions of the character, see Liú Xiàogǎn, *Lǎozǐ gǔjīn*, 286–87, and Henricks, *Lao Tzu's Tao Te Ching*, 56.

3. The six passages are 6, 16, 25, 32, 37, and 39. Four of those also appear in the Guodian materials (17, 25, 32, 37).

4. In addition, chapter 10 has the phrase "heavenly gates" (*tiānmén* 天門). The phrase "heavenly image" (*tiānxiàng* 天象) appears in both the Guodian and Mǎwángduī manuscripts in chapter 41, but that is changed to "great image" (*dàxiàng* 大象) in the various versions of the received text. The Guodian fragment of chapter 16 refers to the way of heaven (*tiāndào* 天道), but the various versions of the received text instead refer to things (*fúwù* 夫物). The Mǎwángduī manuscripts have the strange phrase "heavenly things" (*tiānwù* 天物), although it is possible that *tiān* should be taken there as *fú*.

5. The phrase translated as "do not dare subordinate it" literally says they do not dare make them into ministers or servants (*bùchén* 不臣). The Guodian text has "heaven and earth" (*tiāndì*) as the subject, but both

Mǎwángduī manuscripts and all received versions have "the world," *tiānxià* 天下. That changes the claim from one about cosmology (that heaven and earth are secondary to *dào*) to one about how human beings relate to *dào*.

6. See chapters 1, 2, 14, 23, 25, 32, 34, 37, 41, and 43. Of those, half appear also in Guodian (2, 25, 32, 37, 41).

7. *Pèi* appears in Mǎwángduī B, the Běidà *Lǎozǐ* (strip 90), and in all versions of the received text, but it is missing in Mǎwángduī A.

8. While an argument from silence can never be absolutely decisive, all of these points would represent significant statistical anomalies when compared with either the Guodian materials or the first 66 chapters as a whole.

9. Chapter 57 might also go in this category. Although it begins with advice for using troops (A: 29), it also says that the more sharp weapons there are, the more the state will be disordered (A: 30). Chapter 46 takes the breeding of warhorses as a sign of the world lacking the way. Those lines are missing in the Guodian version of the chapter.

10. D.C. Lau has one of the best statements of this view, claiming that the *Lǎozǐ* should be taken as "no more than a collection of passages with only a common tendency in thought" (Lau, *Lao Tzu Tao Te Ching*, 165). LaFargue refers to passages as "chapter-collages" (LaFargue, *Tao of the Tao Te Ching*, 198). For a more recent examination of how the *Lǎozǐ* incorporates heterogeneous materials, see Richter, "Der Alte und das Wasser."

11. I here follow the interpretation in Gù Bǎotián 顧寶田 and Zhāng Zhōnglì 張忠利, *Lǎozǐ Xiǎng'ěr zhù* 老子想爾注 (Taibei: Sanming shuju, 1997), 15. Stephen Bokenkamp translates the line differently: "When kingly governance turns to destruction and evil, [the Sage] also views the king as a straw dog" (Stephen R. Bokenkamp, *Early Daoist Scriptures* [Berkeley: U of California P, 1997], 82).

12. Gù and Zhāng, *Lǎozǐ Xiǎng'ěr zhù*, 13–14.

13. Ames and Hall, *Laozi—Making This Life Significant*, 183.

14. Chén Gǔyìng, *Lǎozǐ zhùyì jí píngjià*, 322. Similarly, Liú Xiàogǎn explains that in the *Lǎozǐ*, the way of heaven is close to the phenomena and rules of the natural world (*Lǎozǐ gǔjīn*, 726).

15. LaFargue, *Tao of the Tao Te Ching*, 229.

16. I am grateful to a number of people for helpful comments on earlier drafts of this essay: Esther Klein, Paul R. Goldin, So Jeong Park, Lisa Raphals, Robin R. Wang, Brook Ziporyn, and two anonymous reviewers.

Discussion

1. What are the meanings of *dào* in the first 66 chapters? What is the relation here of *tian* to *dào*?

2. How is *tian* conceived in chapters 67–81?

3. What are the differing views of the nature of value and humanity in the two different sections?

Chapter 32

Ritual, Religion, and Naturalism

XUNZI AS A RELIGIOUS PHILOSOPHER

EDWARD J. MACHLE*

Xunzi as religious critic. Xunzi, the great Confucian philosopher of the third century BCE, was a critic of religion. He subjected many religious currents of his time to philosophical criticism. Belief in ghosts, phrenology and similar superstitions, praying in order to cause rain, belief that natural calamities were divine punishments, and determining policies by the flights of birds all felt the edge of his attack. It is no wonder that he has commonly been pictured as a thorough-going secularist and enemy of religion, or, as sinologist Henry Rosemont puts it, an "avowed atheist." [1]

By "religious philosopher" I mean a thinker whose philosophizing has some guiding religious motivation. He is a philosopher rather than a theologian, because he speaks for the "reasonable man" of his culture rather than for some particular worshipping community, but like the theologian, he seeks to make sense of the received religious tradition as a way of continuing to be part of it. For the former reason, he does not shrink from criticizing dearly held practices or beliefs: for the latter, he holds not a purely rational goal of pristine clarity in analysis or neat consistency in system-building, but one of edification of himself and others. [2]

Most contemporary interpretations deny that Xunzi was moved by religious concerns. Marxists claim him as a spokesman for the materialism implicit in the working man's outlook. The Chinese, impressed with the Western scientific outlook, have acclaimed his naturalism, and Western scholars have read his view of Nature as thoroughly secular. It is in connection with Xunzi that Liu Wu-chi remarks that "in the third century BCE the Chinese lost their spiritual soul"; [3] Fung Yu-lan maintains that Xunzi never rises above the merely moral and hence falls short of what he calls "the spiritual." [4]

C.K. Yang attributes this to a response to allegations of Chinese backwardness:

> In the twentieth century, when the dominance of Western influence brought contempt for superstition and magic as the very sign of national backwardness, a new generation of Chinese scholars came forth to defend the dignity of Chinese civilization not only by stressing the rationalistic view of the Confucian doctrine but also by claiming that Confucian orthodoxy had helped develop China into a "rationalistic society" where there was neither a powerful priesthood nor protracted struggle between religion and the state. [5]

Such scholars, stressing the secular and rational character of Confucian thought, treat Xunzi as their antireligious and pro-scientific ally. Western sinologists, reading into Chinese cultural history Western

---

*   Edward J. Machle (d. 2011) was Professor of Philosophy and Religious Studies at the University of Colorado.

Enlightenment biases regarding the relationships of science, nature, reason, ritual, and religion, tended to go along with the trend.

Sima Qian, writing of Xunzi scarcely a century and a half after the philosopher's death, says nothing of his religious views but implies that he was against "attending to magic and prayers, and believing in omens and luck."[6] Since this is the only real biographical source we have regarding him, we cannot go much beyond the guess that his views on religion were not a lively topic of discussion in the second century BCE. While his texts were collected around 76 BCE, there is no study of his work for nine hundred years thereafter. The first serious study dates from Yang Liang in 818. We are thus left with the text itself, general background knowledge, and scholarship from a far later age.

The grounds for painting Xunzi as antireligious seem to be: (1) his criticisms of widespread beliefs as superstitious; (2) his apparent denial of the existence of spirits, particularly spirits of the dead; (3) his treatment of ritual as "mere ornament," which nevertheless had some educational function in molding men's emotional life; (4) his apparent denial of an anthropomorphic Heaven-deity; (5) his belief that man is evil by nature, implying that the Nature that gives man human nature is itself evil, or at best morally irrelevant; (6) his suggestions that nature may be technologically exploited rather than revered; and (7) his widespread, often dominating concern with matters political, economic, legal, and educational.

Whatever "Confucianism" has been down through the centuries, it has always been in some sense *religious* even when not a religion. To quote Yang again, "Modern students of China who maintain the purely rationalistic view of Confucianism are not able to explain away the religious aspects of the doctrine without distorting the meaning of the original texts."[7] Discussion of the preceding seven points revolves around relatively few loci in the *Xunzi* corpus, often without relating them to contrary evidence. The chief issue is whether they are to be given an interpretation which then controls our reading of the entire corpus, or whether they are to be considered as a few items among many, all needing mutual interpretation.

Undermining the received view. The task of reexamining the established position has two steps: we must show both that the received view is without adequate foundation and that there is a viable alternative to it. The former requires analysis of the grounds for the received view, an analysis that itself provides the basis for calling it into question. Only if the received view is shaken can the presentation of an alternative be a serious gesture. Fortunately, attacking one view often suggests, of itself, an alternative.

We pointed out the seven points upon which the idea that Xunzi was antireligious, or at least irreligious, rests. One of these, his absorption with political, economic, legal, and educational matters, can be set aside quite simply, since religious leaders from Moses to Martin Luther King, Jr., have shown their most extensive concerns often to be such matters. Such interests do not of themselves count for or against the existence of such an orientation. Appeal to Xunzi's "scientific" interest is based on an unfortunate collocation of misreadings and Western scientific biases. A psychological account of ritual, when speaking of ritual in nonritual contexts, would be reductionistic only if his psychology were reductionistic. Likewise, his view of man's natural or innate evil may be a religious opposition to Mencius, who held that humans are by nature good, rather than an opposition to religion.

We are thus left with two areas in support of a nonreligious interpretation of Xunzi: his critiques of superstition (including belief in spirits) and his "naturalistic" view of nature. We take these up in order.

Xunzi's critique of superstition. When we turn to his criticisms of superstition, we find two quite different sorts of cases. In the one, there is no disagreement as to what he is attacking, or how, or why. He overthrows physiognomy and related fortune-tellings, for instance, by amassing counterexample after counterexample to show their untenability. His reason for attacking them is not scientific, but moral and practical, since evaluating men by their appearance cannot conduce to a moral, and hence, responsible and successful administration. As he puts it,

> to physiognomize a person's appearance is not as good as to consider his heart; considering his heart is not as good as to select his principles.... When a person's principles are upright and his heart obeys them, although his physiognomy be repulsive, yet if his heart and principles are good, his physiognomy will not hinder him from being a superior man. (Dubs 67, *Xunzi* K 5.1, 5/17/11–13)[8]

Physiognomy is not merely empirically false, it usurps the place of proper moral evaluation.

Such moral criticism of superstition, of course, is not of itself irreligious; it can as easily reflect a critical but deeply religious mind.

What about praying for rain? Consider the following celebrated passage:

> When we sacrifice for rain, it rains. Why? I say, there is nothing to ask "why?" about. It rains even though we don't sacrifice.... This isn't something to be regarded from the point of view of obtaining something we seek, but from a cultured standpoint. Consequently, although the gentleman looks on it as a matter of humane culture, the lower gentry see it as a matter of dealing with spirits. Regard it as a matter of humane culture and good fortune follows; regard it as a matter of dealings with spirits and misfortune follows.

Though this passage is often cited as evidence that Xunzi denied the existence of spirits, that is certainly not what he is doing. The matter of belief that he concerns himself with is belief in the efficacy of rituals to effect some change in events *independent* of their place in the total lives and development of the people involved. It is the business of men to deal with nature only according to 禮 *li*—that is, only through the proper development of their characters and institutions, two things intimately connected in his view. It pertains to man to be related to Heaven wholesale, not piecemeal; as a human world focused in the equality with Heaven that characterizes the Sage. Anything else is counterproductive, and produces just those unfortunate consequences that the vulgar view ritual as the means to avoid.

Compare the passage just quoted with another well-known one.

> A man, having contracted a chill from the dampness, proceeds to beat a drum and make offering of a pig in hopes of effecting a cure. He wears out the drum and loses a pig in the process, that is certain, but no blessing of recovery follows as a result. (*Xunzi* 135, K 21.8, 21/106/15–16)

Both passages deny the physical efficacy of rituals. The first, however, deals with rituals that Xunzi *approves*, rituals which add to the enrichment of communal human life. Such rituals produce in his eyes no ill effects *as rituals*, whatever materials they consume. Ill effects come not from their celebration, but from the expectation of a particular effect, which encourages confusion regarding the proper separation of what is human and what is Heaven.

In the second case, however, two evil results are presented as accruing: ineffectiveness and the waste of the ritual materials. Apparently the folk ritual for illness cannot have the humanizing effect that a prayer for rain may have. One may suspect that Xunzi distinguishes two sorts of rituals; rituals which are not part of *li*, but merely of folklore, are superstitious; rituals which are part of *li* are a proper part of the *Dao* of man, though not to be considered part of the *Dao* of Heaven.

It is worth noting that the example of the man with the chill occurs in a context arguing that men's judgments are unreliable when swayed by emotion. The story is preceded by, and explicitly associated with, the following tale:

> There was a man . . . who lived south of Xiashou. . . . One night he was walking in the moonlight when, glancing down and seeing his shadow, he took it for a crouching ghost. Looking up, he caught sight of his own hair and took it for a devil standing over him. He whirled around and starting running, and when he reached his home he fell unconscious and died. Is this not sad? Always when people see ghosts, it is at times when they are aroused and excited, and they make their judgments in moments when their faculties are confused and blinded. (*Xunzi* 134–35, K 21.8, 21/106/12–14)

Apparently, were the first man well, he would know better than to believe that a drum-and-pig ritual would cure a chill. Sick, he confuses what is of man and what is of Heaven, and so makes a fool of himself. The point being made is that people's judgments, even their perceptions, are impaired when they are emotionally upset. To make this point Xunzi must take for granted that his readers will already agree that claims to have seen ghosts are questionable, and that he needn't bother to establish their dubitability. He is not arguing the falsity of the superstitions; he is using an already established belief in their falsity to make another point. Evidently the process that Mozi objected to so much earlier, that men were giving up their belief in ghosts that punish, had proceeded a long way before

Xunzi's time. What this shows us is that however else Confucianism in his day was still religious, it did not find need for belief in retributive spirits. Nor did it have to. It is already quite clear in Mencius that the good man does right because it is right, and no other reason; Mozi's need for belief in such spirits was already undercut.

If this be sound interpretation, we do not find Xunzi actively denying that spirits exist. Instead, he accepts what appear to be widespread doubts regarding the 鬼 *gui*, the dark, disorderly and at times hungry and vengeful spooks. Here, however, the expectation that his readers share these doubts simply shows he took his place within an already existing tradition of doubt. Similarly, the word for the magical powers of diviners and spooks—靈 *ling*—occurs in his writings only in proper names, in noticeable contrast to the *Laozi* and the *Zhuangzi*. In this, however, he simply agrees with both Confucius and Mencius, and apparently stands well within their tradition.

Xunzi on spirits. What then did Xunzi maintain regarding spirits? A proper place to begin the discussion of the place of spirits within Confucianism is with the famous remark of Confucius in the *Analects* 6:20, "To respect spiritual beings (鬼神 *guishen*), maintaining a proper distance in one's relations with them, may be called wisdom." "Maintaining a proper distance" is a question of *li*, of ritual or propriety. Xunzi here clearly follows his master's example, although probably going beyond it in holding that the expectation of particular results does not accord with *li* and brings about misfortune. Both men would surely hold that truly following *li* brings about only good.

A further note may be sounded. Confucius uses the phrase *guishen*, "spooks and spirits" or "*yin*-spirits and *yang*-spirits" to stand for the whole realm of spiritual powers under Heaven. *Gui* and *shen* are never associated in the *Xunzi*, or for that matter in the *Mengzi* or the *Great Learning* (*Daxue* 大學). Distinction between them is most striking in the *Xunzi*, where *shen* is used nearly forty times, but *gui*, outside of quotations, only four times. Moreover, these four times are all of them highly pejorative in tone, while *shen* appears in contexts of the very highest approval.

It is understandable that the pejorative passages speaking of *gui* are widely quoted to show the sage's rejection of both *shen* and *gui*. But although *shen* may perhaps include both *gui* and *shen*, I know of no instance where *gui* embraces both. We may conclude that Xunzi's opposition to superstitions involving *gui* is not so easily extended to beliefs and practices involving *shen* as many have taken it to be.

An instance of this occurs in his treatment of funeral rites. Contrasting high culture with lack of sophistication, he says,

> The sage understands them, the gentleman finds comfort in carrying them out, the officials are careful to maintain them, and the common people accept them as custom. To the gentleman they are a part of the way (道 *Dao*) of man, to the common people they are something pertaining to the spirits (*gui*), (literally, "ghost-serving"). (*Xunzi* 110, K 19.11, 19/98/2–3)

When he is speaking seriously about the meaning of the rites, however, he says,

> At the internment one reverently lays his form away; at the sacrifices one reverently serves his spirit (*shen*); and by means of inscriptions, eulogies, and genealogical records one reverently hands down his name to posterity. (*Xunzi* 105, K 19.7b, 19/5/17–18)

This sounds as if ordinary folk are superstitious, and think of the rituals as a serving of the *gui* (鬼事 *guishi*), while the sophisticated gentleman speaks of serving (worshipping, or acknowledging) the *shen* of the departed (事神 *shishen*) as part of the true *Dao* of man.

We have a problem, however. In the funeral rites, it is part of man's *Dao* to serve the *shen*, but it is superstition to think one is serving *gui*. In the case of sacrifices for rain, it is superstition to think one is serving *shen*, for the gentleman knows such rites are rather a matter of 文 *wen*, or humane culture. What is one to make of this?

It might be answered: the essay on ritual was written earlier than the one on Heaven, and the author's thought developed in the interim. From viewing only *gui*-ritual as superstitious, he moved to viewing all reference to spirits as superstitious. This would be a solution, right enough, but a purely fiat one. There is no way to establish which essay was written first. Regarding the dates of composition, about all we can say is that the somewhat pejorative reference to the king Chu in the essay on Heaven was probably written while Xunzi was not a resident of Chu. That indicates nothing of the relative priority of the essays. In the absence of a firm chronology of Xunzi's writings, theories about his intellectual development can only be projections of our own assumptions.

The most promising resolution would seem to be this. Funeral rituals deal with the alteration of a close personal relationship, already defined within the rules of propriety. For whatever analogy there may be between one's relation to a loved-one living and the same loved-one dead, there is also a profound difference. Xunzi's whole approach calls attention to the passing from one to the other. The relation to the living is defined by the 孝 *xiao* of family life, that to the dead, in terms of honoring and reporting to the *shen* of one's ancestor, presenting him no more in the flesh, but as resident in the ancestral tablet. Truly humane living requires not only that this transition be lived through, but that it be lived through expressively. The psychology of such living-through can be described, and

Xunzi's essays do that. But effectively to produce the described results, the ritual, and its ritual references, must be *believed in*. Otherwise, one cannot be sincere about the whole transaction, and for Xunzi, as for any Confucian, sincerity is fundamental.

In the case of prayers for rain, or other rituals directed toward nature, there is no such alteration of the relationship involved. The relation of man to Heaven is constant. Xunzi takes for granted that this constancy can be expressed and celebrated in ritual ways. He never criticizes the imperial rites addressed to Heaven and the royal ancestors, or the feudal nobles' sacrifices to the gods of the soil. Prayers for rain, however, are another thing altogether: particular desires and aims intrude into that relationship. This would constitute an imposition upon the powers of nature, an attempt by man to interfere in what belongs to Heaven. Man's place in dealing with drought, Xunzi makes clear, is to so administer his own affairs that he has sustenance enough no matter what Heaven in its mysterious ways sends down.

This also has its reverse side. For coping with drought, there are appropriate administrative technologies, and it is the task of the educated official to acquaint himself with those and to develop sound judgment in applying them. To do anything less is to violate the *Dao* of man, seeking shortcuts that do not fulfill the pattern of *li*. It is this pattern of *li* which constitutes the highest possibility of man's relation to the cosmos, the achievement of a harmonious triad with Heaven and Earth. To depart from it is to regress, to violate it is to cause confusion, to substitute private or local ends for it is obscene.

The outcome is, then, that serving the spirit of the dead has a humane function—it embodies the cosmic *li* in the particular human life. Its ultimate ritual function is to bring the fact of a particular death into the cosmic wholeness. As such, it is a part of *wen*: whatever else it may do is irrelevant. Hence it can be done with that wholehearted seriousness called 敬 *jing*

"reverence." Prayers for rain cannot be so done, for they are, as it were, prayers against wholeness. They refuse to accept the drought Heaven has sent. Xunzi mentions three times those who are "resentful of Heaven," and in chapter 4 says, "He who understands himself is not resentful of men; he who understands the decrees (命 *ming*) is not resentful of Heaven." Lack of rain is not something that lies with man, only with Heaven; he who cannot accept it does not really understand the decrees. This is a mark of the "petty man," the man who is lacking in proper intention.

In saying this, have we done more than to apply to Xunzi's scene Malinowski's distinction between magic and religion? The noted anthropologist writes,

> This difference will serve us as a *prima facie*
> distinction between magic and religion. While
> in the magical act the underlying idea and aim
> is always clear, straightforward, and definite,
> in the religious ceremony there is not purpose
> directed toward a subsequent event.... The
> native can always state the end of the magical
> rite, but he will say of the religious ceremony
> that it is done because such is the usage,
> or because it has been ordained, or he will
> narrate an explanatory myth.[9]

The common people "hope to accomplish something," for they see sacrifices as magic. The gentleman claims no specific efficacy for them, they are just "humane culture," a part of *li* or proper rituals. Although Xunzi discusses in chapter 19 the "historical antecedents" (禮之所起 *lizhi suoqi*) of *li*, their three roots, and their general functionings, he insists that their significance is cosmic, their meaning deep, great, and lofty, and only the Sage can understand them—language surely closer to religious myth than to secular explanation.

The opposition he maintains, then, is not one between sacrifices to *gui* and those to *shen*, but between sacrifices directed toward particular ends (which

Malinowski would call "magic"), and those which are simply part of the profound expressive whole he calls *li*, which is for him not merely the pattern of elegant behavior, but the ground of human organization and happiness and the key to man's place in the cosmos.

So much for the problem of sacrifice. What else does Xunzi say about spirits? Some uses of *shen* are revealing, though not definitive:

> There is no greater godliness (*shen*) than to transform yourself with the Way. (*Xunzi* 16, K 1.2, 1/1/9)

> There is nothing more godlike (*shen*) than to learn to love one thing alone. (*Xunzi* 26–27, K 2.4, 2/6/10)

> The life of a man of perfect sincerity is godlike (*shen*). (*Xunzi* K 14.3, 14/67/1)

> With sincere mind preserve 仁 *ren*, and it will become outwardly evident; outwardly evident, it will become a spiritual power (*shen*); being a spiritual power, it will have the ability to transform. (*Xunzi* K 3.9a, 3/11/5)

These suggest Xunzi had a sense of spirituality, one quite typically Confucian, stressing the possibilities of going even beyond *ren* to a transformed and transforming unity of some sort. Language about transformations and unities is seductive, and one ought to maintain a suitable diffidence toward giving it a specific content. Here we note its occurrence, and look further for more definitional statements.

Xunzi twice approaches definitions of *shen*. In one we read,

> The stars in their course make their rounds, the sun and moon shine in their turns . . . and the myriad things properly receive each its own nourishment so as to reach maturity. We see the efficacy of the entire process while not seeing its actual workings, and so we call it *shen*. Everyone knows the final outcomes, but no one knows the formless antecedents, and so we call it Heaven. (*Xunzi* 80, K 17.2b, 17/80/5–7)

Xunzi's phrase here, 之謂 *zhiwei*, is his usual definitional one. He is not saying, "Folks don't know what it is, so they read a ghost into nature"—though many interpreters, especially the Marxist ones, take him to do so. When he says *zhiwei* he is ordinarily giving a definition. He is saying, in effect, "Nature is properly called spiritual, since, though we see the effects, we don't see the workings; it is properly called Heaven, since, though we know the outcomes, we can't know the invisible causes." This is as close to a definition of "spirit" as a cosmic category as we can find.

In the other definitional statement, he is discussing rather the make-up of man, but of that perfectly developed man, the sage or "holy man" (聖人 *shengren*). Of him he says,

> This *Dao* of his proceeds from his unity. What do we mean by unity? The answer is: laying hold on *shen*, to be firmly established. What do we mean by *shen*? Exhausting goodness and cherishing orderliness is to be called *shen*. To be perfectly established is for there to be no thing in the world sufficient to subvert one. To be *shen* and firmly established is to be a sage. (*Xunzi* K 8.7, 8/31/3–5)

We may have here the outline of Xunzi's view of spirituality. The first quasi-definition given above indicates that in his eyes, spirit in the natural world is characterized by:

1. invisibility in its source or prime workings but productiveness of visible results.

2. the inclusion in these results of remarkable but orderly transformations into higher states of fulfillment.

So far, these characteristics would not go beyond his use of *shen* to mean man's biological life; they do not seem to limit him to merely that.

The second quasi-definition, dealing with spirit in human affairs, adds these further traits:

3. the power to transform morally both individuals and whole populations.

4. a character exhausting all goodness and supportive of true orderliness.

And associates closely with the idea of *shen* still another:

5. the presence of an ongoing unity that cannot be subverted by *things*.

It is apparently in reference to the first of these "definitions" that Chan says of Xunzi, "What he called spirit is but cosmic change and evolution"; it is in reference to the second that Watson speaks of his making *shen* "a quality of moral excellence." In what they affirm, these statements are true enough, but both carry a private element, the first, explicitly and the second, implicitly. Xun surely does call "cosmic change and evolution" *shen*, but clearly does not limit *shen* to that. He does make *shen* "a quality of moral experience," but how this relates to religious sensibilities is not readily apparent. Nor, for that matter, is it quickly settled that his "cosmic change and evolution" is devoid of more-than-secular or more-than-moral significance.

An interesting conclusion follows when we set the preceding five characteristics associated with *shen* alongside other general aspects of Xun's thought. For him, evil consists of disorder, and the primal flaw in man lies in his susceptibility to being turned toward disorder by *things*, as objects of desire or aversion. Since this flaw is characteristic of man *by nature*— but it is typical of the man who lays hold on *shen* that there is no *thing* that can subvert him—*shen* must be, in human affairs, the contrary to 性 *hsing*, or human nature. Since *shen* is in this sense contrary to nature, superior to it, and supervenient upon it, it would not be unjustifiable to call it "supernatural," even though it is not set over against Nature (in another sense). This possibility is in itself a challenge to much current interpretation of Xunzi's whole system of thought.

Xunzi's heaven. So far, he who denies a religious motif to Xunzi could still agree. Watson says of the philosopher's definition of human spirituality that it makes of *shen* "a quality of moral excellence,"[10] just as Fung Yu-lan says Xunzi "never rises above the merely moral."[11] The unity of nature and high culture, at least in the Chinese milieu, could be religious only if nature, that is, "Heaven," retains the transcendent dimensions it shows, in different ways, in Confucius, Mengzi, the *Zhongyong*, Mozi, and the Daoists. Or these cannot be maintained if nature is as desacralized in the *Xunzi* as the received interpretations claim. We can here only outline an argument to show that he may well have had more "natural piety" than he has been credited with.

Xunzi rejects "knowing Heaven" as a proper desire or pursuit of man, except for that "knowing" which consists of developing human potentialities to their fullest. He nowhere gives any clear enunciation of his view of Heaven; even his essay entitled "A Discussion of Heaven" turns out to be an extended exposition of the importance of distinguishing between Heaven's ways and man's ways and of largely excluding the former from our concern. I find it ironic that his resolute refusal to present a theology of Heaven has been turned by interpreters into a full-fledged antitheology. Thus Chinese philosophers affirm that Xunzi's "Heaven" "has no will nor consciousness,"[12] two denials I have been completely unable to find in his works.

Rather than make the futile move of arguing from what he does *not* say, let us note some aspects of his actual talk. In the first place, the received interpretation must treat many of his comments as rhetorical flourish. Consider the following:

1. Rites serve Heaven above and earth below. (*Xunzi* 91, K 19.2a, 19/90/21–22)

2. The Son of Heaven alone performs the suburban sacrifice to Heaven. . . . In this way rites distinguish and make clear that the exalted should serve the exalted. (*Xunzi* 91, K 19.2a, 19/91/2)

3. The very existence of Heaven and earth exemplifies the principle of the higher and lower. (*Xunzi* 36, K 9.3, 9/35/22)

4. The drum is surely the lord of music, is it not? Hence, it resembles Heaven. (*Xunzi* 118, K 20.4, 20/100/20–101/1)

5. The fate of a man lies with Heaven; the fate of the nation lies in ritual. (*Xunzi* K 16.1, 16/75/9, and 86, K 17.9, 17/82/12)

and perhaps

The Kings have Heaven for their first ancestor. (Dubs, 220, but compare the different interpretation in *Xunzi* 91, K 19.2a, 19/91/1)

It is significant that every one of these occurs in a context speaking of ritual, and it is here that Xunzi's heart lies. In fact he claims,

How can *li* not be considered wonderful! Through it Heaven and earth join in harmony, the sun and moon shine, the four seasons proceed in order, the stars and constellations march, the rivers flow, and all natural things flourish. (*Xunzi* 94, K 19.2c, 19/92/4–5)

The perfection of the cosmic *li* has its moral dimension, since it is reflected, in a distinctive human way, in the superior man, for

Heaven has its constant way, earth has its constant dimensions, the gentleman has his constant deportment. The gentleman follows what is constant. (*Xunzi* 82, K 17.5, 17/81/1)

That Heaven supplies a model for men to follow seems quite obvious to Xunzi, as could be shown from other passages.

Loci such as the preceding are frequently discounted, probably on the basis of the following:

Heaven's way of acting has consistency. It did not act as Yao's security nor as Jie's destruction. . . . If you encourage agriculture and are frugal, Heaven cannot make you poor. . . . if you follow *Dao* and are not of two minds, Heaven cannot send you misfortune. . . . but if you neglect agriculture and spend lavishly, Heaven cannot make you rich. (*Xunzi* 79, K 17.1, 17/79/16–19)

and again,

Are order and disorder from Heaven? I reply, the sun, moon, stars, planets and other heavenly auspices were the same under both Yü and Jie. Yü produced order and Jie chaos. Order and chaos are not from Heaven. (*Xunzi* 82, K 17.4, 17/80/21–22)

The latter does not conflict at all with Jesus' remark that God sends his rain upon the just and the unjust, but the former states Heaven's *inability* to perform its traditional rewarding and punishing role. It is this assertion of inability which seems to underlie the widespread belief that Xunzi completely deanthropomorphized Heaven. Surely a purely blind, impersonal, and amoral "heaven" would function as he describes. But so would a thoroughly moral but transcendent Heaven, so long as its *Dao* or *li* did not include the function of rewarding and punishing. In the latter case, Heaven's "inability" to reward or to punish would be its unwillingness to overstep the bounds of its proper *Dao*.

That this is not a fantastic interpretation can be shown through another passage. In chapter 23, we find:

> Why is it, then, that everyone is not able to accumulate good acts in the same way? I would reply: everyone is capable of doing so (可以 *keyi*), but not everyone can be made to do so (可使 *keshi*). The petty man is capable (*keyi*) of becoming a gentleman, yet he is not willing (肯 *ken*) to do so; the gentleman is capable (*keyi*) of becoming a petty man but he is not willing to do so. . . . Hence, it is correct to say that the man in the street is *capable* (*keyi*) of becoming a Yu but it is not necessarily correct to say that he will in fact find it possible (能 *neng*) to do so. But although he does not find it possible (*neng*) to do so, that does not prove that he is incapable (*keyi*) of doing so. (*Xunzi* 167, K 23.5b, 23/116/17–22, parentheses are my own additions)

Xunzi here distinguishes two kinds of impossibility: the abstract impossibility of incapability and concrete impossibility of being unable to bring oneself to choose what he is abstractedly perfectly capable of doing. Thus the gentleman *cannot* become a petty man,

no matter how capable he is of doing it; his moral character does not permit him to do so.

One cannot simply take this distinction neatly and transfer it to the essay on Heaven. It can be argued, however, that it does two things: (1) we cannot treat "Heaven cannot make you poor," as if there is no ambiguity regarding the precise force of the "cannot," and (2) when Xun needed to distinguish "will never take the occasion to do *x*" from "does not have the capability of doing *x*," he used *neng* (or its negation, 不能 *buneng*) for the former and *keyi* (or 不可以 *bukeyi*) for the latter. When we look at the passage ascribing to Heaven the inability to reward and punish, he uses *buneng* exclusively. This at least allows the reading that this inability is not a matter of abstract incapacity but *a consistent pattern of responding to situations*. The gentleman will not consent to becoming a petty man; Heaven will not consent to using flood and drought, heat and cold, as punishments. Such things arrive, but they are not special acts of Heaven directed to special ends; they are Heaven steadily following out its own ritual, its *li*, its *Dao*.

This coheres perfectly with Xunzi's insistence that the crucial problem is not Heaven's action but men's responses—but the proper response to ritual action is a ritual response. Xunzi includes all proper responses to Heaven's action under his rubric of *li*, which is surely better translated *ritual* than any other one term. A ritual response to natural initiative is surely in some proper sense *religious*.

This interpretation seems to me eminently consistent not only with his rejection of looking on rituals as ways of obtaining local and particular benefits, but also with the central Confucian belief in what sinologist Donald Munro calls "model emulation."[13] In the ideal state, men are moved not by hope of reward or fear of punishment but by the attractive example of the perfect Sage-king. As Xunzi argues elsewhere, men are moved toward the goodness they know they themselves lack. How could such a sagely leader be an equal of and copartner with Heaven and Earth unless they, too, operated on the basis of unity, beauty, and profundity of *li* rather than on the basis of reward and punishment?

Xunzi as religious Confucian. I have argued that the widespread treatment of Xunzi as a nonreligious, even antireligious, philosopher is based in part on the biases of Neo-Confucianism and of twentieth-century Westernizers, in part on his rejection of superstition, and in part on his appearance of demythologizing Heaven. I have presented grounds for not extending his denial of *gui*-worship to *shen*, for taking his interpretation of *shen* to be something more than mere naturalism, and for rejecting the interpretation of passages attributing inability to Heaven as denials of Heaven's moral supremacy or religious significance. The picture that emerges is one of a Xunzi who is trying to protect the religious substance of Confucianism from dangers on many sides: from the superstitious who seek to use rituals to obtain special favors or to escape the results of their own foolishness, from Mohists who appeal to heavenly reward and retribution to correct social ills, from Daoists who would downgrade or abolish all *li* as artificial and unresponsive to Nature and substitute disciplines of self-culture which would contribute nothing to high culture and would turn statecraft over to the Legalists; and indeed from followers of Mencius who rely so much on natural processes to produce moral goods that they threaten the Confucian discipline itself.

From his concern for both the consistency of Heaven and the consistency of his own thought, and for the joint primacy of *li* on the one hand and human effort on the other, he was led to deny that the continuity between Heaven and human sanctity lay in the natural processes of production, a principle held by Mencius and the Daoists. Those who could relate men to Heaven only through such a continuity were constrained to find him irreligious. It would be more fruitful to discern his own sense of the sanctities of men and Heaven, and his own principle of their continuity through *li*.

Notes

1. Henry Rosemont, "State and Society in the *Xunzi*," in *Virtue, Nature, and Moral Agency in the Xunzi* (Hackett Publishing Company, 2000), p. 25.

2. A religious philosopher is not a prophet. By this I mean he does not, and cannot, add significantly to the religious materials available to his times. He draws on them, restructures them, reinterprets them, perhaps rejects many of them. When finished, he may claim, "This is what they always really meant." But he is essentially a renovator, not a regenerator.

3. Liu Wu-chi, *A Short History of Confucian Philosophy* (Baltimore, MD: Penguin Books, 1955), p. 96.

4. Fung Yu-lan, *The Spirit of Chinese Philosophy*, trans. E.R. Hughes (Boston: Beacon, 1962), p. 81.

5. C.K. Yang, *Religion in Chinese Society* (Berkeley and Los Angeles: U of California P, 1970), p. 245.

6. Sima Qian, *Shiji* 史記. SBBY ed., vol. 6, LXXIV, p. 46.

7. Yang, *Religion in Chinese Society*, p. 256.

8. Homer H. Dubs, *Hsüntse Works, from the Chinese* (London: Probsthain, 1928), p. 67.

9. Bronislaw Malinowski, *Magic, Science, and Religion and Other Essays* (Garden City, NY: Doubleday, 1954), p. 38.

10. Burton Watson, *Hsün Tzu* (New York: Columbia UP, 1996), p. 8.

11. See note 3.

12. For example, Li Deyong, *Xunzi, gongyuanqian sanshiji zhongguo weiwuzhuyi zhexuejia* 荀子, 公元前三世紀中國惟物主意哲學家 (Shanghai: Renmin, 1959), p. 18, and Zhou Fucheng. "Xunzi," *Zhongguo qingnian* 11.1 (1956), p. 21.

13. Donald Munro, *The Concept of Man in Early China* (Stanford: Stanford UP, 1969), p. 52.

Discussion

1. Why has Xunzi been portrayed as anti-religious?

2. Distinguish *gui* and *shen*. What was Xunzi's attitude toward *shen*?

3. How does Machle understand Xunzi's conception of and attitude towards Heaven (*tian*)?

LI (RITUAL/RITE) AND TIAN (HEAVEN/NATURE) IN THE XUNZI: DOES CONFUCIAN LI NEED METAPHYSICS?

SOR-HOON TAN*

Early Chinese metaphysics. Philosophers working on early Confucian texts are divided on the question of whether there is metaphysics in pre-Qin Confucian texts. Few would disagree that the concerns in the *Analects*, the *Mencius*, and the *Xunzi*, are primarily practical. Passages in early Chinese texts that are apparently metaphysical are dismissed by the anti-metaphysics party as inconsequential for the issues of real concern, and best ignored, especially when they seem nonsensical or indefensible to modern sensibilities. Their opponents disagree, insisting that even when not explicit, metaphysical assumptions are inevitable and necessary. This may be true: one's belief about the kind of cosmos one lives in and human beings' place within that cosmos would have some effect on one's moral vision and commitment. However, such a relationship between metaphysics and ethics does not mean that debates over ethics are resolved by convincing others of one's metaphysical assumptions—indeed what drives the trend against metaphysics in the last century is the irresolvable nature of metaphysics, and the conviction that philosophical debates have a better chance of resolution if one brackets out the metaphysical.

Does the *Xunzi* actually offer a clear and consistent metaphysics? I shall argue that Xunzi's metaphysical assumptions were pragmatic in that Xunzi's main concern was defending his ritual theory and metaphysical assumptions were implied only when needed for that defense. This essay discusses some examples of scholarly attempts at reconstruction of the textual evidence on metaphysical issues. If no specific metaphysics proves *necessary* for ritual ethics, a kind of "metaphysical flexibility," one that might involve a more defensible metaphysics for today, could work to the benefit of the ethics. Could we even dispense with the metaphysics altogether and preserve Xunzi's ritual theory as an ethic that is relevant to contemporary life?

Li 禮 (ritual). The Chinese term "*li* 禮" has been translated as "ritual," among alternatives including "rite," "ceremony," "ritual action," "ritual propriety," "propriety," "code of conduct," "decorum," "manners," "courtesy," and "civility." The earliest written form is believed to depict objects used in practices identifiable today as rituals, with religious, communicative, transformative, and expressive dimensions. The Chinese have paid close attention to li and have emphasized its importance and value since the very beginning of their civilization. Based on archeological evidence, the oracle bones and bronzes from the Shang and Zhou dynasties, the earliest li were probably those in worship of deities identified with the rivers, mountains, or the "four quarters," and in the sacrifices made by rulers to their dead ancestors and other individuals with significant contribution to the dynasty.

The religious root of li as well as its association with Chinese religions is displayed in the 礻 radical of the character 禮, which it shares with the character *shen* 神, used to translate "god." The earliest li could be viewed both in terms of communication with those in a supernatural or sacred realm and therefore as religious activities, and in terms of their sociopolitical functions, particularly those contributing to group bonding, and to establishing and sustaining political legitimacy.

The varied references for the term "li" include religious rituals, state ceremonies, the institutionalized and stylized behavior of the nobility, prescriptions on political institutions and responsibilities of government officials, life-cycle rites, etiquette and manners.

---

* Sor-Hoon Tan is Professor of Philosophy at the National University of Singapore.

The idea became one of the key ethical ideas in the teachings of Confucius in the *Analects*, interconnected with other key ideas of *ren* (humaneness, benevolence or co-humanity), *yi* (appropriateness, what is right and proper), and *zhi* (wisdom). One could understand the Confucian conception of *li* as including all the norms for human actions, roles, and institutions. Such norms are the valued forms of acting and living transmitted from generation to generation—in guiding and governing our actions, they are endowed with the authority of tradition and continued social affirmation and expectation.

Xunzi's ethics of ritual. Ritual occupies an important place in Confucius' teachings about personal cultivation, social harmony, and good government.[1] Xunzi went much further in his emphasis on ritual. Every chapter of the *Xunzi* except two ("Confucius" and "Warning Vessel on the Right") mentions *li*, and one whole chapter is devoted to a "Discourse on *li*." I shall examine what Xunzi believed to be the roles of ritual in various domains of life, from personal cultivation to good government, from making judgments about the world to acquiring or producing knowledge. Xunzi's ethics may be called an ethics of ritual because ritual governs everything ethical and much more.

Xunzi identifies *li* and trustworthiness (*xin* 信) as the "measure of excellence" to be employed in all circumstances "to control the vital breath and nourish life, . . . to cultivate one's character and strengthen oneself" (2/5/11; 1:152).[2] The ancient kings, who "minutely observed ritual so that wherever they went in making the circuit of the world, their acts involved no impropriety" (12/57/27; 2:179), provided models for personal cultivation by showing how "ritual will rectify the warp and woof, the straightaways and byways of one's life" (1/4/2; 1:141). Rituals guide every aspect of a worthy life (2/5/14; 1:152).

Personal cultivation does not happen by chance but requires learning. In Xunzi's understanding of learning, the "proper method is to start with the recitation of the Classics and conclude with the reading of the *Rituals*" (1/3/7; 1:139). Despite his reverence for the classics, Xunzi recognized that book learning is not sufficient: "Learning reaches its terminus when it is fully put into practice" (8/33/11; 2:81). Learning must transform practice, and through practice also transforms the learner's character. "One who is in the process of learning is one who models action on ritual practice."[3] "When rituals have been extended to the individual person, his conduct is reformed" (14/66/18; 2:206; also 20/100/8; 3:84). "It is through ritual that the person is rectified (*zhengshen* 正身)."[4]

A person who is correct, proper, or right, and suitable as a guide or model (that is, *zheng* 正), uses "only those methods sanctioned by ritual and appropriateness" (2/6/16; 1:154). Every aspect of such a person's activities will be ordered wherever he or she may travel or dwell, in any circumstances, in poverty or wealth. Learning must be "perfected in ritual" (1/3/10; 1:139), so that it could fulfill its aim of "first to create a scholar and in the end to create a sage" (1/3/7; 1:139). The scholar (*shi* 士) follows ritual norms "to cultivate his own person" (2/7/6; 1:155). A sage is one who "acts in accordance with the requirements of the indispensable points of ritual and is at ease with them as though he were merely moving his four limbs" (8/30/16; 2:76). Between these two levels of ritual achievement is that of the superior person (*junzi* 君子), "who accumulates ritual and appropriateness" (8/34/7; 2:82).

> The gentleman [*junzi*] is respectful but not fearing and takes strict reverent care but is not apprehensive. In poverty and want, he is not straitened; and with riches and honors, he is without presumptions. When he everywhere encounters changes of circumstances, he is not reduced to extremity. This is due to minutely observing ritual principles. Thus in regard to rituals,

the gentleman scrupulously observes their provisions and finds his security in them. (12/58/1; 2:179)

The *Xunzi* distinguishes among people according to their merits measured largely by their ritual excellence. Xunzi advocated a kind of ritual meritocracy in which those who dedicated themselves to ritual and achieved excellence in ritual performance are raised above others in the social order: "Although they be the descendants of kings and dukes or knights and grand officers, if they are incapable of devotedly observing the requirements of ritual and appropriateness, they should be relegated to the position of commoners" (9/35/4; 2:94). Appointment and promotion to official positions based on ritual and appropriateness applies at all levels through the Confucian advocacy of a general policy of "elevating the worthy and employing the capable" (12/57/15; 2:177). Xunzi gave this ritual meritocracy an ancient lineage, claiming that "men of antiquity" practiced this way of selecting men (12/61/6; 2:186).

In Xunzi's ideal ritual meritocracy, everyone devotes himself/herself to perfecting his/her conduct through ritual and appropriateness, beginning with the ruler, who sets an example and ensures that others practice ritual and appropriateness (8/28/8; 2:70; 11/56/16; 2:169; 10/49/4; 2:138). Ritual and appropriateness are the "mean" the Ancient Kings followed in their conduct (8/28/15; 2:71) that led to good government, since one who governs with ritual "loves his subordinates as if 'tending and caring for a small infant'" (11/54/11; 2:162). When the superior treats subordinates according to appropriate rituals, the latter would reciprocate in a manner that promotes effective government.

> ... if the superior is fond of ritual and appropriateness, if he elevates the worthy and employs the capable, and if he has no mind for avaricious profits, then his subject will also go to

the utmost in offering polite refusals and showing deference, will be loyal and trustworthy in the extreme, and will be attentive to the ministers of government. (12/57/15; 2:177)

Xunzi believed that using ritual and appropriateness enables the rulers to "unify" the people (10/46/20; 2:132).

According to Xunzi, ritual excellence is required to fulfill the responsibilities of various social positions well in order to bring about and sustain his conception of ideal society, structured by roles governed by ritual that provides the ethical norms relevant to each role. Having been elevated to a superior position, one is then constantly subject to evaluation according to the ethical norms of one's role constituted by its appropriate rituals. Just as ritual performance is used to measure the excellence of individual persons in their roles, the appropriate treatment and practice of ritual also provide the criteria for judging governments (which could be conceived as a network of different roles). The king is someone who "enhances every act with ritual and appropriateness" (9/37/19; 2:100, modified). A lord is someone who "employs ritual in dividing the largess, is equitable in every case and unbiased," while a minister is one who "waits on the lord according to ritual principles, is loyal, obedient and not lazy" (12/57/23; 2:178, modified).

Xunzi's ritual meritocracy also solves the problem of social distribution, which if not properly handled, would only result in divisive competition for limited resources and eventually lead to poverty (9/36/2; 2:96). He advocated differential distribution captured by the concept of "*fen* 分" in the *Xunzi*.

> If a society is formed without social divisions [*fen*], strife would result; if there is strife, disorder ensues; if there is disorder, fragmentation results; if there is fragmentation, weakness comes; if there is weakness, it is impossible to triumph over

objects. . . . This is precisely why it is unacceptable to neglect ritual and appropriateness even for the shortest moment. (9/39/16; 2:104)

Xunzi justified the inequality of *fen* through ritual merit. Ritual is specifically the means by which the Ancient Kings created the requisite and appropriate *fen* (9/36/2; 2:96). When people know their place in society, are content with what is appropriate for them, fulfill the responsibilities of their positions, and have their achievements recognized, there is social order. The role of ritual in this social order as conceived by Xunzi is such that it is sometimes identified with that order itself (3/10/12; 1:176), and at other times the beginning of order (9/39/2; 2:103). Either way, ritual plays a key role in sociopolitical order in Xunzi's thought.

Ritual also has a cognitive role in the *Xunzi*. This is already apparent in using ritual as a measure of merit since it implies using ritual to guide one's judgment of people.

Ritual is the inch, foot, double yard, and great yard to the ruler of people for the measurement of his servants. (8/34/18; 2:83; also 12/61/8; 2:186)

Xunzi considered "the sage examining all in terms of ritual," "the acme of humanity and wisdom" to be the highest cognitive achievement (12/58/8; 2:180). How does ritual provide the measure for truth, so that one would not be "fooled by fraud and pretense" as Xunzi claimed (19/92/15; 3:61)? In a religious context, ritual could be the bridge or gateway to knowledge that is not dependent on our physical senses or instrumental reasoning, some kind of direct access to a transcendent realm that, once gained, transforms our understanding of the world we live in and provides the basis for our value judgments. Interpreting Xunzi's claim about ritual as a measure for truth in this way definitely implies a metaphysics. However, there are other ways

of understanding the noetic functions of ritual that do not carry such metaphysical baggage.

Necessity of *Li*. Xunzi did not merely extend and reiterate the importance of ritual in early Confucian teachings about personal cultivation and good government. He sometimes made extreme claims about its necessity for every human endeavor, even human life itself: "a man without ritual will not live; an undertaking lacking ritual will not be completed; and state and family without ritual will not be tranquil."[5] The context for this push towards more extreme claims about *li* is Xunzi's self-appointed role as the defender of Confucian teachings against the criticisms and contending views popular during his times. In this role, he also criticized other Confucian thinkers, including Zisi and Mencius (6/22/8; 1:224), whose views he saw as undermining Confucian learning and ritual ethics.

Xunzi's famous disagreement with Mencius over the question of "*xing* 性 (human nature)," the topic of an entire chapter arguing that "Human Nature Is Bad," concerns the nature of *li* and its role in ethical life. The badness of *xing* renders necessary the learning of *li* with the help of teachers and model practice provided by the sages. Xunzi maintained that "human nature is bad and that any good in humans is acquired by conscious exertion (*wei* 伪)" (23/113/7; 3:151). The most important of human beings' "conscious exertion" is *li*. He pushed the argument further by asking a rhetorical question: if human nature were good (as Mencius had claimed), "what use would there be for sage kings, and what need for ritual and appropriateness!" (23/115/3; 3:155; also 23/115/12; 3:156).

The "Discourse on Ritual" further illuminates the claim that bad human nature requires *li*. Most commentators tend to focus on Xunzi's argument about its necessity for social harmony through its regulation and distribution function of "apportioning things, nurturing human desires, and supplying the means for their satisfaction" (19/90/4; 3:55). Besides stable and valued ways of facilitating social interaction, dealing with conflicting or competing desires in order to eliminate social strife, ritual is also important in effecting mental and emotional harmony at the personal level, as conflicting or excessive desires and feelings sometimes cause confusion and suffering, undermine personal wellbeing and may threaten a person's ethical life. Ritual contributes to personal harmony through its effects on disruptive or harmful desires and feelings, especially during times of personal crises or significant events.

In response to Mozi's explicit attack on "elaborate funeral and extended mourning," Xunzi condemned some of the same excessive funereal practices of their times—starving oneself, competing to appear distraught and emaciated—which, in his view, were neither a "cultivated form" of ritual and appropriateness, nor showed "the emotion proper to the filial son," but rather "done for the sake of effect."[6] Yet Xunzi maintained that elaborate ritual practices served important functions of providing appropriate channels for emotions that people felt on such occasions, as well as displayed the appropriate distinctions that sustain social order. The disruption caused by death gives rise to a yearning for continuity, this emotional need is met by rituals that enable people to display and highlight emotions and attitudes, such as loyalty and filiality, appropriate to their respective relations to the departed (19/93/6–13; 3:63).

According to Xunzi, the extended funeral, with interment only in the third month, is "the expression of the most exalted thoughts of longing and remembrance," and is necessary in order to give the mourners time to come to terms with their loss (19/94/1; 3:64). He drew attention to the function of the various transitions in mourning rites. In "adorning the dead and sending them to their grave in a fashion that resembles the way they lived" (19/95/6; 3:67), funeral rites allow mourners to treat the occasion as no more than "a change of abode" for the departed, and thereby

mitigate their sense of loss, and appease their longing (19/95/12; 3:67). Mixing them with "practices contrary to what is done for the living" (19/95/8; 3:67) and using funeral objects with forms indicating that they will never be used (19/95/11; 3:68) help mourners move towards recognition of the differences and separation between the dead and the living.

An extended period of mourning is justified, indeed necessary, because passage of time is required to deal with the mourners' grief before they can "resume the ordinary course of life." While allowing time to heal the wound of loss, ritual also limits the grieving process; by stipulating a specific end to the mourning period (and specific ritual acts to mark its end), it compels mourners to "return to daily life" (19/96/8; 3:69) by providing symbolic closure. This does not mean that the dead are then forgotten; sacrificial rites take over the purpose of marking remembrance and recollection (19/97/20; 3:72). By having specific occasions for public display of such feelings, ritual limits the negative impact of grief and longing for the dead on the living.

Mourning rituals continue the main function of many rituals of social interaction among the living, which maintain social distinctions by symbolic displays, among others, including those of authority and social prestige.

Thus, the Son of Heaven has the Great Chariot and rush mats to care for his comfort. On either side of the chariot fragrant marsh angelica is placed to care for his sense of smell. In front of him there is the inlaid yoke shaft to nurture his sense of sight. There are the harmonious sounds of the tinkling bells on the horse's trappings; the chariot moves along in time with the "Martial" and "Imitation" music; and the horses gallop in time with the "Succession" and "Guarding" music—all in order to nurture his sense of hearing. There is the dragon banner with nine scallops to nurture a sense of sacredness about him. There are the recumbent rhinoceros, the crouching tiger, back harnesses with scaly dragon patterns, the silken carriage coverings, and yoke-ends with dragons to nurture his majestic authority. (19/90/11; 3:56)

To the more egalitarian minded Mozi, deployment of resources should attend to only utility that remains the same for all, rather than to social distinctions—for example, vehicles only need to be "safe to ride and easy to pull" for everyone, and boats and oars are made only for crossing the rivers, and there is no need for ritual distinctions in their use by people with different social positions.[7]

What critics such as Mozi considered unnecessary extravagance, Xunzi argued is necessary for those occupying positions of authority to discharge their responsibilities and maintain social order and harmony (10/45/16; 2:129). Mozi insisted that the ancient sage-kings abided by a code of simplicity in food and drink.[8] In contrast, Xunzi pointed out that human beings do more than fill their bellies when eating (19/90/4; 3:55). Xunzi's defense of the Confucian ideal of ritually governed life and social order against Mohist attacks is based on a contending belief that merely fulfilling the basic physical need for food, shelter, and security is not enough to make life human. For a human being to "live" is to distinguish himself or herself from the beasts; that is why Xunzi believed that without *li*, "a person cannot live."

The complex social order made possible by qualitative distinctions and other differentiations not only regulates the appropriate distribution of resources but also facilitates achievements beyond the capacity of what appeared to Xunzi to be crude and primitive standards of living advocated by Mozi, who misdiagnosed the problem of the "inadequacy" confronting human societies. Following Mozi's formula for government would make people deprived and produce only social anarchy (10/45/7; 2:128). Ritual is

necessary to prevent anarchy, and appropriately practiced, would increase a society's prosperity. Xunzi defended the Ancient Kings' institutionalizing "sharp divisions, . . . not merely out of reckless extravagance or a boastful fondness for elegance, but rather in order to brightly illuminate the cultivated forms of humaneness (*ming ren zhi wen* 明仁之文) and to make comprehensible the accord with humaneness (*tong ren zhi shun* 通仁之順)" (10/43/11–13; 2:124, modified). From Xunzi's perspective, expenditure on ritual is more than compensated by the social good it delivers. It is the neglect of ritual and appropriateness, preferring profit and worldly achievement instead, which will impoverish a country.

Not only is ritual necessary to solving sociopolitical problems within a state, it is also necessary for interstate relations (10/48/14; 2:136; also 11/49/16; 2:150), and in an imperfect world, even in warfare.[9] Why did Xunzi think that, "if the ruler does not exalt ritual, then the army will be weak" (10/47/19; 2:134)? Xunzi recognized that the ability to motivate people is the key to success in warfare and other cooperative endeavors. He maintained that materialistic rewards and punishment are inadequate to motivate people for really difficult tasks and so commended ritual instruction to "cause them [the people] to make a common effort" (15/70/13; 2:224). Only in a state governed by ritual and appropriateness are the people unified and even willing to die for their ruler because the latter has gained their loyalty and devotion (15/68/6; 3:219). Such a ruler has achieved "the highest and most awesome authority," not by force and terror, but by ritual excellence (16/75/13; 2:239).[10] Ritual is therefore necessary to win the people's support, strengthen their state against other states with predatory interests, and bring order to the world (16/79/8; 2:249).

The metaphysics of ritual. The more extreme of Xunzi's claims about *li* were often a reaction against competing schools of thought or explicit attacks on

Confucian teachings. Most of his defense of ritual focused on the practical functions of ritual. One would expect this, given that Xunzi was trying to persuade a world preoccupied with very real problems, competing with contemporary thinkers offering advice on how to govern well, to win wars, or to live a secure and prosperous life in an age of chaos. However, some intellectual historians have argued that his audience was broader than that; for example, Masayuki Sato maintains that "The quest for metaphysical principles was one of the main characteristics of the intellectual activities of the Jixia Academy in its heyday."[11] As a member of the Jixia academy, Xunzi might also have to address such metaphysical concerns. According to Sato, even before Xunzi's time, the concept of *li* had reached a high level of abstraction and was a "metaphysical principle" in that it "represented the order of the natural, social, psychological worlds."[12] He argues that there is a metaphysical dimension in Xunzi's thought, in the concepts of *tian* and *dao*, although it is subordinate to his interest in social order.[13]

Despite Xunzi's insistence that *li* was created by the Ancient Kings, which points towards ritual being human inventions or social constructions, some passages seem to give *li* a basis beyond human experience, showing how the latter is interwoven into and dependent on, a larger world, often referred to as "heaven and earth" (*tiandi*) or "heaven" (*tian*).

> Ritual has three roots. Heaven and earth are the root of life. Forebears are the root of kinship. Lords and teachers are the root of order. . . . Thus, rituals serve heaven above and earth below, pay honor to one's forebears, and exalt rulers and teachers. (19/90/20; 3:58, modified)

How do rituals serve heaven above and earth below? The answer lies in the conduct of the exemplary person (*junzi*) who, being "the beginning of ritual and appropriateness," "acts with ritual and appropriateness,

actualizes them, accumulates them over and over again, and loves them more than all else" (9/39/2; 2:103).

> Heaven and earth gives birth to the *junzi*, and the *junzi* brings orderly pattern [*li* 理] to heaven and earth. The *junzi* is the triadic partner of [*can* 參] heaven and earth, the summation of the myriad of things, the parents of the people.[14]

Insofar as "heaven and earth" or "heaven" involved some kind of cosmology, these passages point towards some assumed metaphysical basis for Xunzi's ritual ethics.[15]

For the most part, the term "heaven and earth" (*tiandi* 天地) seems to refer to the totality of existence that might be understood as equivalent of a cosmos including the natural world and the world created by human beings, although it remains unclear whether some kind of purpose or value is an intrinsic part of this cosmos.

The statement that the *junzi* "brings orderly pattern" to heaven and earth needs unpacking. How extensive and enduring are the changes the *junzi* is supposed to be able to bring about in the cosmos? The "regulations of a true king" pertain not only to rituals governing social interactions, but they also ensure that all agricultural, fishing, and hunting activities are carried out in the proper seasons, and the use of the myriad things produced by heaven and earth follow an orderly pattern. A sage king "scrutinizes heaven above and establishes on earth below; he fills up and puts in order all that is between heaven and earth; and he adds his works to the myriad things" (9/39/23; 2:105). Under such an ideal ruler, there is harmony not only among human beings, but also between human beings and the rest of the cosmos (11/56/23; 2:170; also 10/45/22; 2:130). The failure of human beings to fulfill their responsibility for order could result in chaos of cosmic proportions: "Heaven and earth exchange places" (26/125/13; 3:202).

The effect of ritual on the cosmos is not without limits. Xunzi rejected the supposed magical or "supernatural" function of rituals common during his time, such as those implied in praying for rain, or "saving" the sun or moon during eclipses. Xunzi insisted, "We do these things not because we believe that such ceremonies will produce the results we seek, but because we want to embellish such occasions with ceremony" (17/82/6; 3:19). Extending his analysis of ritual, we might say that these rituals are ways of working through our feelings, anxiety in particular, and they help us cope with difficult situations and threatening events. Not knowing the limits of human ability to affect the cosmos amounts to a failure to grasp the division between *tian* and human beings, and recognize their respective roles. "Heaven has its seasons; earth its resources; and man his government" (17/80/2; 3:15). What are purely matters of *tian*, such as the seasons, cannot be changed by humans—attempting to do so amount to "competing with *tian* in its work" (17/80/1; 3:15).

The division between *tian* and humans does not mean that human beings should simply ignore *tian*. Some things, even though resulting from *tian*, human nature for example, can be transformed and refined, put to good use, wasted or abused. It is necessary to observe *tian* (9/39/22), to understand *tian* (17/80/15; 3:16) and act in harmony with it. This harmony is often expressed by "orderly pattern" (*li* 理), which stresses the seasonable and timely in ritual performance, for example in "employing familiar foods" (19/21/9; 3:59). One could therefore understand the "triadic partnership" in terms of an interdependence whereby human beings create order in the cosmos, including but not limited to the sociopolitical realm, by responding appropriately to given environment or circumstances not within human control but determined by *tian*. Grasping the division between *tian* and

humans enables one to concentrate on what lies within one's power in order to make progress in ethical living (17/81/5; 3:18), achieve order in the state, and live in harmony with nature, through ritual (17/82/12; 3:20).

If Xunzi's use of the concepts of *tiandi* and *tian* was in response to the metaphysical interests of his contemporaries, to what extent did he share their cosmologies embedded in those concepts? The text devotes a chapter to a "Discourse on *Tian*," in which Xunzi apparently rejected some views popular during his time. Most contemporary scholars credit Xunzi with a view of *tian* very close to the modern, even scientific, view of nature as without purpose or normative content.[16] One reference of "*tian*" in the text is to "the revolutions of the sun and moon and the stars and celestial points that mark off the divisions of time by which the calendar is calculated" and the seasons, spring and summer, autumn and winter (17/80/21; 3:17), which supports an understanding of *tian* as natural phenomena.

The "Discourse on *Tian*" begins with a statement about the "constancy" of *tian* and its apparent neutrality or indifference to human ethical conduct:

> . . . it does not survive because of the actions of a Yao; it does not perish because of the actions of a Jie. (17/79/16; 3:14)[17]

It goes on to deny that *tian* could be responsible for poverty, illness, famine, calamity or misfortune; rather it is human actions that fail to respond appropriately to natural phenomena which bring these about (17/79/16; 3:14). For example, poor harvest need not result in starvation unless one has not stored up excess crops during times of plenty. *Tian* appears to be nature without purpose or value, indifferent to human likes and dislikes (17/80/27; 3:17), neither showing them favor nor bearing them malice. Xunzi rejected as superstition the reading of unusual events in nature—eclipses, unseasonable weather, appearance of new stars—as omens to be feared (17/81/10; 3:18).[18]

Not everyone agrees with the reading of *tian* in the *Xunzi* as a proto-scientific view of nature without purpose and value. While not entirely rejecting that reading, Robert Eno also discerns in the *Xunzi* a second conception of *tian* as nature with ethical significance, providing the basis for ritual in the normative components of human psychology, and serving as a prescriptive model for emulation.[19] Eno argues that the depiction of the human mind creating value and calling it *tian*-like (17/80/10; 3:16) indicate that *tian* is being used as a normative term.[20] This is debatable, as one could argue that calling faculties "*tianguan* 天官" means that they are "endowed by nature," and the fact that the mind judges fortune and misfortune by whether something "accords with its species" means that judgment, even ethical decisions and actions, takes into account (but is not necessarily reducible to) natural characteristics.

Paul Goldin holds that Xunzi sounds like an eighteenth-century deist, for whom reason is the faculty given to human beings by God to discover his will, which means perceiving the laws of nature.[21] Even if God as the author of nature is conspicuously absent in early Chinese thought, a connection between nature and morality could be effected through natural capacities which perceive natural order and create morality on that basis. Goldin notes that "Xunzi postulates a definite order to nature, and maintains that it is not merely *good*, or *profitable*, for us to conform to that order, but *essential to the noble journey*."[22] For Xunzi, the faculties endowed by *tian*, when fully developed and employed with excellence, as they were by the sage kings, enable these individuals to "know heaven" and thereby to create the rituals for future generations to follow.

Although the *junzi* is said to "bring orderly pattern" to *tian*, at times Xunzi seemed to believe that the basis of man-made order lies in "heaven and earth." While human beings create rituals making the distinctions necessary for social order, such

distinctions seem to model a larger natural, possibly cosmic, hierarchy.

> Just as there are heaven and earth, so too there exists the distinction between superior and inferior, but it is only with the establishment of intelligent kingship that the inhabitants of a kingdom have regulations. (9/35/22; 2:96)

Even though the human way, as exemplified by the Ancient Kings following ritual and appropriateness in their conduct, is "not the way of heaven" (8/28/15; 2:71), the "constant way" of heaven nevertheless serves as a model to the *junzi* in its constancy (11/3/4–5; 1:178; 17/81/1; 3:17).[23] One to whom the world would willingly submit because of his great ethical excellence "is as complete as heaven and earth, which embrace the myriad things," since "there are none he does not love, none he does not respect, and none with whom he would contend."[24] The sage is often associated with heaven and with the "greatness" of heaven and earth.[25]

Are these merely metaphorical usages or do they indicate a normative understanding of *tian*, which could point towards a metaphysics of ritual in the *Xunzi*? In presenting the idea of *tian* as "one aspect of Xun Qing's metaphysics" (p. 29), Machle concludes that Xunzi had little interest in the mapping of the cosmos, but adapted some of the conventional cosmological thinking of his time for his own purpose. He judges Xunzi's contribution to the "metaphysics of value" as more significant in reconciling "the orderly value guarantees of *tian* and the disrupted life of the people on earth" (p. 37).

Eno sees the realms of nature and man in the *Xunzi* as a "continuum with a teleological direction," implying "a level above both natural and human dimensions." In his reading, the text comes close to "a systematic metaphysical model hypostatizing this cosmic integration as a transcendental realm of reality" in the ideas of *shen* ("spirit") and *tai-yi* ("Great

Oneness").[26] However, he admits that the latter term is too hazy to even merit speculation (p. 175). For Eno, whether descriptive and natural, or prescriptive and metaphysical, *tian* is not the point, since the text "is not primarily concerned with the philosophical task of formulating a consistent metaphysical theory" (p. 155).

I agree with Eno that whatever metaphysical assumptions there might be in the *Xunzi*, they serve to defend his theory of ritual. If the inconsistencies and ambiguities of the usages of *tian* are any indication, those metaphysical assumptions are unclear and inconsistent. While he might not have been able to avoid metaphysical assumptions, Xunzi did not deem it necessary to have a viable, defensible metaphysical theory.

Ethics and religious metaphysics. Many today reject robust and realist conceptions of God, the afterlife, souls, etc., which render them unacceptable as the metaphysical foundation of ethics (even if they would enliven and inform something like Xunzi's ritual ethics). Moreover, since science assumes a value-free conception of nature, many today would likewise reject even the less theistic conception of *tian* as normative. If one fully affirms the scientific worldview and approaches ritual with the tools of the biological and social sciences, then nature thus conceived lacks purpose and value, and is neither a suitable object for veneration nor provides foundation for any nonnaturalistic morality. For those who find scientific naturalism unconvincing, morality, then, seems to require something beyond science. Something, well, metaphysical. Confucians have often swum against the tide, questioning popular opinions as well as criticizing the powerful. Some Confucians, then, might resist squeezing Xunzi's ritual ethics into modern science and social theories.

Confucians might likewise embark on a new kind of metaphysical inquiry that might be appropriate for recovering Xunzi's philosophy of *li*. Such an inquiry might go as follows. The relation between *tian* and *li* has implications for the fact/value distinction. Working out these implications could be a good starting point for the task of constructing a contemporary metaphysics of ritual. The views of metaphysical import in the *Xunzi* are asserted in defense of the importance of Confucian *li*. Therefore, the metaphysics for Xunzi's ritual ethics would have to be pragmatic in that its theses about the generic character of experience would make a difference to the actual functioning of ritual. The task is not to derive the Confucian ethics of ritual from metaphysical grounds, whether excavated from ancient texts, borrowed from some contemporary sources, or grounded in arbitrary speculations, but rather to inquire into the generic character of experience from the ethical standpoint of Confucian *li* as practice.

The pervasive and fundamental importance of ethical practice in the Confucian worldview implies that ethics would have priority over metaphysics. Because our approach to reality is practice-laden, it is also value-laden, and therefore metaphysics must be grounded pragmatically in ethics rather than the other way round. This endeavor would bring Xunzi into philosophical conversation with Modern Neo-Confucian philosophers as well as Western philosophers rethinking the approach to metaphysics. Quite apart from offering a method conducive to reconstructing Xunzian metaphysics, this opens up an avenue for Xunzi, through the reconstruction of a Confucian metaphysics of ritual, to contribute to the contemporary conversation about metaphysics.

Notes

1. Some passages showing this include *Analects* 2.3; 3.19; 4.13; 9.11; 12.15; 13.4; 14.41.

2. Citation from the *Xunzi* refers to the book/page/line in the Concordance and the

volume: page in Knoblock's translation. D.C. Lau and Chen Fong Ching, eds., *A Concordance to the Xunzi*, ICS Ancient Chinese Texts Concordance series no. 26 (Hong Kong: Commercial P, 1996); John Knoblock, trans., *Xunzi: A Translation and Study of the Complete Works*, 3 volumes (Stanford: Stanford UP, 1988,1990,1994). Knoblock's translations are sometimes modified; e.g., the frequently occurring "*liyi* 礼义," which he usually translates as "ritual and moral principles," is replaced with "ritual and appropriateness," since I share the view that the concept of "principle," with its deontological baggage, is problematic for early Chinese philosophy.

3. 2/8/4; 1:157. Cf. Knoblock's translation of "*fali* 法礼" as "learns of ritual principles and of the model."

4. 2/8/1; 1:157, slightly modified: "individual" replaced with "person."

5. 2/5/15; 1:153. Knoblock's translation of "*guojia* 国家" modified: "nation" replaced with "state and family."

6. 19/94/14; 3:65–66. Cf. Mei I-pao, *Motse* (London: Probstain, 1934), pp. 246, 250, 252.

7. Mei, p. 242.

8. Ibid., p. 240.

9. Knoblock (3:57, 316) notes that one section (15/729 to 15/739) discussing ritual in the chapter on "Debate on Warfare" is included in the *Shiki kaichū kōshō* quotation from the "Discourse on Ritual"; even excluding

that section, ritual is discussed in several other parts in the debate with Lord Linwu about war.

10. 16/77/6; 2:243. Cf. the behavior of the legendary bad kings, Jie and Zhou, who were abandoned by the world, due to their "bringing chaos to the divisions of social functions inherent in ritual and appropriateness, and behaving like wild beasts" (18/84/7; 3:35).

11. Masayuki Sato, *The Confucian Quest for Order: The Origin and Formation of the Political Thought of Xunzi* (Leiden: Brill, 2003), p. 230.

12. Ibid., p. 235.

13. Ibid., pp. 335–36.

14. 9/39/3; 2:103, Knoblock's "provides the organizing principle for" replaced with "brings orderly pattern to." Cf. Sato's "appreciates the principle (i.e., order)" (p. 320).

15. According to Sato, Xunzi was influenced by the Jixia thinkers, for whom the idea of being a triadic partner of heaven and earth signifies an analogical relationship between the natural and human. He argues that Xunzi's "combination of Confucian ethical discourse with a Jixia argumentative framework" provides "pre-Qin Confucianism with a metaphysical conceptual framework." Sato, p. 323.

16. Edward Machle attributed this trend to a desire to link China's quest for modern science with its own tradition. *Nature and Heaven in the Xunzi* (Albany: State

U of New York P, 1993), pp. 7–8. For a recent discussion of rendering of *tian* as "nature", see Lee, *Xunzi and Early Chinese Naturalism*, pp. 22–24. Lee concludes that "the nonpurposive and nonintervening feature of *tian* is revealed in its spontaneous, magical way of working independently from human beings' strenuous and deliberate way of doing. However, the realm of *tian* is not totally inaccessible to human beings because they can participate in the order of *tian* by building a flourishing, orderly society" (p. 24).

17. Cf. Machle's (p. 77) translation: ". . . it did no special act toward Yao's survival, nor towards Jie's fall."

18. Goldin points out that Xunzi was challenging the omenology popular in ancient China, evident in many pre-Qin texts (pp. 39–47).

19. Ibid., p. 132, pp. 157–65. Other uses of *tian* as a normative term do not refer to nature, but adopt conventional uses of *tian* "as god, as ethical precept, or as fate" (p. 133).

20. Ibid., p. 161.

21. Ibid., pp. 51–54.

22. Ibid., p. 53. Cf. Lee's view that, although Xunzi was critical of the naturalism in the thought of early Chinese thinkers such as Mencius and Zhuangzi, his emphasis on human morality being the product of human effort is accompanied by a belief that human morality "reflects the structure of natural order" and that the "isomorphic relation to the way things really are" prevents *li* from being merely conventional and arbitrary (p. 92).

23. Machle (p. 77) draws our attention to the normative connotations of *xing* and *chang* in other usages in the text.

24. 6/23/17; 1:227. See also 10/42/9; 2:122, citing the *Book of Documents*, "How broadly protective is Heaven! Moral power like this will make your own person prosperous."

25. 3/11/9; 1:178, 8/34/4; 2:82 and 19/92/18; 3:61. See also description of the ruler with best kind of authority instilled by the way and its power, cultivating ritual and appropriateness, being "raised as high as heaven" (16/75/14; 2:239, modified).

26. Eno, p. 153.

Discussion

1. Xunzi is first and foremost a philosopher of ritual. How does he understand ritual and its relationship to ethics?

2. What is the concept of *fen* 分 and how does ritual bring about *fen*?

3. Why does Tan claim that Xunzi's metaphysics of ritual is either unclear or unnecessary?

4. Xunzi affirms both highly elaborate rituals and highly structured (hierarchical) society. Can such elaborate ritual and structured society be grounded pragmatically?

Suggestions for Further Study

Denecke, Wiebke. *The Dynamics of Masters Literature: Early Chinese Thought from Confucius to Han Feizi.* Cambridge: Harvard University Asia Center for the Harvard-Yenching Institute & Harvard UP, 2010.

Eno, Robert. *The Confucian Creation of Heaven: Philosophy and the Defense of Ritual Mastery.* Albany: State U of New York P, 1989.

Fung, Yu-Lan. *A History of Chinese Philosophy.* 2nd ed. Princeton: Princeton UP, 1952.

Graham, A.C. *Disputers of the Tao: Philosophical Argument in Ancient China.* La Salle, IL: Open Court, 1989.

Hall, David, and Roger Ames. *Thinking through Confucius.* Albany, NY: State U of New York P, 1987.

Nylan, Michael. *The Five "Confucian" Classics.* New Haven, CT: Yale UP, 2001.

Puett, Michael. *To Become a God: Cosmology, Sacrifice, and Self-Divination in Early China.* Cambridge, MA: Harvard UP, 2002.

Schwartz, Benjamin. *The World of Thought in Ancient China.* Cambridge, MA: The Belknap P of the Harvard UP, 1985.

Slingerland, Edward. *Confucius' Analects, With Selections From Traditional Commentaries.* Indianapolis: Hackett, 2003.

VanNorden, Bryan. ed. *Confucius and the Analects.* New York: Oxford UP, 2002.

Waley, Arthur. *The Book of Songs.* New York: Grove P, 1996.

Permissions Acknowledgements

Adams, Marilyn McCord. "Horrendous Evils and the Goodness of God," from *Proceedings of the Aristotelian Society Supplementary* 63, 1989: 297–310. Reprinted with the permission of Oxford University Press on behalf of the Aristotelian Society, London: www.aristoteliansociety.org.uk. "The Problem of Hell: A Problem of Evil for Christians," from *Reasoned Faith*, edited by Eleonore Stump. Ithaca, NY: Cornell University Press, 1978. Reprinted with the permission of Eleonore Stump.

Adams, Robert Merrihew. "Moral Arguments for Theistic Belief," from *Rationality and Religious Belief*, edited by C.F. Delany. Notre Dame, IN: University of Notre Dame Press, 1979.

Alston, William P. "The Experiential Basis of Theism," from the Leadership U website: http://www.leaderu.com/truth/3truth04.html.

Anselm and Gaunilo. "The Ontological Argument," from *Proslogium; Monologium: An Appendix in Behalf of The Fool by Gaunilo*, translated by Sidney Norton Deane.

Aquinas, Thomas. "The Five Ways," "Speaking of God," and "Whether It Is Becoming to Pray," from *Summa Theologica*, translated by The Fathers of the English Dominican Province.

Baber, Harriet. "Why Feminist Epistemology Sells," excerpted and adapted from "The Market for Feminist Epistemology," in *The Monist* 77 (4), 1994: 403–23. Reprinted with the permission of Oxford University Press.

Bloom, Paul. "Is God an Accident?," from *The Atlantic*, December 2005. Reprinted with the permission of Paul Bloom.

Burns, Elizabeth. "Classical and Revisionary Theism on the Divine as Personal: A Rapprochement?," from *International Journal for Philosophy of Religion* 78 (2), 2015: 151–65. Copyright © Springer Science+Business Media Dordrecht 2014. Republished with permission of Springer-Verlag Dordrecht via Copyright Clearance Center, Inc.

Clark, Kelly James. "Without Evidence or Argument," revised and adapted from "Reformed Epistemology Apologetics," Chapter 5 of *Five Views on Apologetics*, edited by Steven B. Cowan. Grand Rapids, MI: Zondervan Publishing House, 2000.

Clark, Kelly James, and Justin Winslett. "The Evolutionary Psychology of Chinese Religion." Reprinted with the permission of the authors.

Clifford, W.K. "The Ethics of Belief," from *Lectures and Essays*, London: Macmillan, 1886.

Collins, Robin. "A Scientific Argument for the Existence of God: The Fine-Tuning Design Argument," Chapter 3 of *Reason for the Hope Within*, edited by Michael Murray, copyright © 1998. William B. Eerdmans Publishing Company, Grand Rapids, MI. Reprinted with the permission of the publisher; all rights reserved.

Confucius. Excerpts from *Analects*, translated by A. Charles Muller; http://www.acmuller.net/con-dao/analects.html. Reprinted with the permission of A. Charles Muller.

Craig, William Lane. "The Kalaam Version of the Cosmological Argument," from *The Existence of God and the Beginning of the Universe*. San Bernardino, CA: Here's Life Publishing, 1979.

Davis, Stephen T. "Universalism, Hell, and the Fate of the Ignorant," from *Modern Theology* 6 (2), January 1990: 173–86. Copyright © 1990, Blackwell Publishing Ltd. Reprinted with the permission of Blackwell Publishing Ltd., via Copyright Clearance Center, Inc. "Three Conceptions of God in Contemporary Christian Philosophy." Used by permission of the author.

Diller, Jeanine. "Multiple Religious Orientation," from *Open Theology* 2, 2016: 338–53. Used by permission of the author.

Eriugena, Johannes Scotus. "Divine Impassibility," from *Periphyseon: On the Division of Nature*, translated by Myra L. Uhlfelder. Indianapolis, IN: Bobbs-Merrill, 1976. Copyright © Estate of Myra L. Uhlfelder.

Freud, Sigmund. Excerpt from *The Future of an Illusion*, edited by Todd Dufresne and translated by Gregory C. Richter. Peterborough, ON: Broadview Press. Copyright © 2012 by Todd Dufresne and Gregory C. Richter.

Garcia, Laura. "Ontological Arguments for God's Existence." Used by permission of the author.

Hick, John. "The Soul-Making Theodicy," from *Evil and the God of Love*. Palgrave Macmillan, 2010. Copyright © 1966, 1977, 1985, 2007, 2010 by John Hick. "The Philosophy of Religious Pluralism," from *An Interpretation of Religion*. New Haven, CT: Yale University Press, 1989. Copyright © 1989 by John Hick. Reprinted with the permission of Yale University Press.

Howard-Snyder, Daniel. "Rowe's Argument from Particular Horrors," and "Theodicy." Used by permission of the author.

Hume, David. "Critique of the Argument from Design," and "God and Evil," from *Dialogues Concerning Natural Religion*, 1779.

James, William. "The Will to Believe," an Address to the Philosophical Clubs of Yale and Brown Universities. *The New World*, June 1896.

Johnson, Patricia Altenbernd. "Feminist Christian Philosophy?," from *Faith and Philosophy* 9 (3), 1992: 320–34. Reprinted with the permission of Faith and Philosophy Journal.

Laozi. Excerpts from *Daode Jing*, translated by A. Charles Muller; http://www.acmuller.net/con-dao/daodejing.html. Reprinted with the permission of A. Charles Muller.

Leibniz, Gottfried Wilhelm. "On the Ultimate Origination of Things," edited and translated by George Martin Duncan. New Haven: TM&T, 1908.

Littlejohn, Ronnie. "Confucius on Religious Experience." Used by permission of the author.

Louden, Robert. "'What Does Heaven Say?': *Tian* 天 in the *Analects*," excerpted and adapted from "'What

Does Heaven Say?': Christian Wolff and Western Interpretations of Confucian Ethics," in *Confucius and the Analects: New Essays*, edited by Bryan W. Van Norden. Oxford University Press, 2002. Reprinted with the permission of Oxford University Press.

Machle, Edward J. "Xunzi as a Religious Philosopher." Used by permission of the author.

Mackie, J.L. "The Balance of Probabilities," from *The Miracle of Theism*. Copyright © 1982 by John Mackie. Reprinted with the permission of Oxford University Press.

Malcolm, Norman. "The Groundlessness of Belief," from *Reason and Religion*, edited by Stuart Brown. Copyright © 1977 Royal Institute of Philosophy. Used by permission of the publisher, Cornell University Press.

Marx, Karl. "The Opium of the Masses," from *Critique of Hegel's Philosophy of Right*, 1843.

Nietzsche, Friedrich. "Religion as Resentment," from *A Genealogy of Morals*. London: Macmillan and Co., 1897.

Paley, William. Excerpt from "The Watch and the Watchmaker," in *Natural Theology*, 1802.

Pascal, Blaise. "The Wager," from *Pensées* by Blaise Pascal, 1660; translated by W.F. Trotter. New York: P.F. Coller & Son, c. 1910.

Perkins, Franklin. "Divergences within the *Lǎozǐ*: A Study of Chapters 67–81," from *T'oung Pao* 100 (1–3) 2014: 1–33. Reprinted with the permission of Franklin Perkins and T'oung Pao.

Plantinga, Alvin. "Arguing for God," from *Perspectives in Philosophy*. Orlando: Harcourt Brace and Company, 1993. Used by permission of the author. "The Self-Refutation of Naturalism." Used with the permission of the author.

Plato. "Euthyphro," translated by Benjamin Jowett, 1892.

Rowe, William. "The Problem of Evil and Some Varieties of Atheism," from *American Philosophical Quarterly* 16 (4), 1979: 335–41. Copyright © 1979 by the Board of Trustees of the University of Illinois. Reprinted with the permission of Nicholas Rescher, American Philosophical Quarterly.

Stiver, Dan R. "'The Greatest Thing by Far': Metaphor as the Hermeneutical Key to Hermeneutics." Used by permission of the author.

Stump, Eleonore. "Petitionary Prayer," from *American Philosophical Quarterly* 16 (2), 1979: 81–91. Copyright © 1979 by the Board of Trustees of the University of Illinois. Reprinted with the permission of Nicholas Rescher, American Philosophical Quarterly.

Swinburne, Richard. "A Cumulative Case for the Existence of God," excerpted and adapted from "The Vocation of a Natural Theologian," in *Philosophers Who Believe*, edited by Kelly James Clark. Copyright © 1993 by Kelly James Clark. Used by permission of InterVarsity Press, P.O. Box 1400, Downers Grove, IL 60515, USA. www.ivpress.com.

Tan, Sor-Hoon. "*Li* (Ritual/Rite) and *Tian* (Heaven/Nature) in the *Xunzi*: Does Confucian *Li* Need Metaphysics?," from *Sophia* 51 (2), 2012: 155–75. Reprinted with the permission of Springer.

Tidman, Paul. "The Free Will Defense." Used by permission of the author.

van Inwagen, Peter. "Non Est Hick," from *God, Knowledge, and Mystery: Essays in Philosophical Theology*. Copyright © 1995 by Cornell University. Used by permission of the publisher, Cornell University Press, 1995.

VanArragon, Raymond J. "Reconciling Reason and Religious Belief." Used by permission of the author.

Visala, Aku, and David Leech. "Naturalistic Explanation for Religious Belief," from *Philosophy Compass* 6 (8) 2011: 552–63. Copyright © 2011 by John Wiley and Sons, Ltd. Reprinted with permission.

Wainwright, William J. "The Nature of Reason: Locke, Swinburne, and Edwards," from *Reason and the Christian Religion*, edited by Alan Padgett.

Copyright © 1994 William J. Wainwright and Oxford University Press. Reprinted with the permission of Oxford University Press.

Westphal, Merold. "Taking Suspicion Seriously: The Religious Uses of Modern Atheism," from *Faith and Philosophy* 4 (1), January 1987: 22–42. Reprinted with the permission of Faith and Philosophy Journal.

Wolterstorff, Nicholas. "The Silence of the God Who Speaks," Chapter 11 from *Divine Hiddenness: New Essays*, edited by Daniel Howard-Snyder and Paul K. Moser. Copyright © Cambridge University Press, 2002. "Suffering Love," from *Philosophy and the Christian Faith*, edited by Thomas V. Morris. University of Notre Dame Press, 1988.

Zagzebski, Linda. "Does Ethics Need God?," from *Faith and Philosophy* 4 (3), 1987: 294–303. Reprinted with the permission of Faith and Philosophy Journal.

The publisher has made every attempt to locate all copyright holders of the works published in this book and would be grateful for information that would allow correction of any errors or omissions in subsequent editions of the work.

From the Publisher

A name never says it all, but the word "Broadview" expresses a good deal of the philosophy behind our company. We are open to a broad range of academic approaches and political viewpoints. We pay attention to the broad impact book publishing and book printing has in the wider world; we began using recycled stock more than a decade ago, and for some years now we have used 100% recycled paper for most titles. Our publishing program is internationally oriented and broad-ranging. Our individual titles often appeal to a broad readership too; many are of interest as much to general readers as to academics and students.

Founded in 1985, Broadview remains a fully independent company owned by its shareholders—not an imprint or subsidiary of a larger multinational.

For the most accurate information on our books (including information on pricing, editions, and formats) please visit our website at **www.broadviewpress.com**. Our print books and ebooks are also available for sale on our site.

On the Broadview website we also offer several goods that are not books—among them the Broadview coffee mug, the Broadview beer stein (inscribed with a line from Geoffrey Chaucer's *Canterbury Tales*), the Broadview fridge magnets (your choice of philosophical or literary), and a range of T-shirts (made from combinations of hemp, bamboo, and/or high-quality pima cotton, with no child labor, sweatshop labor, or environmental degradation involved in their manufacture).

All these goods are available through the "merchandise" section of the Broadview website. When you buy Broadview goods you can support other goods too.

broadview press
www.broadviewpress.com

The interior of this book is printed on 100% recycled paper.

 PERMANENT 100%   Ancient Forest Friendly™